A Note From

ERIN

among ..re, religion, an eroticism, is a cultural sociologist and professor in the Departments of Religious Studies and Sociology at the University of California, Santa Barbara. He lives in Santa Barbara, California.

...modernist architectu... is the principal of Harold Zellman and Associates, a Los Angeles architecture firm. He lives in Pacific Palisades, California.

© Mark Coppos

Praise for *The Fellowship*

"Just when you thought there was nothing new to be learned about the great American architect Frank Lloyd Wright, [this] massive, gossipy and yet compulsively readable new book proves you wrong."

—*Chicago Sun-Times*

"Remarkable and horrifying. [The authors] tracked down and interviewed dozens of the apprentices who worked at the Taliesin Fellowship. And do these apprentices have stories to tell!"

—*Los Angeles Times*

"An extraordinary and disquieting tale . . . that captures the strange, shadowy and all-too-human world that can gather around genius."

—MARK STEVENS, Pulitzer Prize–winning author of *de Kooning*

"Offers an insider's view of the architect's world that will probably surprise, if not shock, some readers. . . . Fills an important historical gap in the discussion of American arts while reading like high-toned soap opera."

—*BookPage*

"Authoritative and eminently readable. . . . Readers will come away from this book with a deeper appreciation of his genius, but also with a newfound understanding of how peculiar that genius really was."

—ROBERT C. TWOMBLY, author of *Frank Lloyd Wright: His Life and His Architecture*

"This book replaces Wright the demigod with Wright the man. Anyone who admires his architecture will be fascinated. . . . The twenty-first century deserves this new—and truer—picture of Frank Lloyd Wright."

—ALAN HESS, author of *Frank Lloyd Wright: The Houses*

"Biography must be brave, as here. After you read *The Fellowship* you will never be able to look at a Wright building in quite the same way."

—JOHN PERREAULT, ArtsJournal.com, naming *The Fellowship* one of the year's two best art books

The first family of Taliesin, early 1940s. Clockwise from top: Frank Lloyd Wright, Wesley Peters, Iovanna Lloyd Wright, Svetlana Peters, Olgivanna Lloyd Wright.

THE
FELLOWSHIP

THE UNTOLD STORY OF
FRANK LLOYD WRIGHT &
THE TALIESIN FELLOWSHIP

ROGER FRIEDLAND & HAROLD ZELLMAN

HARPER PERENNIAL

NEW YORK • LONDON • TORONTO • SYDNEY

HARPER ● PERENNIAL

FIRST HARPER PERENNIAL EDITION PUBLISHED 2007.

Designed by Kris Tobiassen

The Library of Congress has catalogued the hardcover edition as follows:

Friedland, Roger.
   The Fellowship : the untold story of Frank Lloyd Wright and the Taliesin Fellowship / Roger Friedland & Harold Zellman.
      p. cm.
   Includes index.
   Contents: The masters and disciples—Taking root—The Fellowship—Cult of genius—Behind the lines—The struggle within—Losing ground—Olgivanna unbound.
   ISBN-13: 978-0-06-039388-5
   ISBN-10: 0-06-039388-2
   1. Wright, Frank Lloyd, 1867–1959. 2. Wright, Olgivanna Lloyd. 3. Architects—United States—Biography. 4. Taliesin Fellowship. I. Zellman, Harold. II. Title.

NA737.W7F75 2006
720.92—dc22
[B]   2006049316

ISBN 978-0-06-098866-1 (pbk.)
ISBN-10: 0-06-098866-5 (pbk.)

07   08   09   10   11   WBC/QWF   10   9   8   7   6   5   4   3   2   1

For Debra, the light of whose eyes
still sets my life on fire.
—R. F.

To my wife, Gail, who, with both her love and her
ideas, supported this obsession beyond all reason.
And to Margaret, who so wanted to live to read her
little brother's book, though it was not to be.
—H. Z.

CONTENTS

Wright with his daughter Iovanna

ROSA

"IT'S A MIRACLE YOU FOUND me," Rosa is telling us. "Don't let them stop you. Don't let those bastards stop you. Don't let them tell you I am too ill to talk to."

Insiders from the Taliesin Fellowship had steered us away from her. She was, they told us, incoherent, a lunatic, had spent time in a brothel hotel in Marseilles. Visiting Rosa would be a "waste of time." Nobody volunteered where to find her, and it was clear that it would have been imprudent to ask.

From the outside, Las Encinas, a dark Shingle Style structure surrounded by handsome trees and manicured gardens with fountains, looks like a luxury hotel from the 1920s. It is, in fact, a hospital, a residential treatment center for the depressed and the addicted in Pasadena, California.

Cut into the wooden lintel above the entrance is the admonition *Non est Vivere Sed Valere Vit*: "Life is not being alive but being well." We pass under a low, timbered porte cochere and through the front door. The receptionist calls ahead for clearance, and then directs us back along a pathway toward the building where this longtime Taliesin resident awaits us.

The architecture deteriorates as we leave the elegant old building and move through the gardens toward a complex of buildings that would never appear in the hospital's glossy brochure. We pass a cordon of modest two-story apartment buildings where patients who are well enough live independently. A white, single-story stucco structure stands at the rear of the grounds, a metal grille over its front window; if not for the heavy security door, it might be a laundry facility. A muscular attendant opens the door a crack until we have confirmed who we are.

Rosa is in lockup. Patients who are a danger to themselves, or others, are placed here so they can be observed and controlled. A glass-enclosed nursing station overlooks a bare common room, with a few institutional couches, some chairs, and a single pay phone where patients can receive calls from the outside. The walls are bare, unbroken by decoration or pictures. A bank of doors, always ajar, opens into the patient rooms.

Rosa is the most colorful thing in this sterile, smudged whiteness. She is dressed in a powder-blue robe and slippers, her hair specially permed for the occasion, nails painted gold. Rosa wants to flash.

"You are not afraid to be all alone with me, are you?" she asks as we enter her room. Rosa is angry that the hospital staff has confiscated our tape recorder, angry that she is being kept here against her will, angry that we cannot be in her room with the door closed, alone.

With her gaunt face and a mischievous smile that is more gum than tooth, Frank Lloyd Wright's sole surviving child is strangely fierce and piercingly lucid as she lies in her bed, a skinny but formidable presence. This seventy-five-year-old woman prefers to be called Rosa, not Iovanna, the name her father and mother bestowed upon her.

For her, this is a bad day.

Frank and Olgivanna Wright's only child together was pushed here, she wants us to know—expelled from Taliesin, from the only home she had ever known. Rosa came here more than a decade ago. She had heard that it once attracted glamorous creatures unable to sustain an earthly orbit. It had comforted her that Spencer Tracy had been a patient, that W. C. Fields had spent his last days here. With its lush landscaping, its hardwood-paneled main hall, she tells us, "I thought this would be a nice place to rest." She had no idea, she declares bitterly, that she would not be able to get out. "I have been traveling this road alone."

Rosa wasn't used to being alone. In 1932, she was just seven years old when Wright and Olgivanna, his third wife, launched the Taliesin Fellowship at their home in the isolated wooded hills of southern Wisconsin. Her parents had met at their lowest ebb. Olgivanna had just fled penniless from Paris to America into yet another exile, with no prospect of remunerative work. Wright had recently returned from Tokyo, where he had designed the sumptuous Imperial Hotel—only to find that his latest accomplishment had made little mark at home. "Its originality is so antiquated that it embalms and mummifies the brains of the beholder," the reviewer remarked in *Architect and Engineer*. Most observers in America still believed that the energies of his genius had been spent. His low-slung, open-planned Prairie Houses, the Unitarian church in Oak Park, the Larkin Building were all well behind him. When the Fellowship was founded, Wright was sixty-six years old and almost without clients. In the world of curators and critics, he was a has-been.

Just across the river from Spring Green, Taliesin was Frank Lloyd

Wright's home, and his ideal of what home could be. It was also his architectural practice, around which he and his wife attempted to build a perfect world, a beautiful community that was itself always under construction. The Taliesin Fellowship would eventually attract more than a thousand young men and a few women who were drawn to Wright's creative powers, who sensed his prophetic voice and believed in his vision. They came to participate in its realization, to live in this radiant exemplar, and to glean for themselves the principles by which they might dare design for a new land.

Taliesin, built into a landscape that was itself carefully molded and manufactured, was an encampment for the production of a new particularly American beauty. The apprentices who came to live there—some for a year or two, some forever—were as central to that landscape as its farms, residences, and drafting rooms. Mr. and Mrs. Wright sought to redesign their lives, too. Everything and everyone was to partake of that new, handsome, rugged beauty that Frank Lloyd Wright promoted under the enigmatic term "organic architecture."

For the Wrights, the making of men and the making of buildings were driven by the same vision, the same compulsions. To understand Wright's later architecture, one must understand the extraordinary atelier from whence it came. The Taliesin community was a housing for Wright's imagination, the seedbed where some of America's most important architectural creations were produced. Without the Fellowship, the landmarks for which Frank Lloyd Wright is best known today—Fallingwater, Johnson Wax, the Guggenheim Museum—might never have been created.

Most people who know the name Frank Lloyd Wright know the story of the first tragedy at Taliesin—of what happened in 1914, when his lover Mamah Cheney and several others were murdered there by a deranged servant, and Wright's first Taliesin house was burned to the ground. But that is the least of it. For all its magic, the fealty of its knights to their king of beauty, the cultivated grace of its routine, Taliesin is a haunted house. It has held its secrets, its mysteries and its madness, well. Few know of Taliesin's unsung heroes, the apprentices who gladly sacrificed themselves to make Wright's architecture happen—and fewer still know of its victims, men and women whose lives were irreparably damaged by life in the Fellowship, part of the cost of constructing greatness, of building a cult of genius.

"The house that was once so loved and so lived in is slowly dying," Rosa Wright says, as she warms herself beneath a tattered brown plaid blanket. It is the same blanket in which her father had once draped himself, as he warmed himself before the fireplace in the late afternoons. "And I have no legal power to change it."

*   *   *

IOVANNA LLOYD WRIGHT'S life tracks the story of the Taliesin Fellowship, from its beginnings as a visionary community with the promise to change American life and landscape, to its current status as a beautiful relic whose inhabitants survive off of the residues of her parents' charisma. The Taliesin Fellowship was an extension of the Wrights' home, an extended family fashioned by two powerful personalities, each holding the apprentices to a standard of perfection. Frank Lloyd Wright espoused an all-encompassing philosophy of organic architecture. Olgivanna Lazovich Wright cleaved to a particular strand of esoteric mysticism. The intimate collaboration and titanic conflicts between them set the Fellowship in motion, and shaped its course. An embattled architect staving off the end of his career, and a mystical dancer desperate to find "the way"—the Fellowship was the result of their remarkable union. Each had suffered fiercely, had sought to touch the sacred; each was reaching for immortality. Each brought a passion, indeed a madness, to the place.

Their collision produced both brilliant architecture and a bizarre social order that still inspires—and haunts—many of those who lived by its inscrutable tenets.

THE FELLOWSHIP

Taliesin in the early 1930s

PART I

MASTERS AND DISCIPLES

THE ARCHITECT OF PROPHECY

Frank Lloyd Wright was born in Richland Center, Wisconsin, a small town in a countryside studded with meadows and cliffs and smooth, soft wooded hills. He told me that he had made his entrance into the world on a stormy night and described it to me as though he had witnessed the prophetic initiation. The wind rose over the earth forcing trees low to the ground. Lightning ignited the clouds and thunder struck like a giant in fierce fury. The elements shook the little house which stood up bravely against the attack. "Yours was a prophetic birth," his mother told him.

OLGIVANNA LLOYD WRIGHT

PARIS, 1910. IT WAS A storm locals would long remember. The Seine had flooded its banks. Near the river nothing worked: no electricity, no buses or streetcars. In a café on the Boulevard St. Michel, Frank Lloyd Wright sat alone, sullen, listening to the music.

A cellist picked up his bow and played Simonetti's "Madrigale." Wright used to accompany his son Lloyd as he played the same old Italian tune on the same instrument. On this January day, the sounds opened memory's eye. "[T]he familiar strains now gave me one of those moments of interior anguish when I would have given all I had lived to be able to begin to live again."

The forty-three-year-old architect's "longing and sorrow" had little to do with the wife and six children he had just abandoned in Oak Park, a prosperous

Chicago suburb. "It was not repentance," he recalled. "It was despair that I could not achieve what I had undertaken as Ideal."

Wright walked out into the rainy night, wandering about until dawn, when he found himself "somewhere near where I had started out on the Boulevard St. Michel." The architect was just blocks from the cathedral of Notre Dame, which towered twenty stories above the low-slung city; he could hardly have avoided seeing the Gothic icon.

As a boy, Wright would awaken to the sight of engravings of Gothic cathedrals his mother had hung on his wall. He was only fourteen when he first read Victor Hugo's novel *Notre-Dame de Paris*, popularly known as *The Hunchback of Notre Dame*. Folded into the story of a beautiful woman, a deformed man, and a building was an essay on the fate of architecture. Wright would later describe it as "one of the truly great things ever written on architecture." It was also "one of the grandest sad things of the world."

The would-be architect had been devastated by Hugo's argument that the invention of movable type had enabled the book to dethrone architecture. "Architecture is dead beyond recall, killed by the printed book," he had read. Throughout the Middle Ages, culminating in the Gothic era, the great cathedrals had not only symbolized Europe's great ideas—they were literally encrusted with them. "[A]ll of the intellectual forces of the people," Wright paraphrased Hugo, "converged to one point—architecture. . . . Whoever was born a poet became an architect." Then books grew cheap and ubiquitous; flimsy paper, Hugo noted, became more permanent than granite. The boy whose mother had told him he would be the greatest of architects could now only aspire to become the high priest of a second-rate pursuit.

Hugo had allowed one slim hope. "The great accident of an architect of genius," he wrote, "might occur in the twentieth century as did that of Dante in the thirteenth." Wright took Hugo's hope as prophecy. He would be architecture's redeemer, a T-square-wielding Dante who would dethrone the book and restore architecture to its rightful place. And he would do so in a most unlikely way, by transforming the humble family house into the new cathedral. The printed book was powerful, Hugo had written, because, like "a flock of birds," it was everywhere. Wright would make houses into the birds of architecture.

Now, a quarter of a century later, he was finally in the presence of Notre Dame, the set piece around which his dreams had revolved, the building that embodied the "Ideal." It was the megalith that likely drove him to "despair." How could he ever hope to translate its soaring power into the design of a mere house?

* * *

MARKED BY VIOLENCE and animated by madness, the house where Wright had grown up was nobody's ideal. It was divided between man and wife—divided, in fact, over young Frank. In that setting, the boy struggled to safeguard his sanity and achieve his manhood. Neither task was assured.

Frank's father, William Wright, was a diminutive Baptist preacher and music teacher who had moved to Wisconsin from Hartford, Connecticut, in 1859. A well-dressed polymath, the elder Wright had studied not only music but also law and medicine at Amherst College. He carried his medical satchel on his rounds as a circuit-riding minister.

William had three children with his first wife, Permelia, one of his music students. In 1864, two weeks after giving birth to a stillborn child, she died. Two years later, William married Anna Lloyd Jones, a frontier schoolteacher who had briefly been one of the Wrights' boarders. "Anna would make a wonderful stepmother," Permelia had counseled him just before she died.

Anna had grown up in an extended clan of Welsh Unitarians that eventually ended up near Spring Green, Wisconsin, about forty miles west of Madison. Her brother Jenkin became a nationally known Unitarian minister in Chicago. Unitarians were nonconformist Christians who rejected the trinity—hence the "unity" of God—while emphasizing Christ's humanity, man's natural capacity for moral intuition, and the use of reason to understand scripture. The Lloyd Joneses were known in the valley as pious, serious folk. Some found them pretentious moralists. "God-almighty Joneses," Frank's sister would call them.

Anna was an independent-minded woman; the valley folk remarked that she rode horses like a man, wearing a soldier's cape with a hood and brass buttons. She was also considerably taller than William, who was forced to preach at the side of the pulpit in order to be seen by his congregation. But with his capacious mind and knack for inventing melodies, William Wright must have seemed a catch to the twenty-four-year-old spinster. Men were scarce in the wake of the Civil War, and the intellectual horizons of what men were left in the valley did not extend much beyond the acreage they owned. So Anna gave up her job as a schoolteacher and began to tend to her new husband.

The boy who became Frank Lloyd Wright was born Frank Lincoln Wright on June 8, 1867. (His father, who revered Abraham Lincoln, had delivered a eulogy for the slain president just two years before.) Anna seethed with resentment against her stepchildren, who refused to call her "Mamma." But from the start she poured her energies into her own boy, whom she adored. Frank, she would say, "was to build beautiful buildings."

Anna's boundless faith in her son stood in bitter contrast to her growing disappointment with his father. A Baptist minister, lawyer, classical musician, music teacher, composer, party official, and tax collector, William seemed a dilettante who could barely provide for his family. Unable to afford hired help, she increasingly came to resent the physical labor required of her. William moved the family often—from Richland Center to McGregor, Iowa, on to Pawtucket, Rhode Island, and then to Weymouth, Massachusetts. Returning to Wisconsin, William converted to his wife's creed. With all his talents, Frank's father accumulated no money, no consistent career, not even a solid faith of his own.

Bitter at the way Anna doted on Frank, William directed his rancor at the mama's boy. Frank remembered feeling that his parents' disagreements were all focused on him: "mother always on the defensive, father taking the offensive." He also feared his father. Once, while pumping the church organ's wooden lever as his father played, the seven-year-old's arms and back began to ache. He knew he would be beaten if he didn't pump through to the end of the piece. Bach's heroic chord progressions briefly energized the boy, but Frank soon began crying as he pumped on and on, until finally he collapsed. William said nothing as he led his son home.

While William was severe with Frank, Anna was vicious to her stepchildren. Subject to "tantrums," she beat William's daughter Elizabeth without cause. One Wisconsin winter when she was eleven, Elizabeth recalled, her stepmother "jumped up and down and pumped water as fast as she could and threw it over me and yelled with every jump." Terrified and soaking wet, the girl ran outside, her clothing instantly freezing to her skin. And that wasn't the only such incident. In other confrontations, Anna dragged Elizabeth across the kitchen by the hair, beat her black and blue with a deeply ridged, wooden meat tenderizer, and brought the tines of a meat fork perilously close to the girls' eyes.

Exhausted by her own hysterical ravings, Anna would be bedridden for days at a time. When William discreetly asked her relatives whether there had been insanity in the family, his queries got back to her, only infuriating her further. Fearing for his daughter's life, William finally had Elizabeth sent away to relatives.

MANHOOD DID NOT come easily to Frank Lloyd Wright. He loved beauty—both his own and the world's—a little too much. He had to work at becoming an American man. As a pre-teenager, the boy wore his hair unusually long. "A beautiful head of hair," his mother told him, "was Nature's most beautiful gift to mortals." There were no forts, no Indians, no sports in Frank's early childhood, only drawings, music, and the precocious sensitivity of an aesthete. One day, when he happened on some men plowing a field thick with wild daisies, he was mortified. "Seeing the threat to what he loved," he recalled, he darted in front of the horse-drawn blades to rescue as many as he could. Realizing that most would be buried alive, he "threw himself in the way of the plow and wept."

When Frank was a ten-year-old in Pawtucket, his mother noticed what he later called his "delicate psychology," and feared that he was becoming effeminate. "The mother saw which way her man-child was going," Frank admits, astonishingly, in his autobiography. "She was wise and decided to change it." Convinced that the citified life of the East was responsible, Anna pushed for the family to return from New England to Wisconsin. "She was afraid," Wright recalled, that he "was becoming too detached, dreamy, perhaps too sensitive."

Anna and William returned to Wisconsin, where Anna's brothers gave Frank a job working on their farms and William became an itinerant preacher. Weeping, Anna Wright sheared Frank's blond curls and sent him to Spring Green to labor with his uncles. One day, as the now eleven-year-old trudged hand-in-hand through the fresh morning snow with his uncle John, he was once again seized by nature. Leaving his mitten in his uncle's hand, he broke free and ran about gathering the dry plant skeletons—stems, tassels, flower heads—in his trembling bare hand. But Uncle John spurned his offering. Instead he pointed back at the straight path his footsteps had made through the snow. When Frank looked back at his own "embroidering" path, he was "shamed" by the sight. Beauty and manhood did not lie easily together. "The valley-folk feared beauty," he recalled, "as a snare for unwary feet."

Anna Wright had sent her son to the Lloyd Jones farms to become a man, and eventually the lessons of farm life sank in. Frank herded and milked the cows, shoveled manure, cut and carried wood, repaired fences. He adjusted to the sickening smells of fermented feed, urine, and excrement. In the morning he put on his "sweat-stiffened" clothing. There were times when the teenage boy ran away, exhausted and weeping. But his uncles worked him, teaching him to harness and drive horses, to bale sheaves of grain. By the time he was fourteen, he was being sent out alone to work—and getting paid for it to boot. He gloried in being treated "like a man." At summer's end he returned to Madison, and, although he had since let his hair grow unfashionably long again, he began to make manly things: a catamaran, a bobsled, a cross-gun, an ice-boat, bows and arrows.

And the teenager had also begun romancing girls—imaginary girls, at least. When he was unable to sleep on the farm, Frank sometimes walked barefoot up to the ridge, where he dreamed of a "fairy princess" whose image rose in "pale amber and amethyst nights." After the surge inspired by this dream girl, he felt the "dew [that] came upon the flowers that stood beside his naked legs." He did not, however, allow real girls into this moist dream space. They frightened him. "There was something mysterious," he confessed, "between [my]self and the mystery" of womankind.

The Wisconsin farms of the Lloyd Jones family were a guarantor of Wright's masculinity. On this land he would ultimately find himself shepherding scores of boys into manhood.

ALTHOUGH ANNA WRIGHT had long seen the makings of architectural greatness in her son, Wright himself would take years to distill its precise form. What he would eventually label "organic architecture" began at home, with the Transcendentalist speakers who had wowed his parents when they took him and his siblings back to his father William's native New England.

The Transcendentalists, who saw God in nature's beauty, went beyond the Unitarians' stress on reason and ethical choice. Transcendentalists like Ralph Waldo Emerson—who was much read in the Wright household—sought to fashion a new American culture, seeking inspiration from an inner light found in all creation, including man. Nature's beauty, they were sure, would reveal the principles of form on which both an American democracy and an American architecture could be built. And Emerson declared that "all beauty must be organic." This principle would have a profound influence on Wright's vision: Truly beautiful architecture, he saw, should be designed in Nature's way.

For Wright, Transcendentalism offered a way to love beauty, to be manly, and to be uniquely American, all at the same time. True beauty, he learned, had to be protected from the womanly. Artistic genius, Emerson taught, was a mark of manhood, to be guarded against the "feminine rage" of the "cultivated classes."

The Transcendentalists deplored the sentimental. "[I]t was thought that I was a sentimentalist, and tickled the ears of 'weak women,' who came to delight themselves and be filled full of poetry and love," Francis Parker, one of the great Transcendentalist preachers who inspired Wright's parents, wrote with scorn. To be sentimental was to be overly emotional—unable to engage with reality or to harness the powers of the spirit for the purposes of man. Transcendentalism, rather, involved a romantic quest—though not in the contemporary sense. To be romantic, for the Transcendentalists, entailed a courageous engagement with reality, a heroic struggle to construct a new world. It was this impulse that drove the Transcendentalists to fight for both abolition and women's suffrage.

William Wright did not approve of what he called his son's "sentimentality."

William gave Frank his first lessons in architecture by teaching him about music. A symphony, he explained, was an edifice of sound. But he warned his son that sentimentality could spoil the composition and performance of a piece of music. Frank—who would later find inspiration for his architectural forms in the carefully structured works of his father's beloved Beethoven—would come to identify the sentimental with any architecture that aimed for surface effects, dismissing such design as dishonest, untrue to its materials and structure. In his view, such sentimental architects made pictures, painted two-dimensional scenes; Frank would call their work "erotic foolishness."

WRIGHT ENTERED ADOLESCENCE in verdant Madison, Wisconsin, a small burg tucked between two lakes with its classically domed capitol building hunched over the city's central square. His father soon stopped preaching, turning to music and opening a conservatory. After eight barren years, his musical gift was back and he was determined to use it. Some of William Wright's songs were published, including "The Atlanta Waltz" and "Nymphs of the Woods." Ever the omnivore, William even studied Sanskrit, seeking to grasp the mystical truths of the East in their original language. Learning the mantras and hymns of the Vedic texts, he attempted to replicate sounds that helped man apprehend the aspects of divinity present in the cosmos and the psyche.

William worked hard, but Frank despaired at the sight of his father spending hour after hour scribing notes on staves, the ink smearing his hands, face, even his teeth. Though Frank believed in his mystically inclined father's talent, William's music never brought in enough money to keep up with his mother's spending.

The Wright family found themselves living in genteel poverty, one summer making do on huckleberries, bread, and milk. Anna persuaded her brother James to bring a cow forty miles from his farm near Spring Green. The Lloyd Jones family also sent chickens, barrels of apples, and honeycombs. As desperate as they were, Anna used her grocery money to buy new maple flooring and folding chairs upholstered in Brussels carpet. William was furious. And Anna was humiliated when her husband forced her to take her small children to live on her father's farm for an entire summer, to ensure that they would be provided for.

For William it must have been emasculating to have to depend on the generosity of his wife's brothers. For Frank it must have been fearful indeed. For, while he was his mother's darling, he was more like his father: short, charming, aesthetically inclined, drawn to and capable of multiple forms of expression.

Despite these similarities, young Frank found himself unable to identify with the very man whose failings his mother expected him to redeem.

TRAPPED IN A house divided, Frank retreated into a world of his own. "SANCTUM SANCTORUM. KEEP OUT," read the sign on his attic bedroom door. The room was littered with "things," he remembered, with which he would "'fix up effects' in the childlike desire to make 'pictures' of everything—including himself." In this waking dream space, he manipulated the dry heads of flowers, colored blocks, and even the structure of the toccata and the symphony, playing off their hidden forms. It was a refuge where a vulnerable boy could live in the spaces of his beautiful compositions. Wright's capacity to manipulate these spaces in his imagination would be the source of his fabled ability to conjure a three-dimensional structure before ever putting pencil to paper—an approach he would later urge on his apprentices, though it would prove impossible for many of them to follow.

Wright also read voraciously. Along with Hugo's *Hunchback of Notre Dame*, he devoured *A Thousand and One Nights*—and fancied himself a young Aladdin.

BUT A SANCTUM sanctorum was hard to preserve in the little house. As Frank lay in his attic bed at night, he could hear his father playing Beethoven and Bach, and practicing the recitations he still gave at church. But what would haunt him forever was the sound of William Wright reciting Edgar Allan Poe's "The Raven" as he paced around the room. These eavesdropped moments—particularly this sensuous dirge by his father, who likely loved his first wife more than he ever would Frank's mother—pained him. Frank saw that his father's talents were unappreciated by his mother and unrewarded by the world. The fact that his mother had chosen Frank to outstrip his hapless artistic father—with whom the boy sympathized, but whom he could never quite love—must have been unbearable. All this, Frank would confess, "would fill a tender boyish heart with sadness until a head would bury itself in the pillow to shut it out." In adulthood he camouflaged his sadness, he later told a cousin, by drawing everyone into his beautiful visions, his heroic postures, his irreverent, outlandish claims, even his eccentric dress.

WHEN FRANK WAS sixteen, William crossed a line. One day, in the stable of their Madison home, William was about to thrash him for "some disobedience." But several summers on his uncle's farm had muscled Frank up, and the boy pinned his father on the stable floor, which was saturated with cow urine and horse manure. Frank refused to let his father up until he promised to leave him alone. Frank returned to the house "white, shamed, and shaken," he recalled. " 'Father ought to realize," he told his mother, that he "had grown too big for that sort of thing."

Anna responded by banishing William from her bed, to sleep alone in the coldest room in the house. She also began to attack him physically. Frank's older half-siblings pleaded with their father to leave Anna. And, at long last, he did.

In 1884, William Wright filed for divorce, and the request was granted a short time later. Yet William soon had second thoughts. "I will stay if you ask me," he told Anna, standing outside the door, his violin under his arm.

"I do not ask you to," she replied. He left.

Months later, William happened on his shabbily dressed daughter Maginel on her way home from school. He took her to buy a pair of shoes with copper toes and a straw hat. When Anna—who by now was approaching penury—found out, she stuffed the articles into the stove and let them burn in its purifying fire.

Anna told Frank and his sisters that she didn't really want the divorce, but had agreed to it for their sake. Frank knew she had him in mind. He had already entered manhood by physically defeating his father, an action backed up by his mother's sexual banishment of her husband. That confrontation, Wright believed, precipitated his parents' divorce.

Around this time, Frank replaced his middle name, Lincoln—his father's choice—with Lloyd, a nod to his mother's clan. The fault line had been drawn.

Adding to the understandable trauma of his father's leaving was the shame of divorce—an extraordinary recourse in the days of Wright's childhood. In those times a woman without means would endure enormous abuse just to be assured of survival. William did not provide much, but he did provide. There is no mention of material want in the divorce proceedings. In the late nineteenth century, divorces—relatively rare in themselves—were typically filed by wives, not husbands.

Wright's feelings of guilt and anxiety over his parents' divorce never left him. "Memories," he wrote, "would haunt the youth as they haunt the man." They also haunted his architecture. It was no wonder that Wright devoted his career to designing the architectural casing for the perfect American home—undertaking it as a religious calling, equal parts duty and obsession. He was seeking to rebuild what he never had—and to replace a father for whose failure he held himself partially responsible.

*   *   *

WHEN HE LEFT the family, William Wright took nothing but his clothes, his violins, and a mahogany bookcase, leaving most of his books behind. Anna sold many of them to help pay for a piano for Frank and his sister Jane. But Frank must have made sure she didn't sell the treasure in the lot—his father's favorite volume, a calf-leather bound edition of *Plutarch's Lives.* The book's most heavily thumbed section, he later wrote, was the story of Alcibiades. He would return to this text throughout his life, not only forty years later, when he wrote his autobiography, but also at the end of his life, when he composed his last book.

Wright identified with Alcibiades. While Plutarch's volume is filled with stories of Greek and Roman heroes, scoundrels and kings, Frank was captivated by the story of this Athenian orphan boy who lisped charmingly and who became a warrior, a great general, and eventually a tyrant. Alcibiades was eloquent and cunning, arrogant, impulsive. He was also extraordinarily good-looking, an amorous object for scores of well-born Greek men, each of whom sought to flatter him with "unmanly fondness." For the free men of classical Greece, after all, true love was something that occurred between adult men and adolescent youths, preferably lean and muscled young men whose hair had not yet sprouted on their chins and armpits.

Alcibiades was a scandal, not only in the Victorian America of Wright's time, but also in Alcibiades's ancient Greece. An Athenian boy destined to become a citizen was not to give himself to anyone too quickly, nor to take pleasure in an erotic union with his adult suitor. Young Alcibiades, however, took pleasure in being sought, and in pleasuring the men who sought him. Fortunately he had ignited the ardor of the ultimate mentor, the great philosopher Socrates, who sought "to interpose, and preserve so hopeful a plant from perishing in the flower, before its fruit came to perfection." In battle Socrates threw himself in front of his young wounded lover to save him from death or capture. Nonetheless Alcibiades repeatedly deserted his mentor to pursue all the carnal delights, making Socrates intensely jealous.

Frank read of how Alcibiades loved to have his beauty admired. According to the story, he perfumed his body and wore "long purple robes like a woman, which dragged after him as he went through the market-place." And Frank could relate: At the time he himself was a long-haired dandy who sported skintight pants, "toothpick" shoes, and a mink collar he had his mother sew onto his overcoat. "An incorrigible sentimentalist," Wright later observed in self-deprecation. Yet the Alcibiades he admired was also a figure of manhood, a brave warrior and brilliant military strategist who galvanized his soldiers. This was just the kind of divided soul Wright felt himself to be.

* * *

NOT LONG AFTER William walked out, Anna got Frank a job in Madison working for the University of Wisconsin's dean of engineering, a practicing civil engineer. Frank, who had a poor record in high school, was admitted to the university's engineering school on a trial basis as a "special student." He certainly thought himself special. Just before he enrolled at Wisconsin, with no architectural education or experience whatsoever, he had proposed himself as architect for a small chapel his mother's family intended to build in their valley. (Wright was rebuffed; instead they hired Joseph Lyman Silsbee, an eclectic Chicago designer now working primarily in the Shingle Style.)

While the University of Wisconsin had no architecture school, the civil engineering coursework included structural engineering, a component of architectural training. Beauty, however, is of little concern to the engineer, and Wright, the budding aesthete, found the assigned academic texts a waste of time. Instead, he read widely and voraciously. His mother introduced him to Goethe's *Wilhelm Meister's Apprenticeship,* which they read together. In the novel the young Wilhelm Meister falls in love with an aspiring actress, rejecting his father's "base occupation" as a merchant businessman and leaving home to become an actor and playwright—indeed, a champion of a new national German theater.

The prospect of becoming a kind of Midwestern Wilhelm Meister, daring to seize destiny by the throat, both thrilled and frustrated the bored engineering student. The handsome Goethe offered Wright not only a heroic model of action, but a philosophy for his art and artistry. Goethe, a champion of the Gothic, saw a parallel between the unfolding of the human individual and the development of all living forms, plants in particular. In his vision, a true artist, like a flower, was born to his art.

For those who could appreciate its ineffable force, Goethe proclaimed, nature's beauty provided a sublime aesthetic experience, sensual yet divine. Frank was enthralled by the writer's words, which confirmed the very feelings of communion with nature that had transfixed him from childhood. Aligning oneself with the delicate powers of the natural world—with the structure, beauty, and life force of flowers and plants—could be a path *toward* manly heroism, not away from it. Throughout his career, Wright would train hundreds of male apprentices to love flowers and plants. Learning flower arranging, he instructed them, was an integral part of architectural training.

Wright may have been excited by his outside reading, but nothing he encountered in his university studies captured his attention. During his second term, his efforts in descriptive geometry and drawing—subjects that tested the skills required of an architect—were rewarded with a grade of "average." The fault was not his, he felt; the university had failed him. "Education," he declared, with its "oppressive" rules, was "a vague sort of emotional distress, a sickening sense of fear."

Wright's hero, Goethe, had also despised rote learning and copybook instruction. Goethe was an exemplar of a new kind of romantic hero that emerged in the eighteenth and nineteenth centuries—neither warrior nor king, and still less inventor or entrepreneur, but the new modern aristocrat, the artistic genius destined to design things no one had ever even imagined. The genius derived his artistry not from training, but from birth—and from his struggle to realize and act on his vision. His art was a kind of beautiful madness. The practice of one's artistry, Goethe repeatedly proclaimed, was the real test of one's potential.

After viewing a cast of Goethe's hands on display at the Wisconsin campus, Wright was pleased that his own looked so similar. After a while, however, merely reading Goethe began to frustrate him, "for action, again action and more action was his urge."

FINALLY THE ASPIRING architect could wait no longer. After only two semesters, the eighteen-year-old quit the university. Pawning his father's watch, his mink collar, and some of his father's remaining books (including Gibbon's *Rome* and Plutarch's *Lives*), Wright boarded the train to Chicago.

In 1887, the wind-chilled slaughterhouse city was still rebuilding after the great fire. In the process, Chicago was also just starting to invent the towered skyline of the combine and the corporation. Architecture firms were booming. Here, at last, Frank hoped he would be able to learn architecture by doing it.

He arrived in the city one drizzly spring evening, disembarking at the city's arc-lit Wells Street Station. He had never seen electric lights before. Out on the street, his "supersensitive eyes" were assaulted by more arc-lamps and glaring signs. "I wondered," he recalled, "where Chicago was—if it was near."

In the morning, leafing through the city directory looking for architecture firms, he spied the name Silsbee—the man chosen over him to design the Lloyd Jones chapel. "But I wasn't going there," he recalled. Not wanting to be hired based on family connections, he claimed, he spent the next few days dropping in on architects, misrepresenting himself as two semesters shy of an engineering degree. He was rejected at each office.

On his fourth day, embarrassed but desperate, the teenager finally appeared at Silsbee's office—and was offered a job. The firm had just finished a new church in Chicago for Frank's uncle, Jenkin Lloyd Jones. But that, Wright would have us believe, played no part. "Liked the atmosphere of the office best," he recalled, as if deciding among multiple offers.

With this new position, Wright was finally able to send his mother some money. Anna was so destitute, she wrote him, that she was contemplating suicide. "I have been very sad of late," she added, bemoaning the state of her garden and how expensive everything was becoming. "I am afraid that I cannot pay my debts by fall. . . . What can I do about your debt here?"

AT SILSBEE'S OFFICE, Wright was particularly impressed with one colleague, a "fine looking cultured fellow with a fine pompadour and beard." Cecil Corwin, who was humming the *Messiah*, paused to ask Frank if he sang. "His sleeves were rolled above the elbow," Wright recalled. "His arms were thickly covered with coarse hair, but I noticed how he daintily crooked his little finger as he lifted his pencil. He had a gentleness and refinement."

Wright inquired nervously if he could enter Corwin's office. "I believe we could get along," Corwin answered, looking Wright over. The two became inseparable, and soon they were spending days and nights together. Frank received many invitations from other people; he turned them all down. "I preferred Cecil's company."

Wright (left) with Cecil Corwin

Even though Cecil was extraordinarily handsome, he knew no girls. And neither did Frank. Writing about Cecil more than thirty years later, Wright lovingly recalled being captivated by his older friend. When Frank was hungry, he wrote, nothing ever tasted so good as the corned beef hash to which Cecil introduced him. He never enjoyed a concert as much as those he attended with Cecil. The two danced together "in a friendly tilt" when Frank returned to Silsbee's office after briefly working in another. When they appeared in his autobiography, just as Wright was establishing the Taliesin Fellowship, these passages caught more than one potential apprentice's eye.

JOSEPH LYMAN SILSBEE was an adroit copier of styles, from Gothic Revival to the more modern Shingle Style. But it bothered Wright that Silsbee was just imitating a "style." It wasn't long before Wright heard of somebody in Chicago who was designing something absolutely original. Louis Sullivan, together with his engineer partner, Dankmar Adler, was pioneering what would become the skyscraper, with its steel skeleton and clean-cut windows. This new phenomenon would convince Wright that Hugo's predicted revival of architecture had begun. When a fellow Silsbee draftsman told him that Sullivan was hiring, Wright recalled, "[m]y heart jumped." The only thing that seemed to concern him was leaving Cecil behind, but Corwin, who had previously worked with Sullivan, urged him on.

Sullivan was also drawn to the Gothic, not the Greek and Roman imitations that had begun sprouting up in every American city. Rather than mimic Gothic tropes, however, Sullivan was trying to use its underlying principles to make something radically new. And Sullivan also followed the theories of the

great English critic John Ruskin, believing that what elevated a building to the status of architecture—rather than a utilitarian structure like a "wasp nest, a rat hole, or a railway station"—was the addition of something "useless": ornamentation.

Louis Sullivan was the undisputed American master of ornamentation. The efflorescent tendrils and blooms that snaked their way along his arches and capped his capitals were delicate, yet stunningly powerful. When Wright arrived in Chicago, Sullivan was designing one of

Louis Sullivan

his extraordinarily ornamented projects, the Auditorium Building. Combining an office tower with what would then be America's largest theater, the Auditorium's interior boasted ornamentation that was likely derived from Eugène-Emmanuel Viollet-le-Duc's drawings for the nineteenth century restoration of Gothic buildings—most prominently Notre Dame de Paris, Wright's "Ideal" since childhood.

If Frank was excited about the chance of working for Sullivan, his mother was adamant that he stay just where he was—with Silsbee. "Father used to tell me always," she wrote him, "stick to the same place if you can, even for less money—for that shows character, and there is much in it, Frank. . . . I cannot bear the thought of your changing." Wright's mother was terrified that her son would shame her in the eyes of her brothers. "Don't let our enemy get the victory by seeing you go bad."

But her son wasn't listening. Instead he accepted an invitation from Sullivan to show him his work, making drawings of ornamental details, some of them Sullivan-like and others based on Gothic motifs. Frank, who was little more than a decade younger than the thirty-two-year-old Sullivan, felt rather unnerved when the architect first turned his big brown eyes on him, seeming to grasp even his "most secret thoughts."

Sullivan, a short, bearded man who dressed impeccably, looked at Wright's samples; then, without a word, he removed the cover sheet from over his own work and resumed drawing. Wright "gasped with delight." Watching the touch of Sullivan's pencil, the languid lines coursing through his ornamental detailing, seemed to Frank like that of the "passion vine." The sight so entranced the young apprentice that he was ashamed by his own pleasure.

"You've got the right kind of touch; you'll do," Sullivan finally said. Wright was hired to draw foliage for the Auditorium's interior.

Wright's mother was not pleased. "Oh, my boy, stop where you are now. I thought you were doing well. You are too much in a hurry. Why do you ignore all my advice. I told you not to leave Silsbee until you get more experience. Of course, my boy, you have not yet the experience. You are not yet twenty."

AS A STUDENT, Wright had been a failure; as an apprentice, he was a stupendous success. A quick study, he soon became Sullivan's closest assistant, with a private office right next to the master's. And there was much for him to learn—about both architecture and the world at large. Dankmar Adler, Sullivan's engineer partner, was a Jew—something Wright had seldom, if ever, encountered in his sheltered life. So were many of Frank's fellow draftsmen, as well as many of Sullivan's clients.

As an inexperienced apprentice who rose dramatically in the firm, Wright was resented by some of the others. Anxious about defending himself, he secretly began taking boxing lessons—which came in handy when one of his colleagues, a man named Ottenheimer whom Wright described as "a heavy-bodied, short-legged, pompadoured, conceited, red-faced Jew, wearing gold glasses," began goading him. Wright beat Ottenheimer to a pulp; nobody bothered him after that.

In after-hours sessions, Sullivan revealed to his young assistant the philosophy underpinning his architecture. Much of it, a variant of Ruskin's organicism, would have already been familiar. Wright had read the theorist's *The Seven Lamps of Architecture* years before with his mother. Ruskin, like Goethe, believed that God's law could be discerned in nature. Biological organisms—birds, trees, flowers—weren't "designed" to be pretty, Sullivan explained. Their forms evolved in response to their environment, in whatever way was necessary to best perform specific functions. Buildings, he told Wright, should be designed the same way. The greatness of Gothic architecture, for example, came from the fact that it was designed from nature's template. This principle gave rise to Sullivan's famous dictum: "Form follows function."

Wright was soon calling Sullivan his *lieber meister*, or "beloved master." Sullivan instructed him about not only architecture, but also art, poetry, philosophy, and music. The chubby-cheeked, bearded architect sang from Wagner's operas while he sat with Wright at the drawing boards, conjuring up the scenes as they worked. Sullivan, whose own photographs of roses inspired his ornamental designs, also taught Wright how to take pictures. It could not have escaped the young man's notice that Sullivan was as multitalented as Wright's father, with one difference: He was a success.

In private moments, Sullivan also bragged to his young apprentice about his sexual gymnastics. Although he had many casual liaisons with women, however, he loved none. Rather, the evidence suggests that Sullivan was animated by homosexual desire. As a younger man, he had been a member of the Lotus Club, a group of intellectual men who loved flowers and developed their bodies by rowing, body-building, and racing. The *Lotus Club Notebook* was largely composed of drawings of naked men wrestling and swimming. Sullivan himself sketched male bodies in loving detail; his drawings of women, in contrast, were few and unflattering.

In the same year Sullivan hired Wright, the architect also wrote an adoring letter to the poet Walt Whitman, whose poetry and life bespoke a new model of manly, homosexual love. In *Leaves of Grass* and elsewhere, Whitman conjured not the effeminate "fairy," but the man whose love for other men was manly, an eroticized intimacy between comrades that he saw as democracy's emotional core. "I, too," Sullivan penned Whitman, " 'have pried through the strata, analyzed to a hair,' reaching for the basis of a virile and indigenous art."

Frank Lloyd Wright had found his Socrates. Though Sullivan's sensuousness made him uneasy, Wright's relationship with him was his template for what apprenticeship could mean: a relationship with an older man that went far beyond the technical aspects of architecture, embracing all the arts and perhaps more, and energized by passionate identification.

VICTOR HUGO NOT only provided the plot line for Wright's architectural career, but his characters also played a role in finding young Wright his first love. It all started when the Victor Hugo Club at All Souls Church, his uncle's parish, decided to stage a *Les Miserables*–themed costume party. Frank dressed up as Enjolras, the novel's tall, bourgeois young leader of a secret revolutionary student club in Paris. The character of Enjolras, Wright read, is not "aware there was on earth a thing called woman. He had but one passion—the right." When Enjolras is captured, he offers his breast to the guardsmen. The guardsmen hesitate; one lowers his gun. "It seems to me that I am about to shoot a flower," he says.

With Cecil Corwin's help, Wright threw himself into the role, donning tight white trousers and a scarlet military jacket with gold epaulettes, a sword with a leather scabbard at his side. He begged Cecil to join him at the church, but Cecil declined. At the party, it was the girls who approached Frank and asked him to dance. And Frank had trouble controlling his sword. "[T]he infernal slab-sided sword was slung so low that if I took my hands off it, it got between my legs. . . . I tried a dozen schemes to control it for I wouldn't spoil the fine figure I was making by taking it off! I was going to hang on to that swinging, dangling, clanking thing if I mowed the legs off the whole 'Les Miserables' tribe and broke up the party."

That night, Frank literally bumped into Catherine Tobin by accident; they would spend the rest of the evening together. Thus, to his mother's dismay, began a two-year courtship with the Victorian beauty, a woman Wright described as having "a frank, handsome countenance in no way common."

In 1889, when the couple decided to marry, Cecil Corwin was crestfallen. He argued with Frank about it. "She's awfully fond of me, Cecil," Wright reassured his friend. "Well," Cecil replied, "so am I." He wasn't the only one disturbed by the marriage: Anna Wright fainted at the wedding.

Catherine became pregnant immediately, and Wright convinced Sullivan to offer him a five-year contract with the firm. He also persuaded his employer to lend him money against the contract, and to hold a mortgage on the new house Wright had designed and constructed for himself and his family in the Chicago suburb of Oak Park. In the living room, he incorporated flowery ornamental pieces derived from Sullivan's Auditorium designs.

On March 31, 1890, precisely nine months after the wedding and shortly after moving into their new home, Catherine gave birth to a son, Frank Lloyd Wright Jr. Wright's mother moved in next door.

It was also a productive year at the office. Frank was in the office when Sullivan sketched the Wainwright Building, the first true skyscraper, in a matter of minutes. Its façade was inspired by Reims, another of the great French Gothic cathedrals.

Within the next few years, Wright is said to have become the highest-paid draftsman in Chicago. But in 1893, near the end of his contract, Sullivan fired him. Always in need of money, Wright had been taking freelance commissions on the side. Sullivan claimed that this violated the terms of their agreement. "I was scared to death," Wright would later confide to his apprentices about the rupture. "I thought to myself—this is awful—how can I do it."

Wright's departure wasn't the only change for Sullivan that year. For some time the architect had been moving in a radically more florid, ornamental direction. The Golden Doorway he designed for the Transportation Building at the 1893 World's Columbian Exposition in Chicago—its interior inspired by Notre Dame—sported a multicolored façade in reds and golds, its arches ornamented with Islamic motifs, a wild contrast to the bleached, neoclassical forms of the "White City" exposition. The spectacle initiated Sullivan's fall from public favor. At a time when the stern white columns of Beaux Arts architecture seemed to capture the nation's burgeoning power, Sullivan's architecture suddenly appeared womanly, its façade crowded with intricate flowers, right there for everybody to see.

WRIGHT HAD HAD help in his moonlighting from Cecil Corwin, and now he and Cecil opened an office together—in Sullivan's Schiller Building, no less. But Corwin soon left, discouraged that Frank had so little time for him and unable to compete with his young friend's astounding creativity. Indeed, Corwin left architecture altogether. "You *are* the thing that you do," he told Wright. "I'm not and I never will be." Wright pleaded with him to stay, but to no avail. When Corwin left, Wright was miserable. "That place . . . soon seemed nothing at all without him," Wright later said. The two men would never see each other again.

Wright was now on his own—free to begin his quest to transform the lowly American residence into a cathedral. Opening his own practice in Chicago, he began searching for clients who needed houses.

*   *   *

"TO DENY THAT men of genius yet to come may be the peers of the men of genius of the past," Frank Lloyd Wright was telling an audience at Northwestern University, "would be to deny the ever-working power of God." In 1896, three years after going out on his own, the twenty-nine-year-old architect was standing before the University Guild of Evanston, giving one of his first public lectures.

Having left the drawing board—"to play the role of preacher," as he put it—Wright seized the moment and declared himself the genius architecture needed if it were ever to recapture its lost glory. Throughout his long career he would remind his audiences of the powerful impact *Notre Dame de Paris* had on him. But only on this occasion, his first lecture, did he explain so forthrightly just how he intended to overcome architecture's death sentence.

"[I]f great architecture in the old sense no longer exists," he announced, "in domestic architecture today we have finer possibilities and a measure of salvation." The architect should translate the cathedral's beauty "to the homes of the people," he instructed, transforming average homes into "sermons of stone."

Hugo had predicted that if architecture were to somehow revive, it would have to "bow to the sway of literature." Wright took this as a practical injunction; he would make architecture into a book, designing according to his reading of the souls of its inhabitants. The homes of the future "will be biographies and poems," he declared, "appealing to the center of the human soul. . . ." There should be as many types of houses as there are types of people.

The Northwestern speech also marked Wright's first public use of the term "organic" in describing architecture. Organic architecture, he said, offered Americans a new beauty through which they would be redeemed. "There is not, nor ever was," he later preached to the Architecture League of Chicago, "room in right living for the ugly. Ugliness in anything is the incarnation of sin, and sin is death—ugliness is death."

It was a critical moment in Frank Lloyd Wright's ascendance from architect to public visionary. For the rest of his life, Wright would variously cast himself as preacher, prophet, sometimes even messiah, striding forth to save the American home from the sin of ugliness. But to fulfill this mission, he needed disciples.

IN 1898, TWO years after presenting himself as the genius of Hugo's prophecy, Wright built an architecture studio alongside his Oak Park house. A bas relief image on the columns forming the entry says it all: a floor plan of an ancient cathedral connected by a short corridor to an octagonal baptistery. The plan embossed on the columns bears a remarkable resemblance to the studio beyond.

The studio's portico is a miniature version of the entry to the building carved on the columns, a design familiar to anyone who has visited Europe's great cathedrals. Rather than walk straight into the building, the doors are likewise located to the sides. A short hallway to the left of the studio leads to a drafting room flooded with sunlight from its high clerestory windows, as in the nave of a cathedral. Just beneath the windows, an octagonal mezzanine hovers over the wood drafting tables below. Wright suspended it on heavy chains, an old trick of the Gothic builders. Even more remarkable is the octagonal room found at the end of a short hallway to the right of the studio, clearly modeled after a baptistery, the place of initiation into Christianity. Wright used this space, among other things, to deliver the gospel of organic architecture to his draftsmen.

Such cathedral elements, including cruciform floor plans and clerestory windows, soon began to find their way into the houses he designed for his clients. Wright placed living rooms—along with their high "cathedral ceilings," as we now call them—on the second floor. He even treated the furniture for his houses as though he were designing for a church, fixed in place like old wooden pews, "built-in, in complete harmony, nothing to arrange, nothing to disturb"—and almost invariably uncomfortable.

In the medieval world—as another of Wright's inspirations, the great scholar of the Gothic Viollet-le-Duc, had written—clerics functioned as architects. If the cleric could become an architect, Wright would have reasoned, the architect must become a cleric for architecture to be restored.

WRIGHT CALLED HIS revolutionary new designs "Prairie houses," a term he applied to most of the dwellings he worked on for the next two decades. While Wright's Prairie house designs varied widely, all were based on common principles he folded into his evolving theory of "organic architecture." The first principle is the primacy of the interior. In contrast to Renaissance buildings, which are said to draw the eye to their surfaces (often covered with frescoes), the Gothic was designed from the inside out, giving rise to massive volumes of interior space flooded by exterior natural light through enlarged windows. This awesome inner space is the defining substance of the architecture, a site of transcendence, an intimation of the heavenly city here on earth. Architects, Wright believed, should compose with space, not surface and mass.

The primacy of the interior is related to a second principle: "honesty" of structural expression. The Gothic cathedral's vaulted roofs and exterior flying buttresses allowed for a thinning of the walls, a dramatic increase in window size, and extraordinary flexibility in terms of interior composition. The ribbed vaulting of the cathedral gathered the vertical weight and horizontal thrust of the roof into the walls and columns inside and, most dramatically, into the unique flying buttresses. The flow of forces was right there for the eye to see, making a finished building into a diagram of how the structure resists gravity. Visible form and structure are one.

The Gothic inspired Wright's architecture in another way. These cathedrals, with their vast interior spaces, appeared to do the impossible. How could stones piled upon stones rise to such heights? The windows seemed so large, the walls incredibly delicate. The architecture evoked the miraculous. Like his Wisconsin contemporary Harry Houdini, Wright would make defying the laws of gravity and physics a lifetime quest.

FRANK AND CATHERINE'S household grew steadily. Now in her late thirties, Catherine was a lovely woman with auburn hair, a sensible yet spirited wife, a confirmed teetotaler, a regular churchgoer, and a devoted mother. Literate and progressive, she was also active in Oak Park's literary and civic clubs, occasionally giving public talks on theater and poetry. Yet Catherine Wright kept her ventures well within the boundaries of compliant domesticity, appearing in public only when her husband approved. Frank even designed the dresses she wore.

Wright was a reckless spender, and Catherine struggled to keep the family afloat. It was her level-headed money management that enabled the Wrights to enjoy a respectable bourgeois life. Unlike his wife, Wright rarely appeared in church. He dressed more as a gentleman rogue, à la Oscar Wilde, than as a bourgeois architect. And, as Wright's reputation grew, his wife seemed insufficient to reflect his increasing light. Her quiescence steadily eroded his interest in her.

Catherine Wright

* * *

IN DECEMBER 1900, Wright had a very special visitor. Charles Ashbee, an English architect-designer, had established a kind of fellowship, a working community of artisans under his direction. Ashbee made beautiful things for the market, and taught young apprentices to do the same. This man and his enterprise would shape Wright's vision of what a community of apprentices might become, just as Wright's own ideas also influenced his British colleague.

A wiry man with a captivating smile, Ashbee was a leader of the English Arts and Crafts movement, whose designs, community, and published writings were well-known in Wright's Chicago network. Ashbee had founded the Guild of Handicraft in 1888 in London's East End as a cooperative workshop into which he sought to integrate a school where boys were taught crafts. By providing a space where craftsmen could work together to fashion beautiful things of their own design, he was attempting to save art from the deadening uniformity of the machine, and in the process to create a democratic workplace. The Guild produced singular pieces of furniture, jewelry, glassware, and books that were sold in shops, and it also designed and produced the interior decoration for the buildings Ashbee designed.

Ashbee's work soon became known around the world. The Guild of Handicraft inspired the formation of the Wiener Werkstätte in Vienna in 1902. And years later it would prove a formative influence on Wright's own community of apprentices, the Taliesin Fellowship.

Ashbee and Wright were a matched set, their bond instantaneous. Estranged from their fathers, the polymath sons of doting mothers, both men made a religion of beauty and wanted to make it a political program as well. Both revered the Gothic and had first apprenticed to architects experienced in that style. Both saw themselves as heirs to John Ruskin and William Morris, founders of the Arts and Crafts movement, who idealized the medieval craftsman and condemned the Renaissance for creating a false divide between the high and decorative arts. Both were enamored of Walt Whitman, his espousal of a democratic beauty located in the solidarity of men.

Charles Ashbee, in a photograph taken by Wright.

Both were handsome and dressed with flair, supreme aesthetes wrestling with the leveling powers of the capitalist machine.

There was one major difference: Though married to a woman himself, Ashbee was an open advocate of what he considered the superiority of homosexuality, or "comradeship," as he called it. Indeed, he founded the Guild of Handicraft in the belief that utopian socialism and this "more genuine" love between men depended on each other. Ashbee looked to manly love for the energies that would enable his apprentices to break down class barriers, to build a democratic community of comrades. "It is not new in itself," he wrote, "this, the feeling that drew Jesus to John, or Shakespeare to the youth of the sonnets, or that inspired the friendships of Greece, has been with us before, and in the new citizenship we shall need it again. The Whitmanic love of comrades is its modern expression; Democracy—as socially, not politically conceived—its basis."

There had been an immediate mutual attraction between Ashbee and Wright. "The burning activity of Chicago kindles such a brotherhood with a flame peculiarly its own," the Englishman wrote in his private journal after Wright toured him around Chicago. These feelings were reciprocated. When Wright heard that Ashbee would be back, he wrote him, "I know of no one whose coming to Chicago would be a greater event to my little world."

Indeed, on the boat sailing back to England following this last trip, Charles and Janet Ashbee decided to move their Guild in its entirety from the East End of London to the countryside. It was probably Wright who inspired them to move out of the city. Although craft utopianism had always had a rural disposition, Wright's own persuasions would have been fresh in their minds. Wright had railed to the Ashbees against the city, no doubt repeating the arguments of his recent lecture on the education of an architect. Young architects, he urged, could not go into the world penniless and be expected to produce new forms. To steel young men for creative battle, one had to assure their board and lodging for life. Only in the countryside, where land came cheap and the community could grow its own food, would that be possible.

The countryside was also the only place where young men could truly be intimate with nature, the mother teacher. Only by working under "a catholic-minded, nature-wise loving Master," Wright proclaimed, could creators be created. A young architect "should be brought into contact with Nature by prophet and seer until abiding sympathy with her is his."

In 1902, the Ashbees were finally able to move the assorted Cockney cabinetmakers, silversmiths, printers, blacksmiths, and their families from London to an abandoned silk factory in the countryside village of Chipping Campden. The hundred-and-fifty guildsmen and their families who eventually gathered there, Ashbee thought, should be able to produce much of their own food on their own small holdings. In the evening hours, they would put on their own plays and musicals for the public. Ashbee put his wife in charge of the day-to-day household operations.

Here at their rural colony, Ashbee found himself living among mostly men, some young and single, others with wives and children. During the summers, he would take groups of these guildsmen boating on nearby rivers, the Wye, the Thames, or the Severn; one sometimes rowed naked, a wreath of flowers in his hair. Sometimes Ashbee would go alone with one of his favorites, swimming, reading Plato. Janet Ashbee became a well-loved "house-mother" at the Guild, not interfering, as she put it, with his powers of "seeing and knowing the human boy . . . of loving him, and begetting love in return." She did not expect to rouse her husband's sexual interest. "It is like asking a horse to be a stag," she wrote in her journal.

WRIGHT, HOWEVER, WAS quite the stag.

Throughout the first decade of the twentieth century, his practice burgeoned. He designed a slew of Prairie houses, experimenting with new forms. In 1903, he designed the Larkin Building, a completely new kind of office complex. Two years later he revolutionized architecture with his Unity Temple in Oak Park, a landmark design based on a Japanese model and boasting the first use of raw concrete by a major architect. He was a celebrated American form-giver, with a future that should have been as promising at his past.

And then, in September 1909, the forty-two-year-old architect abandoned it all—his successful practice in suburban Chicago; his wife, Catherine, and their children; and his status as a gentleman who lectured women's clubs on the future of house design.

As Wright's five-year-old son, Robert, held his mother's hand tight, unable to understand why she was crying, his father smiled, waved, and drove off from his Oak Park home to meet his lover in New York.

Wright had met Mamah Cheney quite by chance. In 1903, the architect had been examining Japanese prints with a friend in a Chicago gallery when he spied an attractive, dark-haired woman peering in through the window. Without a word, he went outside and began talking to her. He left his friend inside, and the two walked off together. At Wright's urging, Cheney soon persuaded her husband, a balding electrical engineer, to hire him to design a house in Oak Park for the Cheneys and their infant child.

Wright's brick Cheney house, with its low ceilings and open spaces, its many windows sheltered by a deeply eaved hip roof, was designed to guard a family's intimacy. His goal was to make the middle-class house into a handsome space for a vibrant, yet informal, domesticity. In this case, however, the architect ultimately destroyed the family his architecture was intended to protect. As his cousin Richard Lloyd Jones wrote him, he was a "house builder and a home wrecker."

UNLIKE THE MORE quiescent Catherine, Mamah Cheney, two years Wright's junior, was an independent-minded intellectual with literary ambitions. A strong-willed, handsome woman with a kind of severe grace, Cheney was a postgraduate student at the University of Chicago who knew German, French, and Italian, as well as some Latin and Greek. She had translated Goethe from the German. Cheney had little patience for the conventional rites of female society. She was not particularly invested in motherhood, either: She delegated her maternal duties to a governess, and sent her children to a boarding school.

Cheney became a follower of Ellen Key, an influential Swedish feminist. She was taken by Key's progressive theories of childhood, her notion that schools destroyed children's creativity and individuality. And she was attracted by Key's belief that freely given love was the highest form of expression between equal men and women. Love, Key argued, was not property; marriage that was not mutual should not be sustained.

At first the Cheneys and the Wrights were friends. The house Wright designed for them was just blocks away from his own. The Cheneys and the Wrights went to concerts and parties together. Mamah and Catherine were both members of Oak Park's Nineteenth Century Club, a progressive women's club whose membership included Ernest Hemingway's mother, and the two became friends. In 1907, Mamah and Catherine even delivered a lecture together on Goethe's life and poetry at the Scoville Institute, Oak Park's first library.

Mamah Cheney

Yet it was also in 1907 that Mamah and Frank began their affair, and soon it became a scandal in the community. The two drove the suburban streets together in Wright's bright yellow Stoddard Dayton convertible roadster, and made out on the couch in the library he had designed for his paramour's family.

WRIGHT'S AFFAIR WITH Cheney was well under way when Charles and Janet Ashbee came to spend Christmas with the Wrights in Oak Park in 1908. Ashbee had recently been forced to liquidate the Guild as a corporate entity, though many of the workshops were still operating independently in their countryside retreat. Ashbee's Guild had produced too many individual works of art, rather than more standard items that could be sold to the trade in greater volume. Retail stores had undercut sales of its craft products, and in the down times, the men could find little alternative work in the sparsely populated countryside.

Janet Ashbee knew what it was like to be married to a man who looked elsewhere for his pleasures. She was just then recovering from a nervous breakdown from her husband's lack of sexual interest and her unwillingness to take another man. Janet, who had little fondness for either Wright or his architecture, identified with Catherine's pains. "I feel in the background somewhere difficult places gone through," Janet wrote in her diary. "[W]hen she laughs, you forget the tragic lines about her mouth. But people do not kiss one in that way unless they are lonely in the midst of plenty."

Ashbee and Wright, as usual, got on famously. Wright took him to visit Louis Sullivan, who read to him from his Whitmanesque prose epic, *Democracy—A Man Search*. The two men undoubtedly understood each other as Ashbee's ideas on "comradeship" were themselves inspired by Whitman. Before the Ashbees took their leave, Charles invited Frank to Sicily to see the villa he was building at Taormina and then return with him to Chipping Campden. It was there in Sicily where Ashbee was building a house for Colonel Shaw-Hellier and the colonel's young Sicilian lovers. "No temptation to 'desert'," Wright replied, "was ever so difficult to resist. . . ."

JANET ASHBEE UNDERSTOOD what was coming. Nine months after the Ashbees' visit, in September 1909, Wright announced his decision to abandon his home for Mamah Cheney. His eldest son, Lloyd, a nineteen-year-old who towered over him, socked his father so hard he knocked him to the floor. But Wright was undaunted: "I am leaving the office to its own devices," he wrote his friend and client Darwin Martin, "deserting my wife and children for one year, in search of a spiritual adventure. . . . You will probably not hear from me again, so here is a good-bye to you and the wife and the children." Martin was appalled.

Until then, Wright had lived the life of an eccentric, but ultimately bourgeois, family man. His radicalism was confined to his work. His horizontal, hearth-centered Prairie houses had revolutionized house design, integrating delicate post and beam structures with traditional load-bearing walls, enabling him to open the walls between rooms inside the house, and open the house itself to the site on which it stood. Dubbed the "open plan," the style was epitomized by the Robie House in Chicago, where the living room and dining room were less "rooms" than one large volume separated by an ingenious fireplace whose chimney was discreetly off to the side, allowing, as if by magic, open sight lines over it from one area to the other. His architecture, widely recognized in Chicago, was on the cusp of having a vast influence. Europe's architects were the first to take serious notice of his work, but his American profile was growing as well. At just the moment he was deciding to leave his personal life behind, he was considering a major commission to design an estate for Henry Ford.

But Wright turned down the commission and joined his lover in New York City, where they checked into a room at the Plaza Hotel. Within a day or so, Frank and Mamah boarded a ship for Europe. Wright had never seen the Old World. Cheney visited her feminist mentor Ellen Key in Sweden and spent some time translating her works into English. Wright worked with a German publisher in Berlin on the first book devoted to his architecture, *Ausgeführte Bauten und Entwürfe von Frank Lloyd Wright*, known after its publisher as the Wasmuth Portfolio. Lloyd, his fury abated, later came over to help with the project.

· Frank and Mamah eventually moved in together in a mountainside villa in the Italian village of Fiesole. Just a short tram ride away, the tiled roofs of Florence could be seen from the villa's terraces. The region's simply structured peasant houses, built snugly into the wooded terrain, caught Wright's eye. The two wandered the Italian countryside hand in hand, translating Goethe; Mamah spent time preparing Ellen Key's text—with its declaration that a marriage that was not mutual was no better than slavery—for publication in English.

Wright was not without remorse, however, and he chose Charles Ashbee as his confessor. "I think you will believe that I would do nothing I did not believe to be right," he wrote Ashbee, "but I have believed a terrible thing to be right. . . . I have never loved Catherine—my wife—as she deserved. . . . I know what a blow this will be to you—to all who believed in me; what a traitor I seem to . . . the cause of architecture.

"I would give much to feel you my brother still; that would help. Your friendship has been one of the lovely things of my life."

Wright's choices, Ashbee assured him, would make no difference to their personal friendship. There were things Ashbee just couldn't say to him—things that depended rather on "a look of the eyes perhaps or a touch of the hand." Again he invited Wright to come and see him.

After a year spent walking among the olives, watching the clouds billow and spill their contents in the rich soil below, Wright was ready to return home. On his way back, in September 1910, he finally took Ashbee up on his invitation to visit Chipping Campden. Ashbee and Wright discussed architecture, Japan, and the machine. They must also have talked about the promise of the Guild, whose workshops were still operating independently there, along with Ashbee's flourishing Campden School of Arts and Crafts, and his plan to open a gallery where craftworkers could sell their wares without commercial competition. Wright admired Janet Ashbee, "the rare lady that is your helper," and the managerial role she played. Although his larger rural collective had failed, Ashbee hardly took notice; his idealism was undimmed. This belief in a broader mission—even in the face of financial ruin—must have made a strong impression on the free-thinking architect.

Wright asked Ashbee to write the introduction to the Wasmuth volume. It was, he admitted, "a pure bit of sentiment on my part—because I liked you and I turned to you at the critical moment." Yet the result, drafted while Wright was still Ashbee's house guest, was hardly an unmixed endorsement—for Ashbee found his friend's architecture lacking in what Wright himself might have called sentiment. Ashbee's own designs—for jewelry, furniture, and glassware—were by far the most delicate and sensuous in the English Arts and Crafts tradition. In contrast, having sat on Wright's austere high-backed chairs, having seen his geometric tapestry and window designs, Ashbee found his friend's designs too severe. "I have seen buildings of Frank Lloyd Wright's that I would like to touch with the enchanted wand," Ashbee wrote, "not to alter their structure in plan or form or carcass, but to clothe them with a more living and tender detail." That was precisely the kind of ornamental detail, Wright knew, that his old mentor Louis Sullivan would have brought to such projects.

Wright had informed Ashbee that he was returning to Oak Park "to work among the ruins—not as any woman's husband but as the father of my children." He arrived back in the Chicago suburb on October 8, 1910, remodeling his studio to house his family while he lived and worked alone in the house. Mamah Cheney had returned as well, living nearby.

Catherine found the situation impossible. "Each morning I wake up hoping it to be the last," she wrote Janet Ashbee. "Womankind seems to be so moveable a 'feast.'" Tending to their children and waiting for her husband to come to his senses, Catherine refused to entertain the idea of divorce. Yet Frank did not remain long with his family.

IT WAS DURING his Italian sojourn that Wright began dreaming of a country retreat in Wisconsin. The prospect—and its dangers—had been reinforced by his visit to Ashbee's rural colony. In any event, Wright and his lover needed a refuge from the wagging tongues of bourgeois Chicago. And so the unmarried couple looked to the remote valley inhabited by Wright's mother's family, the Lloyd Joneses.

It was in this valley that Wright had learned to work the land, where he had first studied nature's forms. And it was there that Frank's maiden aunts, Anna's sisters Ellen and Jane Lloyd Jones, had founded the progressive Hillside Home School on their father's land in 1886. Wright had designed most of the school's physical plant; its dormitory in 1887 was his very first commission, and in 1902 he added a slightly cruciform assembly hall. He also designed a wooden windmill, dubbed "Romeo and Juliet," used for pumping water. His uncles, Wright loved to recall, were sure it would collapse in the first winter storm. Many of Wright's family members had been involved as students and teachers in Ellen and Jane's progressive venture. Even his mother had worked there as a dormitory matron.

The Hillside Home School, which took pupils from kindergarten through high school, was one of America's first coeducational schools. The school had been a working farm; its students did agricultural work, calling the horses and cows by name, tending vegetables on their own small plots of land. It was also a home whose domestic order was put to pedagogic purpose, including the instruction of boys in womanly tasks like stitching. Its pupils studied nature as well as books, woodworking in addition to Latin and Greek. There was also fun to be had, from picnics and dances to theatrical productions. Initially intended for Wright's cousins in the valley and some local children, the school soon attracted the wealthy of Chicago and beyond. It was both well-known and profitable, with scores of teachers ministering to its students at the school's height of popularity.

In 1909, though, just before Wright left Oak Park for Europe, the school had been forced into bankruptcy—not because of school economics, but because Wright's aunts had helped guarantee their brother James's ill-advised land acquisition schemes. But Ellen and Jane were eventually able to recover.

For a time, it appeared that another family member would be joining them in the valley. On April 10, 1911, six months before her son returned home, Wright's mother, Anna—who had just sold her Oak Park home at her son's suggestion—purchased thirty-one acres of land near her sisters' school. Anna understood her son's need for a refuge. Indeed, in buying the land, she was likely executing his instructions; even before leaving for Europe, Wright had already done conceptual work for a house on the site.

Now that he was back from Italy, Wright began turning that concept into a set of plans. Having gone a year without working, neither he nor his mother had enough money to build a house or even to finish buying the land. Wright secured funds from his friend and former client Darwin Martin, imploring him to help "bring mother out of a tight real estate situation closing Saturday." Anna Wright, he explained, had purchased "a small farm up country," hoping to sell her home in Oak Park. "I went up with her to close it and see about building a small house for her."

Wright was lying. His drawings show that the living room he envisioned was huge, about twenty feet wide by forty feet long, many times grander than the one Wright had designed in Oak Park for himself, his wife, and their six children. The architect's plans even included space for a large drafting studio. This was clearly no "Cottage for Mrs. Anna Lloyd Wright," as the drawing's title proclaimed. Whether he knew it or not, Darwin Martin had underwritten a working villa for Wright and Cheney, of whose relationship he disapproved. Putting the property in his mother's name merely enabled Wright to shield it from the divorce settlement he expected to face.

The property included the hill where young Frank had retreated barefoot in the moonlight, escaping his exhaustion and his horror at the rutting animals—"sex slaves," he called them—to dream of his "intimate fairy princess." But its highlight was the new house Wright envisioned—a house that wrapped itself around the hill, just below its crown. This was the house he would call Taliesin, and he designed it to evoke a vision of himself and his lover in hidden embrace—between the masculine building itself, which he called "flesh," and the feminine hillside beneath.

Taliesin was Wright's heroic attempt to produce an American architecture as great as that which Goethe had discerned in Germany's Gothic cathedrals. Taliesin's architecture, he wrote in his oblique style, was "something of the prayerful consideration for the lilies of the field that was my gentle grandmother's: something natural to the great change that was America herself." But it was also, in its way, his American version of a Tuscan villa, with its hillside site, its use of terraced gardens as a transitional buffer between house and the working farmlands beyond.

Wright believed himself to be the inventor of what he called "the natural house," the merger of architecture with the Lord's spirit as revealed in nature. "Now," he declared, "I wanted a *natural* house to live in myself." In designing Taliesin, he sought to align it with its natural environment, and to work nature's forms, colors, and textures into the house itself. Its roof lines paralleled the lines of the surrounding hills. Unlike the tight interlocking geometries of his Prairie School designs, this house was loosely laid out, informal, asymmetrical, irregular, designed to follow the hill's contours—to become another of the hill's ragged ledges, located as it was where, Wright declared, "the rock came cropping out in strata to suggest buildings."

In its construction Wright used materials found nearby, often on the property itself. Half a mile away, he discovered an outcropping of "yellow sand-limestone" and used it to build the base, a horizontal band that was both of the house and of the hill. He had an old Norse stonemason blast and quarry the stone out in "great flakes." Men from the neighboring farms helped haul numerous cords of stone over the hill to the construction site. The stones were quarry-faced and set irregularly, like the natural ledges near the site. These stone walls,

Taliesin

he noted lovingly, brought the new house down to the ground; he recalled plea-
surably that it was difficult to see where the stone ledges ended and the walls began. Stretching horizontally along its narrow perch, the roof's broad eaves gave
shelter from the elements—eaves Wright designed without gutters so that icicles, some as long as six feet, would grow there in winter. Where Wright could
not use local materials, he made reference to them. The roof shingles were allowed to weather "silver-gray like the tree branches spreading below them."

Once the walls, roofs, windows, and great stone fireplaces were in place,
the building was secure enough from the weather that interior finishing
could begin. For the floors, he used both stone and wide, dark-streaked cedar
boards. The plaster for the walls was mixed with raw sienna, drying out
"tawny gold." The house had no attic; its ceilings conformed to the slopes of
the roof, which Wright saw as the "chief interest" of the whole house. (This

architect who had spent his boyhood in an attic bedroom later denounced the attic in general as a morally degenerate space.)

Alongside the house Wright built a series of courtyards, each leading to the next, that featured flower and vegetable gardens, orchards, and fountains, all irrigated by water pumped up by the force of a waterfall he created by damming the stream below. This also raised the stream's water level, making it visible from the house. Equipped with a large studio, as well as residential space for draftsmen, the complex was designed to be self-sufficient, over time providing its residents not only shelter but also food, clothing, and their own water and electric power. In this new compound, Wright envisioned a colony even less dependent on the market for survival than Ashbee's guild at Chipping Campden.

Wright named his house on the brow of the hill "Taliesin," after the sixth-century Welsh bard and poet whose name means "shining brow." Wright had been captivated by Richard Hovey's *Taliesin*, in which only the impure bard at King Arthur's court, who has the divine gift to "fashion worlds in little," is able to see into the Grail. In his own creativity, the architect felt a greater kinship with poets than painters or other visual artists. But the name was also a sly gesture of appropriation: Given his family's use of Welsh names for their places, and the straight-laced Lloyd Joneses' scorn for his immoral personal life, choosing Taliesin as the name for his extramarital trysting place may have been Wright's way of thumbing his nose at their Welsh pride.

Taliesin, which would be the site of Wright's professional rebirth, was aptly named: The Welsh bard of legend had himself been the product of a miraculous rebirth, a boy who was remade into a handsome sage. In the legend, a witch goddess seeks to transform her ugly biological son into a figure of beauty. Yet the witch's hapless assistant accidentally swallows three drops of "the grace of inspiration" meant for the witch's son, transforming him into the greatest sage on earth. Fleeing the enraged witch who relentlessly pursues him, he successively becomes a hare, a fish, a bird, and then finally a grain of wheat, consumed by the witch herself, who has taken the form of a hen. After nine months in the witch's stomach, the assistant is reborn as Taliesin, now a beautiful man with a radiant brow—so beautiful that the witch is unable to kill him. Instead she places him in a bag made of skin and throws him into the sea, where he floats for years until he is found by a king who is struck by the beauty of his shining brow.

Legend has it that Taliesin was a member of the court of King Arthur and his Knights of the Round Table. Tennyson's epic poem of Arthur, *The Idylls of the King*, with its "goodliest fellowship of famous knights," had been a classroom staple in Wright's boyhood. The resonance of the Round Table stories could not have been lost on an unrepentant Wright, who had sacrificed his prestige and his work for a scandalous love affair. Taliesin would be his redoubt, a place where he could "get my back against the wall and fight for what I saw I had to fight." Twenty years later, when Wright's Fellowship was finally ensconced there, more than one of the young men who joined their master's battle would call the place "Camelot," recalling the spirit of knightly "fellowship" described in Tennyson's famous poem.

Wright immersed himself completely in the construction of Taliesin, and in his new life with Mamah. A letter from his daughter Frances, now twelve years old, begged him to "*Please* write *Please*," but it went unanswered. In subsequent letters, she pleaded with him to visit his family in Chicago. "Please be here for Christmas. *We* all want you to be here." She was speaking for the whole family. After signing it formally "Frances Barbara Wright," she let loose, adding, "Please! Please! Please! Write! Please! Please! Please! Come home!! For Christmas!" The word "home" was underlined five times.

But her father *was* home—at Taliesin.

IN 1913, MORE than three years after she had been abandoned, Catherine Wright had still not given up hope that her husband would renounce life with his mistress at Taliesin and return to Oak Park. "[I]t is like living on the edge of a volcano," she wrote Janet Ashbee. "It is beyond me to make even the smallest prophecy but as his road grows more difficult mine seems to grow broader and freer."

But Wright's road would soon be rutted with horror. On August 15, 1914, Wright was away in Chicago supervising the construction of the Midway Gardens, a pleasure palace for the city, when he received a call. Mamah was dead; Taliesin was burning.

Julian Carlton, a Wright family servant from Barbados, had served lunch that day to Mamah, along with her son, John, and her daughter, Martha, ages eleven and nine, who were spending the summer there. Carlton asked for gasoline to clean a rug. Instead, after nailing shut all of Taliesin's doors except the lower half of a single Dutch door, he splashed the gasoline on the floor and set it on fire. He then stood outside the single escape hatch and slaughtered the inhabitants one by one with an axe as they crawled through the low opening. Mamah was the first to be hacked to death. All her children perished. Only two people inside survived: A skilled gymnast named Herb Fritz, who was working there as a draftsman, was able to dive out of a window, rolling to break the fall. So was Wright's foreman, William Weston, though Weston lost his thirteen-year-old son, Ernest, in the conflagration. Carlton killed himself several months after being arrested.

Why had he done it? Shortly before Carlton's murderous rampage,

Mamah had given him notice. But the reason for his firing likely went beyond some shortcoming in his work. One of Wright's draftsmen, Emile Brodelle, who was also murdered, had asked Carlton to do some work on his own house. When Carlton had refused, Brodelle had shouted at him: "You black son of a bitch." Now, in the wake of the murders, a great fear of black men seized the valley.

WRIGHT RETURNED AT once to his ruined homestead. He had his own carpenter fashion a simple pine box for Mamah's body and filled it with flowers he cut himself from her garden. Wright walked beside the wagon that bore her to the Lloyd Jones family cemetery, next to Silsbee's low-slung Unitarian chapel. No one was there to meet them. When the box was lowered, Wright did not cry. "His face," remembered his son John, who watched from afar, "bore the expression of one not on earth. . . . The air itself seemed to be afraid to break the silence. I watched him, but he made no sound."

The fire had spared Taliesin's studio workshop, and in the wake of the murders Wright took up residence there. Alone at night, except for a watchman who sat on the steps with a gun across his knees, Wright sat trying to coax music from a legless piano that had been thrown from a window to save it. In the weeks that followed, his sight degenerated so much that for the first time he required glasses. He lost weight. Boils appeared on his skin.

In the gossip of the day—and even in newspapers like the *Chicago Tribune*—it was hinted that the massacre was a judgment on Wright's sinful compound. Mamah escaped most of the scorn; before her death, she had actually won the respect of the locals. In an open letter Wright praised his neighbors who had "rallied so bravely" to fight the fire, and thanked them for the "courtesy and sympathy" shown to Mamah. "[A]ny other community . . . would have seen her through the eyes of the press that even now insists upon decorating her death with the fact, first and foremost, that she was once another man's wife, 'a wife who left her children.' " The writer for the *Chicago Tribune*, Wright declared, "belongs with the mad black [Carlton] except that he struck in the heat of madness and this assassin strikes the living and the dead in cool malice."

Revived by anger, determined that this blood sacrifice should not be in vain, Wright turned his mind to rebuilding Taliesin. And rebuilding, of course, meant designing it anew. Now, as always, intense immersion in work would be his therapy. "More stone, more wood, more work, and more harmonious use of them all," he reflected. "More workmen, more sacrifice, more creative work on my part and efforts to find and earn the necessary money."

IN 1916, AN envoy arrived from a faraway land, bearing an invitation that would change Wright's architecture and contribute to the sensibility of the Taliesin Fellowship. Aisaku Hayashi, the manager of the Imperial Hotel in Tokyo, came with his wife to Taliesin on behalf of the hotel's owners to secure Wright to redesign the city's most important hotel. The emperor of Japan had even approved the choice. Before Mamah's death, Wright had already been to Tokyo with her to discuss the preliminaries. Now he jumped at the chance to escape—Taliesin, America, and, as he thought at the time, himself.

He did not, however, go to Japan alone. A few months after the murders, he received a sympathetic letter from an admirer named Miriam Noel. "Rejoice," she wrote, "that you are worthy to bear so great affliction. . . ." After receiving his reply, her opening gambit could not have been clearer: "There are some rambler roses in a silver bowl on my table—they make my throat palpitate with their beauty."

That was all it took. Facing Christmas alone, his grown children at his wife's house in Oak Park, Wright responded to Noel's bold and sensual invitation. Such a woman was likely to be neither young nor pretty, he ventured in his response. No matter. "I hunger," he wrote her three days before Christmas 1914, "for the living touch of someone—something, immediately peculiar to myself—inviolably 'mine.' Yes—at times almost *anyone* or *anything*."

And then, on Christmas day, Miriam wrote back with her inadvertent *coup de grace*: "Let me crown your head with a wreath of violets and bind your hair with fillets of gold, like Alcibiades at the feast of Agathon." She could hardly

Miriam Noel

have known of Frank's childhood fascination with the Greek warrior, whose warship fought under purple sail. "I kiss your feet with my trembling lips," the sculptress wrote. "I will come into your life for a little while," she warned him, "and then I will lose you because you will never understand, and then like Hagar I will go forth to hunger and thirst in the wilderness, alone with my Ishmael, the poor frail child the world calls love."

Poor frail child: It was a telling phrase. When they finally met, Wright discovered that Noel's health "had been broken" by a failed love affair. But she was a vision nonetheless, appearing at his Chicago office wearing leopard and a monocle. Wright was wearing Chinese trousers and a black velvet dinner jacket. Soon Noel, who had recently been driven from Paris by the outbreak of World War I, was living with Wright at Taliesin. Her money allowed the architect to rebuild Taliesin.

Charles Ashbee came to visit the pair. Taliesin now struck him as "an immense aeroplane at the moment before flight." It was early 1915, and America had not yet entered the European war; as Wright traversed the Taliesin grounds on a wild brown horse he called Kaiser, he made his pro-German sympathies perfectly clear to Ashbee.

To Ashbee, the gray-haired Wright looked much older than his forty-eight years. Ashbee's wife, Janet, didn't think Wright merited her husband's attention. Janet now admitted that she actively disliked Wright, "his poses and all his talk and gas, and *parade* of it all." Catherine, she felt, was "silly" not to divorce him. After five days with Wright, looking over his drawings for the Imperial Hotel, Ashbee thought otherwise. "I love your work," Charles told Frank in his thank-you note. He hoped to be invited back again soon.

WHILE WRIGHT WORKED away on his hotel plans, the Japanese ambassador to the United States sent him a copy of Okakura Kakuzo's *The Book of Tea*. In this elegant treatise on the philosophy of the Japanese tea ceremony, he read of the great Chinese philosopher Laotse, the founder of Taoism. Laotse, Wright learned, had understood long ago that the reality of a building was found not in its walls and roof, but in the empty space they contained.

Wright was devastated: His long-treasured original insight had been discovered by another, and centuries before. Just as he had upon his first exposure to Notre Dame, Wright felt his confidence collapse. "Instead of being cake," he recalled after reading the book, "I was not even dough."

Wright went out to break stones on the road, "trying," he recalled, "to get my interior self together." But the work provided no relief. "I was like a sail coming down; I had thought of myself as an original, but was not." His depression lasted for days—until he happened upon the thought that saved him. Laotse may have hit upon the idea first, he realized, but the philosopher had never "*built* it." Nor had anyone else. "Well then," he thought to himself, "everything is all right, we can still go along with head up." His calling as the savior of architecture was intact.

THE GENERAL'S DAUGHTER

OLGA IVANOVA LAZOVICH HINZENBERG—DARKLY elegant, even aristocratic—sat alone in the hard wooden pews of Notre Dame. It was October 1924, and the twenty-seven-year-old was at a turning point of someone else's making.

She and her master, Georgi Gurdjieff, had just met at the Café de la Paix, where he held court as always among those who sought his esoteric counsel and cures. She had only wanted to remain with him, tending to his estate, dancing the spiritual dances in which he directed her. Now Gurdjieff had made it clear that she could not stay on at his Institute for the Harmonious Development of Man. Her future, he suggested, was in America, but it was she who must decide where to go.

Here, in this Gothic reservoir of ancient mysticism, she hoped to find her way.

OLGA LAZOVICH—OR Olgivanna, as she came to be known—had followed a tortuous path from Montenegro, where she was born in 1897. Even for the Balkans, the once-independent kingdom of Montenegro, the "Black Mountain" nestled within the Serbian Empire, was notorious for its warring tribes and blood feuds. Olgivanna was raised there as the last of nine children of Iovan Lazovich, Montenegro's first chief justice, who read his verdicts aloud to the crowds that gathered in Cetinje's town square.

Olgivanna's mother, Melena, was as abrasive as her father was gentle, a woman who should have been, and tried to be, a man. Melena Milianov was the third and youngest daughter of Marco Milianov, a fierce sharpshooter general who had led the Montenegrin and Serbian armies in their successful drive to push out the Turks in 1878. Only a fatal bullet wound to the chest denied him the role of sovereign, for which he had believed himself destined.

Enraged by his wife's failure to provide him a son, Marco had raised Melena as a boy, teaching her to fire a rifle and slash with a saber, even carrying her on horseback behind enemy lines. Her early training took; Melena later joined the army and rose to the rank of general. Olgivanna's mother was an imperious woman who threw rocks through her neighbors' windows when she disapproved of their behavior. A frequent traveler on political missions, she was rarely at home during her daughter's childhood.

Melena was an imposing sight, wearing her white hair tightly braided upon her head like a crown, covered always with a black silk mantilla; Olgivanna looked on her with an awe tinged by fear.

For her father, however, she felt only tenderness and love. By the time she was born, Iovan Lazovich was already blinded by glaucoma. Only the chief justice's prodigious memory allowed him to continue rendering judgments.

Olgivanna would walk hand in hand with this tall, gaunt man, describing the flowers and the clouds to him. When the two were accosted by a beggar, he would ask his daughter if the man was blind, and always gave to those who were. Every Sunday, Olgivanna accompanied her father to the Serbian Orthodox church, where they stood together for the service. From an early age, she read newspapers and books to him; in turn, he explained the stories a young girl might not understand, expanding her horizons beyond her years. Iovan Lazovich tracked the growth of his daughter by the strength of her grip and the timbre of her voice. And Olgivanna prayed nightly, in vain, for her father's sight to return.

In 1911, at the age of fourteen, Olgivanna was sent to Batum, a humid subtropical town on the Black Sea coast, to live with her older sister Julia, the wife of a wealthy tea plantation owner, and a friend of the writer and mystic Leo Tolstoy. One day, Olgivanna wrote in her autobiography, she and a girlfriend visited a fortune-teller. Staring into her crystal ball, the thin, blonde woman told Olgivanna that she might marry early, but it would not be a happy life.

Then, Olgivanna claimed, the seer became uncertain. "Someone keeps interfering," she said. Finally, another message came through: If Olgivanna seized the opportunity, she would have a chance to change her life and marry "a very famous man." He would have something to do with geometry. The soothsayer was not sure who he might be. She saw triangles, circles, and squares. That was all.

Olgivanna Hinzenberg in the 1920s

When Olgivanna was eighteen, a likely candidate appeared. While visiting a friend in Tiflis, the capital of Georgia, she met an architect named Valdemar Hinzenberg, ten years her senior. A chain-smoking Latvian now living in Moscow, Hinzenberg was passionate about Picasso and the other modernists who were shocking European sensibilities at the time. Olgivanna was flattered by the attentions of the wealthy architect and interested in his artistic world. And Moscow, with its exceptional music, art, dance, and theater, beckoned to the young woman, who longed to study drama there.

After Olgivanna moved to Moscow, Valdemar began courting her anew. But as she got to know him better, her initial enthusiasm waned. He was neither particularly intelligent nor creative, the eighteen-year-old student concluded; in fact, the older architect seemed rather beneath her.

Valdemar invited her to his family's country home, where she met his mother. In her, unlike the son, Olgivanna sensed "greatness." She was everything her own mother wasn't. Where Melena Lazovich carried a cane and wore austere black dresses—when she wasn't in uniform—the elegantly feminine Mrs. Hinzenberg ordered her gowns from Paris. Olgivanna quickly came to love the woman, spending a great deal of time telling her stories, even acting them out to make her laugh.

And, unlike Olgivanna's own mother, Valdemar's returned her affection. Indeed, she hoped to see Olgivanna become her daughter-in-law. Olgivanna remained unconvinced, until one day Valdemar's mother suffered a massive heart attack. As Olgivanna tended her sickbed, Mrs. Hinzenberg made her promise to marry her son. Two hours later she died.

After the funeral Valdemar took Olgivanna to Kursk, where the two were married in a midweek civil ceremony on January 31, 1917. The bride cried throughout the ceremony.

By the time the newlyweds returned to the capital, there was violence in the streets, and bread lines were forming. The revolution had moved into Moscow. Worried for his new wife's safety, Valdemar told her to return to Batum, a port city at the western edge of Georgia, a fiercely independent region with its own language and culture. He would follow later. The teenage bride took the last train out of the city. Hinzenberg left for Karkov, his family's home, where he evidently had business.

As the train carried her away from her new husband, Olgivanna Hinzenburg was already pregnant.

FRANK LLOYD WRIGHT, meanwhile, was in Japan. With his Imperial Hotel drawings in hand, he and Miriam Noel had arrived there in 1916 to get construction underway. In Tokyo he discovered that for many years Miriam had "been the victim of strange disturbances." "All would go happily for days," he recalled, "then strange perversions of all that." Noel's nervous condition was "tearing her to pieces."

Japan, on the other hand, seemed flawless, with its disciplined aestheticism that suffused every aspect of life. In the way of Shinto, its people lived a life that seemed clean—not just of dirt or waste, but in terms of spiritual purity. Wright marveled at the feet of the Japanese, clad in pristine white *tabi*, as they walked shoeless across the tatami mats whose organization determined both the size and the shape of Japanese homes. Their interiors were never cluttered with ornament or appliances; each item was designed to be taken out, used, and stored away in its proper place. Art was inscribed into the partitions. Choice paintings and sculpture were displayed in alcoves like sacred objects.

"The truth is," he wrote, "the Japanese dwelling owing to the Shinto ideal 'be clean' is in every bone and fiber of its structure honest." Everything in Japan seemed to be reduced to its basic principles. Buildings, like people, were what they appeared to be. For Wright, it was a revelation. Modern architecture, he was convinced, should look to these Japanese structures for inspiration. Wright's own certainly did, as Ashbee had noticed: With its low eaves and exposed beams, its incorporation of the literary into the architectural, its asymmetry, modular geometry, and its very spareness, Wright was already reaching for what he called the "elimination of the insignificant."

Wright also experienced a "new" way of working in Japan, one that offered him a taste of the respect, even adoration, he had always craved: He had apprentices. "His genius is just unbelievable," the long-haired, bearded Arato Endo, the first of Wright's apprentices, wrote in his diary upon meeting Wright. "[T]he fact that he is alive is even more unbelievable. To me personally it is unbelievable to be in a close position to care for each other."

While Wright had clearly respected and even adored his own master, Louis Sullivan, he found in Endo a deference beyond the imagination of young Americans. And there were others, all handpicked by Endo, all similarly worshipful. Wright, who could never have enough praise, was in heaven. In Endo he had found not just a loyal assistant, but a window into Japanese culture, and a teacher in the ways of the samurai.

As construction on the hotel began, Wright was equally impressed with the Japanese builders. "I never expect to see again such forbearance on the part of anyone so absolute as these boys and their Japanese workmen displayed, nor such universal gentility of conduct."

ON MARCH 16, 1917, two months after she last saw her husband, Olgivanna was sitting with friends in a Batum café when a friend suddenly ran in brandishing a newspaper. "The Great Bloodless Russian Revolution," the headline read. Nikolai II had issued a public declaration abdicating the throne. Obey the Czar, he beseeched the Russian people. "May God help Russia."

For the moment, daily life in Georgia was largely unaffected. Olgivanna moved east from Batum to Tiflis, the Georgian capital, where Valdemar had an apartment and had also lined up some work. In late September, after eight months of marriage—only a few weeks of which they spent together—Valdemar joined his wife just before her labor began. On September 27, Olgivanna gave birth to a girl; they named her Svetlana.

A month later, the Bolsheviks seized power in Moscow. Nationalists and revolutionaries were still vying for influence in the provinces. Hordes of refugees fled south from the violence. Georgia was no longer safe. The social bases of restraint were steadily giving way. One learned to walk in groups; people were hungry for bread, and a man could be killed for his overcoat.

As Hinzenberg's wife, Olgivanna had become a woman of means. She had a beautiful apartment, a box at the opera, and front row seats at the symphony. But she didn't love her husband.

Repulsed by the violence of the revolution and unattracted by its politics, she looked to philosophy for solace. Olgivanna devoured the works of Schopenhauer, Kant, and the Hindu writers. But most of all she was drawn to Nietzsche. "I teach you the superman," she read in *Thus Spake Zarathustra*. From Nietzsche, the young mother learned that man is "something that is to be surpassed." His call for an elite group of supermen to use their will and creative power to surpass the resentful common man, she recalled, "struck something deep in me. I began to think that there must be a supersoul in our life. I understood it in the sense of an inner kingdom, of being the master of oneself. I wanted to find the way to achieve it."

IN TIFLIS, VALDEMAR was designing a cabaret restaurant, the Peacock's Tail, which he co-owned. Olgivanna, whose theatrical studies had ended with her hasty escape from Moscow, occasionally performed on its small stage. For a scene based on *Pagliacci*, she was joined by Luigi Valazzi, an old childhood friend, two years her junior. The pair fell in love. When Luigi's parents learned of their son's relationship with a married mother, they were horrified. The couple was actually considering running away together, but Luigi's parents stepped in and sent their son away. Olgivanna was shattered.

The Red Army was now on the outskirts of Tiflis, and revolutionaries were operating within its limits. The Bolsheviks had begun organizing there

several years before, led by a man who had once been a student at the local
Jesuit seminary and was now a rising Soviet commissar. Born Iosif Vissa-
rionovich Dzhugashvili, he would soon be known as Joseph Stalin. As life in
Tiflis rapidly deteriorated, Olgivanna stood in line with the others to receive
her ration of black bread adulterated with straw. To feed her child, she traded
a pair of diamond earrings for a loaf of bread.

Surrounded by danger, pained over the loss of Luigi, Olgivanna withdrew to her apartment and the comforts of philosophy. It was then, when life
seemed most desperate, that she found a new way forward. In the winter of
1919, humoring a friend, she left her apartment to see a visiting Armenian-
born mystic, a man who was said to teach dances that could develop the
will. She was, she recalled, "looking for something beyond the limits of my
senses."

MEANWHILE, WRIGHT'S EXPERIENCE with Japanese adulation had
worked its magic. He traded in his Wildean wardrobe for one of his own design, affecting double shirts, both with collars, and a cape, a staple for men
during the Middle Ages. *Wright-san*, as the Japanese honored him, now cut
an even more conspicuous presence in the streets of Tokyo, his unique collar
suggesting clerical garb.

Wright had always drawn young men, and a few women, who wanted to
work specifically with him. But the Japanese apprentices and craftsmen were
different. Their ancient tradition had produced a culture of extraordinary
discipline and refinement. With an unquestioning obedience to his master,
each worker spent years perfecting some small part of the task at hand before
graduating to another part. Puppeteers, for instance, spent years learning to

Wright (center, seated) with his Imperial Hotel team. Head apprentice Arato Endo is seated fourth from left.

work the left leg, then the right, then one hand, then the other, until finally they were allowed to manipulate the head. One moved slowly closer to mastery, with the expectation that one gave one's life to the work organized by the master.

Though still embittered by his own university experience, Wright found his interest in education renewed by the Japanese apprentice tradition. And it was in Tokyo that he began to think about setting up his own institution using the abandoned buildings from his aunts' school at Hillside, now permanently defunct. His plans became quite specific: The school would house thirty young men, and offer a theater and even a lecture center for the locals.

Hearing of the idea, his mother was elated. "Great things for the world are in your hands. Your scheme to restore Hillside is very near my heart."

Wright had come into ownership of the Hillside property the year before he left for Japan, in exchange for agreeing to pay off his aunts' debts. The gesture may have been an attempt at making amends, for Wright himself was partly to blame for their ruin. Parents had begun withdrawing their children from Hillside when he and Mamah Cheney set up their scandalous love nest next door. His uncle, Reverend Jenkin Lloyd Jones, had declared his nephew a "blinded egotist" whose "Haven of Pleasure" was the "deadliest blow of all" to the school's fortunes. The murders and fire of 1914, followed by Wright's return to Taliesin with his new mistress, Miriam Noel, sealed Wright's scandalous reputation and the school's fate: Frank's aunts barely finished the next school year.

Now the place was his. And, as if his aunts Ellen and Jane hadn't suffered enough, Wright later reneged on the $250 annual payment he owed each of them as part of the deal. Jane Lloyd Jones thought her nephew had become "a mad man."

A SCHOOL OF sorts had just opened in Tiflis. And more than one observer thought its proprietor mad—but not Olgivanna. Georgi Ivanovich Gurdjieff was a bald, mustachioed, charismatic trickster, a man able to address large crowds and convince many that he was speaking directly to them. He seemed to deploy an electromagnetic and tactile power that was said even to draw out disease. His eyes, many claimed, could penetrate one's psyche. They could even bring a woman to orgasm from across a room. At fifty-three, he was also a quick-witted, canny entrepreneur with a feline yet powerful body.

Like Olgivanna, Gurdjieff had fled Moscow for Tiflis, a city he knew well. Born in Soviet Armenia, he had first moved to the Georgian city at the age of seventeen in 1883 to enroll in the local Jesuit seminary, the same one attended by the young Joseph Stalin. Although Gurdjieff later claimed the two were classmates, Stalin matriculated about ten years after Gurdjieff, who by then was living in Alexandropol. And there was another untruth in Gurdjieff's claim: He had never actually enrolled in the seminary.

Gurdjieff may have fabricated his personal encounter with Stalin, but members of his family had actually known the future dictator—much to their misfortune. As a seminary student, Stalin had rented a room in their house. After being expelled for conducting study groups on Karl Marx's *Das Kapital,* he joined the Bolshevik underground and moved out of the house, stiffing the Gurdjieffs for a substantial amount of rent.

In 1895, the year Stalin discovered his atheism among the Jesuits, Gurdjieff went on his own journey of discovery. He began traveling with the Seekers of Truth, a group of men who were scouring the East for esoteric knowledge. Their search had been inspired in part by Theosophy, a movement founded in New York in 1875 by the Russian spiritualist Madame Blavatsky. Despite the fact that Blavatsky's movement was banned in Russia and the Caucasus, Gurdjieff imbibed the Theosophical doctrine. Theosophy was a catchment basin for the occult revival that had begun in the late nineteenth century. No matter what aspect of esoteric doctrine—astral bodies,

Georgi Gurdjieff

secret masters, the ray of creation, arithmology, astrology, the seven centers in man—Blavatsky's so-called "secret doctrine" seemed to embrace it.

During one sojourn in 1898, Gurdjieff entered Afghanistan. There, guided by a monk said to be 275 years old, Gurdjieff was allowed to enter the innermost courts of a Sufi monastery. In the center of the fourth court, he came upon a group of young girls training to be priestess-dancers. He was stunned by the "purity of execution" with which they assumed various positions, guided by a complex apparatus of ebony and ivory shaped like a seven-branched tree, each branch divided into seven joints of decreasing size. The sacred dances were composed of sequences of these postures, each representing a different truth. Gurdjieff recognized the dances immediately as an ancient form of book, a kind of choreographic text passed down for centuries.

Seven years later, around 1905, Gurdjieff made his way to Tashkent, Uzbekistan, where he took a position as a professor-instructor in the supernatural sciences. He studied with Sufis, who taught through the secret symbols in their dances what others taught through books. These dervishes, he later explained, "teach dancing same as put seed in the ground, but seed very hard, this green plant grow slow because need much time to grow."

Seven years after that he made his way to Moscow, where he began to teach and choreograph his own sacred dances. Through dance, he maintained, one could attain knowledge once known to the ancients that was now lost to the modern world. Modern man, he taught, was little more than a machine, moving through life in a state of perpetual sleep, of unthinking habit and no self-awareness. The sacred dances were part of a system of techniques designed to awaken him. Under his guidance, he claimed, his students might achieve a kind of super-consciousness—and, if they were willing to struggle and suffer enough, even immortality.

Gurdjieff's dances were unlike anything found in Russia's renowned classical ballet. Underwritten by and performed for the czars, Russian ballet largely explored royal themes, stories in which the monarch usually wins the day. Gurdjieff's were based instead on cosmic mathematics, visual enactments of the laws of the universe. And also unlike ballet, his movements were centered on the pelvis. "Ass is projector for understanding all other parts of a person," he would say. "Ass is root."

Gurdjieff began to attract devoted followers. By 1916, his exotic dances had also captured the attention of major artists. Thomas de Hartmann, once a page in the Czar's court, now a well-known young composer, was enthralled. De Hartmann had written the music for *The Pink Flower*, a ballet choreographed by Sergei Diaghilev; its premiere in 1907 was Vaslav Nijinsky's first public performance, and also featured the ballet greats Anna Pavlova and Tamara Karsavina. After falling into Gurdjieff's orbit, de Hartmann began working on the music that accompanied the sacred dances. He listened for hours as Gurdjieff whistled themes or played them on the piano, scribing Gurdjieff's notes into musical notation, then turning them into full piano arrangements.

As the Russian monarchy crumbled, Gurdjieff fled southward from Russia with a dozen or so followers. Their trek across the Caucasus Mountains tested their physical limits. Some thought they were mad; others even accused them of harboring Lenin and Trotsky. Once out of the mountains, the group headed for the Black Sea port of Sochi, and from there to Tiflis.

IN A BARREN room in Tiflis, Olgivanna watched Gurdjieff as he watched five women execute his dances, which he called "the movements." Their structured geometry captivated her; here was a man with the knowledge she craved.

When she returned the next day, Gurdjieff set her to work, sculpting her own hand out of clay. After hours of silence, he asked her if she had a wish.

"Georgivanitch, most of all I want immortality," she replied. "There is so much injustice in the world and Christ speaks such marvelous things. If it is that way, through his words, that I can reach immortality, could you help me?"

Yes, he told her.

Gurdjieff taught that man is capable of developing three higher bodies in addition to his prosaic physical one—bodies that could survive death. He likely absorbed this notion from the Tantric tradition undergirding Tibetan Buddhism and certain streams of Hinduism; Theosophy pointed to the same phenomenon. These bodies, he taught, could be built by capturing a greater quantity of what he called "finer hydrogens"—unknown to physics—that were absorbed from the planets, the sun, and beyond the planetary system. Gurdjieff named the first "astral" body the *kesdjan* body, after the Persian word meaning "vessel of the soul." The rudiments of this body were necessary to absorb reason. A second, "higher being body" allowed one to participate in the cosmic process.

The work involved in developing these additional bodies, and therefore the possibility of immortality, was arduous, involving conscious will, voluntary suffering, and a technique he called "self-remembering," by which one produced the subtle energies of which these other bodies are composed. Though Olgivanna may not have known it at first, Gurdjieff also taught that Christ had an "astral body," which enabled him to communicate with the living even after his own death. During the Last Supper, Gurdjieff claimed, Christ's followers had actually eaten bits of his flesh and swallowed his blood.

After Olgivanna revealed her wish for immortality Gurdjieff looked at her for what seemed a long time. It would be a long road, he told her. Was she ready to make any sacrifice?

She looked into his eyes. She was, she replied.

Did she know how to cook, he asked?

Olgivanna was taken aback. She did not. Her two maids took care of the house, she explained.

Fire the servants, he told her. She should learn to do everything herself.

As instructed, Olgivanna dismissed her servants. She returned the next day, bringing Svetlana, now three years old. Gurdjieff directed her to prepare a meal for many guests, including himself and his wife, Julia. He escorted her to the market, instructing her in the purchase of meat, vegetables, and fruit. Back in her apartment, he supervised as she cooked a complete meal, featuring a lamb roast. The kitchen lessons she learned that day stayed with her for the rest of her life.

It was a superb dinner. Among the guests was Alexander de Salzmann, her husband Valdemar's partner in the Peacock's Tail, an artist, set designer, and former student of the dervishes himself. Also in attendance were Gurdjieff's composer Thomas de Hartmann and his wife, an opera singer. Not long after, the de Salzmanns joined the de Hartmanns as Gurdjieff's followers.

Olgivanna began her journey toward immortality in the kitchen. Gurdjieff, a master chef, maintained that the choice of ingredients, their cooking, and the elimination of waste, were all part of a spiritual discipline. These ordinary activities, if conducted according to the correct principles, provided deep knowledge. In his system, different elements—carbons, oxygen, nitrogen—carried different energies, which were equivalent to notes on the octave. By changing the impressions one took in with one's food, one could transform ordinary foods into ever higher, finer, more energy-rich forms of matter. Cooking and eating were alchemical practices. "If one knows how to eat properly," Gurdjieff insisted, "one knows how to pray."

With her first test behind her, Olgivanna was allowed to start training in the sacred dances. Gurdjieff's movements were intended to "correlate" the body, training the body's own intelligence to free itself of its machine-like habits. Like any practitioner of yoga, he held that particular bodily postures are associated with particular thoughts and feelings. Realizing one's true essence requires systematic bodily manipulation.

Gurdjieff referred to his total program—from food consumption to physical and psychical training—as "the work." Behind the work, Olgivanna learned, was an arcane and complex series of cosmic laws. The "Law of

Three," for example, stated that all phenomena, whether a molecule, a human, or the cosmos itself, are the result of three forces: the positive, the negative, and the neutralizing. In man, Gurdjieff maintained, the positive is located in the brain, the negative in the body, and the neutralizing in the emotions. In the normal mortal, these three forces are not unified and frequently cancel one another out. It is this sorry, fragmented formation that one calls a personality. When combined with something he called the "Ray of Creation," Gurdjieff taught, the Law of Three allowed his students to determine their places in the universe.

Gurdjieff shared with Olgivanna many such theories, some more abstract than others. One's inner soul and the larger cosmos were the essential sites for knowledge and action, he explained; everything in between—history, politics, war, revolution—was ultimately irrelevant. The true struggle, the one for immortality, was located inside the soul. There one could also observe and work with the laws of the universe. Gurdjieff claimed that he was developing a technique for releasing the energy of the universe in order to transform the world.

Gurdjieff believed that, by correlating a dancer's motor and emotional centers, his movements could integrate the forces found in the Law of Three, creating an "indivisible trinity," and hence what he called a "true I."

Olgivanna had much to learn.

EXECUTING THE MOVEMENTS demanded a high level of self-consciousness. The dancers were required to make complex internal counts, while moving different parts of the body according to different rhythms. Gurdjieff told them that his training of the body would help them make a willful break with their unconscious mental and emotional routines, which had been conditioned by decades of bodily habit. Only thus could they develop their own essence, and shed the personality they had fashioned unknowingly from the culture in which they happened to grow up.

Gurdjieff's "stop exercise" was intended to achieve the same result, but with an element of physical risk. At any given moment, whether during the movements sessions or at any other random moment of the day, the master might cry "stop!" On hearing the command, the students were required to freeze their bodies in place, no matter how painful their position might be. Everything, from the position of one's eyes to the thoughts in one's head, must remain just as it was at the moment the command was issued. Even smokers who had just inhaled were required to hold the smoke in their lungs until the exercise was over. The students would wait in agony—sometimes only a few seconds, sometimes long, agonizing minutes—before the master shouted "*Davay!*" or "Continue!" Occasionally a student would faint from the physical strain.

Olgivanna worked hard on the sacred dances, and Gurdjieff was impressed with her progress. But her primary goal—immortality—posed a bigger challenge. "You can be God-like," he told her. "You can do things that plain mortals cannot do, provided you struggle with yourself to overcome your weaknesses."

That struggle, according to Gurdjieff, involved two techniques: self-remembering and voluntary suffering. The first was a detailed monitoring of one's life as it was lived. It was a maddeningly difficult task, demanding extraordinary concentration. Its aim was to show each student that the self was not a single entity but a collection of sometimes conflicting centers, from which a unified self—the "I"—could be refashioned. If they could "correlate" their mental, emotional, and physical centers, Gurdjieff argued, Olgivanna and the others would become their own masters, able to act in the world rather than merely react. A correlated self had the added advantage of preventing leakage of vital energies.

"Voluntary suffering" was another key to the master's vision. A hungry man achieved nothing through his suffering, he said, if it was caused by external circumstances over which he had no control. To have food and not eat it, in contrast, was to endure voluntary suffering, which helped one develop the finer inner substances necessary for a soul, and thus achieve immortality.

If Olgivanna could achieve all this, Gurdjieff claimed, she would no longer be a prisoner to external circumstances. With Tiflis still mired in revolutionary chaos, this promise was seductive indeed.

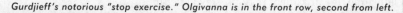

Gurdjieff's notorious "stop exercise." Olgivanna is in the front row, second from left.

* * *

OLGIVANNA HINZENBERG CAME to be seen by the group as someone who was tough and respected toughness. But the others—women in particular—found her too independent, even arrogant. Beneath her determined exterior, she appeared desperate, hungry for communion with a worthy authority. Her touchstone had been her father, the vulnerable blind man whose respect derived from his absolute command of the law. Only a man who lived by force of principle would hold her. It was this hunger that allowed Gurdjieff to capture her devotion so completely.

Like many, Olgivanna found that her master's understanding of the world disrupted her sense of reality. And his psychological interventions, whose secrecy she swore to protect, could be difficult to endure. But he had a commanding power, a remarkable ability to discern a person's fundamental character. Many said he could look right into them and see their innermost fears and desires. Some went mad under his regimen; a few took their own lives.

Certain that Gurdjieff controlled the path to a secret knowledge, Olgivanna endured her master's psychological blows, his excavation of her conceits and illusions. She wanted only to be in his presence, to pass his tests, to go where he pointed.

After a year in Tiflis, with the Bolsheviks closing in, Gurdjieff decided once again to flee. Over the objections of Valdemar and her family, Olgivanna resolved to go with him. In May 1920, Gurdjieff and his thirty acolytes traveled on foot to the Black Sea port of Batum, a rugged 200-mile trek. From there they left the contested Russian territories and headed west for Turkey.

Olgivanna, for unknown reasons, stayed behind.

CONSTANTINOPLE WAS A city of roughly a million people, whose streets still turned to mud in the rainstorms. Soon after Gurdjieff and the group arrived, he rented a building in the drab new district outside old Istanbul, home to desperate Russian refugees, Jews, and dervishes. In addition to sleeping rooms, the building contained a large hall. What used to be Istanbul's Grand Rabbinate he now dubbed the Institute for the Harmonious Development of Man.

Wearing his astrakhan cap, Gurdjieff, the Institute's leader, held court in the Black Rose, a café frequented by White Russian officers, prostitutes, and drug addicts. Twice weekly he gave lectures, speaking in Russian, Greek, Turkish, or Armenian, depending on his audience. In his lectures he frequently warned of the limits of science, claiming that he had cracked the codes revealed by Einstein and Freud by employing magic, fortune-telling, and hypnotism, all of which pointed to other forces that elude empirical observation and scientific representation. Gurdjieff also set his students to studying Kabalah, numerology, Asian myths, and magic. And he began to plan an elaborate public performance of a ballet, *The Struggle of the Magicians*, based on his sacred dances.

Still stuck in Tiflis, Olgivanna befriended some Scottish troops who helped her and her daughter escape the city and make their way to Constantinople and the Institute, where they took a room on the ground floor. Valdemar came too, although it is not clear whether he was staying with his wife and daughter. Olgivanna joined the others in practicing for the ambitious performance, moving her lithe body across the black-and-white tiled floor of the Institute's large hall. Under Gurdjieff's watchful eye, she was quickly becoming skilled at the complex movements.

Based on the dances of the Tibetan monasteries and the music of the Whirling Dervishes, *The Struggle of the Magicians* told a story of good and evil. The same dancers enacted both the harmonious movements of the White Magician and the jerky, hostile movements of the Black. Gurdjieff, who dressed in black for the rehearsals, believed that the rival forces within each of us determine our future. Evil enters the world through the gate of unawareness, which he saw as a failure of will.

One morning, before dawn, Gurdjieff invited a delighted Olgivanna for a walk in the rocky islands at the edge of Constantinople. Along the way he spoke to her of the nature of time, and of the substantial unity of all life. At first she picked flowers and smelled the herbs, but she stopped when he advised her that she should control her thoughts and sensations with great care. The sun rose and the villages slipped away as they tramped farther and farther from the city, carrying on though her arms were cut and her dress torn by branches. Eventually Olgivanna's throat grew so parched she couldn't swallow; her feet blistered and bled, but still they walked on. Sunburned and filthy, Olgivanna wanted to die.

As darkness fell, she saw lights ahead, and picked up the smell of roasting meat. They had arrived at the edge of a village. Was she ready to return to the wilderness? Gurdjieff asked. Yes, she somehow managed to say. Through her voluntary suffering, it seemed to her, she had at last touched a self beyond her body. Perhaps, she thought, access to eternity was indeed right here in this world.

But they did not go back. Instead Gurdjieff brought her to an outdoor taverna. Everything around her seemed extraordinary—especially Gurdjieff, who was apparently unfazed by the ordeal. Her exhaustion, he told her, was a function of her dependence on her "small accumulators." Each of the three major centers—physical, emotional, and intellectual—had two of these energy accumulators. The small accumulators were connected to a large accumulator, a kind of reserve tank. Like nearly everyone else, Olgivanna drew only from her small accumulators. Gurdjieff, however, was able to tap directly into his large accumulator. With proper guidance, Olgivanna could learn to do it too. Their all-day ordeal was an attempt to push her to that point.

CONSTANTINOPLE WAS BECOMING less tenable. Gurdjieff had entered the city the very year that the Turkish nationalists allied themselves with Lenin, and in the face of French and British military occupation, declared an independent Muslim Turkish state. The Ottoman empire was fracturing; independent warlords and bandits were operating everywhere. And Bolshevik agents were moving in.

As the mystical son of a Greek father and an Armenian mother, Gurdjieff was caught between the Turkish nationalists, whose hatred for both sides of his heritage seemed boundless, and the Soviets, whose ruthless revolutionary violence and hostility toward religion were anathema to him. With his contention that all human suffering was determined by planetary forces, it's no surprise that Gurdjieff found it difficult to interest the Constantinople locals in his work. In 1921, after only three months in Turkey, he decided to move once again, this time to Hellerau, Germany. A cradle of the progressive urban-planning theory known as the Garden Cities movement, Hellerau had become a mecca for the Russian and European avant-garde.

Hellerau was also the home of Émile Jaques-Dalcroze's school of what he called Eurythmics, a "rhythmic gymnastics" that sought to galvanize and unleash the expressive powers of the unified senses. Olgivanna's friends Jeanne and Alexander de Salzmann were among a number of Gurdjieff's followers who had migrated to him after first participating in Eurythmics. While there was a certain kinship between the two teachers, Gurdjieff's interest in Hellerau had little to do with Jaques-Dalcroze himself. Gurdjieff had fallen for his building, the Festspielhaus, a neoclassical gem where Jaques-Dalcroze had taught until leaving for Geneva. He wanted the place as a home for his Institute.

Olgivanna and her daughter accompanied Gurdjieff and the others to Hellerau. Her husband, Valdemar, however, had decided to sail to America. He asked his wife to join him, but she preferred to remain with Gurdjieff. Their parting was apparently friendly. She would always be welcome, he told her, if she wanted to join him in America.

Unable to make a deal on the Festspielhaus, Gurdjieff set his sights on an even greater cultural center—Paris. Olgivanna was delighted. Before they left,

Gurdjieff sent her to visit her mother, hoping they might repair their tattered bond. The visit ended in failure. She returned in agony—only to discover that Gurdjieff had yet another test for her.

Had she not, he reminded her, once declared her willingness to make any sacrifice to achieve immortality?

Yes, she replied. It was true.

"Even that?" he asked, gesturing toward her five-year-old daughter, Svetlana, who was playing with a ball nearby.

Olgivanna began to cry.

"You see," was all he said.

Olgivanna fought to say yes. Voluntary suffering, she knew, would enable her to see her personality—her maternal self—for the reactive machine it was. Such knowledge, she knew, must be paid for.

Her brother Vlado was preparing to move to America with his wife, Sophie, and now he came to Berlin to pick up his niece. Dejected after the death of his elder brother, Vlado hoped that a child would cheer up the childless couple. On April 26, 1922, Vlado and Svetlana boarded the SS *Orbita* in Hamburg bound for America.

TWO MONTHS LATER, on July 22, with the Tokyo hotel nearly completed, *Wright-san* and Noel left for America. As the car started down Hibiya Street to Tokyo Station, the craftsmen of the Imperial Hotel ran after it crying "Banzai Wright-san!" *Long live Mr. Wright!* At Yokohama Harbor, they were met on the deck of the *President McKinley* by a line of about twenty apprentices. Wright went down the line shaking hands and exchanging good-byes. At the end of the line, he reached Arato Endo. They shook hands wordlessly; both men cried. Then the apprentices descended to the dock, and the ship departed for Seattle.

Although he would never return, Japan had forever changed Wright, providing templates that influenced both his architecture and the organization of his architectural practice. But *Wright-san* knew that coming home to America would mean a painful return to his tarnished status. And once again he would be living in sin at Taliesin—only this time with an emotionally unstable woman. Four months later, he was granted a divorce from Catherine. If he wanted to marry Miriam, he would legally be required to wait one year.

WITH OLGIVANNA NOW encumbered by neither husband nor child, Gurdjieff briefly made her the manager of the Institute, allocating rooms, purchasing, keeping inventory, making up work lists, and observing his interviews with prospective students, who were now streaming in.

From the outset, Paris proved more hospitable to the Institute. Gurdjieff suceeded where he had failed in Germany, renting the local Eurythmics studio. And he attracted some of Jaques-Dalcroze's best rhythmicians to his work, including Jessmin Howarth, a dance teacher at the Paris Opera, whom he recruited to teach his own movements.

It had been two months since Vlado had taken Olgivanna's daughter, Svetlana, away to America. Olgivanna cried at night, cried whenever she saw children playing in the park. Christmas was an agony. To make matters worse, Gurdjieff purposefully put her in charge of the half-dozen children now at the Institute. She would sneak out to a café, hoping to calm her emotions with a cup of coffee and a piece of cake. When he found out about her visits, though, Gurdjieff made her sacrifice them, too. She forced herself to give up sweets for a year. To test her will, Gurdjieff made her keep sweets in her room.

THERE WAS BIG news. Sight unseen, Gurdjieff had leased the Prieuré des Basses Loges in Fontainebleau, an estate forty miles outside Paris. Originally bestowed by Louis XIV on his second wife, the property had recently been owned by the family of Captain Alfred Dreyfus, the Jewish captain who had been falsely accused of passing secrets to the Germans. After his exoneration in court, Dreyfus had given the estate in payment to his lawyer. The lawyer's widow first leased the property, and later sold it to Gurdjieff for 700,000 francs—money he was said to have obtained in part by establishing and then selling two Montmartre restaurants, and in part by selling shares and options for the Azerbaijani oil fields. The rest of the funds he appears to have borrowed.

The forty-five walled acres of the Prieuré contained a three-story chateau with a slate mansard roof, oak-paneled walls, formal gardens with fountains, and an orangery. Although the building housed a beautiful paneled library, Gurdjieff brought not a single book there, relying instead on his usual blend of aphorisms, personal counsel, and rambling talks. He and his most honored guests lived on the second floor, known by his students as "the Ritz," which featured well-appointed bedrooms and murals by Valdemar's former café partner Alexander de Salzmann. Olgivanna and most of the others lived in what became known as the "Monk's corridor," a row of tiny third-floor rooms originally intended for servants.

Gurdjieff posted new directives daily. "The breaking of all ties was demanded," Thomas de Hartmann recalled, "meaning that one must not be identified—blindly attached—to one's husband or wife, parents, children, friends, and so on." Another notice demanded that everyone give up all material possessions, which they were expected to enumerate in writing.

Soon after moving in, Gurdjieff took Olgivanna to the estate's huge pantry. "This will be the high school of your new birth," he told her. Then he ushered her into the kitchen, with its copper pans hanging overhead. "[A]nd this, Olgivanna, will be your university." Gurdjieff maintained a bounteous kitchen. Meals included herring with onions, grilled sardines on toast, Russian cutlets, hearty stews, whole baby pigs roasted in the oven, various rice dishes, and stuffed cabbages, all washed down with bottles and bottles of Chateau de Larresingle Armagnac. One day he decided to have his pupils cut off the tops of the hundreds of empty Armagnac bottles to make planters. He did not provide them with proper tools, and many bled profusely by the time the bottle garden was finished. No one thought to complain.

At six o'clock every morning, Olgivanna and the others were awakened by a student assigned to run up and down the corridors ringing a small bell. During the day Gurdjieff put his charges through a series of work tasks—from tending the chickens to hewing limestone and rough-sawing timber. As soon as they mastered one job, they were transferred to another. Physical labor was supposed to be as conscious as possible, occupying all of one's mental and emotional energies.

Indeed, a disciple's labors were often purposeless—intentionally so. Gurdjieff had them dig holes in the earth, only to fill them up again. He called this "dulio-therapy," or the "slave cure." Only through voluntary submission to the teacher, by freely being a slave, he claimed, could one learn *not* to be one. Jesus, after all, had submitted to God as the pathway to resurrection.

In addition to her regimen of dulio-therapy, Olgivanna washed dishes, tended to the children, took care of the pigs, and did the laundry—by hand of course—for everyone at the Institute. As the students performed their tasks, they were expected to practice certain mental exercises, learning Morse code or lists of Tibetan words.

Gurdjieff napped each afternoon at three o'clock, rising at five for tea. Olgivanna worked with the others until six in the evening. When a large bell called them to dinner, they were expected to appear in suits and dresses. At eight or nine in the evening, after changing again, they gathered to perform the movements. This often went on until midnight, at which point Gurdjieff called out, "who want sleep go sleep." But no one did. They all knew that in these after hours, he was most likely to reveal something especially interesting. The sessions often continued for another hour or two. Many awoke the next day after only sleeping four or five hours. Most sleep, Gurdjieff maintained, was wasted time anyway.

The disheveled state of Gurdjieff's own rooms in the morning, with coffee spilled everywhere—including on the sheets of his huge bed—suggested that the master did more than sleep. He was, in fact, having sex with many, if

Olgivanna working on the
"study house" at the Prieuré

not most, of his younger female followers. He sired at least six children with women in the community, some of whom were married to other followers. Fortunately for Gurdjieff, it was considered an honor to bear the master's child. Gurdjieff explained that he chose particular women to impregnate in order to provide the earth with "seekers for truth." According to Paul Taylor, an American member of the community whose sister, Eve, was one of Gurdjieff's daughters, two such husbands—Thomas de Hartmann and the psychiatrist Dr. Leonid de Stjernvall—"were proud that their wives were bearing Gurdjieff's children."

ONE OF OLGIVANNA'S projects was to assist in constructing a new "study house." Gurdjieff had purchased a skeletal old French air force hangar for the purpose; she and the others covered it with planks, and then shoved dried leaves mixed with earth and clay between the planks as insulation. Holes were punched into the walls to make windows on which they painted Gurdjieff's aphorisms, translated from Russian and English into Gurdjieff's secret code. Finally, the pounded and dried earth floor was covered with goatskins and Oriental carpets. Two fountains were eventually installed, whose waters Gurdjieff had scented with central Asian perfumes.

The "study house" was used for practicing the movements. On Saturdays, Gurdjieff staged performances there for visiting guests. The evening would begin with a feast, with suckling pigs, roast lamb, their skulls split open with the gray brains exposed, even jerked bear meat. Sometimes Gurdjieff ripped apart the mutton with his hands and tossed pieces to guests. At other times he speared the roasted sheep eyes, which were like dark crusty raisins, and passed them to special guests. The children were favored with the cheek or the brain. In the town, it was rumored that Gurdjieff ate children's heads.

The feast was followed by dance performances for visitors, most of whom came down from Paris. De Hartmann's former collaborator Serge Diaghilev, the founder and choreographer of the Ballet Russe, became one of many weekend regulars. He was so impressed, he asked Gurdjieff if he could include some of the dances in his repertoire. Gurdjieff refused. The dances, he explained, were intended to instruct the performers, not entertain an audience.

The movements drew other dance aficionados as well. Lincoln Kirstein, a willowy American visiting the Institute for the summer, was as impressed by Gurdjieff's dances as he was appalled by his food. "As far as I could tell," he recalled, "apart from the cleanly cut and prepared crudités, there were interspersed bits of boiled leather, wax flowers, clippings of sponge on rubber, and some glazed knots of rope, varnished in blood."

Kirstein's perseverance was well rewarded when they later moved from the dinner table to the study house. Kirstein, who would profoundly shape American dance as founder of the New York City Ballet, came to see Gurdjieff's movements as an awakening to a new order, a "geometrically poetic constellation," a physical praise poem to what other people called God. By physically reworking the body's habits, by playing at the limits of its pains, he believed that one could indeed become truly self-aware. Gurdjieff, Kirstein later wrote, influenced him more than anyone else, including his parents.

On the ceiling of the study house, Gurdjieff had painted an enneagram—a geometric diagram (from the Greek *ennea*, or nine, and *gram*, or point) composed of two superimposed forms inside a circle. The forms were a six-pointed Star of David whose components were rotated so that two of its points coincide, leaving an opening at its base to its center, and an equilateral triangle. Gurdjieff had first seen an enneagram at the Sarmoung monastery, whose priests and priestesses used it in their esoteric exercises. The symbol could be traced back to the mystical geometries of the Pythagoreans, the Sufi orders, and the Jewish Kabbalah, with its Tree of Life.

Gurdjieff maintained that the nature of "all and everything" was contained in this symbol. The geometric form of the enneagram laid out the sequence of vibrations emanating from the cosmos, the great "ray of creation" that carried its energy and its information to Earth. The enneagram expressed Gurdjieff's two treasured cosmic laws—the Law of Seven and the Law of Three. The Law of Seven governs the progression of cosmic vibrations from "the Absolute," a progression on which the structure of the octave, the order of creation, the days of the week, the periodic table, the scale of light, and the transformation of food into vital substances are all based. The separate triangle is made up of the three missing numbers—nine, three, and six. From this triangle Gurdjieff derived the "free trinity" of the enneagram, a manifestation of the Law of Three. And the circle that contained both the star and the triangle represented the zero, which contained everything necessary for its own existence.

Gurdjieff believed that every world, every plant, and every organism was an enneagram. Its points corresponded to foods, musical notes, and planets. To understand the symbol fully, he claimed, his students must literally put their bodies through its geometry via the movements. The goal, Gurdjieff instructed Olgivanna, was for her to become a six-pointed star, a self-contained being with the ability to insulate herself from mechanical reaction to what Gurdjieff dubbed external "shocks." Gurdjieff believed there were two discontinuities in the musical progression of cosmic vibrations, one between *mi* and *fa*, the other between *ti* and *do*. These dangerous "intervals" allowed random shocks to transform one's "line of force," to change its direction, to push human beings and their history in a direction different from what was intended. He called this six-pointed star the Seal of Solomon, and Olgivanna strove mightily to embody it.

Olgivanna danced nightly in the study house, with its enneagram hovering overhead. On either side of the inner triangle, Gurdjieff had painted an angel and a demon. To move beyond their grasp, he told her, she must learn to master both. Only then would she be able to use their energies to regenerate her own life.

AS ONE OF the Institute's best dancers, Olgivanna also became one of its dance teachers. By far her most important student was the antifeminist English writer Alfred Orage, twenty years her senior. Hailed as London's best literary critic by no less than T. S. Eliot, Orage had been the editor of the avant-garde literary magazine *New Age* before renouncing the life of letters to study with Gurdjieff.

An advocate of William Morris and the Arts and Crafts movement, Orage despised commercial competition for having destroyed the arts. A Theosophist, he believed that every individual had the spiritual potential to evolve toward God, the perfect man. He was also a guild socialist, who (like Wright's friend Ashbee) believed that associated workers, not state planners, should make decisions on political and social matters. For Orage, matters of politics and spirit were of a piece; in his writings he advocated both an economy based on socialized credit and a new civilization based on the desire to "pour out life...."

"I am going to find God," Orage had told his secretary as he left his editorial post to join up with Gurdjieff. Always open—too open, some said—to new ideas, Orage was famous for his lucid speech and his rapid ideological shifts. Orage, one critic carped, "knows the

Alfred Orage

shape of everything and the weight of nothing." To his literary colleagues, his decision to abandon his brilliant career only confirmed that impression.

When Orage arrived at the Prieuré, Gurdjieff put this man of letters through months of endless physical labor designed to crush his personality and open access to his essence. Gurdjieff commanded him, for instance, to dig on the grounds right through the night, to the point where he could no longer stand and was ready to flee the place. In the depths of despair, Orage vowed to make an extra effort to complete the tasks Gurdjieff required of him. "Soon," he recalled, "I began to enjoy the hard labor, and a week later, Gurdjieff came to me and said, 'Now, Orage, I think you dig enough. Let us go to the café and drink coffee.' From that moment things began to change." The master's dulio-therapy was working.

The tall, big-framed Orage actually hated the movements Olgivanna taught him. "But it is a wonderful experience," he wrote to his wife, "to have the strength to do what is disagreeable." Orage also gave up smoking at Gurdjieff's insistence, though the master puffed on Russian cigarettes in his presence. After months under Gurdjieff's guidance, his friends observed, Orage was calm and glowing. The work regime at the Prieuré had made him lean, muscular, and agile. His artistic ambitions now seemed to him like pretensions and illusions. Contemporary literature, his longtime passion, no longer seemed important. He had, he claimed, found his way.

ORAGE'S ARRIVAL AT the Prieuré coincided with the introduction of a new theory Gurdjieff called "the science of idiotism." Raising a glass of Armagnac or vodka, Gurdjieff introduced a new dinner table ritual, "the toasts to the idiots." *Idios*, in Greek, refers to a simple person, a private, unlearned plebian. For Gurdjieff, though, an idiot was somebody who was in direct contact with reality, including his own. There were, he explained, twenty-one grades of idiot.

Gurdjieff's "work" was a conscious struggle to break the hold of illusion. In his cosmic scheme, human beings had an organ at the base of the spine that he called the *kundabuffer*, which both heightens our sense of pleasure and prevents us from seeing reality. The work allowed one to overcome the effects of the *kundabuffer* and move through the ranks of idiots—first down to the level of the "ordinary idiot" to recognize one's nullity and then up the ladder of reason toward God. There were ordinary idiots, true and false hopeless idiots, compassionate idiots, squirming idiots, square, round, and zig-zag idiots, swaggering and enlightened idiots.

Alcohol was required to help people "strengthen their power to wish" to die at one stage and be reborn at a higher one. For the toast, the followers were instructed to draw on their intuitive self-knowledge and choose which kind of idiot they thought they were. Adapted from a feast custom Gurdjieff had picked up in Turkestan, the sequence of toasts actually traced the spiritual evolution of man. Gurdjieff had ascended as far as the eighteenth grade of idiot. The last three stages, beyond what ordinary human beings could achieve, were reserved for true sons of God—culminating in the twenty-first idiot, who he called "The Unique Idiot" or "Our Endlessless."

The eloquent Alfred Orage, whom Gurdjieff dubbed his "super idiot," brought others to the Prieuré from his network. One was a woman who became Olgivanna's most important responsibility: the New Zealand writer Katherine Mansfield. Orage had published Mansfield's first stories in his literary journal and tutored her on her writing; now he began introducing her to Gurdjieff's ideas.

With her fine-boned, slightly severe face and close-cropped hair, Mansfield was acutely sensitive and highly ambitious. Her book *The Garden Party* had just been published to critical acclaim. But she was also dying of tuberculosis. In search of helpful therapies, Orage had pointed her toward the occult doctrines of "cosmic anatomy." She had submitted herself to more than a dozen sessions of radiation of her spleen by a Parisian spiritualist doctor, who claimed the concentrated rays would change her blood. But the regimen didn't work. By 1922, she was keeping two old apothecary jars on her dresser. One was for her ashes.

Yet Mansfield kept searching for unorthodox solutions. "I have a suspicion," she confessed in her journal, "sometimes a certainty—that the real cause of my illness is not my lungs at all, but something else. And if this were found and cured, all the rest would heal." With Orage's encouragement, she agreed to take the next step and put herself in Gurdjieff's hands. "You remember," she wrote to her husband, "how I have always said doctors only treat *half*. And you have replied: 'It's up to you to do the rest.' It is. That's true. But first I must learn how. I believe Gurdjieff can teach me."

Gurdjieff employed extraordinary techniques for bodily cures. When a pot of boiling fish stock at the Prieuré kitchen spilled on his nine-year-old niece, Luba, he swabbed her arm with oil and put it back over the fire, burning her again, sending the girl into screams of agony. The next morning, it was said, her skin was free of pain and blemish. Apparently, she was not the only one for whom such treatments were successful. In the master's view, it was a matter of increasing the source of the pain in order to take it away—that is, of teaching the body who was boss.

Word of these and other incredible interventions was widely circulated in those years. At times, Gurdjieff's ministrations to alcoholics, drug addicts, depressives, and homosexuals provided him with a significant source of income. It was even said by his intimates that a wheelchair-bound Franklin D. Roosevelt made a secret visit to the Prieuré—and that Gurdjieff had him standing.

On October 17, 1922, at the age of thirty-four, Katherine Mansfield arrived at the Prieuré with her friend and lover Ida Baker. Olgivanna was immediately drawn to the writer's "wonderful face." Mansfield's back now ached with sciatica; her face was the color of chalk, her fingers so bony she hid her hands under the table. Her husband had more or less abandoned her to her own devices.

Mansfield had come to Gurdjieff as a last resort. "I want to learn something that no books can teach me, and I want to try and escape from my terrible illness," she wrote in her first weeks there. She still hoped for a cure, and many in Gurdjieff's community were sure it would come to be. "I do feel *absolutely confident*," she wrote her husband, "he can put me on the right track in every way, bodily and t'other governor."

Olgivanna was entranced by Mansfield—especially her eyes, "avid for life, for impressions"—and Mansfield was similarly impressed by Olgivanna, though on their first meeting no words passed between them. Standing before her new guest with a white kerchief around her head, her arms filled with wood, Olgivanna seemed to understand neither French nor English. "But her glance was so lovely," Mansfield wrote, "laughing and gentle, absolutely unlike people as I have known people."

Olgivanna entreated Gurdjieff to allow her to work with the ailing new guest; the master consented, and Mansfield sent her companion away. Olgivanna built fires for Katherine, who was so cold that she wore her fur coat night and day. She stole flowers from the garden for her, watched the dances with her, and, after a hard day of work, stayed at night in her room until two and three in the morning, when her charge finally fell asleep. "Friendship," Mansfield wrote to her husband, "the real thing that you and I have dreamed of. Here it exists."

Olgivanna imparted Gurdjieff's teachings to the writer. "Your body," she told her, "is only a medium through which you receive the thing you love most." Indeed, she added, "there is no death for one like you who perceives the possibility of sweeping death aside when the time comes as an unnecessary phase to go through."

At first, the experience seemed to have a positive effect. "At your very approach," Katherine told Olgivanna, "I feel better and stronger. And when you go I am left with so much energy that the legion of doctors could not give me a tiny drop of it with all their prescriptions and pretensions."

Olgivanna paid no heed to the contagiousness of Mansfield's disease. For a month, she and Katherine shared a small room together in the

Monk's Corridor. She also tended to her in a converted hayloft with a gilded balustrade above the cow stable, where Gurdjieff set up the area with Oriental rugs and cushions so that she could inhale what he considered the stable's restorative vapors, as well as watch the milking and slaughtering of the animals. As in the Prieuré itself, an enneagram was painted on the ceiling.

Mansfield gave herself over fully to Gurdjieff. "[I]f we're allowed a single cry to GOD," she wrote to her husband, "that cry would be: *I want to be REAL*." For the first time in three months, he came to visit. "I have never seen any one so beautiful," he remarked. Indeed, she was doing so well that she was actually planning her next book.

Katherine had become completely dependent on Olgivanna. "Oh, don't you know how much I love you!" Katherine told her after Olgivanna had spent just a day away. "This was the most terrible day I've spent in the Institute. . . ."

One evening, Katherine watched Olgivanna in the salon as she danced *The Initiation of the Priestess*. When Katherine returned to her room, she began to hemorrhage, the blood flowing from her mouth. She died shortly thereafter. The next day, Olgivanna approached Gurdjieff in desperation: Had Katherine had enough time to develop a soul?

At Mansfield's funeral, Gurdjieff distributed cornets of nuts and raisins, casting handfuls into her grave. They contained, he said, the germs of renewal.

THE FAMOUS WRITER'S death, coming as it did under Gurdjieff's care, became something of a scandal in and around Paris. There were cries of charlatanism. But the Institute for the Harmonious Development of Man faced problems more dire than that. Following the purchase of the Prieuré and the costs of restoration, Gurdjieff was now heavily in debt. To make matters worse, he was also supporting the remnants of his family, who had fled Georgia to come and live with him. Neither the tuition from his pupils nor money he was earning in Paris as a healer could cover his expenses. By the fall of 1923 the Institute was close to insolvency, and Gurdjieff was physically exhausted, his large accumulator apparently drained.

Pressing himself into intense "mentation," Gurdjieff came to a conclusion: "If within three months I did not have a least one 'cool' million francs, I would go up the chimney . . . forever."

But money was coming in from at least one direction: west, from the United States. One American couple in Paris, convinced that Gurdjieff had cured their son, had volunteered to pay double the fee they'd previously agreed. The French, Gurdjieff concluded, were tapped out; now he would turn to America, a wealthy land of hungry souls—an "infant nation" he called it, filled with unsophisticated, but open, people. As far back as Constantinople, he had told his followers of the possibilities in America, expressing his wish to establish branches in New York and Chicago. He told his followers in Moscow to "discover America," by which he meant that they must incorporate the country within their true selves. Now, he told them, it was time to bring their physical selves to the States.

For Olgivanna, this was reason to be ecstatic; at last she would see her daughter again. But there is no evidence that Gurdjieff intended to relocate the Institute itself to the United States. His plan seems to have been to travel there, stage demonstrations, raise a lot of money, then return to Europe, leaving American pupils behind to keep the branches going without him.

The venture would be a high roll. To finance it, Gurdjieff put up money he needed for an upcoming payment on the Prieuré. If the American windfall failed to materialize, he would lose the estate.

Before leaving, Gurdjieff wanted to stage a dry run in Paris, hoping that his students—many of whom were shy about performing in public—would get over their stage fright. Making his finances even more precarious, he spent a considerable sum renting the Champs-Elysée Theatre for a few performances in December.

Olgivanna and the other dancers began an intense regime of rehearsals. The performance included the movements, bits of ritual from the "ancient East," sacred dances like "The Initiation of the Priestess," and the extraordinary "stop exercise." But there was more than dance; the troupe even began practicing conjuring, memory, and telepathic tricks.

It was a spectacular event; even Émile Jaques-Dalcroze, the inventor of Eurythmics, was in attendance. For the occasion, Gurdjieff had the fountains from the Prieuré carted into the theater's foyer, scrubbed clean, and filled with red wine. Olgivanna ladled out wine to the guests, terrified that she might stain her white costume in the process. Other costumed pupils served Middle Eastern delicacies, and plied the guests with trays of perfumed wines.

The performance was a success.

IN THAT NOVEMBER of 1923, tormented by the unstable and morphine-addicted Miriam Noel, Frank Lloyd Wright did the seemingly unthinkable: He married her. It had been precisely one year since his divorce, the legal minimum waiting period. If he expected the marriage to have a calming influence on their relationship, he was wrong. "There were no longer carefree walks over the friendly hills," he remembered, "nor swimming in the river below." Taliesin, he confided in his autobiography, "had encountered disintegration from within." What he didn't reveal was that, on at least one occasion, he beat his new wife black and blue; she in turn drew a knife on him and threatened to get a gun.

GURDJIEFF'S FINAL PERFORMANCE in Paris was on Christmas Day. As Olgivanna helped the little girls of the Institute put on their special white dresses, she ached for her own daughter, Svetlana, who wouldn't be there to rush to the huge Christmas tree and the presents in large white hat boxes underneath. Despondent, Olgivanna refused to appear for dinner. But Gurdjieff threatened that failing to appear would prove she had learned nothing from his teachings.

When Olgivanna entered the dining room, a hundred or so students and guests were seated at long tables. At the end of the meal, everyone was served pudding. Gurdjieff announced that one of the servings contained a gold coin. Whoever got it, he said, would be marked with a symbol of goodness. The lucky winner would also be given a calf born two days earlier. Olgivanna put her fork into the pudding and immediately struck the coin.

"I got the gold coin," she said. "So what?"

Gurdjieff fixed her eyes with his. "Oh, Olga, you don't know what you got." His face, she recalled, looked like that of a prophet. He saw that she was "marked," he told her, even as she reluctantly entered the dining room.

Holding tightly to the coin, Olgivanna followed Gurdjieff numbly to the stables. As he held a kerosene lantern, she bent down and touched the newborn white calf, smelling its sweet breath. Suddenly she was overcome with the feeling that this was a gift from elsewhere. Sensing a divine presence, she concluded that she was now "part of the universal order."

And her mind turned to thoughts of Svetlana, and America.

PARALLEL LINES

LOCATED AT THE BASE OF the New York's Yale Club building, at the corner of West Forty-fourth Street and Vanderbilt Avenue, the Sunwise Turn bookstore attracted a clientele of activists and freethinkers—readers who sought change both in the world and in themselves. It was a place where people with an interest in Picasso, socialism, Eastern religions, or psychoanalysis went to talk and hear lectures. And the store became a popular destination: In the aftermath of the Great War, after the laws of history had gone so awfully wrong, more than a few American intellectuals were drawn by the promise of more timeless secrets of the universe.

One day near the end of 1923, twenty-two-year-old Jessie Dwight, the store's beautiful and wealthy co-owner, happened on an attractive stranger browsing there. Who is that man? she asked an associate. The clerk didn't know his name, but said that everyone was excited about his upcoming lecture on Georgi Gurdjieff. The man, Dwight soon discovered, was Alfred Orage. As a proponent of modernist literature, radical politics, and Eastern mysticism, Orage was a natural match for the Sunwise Turn.

Orage was a consummate seducer who made an ideal frontman for Gurdjieff. Working his network of literary connections, the inveterate womanizer made sure to stop at the offices of two women who wouldn't be sexually interested in the least. Jane Heap, who wore her hair closely cropped and preferred men's clothing, and her former lover, the exquisitely feminine and hyperrational Margaret Anderson, offered Orage the perfect entrée into the city's literary and artistic elite.

As editors of the small but influential literary magazine *The Little Review*, Heap and Anderson had been publishing the avant-garde before the cultural nabobs even knew enough to put up their guard. William Butler Yeats, Ezra Pound, Ernest Hemingway, Djuna Barnes, and Sherwood Anderson had all made early appearances in the magazine. After being convicted of obscenity for serializing the then-unknown James Joyce's *Ulysses*, they fearlessly arranged its first publication in book form. In America, Anderson and Heap were literary modernism's greatest midwives.

Anderson had first launched *The Little Review* in Chicago in 1914, bringing in Heap two years later as her coeditor and lover. Frank Lloyd Wright, then at work on the city's Midway Gardens, was one of the journal's early patrons. After donating the substantial sum of one hundred dollars, he admonished the apparently discomfited Anderson never to "be ashamed to ask help for good work." The next year he made another kind of contribution to *The Little Review*, publishing in its pages a translation of Goethe's "A Hymn to Nature" that he had worked on with Mamah Cheney.

Alfred Orage, who himself had contributed an essay on Henry James's ghosts to the magazine, now arrived at its Twenty-eighth Street office to make an announcement. A transforming event was about to hit America, he told Jane Heap with his typical casual eloquence. The country, he explained, was ripe for revolution—a revolution that would blend the scientific and the spiritual.

LONDONER STANLEY NOTT was working at the Sunwise Turn when Orage showed up to give his talk. Nott had been in the city only a few weeks

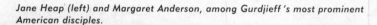

Jane Heap (left) and Margaret Anderson, among Gurdjieff's most prominent American disciples.

when he took the job. Joining the audience packing the small room, Nott was about to become one of the transformed.

"The Institute for the Harmonious Development of Man," Orage began, "which is based on the system of G. I. Gurdjieff, is really a continuation of the society called the 'Seekers of Truth,' which was founded in 1895 by a group of doctors, archaeologists, scientists, priests, painters, and so on, whose aim was to collaborate in the study of so-called supernatural phenomena, in which each of them was interested from a particular point of view."

One of these men, he declared, was Mr. Gurdjieff.

Orage brought his audience up to date, tracking Gurdjieff's life from his dangerous trek out of Russia with his followers to his establishment of the Institute at the Château du Prieuré. For the rest of the evening, he regaled the crowd with Gurdjieff's theories. And he invited the interested to attend further such gatherings, "the time and place of which," he promised, "will be announced shortly."

Jane Heap sat in the audience electrified. The experience, she recalled, was "superreal." Gurdjieff's theories seemed to offer her, and the other attendees, a chance to become a real human being for the first time. "I am in on the front row of the show," she effused in a letter to a friend. "I don't rave about this," she later wrote. "I have been waiting for it."

Soon after Heap received the word, writer Gorham Munson's doorbell rang. It was his friend, the poet Hart Crane, who lived above *The Little Review* offices.

"Gurdjieff is coming!" Crane announced. "He is the master Ouspensky found."

P. D. Ouspensky, a stern, stout, bespectacled Russian physicist, was arguably the most celebrated intellect to declare himself a Gurdjieff disciple. Ouspensky's lectures on physics and metaphysics, past lives, Tarot, and the Yogis had drawn thousands in Moscow and St. Petersburg. In 1915, he had met Gurdjieff in Moscow, adopted him as his teacher, and followed him down to Istanbul. Ouspensky now ran his own group in London devoted to psychological study, an enterprise financed by Jane Heap's friend and current lover, the English literary patron Lady Rothermere.

It had been through Ouspensky that the likes of Alfred Orage and Margaret Anderson had first become interested in Gurdjieff. Many among the Sunwise Turn crowd, Hart Crane included, had been mesmerized by Ouspensky's book *Tertium Organum*, its title referring to his claim that human beings possessed a "third organ of the senses." Even the supremely confidant Alfred Orage had felt humbled by the physicist. "I may find that all I have regarded as the real me, the literary man, the artist, the philosopher," he had declared, "all is artificial. Perhaps my real bent is cobbling old boots."

* * *

FRANK LLOYD WRIGHT was now spending much of his time traveling from Spring Green to Chicago's seedy Warner Hotel, where he comforted his *lieber meister*, Louis Sullivan. They had corresponded but hadn't seen each other since two decades before, when their estrangement ended with Wright attending one of the old man's lectures. When he greeted his master afterward, Wright wept.

Sullivan was now reduced to a bedchamber and a bathroom, his books kept on a bathroom shelf, the bedroom walls decorated with prints from magazines. He was tended to by an auburn-haired milliner woman who visited him regularly. When he could no longer pay the rent, he wrote to Wright, "I have much to tell you that I cannot write. . . . I am desperately in need of the right kind of companionship. No doubt you understand." The man who had invented the modern skyscraper had fallen into oblivion.

Penniless, living off of donations from friends, Sullivan had turned to writing and to drink. To raise cash, he even sold to Daniel Burnham, the legendary Chicago architect, the bound and inscribed copy of the Wasmuth portfolio Wright had presented to him. Wright, who began sending his *lieber meister* money regularly, happened upon him while taking his son Llewellyn to buy a tuxedo. Llewellyn was shocked to discover that the man his father so revered was "a down-and-out alcoholic." Wright swept Sullivan along with them into the store and bought the old man an overcoat.

WRIGHT WAS NOT Sullivan's only visitor at the Warner. Claude Bragdon, an architect, architectural critic, and publisher from Rochester, New York, also visited frequently. Now largely forgotten, Bragdon was Sullivan's second most important protégé. Bragdon and Sullivan had much in common: Both understood architecture as more of a religion than an art. Both, as Sullivan acknowledged, were cosmic seekers as well.

One might think that Bragdon and Wright would get along famously. Bragdon even embraced the term "organic architecture" for his own work. But, while Bragdon much appreciated Wright's architecture, he couldn't stomach him personally. For one thing, he believed that Wright had misrepresented his true inspiration: In Bragdon's eyes, the real credit for Wright's success belonged to Sullivan's partner, Dankmar Adler. "[I]t was the great good fortune of Wright and Sullivan," Bragdon wrote, "creative artists both, and therefore in the large sense feminine, to have been impregnated, so to speak at their most formative period with the virile and essentially male ideation of Adler, one of the greatest structural engineers of his time."

While Wright apparently bore no ill will toward Bragdon, he had absolutely no use for at least one aspect of his colleague's approach to architecture. Bragdon was a Theosophist—a leader of the movement, in fact—and as such he believed that mathematics held the key to the divine code that governs nature's forms. Bragdon even devised a complex calculation-based system for generating architectural ornament, intended to translate "mathematical truth," as he put it, "into visible beauty."

For Wright, this was so much nonsense. "You don't cut open a drum to see where the sound came from," he once observed: The truth of art could never be revealed through science.

CLAUDE BRAGDON'S IMMERSION in cosmic matters led him to one place where neither Sullivan nor Wright had gone—the world of Gurdjieff. The appeal was natural, inspired as he was by Theosophy, the same movement that had first set Gurdjieff on his spiritual journey.

Bragdon had had a huge success publishing the American edition of Ouspensky's *Tertium Organum*, whose English translation he edited. A strange thing had happened on the day of its publication. Bragdon's wife, Eugenie, was a mystic herself who claimed to channel through automatic writing the long-dead Zanner, daughter of Humas, among others. On January 19, 1920, the day Bragdon published *Tertium Organum*, Eugenie's hand began transcribing a message about the book from her chief oracle in the spirit world. It was an endorsement from heaven. "It is destined," the message said, "to have a profound influence on many men whose work would be sterile without this new light." Eugenie died of stomach cancer a few months later.

Ouspenksy's book sold 150 copies per week during its first year—a best-

seller in those days. Partly rooted in Theosophy, the treatise sought to reconcile the physical and metaphysical, to build a logical bridge from man's subjective consciousness to what he termed "cosmic consciousness," a state where time no longer existed. Those fortunate enough to achieve this, he claimed, experience the past and the future as if in the present. They were, in his parlance, "supermen," the same elite Orage referred to as the "few humans" who might emerge from the "multitude of apes."

When Ouspensky had first discovered Gur-

Claude Bragdon

djieff in Moscow in 1915, he thought the teacher's training system might finally offer a way to nurture these fledgling supermen. But the severe Russian intellectual had never really understood the movements, and in 1921 he left the Prieuré for London, having decided to proceed on his own. He attempted several reconciliations with his former master, but it was not until now, when Gurdjieff set off to join Orage in New York, that Ouspensky finally made a complete break. This new public razzmatazz was just too much for him.

ON JANUARY 13, 1924, Olgivanna watched from the *S.S. Paris* as the New York docks came into view, knowing that somewhere down below would be Svetlana. She hadn't seen her in two years.

The six-year-old girl was there waiting, along with many who had come to witness the arrival of Georgi Gurdjieff. The gangway lowered, and out came Gurdjieff and his entourage of twenty-one students, along with a thousand other disembarking passengers. The students' immigration papers bore strange anomalies: While Gurdjieff listed his race as Greek, half of his group listed theirs as "Hebrew," including Gurdjieff's wife. In fact, few Jews had been drawn to the Institute. Perhaps Gurdjieff thought Jews would gain easy access to the city, or perhaps it was a statement that his small, misunderstood band of followers were like Jews in "Exodus." Olgivanna, who listed her occupation as "student," noted on her papers that she spoke Russian, German, Polish, and French.

On the dock, Olgivanna pushed through the crowd, and past the customs officials, looking for her daughter. Then she saw Svetlana, accompanied by Vlado and Sophie. Valdemar had earlier applied for a transfer of custody, but his bid had failed.

"She looked lovely and sad, but distant," Olgivanna recalled of her daughter. "She had grown away from me."

THE NEWS OF the master's arrival surged through the city's intelligentsia. Orage's advance work had paid off. On the snowy evening of January 24, 1924, a large crowd gathered to hear Gurdjieff in his first American appearance. Arriving at the venue prepared to give the introduction, Orage ended up giving the lecture: Gurdjieff never showed. (For Orage, at least, the evening was not a complete loss: After the lecture he walked Jessie Dwight home, and that night the literary lion began a relationship with the young co-owner of the Sunwise Turn, nearly thirty years his junior.)

Two days later, Orage stood before an even larger audience to introduce Gurdjieff. This time the master showed. He addressed the group in

Russian, but often interruped his interpreter to suggest more precise translations. The audience was stunned by his presence, especially his penetrating eyes.

The following Saturday night, "all New York," as Margaret Anderson put it, showed up to see Gurdjieff at the Neighborhood Playhouse, where the Sunwise Turn had a small branch store. This time, Gurdjieff's talk was enhanced by the first American demonstration of the sacred dances. Among the many notables in attendance were writers Hart Crane, Theodore Dreiser, John O'Hara, and Rebecca West. Margaret Anderson was there, of course, as were actresses Gloria Swanson and Georgette Leblanc.

The audience saw something that night that was unlike anything they had ever experienced. Barefoot, dressed in white tunics and loose-fitting pants with dark sashes at their waists, Gurdjieff's pupils went through their precise, seemingly automatic movements. As one of the three lead dancers, Olgivanna performed in the front line.

With Orage introducing each dance with an explanation of its meaning, Gurdjieff's presence went largely unnoticed. "From my seat down in front," Anderson recalled, "I saw him for a moment in the wings, commanding his pupils, exhorting them to greater, and ever greater, precision." His general appearance, writer Llewelyn Powys observed, "made one think of a riding-master," though "there was something about his presence that affected one's nerves in a strange way." This was especially true during the dances, when his pupils performed "like a hutchful of hypnotized rabbits under the gaze of a master conjuror." When not directing, Gurdjieff, who claimed to be able to read a person's desires just by examining his posture, prowled the aisles or the foyer, surveying the audiences, looking for prospects.

At the end of the demonstration, Margaret Anderson went backstage to look for Orage. There, for the first time, she saw Gurdjieff up close. His life, she recalled, "seemed to reside in his eyes. . . . He had a presence impossible to describe because I had never encountered another with which to compare it." In Gurdjieff she felt she had witnessed a great man, a seer, perhaps even a messiah. Her partner, Jane Heap, was similarly transfixed. "Now dear," she later wrote a friend, "it doesn't matter whether there is a Swedish ballet or a Russian Art Theatre or any of those things. Gurdjieff is the thing. . . . The intelligentsia is kookoo and dazed. . . . No advertising—no admission—and people go about with their eyes fixed and their tongues out—trying to get an invitation."

The reviews were excellent. It was "the most amazing dancing I had ever seen," gushed the correspondent from the *New York Times*. "In comparison the best of the Russian ballet seemed child's play."

* * *

MEANWHILE, FRANK LLOYD Wright had his eye on another woman. While living in Japan with Miriam Noel, Wright had read an American play, *Lulu Bett*, written by a woman who lived not far from Taliesin, in the small farming town of Portage, Wisconsin. Wright had known playwright Zona Gale's family back in his Oak Park days, when he designed her uncle Thomas and aunt Laura's house down the street from his own, and later another house and a summer cottage for Laura after her husband died. The second house, with its two jutting parapets, would provide the basis—as he liked to point out—for his masterpiece, Fallingwater, more than two decades later.

Gale's play dealt with a spinster's confrontation with the dull constraints of small-town life. He had met its author at Taliesin, and recalled her chiseled beauty and the intensity of her eyes. Now he resolved to pursue her: "Straightaway I made up my mind to know Zona Gale better when I got home; if not, to know the reason why." It was a decision that would change his life, though not for years, and in a way he could never have expected.

By the time Wright rediscovered her, the young woman with the intense eyes had become a literary sensation. Her play, which she adapted from her own novel, had won a Pulitzer Prize, making her the first woman to win. She was a feminist beauty, not unlike Mamah Cheney. And now, though he was still involved with Miriam Noel, Wright began courting Zona.

Miriam unleashed jealous tirades—sometimes, to Wright's mortification, on the common rural telephone line the Wrights shared with neighbors. He scolded Miriam in letters as a "poor tortured soul whose crying for the moon resolves itself in a wail over a round green cheese." He had no reason to be ashamed, he protested. "I can not even promise to be 'true' to you whatever you mean by it, I can only be true to myself. . . . But perspective is gone!

Zona Gale

Reason is gone! Charity is gone—now comes Fear—Hate—Revenge—Punishment. Then Regret—Shame, Humiliation—Ashes. . . . Hear me! Sex is the curse of Life."

Wright drove up river from Taliesin to visit Zona in Portage, where she lived with her aged father in a house dominated by a two-story Ionic-columned portico (which predictably displeased the architect). Wright arrived at her house with his arms full of wildflowers he had gathered along the way. "[S]he was always glad to see us," he remembered, "asking me to come. . . ."

On one occasion, in the spring of 1923, Wright brought his Japanese apprentice, Kameki Tsuchiura, and his wife, Nobu. Posing them on the lawn in traditional Japanese clothing, complete with parasol, he readied his camera and began "making pictures for Zona." She made suppers for him and his guests in her home. But she refused to be seen in public with him; she was, after all, a Regent of the University of Wisconsin—not to mention a Daughter of the American Revolution—and he was a walking scandal.

Frank wanted Zona. To him, she was "like something exquisitely carved out of ivory." He hoped to bring her back to Taliesin. Still unmarried at forty-nine, Zona Gale was available. But she did not want Frank. And this was one maiden, it turned out, whom Wright didn't know how to pursue. It wasn't that Gale didn't believe in love. "Loving," she wrote, "like prayer, is a power and a process." "Perhaps," Wright later revealed, "I had always expected the women to make love to me. I just didn't know how to make love to Zona Gale."

ONE WHO EVIDENTLY did have the power to entrance Zona Gale was Georgi Gurdjieff. Fresh from the publication of her new novel, *Faint Perfume*, Gale was at the Neighborhood Playhouse on the night when the master debuted his sacred dances. Long interested in Theosophy, Gale inherited a taste in the occult from her mother, whom Gale believed to have been clairvoyant. When she discovered Gurdjieff, she was still grieving her mother's recent death; she claimed to have received hundreds of "spirit messages" from beyond the grave.

Gale threw herself into Gurdjieff's cause, volunteering to organize the publicity campaign for the master's next demonstration, a major event at Carnegie Hall. Four days before the performance, she wrote a letter to the editor of the *New York Times*: "The Asiatic dances are very beautiful, but these are merely an introduction to the technique developed by Mr. Gurdjieff, whose Institute, now established in the chief European cities, may in another year have an American branch."

*   *   *

ON MARCH 3, 1924, Carnegie Hall was packed with New Yorkers—spiritualists, Theosophists, artists, intellectuals—eager to find out what this Gurdjieff business was all about. And this time, they actually had to buy a ticket.

The evening's dance demonstrations, accompanied by Thomas de Hartmann's percussive piano, followed what some had already seen at the Neighborhood Playhouse—until, that is, the dancers lined up at the back of the stage for what appeared to be a repeat of the "Stop exercise." As Gurdjieff seemed to direct the dancers with his eyes alone, his students raced forward toward the audience . . . and the edge of the stage. Instead of yelling "Stop!" Gurdjieff calmly turned his back and lit a cigarette as the dancers hurtled through the air into the orchestra pit in a fearful crash, leaving a pile of human forms strewn about in front of the stage. Only then did he yell "Stop!" freezing them where they lay, silent in collapse. When Gurdjieff gave them permission to rise—and it was clear that no one had broken anything—the audience broke into resounding applause.

Claude Bragdon was also in the audience, but he didn't share the general enthusiasm. He found the students' memory feats unimpressive; having undertaken memory training himself, he knew that such tricks could "be learned by anyone without much difficulty." Neither did he like the dances, thinking them remarkable for their precision but "lacking in beauty." And while he recognized Gurdjieff "as a man of power," Gurdjieff and his adepts repelled him as human beings.

Others from America's avant-garde were more impresssed. Writer Waldo Frank, a leading figure of New York's thriving modernist literary movement, was one. Wowed by Bragdon's edition of Ouspensky's *Tertium Organum*, Waldo Frank had declared in his recent book *Our America* that he and his contemporaries were the first generation of spiritual pioneers. His circle included Jean Toomer, the Harlem Renaissance writer he mentored; the novelists Sherwood Anderson and Hart Crane; and Frank Lloyd Wright's most important advocate, the architectural critic Lewis Mumford. Waldo Frank's own wife, Margaret Naumberg, the founder of New York's progressive Walden School, was also part of the circle.

With the apparent exception of Mumford, they had all caught the Gurdjieff fever. Toomer, who once identified himself as an "American with Negro blood in his veins," saw Gurdjieff's work as a potential pathway toward a spiritual brotherhood beyond race. While Waldo Frank and Margaret Naumberg's standing in the New York scene made them big catches for Gurdjieff, no one could have foreseen the role they would later play in the life of Frank Lloyd Wright.

*   *   *

IN MARCH GURDJIEFF mounted a second Carnegie Hall demonstration, and once again the city's cultural elite were there in force, including many repeat customers like Dreiser and O'Hara. Word was spreading; the new event drew such luminaries as T. S. Matthews, later the editor of *Time*, and Herbert Croly, founder of the *New Republic*, who had been the editor of the *Architectural Record* during the remarkable six-year period when Wright produced the Larkin Building, Unity Temple, and the best of the Prairie houses.

Gurdjieff also made the rounds of the city's literary salons. One of the most important was led by the wealthy and much married patron Mabel Dodge Luhan. Luhan was a friend to many literary greats, especially D. H. Lawrence, to whom she had recently given another of her properties, a mountain ranch twenty miles outside Taos, New Mexico. Lawrence's wife, Frieda, reluctant to accept the ranch as an outright gift, gave Dodge the hand-written manuscript for *Sons and Lovers* in return.

Lawrence had warned Luhan about Gurdjieff. He had heard enough about the Prieuré "to know that it is a rotten, false, self-conscious place of people playing a sickly stunt." Luhan was not only undeterred, but also soon wondered if Gurdjieff might want to obtain her own compound in Taos for a second Prieuré.

Luhan's friend Muriel Draper, a close friend of Henry James and Gertrude Stein, ran the other major salon that was drawn into the Gurdjieff movement. An interior designer, Draper soon became the architectural editor for the *New Yorker*.

Alfred Orage worked to transform these literary networks into Gurdjieff study groups around the city. For some, the Institute was a part-time interest; others became consumed by it. Explaining her complete conversion, Margaret Anderson claimed to speak for the others: "Gurdjieff's statement was that there does exist a super-knowledge, a super-science . . . and what he had to say about it convinced us that we would never hear anything else which could illuminate the great texts to which we had always wanted to give a reverent investigation."

THE SECOND CARNEGIE Hall event, on March 3, 1924, was packed, and Zona Gale's publicity campaign was given much of the credit. About a week later, Gurdjieff sent Orage to Boston and then on to Chicago to make arrangements for additional public demonstrations. The Englishman's reception at Harvard and Boston was tentative, even frosty—but faculty at the University of Chicago and Northwestern University, and the intellectual society surrounding them, were decidedly intrigued. "It's surprising," Orage wrote back to Jessie Dwight, "what a splash a little Gurdjieff makes when it drops into a university pool."

Gale came to Chicago, her home turf, to help Orage organize the demonstration. "Zona is still very ardent," Orage wrote Dwight. She has "many friends here and is thought much of." If necessary, Gale offered, she would cover the entire troupe's train fare back from Chicago.

There were others with the wealth and commitment to help out. Julie Rublee, birth control pioneer Margaret Sanger's closest associate and the wife of a wealthy attorney, was one. Sanger, like Gale, was a friend of Wright's. Thanks to Rublee, Gale, and others, two Chicago theaters were booked; box seats were priced at fifty dollars, quite a sum in those days.

The Chicago demonstrations were a success. The *Daily News* reported that the audience was enthralled and appreciative. "Ancient esoteric rites, group dances taken from the monasteries of the Far East and native music," the article read, "comprise the unique program." The story was accompanied by a photograph of three female dancers, the caption identifying one as Olgivanna Hinzenberg.

The chances of establishing a branch of the Institute in Chicago looked promising. Before leaving, Gurdjieff and Orage appointed a small committee to explore the prospect of setting up groups there. In fund-raising terms, however, the city was a disappointment. After paying the bills, the troupe found that they were broke. Olgivanna and the other dancers—one of them now pregnant by Gurdjieff—were unable to purchase train tickets back to New York. Although she had picked up Orage's hotel bill, Zona Gale hadn't come through with the windfall the master had expected. Some members of the Community Chest charity organization took pity and raised the money for the group's fare back east.

By the time they joined Gurdjieff in Manhattan, he had made some major decisions about the future of the Institute in America. Alfred Orage would stay in New York to expand his network of groups, deliver lectures to attract more people, screen candidates to be sent on to the Prieuré, and, of course, raise money. On April 8, 1924, in the East Side apartment of Juliet Rublee, Gurdjieff founded a New York branch of the Institute for the Harmonious Development of Man. Gurdjieff planned to split his time between the French and American branches, wintering in New York.

The three-month American campaign had been a recruiting success. Gurdjieff had signed up an enthusiastic core of influential New Yorkers and Chicagoans. Some money had been raised, at least in New York—enough to make the next payment on the Prieuré, but evidently not enough to book passages for everyone back to France.

Olgivanna was among those left behind.

* * *

BY NOW LOUIS Sullivan was failing, his eyes sunken; he was unable even to traverse a crosswalk without pausing for breath. Wright would sit by his bed, listening to him read from the manuscript of his book *The Autobiography of an Idea*. Wright had declined to write the preface, so Sullivan had gotten Claude Bragdon in his place. "The book," Frank remembered, "meant life to him now." In his text, Sullivan recalls his thrilling discovery that function created the form to fulfill it. Indeed every function, including that of man, was a power, and all such powers derived from "the all-power of Life." There was, he contended, a truth to beauty, a beauty that could only be had by cleaving to that truth.

Wright came once a week. Sullivan's condition steadily worsened, to the point where "his breath was so short he would have to take my arm to walk— even very slowly." As his mentor declined, Wright increased his visits to several times a week. One day, as Wright got up to leave, Sullivan begged him, "Don't leave me, Frank, stay." Wright waited into the evening, when Sullivan had fallen asleep. Before the long trip back to Taliesin, he made the nurse promise to call him if he was needed.

On his next visit, a few days later, Sullivan seemed better. A finished copy of *The Autobiography of an Idea* was on the table by his bed. Its publication, by the American Institute of Architects, meant a kind of ratification of Sullivan's life by the very gatekeepers he had reviled and who had blocked his way. "There it is, Frank," Sullivan said as he looked over to the book. "I was sitting by him," Wright recalled, "my arm around him to keep him warm and steady him. I could feel every vertebra in his backbone as I rubbed my hand up and down his spine to comfort him; and I could feel his enlarged heart pounding."

Sullivan asked Wright to hand him the book. "The first copy to you, Frank! A pencil?" At first Sullivan couldn't raise his arm to write. Finally, as he inscribed the book, he said, "Frank, it is you who has created the new architecture in America, but I do not believe you could have done it without me."

Less than a year earlier, in 1923, shortly after learning with Wright that the Imperial Hotel withstood the huge earthquake and fire that engulfed Tokyo, Sullivan reviewed Wright's Imperial Hotel in the *Architectural Record*. Wright, he proclaimed, had performed a "high act of courage"; he had managed to "penetrate" the "genius of another people," offering them a building that, while containing no form that was particularly Japanese, nonetheless captured "their innermost thought. . . . [T]he Imperial Hotel stands unique as the high water mark thus far attained by any modern architect. Superbly beautiful it stands—a noble prophecy." Frank Lloyd Wright had been anointed.

But Sullivan's autobiography itself must have hurt Wright. Although the book argues for the importance of nurturing young genius, Sullivan never even mentions Wright by name. A quarter of a century later, in Wright's testament to his master, *Genius and Mobacracy*, he would write, "I could never regard the book without a strange resentment. I know of it only by what he read to me himself."

Louis Sullivan died that April. Wright, who missed the funerals of both his parents, resolved to be there for his *lieber meister*'s. And he was—at least partially. When the service began, he stood outside, unable to share a room with the remains. In his eulogy, published later, Wright railed against an America that spurned his "beloved master," one unable to recognize beautiful form. Sullivan's "fertility," he declared, was "great enough to scatter seed no matter the obstruction."

When Wright left his master for the last time, Sullivan had pressed into his hands a thick sheaf of architectural drawings, including his latest floral illustrations, as well as nudes he had executed as a student in Paris. "Frank," he asked, "you will be writing about these some day?"

"Yes, *lieber meister*," Wright replied, "I will."

Wright, who always suspected he was ugly, had seen his own beauty through Sullivan's "beautiful eyes." "To know him well was to love him well," he wrote. "I never liked the name Frank until I would hear him say it, and the quiet breath he gave it made it beautiful in my ears. . . ."

STILL IN NEW York, Olgivanna spent her time with Jane Heap. Heap was a woman who got what she wanted, and she wanted this supple and resolute dancer. The anarchist Emma Goldman, whose cause *The Little Review* had championed, had found Heap's amorous advances too aggressive; Olgivanna evidently found her just right.

Before sailing back to France, Olgivanna spent her last night in passionate embrace with Jane Heap. In her diary, Heap wrote that she "played" with Olgivanna in New York, her slang for casual sex. Yet their relationship must have been more than mere play, for on that last night, she passed up bidding farewell to another lover, Lady Rothermere.

Others had noticed Olgivanna as well. The movie director Cecil B. De-Mille, whose brother had directed the movie version of Zona Gale's *Lulu Bett*, offered her a job as a dancer in Hollywood films. But she declined De-Mille's invitation in favor of the chance to bring Svetlana to the Prieuré to be with the master. After nearly two years apart from her daughter, it seemed Olgivanna had finally passed Gurdjieff's brutal test.

A week after Olgivanna set sail, Jane Heap was aboard a Cunard liner, steaming toward France and, as she put it, "my Olgivanna." Alfred Orage, who hoped to recruit Heap to work with him at the Prieuré, remained, for now, in New York. The two editors would make a powerful team. Orage had confided in Heap his low opinion of Olgivanna. "Orage said many harsh things about my Olgivanna," Heap wrote a friend from on board the *Beregania*, "but they were the things that one could easily say about any woman of that type. I happen to like the type. . . ."

Perhaps Orage was put off by Olgivanna's air of superiority, especially around the English. But more likely he was galled that she had rejected his own seductions during the New York visit. Her reason—that an affair between members of the Institute would be unwise—apparently did not apply to affairs with women.

By the end of the voyage, however, Orage's hectoring about Olgivanna had gotten to Heap. "You are in the power of a despot," he told her, "which is the sum of your personalities which says 'Won't' to everything." Olgivanna, he convinced her, was part of that negativity. "I'll have to give Olgivanna up," she wrote a friend just before landing at Cherbourg.

Jane Heap, Margaret Anderson, and Anderson's new lover, the actress and singer Georgette Leblanc, encamped at the Prieuré and were assigned to the Monk's Corridor. There they met up with an old friend, the pianist and modernist composer Carol Robinson, whom they had promoted as America's "foremost pianist" in *The Little Review*. The doe-eyed Robinson, who had moved from Chicago to New York following Heap and Anderson, was part of their lesbian circle. Whether as friend or lover, the tall, slim pianist with cat-

Carol Robinson, Gurdjieff's pianist and Olgivanna's lifelong friend

tail eyebrows had shared Jane Heap's apartment at least since 1922, the year Heap and Anderson broke up.

Robinson had been performing with the Boston Symphony when Gurdjieff arrived in that city to give a lecture. She attended, and Gurdjieff, who was always adept at spotting likely converts, singled her out in the audience. Gurdjieff invited Robinson to be one of four lucky prospects, two men and two women, whom he had selected as four different types to come spend the summer at the Prieuré. Although everyone assumed the master was nearly penniless, he offered to pay their way. Robinson, who had contracts to teach master classes at three universities, cancelled everything to go.

At the Prieuré, Carol Robinson did physical labor with the others during the day and accompanied the movements on the piano at night. Gurdjieff loved hearing her perform. And Robinson, acutely conscious of the physical aspect of playing the piano, was enthralled by the possibilities of working music and dance through one another, a subject she explored for the rest of her career. Olgivanna was her movements instructor that summer. She also became Olgivanna's new roommate, and the two became lifelong friends.

Orage's warnings on the ship failed to squelch Jane Heap's attraction to Olgivanna. "Olgivanna was in the kitchen—and couldn't play with me," she recalled to a friend, "and is too much under the Institute rule to be herself . . . all changed from New York." Part of it was that Olgivanna, who spoke a rough English, felt threatened by Jane's long-hewn intellectual intimacies with the eloquent Margaret Anderson. Anderson found Olgivanna good-looking, but was offended by what she perceived as the young woman's studied indifference.

If Olgivanna was subservient to Gurdjieff, Jane Heap deferred to no one. She could never be just one of the girls, even refusing to take steam baths with them. Gurdjieff's all-male Saturday night feasts irritated her so much that she helped organize a women-only counterpart in one of the bedrooms. "Never such thing again in my house," Gurdjieff declared when he found out. From then on, all the major feasts included both women and men.

THE "SHOCKS" THAT can change one's life aren't always predictable—even to Gurdjieff, the master of what he called the "vulnerable interval," the precise moment when such a shock can have maximal impact on a human being. Gurdjieff liked to drive fast, and he was a very bad driver. On July 8, 1924, after a huge Armenian lunch on a sultry Parisian afternoon, he was driving his Citroen at ninety kilometers per hour when he had to swerve to avoid another vehicle entering from a crossroad. His car slammed into an embankment and then into a large tree; the collision snapped the steering column, sheared the engine off its seating, and smashed all the windows and doors.

Carol Robinson had just come back from a night with Jane Heap in Paris when a gendarme appeared at the Institute with the shocking news. Somehow, the policeman reported, Gurdjieff had managed to get a blanket and seat cushion out of the car and was found lying covered on the ground, unconscious, badly lacerated, with a severe concussion. The doctors didn't think he would survive.

But he did. His head heavily bandaged, Gurdjieff was taken by stretcher and driven back to the Prieuré, where he lay unconscious for five days with Olgivanna, among others, tending to him. When he finally awoke, he couldn't see properly, and didn't recognize people he had known for years.

"[I]t was hushed and sad there," Heap recalled. "I talked a few moments to Olgivanna—something had gone wrong." She couldn't decide whether it was fearful grief or jealousy about Jane's other liaisons. "[S]he is 'afraid to bring life into institute' she says—but I think something had made her jealous or angry—or unhappy—she acts very strange and is very appealing." (If Olgivanna was jealous, Heap shouldn't have been surprised. Between sojourns with James Joyce, who explained his new novel to her, and Gertrude Stein, whom she was arranging to publish, Jane was having affairs with the girls of Paris, as well as Djuna Barnes and Lady Rothermere. "I've so many heart affairs that I get tied up all around the place," she wrote that summer.)

Olgivanna and the others were profoundly traumatized by Gurdjieff's accident, and not just because Gurdjieff was hovering near death, his lungs fed by oxygen tanks. The very goal of his teaching was supposed to avoid accident, to develop a will that chose a direction and stayed on the path. Gurdjieff, in fact, had asked a mechanic to check his car just before the accident—particularly the steering wheel, the very part that caused the accident. And, unaccountably, he had asked his secretary to take the train rather than to drive with him, as she always did. Was the master himself subject to his law of accident? Some concluded that he must have chosen the path that left his body nearly lifeless. Visiting the crash site, his visibly shaken ex-disciple Ouspensky anxiously declared, "I still wonder whether it's really an accident? . . . Has he not gone too far?—I tell you, I'm terribly afraid."

As he lay awaiting his fate, Gurdjieff called for his students to light fires outside the Prieuré, perhaps to draw their energies. With Olgivanna working away at a crosscut saw, the students felled the huge trees on the property to keep bonfires going on the lawn. Gurdjieff sat outside in the summer heat dressed in a heavy black coat and astrakhan hat. During his long and painful recovery, his followers spoke in hushed tones, some huddled on the floor in front of his closed bedroom door. And the money stopped coming in. Each did what he or she could to earn some revenue.

In the solemn aftermath of the accident, Olgivanna appeared to warm again to Jane Heap. "Olgivanna liked me yesterday," Heap wrote a friend a month after the crash, "but I haven't tried to see her for two weeks, she hurts me, I left her last night when she wanted me to stay and I couldn't sleep—for unhappiness."

*   *   *

WHAT APPEARED TO be an accident, Gurdjieff proclaimed, was nothing of the sort. "It was the last chord of the manifestation toward me of that 'something' usually accumulating in the common life of people, which . . . was first noticed by the Great, really Great King of Judea, Solomon, and was called 'Tzvarnoharno.'" This great shock, he contended, had been sent to show him that his pupils' vanity would prevent them from ever being truly able to disseminate his teachings.

Gurdjieff had always resisted the idea of writing anything down himself, allowing Ouspensky to record his teachings. Now, in the wake of the accident, he decided to preserve his wisdom on the printed page.

"It was in the year 223 after the creation of the World, by objective time-calculation, or, as it would be said, here on the 'Earth,' in the year 1921 after the birth of Christ." So began his sprawling interplanetary narrative, *Beelzebub's Tales to His Grandson*, written from the perspective of Beelzebub, a fallen figure who was exiled to Earth after his rebellion against God. In the story, Beelzebub—a derisive Hebrew term for the Canannite god Baal—arrives on Earth from the "trans-space" ship, Karnak, in the year 1921. Beelzebub's tales, told to his grandson Hassein on their return from exile, lay out the structure of the universe, the fallen state of man, and the path to redemption.

Having embarked on such a massive project, Gurdjieff now grew concerned that his disciples' presence was sapping his limited energy. One morning, Olgivanna and the others were called to the Study House. Too weak to speak, Gurdjieff had his secretary read a prepared statement. The "work" at the Prieuré, he declared, had come to an end. Few of the students, he read on, really understood it. Some had even betrayed him—a clear allusion to Ouspensky. "Now, inside of me everything is empty."

Moreover, Gurdjieff had decided to sell the Prieuré. "In two days everyone must be gone from here, only my own people stay." A list would be posted. "Everything now stop—dances, music, work. You all must go in two days." All, that is, but his closest disciples. "For a long time I live for others, now I begin to live for myself."

Olgivanna and the others were dismayed.

There were no more movements, no more exercises. Day and night the master worked away on *Beelzebub's Tales*, scribbling on pads in Armenian, dictating to Olga de Hartmann, occasionally breaking to compose music. His only teachings now came at day's end, when he read from the manuscript, often in poor Russian; his audience listened in reverent silence, their eyes lowered. He composed short new musical pieces to be played just before the reading of specific chapters, to condition their reception, and watched the listeners' faces to gauge the effect of his writing.

Gurdjieff periodically posted lists of those he still considered members of the Institute. One night, when Olgivanna checked the latest list, her name had disappeared. To make matters worse, she recalled, some on the list were "fools" compared to her. One of them was Bernard Metz, a young Englishman whose responsibilities included serving as Gurdjieff's valet and auto repairman.

At midnight, distraught, she made her way to Gurdjieff's room. She was indignant, she told him; this was unfair.

The master didn't mince words. Metz, he told her, worked harder than she had. He was tougher. "He would strike anyone for the Institute," Gurdjieff chastised, whereas she would not. And there was more: "Those who became her friends," he continued, "became the enemies of the Institute." She protested further, but Gurdjieff had made up his mind. Olgivanna would have to leave the Institute. She had failed, she was told. She had not worked hard enough.

"His words struck me," she later confessed, "reverberating through my being." Within weeks Olgivanna was in Paris, working as an attendant in a women's lavatory.

A MONTH AFTER her departure from the Prieuré, Gurdjieff met Olgivanna at a small sidewalk table at the Café de la Paix. The master's once-promising pupil was still floundering. She should start a new life, he told her. It was time for her to leave France.

Olgivanna didn't know where to go, she confessed. Russia, perhaps? She missed the Caucasus, and her sister, a believer in Lenin, still lived there.

Gurdjieff had other ideas. Olgivanna should go to New York and connect with members of the Institute there, including Carol Robinson, who had just returned to the States from the Prieuré. From there she should go to Chicago, the Institute's next target city, where Jean Toomer was expected to take the lead. He reminded Olgivanna about her husband, now an architect in Chicago. "[Y]our daughter needs a father."

"But I need you," Olgivanna protested.

"I have taught you everything that I have to teach you. You will never be lost now. Make a new form of life for yourself. I will see you again."

"You are my true student," Olgivanna recalled him adding. "You remember the gold coin you found on Christmas? I told you then you were the chosen one. But still you must make your own decision."

Olgivanna must have been bewildered. Gurdjieff had declared her chosen and then ejected her. Perhaps he was trying to crack her ego, to counter her oft-observed air of superiority, which could have only gotten worse after she received that extraordinary Christmas present. Whatever the case, now he was offering redemption—apparently in exchange for meeting his expectations in America. The message would have been clear: The gold coin was still to be earned.

"From the rue de la Paix," Olgivanna recalled, "I went by myself to Notre Dame to feel the powerful silence of that ancient cathedral I loved. And it was there that I felt inner agreement with the directive that Georgivanich had given me."

She returned from the cathedral and told Gurdjieff of her decision. He promised to take care of her passport, her transportation, and all of her expenses.

Once again, Olgivanna spent her last nights before departing with Jane Heap. At one point, Heap gave a drunken monologue before passing out in bed. "O she talked all sad things of our lives," Olgivanna described it at the time, "like Gertrude Stein, repetition—and beautiful face with beautiful words and gentle tears."

On October 21, 1924, Olgivanna Hinzenberg and her daughter traveled to Le Havre, where they boarded the *Rochambeau* bound for New York. As she unpacked their belongings, Jean Toomer, the other student assigned to Chicago, was in another cabin on the ship, doing the same.

IF FRANK LLOYD Wright was the genius of Victor Hugo's prophecy, he was fortified with Louis Sullivan's mystical seed. On his final visit to Sullivan's bedside, Wright learned that his master had just published not one, but two books. In addition to his autobiography, Sullivan had written a very slim volume on architectural theory: *A System of Architectural Ornament According with a Philosophy of Man's Powers*. Here, in a work he considered one of his greatest achievements, Sullivan revealed the mystical dimension of his organic architecture, proclaiming it a "new faith." Architecture, with its transformative geometries, had powers "to control by means of formulas and secret ritual, the destiny of man."

For Sullivan, that destiny was determined by a "germ of a seed" within every man that was the locus of his power. Indeed, if man could grasp the germ's powers as the source of his own, he could finally realize his potential as a "super-manipulator who materializes his dreams in the every-day world." He would finally recognize that he possesses the power to partner with God. Man, he declared, could claim his place with God as "co-creators."

And Louis Sullivan saw Frank Lloyd Wright as just such a man.

Wright soon took Sullivan's message one step further. In the same month that Olgivanna Hinzenberg left Europe for New York and Chicago, the German architect Erich Mendelssohn visited Wright at Taliesin. Wright revealed to him his vision of a new marriage between religion and architecture. "I think," Wright told him, "the old separation between God and man is disappearing. Man today is becoming a god."

Wright's first wife, Catherine Tobin, had brought him into bourgeois family life. Mamah Cheney had instigated his transformation into a bohemian renegade. He was now only weeks away from meeting the woman who would stir him to reach for divinity.

THE MAD GENIUS OF THE PIG BRISTLES AND MR. BELLYBUTTON

FRANK LLOYD WRIGHT WAS ALONE. For months he had ferried back and forth from Taliesin to the tawdry hotel room in Chicago to succor his *lieber meister*. Now Louis Sullivan was dead. A month after the funeral, Miriam walked out on Wright. Their rancorous five-month marriage had turned violent. After taking the unprecedented step of seeing a psychiatrist, Wright recognized that the relationship was hopeless, although it would be more than a year before he filed for divorce.

No one will ever know just what Wright told the doctor, but by his own admission, he needed women like Miriam Noel—women who pursued him. And she was barely out the door when another such woman slipped into his life. As he told the story, it all seemed so innocent, almost childlike.

It began on the morning of November 30, 1924, a day he would never forget. The fifty-seven-year-old architect was encamped at his favorite Chicago hotel, the Congress on Michigan Avenue—a pretty posh place for a man who had recently written his son that he had "less than none by forty-seven thousand dollars." Sullivan had consulted in the hotel's design at the height of his success, in the same year that he fired Wright for moonlighting.

"I am learning to be alone by degrees," Wright wrote his son Lloyd at the time. Later he recalled feeling "lower down in my [own] estimation than I had ever been in my life." But Wright now had his eye on a big one. He had a contract for preliminary sketches for an enormous project in the city, a skyscraper for the National Life Insurance Company. "All his hopes," a guest at Taliesin at the time recalled, "were based on this." It would have been the largest commission he had ever taken.

Frank Lloyd Wright was finally emerging from the Wisconsin woods. Before arriving in town, he announced in the *Chicago Tribune* that he was opening an office in the city to accommodate twelve draftsmen. He would be devoting his practice to commercial projects—a gesture sure to convince National Life that he was committed to being a straight-and-narrow businessman's architect. And that wasn't all. The announcement promised that he would be moving his home to Chicago as well. In just four weeks, it seemed, Taliesin would become vacant.

At that very moment, there were others looking for just such an estate.

A MONTH EARLIER, the French liner *Rochambeau* had docked in New York Harbor. Among its passengers was a lanky twenty-five-year-old woman, wearing a short squirrel jacket, her seven-year-old daughter. Along with Olgivanna and Svetlana Hinzenberg, the passengers on that voyage included another noted Gurdjieffian, the handsome Jean Toomer.

"As directed by Georgivanich," Olgivanna wrote in her memoirs, "I stopped in New York." After contacting Institute members there, she was to go to Chicago. Gurdjieff suggested she reunite with her husband there, and on the ship's alien passenger list, she did list Valdemar's address as her destination.

Olgivanna was on assignment. Her master had instructed her to help start an Institute group, apparently in Chicago. Though she later claimed that the group was to be her own, the evidence suggests that Gurdjieff and Orage expected Toomer to be the leader. Olgivanna would be responsible for teaching the movements, just as she had done at the Prieuré. Whatever her mission, she believed Gurdjieff had prepared her well. She was, she recalled, "ready and fearless."

Mother and daughter checked into New York's Hotel Brevoort, a few blocks off Washington Square in Greenwich Village. Rather than stay with her brother on the West Side, Gurdjieff booked her into the hotel, across the street from the apartment where Mabel Dodge Luhan hosted her avant-garde literary salon and her Gurdjieff groups.

Olgivanna was in no hurry to get to Chicago. She spent a month in New York meeting with members of the Institute. Just two days after her boat docked, Alfred Orage gave his first public lecture as head of the Institute's American branch, at the Lenox Theater. He was also holding weekly groups, charging ten dollars a month, at the homes of Luhan, Muriel Draper, and Jane Heap, as well as at Margaret Naumberg's Walden School. "Little knots of people scattered about town in comfortable places," Waldo Frank wrote in the *New Yorker*. "Here were true intellectuals who despised Greenwich Village. Here were [the] socially elect who looked down upon Park Avenue as a gilded slum." Orage, he wrote, "drops spiritual bombs into the laps of ladies who adore him."

Orage's public lectures were weekly affairs, and among the luminaries who attended were a number of Wright's friends—Georgia O'Keefe and her husband, Alfred Steiglitz; Claude Bragdon; and, likely, Zona Gale. Orage told his audience at the Lenox talk that Gurdjieff groups would soon be springing up across the nation. But his leader expected more. It had been eight months since Zona Gale had announced in the *New York Times* that Gurdjieff wanted an American center, a second Prieuré, up and running in a year. But no site had yet presented itself. Olgivanna, the evidence suggests, found a way to help. Three months after moving to America, she, along with Zona Gale, Alfred Orage, and Jean Toomer, would have a business proposition to discuss with Gale's old suitor, Frank Lloyd Wright. That proposition almost certainly involved using Taliesin as the Institute's Chicago-area center.

The complex chain of events leading to that meeting began just a week after Olgivanna arrived in the city, when she made her way uptown to the apartment of novelist Waldo Frank, by now a serious participant in the Gurdjieff groups. The event would have included numerous other writers and artists caught up in the nascent American Gurdjieff movement. The most important guest, as things turned out, was the American painter Jerome Blum.

Jerry Blum was a brilliant colorist whose work had been exhibited at the Chicago Art Institute and the Whitney Studio Club. His good friend Sherwood Anderson said of one of his paintings, "I would ask for nothing more than to live with a little canvas like that for the rest of my life." Blum was well connected to Olgivanna's Gurdjieff circle, including her close friend Carol Robinson, to whom he had given one of his paintings.

Blum also knew Frank Lloyd Wright, having gotten to know the architect well ten years before, when he worked on the murals and color scheme for the architect's Midway Gardens. Like Wright, Blum was a man who noticed women and was noticed by them. He took chances, once voyaging to Tahiti to convince its queen to sit for a portrait. With his oversize, commanding eyebrows and a pungent Havana cigarette hanging from his sensuous lips, he projected both toughness and sensitivity. Women did not forget his face, his husky voice, the way he talked about them.

Olgivanna and Jerry, who met that night at Waldo Frank's, had much in common. Both had recently lived in France; both were preparing to leave for Chicago to deal with pending divorce arrangements. In mid-November, within a week or so of their first meeting at Waldo Frank's, Jerry Blum and

Olgivanna Hinzenberg each left for Chicago. By then, she later told a confidante, the two had become friends.

Though Olgivanna had other friends in Chicago, she and Svetlana stayed
at Valdemar's apartment. That first week went poorly. There was nothing—
not even physically—between them. And then there was the metaphysical.
Valdemar, she moaned, "rejected the interior life with its infinite riches. . . . I
had to have more in my life."

Even in New York, Olgivanna had already known her marriage was over.
The day before her departure, she had stood at the window of her Manhattan
hotel room watching the rain sheet down the glass. "God," she prayed, "help
me to find a man some day whom I can love and respect and create life with
deep content, full of rich experiences of working together, thinking and feeling together. God, please help me."

EIGHT DAYS LATER, on the afternoon of November 30, Wright heard a
knock at the door of his room at the Congress. He wasn't expecting anyone—
and certainly not Jerry Blum. Wright hadn't heard from Blum for a decade,
since the Midway Gardens project was completed. Although the two had
much in common—sensitive boys who became avant-garde artists, boys

who hated school and whose
fathers beat them—they were
not close friends. Wright found
the painter intense, perhaps a
little too intense; he called
Blum the "mad genius-of-the-
pig-bristles," a reference to the
brushes preferred by oil painters. In his autobiography, he
described Blum as "rather terrifying." And with good reason:
Whether Wright knew it or
not, Blum was packing a gun in
the city, concealed in a deep
vest pocket, where, he noted, "it
could be taken out again with
ease."

After trading stories of
marital misery, Jerry suggested

Jerry Blum

that they take a short walk to the Eighth Street Theatre for the three o'clock matinee. Thamar Karsavina, the great Russian ballerina, was there, making her only Chicago appearance. "All unsuspecting," as he later recalled, Frank agreed. The twelve-hundred-seat theater was sold out that afternoon. But Blum just happened to have two tickets.

The performance had been arranged by Adolph Bolm, a noted dancer and director who starred in the 1910 premiere of Igor Stravinsky's *The Firebird*. Bolm had helped Gurdjieff and his troupe stage a demonstration at Chicago's Blackstone Theater seven months before, working with Olgivanna's friend Juliet Rublee on the event's sponsoring committee, booking the venue, and providing the studio for Institute rehearsals. Gurdjieff found the choreographer "very amiable and obliging," dubbing him "Mister Bellybutton," presumably inspired by the fact that dance costumes often left the navel exposed.

Bolm later became the first director of the San Francisco Ballet. But a greater contribution to American art may have been a small kindness he apparently granted to Gurdjieff—offering the master his private balcony box on that November afternoon.

Wright remembered the moment in exquisite detail. "Our tickets landed us near the stage in two balcony box-seats, by the rail," he recalled. "A third seat in the box was empty: apparently the only unoccupied one in the big overcrowded house." The seat remained empty through appearances by the Eric DeLamarter Solo Orchestra and Bolm's Ballet Intime, performing his *Foyer de la Danse*, based on the painting by Edgar Degas.

Then, after another short intermission, Karsavina began dancing to Mozart's "Elopement" along with Bolm himself, who had choreographed the piece a year earlier. It had just begun, Wright recalled, when "an usher quietly showed a dark, slender gentlewoman to the one empty seat in the house," the one next to Jerry.

Olgivanna Hinzenberg had arrived.

Just as the evening's star began to dance, Olgivanna settled into her seat. For Frank, at least, her entrance upstaged Karsavina. "I secretly observed her aristocratic bearing, no hat, her dark hair parted in the middle and smoothed down over her ears, a light small shawl over her shoulders, little or no makeup, very simply dressed. French, I thought—very French . . . and yet perhaps Russian?"

According to Wright, Jerry too was more intent on the "dark, slender lady with the graceful movements" than on the great ballerina below. When Blum leaned toward her as if to speak, she unexpectedly moved away. Frank attributed the gesture to fear.

But Blum was determined to connect with Olgivanna. "He addressed

a remark to me," Wright remembered, "intended for her, foolishly compli-
menting Karsavina, so I gave him one also intended for the gentle stranger."

"No, Karsavina won't do. She's dead." Wright announced. "They are all
dead," gesturing with his hand to the audience below. "The dead is dancing to
the dead."

The beautiful stranger gave Wright a "quick comprehending glance."
Gurdjieff, after all, had taught her that most people live their lives as if they
were dead—automatic and unthinking. A "strange elation" stole over the architect. "Suddenly in my unhappy state," he recalled, "something cleared
up—what had been the matter with me came to look me in the face—it was,
simply, too much passion without poetry. Starved for poetry . . . that was it,"
he went on, "the best in me for years and years wasted—starved! This strange
chance meeting, was it poetry? I was a hungry man."

During the next intermission, Blum made the first move. "Pardon me,
Madam," he said, approaching Olgivanna, "we have met somewhere before?"
She seemed "unconvinced and unimpressed," Wright noted.

Blum pushed on. "In New York, at Waldo Frank's perhaps?"

Olgivanna gave a startled look—but to Frank, oddly, not Jerry. Indeed,
she replied, she knew the writer's wife, Margaret Naumberg. "A long shot,"
Frank thought. But then Jerry dropped a few more names, and it turned out
the two knew several people in common.

Frank thought Jerry a "clever knight," and Olgivanna "the emissary of Fate."

Once the dance of mutual recognition was over, Jerry introduced Frank.
"My friend," he announced, "he is Frank Lloyd Wright, the famous architect.
You may have heard of him."

She said she hadn't, but Frank thought she looked at him as though
she'd seen him before. "So much so," he recalled, "that I thought she had for
a moment."

Olgivanna introduced herself.

"I was in love with her," Wright recalled. "It was all as simple as that.
When Nature by hand of Fate has arranged her drama all else is besides the
mark. It is as it should be."

PROVIDENCE, OLGIVANNA WROTE in her only published account of the
meeting, "usually comes to help those who live for an ideal." She saw herself
as that providential gift to Wright, a man "searching for an expression of life
that placed the spirit above all else." In her unpublished memoirs, she offered
that "God had heard my earnest wish to meet a man whom I could love and
respect."

If it was God's work, he had a lot of helpers—all in some way connected to Gurdjieff, all suspiciously left out of Olgivanna's version of events. For one, she never mentioned the role of Adolph Bolm, the man who arranged the Chicago space where she danced the year before, and likely provided the penniless Olgivanna one of the most expensive boxes in the house. Nor did she mention Jerry Blum, the man who brought Wright into that box, whom she actually sat next to, whom she had recently spent time with in New York—the man, she privately confessed years later, who was actually a friend of hers.

AFTER THE BALLET, Wright invited Olgivanna and Jerry back to his hotel. She bowed her head in acceptance, Wright recalled, in "perfect ease without artificial hesitation." As they sipped their tea, Wright shared stories of his professional and personal life—from his struggling architecture practice and the murders that took Mamah Cheney and her children, to the triumphs of his revolutionary architecture and his Imperial Hotel's miraculous survival in the face of an earthquake.

"But now," he said after what must have been a long monologue, "tell me about yourself."

Olgivanna talked of art and philosophy. "She held her own in either," Wright quipped, "and 'her own' was a famous architect." She told of her child, her years with Gurdjieff, the movements he had taught her, the extraordinary powers to which they gave access. She told Wright that she was one of the Institute's five "star leaders," putting herself in the same league as Gurdjieff's composer Thomas de Hartmann and Dr. Leonid Stjernvall.

Wright had already heard—perhaps from Claude Bragdon or Zona Gale—about Gurdjieff and his Institute. And the mystic's ideas resonated with theories that had long intrigued him. Just weeks before his death, Sullivan had been regaling him with stories of ancient visionaries who were able to give "occult powers" to geometric forms, trying to master nature "by means of formulas and secret ritual." Wright shared Sullivan's belief that man already had these powers in his own nature. Wright was also knowledgeable about dance. Gurdjieff's movements reminded him of Jaques-Dalcroze, he observed, but "more profound." Olgivanna seemed impressed. "Between us across that tea table went more from each to each than I can ever describe," Wright recalled. Both he and Blum wanted to see her again. But only Jerry wrote down her address; the architect didn't have a pencil.

Wright had to go east for a week. He sent Olgivanna a note from the train. On his return, he discovered that Jerry had been spending time with her. But he needn't have worried. "[S]he only wanted to talk about you and that bored me," Jerry told him.

The would-be lovers spent much of that December apart; Wright had business in New York and a studio to maintain in Wisconsin. Passing through Chicago, he invited Olgivanna to the theater, and she took him around to meet her Institute friends. One of them, Carol Robinson, joined them for lunch. "He liked her," Olgivanna told another Gurdjieff associate at the time. "I tell him he will like my friends." Now and then Wright dropped by her apartment unannounced, presumably when Valdemar was at work.

With Orage and Toomer still in New York, Olgivanna decided to start "the work" in Chicago on her own. Neither Gurdjieff nor Orage considered her competent to run adult groups independently, so Olgivanna turned to recruiting teenagers who might want to learn the movements. Carol Robinson wrote her a letter of recommendation to her former piano teacher, who she thought could help identify prospective pupils. But getting started wasn't easy for Olgivanna. She telephoned everyone she'd met in Chicago, asking to teach their teenage children. Some agreed, but no one was willing to pay. She ended up teaching free. The parents, Olgivanna recalled, were satisfied. "Yet I had to have more than that in my life."

FRANK LLOYD WRIGHT certainly promised more than a life spent teaching adolescents. Olgivanna was still living with Valdemar when Wright began courting her. Valdemar didn't know about this new architect in his wife's cir-

A concert in Taliesin's living room. Seated next to Wright is Richard Neutra; his wife, Dione, is playing the cello.

cle, and Olgivanna knew he would not be pleased by the news. As she told a friend around this time, Valdemar had fallen in love with her all over again. For his part, Wright was under the impression that Olgivanna had already begun the process of divorcing her husband. She had not. It took a month after meeting Wright at the ballet before Olgivanna approached Valdemar and got him to agree to a divorce. They separated, for the last time, on New Year's Day, 1925. With Svetlana in tow, Olgivanna left Valdemar's place and went to stay with friends.

Frank invited Olgivanna to visit Taliesin—and she was awed by the sight. In her native Montenegro, where blood feuds between clans still passed for justice, an estate like this might have been a fortress. Taliesin was quite the opposite. Instead of thick stone walls rising high to crenellated parapets, Wright's broad low eaves hovered over wide, vulnerable glass windows. The architect had built no walls or gates between the highway and his living room, just a short drive up a winding gravel road to a wooden door.

There were other Europeans at Taliesin to greet Olgivanna—among them Richard Neutra, a young Viennese architect who had asked Wright for a job when they met at Sullivan's funeral. Neutra was getting ready to leave for Los Angeles to join another former Wright draftsman, Rudolph Schindler. But before his departure he stopped at Taliesin with his wife, Dione, a talented singer and cello player Frank fondly called his "songbird." Frank offered to design an evening gown for Dione, suggesting that she paint her cello to match it—a heresy to anyone familiar with instrument acoustics. Dione declined.

That wintry evening Olgivanna danced before the flames of Taliesin's huge living room fireplace as Dione Neutra played and sang Schubert's *Der Erlkonig*, a musical setting of a Goethe poem that Wright undoubtedly knew from his days with Mamah Cheney. As she sang, Dione must have bowed furiously to emulate Schubert's maniacal piano score, miming the pounding of a horse's hooves as a father rushes his fearful son home on a winter night. The beautiful boy hangs in his father's arms, hearing the seductive call of the "elf king." "I love you, charming boy," the elf king calls, "and if you don't come freely, I will take you by force!" When the anguished father arrives home, his son is dead in his arms. Olgivanna danced the composition's many roles—the protective father, the frightened son, the demonic tempter-king.

Olgivanna didn't stay long on that first visit. But by the end of January 1925 she had returned to Taliesin, this time to stay. Wright hired a chauffeur to pick her up in Madison. The two of them took off in a sparkling Cadillac, the chauffeur sporting a "special fur cap" for the occasion. At the end of the two-hour drive, Olgivanna passed through what was to be her new hometown, Spring Green—the village that was little more than one main street, Jefferson Street, with its Post House hotel and the few stores essential to any farm town. Continuing south on a two-lane road, within minutes they crossed the wide meandering Wisconsin River and entered the valley of the God-almighty Joneses, its snow-covered hills rising on either side of the road.

When Wright's car finally sped up the gravel lane toward the house, a young dog ran across its path. "The Cadillac which raced towards Taliesin drove over the head of poor Tatters," Neutra wrote his mother-in law, "you remember the funny puppy—and thus ended all further fun for him." Taliesin was now down to a single dog.

Falling back on a ruse he had first attempted when Miriam Noel moved in, Wright officially presented Olgivanna as the new housekeeper, an unconvincing charade to anyone who witnessed her chauffeured arrival. He even gave her an alias—Mary. Neutra was not impressed with the newcomer. "Mary whom you liked so much," he wrote his mother-in-law the next day, "is a WEAK female. Unfaithful to the Armenian poet," an apparent reference to Gurdjieff, "she can be considered as Wright's present sweetheart."

Olgivanna was entranced by Taliesin. "Such beautiful things, collections of lovely things he has at his place," she told a friend a few weeks later. There was a bronze Buddha and ceremonial gongs from China. From Japan, Wright had collected "magnificently painted screens in gold and silver on which were painted either colored flowers or clouds with birds or dark green fir boughs" as well as "magnificent embroideries" and "marvelously colored fabrics." He also had a photograph of Potala, the Dalai Lama's residence in Lhasa, Tibet—the only image on display at Taliesin of a building that Wright hadn't designed. Olgivanna knew well that Gurdjieff had visited there and studied its rites. She was taken as well with Taliesin's surroundings; she took eagerly to the country life, even braving the cold to run for hours in the country.

Wright marked her arrival at Taliesin with a promise that her life was now poised to take off. "Olgivanna, from this time on you won't be seen for the dust." Both were still married; Wright hadn't even filed for divorce from Miriam. But none of that mattered. "Waiting was not in our natures—never was," he recalled. Reeling in this lovely twenty-six-year-old woman was quite an accomplishment for the fifty-eight-year-old architect. "Olgivanna," he crowed, "was mine." And now she was at Taliesin to stay.

So, it appeared, was Wright. Despite the architect's published notice that he was abandoning Taliesin for Chicago—an announcement that may very well have gotten the attention of Gurdjieff's people seeking an American Prieuré—he was probably never all that serious about the idea. Taliesin meant everything to him. But the huge National Life Insurance skyscraper project meant something equally precious: financial security, at least temporarily. And so, before meeting Olgivanna, he expanded Taliesin's drafting room to accommodate twenty more people, in preparation for a visit from the company's president. When the executive arrived, Wright's desperation was palpable. "It was somewhat painful," Dione Neutra recalled, "for us to see such an outstanding man humbling himself by being amiable, offering hospitality in order to get a commission."

Wright was far happier offering his hospitality to Olgivanna. "My life in a worldly sense started then," she recalled. She always maintained to outsiders that everything changed after moving in with Wright, that she became a woman devoted to her man and his genius. But Olgivanna also had an "unworldly" life, one that was still ruled by Georgi Gurdjieff. Her loyalty to him, she revealed after Wright's death, was "unfaltering." As one confidante later put it, "she never lost sight of the objective for which she had migrated to America in the first place."

BACK IN NEW York, just a day or two after Olgivanna moved into Taliesin, Alfred Orage and Jean Toomer held a series of meetings on February 1 and 2, 1925. The general and his lieutenant had already been conferring regularly, strategizing on how to launch Gurdjieff in America. But on this occasion they were joined by Zona Gale—an unusual addition, for Gale had recently been somewhat inactive in the Institute. Just days before, Orage's lover Jessie Dwight had been forced to insist that Gale attend Orage's lectures. So why was Gale invited to this meeting? Undoubtedly because she was the Institute member who knew Frank Lloyd Wright the best—better, at this point, than Olgivanna herself. More to the point, she knew his estate, Taliesin, firsthand.

"Olgivanna   Hinzenberg was discussed" at both meetings, Dwight noted in her diary.

Orage didn't particularly cotton to Wright's new lover; af-

Jean Toomer

ter all Olgivanna had rebuffed his own romantic advances, and there were still "troubles" between them over it. But now, two days after she moved in with Wright, Orage was holding multiple meetings about her. Whatever his personal feelings, he and Toomer now needed her—or, more precisely, her new lover.

But why? In some respects Frank Lloyd Wright was no big catch for the movement. There were plenty of renowned artists and writers on board already, and the architect came with a lot of baggage. Living in sin once more with a married woman, Wright was again a scandal, just as he was less than two years before with Miriam, when Zona Gale had refused to risk her reputation by being seen with him in public.

Wright, however, had two big drawing cards for the Gurdjieffians: He was in love with Olgivanna, and he had an estate he had already announced his plans to vacate. Though Olgivanna later acknowledged that she found his Taliesin land appealing from the start, she never revealed exactly why. Yet any member of Gurdjieff's circle would have understood: The master needed a place to write his opus and his American leadership a base of operations. Zona Gale had announced the previous February in the *New York Times* that Gurdjieff hoped to have a new American center running within a year. And Taliesin would be perfect for the role. Like the Prieuré, it was isolated in the country and spacious, yet only a day's drive from a major city. The Gurdjieffians—even those with little confidence in Olgivanna—surely hoped she could deliver Taliesin for the Institute.

JUST TWO WEEKS after these meetings, Olgivanna left Taliesin for New York, bringing Wright with her. As the train clacked eastward across the plains, he read her to sleep with "Carl's fairy tale of *The White Horse Girl and The Blue Wind Boy*." "Carl" was his friend Carl Sandburg, who had written for his own daughter the story of a girl who rides her white horse and the boy who walks the hills listening for the "blue wind." "Of course," Wright read to her, "it happened as it had to happen, the White Horse Girl and the Blue Wind Boy met." Sandburg's young lovers go off together without telling anyone, leaving behind only one short letter:

> To All Our Sweethearts, Old Folks and Young Folks:
>
> We have started to go where the white horses come from and where the blue winds begin. Keep a corner in your hearts for us while we are gone.
>
> The White Horse Girl.
> The Blue Wind Boy.

Olgivanna, born just a year before Wright's daughter Frances, listened to the fairy tale and fell asleep.

But Olgivanna was a big girl. Shortly after arriving in New York, on Tuesday, February 17, she left Wright to meet with Orage, Toomer, and Gale. The meeting was very long; something big was clearly in the works. Afterward, Wright joined the group for lunch—and in doing so was confronted with Zona Gale, the woman he had once wanted more than any other. If this lunch was part of Orage's strategy to secure Taliesin, it was a brilliant touch. How could he say no to Zona Gale?

If the Gurdjieffians approached Wright directly that day about the possibility of using Taliesin as their new center, he must have been intrigued—if only for financial reasons. Wright's huge insurance company project hadn't come through, and he had little else on the drawing board. And he was still $47,000 in debt. Alfred Orage, however, was by then garnering enough donations in New York to support his operation and send thousands of dollars back to Gurdjieff in France. There was no shortage of spiritually inclined wealthy Americans. Sharing the cost of the estate with Olgivanna's friends would have been tempting.

Beyond the monetary lure, Wright would certainly have wanted to please his new love. But he was also attracted to Gurdjieff's philosophy. There were many uncanny correspondences in their thinking. Wright, like Gurdjieff, believed in the unity of all life, in the correspondences between nature, as the book of God, and the soul of man. Nature's interior order was Wright's religion and his most profound design inspiration.

Although Gurdjieff looked beyond nature to cosmic forces, he also placed enormous importance on "organic life," which he understood as the Earth's organ of cosmic perception. What Gurdjieff called the "cosmic octave" could be discerned, he believed, in the outlines of a human body—or even a tree, like the one at the Sarmoung monastery that inspired him to design his movements. Wright looked to trees, and all of nature, in much the same way.

For both Wright and Gurdjieff, beauty had a timeless interior structure, a subtle, immanent order that was present in music and movement just as in architecture. Both men saw their art as a means to reveal and express that order. "Real art," Gurdjieff had said during Olgivanna's residence at Fontainebleau, "is based on mathematics. It is a kind of script with an inner and outer meaning." He viewed his own dances and the music accompanying them as "objective art," which he identified with Gothic architecture—the very same architecture that inspired Frank Lloyd Wright.

*   *   *

WHATEVER WAS DISCUSSED at Wright's meeting with Gurdjieff's American leaders was no small matter, for the subject—even the fact that the meeting took place—was understood by the participants to be a secret, one to be kept even from others in the Institute.

But there was one Gurdjieff follower, not a party to these meetings, who knew a good deal about Olgivanna's personal life, including the goings-on with Frank Lloyd Wright. And she had already done some talking. The pianist Carol Robinson, who had met the besotted couple in Chicago, was now in New York for a few days performing in a club. On February 18, the day after Olgivanna and Frank met with the Institute leaders, Robinson and Margaret Naumberg saw each other, almost certainly at Orage's regular Wednesday meeting. When the subject of Olgivanna came up in conversation, Robinson disclosed some very intimate details of her friend's life—probably more than Olgivanna would have liked.

The next day, Olgivanna picked up some red roses and headed for Naumberg's apartment. Thirty-five years old, dark-haired, with the start of a double chin, Margaret Naumberg was best known as the founder of the Walden School. She had recently been divorced from Waldo Frank, in whose apartment Olgivanna had first met Jerry Blum. Naumberg was still in the midst of

a long affair with Jean Toomer, her husband's protégé. One of their earliest outings had been Gurdjieff's first American demonstration of the sacred dances—a performance, of course, that had featured her visitor.

Naumberg was surprised by Olgivanna's unexpected arrival; the flowers seemed out of character, and the visitor offered no explanation for her visit. While Naumberg went in search of a vase, Olgivanna chatted with Tom, Naumberg's two-and-a-half-year-old son. She returned to overhear Olgivanna asking Tom whether he liked her.

Yes, the child replied.

Olgivanna, probably a few years after meeting Wright

Olgivanna then asked him if he liked everybody.

"Yes, like everybody."

Olgivanna disapproved of the little boy's answer, and told him so. To Naumberg, it struck her as a "very typical and significant little by play." Olgivanna, she observed, was "always seeking and wanting to be liked."

Naumberg noticed that Olgivanna was wearing expensive jade earrings—so expensive that there must have been a dramatic change in her financial state. Olgivanna wanted to explain, she teased, but she was "afraid she couldn't tell one friend without [telling] the other. . . ." Instead, she pressed Naumberg to tell her what Carol Robinson had revealed the day before. Margaret conceded that the pianist had shared a piece of gossip: That Valdemar had agreed to a divorce.

Now that she knew her friend had been talking, Olgivanna moved to defuse the possibility that Robinson had revealed anything about their plans for Wright, or that Naumberg would compromise them. As the two women walked down the street, she told Naumberg that she had "completely cut herself off from all the institute life. All thought of her connection with it." Given her meetings just two days before, of course, this was a lie—one that might well have been arranged in advance by the others at the meeting.

Olgivanna then described her new life. "I feel as though I had been born again," she said. "I have found love. It is six years since I went to the Institute that I have not felt this. But it is all very different from before. I see and feel life differently. But I have been able to be happy like a little child again. He is much older man." She then revealed Wright's identity. And again she lied. "You are the only one," she said, "who knows." And then another untruth. "I wish you and J could meet him." "J," in Naumberg's shorthand, could only have been her lover, Jean Toomer—who had lunched with Wright just two days before.

Olgivanna went on to tell Naumberg that she wanted to get Wright interested in Orage's groups, and asked for Orage's telephone number. It was another ploy, for surely Olgivanna already knew how to contact Orage.

When Naumberg happened to mention Bernard Metz, the English Jew who served as Gurdjieff's unofficial valet, car mechanic, and writing assistant, Olgivanna suddenly darkened. She then revealed a humiliating truth—something, she told Naumberg, that she had never told anyone: Three months before, she had been ejected from the Prieuré. When she discovered that Gurdjieff wanted her gone—but was retaining "fools like Metz"—she was furious. "She had given up her life, every thing," Naumberg recorded, "following G to the Caucuses, Tiflis, all over Europe. Broken up her whole life. . . . She did not see why she had been pulled down so."

Clearly Olgivanna was going somewhere with all this. She would never "do things just off hand to hurt people," she insisted cryptically—at least not "without questioning." On the other hand, she didn't want to be seen as soft. If she was sure it was necessary to do "the painful thing," she declared, "she would."

Now Olgivanna arrived at a potentially damaging secret. From the moment she met Frank Lloyd Wright, she had represented herself as a "star" of the Institute. It was one of the reasons he held her in such high regard. And Wright knew nothing of her ejection from the Prieuré. It would be a serious indiscretion, Olgivanna told Naumberg, if anyone were to enlighten him. Afraid that she had revealed too much, Olgivanna prevailed upon Naumberg to preserve her confidences—including the very fact of her involvement with Wright. Her friend assured her that her secrets were safe. Olgivanna could only have hoped that Naumberg's reassurances covered whatever Carol Robinson might have told her as well.

By this point, the official legend has it, Olgivanna Hinzenberg had shifted her allegiances once and for all from Gurdjieff and the Institute to Frank Lloyd Wright and Taliesin.

The real story was far more complex, and she would take it to her grave.

WITH THEIR NEW York business complete, Frank and Olgivanna returned to Wisconsin. About a month later, she was in Chicago for a court date with Valdemar. A week later, their divorce was granted. Olgivanna was granted custody of the seven-year-old Svetlana. If she had appeared before the judge just a few months later, the question of custody might have turned out very differently.

Olgivanna was pregnant, the father the notorious libertine Frank Lloyd Wright. The baby was likely conceived during the first few weeks following her meeting with Orage, Toomer, and Gale. It could scarcely have been an accident: Frank hadn't impregnated a woman in twenty-six years, and Olgivanna hadn't conceived in eight. The couple—both acquainted with birth-control pioneer Margaret Sanger—surely knew how to avoid it.

FRANK LLOYD WRIGHT was intrigued with the Gurdjieff system. He was also desperately in love with this lithe Gurdjieffian dancer. Whether or not he agreed to house the Institute's American branch during his New York visit, we may never know.

In any event, a stuck door buzzer precluded the possibility, at least for now.

About a month and a half after returning from New York, on April 20, 1925, Wright was eating dinner in a small detached dining room he had built on the hill above the main house at Taliesin. His housekeeper came in to tell him that the door buzzer in his residence had been ringing for twenty minutes.

"Thinking he had pushed a button and it had stuck," a newspaper reported, "he returned to his bedroom to find the telephone stand in flames, the curtains burning and flames shooting up the inside of the slanting ceiling." There had been a short circuit in the wiring. Aided by his neighbors, he "fought back the flames with buckets of water from the huge fish tank at the entrance to the dwelling and from a fountain at the end of the courtyard."

In spite of their furious efforts, Taliesin burned to the ground again; only the drafting room was spared, due to a providential downpour. Nobody was hurt, but along with the structures went Wright's valuable tapestries, screens, and bronzes. The art, he claimed, was valued at half a million dollars. "A poor trustee for posterity, I," Wright lamented. "But they should live on in me, was the thought with which I consoled myself. I would prove their life by mine in what I did. I said so to the suppliant figure standing on the hill-top in the intense dark that now followed the brilliant blaze." That figure was Olgivanna.

"The fire knocked me flat," Wright wrote. "My Tokio earnings all went up in smoke." With most of his Asian art collection lost, all hope of getting out of debt had evaporated. Wright was already behind on his mortgage payments, and the Bank of Wisconsin was on the brink of foreclosing. To reconstruct, he would have to take on even more debt. Even if the architect were to agree to house the Gurdjieff center—to mollify his new love, or to secure their financial support, or both—the estate Wright could have offered Alfred Orage was now in ruins. The Gurdjieffians would have to look elsewhere.

OLGIVANNA WAS A little less than two months pregnant when she visited her doctor in Spring Green. There was madness on both sides of their family, she told him; fearing that the child would inherit insanity, she wanted an abortion. It was a risky request: Not only was the procedure itself fraught with danger, it was also illegal. Furthermore, as Frank Lloyd Wright's latest live-in lover—and a foreigner to boot—Olgivanna was already the subject of nasty local gossip. How could she know the doctor would keep her secret?

Predictably, the doctor refused her request. But she might not have expected his reasons. "It is people like you and Mr. Wright," he counseled, "who *should* have children."

* * *

TALIESIN HAD BURNED before, and under far more grisly circumstances. Wright's reaction then, and now, was to immerse himself in rebuilding. He and Olgivanna set to work restoring the stone walls, inserting scavenged bits and pieces of his Tang Dynasty marble heads and Ming pottery as they went along.

The architect also began to write again. Since Louis Sullivan's death a year before, he had written only two brief eulogies to the dead master. Just before he met Olgivanna, the Dutch architect Hendrik Wijdeveld had begun assembling a special issue of his magazine, *Wendingen*, devoted entirely to Wright. Wright himself had provided a short essay. But soon after Olgivanna moved in, he informed Wijdeveld that he wanted to withdraw the piece in favor of something "more philosophical."

The revised essay was unlike anything Wright had ever written before. At just the moment that the Wisconsin architect was entertaining a partnership with the Montenegrin mystic, he proclaimed in exuberant cosmic terms a unity of purpose between the " 'new world' that is America" and the "old world" of Europe.

> The artist is in no trance. His dream finds its work and finds its mark in the Eternity that is Now. Life is concrete—each in each, and all in all although our horizon may drift into mystery. In harmony with Principles of Nature and reaching toward Life-light, only so are we creative. By that Light we live, to become likewise. And all that need ever be painted or carved or built—are significant, colorful shadows of that Light.

To the knowing reader, it was clear: Frank Lloyd Wright had found a place in his world for Gurdjieff.

WITH HIS INSTITUTE activities more or less suspended, Gurdjieff devoted all his energies to completing his book. In two years' time, he announced to his few remaining followers at the Prieuré, *Beelzebub's Tales* would be read all over the world. Translations in many languages were already underway.

It had been four months since Olgivanna's meetings with the Institute's leaders in New York. But now, as far as they knew, she had dropped off the map. In June 1925, her brother, Vlado, visited Paris, where he became the source of a rumor that Olgivanna "was happily married to a millionaire." Margaret Naumberg, now living at the Prieuré, relayed the news back to her lover, Jean Toomer. When the rumor reached Madame de Hartmann, the opera singer who had become Gurdjieff's secretary, she was indignant. Olgivanna had married for money, she sneered to Naumberg; eventually she would appear at the Prieuré "showing off her fine clothes."

Married and to a millionaire—both were patently false, as Vlado must have known. The Miriam Noel soap opera was a regular feature in American newspapers by this point, and anyone who followed it knew that Wright hadn't even filed for divorce. The idea that Olgivanna was involved with a millionaire is just as hard to explain. Perhaps Vlado was jumping to conclusions based on Wright's impressive estate. But if Olgivanna hoped to keep the prospects of a Taliesin Prieuré alive during reconstruction, a rich husband would have been a good rumor to spread, one that might persuade a beleaguered Gurdjieff to believe in Taliesin as a potential life raft.

But the rumor seemed to have exactly the opposite impact. For Naumberg, it explained why Olgivanna had disengaged from the Gurdjieff network. "Well that's that," she wrote Jean Toomer. "Its strange she never let any of us in N.Y. hear another word."

Ten days later, Wright finally filed for divorce. Under state law, he had to wait a full year before he could marry Olgivanna.

Around November, Jean Toomer showed up in Chicago, where he met with Olgivanna and tried to reengage her with the Institute. Recalling the meeting later, Toomer noted that he was looking for help with his dancing exercises and names of potential pupils. But he may also have been hoping to keep the prospect of Taliesin on the table. Whatever the case, by now Olgivanna was in her ninth month of pregnancy and too ill to help.

IF ANYONE HAD ever believed it, Olgivanna's pregnancy dealt a final blow to her cover as Mary the maid. And now the media began to jump on the story of the Montenegrin dancer who was living with Wright and carrying his child. When an editor from the *Herald Examiner* called Wright at midnight to confirm the story, Wright agreed to come to his office, bringing with him his most trusted friend, University of Chicago history professor Ferdinand Schevill.

If Wright and the Renaissance professor hoped to dissuade the editor from the running the story, it didn't work. When the piece reached the newsstands, Wright and Noel were on the verge of a divorce settlement that would have paid her $250 per month plus a $10,000 lump sum. Now she refused to settle, seeking instead to have the Federal Bureau of Investigation deport Olgivanna for violating immigration laws. Noel no longer wanted money; she wanted vengeance.

In spite of Wright's best efforts, word got out that Olgivanna was about to give birth at Chicago's West Side Hospital. As the reporters lay in wait, Frank camped out at the Congress, convinced that the press had tapped his hotel phone.

On December 2, 1925, at about six o'clock in the evening, Wright received the "anxiously awaited call" from Dr. Anna Blount, the obstetrician. Wright evaded the photographers by entering the hospital through the rear. "Dr. Anna Blount herself let me in," Wright recalled, "and proudly led me to the room where a little white bundle lay. A delicate pink face showing in the hollow of her mother's arm." Holding his newborn daughter to the light, he declared, "You're as big as a minute."

The baby was given the name Iovanna—a name, he explained, "made from her maternal Grandfather's—Ivan, or John, and her paternal Grandmother's Anna." But Olgivanna's father's name was Iovan, not Ivan; the baby's name was actually the feminized form of her father's name, not the blending her future husband imagined. As Olgivanna may well have known, "Iovanna" was also the Russian feminized form of the Greek "Ionnas," the name of Gurdjieff's father.

The new parents had little respite. Three days after the birth, Miriam Noel Wright burst into the hospital, found Olgivanna's room, and began haranguing the new mother in her bed. Frank and Olgivanna had to flee. They decided to leave for the small town of Hollis, New York, where they could hide out at Vlado's place. Svetlana, now eight, remained in Chicago with her father.

With the reporters staked out at the hospital's entrance, the architect planned an escape worthy of his Wisconsin-born contemporary Harry Houdini. Olgivanna left in a wheeled stretcher through the rear elevator and from there was taken by ambulance to the station. With a cadre of reporters waiting on the platform, Wright arranged for Olgivanna to be secreted to the "back" side of the train, where she was slid through the open window of their compartment. "Alma, the nurse, uniform covered up, got onto the proper car with a basket on her arm." Wright recalled, "Iovanna was in it and was safely put to bed in the stateroom next to her mother."

Frank didn't board in Chicago. "I myself got on at Englewood, next city stop down the line, the porter on the lookout for me on the side opposite the boarding side. And we were all safe en route to Vladimir and Sophie. Iovanna was not quite three days old."

WHATEVER WAS HAPPENING with Taliesin, Jean Toomer was still scouting other locations for Gurdjieff's Institute. He and Alfred Orage held a series of meetings in New York with Mabel Dodge Luhan, the wealthy muse and Gurdjieff enthusiast, who had fallen under the handsome Toomer's spell. As Olgivanna was in the hospital awaiting Iovanna's birth, Luhan was inviting Toomer to Taos. "I need you," she wrote him, "*Need* to love you the way I do." Within days of Olgivanna and Frank's departure for Hollis with the baby, Toomer left for New Mexico. Luhan told him that Gurdjieff could have her ranch in Taos for his Institute. She had even promised a $14,000 loan. All of this was assuming, of course, that Toomer would be living at the new Taos Institute.

Luhan's letters strongly suggest that she and Toomer had an affair during his visit. Tony Luhan, her quiet yet powerful Pueblo Indian husband, felt threatened. "He crushes me under boredom," she confessed to Toomer, "for I am no longer interested." Tony, describing himself as Mabel's "captive Indian," threatened to kill her with a hammer. But Tony Luhan had little reason to fear Toomer; still very much involved with Margaret Naumberg, he was hardly interested in a long-term relationship with Mabel.

He was, however, interested in the Luhan estate. Though Taos itself was remote, Toomer wrote Gurdjieff, and lacked the café society his master treasured, it was an "opportunity for exercising the instruction centre that is categorically imperative." Here in the high desert of New Mexico, he wrote, there was a "naturalness of function" that recommended it as a site for the master's work.

The Taos estate was indeed commodious, with a large room for dancing and hot springs nearby. The very atmosphere, Toomer reported, "tends in itself to awaken the sleeper—to prod the lazy." Besides its isolation, the only real drawback was its mistress: Mabel Luhan had energy in abundance, but she was a supreme egotist and mercurial. Still, he was sure Gurdjieff would be able to work with her.

Yet Toomer's work was in vain. "I regret," Gurdjieff wrote Luhan directly, "that at the present moment I cannot take advantage in any way whatsoever of this amiable and kind offer of yours." His mind was now elsewhere—not just on his writing, but also on his wife, Julia, who was rapidly losing her battle with cancer. Gurd-

Mabel Dodge Luhan

jieff was trying to keep her alive as long as possible, by using his powers and feeding her large quantities of blood pressed from specially selected meats.

For now, at least, the search for the American center was on hold.

NOT ALL OF the problems surrounding Iovanna's birth were caused by the scandal-hungry press. Just hours after the little girl was born, Olgivanna began to experience what would likely be diagnosed today as postpartum depression, or, even worse, postpartum psychosis. "I lost what I knew as myself," she later wrote to a friend. "If you knew how I called to it, how helpless I felt without it, how strange it seemed to keep up only the appearances of what I knew as myself. But so it was." Two months after the birth she had improved little, and was eating almost nothing.

Frank and Vlado thought a warmer climate might help, and the couple took the baby and boarded a boat to Puerto Rico. The trip was cleverly timed: Travel to Puerto Rico required no passport, and Wright's attorney had advised him to disappear for a month or so. Miriam had the immigration authorities on the verge of deporting Olgivanna as an undesirable alien, and the Department of Justice was about to indict Wright for violating the Mann Act, which made it illegal for a man to take a woman across state lines for immoral purposes.

Frank and Olgivanna, along with the baby and a nursemaid, spent two months on the island under the alias of Frank and Anna Richardson, a pseudonym likely inspired by the pioneering architect H. H. Richardson. Yet the warmer climate worked no magic on Olgivanna, who by now was almost "a shadow."

"We needed a home," Wright recalled. "Anything was better and safer than this equivocal, dangerous migration from place to place." They decided to return to Taliesin, and, as Frank put it, "take the consequences."

Svetlana was plucked back from Valdemar in Chicago, and the reunited foursome made their way to Spring Green. They had barely unpacked when Miriam Noel attacked. Her lawyer had advised her that Taliesin was community property and she had every right to live there. "I am still his wife and Taliesin is still my home," she told the press. "If I can have just a corner of the bungalow to myself I will be satisfied." With newspaper reporters and photographers in tow, she marched up to the front gate of Taliesin to take possession, an arrest warrant for Olgivanna in hand. The gate was locked. Her press entourage was delighted when she ripped a "No Visitors Allowed" sign off the gate and heaved it away.

The next day, Miriam returned. This time she actually had Wright arrested and briefly jailed, though Olgivanna eluded her. When Wright was released, Miriam renewed her assault on the estate. This time the county prosecutor met her with an offer from Wright: $125 a month if she would stop her campaign. She agreed.

IN HIS STRUGGLE to fend off Miriam's financial demands, Wright got himself into even more trouble. He had claimed insolvency, and now his mortgage carrier, the Bank of Wisconsin, officially declared his loan in arrears. Convinced by his lawyer, Wright offered everything he had—his farm, all his land, his house and studio, his drawings, his print collection—as collateral for a new loan. Now, if he should fall behind again, he would lose everything.

On August 30, 1926, Miriam struck again, filing a $100,000 alienation-of-affection suit against Olgivanna. Wright countered with an "open letter" in Madison's *Capital Times* announcing that he was going abroad. His lawyer suggested that he head north to Canada, but it seems unlikely that the filing of a lawsuit sent the couple out of the country. More likely, Olgivanna was facing the threat of deportation.

The four of them piled into Wright's Cadillac, leaving the dining table still set for a meal. Their immediate destination was Lake Minnetonka, near Minneapolis. Crossing the state border with Olgivanna in the car, however, was a serious mistake, leaving Wright vulnerable again to arrest under the Mann Act. Had Olgivanna merely stepped out of the car and walked alone across the border, no crime would technically have been committed. And indeed their crossing did not go unnoticed. But the foursome drove on to the lake momentarily unchallenged, checking in again as Mr. and Mrs. Frank Richardson, though they kept forgetting to use their aliases.

During their time at the lake, Frank began work on an autobiography. The project was Olgivanna's idea; in fact, she helped write some of it, likely inspired by Gurdjieff's advice about close self-observation. Frank was sure it would bring in money. They hired a stenographer, Maude Devine, who quickly became close to Olgivanna.

They were also contending with a custody battle over Svetlana. When Valdemar Hinzenberg heard that Wright and his crew were heading out of the country with his daughter—a drama covered faithfully in the newspapers—he was terrified that he would never see her again. Using Olgivanna's out-of-wedlock baby as grounds, he secured a writ of habeas corpus to gain custody of Svetlana. He also offered a $500 reward for information leading to Wright's capture. Then, following Miriam's lead—he even retained her attorney—he sued Wright for alienating the affection of both his daughter and his former wife.

Soon after the reward was posted, Wright and family were in Minneapolis when a local who had been following the news overheard the "Richardsons" call their older child Svetlana. Late in the evening of October 20, 1926, the local sheriff, accompanied by reporters, drove up to Lake Minnetonka and arrested Wright just as he was dictating the last pages of the first book of his autobiography. The whole family, including Svetlana and the infant Iovanna, spent two nights in the Hennepin County jail. For a while, eight-year-old Svetlana was placed in a solitary cell, with Olgivanna calling out to her, "Svet, Svet, it's all right." The warden refused to provide milk for the baby. Wright was placed at "the far end," where, he noted, "the 'better element' of jaildom, the high-swindlers and bootleggers were kept." The dirty mattress, the filthy toilet, the small cell—it all made him want to retch. But at night he was mesmerized by the rich baritone voices of prisoners singing until nine o'clock, after which silence was mandatory. "They made me feel ashamed of my shame because, after all, I was there for a passing moment while they were there for years, maybe for life."

A preliminary hearing was scheduled for the following week. When they were released, Wright railed against the Hearst newspapers, which had kept the heat on the story. From then on, Iovanna recalled, Hearst was never Mr. Hearst, only "Hearst the Bastard" or "Sewer Hearst." Perhaps influenced by her mother, Svetlana put the blame on her father, Valdemar.

Olgivanna took it the hardest. She even thought of killing herself. The day before the hearing, she collapsed and was taken to a local sanatorium. This too, of course, made it into the Hearst newspapers.

JEAN TOOMER WAS now in charge of all Gurdjieff's American operations outside of New York, and the master had instructed him to start a group in Chicago. He still hoped that Olgivanna would play a role in "the work." He was also lobbying Gurdjieff to abandon France and permanently relocate himself and the Institute to the United States. An American Prieuré at Taliesin would still have been appealing, but Toomer grew concerned when he heard that Olgivanna had been hospitalized. A few days later he contacted Jessie Dwight, who relayed the message to her new husband, Alfred Orage. The "Olgivanna business is nothing," Orage responded. He should sustain himself by concentrating on his writing and "the work."

Nonetheless, the weeks after Olgivanna's collapse saw Toomer escalate his efforts to find a site for the center. Toomer renewed his pursuit of Taos, and this time Gurdjieff was on board. Finances were getting increasingly worrisome at the Prieuré and interest in New York and Chicago was waning. "I've never for a moment lost the sense of basic relationship and joy in being with you," Toomer wrote Luhan. Her estate, he revealed, was one of only three in the world under consideration. He didn't name the other two. By now, though, Luhan had lost interest. "Do you still love yourself as much as ever?" she sniped to him in a letter.

OLGIVANNA'S HOSPITALIZATION WAS brief. Toomer arrived in Chicago in November 1926. Olgivanna must have been highly persuasive about the possibilities of a Prieuré at Taliesin, for Wright traveled to the city soon after Toomer's arrival to meet with him about his new group. In December 1926, still prevented by the bank from returning to Taliesin, Frank whisked Olgivanna and Iovanna, now a year old, off to New York City. In Manhattan the little family was taken in by Wright's sister Maginel, who worked there as a children's book illustrator.

Svetlana wasn't with them. Valdemar had dropped all charges after being assured that Olgivanna wasn't going to take her out of the country. Now, with her status as Svetlana's sole legal custodian confirmed, Olgivanna put the nine-year-old in a Chicago boarding school. Valdemar paid all the girl's expenses. "Whenever I go in the street or in the stores and see people and children hurrying with packages in their hands," Olgivanna wrote her daughter, "I think of you, of my big little daughter. . . . My, my, my Svetlana kiss you thousands times."

But Olgivanna's kisses were hardly a substitute for real family life. Abandoned by her mother at age four, reunited with her two years later in New York, and sent off again after another two years, the little girl was thrown "out of step," according to Wright's friend Ferdinand Schevill, who monitored the young girl's well-being for her on-again, off-again mother.

Olgivanna's mysterious sense of self-estrangement, which first surfaced after Iovanna's birth, still haunted her in Manhattan. All her Gurdjieff training seemed useless in the face of her disaffection. "Why since the baby was born," she asked Maude Devine rhetorically, "I stopped to exist?"

And then, just as suddenly as she had lost it, Olgivanna found her missing "I." A week after arriving in New York, she explained in her still imperfect English, "I went to see one of my pupils in movement. I told her about my happenings—all was interesting lively. Then I asked about those I knew." One of those was her beloved Julia Ostrowska, Gurdjieff's wife.

"Why, Olgivanna, don't you know she is dead?" the pupil replied.

Gurdjieff's efforts to cure Julia's cancer had failed; she had died the previous June. Olgivanna was stunned. "And [it] seemed," she wrote Maude, as if "I got a blow right in the middle of my forehead and then a sharp pain in my heart and tears, tears—all in one second—*I was there, right there, I that was* lost saw everything that passed for [the] past two years clearly and simply, saw it together with my dear friend. She was with me in me with all her love and understanding. Such happiness and quiet she brought to me. Such rest and relief after the storms that passed. She woke up the life within myself and the capacity to communicate with outside life."

It was no memory, no mournful recollection. It was, Olgivanna believed, a visitation. "It was first time in my life, *my first experience*—I knew, felt, understood, that she did not die. First human being I know that did not die. . . . She stayed within me for a few days . . . and left leaving the light and life."

After this moment of communion with Julia's "astral body," Olgivanna was revivified. Within days she had reconnected with some of her former dance students from the Prieuré, now full Institute members. "They are happy to see me again." And she was happy to see them, slipping eagerly into the New York scene. She loved "being in the whirle [sic] of social life." And she loved the exposure to a broad range of new ideas. "There has been much of intellectual life lately through talks, conversations that sometimes lasted hours." She began to study Yogic philosophy, the new rage among the intellectuals. Wright's sister Maginel was similarly intrigued.

Happy to be back in the world, Olgivanna often walked Iovanna through the streets of Greenwich Village in a carriage. On one occasion, with Frank along, they ran into one of his old Prairie house clients, Queene Ferry Coonley. Frank introduced Olgivanna as his wife; then, with a sweeping gesture toward the carriage, he declared, "And this is my crime!"

OLGIVANNA'S NEWFOUND CONTENTMENT would soon be tested. As Svetlana's first year at Chicago's Elmwood School progressed, the ten-year-old stopped writing to her mother. Perhaps Olgivanna shouldn't have been surprised. After all, she neither sent for her daughter to come home for Christmas nor came to visit herself.

"I wish I could see you!" Olgivanna wrote her daughter three days before Christmas. But she couldn't afford to bring the baby and her nurse. "[Y]ou know how difficult it is to do what you want to do. One must do what is best for all—so this time I must do what is best for all—not only for you and me—and that is to stay right here where I am now. But just the same I will be with you . . . in my imagination." Under her Christmas tree, she promised, there would be a gift for Svetlana, wrapped so lovingly that Svetlana would be able to feel that "mother is right there with you."

Svetlana couldn't feel it. Ferdinand Schevill, who telephoned the headmistress at Elmwood School, reported back to Olgivanna that he had negotiated a deal: The headmistress would "see to it that Svetlana would write at once," and on every Sunday after that. Sunday, Ferdinand informed Olgivanna, was the day her daughter spent with her father. Then, to Svetlana's dismay, her mother had her transferred to another school up in Wisconsin, far from her father. But she still didn't write to her mother. Of course she does not like to write, Olgivanna wrote Schevill; "every child is like that."

But mother-daughter issues were the least of Olgivanna's problems. While she was in New York awaiting resolution of Taliesin's mortgage crisis, Olgivanna was arrested by immigration officials at Maginel's home and threatened again with deportation for traveling to Puerto Rico. Frank was forced to cash his last fifty-dollar Liberty Bond to bail her out. Though his lawyers advised him to send Olgivanna and the children away until things could be set right, Frank took Olgivanna right to Washington, D.C., to reason with the authorities. Frank's close friend, the writer Alexander Woollcott, sent a personal appeal asking Colonel William Joseph "Wild Bill" Donovan, a hero of the Great War and now a federal attorney, to intervene. The government gave Wright six months to resolve the issue.

Meanwhile, Wright was desperate to return home. He had sold off all his livestock in an effort to pay off the bank, but after his arrest they also demanded that he sell what remained of his collection of rare Japanese prints. He was forced to put them up for auction in a depressed art market. New York's Anderson Gallery, to whom Wright owed money, handled the sale— and the measly take barely covered his debt to the gallery.

Now essentially broke, with no commissions in the works, Wright nevertheless seemed unfazed. The critic Lewis Mumford met him at the architect's favorite bar at the Plaza Hotel. "His ego," Mumford recalled, "was so heavily armored that even the bursting shell of such disastrous events did not penetrate his vital organs. He lived from first to last like a god: one who acts but is not acted upon."

The great architect couldn't be kept down for long. His friend Philip La Follette, a Hillside Home School alumnus and the son of a legendary Wisconsin governor, made him a proposal: The famously antibusiness architect should incorporate himself. For $7,500 each, investors in Frank Lloyd Wright, Inc. were promised a share in his future earnings. Wright agreed, and ten investors signed on, including his friends Schevill and Woollcott. The corporation's board of directors was made up of friends and supporters, all influential and credit worthy. Wright thought it "so natural and reasonable . . . that most anyone would let me have that much—and there would be no trouble getting all I needed and more too."

La Follette, soon to be governor himself, and the corporate directors pressed the federal attorney to drop the charges against Wright. They also began negotiating a repayment plan with the bank—one, they hoped, that would allow Frank and Olgivanna to move back to Taliesin.

AMID ALL OF this, the baby Iovanna was thriving, "talking and laughing, and exclaiming out loud [as] if she wanted to tell the world that to live is a great fun," Olgivanna wrote. The child was taking her first steps and soaking up the attention when they strolled through the park. New York seemed to agree with mother and daughter alike. "It was a happy thought to come here," Olgivanna told Maude Devine.

But Wright felt otherwise. "For four months I've been marking time in New York," he wrote, "dying a hundred deaths a day on the New York gridiron in the stop-and-go of the urban criss-cross." He felt oppressed by the crowds, the traffic, always having to wait for something—a traffic light to change, an elevator to arrive. He even felt oppressed by the quantity of printed matter thrust on him daily, "stacked in every lobby, waiting at the gates of every train, waiting on the floor of outside the hotel bedroom door."

Olgivanna with Iovanna

And then there was sex. Wherever he turned on Manhattan's sidewalks, Frank saw women's exposed, "silken legs." When he and Olgivanna went to the theater, he found himself confronted with "plays of sex appeal, sex intrigue: sex satisfaction. Plays on sex triumphant, sex foiled, or sex despoiled—until the one passionate interest evident as the living nerve in pictures and 'shows' is sex." Sex, he lamented, was everywhere; there was no escape.

The architect felt trapped in this titillating grid; his descriptions recall the tales of Edgar Allan Poe, who wrote "The Fall of the House of Usher" in a house just blocks from Frank and Olgivanna's hotel. Wright hungered to return to Taliesin's beautiful safety.

For Olgivanna, however, being in Manhattan meant being back in touch at last with the Gurdjieff scene. Alfred Orage, in addition to his lectures, was giving weekly readings of Gurdjieff's massive *Beelzebub's Tales* manuscript to rapt students. "It is not plain sailing to interpret G.," he confessed to Toomer. "I'm usually in despair before the lecture and in a state of self-disgust after it." But he continued his efforts to start more new groups and raise more funds. "*Money* is our object," he wrote his wife, Jessie.

ON MARCH 3, 1927, Orage sat down again with Frank and Olgivanna. It had been two years since their first meeting after Olgivanna's move into Taliesin. This time the meeting was Wright's idea. He wanted to learn more about the Institute's program. He also inquired about Toomer's credentials. Olgivanna thought Toomer was weak in his understanding of the movements. The architect and Gurdjieff's waggish emissary talked for quite a while, their conversation ranging from the work of the Institute to Orage's social credit theory, an idea Wright would adopt as his own.

Though it isn't certain that Wright put Taliesin on the table at this meeting, the timing is very suggestive. As Wright surely knew, on the following day it would be announced in public that the Mann Act charges against him were being dropped. That would remove a major obstacle to his returning to Taliesin—if, that is, he could cover his mortgage payments. But even his new corporation, with its prestigious board, hadn't managed to rescue his desperate finances. Wright hadn't worked since he fled with Olgivanna to Minnesota, and he must have feared that the pool of clients willing to take a risk on him was small indeed. If there was ever a time when he would have considered making a deal to share Taliesin with the Gurdjieffians, it was now.

What Wright apparently didn't know was that the cash Orage was collecting from his groups was all being siphoned back to Gurdjieff in France. And Olgivanna herself may have led her husband on when it came to Gurdjieff's financial situation. In fact, Gurdjieff had been forced to give up his flat in Paris and return to the Prieuré, where he reversed his policy and agreed to take in new American students in exchange for one hundred dollars a week. The Institute was almost completely dependent on Orage's American fund-raising—but with fewer and fewer new applicants, it was all the writer could do just to meet Gurdjieff's own needs.

Orage's notes don't reveal whether anything was resolved at his meeting with Wright. But one thing is clear: Wright's interest in the Institute was piqued. He asked about Jean Toomer's Gurdjieff group in Chicago, which would have been key to a new Institute center in Spring Green. And at the end of the discussion, Orage and Wright were joined by e. e. cummings and John Dos Passos to see a demonstration of the sacred dances. Dos Passos and cummings were impressed; Wright must have been as well, for soon thereafter he visited Toomer in Chicago.

The next day, the announcement about the Mann Act made national news. "The top o' the morning to you, dear Frank," Schevill wrote to his old friend. "This is the turn of the wheel which opens a new chapter. Crowd your sails with all the winds that blow and show 'em how a good ship takes the waves when its keel isn't fouled. I expect great things of you."

But one obstacle still kept Frank and Olgivanna from returning to Taliesin: They were not married, a little detail that put them in violation of the bank's ruling. The pair decided to leave New York anyway. "I don't know where we are going to stay," Olgivanna wrote Maude Devine in April. "Frank may lose Taliesin." It was only because he was a "great man," she added, that he could handle it.

La Follette came through just in time. In May he worked out a plan with the bank that allowed Wright to return to work at Taliesin. He also secured a one-year grace period on the loan payments. Wright took the deal and returned to Taliesin. To conform to the bank's dictates, he kept Olgivanna hidden from view in his sister Jane Porter's adjacent property. But Jane's help only went so far: She refused a solicitation to invest in her brother's corporation. Why, she responded, throw good money after bad?

With no work in sight, Wright needed income—and quick. "Mr. Wright is leaving for Chicago today," Olgivanna wrote Maude Devine on May 13, 1927. "It will be his last chance to save Taliesin." While in Chicago, he visited one of Toomer's groups. Wright both needed and dreaded the courtroom showdown with Miriam that followed. Her opening gambit was that she would agree to a divorce if Frank promised to give up Olgivanna. No deal. Miriam struck back, alleging that she had walked out of the marriage because Wright abused her—both verbally and with his fists, rendering her black and blue. Wright didn't deny it. "All the wrongs that can be done to a woman by a demon in human form," she later told the press, "have been done to me. My husband hid behind his talent and let unspeakable things occur at Taliesin."

The Wrights' housekeeper, a black woman named Viola, who apparently witnessed at least some of Wright's "unspeakable" behavior, testified in court. There is no record of what she said, but Frank and Olgivanna's fury with her suggests that it must have been devastating. Shortly after the hearing, Wright mused to his friend Harold Kemp in a letter that "all history is the dirty product of the servant-mind." Frank and Miriam's household had had at least one other servant, an English woman; Wright referred to the two as "black and white" or "Blanche et Noire." "There's a nigger in this wood pile, boy, 'sho's you bohn," Wright wrote of Viola.

After leaving the Wrights, Viola went to work for their friends the Thayers; the Englishwoman went to work for Kemp. Kemp complained about "Blanche," and wrote a letter to Wright in which he gloated over attacking her bodily.

"I am glad," Wright replied, "you struck old obstinate le-Blanche as many times and in the precise places you said you did. . . . Plenty of times I wanted to do what you finally had the courage to do. For one I am glad you did kick her sixty-seven times. You are a man after my own heart. Olgivanna is not sorry either. And we are both glad you let us 'in on the business'. . . . If she should die of her bruises I shall defend you, never fear. The sample you already have here of my capacity should assure you of protection and comfort you."

ON AUGUST 26, 1927, Frank Lloyd Wright was granted his long-sought divorce. But the judge, no doubt influenced by Wright's brutality, hit him hard. Olgivanna worried that half their "salary" would go toward paying Miriam. The reality was far worse. Wright was ordered to pay her $6,000 up front, provide a $30,000 trust fund, and come up with $250 per month in alimony for the rest of her life—enormous sums in those days. The capital La Follette and his fellow investors plowed into Wright, Inc., would end up in Miriam Noel's pocket.

The divorce decree also stipulated that Wright could not live in an "immoral situation"—meaning with Olgivanna—for one year. Yet that, of course, is exactly what he did. "We found everything in order," Olgivanna wrote Svetlana on her return to Taliesin. "Nellie has two puppies. . . . The birds are leaving us. The frogs are not singing any more—the winter is coming fast. . . . Your room looks lovely. And the little Japanese doll is still sitting on the stone wall leaning on her hand and waiting for you to come back."

* * *

WHEN WRIGHT FINISHED the first draft of his autobiography, he sent its extraordinarily intimate text to his friend Alexander Woollcott, the witty and acerbic writer, critic, and member of the Algonquin round table, and a gay man. But Woollcott declined to read Wright's work. "A primitive instinct of self-preservation has given me only two rules of life." One was to stay off of all committees. The other was "never to look at anybody's manuscript except my own, at which I stare with a mixture of nausea and infatuation from dawn to dusk."

"Damn the manuscript," Wright wrote back. "I understand you—and like you for pushing it away. I don't think I can write[s] or ever will, well enough to know my effects. More and more a stranger, in my own land—Alexander. I should to love to see you again—Here's hoping. And dear, Alex, feel this, just the same. I love and admire Alexander Woollcott—his sorrow is my sorrow and any joy that come to him my joy too. If the time should come when he needs me he has only to let me see it or hear it."

THE BANK OF Wisconsin soon caught on that Olgivanna was back at Taliesin, though she was technically installed next door. Their mortgage had been "outraged," the bank claimed. Wright was forced to leave the premises on January 13, 1928; moreover, the bank insisted that he pay off the loan, or they would sell the place.

Less than two weeks later, Wright received a telegram from Albert McArthur, one of his draftsmen from the Oak Park days, informing him that he had a commission to design a two-million-dollar Arizona Biltmore hotel in Phoenix. Would Mr. Wright join him as a consultant? McArthur wanted to use the inexpensive textile-block system Frank and his son Lloyd had developed in California. In an instant, Frank and Olgivanna had found both a source of income—$1,000 per month—and a place of refuge. In the face of this new cashflow, the bank even agreed to postpone the auction.

It was soon after he answered McArthur's call and arrived in the Arizona desert that Wright began plotting a strategy to reclaim Taliesin, one that hinted at the Fellowship he and Olgivanna would found four years later. To resurrect his practice, he figured he would need housing and a studio for four or five draftsmen and their families. In exchange for their architectural services, draftsmen would be entitled to room, board, and—needless to say—the privilege of working with him.

"The economy of Taliesin," he wrote to the directors of Frank Lloyd Wright, Inc., "would depend upon making it able to produce what we eat. We should make our own butter." Those who were willing to help with farming or typing would receive twenty-five dollars per month. It wasn't a bad deal, Wright opined. "The 'living' provided at Taliesin goes a long way on draughtmen's salaries most of them having nothing left in the city after their living is paid especially if married and have children."

There were plenty of candidates, Wright claimed, who were anxious to work with him. "I have fifteen letters from young men in all parts of the country applying. . . . I shall correspond with this group." The proposal was typed up and sent to his overlords, La Follette and the officers of Frank Lloyd Wright, Inc. There is no record of the attorney's response—except that La Follette was furious to learn that Wright had left for Arizona without notifying him.

HILLSIDE HOME SCHOOL

FRANK LLOYD WRIGHT A

STYLE CENTER.

PART II

TAKING ROOT

CRANK LLOYD WRIGHT, SCHOOLMASTER

SAVING FRANK LLOYD WRIGHT FROM himself was becoming a cottage industry. Attorney Philip La Follette, for one, as chairman of the board of Frank Lloyd Wright, Inc., was constantly hectoring him to behave like a working businessman, demanding an account of every penny the architect took in and spent. But rather than being grateful that La Follette was trying to save Taliesin—and arranging to provide him an extraordinary $500 weekly salary—Wright bristled at the thought that Taliesin might become a corporate acquisition, and he just another salaried man.

Wright also didn't appreciate being lectured to by his cousin "Dickie"— Richard Lloyd Jones, a newspaper publisher and editor in Tulsa, Oklahoma. Although he had recently asked Wright to design him a new house, Lloyd Jones couldn't bear Frank's presumption in trying to have his life just the way he wanted it. When Wright came to visit in 1928, they got into a ferocious argument. On Wright's return, he wrote a letter calling his cousin a "puritan and a publican of the worst stripe."

Lloyd Jones replied with a raging broadside. "You covet attention," Lloyd Jones charged, scorning his outlandish wardrobe. "You are always out of step, marching by yourself, scoffing at all others, calling everybody and everything ridiculous, speaking only in words of contempt for your country and your countrymen. You tell organized society to go to hell, and then expect it to honor and praise you." As a journalist—and someone with firsthand knowledge of his cousin's family history—he damned the autobiography Wright had recently begun as "at least half pure hooey."

(Dickie's own idea of an "organized society" was not beyond criticism.

Seven years earlier, after a young black man in Tulsa was charged with assaulting a white woman in an elevator, Lloyd Jones had penned an inflammatory editorial in his paper; the headlines screamed "Nab Negro for Assaulting Girl in Elevator" and "To Lynch a Negro Tonight." A white mob later burned down thirty-five square blocks of the prosperous black neighborhood, murdering four hundred African Americans.)

"Did you ever stop to consider the cause of all the troubles you have ever had?" Lloyd Jones now demanded. "Every one has grown out of your insistent appetite for a woman, a purely selfish wish to follow your own selfish interests in utter self-indulgence." He called Wright "a house builder and a home wrecker" who had "wrecked three homes in your heroic effort to work out your own salvation with honesty and freedom from hypocrisy." And to top it off, he chided, "you picked out a perfectly crazy woman to live with, and she gave you a full dose of her own selfishness."

If Lloyd Jones had little sympathy for Miriam Noel, he rose to the defense of the still-fragile Olgivanna. He was incensed at Wright for moving her into Taliesin before the way was legally clear, accusing him of not loving her enough to protect her. "There was no reason in the world why she should have been subject to the humiliation and anguish and worries which you subjected her to. . . . You thought only in terms of yourself. She foolishly trusted you. . . .

"You are the most conspicuously selfish person I have ever known," he continued. "[Y]ou expect all your friends to make personal sacrifice to stand by you, and if need be, to go to hell for you.

Lloyd Jones advised his wayward cousin to change his ways. "What you need is a Hart, Schaffner & Marx suit of clothes, a four-in-hand tie, a Dobbs hat and a chance to learn how to be unseen in a crowd." And he could use a dose of jingoistic spirit while he was at it: "If you are going to stay here, pull up the children's chairs to the table, buy the Stars and Stripes, tack a flag-staff to your bungalow and fly the colors and learn to love it."

Richard Lloyd Jones

* * *

BUT WRIGHT DIDN'T need a four-in-hand tie or a Dobbs hat; he needed only to find someone brave enough to sign on as his client. And Alfred Chandler, an ex-veterinarian, turned out to be that person. While consulting on the Arizona Biltmore, Wright had been contacted by Chandler, one of the state's self-made magnates, a man who had developed his own canal system that now irrigated thousands of desert acres. He had also founded his own town, modestly named Chandler, which he hoped now to make over as a mecca in the dusty Southwest.

Chandler's dream, as Wright put it, "was an undefiled-by-irrigation desert resort for wintering certain jaded eastern millionaires who preferred dry desert to green, wet fields." The doctor had a 1,400-acre site in the middle of the Salt River Mountains and an idea for a stunning hotel. He lacked only the money to build it. But the two men liked each other, and Wright certainly understood the idea of taking on a big project without the funding to cover it. Moreover, he loved the pristine site, relishing the prospect of designing an American counterpart to his Japanese hotel.

Wright agreed to do the project at a reduced fee, starting with beautiful preliminary drawings seductive enough, the two men hoped, to secure the financing. For its motif Wright chose the saguaro cactus. The year before, he had completed concept drawings for an apartment tower in New York City called St. Mark's in the Bouwerie. This one would be called San Marcos in the Desert. When the deal was done, on April 6, 1928, Wright cabled his friend Darwin Martin, now director of Wright's corporation. "Ideal commission settled," it read, "will build and furnish San Marcos in the Desert[,] a perfectly appointed half million dollar hotel." If financing came through, Wright stood to earn a $40,000 fee. And not a moment too soon: The one-year grace period on the Taliesin mortgage was just about to end.

In late June, Frank and his family, minus Svetlana, escaped from the Arizona heat and moved into an oceanfront house in La Jolla, California. Soon they were visited by Richard and Dione Neutra, who drove down from their new home in Los Angeles with their two sons.

Wright "greeted us warmly," Dione recalled. She found Iovanna a "completely self-sufficient child [who] has her own strong will." When one of the Neutras' sons reached for the cutlery on the table, Iovanna whispered, "Don't touch, Daddy makes spanky, spanky," giving the little boy a few smacks to demonstrate.

On July 14, Wright and his brood left home for the day. Soon after, the phone began ringing in the empty house. It was Miriam, calling to make sure no one was there. She had just sought a warrant for Frank and Olgivanna's

Wright and Iovanna at the beach, probably near their house in La Jolla, California

arrest as "lewd and dissolute persons," but apparently that wasn't enough to satiate her fury. "I decided," she later explained, "to get on the front page of the newspapers and see what effect publicity would have upon the situation. I thought the happy home belonged to Frank, so I wrecked the place inside, and as a wreck it was a perfect success."

Miriam got her publicity, along with a thirty-day suspended sentence.

TO READERS OF the *Chicago Tribune*, the ad needed no address. "For sale: One romantic, rambling famous picturesque home on a hill with 190 acres of farm and park, known as a 'love nest,' murder scene, fire scene, raid scene and showplace." The grace period on Taliesin's mortgage was now two months past, and Wright had failed to come up with the $43,000 he owed. The bank had already auctioned his farm machinery and art pieces. On July 30, 1928, they put Taliesin up for sale. When there were no takers, the bank sold it to themselves.

Back in Wisconsin, La Follette was busy whittling down Wright's debts with merchants and workers by converting them into long-term notes. He also reorganized the corporation and gave it an abbreviated name, Wright, Inc. It was a change the architect loathed. "I hesitate to inform any of my clients here," he wrote La Follette, "that I am 'WRIGHT INCORPORATED' for fear they might expect a truck to back up and dump something dead in their backyard."

On August 25, with his divorce from Miriam exactly the legally required full year behind him, Frank married Olgivanna in Rancho Santa Fe, just north of San Diego. There was nothing now to keep them from returning to Taliesin—if, that is, they still owned it. And two days later they did, practically speaking. La Follete had managed to buy it from the bank in the name of Wright, Inc. Taliesin, Darwin Martin announced in a telegram, is "open for your return." In "playing second fiddle to La Follette," an elated Schevill told Wright, he had won a "heroic victory" over himself. "Your reward," he added, "is coming."

As the honeymooners headed home, they stopped in Phoenix, where Wright handed Chandler a set of gorgeous presentation drawings of his proposed new hotel. The doctor, in return, handed the architect a signed contract to complete the design and prepare detailed construction drawings. But the bulk of the fee was still contingent on finding financing. Still unable to count on architecture to support Taliesin, Wright desperately needed another source of income.

* * *

IN LATE OCTOBER 1928, just weeks after the Wrights' return, Siegfried Scharfe visited Taliesin. An art history professor at the University of Wisconsin, Scharfe was a scholar of German church architecture and an admirer of Wright's work. Back in Japan, Wright had conjured an idea for resurrecting the Hillside Home School as a place for teaching architecture. The subject must have come up with Scharfe, for when the professor suggested bringing his students to visit Taliesin, Wright replied, "I think you understand what Taliesin is for and you will be entirely welcome to bring your students."

Before Wright's personal meanderings had dragged it down, the Hillside Home School had provided his aunts a living. Now he hoped it might do the same for him.

Just one day after the students' visit, Wright was already promoting the idea. That day Wright entertained P. M. Cochius, the director of the Royal Dutch Glassworks at Leerdam, at Taliesin. Ushered into the living room, Cochius saw for the first time the heart of Wright's prototype for the "natural house." With its high, double-pitched open ceiling, rough-hewn stone from the exterior spilling in judiciously, unpainted wood, warm-hued plaster, and numerous Buddhist sculptures, this showpiece room—the jewel of Taliesin—was the antithesis of the brand of modernism that was taking hold back in Europe. "This is the most beautiful room in the world," he told Olgivanna. "Your husband is a great mystic." Cochius had come to commission Wright to design glass blocks based on the concrete ones he had made for his California houses in the 1920s. Before long, though, the architect had incorporated his guest's vocation into his own plans. He told him of his idea to open a school of architecture and other arts, including the design of manufactured products. The glassmaker was enthusiastic, even offering to set up a manufacturing facility at Taliesin as part of the program. Wright must have immediately seen the possibilities of building Taliesin into a community not unlike the one his friend Charles Ashbee had founded.

The day Cochius left, La Follette arrived to discuss, as Wright put it, "urgent matters" whose solution would make the work at Taliesin "both economical and desirable"—no doubt hoping to convince La Follette to release Wright, Inc. funds for the school scheme. If so, he made little headway.

Before long, though, he—or perhaps Professor Scharfe—quickly came up with a possible source of funds. The University of Wisconsin had an innovative program they called "experiment stations," a way to test new ideas by setting up small satellite institutions around the state. Wright began drawing up a proposal to make Taliesin effectively an adjunct campus of the university—an enormous irony, given that this was the very institution that had soured him on formal education in the first place. If the proposal were accepted, however, the financial windfall could make Wright, Inc., and its overlord La Follette, immediately irrelevant.

* * *

WRIGHT'S PROSPECTUS FOR the Hillside Home School of the Allied Arts was everything Richard Lloyd Jones would have expected: arrogant, self-serving, and dismissive of America's virtues. The American people, it claimed, are "ingenious, inventive, scientifically, commercially progressive and, as the whole World has occasion to know—uncreative." *Artistically* uncreative, that is: America was an ugly place, he told the university. The creativity he would nurture at his new school would serve to change that.

Wright's prospectus was explicitly inspired by his English friend Charles Ashbee. In its opening page, Wright invoked Ashbee as a "sympathetic critic" of America's ugliness. In choosing to work from the countryside, Wright was following Ashbee's lead. Yet he disagreed with the Englishman in one important respect: Instead of an Ashbee-style guild of handcrafted work, Wright envisioned his new school as "an integral part of the great industrial system of America," a place where machinery and art could each shape the other from the very beginning. His school of fine arts, he wrote, "would serve machinery in order that machinery itself . . . [and] in the future might honestly serve what is growing to be a beauty-loving and appreciative country now borrowing or faking its effects because it knows no better and has none other."

Like Ashbee's Guild, the school would produce all manner of glassware, jewelry, tapestries, furniture, light fixtures, sculptures, and flower pots. Where Ashbee sold his workers' products in boutique craft shops, though, Wright intended his to be mass-produced for a wider market. Wright believed that Ashbee had failed because he was trying to compete, rather than collaborate, with industry. The alternative, Wright believed, was to create an American capitalist answer to the Bauhaus, the bastion of socialist modernism in Germany established in 1919. "There should soon be a substantial profit to show on production," he promised in his prospectus.

Wright was proposing to transform Taliesin into a design shop for American industrialists' mass production. But the idea went well beyond that: In exchange for putting up a quarter-million-dollar endowment, these magnates would own the school's designs and be able to hire its graduates. Even more remarkably, the industrialists would receive ownership of a significant portion of his buildings and land—the Hillside parcel. La Follette must have been stunned. The creative iconoclast Frank Lloyd Wright—who had just railed at him that the very sound of "WRIGHT INCORPORATED" was likely to scare away clients—was offering up the fruits of his genius to all corporate comers.

Wright quickly sought to line up his friends in academia behind the school scheme. Franz Aust, a friend and former client who taught landscape architecture in Wisconsin's agriculture department, responded enthusiastically and agreed to promote the idea to the university hierarchy. Ferdinand Schevill, at the University of Chicago, also agreed to help.

After years of running from the banks, deferring to lawyers, and pandering to his clients, Wright seemed a man of action at last, with a clear vision of his future. But it was not the kind of action La Follette had in mind. On November 9, frustrated by Wright's persistent attempts to circumvent their agreement, La Follette came to Taliesin to lay down the law. From now on, he insisted, Wright was to pay everything with cash, not credit, submit to him itemized statements of his expenses (which would be "promptly audited"), and incur no debts or obligations without prior authorization. The world's greatest architect soon found himself asking his lawyer for permission to

purchase basic materials he needed to maintain Taliesin's grounds. "You are authorized to order 60 yards of gravel at a cost of $2.15 a yard," La Follette wrote him. "No other items have been or will be incurred by you until and unless we have conferred and agreed upon them."

A WEEK LATER, the esteemed landscape architect Jens Jensen came to dinner at Taliesin. The school idea was still their main topic of conversation, but now Olgivanna and Frank were arguing over the basic philosophy behind the plan. She was remarkably assertive—

so much so that Wright later wrote to Jensen to clarify his vision, in a letter that was extraordinarily deferential to his wife's views.

Wright acknowledged that it had been Olgivanna's idea to make Taliesin a place where they could create creators. But they differed on how much an education—even an unorthodox education at Taliesin—could accomplish. Creativity, Wright argued, was the quality that distinguished man from "the brute," and as such, it should be the goal of education. But only in those who already had it. "This creative-instinct [is] dead in most," Wright argued. "[P]erhaps three-fifths of humanity lacks any power of that kind." And once it was lost, he felt, creativity could never be regained.

Olgivanna disagreed. "She believes," Wright wrote Jensen, "that the creative instinct is the original birthright of mankind . . . and that by proper treatment it may be revived." Finding that "proper treatment," of course, was a matter for Gurdjieff's techniques. But to Wright the task ahead had little to do with awakening lost souls, as Olgivanna had argued; instead, it involved identifying those few who still retained that creative spark, and saving them from further damage.

Even in their earliest conversations about the school, then, Olgivanna was already putting Gurdjieff on the table. Having taught her husband the movements—which the couple practiced with Svetlana and little Iovanna—she now convinced him to let her teach them, at least in modified form, at the school. The prospectus called for one of the school's five central directors to be a "teacher of rhythm by Dalcroze at Hellerau, or by Gurdjieff at Fontainebleau, France." The document even sounded Gurdjieffian, advocating the importance of "the natural correlation of the whole man" as the path to creativity and rebirth—a means to capturing "the gods if not God."

A few weeks later, Wright received a letter from Professor Franz Aust, their faculty connection at the university. Science "has been tried and found wanting," Aust wrote. Why not "put in a department of religion in your Hillside School?" Wright modified the prospectus accordingly. It was another opening for Olgivanna.

THE ONLY INSPIRATION to which the Wrights never admitted was money. Nonetheless, the prospectus paid considerable attention to the financial side of the school. They planned for around sixty students, each of whom would pay an annual tuition of three hundred dollars—while shouldering the burden of farming, feeding, and cleaning the community without compensation. The school would give no exams and offer no degrees—just a letter of reference sent to the lucky firms vying to employ those who had trained there.

The name Wright proposed—Hillside Home School of the Allied Arts—
hardly suggested a forward-looking merger of industry and beautiful design.
But it did hint at one thing Wright was keenly interested in conveying: pro-
priety. Wright's maiden aunts had been known far and wide as caring educators. Only a year had passed since newspaper readers in Madison had read
Miriam Noel's column labeling Wright "a demon in human form" and alleging that he had done "unspeakable things" to her at Taliesin. By appropriating
the name of his aunts' school, Wright surely hoped to send a signal of newfound moral probity to the university. A few weeks after first conjuring the
school idea, he conceded that the university president, with his "great moral
obligation . . . as the mentor of 10,000 youths," could only view the Hillside
School proposal as "a delicate matter."

To make it even more delicate, the new school was intended to admit
both sexes, though Wright was unmistakably reluctant on this point. "I suppose it would have to be coeducational," he wrote Schevill, because the university was committed to coeducation. In fact, while Frank's aunts had
originally housed boys and girls, they had ultimately dropped the girls after
the number of teenage romances taxed their capacities for supervision and
threatened to stain the school's reputation.

ALTHOUGH WRIGHT PROPOSED himself as chairman of the board, at
first he had no intention of actually running the school, as an administrator
or even a teacher. As director, he proposed another architect: Hendricus
Theodorus Wijdeveld.

Wijdeveld was the founder of the Amsterdam School, not literally a
school but a Dutch modernist movement that was strongly influenced by
Wright's work. In 1925, Wijdeveld had sent Wright a copy of his recently
published A Life-Work of the American Architect Frank Lloyd Wright
with the inscription, "Some Flowers for Architect FLLW." It came at a time
when Wright's career had dwindled to a few houses in Los Angeles. Wijdeveld's inscription, Wright replied, was "a charming and graceful compliment of highest value and I hope some day to be able to return it in some
fashion."

Now, three years later, Wright turned to Olgivanna and said, "Perhaps
Mr. Wijdeveld would be the man to come out and help rebuild the Hillside
Home School." The next day he wrote to Cochius, a friend of the Dutch architect, informing him that he wanted Wijdeveld to head the school and asking him to forward a copy of the prospectus. As Wijdeveld must have been
surprised to discover, Wright had already taken the liberty of listing him as
the school's director.

* * *

IT WAS A bitter cold Wisconsin December. Takehiko Okami, a Japanese archi-tect living at Taliesin and drafting for Wright, got up early one morning to dis-cover that the water had frozen in a beautiful vase of flowers; the sight almost made him cry when he described it to fellow draftsman Vladimir Karfik. With little architectural work to do, Karfik, Okami, and the others were killing time doing "busy work." Their master, in contrast, was in high gear, writing letters, finishing drawings, pushing hard to make the school scheme fly with the university—even as he fought off the flu.

"[C]ome along dear Ferdinand, put your shoulder to the wheel," he en-couraged Schevill in one letter. "If we all do we will win." But Schevill, who plotted the campaign for the university's approval like a military assault, was dismayed by Wright's idealistic assumption that the university would fi-nance the plan. "Oh, Holy simplicity of the artist mind!" he responded to Wright. "Unless the University of your grand and glorious state is run on an entirely different basis from that of the other higher institutions of this land, it will, immediately after acceptance of your School in principle, de-mand the necessary war fund."

FOR WRIGHT THE school prospectus was a call to war—one to create an authentic American culture. He made sure to send a copy of the prospectus to critic Lewis Mum-ford, who had first joined Sulli-van and Wright's organic camp of architecture in 1918 after reading Claude Bragdon's *Architecture and Democracy*. Mumford was urging America to look to its dis-tinctive forms, its "usable past," in order to generate its own modern architecture. He appreciated Wright's sense of place, his use of materials, the warmth of his modernism. Mumford became a frequent correspondent and a

Lewis Mumford

good friend to Wright; both he and Bragdon were listed in the prospectus as visiting lecturers.

The prospectus was a grab bag of Wright's obsessions. European architects, he charged, were now laying claim to designs that properly belonged to America—by which, of course, he meant *his* designs. Wright was furious over the way his ideas had been regurgitated by the European modernists and served back to America as something new. It was a bitter point, but not without validity. And it drove him into a frenzy that the American cultural avant-garde was now adopting the European version—their "stark and naked and severe" glass boxes—as its own imported standard.

As his prospectus for the Hillside Home School built to its climax, Wright's grandiosity soared. He predicted that the European's "exploitation of this original source"—himself—"would set American culture back again another thirty years, at least. Perhaps poison its culture permanently."

WRIGHT EITHER MISUNDERSTOOD the stated mission of the University of Wisconsin, or didn't give a damn about it. Created by one of the country's most progressive states, the university was committed to democratizing higher education. Yet Wright's proposal concluded with an attack on American democracy, all in the name of saving the creative impulse of the genius from the masses. "Enough mischief has already been done in the name of misconceived and selfishly applied *Democracy*," he wrote. "Even the 'best' of us may now, all too plainly, see in our country the evil consequences of a sentimentalized singing to the Demos as a god. We see the evil consequences of this patting of the 'common denominator' on the back and ascribing to him the virtues of deity."

The decision makers at the university must have been taken aback. Chicago's Ferdinand Schevill, understandably embarrassed to be associated with these ideas, decided to write his own innocuous version for the university to accompany the original—"a kind of digest," he told Wright, "to be studied side by side with your own rhapsodic exposition."

The professor knew his audience. Gone, in his version, was Wright's heated condemnation of America and its failure to educate its youth properly. And gone was Wright's thinly veiled claim to being the source of everything right and good in the world. Wright's Hugo-inspired harangue on the superiority of architecture was, in Schevill's account, bureaucratized by a "Division of Architecture" with "sub-divisions of Landscape and decoration," and "a selected number of Industrial Arts."

Lloyd Wright, the architect's nearly forty-year-old son, was less accommodating when he received an early draft. "I was so disappointed," he wrote his father from Los Angeles, "that I could hardly bring myself to the futile task of expressing my opinion. However I have given it, fruitless [though] it undoubtedly is." Among the "goofy details outlined in your prospectus," Lloyd singled out his father's idea for a "small Kindergarten" as the most ridiculous of all. Abandoned by his father along with his five siblings, Wright's son could hardly be blamed for blanching at the thought of his father overseeing a brood of young children.

Wright did incorporate some of his colleagues' suggestions into his final prospectus, and submitted it to the university along with a portfolio of drawings. Now, as his financial situation continued to deteriorate, all he could do was wait.

WITH THE HUGE San Marcos in the Desert project still a go, Wright had enough work to hire an additional draftsman. Wright found him in Henry Klumb, a young German with intense eyes and a grave bearing. Actually, it was Klumb who found him: Wright wasn't lying when he boasted to La Follette that there were hordes of young men dying to work for him. After graduating from the University of Cologne, the neophyte architect had sailed to America with the specific hope of landing a job at Taliesin. "I have . . . considered your wonderful work," he wrote to Wright from St. Louis, where he found temporary work in an organ factory, "with a deep longing to have someday the opportunity to work for an architect who creates things like you do!"

When Klumb arrived at Taliesin, at Wright's invitation, the new hire discovered that his expected duties went beyond the drafting table. Wright raved to him about the new school he envisioned, making it clear that Klumb would be expected to contribute to its development. With the exception of two Americans, Klumb's coworkers in Wright's

Henry Klumb

drafting room—these men working to realize Wright's dream of a uniquely American architecture—were either European or Japanese.

THE FIRST WEEK of 1929 brought Frank another upbeat greeting from Ferdinand Schevill. "This is the year of great achievements, which will see you with your feet on an ascending road. The goal is distant but not so distant as not to make a splendor in the sky."

Although Wright, Inc. was down to its last two thousand dollars, things were looking up. Dr. Chandler had summoned Wright and his draftsmen back to start work on San Marcos in the Desert. The Arizona landscape, Wright wrote his friend Alexander Woollcott, was "the most beautiful part of this earth and the most unspoiled. . . . It is entirely possible that I may build a good many [buildings] out there and that we will have an Arizona extension of Taliesin waiting to receive you and yours in the desert in a year or two."

Wright had also just signed a lifetime contract with Cochius's Leerdam Glassfabriek to design glass products on a royalty basis. He sent Lewis Mumford a snapshot to reassure him that he was "battered up but still in the ring." As he told Philip La Follette, "we [had] coke to burn. We had Taliesin. It was enough. We were in luck."

* * *

Ocatillo drafting studio. Draftsman Vlademir Karfik is in the foreground.

AT THE END of January, Wright and his company of fifteen left Taliesin for Arizona to work on the hotel. Dr. Chandler had offered them a small parcel of his desert land to stay on while they worked on the massive, half-million-dollar resort project. Their first task was to build a desert compound, to include housing, a drafting studio, and an office. They named it Ocatillo after the omnipresent cactus.

This was no ordinary campsite. Wright stretched canvas roofs over elegant, low wood-sided bases. The largest of these "tents," their floors covered with Navajo blankets, enclosed rows of drafting tables whose ranks ended with a grand piano. When the final chord of one of Wright's beloved sonatas decayed in the desert air, the sound was replaced by the night howls of coyotes and other predators.

By some accounts, Dr. Chandler had agreed to pay Wright $60,000 once the half-million-dollar construction loan was secured. If things went according to plan, the architect would be out of debt for the first time in almost twenty years.

BY THE END of February 1929, three months had passed since Wright extended his invitation to Wijdeveld to come and be the director of his school. There had been no response from "Dutchy," just a note from Cochius that Wijdeveld was "delighted" with the idea. Finally Wijdeveld cabled Wright to explain: He had been planning to start his own school in Amsterdam, and

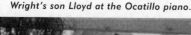

Wright's son Lloyd at the Ocatillo piano.

was trying to decide whether to abandon that plan and throw his lot in with Wright.

Wright didn't reply for six weeks. Wijdeveld wrote Wright again, this time leaving no doubt of his enthusiasm for joining him. "If your plans to erect a school for architects, a home for young people, an atmosphere of real living . . . which is Life, Work, and Repose in One, are in an advanced state . . . then I know that I would be next to Wright—the *wright* man in the *wright* place! . . . To organize, to build and lead with you this new school for the study of architecture and the decorative arts in Harmony and International understanding would mean to me the realization of a long-cherished—DREAM."

Wijdeveld saw their shared desire to create schools as an instance of cosmic synchronicity—two "great renewals" emerging independently at the same time, an ocean apart. He enclosed a brochure for his own institution, referring to it as a *werkgemeenschap*, a "work fellowship." "Why not remove this idea, this work, to America," he wrote, "to the land with the nation of promise, to Wisconsin . . . to YOU.

"Write Soon," the letter concluded, "and. . . . We come!"

Wright's response was timely but tepid. He was now uncomfortable asking the Wijdevelds to uproot themselves, he explained, before resolving his own financial concerns. Though Wright didn't foreclose the idea altogether, he conceded that it was "still some distance away, I am sorry to say."

In the past, Wright had rarely allowed a lack of funds to stop him. But he was severely constrained by La Follette's oversight of Wright, Inc. Wright complained to the lawyer that he was "totally without money" to finish the drawings for Chandler, or even to keep his family and staff fed. Shortly after his letter stalling "Dutchy," Wright lashed out at his overlord. "Clearly, under this contract," he wrote La Follette, "I cease to exist as an individual either personally or in relation to my work. I have already worse than lost everything in connection with either as it reads. Taliesin is responsible. That is to say, loving it too much and trying to hang on to it at this price."

While money may have played the larger role, the Dutchman's brochure for his own school, his "work fellowship," had also given Wright pause. Wijdeveld's earlier work had been clearly in the Wright idiom, but his new drawings of his proposed Amsterdam school, Wright wrote Lewis Mumford, were in the mode of the European functionalism of Le Corbusier, Walter Gropius, and Bruno Taut. Wijdeveld's vision was "more shallow than it should be," Wright felt, "and its form too much iteration and reiteration."

Olgivanna was likely also a factor. About a week before Wright wrote Wijdeveld not to come, he received a letter from Richard Lloyd Jones suggesting that he already had a capable manager—in house. "You have in Olgivanna," he wrote, "a mighty fine woman. Both George [Lloyd Jones's wife] and I have been much pleased by her and impressed with her. I think she is a woman with a lot of sanity and ability and balance and poise and [who] could develop business sense as fast as business responsibilities were imposed upon her. Now if I were you, I would employ Olgivanna as my business manager just as soon as I found it possible to get out of this La Follette tie. Let her take in all the money, run a bank account, finance your enterprises and then you go to work and think of nothing but your job."

While Wright would never have considered his wife capable of directing the pedagogy at the Hillside School, he might easily have seen her as its administrator, organizing work and assigning tasks as she had done for a brief period at the Prieuré. This had been Ashbee's wife's role in his Guild of Handicraft, after all, and Wright had been impressed by her. If Olgivanna saw the very complementary letter from Jones, as it's likely she did, she may well have suggested it herself.

WRIGHT HAD AGAIN summoned his architect son Lloyd to work with him on the huge hotel, with its thousands of zigzag, molded concrete blocks stacked up in steps until they all somehow came together against the mountainous horizon—somehow suggesting both a city skyline and a pueblo. At dinner, Lloyd recalled, his father lambasted the city. "The city is a prison," he intoned. "There is no place to breathe. There's no sun and light. No place for a man's spirit to grow. . . . The desert is more inviting. It's a challenge and an opportunity. Remember what Victor Hugo said: 'The desert is where God is and man is not.'"

To the six draftsmen accompanying him, though, Ocatillo was hell, not heaven. In late April, the temperature was already over 100 degrees Fahrenheit. Most of them couldn't even work. Lloyd Wright and Henry Klumb were the only ones able to draw and then only after swimming in the irrigation channels two or three times a day. Fed up with the heat and mosquitoes, the draftsmen dogged Wright with pleas to return to Taliesin. "Don't worry," he told them, "we will go very soon." By the end of May, the conditions were so unbearable that the group was forced to leave for Taliesin before the San Marcos drawings were complete.

Now the task would be even more difficult. Having spent the fees from Chandler unwisely—on the grand piano in the tent, among other things—Wright was out of cash to pay his draftsmen. It was an excruciating bind: Chandler needed the drawings to get the investor funding needed to pay Wright the balance of the fee—but Wright needed the fee to complete the drawings.

As they made their way back east, La Follette sent a letter to the other directors of Wright, Inc. The corporate treasury was depleted, he reported, the taxes still unpaid. A notice from the bank, informing them that they were about to breach the terms of the mortgage, could be expected at any moment. And now Wright was requesting a modification to his contract allowing him to buy out the Wright, Inc. stockholders, claiming that he never understood the contract in the first place.

That Wright, by definition as broke as his corporation, would ever be in a position to buy out the stockholders must have seemed like a joke to its directors. Yet dreams of potential windfalls from Chandler and the University of Wisconsin still danced in his head—though each grew less likely with each passing month.

Three months later, on October 29, 1929, both hopes evaporated with the crash of the stock market. That day, Wright wrote Lloyd—who had little work of his own, and was still waiting to be paid for his work in Arizona—that his friends were trying to cobble funds just "to keep the wolf from the door." Wright told his son to "keep a stiff upper lip. You have real ability and enough character to make it count. . . . If the San Marcos goes on, I shall be glad to hook you up with it if you want to be so hooked." He also wrote Wijdeveld that the university can "do nothing within years—if at all." Private funding, he added, was looking like their last hope.

He was wrong. Less than three months after the crash, Wright's presence was requested at a meeting of the faculty committee assigned to deliberate the Hillside prospectus. On December 16, 1929, precisely one year after he first drafted the proposal, he drove into Madison. When he arrived, though, he discovered—to his "surprise and chagrin"—that the plan being discussed differed sharply from the one he had submitted. The university had modified it by, among other things, rejecting the idea that Wright or anyone else should "dominate" the school as chairman. At least as disturbing, they rejected the notion that architecture would dominate the other arts. The academics were tampering with his "Ideal," his mission to reestablish architecture as the foundation of all culture. Worse yet, the hapless faculty committee treated him as though he were an ordinary man. The revised proposal was out of the question.

Wright was also outraged to discover that his friend and faculty ally, Franz Aust, had been complicit in the university's revisions. The fundamental concept of the school, Wright scolded the professor, was not some experiment, but an "accomplished fact" of superior culture for which he had fought single-handedly for the last thirty years. Only his uncompromised work would command the world's support; after all, it had "already changed the thought and remodeled the forms of the entire European modern world." He accused Aust of either not understanding this fact, or intentionally concealing it.

Wright wrangled with the committee, with what he called its "inane fiddling with philosophy" and "insane presumption of science to creative power."

Architecture had to have primacy, and he, Frank Lloyd Wright, had to have creative control. His rhetorical efforts were not without effect: Three of its members changed their minds. But it was not enough. And for Wright, it was all or nothing. What the university wanted was "too much apiece with the ignorant-prejudice of the academies to deserve more than contempt."

He would have to start anew.

BUILDING IS INHERENTLY an act of optimism. In the wake of the market crash, T-squares across the country were still. In his way, Wright was better prepared than many architects to weather the downturn. With his scandalous ways and unorthodox ideas, he had been forced to learn to survive without clients during even the boom years, getting by on writing and lecturing.

Wright's response to crisis, economic or otherwise, was to get busy. This time, though, fate was also on his side. On January 3, Miriam Noel died. Aside from his now very old debt to Darwin Martin, Noel's divorce settlement was his largest financial liability. Her death not only canceled out that debt, but it also allowed Wright to reclaim funds he had put into a trust account for her. Four weeks later, he cut a check for $15,000 to pay off the mortgage on the Hillside School property.

The following month, another architect-turned-educator visited Taliesin. Eliel Saarinen, the great Finnish designer, was working on a campus for a girl's school for the Cranbrook Foundation in neighboring Michigan, drawing on Wright's Prairie School architecture. He was also working on a design for the Cranbrook Academy, an art school he directed. The two architects were both seeking to become educators. With Wright's architecture income "practically nil," and Chandler's ongoing inability to fund San Marcos now a permanent and "somewhat staggering blow" (in Wright's words), the two men surely compared notes on their respective school projects. Wright came away from his day with Saarinen with renewed energy for the school scheme.

Saarinen must have come away with something else. "Frank Wright," he later quipped, "was neither."

IN MAY 1930, less than two months after Saarinen's visit, Frank and Olgivanna traveled to East Aurora, New York, near Buffalo, to visit Roycrofters, a remarkable Arts and Crafts community inspired by founder Elbert Hubbard's travels to England to meet William Morris. Roycrofters began as a Morris-influenced book design and printing facility and farm, later adding manufacture and mail-order sales of metal products to its operations.

A born salesman, Hubbard had worked as a young man for the Larkin Company, the mail-order business that also employed Darwin Martin. Hubbard left Larkin in 1893, the same year Wright left Sullivan. Wright and Hubbard had been good friends since 1902, when Darwin Martin invited Wright to Buffalo—a trip that resulted in commissions for Martin's own house, the Larkin Building, and another house for Hubbard's sister. It must have thrilled Wright to see Hubbard's followers—eight hundred at the community's peak—burst into applause as their leader entered the dining hall. Hubbard had been a frequent visitor to Frank's home in Oak Park. Indeed, his Wildean wardrobe may have been a model for Wright's.

Frank and Olgivanna likely learned much about creating an arts-oriented community, if not a school, from visiting Roycrofters. The Hillside School prospectus appears to reflect at least some of Hubbard's innovations, among them a child care center to liberate the community's women for other work. Cochius had already offered to set up a glass-manufacturing facility at the proposed school; Wright would surely have been encouraged by how the Roycrofters factories had made Hubbard's community self-sufficient. The only thing missing was Hubbard himself. Fifteen years before, in April 1915, Hubbard—who often wrote pieces for the Hearst newspapers—was sailing toward a hoped-for interview with Kaiser Wilhelm when his ship, the *Lusitania*, was sunk by a German submarine.

Wright's return to Roycrofters in 1930 coincided with a trip to Princeton University to deliver a series of prestigious lectures tied to a traveling exhibition of his work. Henry Klumb suggested to Wright that his most important buildings be redrawn for the lectures, using his own stark black-and-white rendering technique, which revealed the three-dimensional character of the buildings at the expense of a complete elimination of surface detail and subtle color—hallmarks of Wright's elegant and wispy colored pencil drawings. "Do it," Wright replied. Klumb had them done in ink on white roll-up window shades. "Nothing that International Style had to [offer] could equal it," Klumb recalled.

WRIGHT USED THE occasion of the Princeton lectures to make his first public statement of the core ideas behind his new school. Calling it a "style center," he told his audience that his school would take "sensitive, unspoiled students"—presumably excluding Princeton types—and prepare them for the day when "art must take the lead in education."

But the bulk of the four sessions were devoted to his ideas on architecture. It was likely not the kind of talk that the Ivy Leaguers had ever heard, at least not outside of church.

"The first thing to do," he lectured the students, "was to get rid of the attic and, therefore, of the dormer and the useless 'heights' below it. And next get rid of the unwholesome basement—entirely, yes, absolutely—in any house built on the prairie." Wright was describing his revolutionary Prairie house designs, which eliminated a house's most hidden spaces—places where memories and the material detritus of the family are stored. But he was also opening an extraordinary window into the fundamentals of his aesthetic— and, beyond that, into his very psyche.

In his Princeton lectures, Wright likened the traditional house to a medieval prison, with its places of unobserved torment, its dungeons and closed cells. The conventional attic, in his view, was positively malevolent. "Chimneys were . . . sooty fingers threatening the sky. And beside them, sticking up by way of dormers through the cruelly sharp, sawtooth roofs, were the attics for 'help' to swelter in." To Wright, getting rid of the attic and basement—secret spaces where things could happen unobserved by the family—meant erasing a family's past, or at least its depositories. Wright was not speaking architecturally or even aesthetically about these spaces. His language was moral.

In Wright's experience, of course, the attic and basement were more than mere symbols of danger; in his own youth, they were actual sites of terror. It was in the attic where he closed himself off against his father's judgment and his violence. And it was in the basement kitchen where his mother took fork-tines to his sister's eyes. In the tornado-prone Midwest, the basement was a source of refuge; for Wright, it had been a place of danger.

Wright is justly famous for originating the open plan, rendering the ground floor rooms observable to one another, replacing walls with partitions and screens, making living room, dining room, and kitchen all flow into one another. What is remarkable about his Princeton lectures is how clearly he expressed his vision as a defense against the perils of American family life—at the very moment when he was planning to expand his own domestic sphere into an all-encompassing community.

Anna Wright, reading John Ruskin to her young son as cathedral engravings hung over their son's bed; William, introducing him to a life of arts and letters—each of Wright's parents took extraordinary, and quite conscious, steps to mold him into a great architect. But the madness of Frank Lloyd Wright's family—the uncontrolled violence and the terrors they set in motion—may have been even more powerful contributions to his creative universe. His unprecedented houses were sites of shelter, designed to produce domestic harmony. With their open plans—and particularly the open kitchens Wright championed later—they allowed mothers to keep their children in constant view and rendered it difficult for a father or a mother to abuse a child unobserved. They fulfilled Wright's clear intention to preserve and protect the form of family he had been denied in his own youth . . . and had such difficulty sustaining in adulthood.

AFTER THE PRINCETON exhibition closed, Wright arranged for it to tour to a number of American cities and then asked for Wijdeveld's help in bringing it to Europe. Eager as always, Dutchy agreed, putting in an enormous effort to arrange venues and personally design the exhibition layouts. Wright sent Klumb to Holland to help Wijdeveld mount the exhibition.

"Your ways are Wright's ways," Klumb told Wijdeveld when he arrived. "His longings are yours." Their shared vision of a school at Taliesin, he assured Dutchy, was still intact. Wijdeveld was ready. He notified Wright that he was now professionally and financially prepared to move with his family to America. If he sold everything, he wrote the architect, he would have ten or fifteen thousand dollars left when he arrived. The school, he assured Wright, could be self-supporting in a year.

Wijdeveld's devotion to Wright made a strong impression on Henry Klumb. When the exhibit opened in the Netherlands after nearly six months of planning, the young architect wrote a gushing letter describing the event. "A stream of joyful words about your work was flowing," Klumb reported. "Nobody dared to breathe. I will remember all the time the things [Wijdeveld] said, I still see the astonished faces, the wondering eyes of those who listened." Thanks to the Dutchman's efforts, the European artistic community would all know that Wright was the source of the continent's burgeoning modern architecture movement, Klumb wrote—and, not incidentally, that he was still working.

"Mr. Wijdeveld would give his life for your ideas, for your work," Klumb advised Wright. "He is living in it and with it even though he does not know you. His appreciation is the deepest and the purest of all I know. He would leave his work and home behind, would come to Taliesin and help to make your dream—the Hillside School—reality." There could be no better choice to direct the school. "*His life would make it live*," he wrote, "his energies and work would leave you free, so you could give the world still more and greater buildings of a higher sphere." Klumb himself, of course, also hoped to be a part of that higher sphere.

And then there was a bit of personal news, news Klumb assumed would be well received: He was about to be married.

BACK IN WISCONSIN, Wright received a portentous letter from Mumford. The Museum of Modern Art was putting together an architecture show, and they wanted Wright to be represented. Just two years old, MoMA had been founded by capitalist patrons of post-impressionism. The museum's director, the twenty-seven-year-old art historian Alfred Barr, had tapped the heavyset and mustachioed Henry-Russell Hitchcock, America's most eminent historian of architectural modernism, to curate the exhibition. To assist Hitchcock, Barr chose one of his intimates, the lanky, debonair Philip Johnson, a wealthy young Harvard philosophy graduate enthralled with Friedrich Nietzsche's apotheosis of artistic creation.

Philip Johnson "will come West to talk things over with you, I think," Mumford wrote, "if you feel this is necessary."

This was a surprise. In his recent volume of architectural history, *Modern Architecture: Romanticism and Reintegration,* Hitchcock had heralded the emergence in Europe of the "New Pioneers" with their "international style." Hitchcock and Johnson had subsequently decided to write a new, more popular book about modern architecture, and it was their research for this book that led them to conceive the exhibition. Its subject, Johnson announced, would be "the style and nothing but the style." But Hitchcock and Johnson's regard for Wright's work was distinctly limited: When it was published the following year, their new book, *International Style: Architecture Since 1922,* would declare Wright to be "more akin to the men of a hundred years ago than to the generation which has come to the fore since the war." Hitchcock chose not even to include Wright's work in the book.

Even before the volume appeared, Wright knew whom he was dealing with—the enemy. To Mumford's triumphant announcement, he responded acidly that Hitchcock was an agent of the "surface and mass" party, part of the "coroner's jury" sitting in judgment of him.

But Wright also recognized that this architectural exhibit at MoMA would mark America's first exposure to European modernism. He was terrified that the curators' view of him would prevail, that the new men were preparing to dominate the stage

Philip Johnson, Wright's nemesis, champion, and friend

and eclipse him forever in the public eye. It was bad enough that two architectural curators at the Museum of Modern Art were christening the Europeans, with their flat-roofed, white machined boxes, as "new pioneers." But the
prospect that the show would also fail to mark his paternity galled him even
more.

While Wright had pioneered modern architectural forms with open
asymmetrical plans and new geometries, he sharply distinguished his work
from the European modernists, whose designs were already galvanizing
young architects on both sides of the Atlantic. For many of these Europeans,
ornament had become something criminal, degenerate. Wright called their
complete rejection of ornament "the bastard begotten by intellectualists out
of the dogma 'form follows function'; begotten because the abuse of a noble
thing was mistaken for the thing itself." Wright was no classicist, but his apprenticeship with Louis Sullivan had been a lasting influence; the subtle ornamentation of Wright's designs was integrated carefully with the materials
and methods of construction he employed throughout his career.

There were other significant differences between Wright's vision and the
International Style. The European modernists' structures typically had flat,
nonprojecting roofs. Wright's extended roofs, by contrast, conveyed a powerful sense of shelter. Many of the Europeans' houses looked like they could be
anything—an office building, a doctor's office, a shop. Wright's, although eccentric, were obviously family homes, not abstract universal solutions that
might suit any function, or, for that matter, any site or climate.

And then there was the role of the machine. Led by Le Corbusier in
France, who subtly fashioned buildings in the image of steam ships, the European modernists made an aesthetic out of the machine itself, in the belief
that industrial production should provide not only the techniques of production, but also the very forms of architecture. Wright, in contrast, had
maintained as early as his 1901 lecture at Hull House that architects should
master the multiplying powers of industrial machinery, not mimic them in
their art.

It was Wright's partisan Lewis Mumford, who was in charge of the collective
housing element of the MoMA exhibition, who pushed Hitchcock and Johnson
to include Wright in the International Style exhibition. Immediately after the
idea for the show was first floated, Johnson wrote to him that Wright had nothing to say to "the International Group." Two years later, he wrote Mumford that
Wright "was a great pioneer but he is a romantic and has nothing more to do
with architecture today."

Mumford, however, was a strong believer in Wright's organic architecture. Compared to the houses of the Europeans, he wrote, who "fall into rap-

tures over the articulated skeleton, and despise the flesh," Wright's work "has skeleton, flesh, and all necessary organs, and so will be, I hope, the mold of all our new architecture."

Somehow Mumford must have prevailed, for the two curators ultimately decided to include Wright in the New York show. The only question was whether, side by side with his younger challengers, he could hold his own.

NEW YORK WAS also about to receive Gurdjieff. But much had changed in the seven years since he had been the talk of the city. This time he was coming to save, not expand, his enterprise. Donations from New York and Chicago were keeping his Institute afloat, but with the Prieuré on the brink of foreclosure, he needed more. He decided to run the American operation himself. Alfred Orage had to go.

Calling all Orage's New York groups together, Gurdjieff denounced their members as "full-aged unfortunate people vegetating in American-scale organized 'lunatic asylums.' " They were, he told them, to renounce their loyalty to Orage. By the time the magus boarded the ship back to France in mid-March, he had so alienated Orage that his American leader also sailed for England, never to return again.

Orage's departure left the Chicago-based Jean Toomer as Gurdjieff's only trusted lieutenant in America. Having built up a large following, Toomer regularly sent both pupils and money to Gurdjieff in France. Gurdjieff himself traveled to Chicago twice, in the winters of 1930 and 1931, to maintain the membership's loyalty and flow of cash. And his helpers in the enterprise included a number of Frank Lloyd Wright's closest associates: Ferdinand Schevill, his dearest friend; Baker Brownell, a friend and later coauthor; and Zona Gale, who all sponsored lectures by Toomer.

But Toomer was shaken by Orage's decision to part with the Gurdjieff movement. Toomer had been developing his own spiritual ideas, and now he too chose to go his own way. And Zona Gale was willing to back Toomer all the way, whatever the cost to Gurdjieff's fortunes in America.

Gale knew well what a formidable force Gurdjieff could be. The previous spring, she and Claude Bragdon had been subjected to an extraordinary display of the master's powers. The two were eating in a Manhattan restaurant when Gurdjieff and his party entered. Sitting at a table across the room, Gurdjieff caught Gale's eye, then began to inhale and exhale "in a particular way." Bragdon noticed that she was turning pale, as if she might faint at any moment. What was wrong, he asked her? "Something awful happened," she responded—something "uncanny." Gurdjieff's gaze was so powerful "that within a second or so I suddenly felt as though I had been struck right through my sexual center. It was beastly!" Gurdjieff had apparently aroused Gale to orgasm just by staring at her.

But Gale was undeterred by Gurdjieff's powers. She agreed to provide Toomer with a five-room farmhouse near Portage, her Wisconsin hometown, where he could house the eight core members of his offshoot organization, supplemented by weekend visitors from Chicago. The "Portage experiment," as it was known, was launched in the summer of 1931. Toomer wanted to get back to the natural child, to create a kind of nursery school for adults. And the residents paid for their enlightenment, just as they had with Gurdjieff. Toomer had them all working—the women cooking and cleaning, the men doing heavy labor outside. In marathon discussions, the members revealed how they "really" felt about one another. They also studied Gurdjieff's movements, went swimming in the river, and played croquet and deck tennis; Toomer climbed trees so that he could observe them closely. He even assigned each of them a unique type of "tail," just as Gurdjieff had his typology of "idiots."

Only sixty miles from Taliesin, Toomer's spiritual community would certainly have caught Olgivanna's eye. Indeed, it captured the nation's attention—though for reasons Toomer would surely have preferred to avoid.

During his time in Portage, Toomer—a light-skinned African American—fell in love with Gale's beautiful literary protégée Margery Latimer, whose heritage went back to Cotton Mather. The couple married in October 1931. Gale, who had tried to convince Latimer not to marry a man she knew to be a Negro, did not attend. The bride wore black.

On their honeymoon, the newlyweds traveled first to Santa Fe, near Mabel Dodge Luhan's Taos estate, to see about forming a group there. From there they went on to Carmel, where Toomer established a Portage-like experiment.

In Portage, Toomer had passed for East Indian. In Carmel, he wouldn't be so lucky. A reporter there discovered Toomer's work in the famous 1925 anthology of Negro writers, *The New Negro*. When asked if he was a Negro, Toomer denied it. But the word was out. "Negro Poet and White Bride in Honeymoon at Cottage in Carmel," the *San Francisco Examiner* blared. Even *Time* picked up the story of the race-mixing literary couple. "As I see America," Toomer declared in *Time*, "it is like a great stomach into which are thrown the elements that make up the life blood. From this source is coming a distinct race of people. They will achieve tremendous works of art, literature and music. They will not be white, black or yellow—just Americans."

From Portage, Toomer received a letter that he was liable to be lynched if he ever showed up in town again. In the wake of the story, the Portage experiment became a national scandal. There were charges of communism, nudism, and sexual license. Unmarried men and women were living, unsupervised, under one roof.

Toomer was in serious trouble, and Olgivanna knew it; at least one Portage participant visited Taliesin at the time. But the writer's public image would have interested Mrs. Wright less than his standing within the Institute, which had plummeted. His commune was seen as a misguided, "rash Prieuré-style experiment." Toomer had been reading his own writings to his pupils, making liberal interpretations of Gurdjieff's movements, engaging the students in whimsical collective activities rather than individual projects involving hard physical labor.

Both Alfred Orage and Jean Toomer, Gurdjieff's main men in America, were now out of the picture. Yet America was still his best hope. He even began telling people that he intended to move permanently to New York City. Somehow, through it all, Olgivanna managed to remain in his good graces; she had just signaled her commitment by publishing an essay, "The Last Days of Katherine Mansfield," in *The Bookman*, a respected New York journal. And she had reason to believe that she was finally about to become the matron of a school—one with spiritual studies on its agenda.

Gurdjieff believed that women were incapable of the same level of self-development as men. With her talent for teaching the movements, her estate, and her pending school, though, Olgivanna must again have seemed a promising field asset.

OLGIVANNA'S FUTURE WITH Gurdjieff was a matter of conjecture, but the fate of Wright's school seemed bright. In May 1931, Wright wrote Wijdeveld that he had discovered a possible new source of money—lots of it—for the Hillside school. "A school is forming in Chicago," he wrote, "known as Allied Arts and Industries similar to the plan I had in mind with an endowment of 2½ Million Dollars. They wanted me to take direction but I suggested you with me as Chairman of the board." He told Wijdeveld that he would be getting a ten-year contract with a salary of ten thousand dollars per year. A year and a half into the Depression, the offer was miraculous. Wright suggested that Wijdeveld come the following fall.

"Chicago school overwhelming," Dutchy wired back, "Accept directorship willing to cross immediately for short stay."

A few days later, Wright received a letter Wijdeveld wrote before hearing about the Chicago deal. Indeed, calling it a mere letter hardly does the eighteen-page production justice: In its carefully composed pages, Dutchy wove together photographs of himself and his family, snippets of poetry, and short biographies of his wife and children. At the bottom of its last page, Wijdeveld laid in a cut-out photo of himself looking up, shading his eyes with his hand, gazing up at a star drawn at the top. And along the line of sight between Wijdeveld's eyes and the star, as if carried along by a ray of light, were written the words: WRIGHT, TALIESIN, WIJDEVELD, ART-SCHOOL, FUTURE, CULTURE.

Alas, it was all a mirage. There was no such deal with the Chicago organization. The year before, Frank and Olgivanna had had lunch with a woman named Norma Stahl, the executive secretary of the Association of Arts and Industries, a group looking to start a school similar to Wright's. After reading Wright's Hillside prospectus, though, Stahl wrote Wright that their projects had significant differences. And hers was committed to Chicago. Although Stahl did suggest the name of a Chicago socialite who might be able to finance his venture, she shut the door on any collaboration with Wright.

Yet somehow Wright believed that the door remained unlocked. The day after receiving Dutchy's telegram, he wrote to Stahl urging her to come for a visit. "I want you to see Hillside in its present state."

A page from Wijdeveld's illuminated letter to Wright. (The swastika here is unrelated to Nazism.)

* * *

TWO MONTHS PASSED without Wijdeveld hearing a word from Wright. On June 10, the Dutchman took the initiative, sending Wright a letter announcing enthusiastically that he was preparing to join the master at Taliesin. "With my letter," he announced, "a spirit crosses the Ocean."

In a sure sign of Wright's discomfort, Wijdeveld's rhapsodic letter was answered by his secretary, Karl Jensen. There was no deal as yet, he admitted, but Wright was going back to Chicago to try to make it happen.

Wijdeveld's life was back in suspension.

After two months he finally received a letter from Taliesin, this time from Wright himself. "I have only been unwilling to encourage you to come here," he wrote, without apologizing for his silence, "until I had some assurance myself that your effort would not be sunk in vain in this great commercial engine we call the United States." He now had that assurance, if only moderately: He had "enlisted the cooperation of the woman who is really responsible for the Chicago Allied Arts and Industries to make our School here the small head and beginning of that greater school which will be built in the next year or two." The Hillside school, he explained, would become a modest pilot project "to determine just what and how the Chicago enterprise should be planned." There was no mention of funding.

As usual, the truth was a little less sanguine. Norma Stahl had indeed visited Hillside at Wright's invitation. But what Wright represented to Dutchy as an offer was no more than a suggestion that Wright's school might someday— perhaps years frow now— merge into her projected Chicago institute.

Still, Wijdeveld took the bait. Wright reminded Dutchy that he only wanted to be chairman of the board, and Wijdeveld would be the school's director. Still, Wright made it clear that he expected to have "a deciding voice from 'behind the throne' for some years." Moreover, he warned Wijdeveld that he was "unused to working *with* anyone."

Could Wijdeveld visit Taliesin in November?

Now it was Wijdeveld's turn to grow uncertain. "I feel the burden of a great responsibility coming over me," he replied to Wright. His own school proposal received encouraging letters from the likes of Albert Einstein, William Butler Yeats, Leopold Stokowski, Le Corbusier, Max Reinhardt, and Wright's own friends Lewis Mumford and Eric Mendelsohn. Nonetheless, he told Wright, starting his own school looked like "an infinity of trouble and work."

A dedicated Theosophist, Wijdeveld sought advice from the movement's onetime boy wonder, Krishnamurti. After a long meeting, the Indian mystic told him, "Where you start is of no importance . . . just start!"

The Dutchman was leaning toward Taliesin. "I am longing," he wrote

Wright, "to renew life and start in a 'wider-field,'" a play on the translation of his name. "I feel a change coming over me," he concluded.

> *let it come*
> *as it comes.*
> *let fate reign.*

Wijdeveld then left Amsterdam for a long walking tour of southern Europe to deliberate "in the solitude of nature." Ten days later, he was back in Amsterdam with a decision. "Consider earnestly proposal," he cabled Wright, "ready crossing first alone for short meeting you to settle matters."

At the end of October 1931, Hendricus Theodorus Wijdeveld descended a gangway in the harbor of New York. From there he headed west to Chicago, where Wright would pick him up for the drive back to Taliesin. The two had never met face to face.

A STATION FOR THE FLIGHT OF THE SOUL

"THAT COUNTS YOU ONE," WRIGHT told Wijdeveld, greeting him with a handshake. Being "counted one" was the ultimate compliment. And Dutchy had earned it by publishing his book on Wright. "It doesn't matter how many errors you commit now," he went on, "that will always count you one."

The next day the two men crossed the gentle hill separating Taliesin from Hillside to survey the abandoned, dilapidated wood and stone school building. Dutchy was overwhelmed. "Could life undergo a transposition," he wrote to his wife, Ellen, that night, "how willingly would I take it at Taliesin. . . . Here I increase my knowledge and appreciation of life."

The two architects had known each other only by correspondence, and in his letters Dutchy had been adoring and deferential. In the flesh, he was different. His International Fellowship idea had just been ratified by some of the greatest minds of Europe. "I will propose this scheme to Wright," he wrote his wife that first night, "and we'll see what he says about it."

The next day he did just that. Wright was surprised to discover that the Dutchman—far less famous and eighteen years his junior—was so willful and self-possessed.

Dutchy's scheme bore little resemblance to Wright's Hillside Home School of the Allied Arts. His International Fellowship was instead a return to the spirit of the medieval guilds. In the old guild system, he declared in his Amsterdam proposal, "all found recognition, all creative fellow-workers, members of one great body, in which they were united by their mutual aim, not merely that of their daily bread, but of their vision of a common ideal." And it was the creative artist, he argued, who led the way. But over time the workshop had been replaced by the school, skill replaced by theory—and in the process, he argued, the creative faculty had been lost. So was the people's grasp on the "cultural foundations of their own race."

Wijdeveld's fellowship idea, in fact, was more Frank Lloyd Wright than Wright's own. And Wright knew it. What his European colleague proposed was akin to what Wright saw at Charles Ashbee's guild in the English countryside, while working on the Imperial Hotel in Japan, and at Roycrofters just the year before. What's more, Wijdeveld's approach—jettisoning classroom pedagogy for something closer to medieval apprenticeship—was far better suited to his nature. No formal curriculum, none of the reading and regurgitation he had reviled as a university student. Indeed, Dutchy's idea could be seen as an expansion of his existing architecture practice, with one difference: Rather than Wright paying his workers to draw and farm, they would be paying him.

WRIGHT'S DRAFTSMAN HENRY Klumb returned to Taliesin with Wijdeveld. He had worked on Wright's exhibition as it traveled from Holland to Germany and Belgium. Wright had paid him $800 plus expenses to act as his agent. But the young German had also given a series of well-received lectures on his journey, and now Wright upbraided him for garnering so much attention. To make matters worse, Klumb had returned with a wife, a weaver named Else. Wright berated him for marrying without his permission. Else was grudgingly accepted into the community. But Henry Klumb remained irked by Wright's treatment.

INSIDE WRIGHT'S SMALL office, its plaster ceiling inlaid with dark wooden boards forming a subtle abstraction of branching tree trunks, Frank and Dutchy worked side by side on the design of their new "institution." Olgivanna, who was quite ill at the time, likely played little if any role in the deliberations. Iovanna, nearly six now, made a game of the proceedings—and a pest of herself—by throwing pebbles at the earnest Dutchman through the breezeway door.

Within a week the two architects agreed on a new draft prospectus. Frank's "Hillside Home School of the Allied Arts" gave way to the "Taliesin Fellowship," echoing Wijdeveld's now abandoned International Fellowship. The new name reflected a complete rethinking of Wright's plan. This was no school. The current group of draftsmen, referred to in the document as "associates," would be supplemented by one hundred apprentices, each paying a yearly tuition of $500, and each agreeing to labor over Taliesin's fields and buildings—all in exchange for "the privilege of participation." In one feature carried over from Wright's earlier scheme, the huge coterie of new apprentices would be expected to design and manufacture "art objects" to be exhibited and sold. In return, each would receive a share of proceeds at the end of the year.

This typed document, which resides today in Taliesin's archive, was clearly the work of Wijdeveld, but it contains edits in Wright's hand, corrections that deflect Wijdeveld's more universalist urges. Wright changed Dutchy's global aim of directing "the course of culture" to "the forming of a native culture." In place of Dutchy's declaration that all the arts would "emanate from the philosophy of modern life as we are living it," Wright wrote that it would emanate from "the organic philosophy of an organic architecture for modern life as we are living it at the present time."

While architecture and product design would dominate the new Fellowship, the "lesser" arts would also have their place. There would be plays, musical evenings, and cinema. And there would be lectures by musicians and "literary men," some open to the public. The members of the Fellowship would experience the intimacy with nature that only the countryside could offer, without sacrificing the cultural sophistication of the city.

Underlying the revised plan was another agenda, one so complex and grandiose that it couldn't possibly be contained in a mere proposal. A little more than two weeks after the architects finished their prospectus, Wright signed a contract for a book, one that left no doubt that the Taliesin Fellowship was intended to be a far-reaching social experiment—a prototype, in fact, for a new form of American community.

The book's title, *The Disappearing City*, was not intended as metaphor. The modern industrial city, Wright's manuscript declared, had become an overpopulated, dangerous, and polluted relic. Just as Charles Darwin had foreseen the disappearance of unfit organisms, Wright predicted that the city itself was near extinction. A few weeks after Wijdeveld arrived, in a lecture at Manhattan's New School for Social Research, Wright declared the just-completed Empire State Building "a tomb that will mark the end of an epoch."

Wright proposed to replace America's urban centers with something he called Broadacre City, a network connected by modern transportation and communications that would be neither countryside nor city. Its modern villages would be close to nature and the farm, harbor environmentally benign industry, and provide their citizens with the best of the arts and letters without forcing them to travel to New York or Chicago.

Wright had begun working on his Broadacre City idea before Wijdeveld's arrival, but the brassy Dutchman's influence showed through in both the

book and the final Fellowship prospectus. Utopian schemes integrating nature and the city had been one of Wijdeveld's great passions, as far back as
1919 when he proposed extending Amsterdam's Vondelpark all the way to the
coast. (In Wijdeveld's plan, the main entry to the park, a landmark in erotic
architecture, was to be shaped like a giant vulva.)

But one important feature of this new utopian vision was all Wright, and
it astounded some critics: The management of these modern villages would
be turned over to architects. Political power, like everything else, was to be
decentralized and handed over to the practitioners of organic architecture—
a "group" that, in 1932, essentially counted Frank Lloyd Wright as its only
member.

The Taliesin Fellowship was designed as a harbinger of Broadacre City.
"Creative impulse," Wright and Wijdeveld wrote in describing the Fellowship,
"should have a chance at fresh life under fresh conditions un-contaminated
by conditions and expressions already dead or dying. The city is such a condition and such a dying or dead expression."

APPRENTICESHIP, AS OPPOSED to academic education, was a matter of
assisting a master in real-world projects. With almost no clients, and the
stock market at its lowest ebb since the crash, it was not at all obvious what
the hundred neophytes in Wright's program would be doing. But one thing
was clear: If one believed the calculations Wright made in the margins of the
prospectus, the Taliesin Fellowship would be amazingly profitable. It would
bring in $52,000 a year from tuitions, plus three hours a day of free labor
from each apprentice—time they would spend farming Taliesin's two hundred acres and repairing and expanding its buildings. The aggregate "donated" labor alone, over two thousand hours per week, would have been
worth more than the tuition, bringing Taliesin's effective yearly income to
around $120,000—at at time when anyone lucky enough to have a job was
glad to earn $1,200 a year. Even adjusting for expenses—which were mini-
mal, since the apprentices would be growing their own food and building
their own housing—the Fellowship penciled out as potentially one of the
Depression era's few successful businesses, easily eclipsing what Wright
might earn as an architect if he should ever find new clients.

If it got off the ground, the Taliesin Fellowship would solve Wright's most
urgent needs: money for the mortgage, labor to restore and expand Taliesin,
and a huge supply of farmhands. Even better, it would allow him at last to
drop the humiliating baggage of Wright, Inc.

As with his earlier Hillside School proposal, Wright sent the Taliesin Fellowship prospectus to Lloyd. This time his son was even more aghast. "It is in

fact and principle a very sorry business all around. And the sorriest part of it is the feudal business of your students. That will make them ashamed of themselves and you if they think and have any perspective and if they don't they will go thru life . . . as cowards and fools. God help your school if this is what it turns out. You['ll] wonder why your pupils are such washouts."

IT WAS THE rainiest November in fifty years. Great sheets of water shot off Taliesin's gutterless eaves as Wright and Wijdeveld sat inside drawing up an agreement. Each of them would invest $3,000 of their own money for the restoration of the buildings. Two thirds of the Fellowship's income, and one third of the old Hillside Home School's ten acres, would go to Wijdeveld. Wright still saw himself filling the surprisingly passive role of "founder and trustee." Wijdeveld would be the "leader."

For a man who refused to share creative authority with any man, Wright was offering Wijdeveld extraordinary control. "The various enterprises of the Fellowship," the contract read, "and such collateral enterprises as may directly grow out of the Fellowship shall be subject to mutual agreement between Wright and Wijdeveld." Wright did, however, retain a critical role—landlord of the larger property. Unlike the Hillside land, which they would own jointly, the two hundred acres comprising the Taliesin farm was to be rented to the Fellowship, albeit at a modest rate.

The deal relieved Wright of most of the costs of owning, restoring, and maintaining his property, while demanding little of his personal time. In return Wijdeveld would gain a base of operations from which to pursue his idealistic agenda, and a partnership with the master. But the contract offered the Dutchman no guaranteed income. Instead he would receive the majority of the money raised from apprentice tuitions—after substantial expenses, including the cost of operating the farm and even his own room and board, were deducted.

While Wijdeveld seemed to have handled himself quite well, he did make one serious misjudgment, at least as far as Wright was concerned. At a paid lecture Wright secured for him at the University of Wisconsin, he presented himself as one of the founding fathers of the "modern movement" in Europe. Although he ended his lecture with a paean to Wright, the damage was done: He had cast himself as a progenitor of the master's enemies. Wright sniped about the transgression in a letter to Mumford. "The thing has as many pedigrees now floating from banners on the band-wagon," he wrote, "as there are peddlers."

On December 5, Dutchy cabled his wife. "Settled plans and contract with Wright, but decide only with you." Three days later, accompanied by Wright, he left Taliesin for New York to board a steamer to Germany. On his first day at sea, he wired Wright to thank him for a "beautiful time at Taliesin."

"Dutchy has gone home," Wright wrote Mumford the same day, enclosing the school prospectus. "He is too much of a lyrical egoist to be ideal for the school, but he has enough good qualities to make it worthwhile to try."

IT WAS A lean holiday season at Taliesin. "We have done nothing at all this Christmas for anyone," Wright wrote his son Lloyd, who was struggling to maintain his own architectural practice in Los Angeles. His publisher, Longmans, had sent Wright six copies of the just published *An Autobiography*, but the master didn't have enough money to send each of his children a copy. "Unless they can buy it they must wait to read it," he confessed to Lloyd. "But I'll send you one of the six because I imagine you are as 'hard up' as I am."

Whenever they were finally able to read it, Wright's six children with Catherine were no doubt dismayed to discover that the book barely mentions any of them. He listed their names and their occupations, but that was it. With Iovanna, however, Wright clearly hoped to redeem himself as a father. She accompanied him everywhere, he boasted in the *Autobiography*, even in his work. He had even invented a game for them to play together with brightly colored inch-square blocks: Father and daughter took turns placing their blocks in a jointly composed geometrical figure, which they then evaluated together, just as his mother had with the Froebel blocks of his own childhood. Frank Lloyd Wright was giving his daughter an education in architectural imagination.

"I HAD A wonderful time in America," Wijdeveld wrote Wright on his return to Holland. "I found more and better than I expected." There was, he continued, "a great longing in me to join you and stay and help to build up and be one with you and you with me. . . . Keep a place in your mind, your heart, and your country for H. TH. Wijdeveld and his little family."

Two weeks later, on January 26, Wright wrote a letter, but not to Wijdeveld. It was a mass mailing to every notable who might be counted on to endorse and/or fund the Fellowship, including old friends and acquaintances like Jane Addams, Georgia O'Keefe, Edward Steichen, Alfred Stieglitz, Leopold Stowkowski, Norman Thomas, and Albert Einstein. Also included were at least two members of Gurdjieff's Institute. "I am sending you a copy of the prospectus of the Taliesin Fellowship," the letter began, "founded and being conducted by myself."

Dutchy had been told nothing.

* * *

THERE WAS MUCH for Olgivanna to dislike about her husband's deal with Wijdeveld—not least of which was that Dutchy's wife was named as "the matron of the entire establishment." With the strong-willed Wijdeveld and his wife in charge, her plans to teach Gurdjieff at Taliesin were suddenly in jeopardy. Where her husband's Hillside School proposal had referred to the "work," the one he drew up with Dutchy never mentioned it. Worse yet, the contract mandated that—for the three-year duration of the contract—anything "affecting the growth, stability or character" of the Fellowship would be decided between her husband and Wijdeveld. Olgivanna would have no authority.

Olgivanna's protracted illness in this period left her so exhausted that she could barely walk, much less attend to her husband's business dealings. After Wijdeveld left, she was concerned enough to travel all the way to Chicago see a doctor, who saw ominous spots on her chest X-ray. She had tuberculosis, not surprising given her intense exposure ten years before while nursing Katherine Mansfield at the Prieuré. TB bacteria can remain alive, but inactive, in the body for many years before triggering the disease.

Olgivanna returned from Chicago with a dietary cure—two quarts of milk, five raw eggs, raw cabbage, and orange juice, not exactly what a doctor would have prescribed. While there she had surely seen Gurdjieff: The mystic was in Chicago around this time trying to raise money to stave off foreclosure on the deteriorating Prieuré, whose "Study House" rugs were now gnawed by rats and covered with dog remains. When it came to donations, Gurdjieff groused, Toomer's group had proven "a ball of shit." And with Toomer himself long gone from Chicago, the group would soon suspend its activities.

With Toomer out of the picture, the Portage experiment over, and the Prieuré about to follow, Olgivanna must have sensed an opportunity. Although she was in no position to present Taliesin as a secure financial bastion to Gurdjieff, she suspected she could make some headway for him there—as long as Wijdeveld was out of the picture.

Frank and Oligvanna now revised the prospectus, deleting all mention of Dutchy. "I had certain qualifications; Olgivanna had others to add to mine," he wrote in describing their collaboration. With Wijdeveld's disappearance came some telling changes in the document's language and emphasis. "The Fellowship aims first of all," it began, "to develop a well correlated human individual. It is this correlation between the hand and the mind's eye that is lacking in the modern human being." "Correlation of one's centers," the core of the Gurdjieffian program, was now being declared the Fellowship's primary objective. While molding individuals was never Frank's strength, he also recognized it as a practical proposition given the times. "Why not build the builders of buildings," he wrote of founding the Fellowship, "against the time when buildings might again be built."

Whatever its other benefits, the new document would send an unmistakable signal to Gurdjieff.

Years later, Olgivanna recalled that it was she who persuaded Wright to replace his professional draftsmen with young apprentices. Though she never said so directly, it was clear to her confidante that she had seen the nascent Fellowship as "an inexhaustible supply of young people who could become candidates for Gurdjieff's teachings."

The Fellowship now represented a joining of the ambitions of Frank and Olgivanna. Ten years later, when he penned his first detailed account of the Fellowship's founding for his revised autobiography, he left little doubt that spiritual growth was at the core of the idea. The section bore the title, "A Station for the Flight of the Soul."

THE WEEKS AFTER Wijdeveld's departure were a propitious time for Olgivanna to shoulder him aside. Her husband was enjoined in a battle over the Museum of Modern Art exhibition, with its premise that the European modernists represented the future of American architecture. Wijdeveld's recent drawings for his own International Fellowship had been perilously like the work of these "inorganic" foreigners. Even a subtle suggestion by Olgivanna that Wijdeveld was one of "them" might easily have turned her prickly husband against the Dutchman.

Betrayal by Europeans was fresh on Wright's mind. Just months before, Lloyd Wright had alerted his father that Richard Neutra and Rudolph Schindler were trading on their experience with Wright and "pushing themselves forward at your expense." Without asking his permission, the two Austrians were putting together an exposition in Los Angeles that would feature their own work together with Wright's. Lloyd thought the show a "perversion."

"Both of you have betrayed any and whatever confidence I placed in either of you," Wright wrote Schindler, "when you might have supported me. . . . Do you both want to go on record as both liars and peddlers with the foreign thrift at the calling that thrives on this country and gives back nothing to it of honor and virtue? Why stick foolish heads in the hot sands of the Los Angeles district, imagining yourselves unseen?"

Meanwhile, another show—the MoMA exhibition—loomed far more threatening on the East Coast. Wright had reluctantly consented to participate in the show, but Lloyd saw it as part of a plot. "The internationalists," his son warned, had "set to work evidently to sell you out."

Before heading to New York, though, there was business to do. On January 17, Wright boarded the *Santa Fe* for Los Angeles, where Lloyd had booked him a series of paid lectures. The new project at Taliesin was on his mind. Before leaving for dinner with Albert and Elsa Einstein, he cabled Olgivanna: "Will try to get them for the Fellowship." Before the end of his California tour, Frank too was ailing. "Leaving Los Angeles for San Francisco tonight. Getting strong slowly," he wired Olgivanna. "Give my love to the Fellowship and my best to my own little three." By now the "Fellowship" and his current crop of draftsmen were one and the same, at least in Wright's mind.

EVEN WITH THE cash he earned from his lectures, the upcoming MoMA show put Wright in a foul mood. He was working with his small staff on a presentation of a project he'd hoped to get in Denver, Colorado. Wright had already sent the curators photographs, drawings, and a model of his House on the Mesa, a luxurious set of pavilions with a three-car garage, a maid's room, a billiard room, and an artificial lake with a swimming pool. The estimated construction cost was $125,000, almost twenty times the average cost of a house at the time. Although the house (which was never built) was remarkable, its flat-roofed design was hardly a counterpoint to the European approach; in fact, it showed Wright to be one of its most skilled practitioners.

While he had arguably bested them at their own game, Wright was not happy. With the exhibition set to open in just a few weeks, he wired curator Philip Johnson announcing his withdrawal. "My way has been too long and too lonely," he wrote, "to make a belated bow as a modern architect in company with a self advertising amateur and a high powered salesman"—the latter being Neutra.

The next day he followed up with a long letter. "I am going to step aside and let the procession go by with its band-wagon," he wrote Johnson. "I find myself rather a man without a country, architecturally speaking, at the present time. If I keep on working another five years, I shall be at home again, I feel sure."

On the same day, he complained in a letter to Mumford that Richard Neutra had been "worthless here @ $30.00 per week" as a draftsman in Wright's stable. Neutra had "left after nine months . . . . He went to Los Angeles to join Schindler. I think both are half-baked jews and were friends in Vienna." It was a sad turn of events: Wright had liked Neutra and his work, had even appealed to him to stay on. Neutra had even named his firstborn son Frank after the master.

Wright tempered his language a bit with Mumford, himself of Jewish parentage. Just two weeks before, Lloyd had sent him a monograph with a page containing two photographs, one of Schindler and one of Olgivanna. Wright was livid, he later told Lloyd, to see "Olgivanna alongside Schindler, 'the kike.'"

But Mumford wouldn't accept Wright's decision to withdraw from the exhibition. He had fought too hard to have Wright included to let him pull out over the inclusion of a former draftsman. And he knew just how to couch his appeal. "As for company," he cabled him, "there is no more honorable position than to be crucified between two thieves." The telegram was sent on the morning of January 21; by early afternoon, Wright relented.

Lloyd Wright heartily agreed and admonished him to hire American draftsmen from now on. "For God's sake lay off these international youths. They're just sad fools."

THE HISTORIC "INTERNATIONAL Style" show at MoMA opened on February 9, 1932, including a room displaying Wright's model of his House on the Mesa, among other projects. But, as Wright no doubt feared, it was the young upstarts, including Neutra, who got most of the attention. In the catalog, the curators even opined that Neutra's Lovell "health house" was "without question, stylistically, the most advanced house built in America since the war."

Wright couldn't bear it. "Believe me, Philip, I am sorry," he wrote Johnson of his decision to stay in. "Give my best to Russell Hitchcock and I expect to see you both here at Taliesin early next summer with your wives. If you haven't got them now you will have them by then?" It was a pointed jibe: Frank understood that he, a real American male, had been shoved aside by two homosexuals.

"In short, Philip my King," he wrote Johnson in a short-lived tempest after the show, "a strange undignified crowd you are, altogether, all pissing through the same quill or pissing on each other. I am heartily ashamed to be caught with my flap open in the circumstance. But I am caught in this crowd as I was caught in the show."

ARCHITECTURE WAS OFTEN sexual for Wright. Just days before leaving Spring Green for his California tour, he wrote a short essay excoriating the European modernists. In it he cast architecture as an erotic discipline, one that drew on an architect's capacity for romance. The International Style architects, after all, were not real "men." He called his unpublished screed "To the Neuter," an unmistakable play on "Neutra."

In the essay, Wright compared the International Style modernists to eunuchs whose procreative energies had been degraded into sterile abstraction. There was a lack of "virility" about them, he ventured; they had lost their potency as the result of "over-indulgence = sentimentality, or the practice of self-abuse (eclecticism)." The international style boys, in short, had converted their aberrant lusts into formula. Architecture, Wright declared, should involve neither the excesses of what he considered the "prostitution" of the nineteenth-century Beaux Arts movement, nor the unnamed sexual aberrations—undoubtedly homosexuality and masturbation—that he identified as the source of European modernism. Architecture, rather, was a "true love-affair." And for his lover Wright would take Nature herself; he was the one who could penetrate her secrets, who could fructify the earth and create habitations amidst her folded skin. Beleaguered by homosexual curators and foreigner architects, Frank Lloyd Wright was recasting himself as the American pioneer who would husband a truly American modernism.

THOUGH BY NOW he had declared himself the Taliesin Fellowship's leader, Wright still wanted no part of running it. He continued to solicit candidates for the directorship, but this time only Americans, real Yanks. "To tell the truth if I could keep the fellowship primarily our own on our own ground I would like it better," he wrote Mumford. "I am growing suspicious of 'internationalism.'" A week before the MoMA show opened, he asked Mumford, not for the first time, if he would take the position. "We have at this time," he wrote, "approximately 25–30 applications from young men who would like to come. And this on the strength of the *rumor* abroad that such a school would open!"

Mumford declined, suggesting that the job should go to a professional administrator. "Creative people," he wrote to Wright, "are usually rotten in the details of administration, unless they cease to be creative."

Ignoring his friend's warning, he then asked painter Georgia O'Keeffe and writer Alexander Woollcott. They too turned him down. Wright, by default, remained the leader.

WHILE UNSOLICITED REQUESTS to join the Fellowship were already coming in, the architect was not beyond missionary-style proselytizing. All across the country there were Beaux Arts–oriented academies filled with students who needed to be saved. Wright sent a mass mailing to the heads of these schools, asking them to post it where their students could see it. "Everywhere Youth is rocking in an old academic boat no longer seaworthy," the letter proclaimed—no doubt much to the horror of the administrators, many of whom likely threw it away. If they really loved architecture, the posting went on, they should consider learning "the principles that make 'modern architecture' so objectionable to the Beaux Arts." Where to learn them? Taliesin, of course, a place that has "already established a living, world-wide Tradition," a "new reality" that "youth everywhere" hungered to embrace.

WHAT RESULTED FROM the Beaux Arts postings, no one knows. But press notices announcing the Fellowship immediately yielded letters from eager applicants. "The articles in the paper concerning the school you plan to open, interests [sic] me greatly," wrote Alice Warner of Antioch, Illinois, the day after Wijdeveld arrived in Holland. Two weeks later, Louise Dees-Porch's inquiry was returned with an official application form for membership in the Fellowship. It asked her to indicate her "Predilection for what particular art expression: building, music, painting, sculpture, crafts." A school librarian in Honolulu received the following reply to her query: "The new prospectus of the Taliesin Fellowship is now at the printers and we shall forward you a copy as soon as we receive it." The return address, for the first time, included under Wright's name the words "Taliesin Fellowship."

The final printed prospectus soon appeared in the young people's mailboxes. "Apprenticeship will be the condition and should be the attitude of mind of all the Fellowship workers," it read. "The leader" would now oversee seventy such apprentices, who would also be served by three "resident associates"—a sculptor, a painter, and a musician—and three "technical advisers trained in industry." There would be special studies of typography, ceramics, woodworking, and textiles. With no real expectation that it could eke out many architectural commissions in the moribund economy, Wright announced in the prospectus that the Fellowship would initially have to survive primarily on apprentice tuitions, which were set at $675 per year—a third more than the amount set with Wijdeveld, and more than Harvard charged at the time. Wright apparently believed that industrial contracts for Taliesin's products and services would eventually enable him to reduce, if not eliminate, the tuition.

"The home life will be simple." There would be common meals and fixed hours for work and rest. Each "worker" would have his or her own room. There would be plays, musical evenings, movies, lectures by visiting writers and scientists. Each apprentice would be expected to work for three hours each day "on the ground or buildings or farm for the privilege of participations in the experimental work in the studios and shops."

Taliesin, the prospectus promised, would be a hothouse for nurturing what "creative impulse" remained in America, creating creators by "up-build[ing] spiritual forces." The apprentices would have their creative spirits nurtured not only by "the inspirational fellowship of the genuinely creative artist," but also by their "constant contact with the nature of the ground," growth in nature being the most "valuable text" from which to learn Wright's organic architecture.

Wright's January 26, 1932, mass mailing of the prospectus marked the official announcement of the Taliesin Fellowship, and of Wright's role as leader. Two weeks later, an oblivious Wijdeveld penned a letter to Wright announcing his plans to move to America. He would begin, he wrote, with a series of university lectures. "After that we might start at Taliesin."

Wright was finally forced to act. On February 13, 1932, four days after the opening of MoMA's "International Style," he sent the Dutchman a painful letter. "Much as I like you and hard up for help as I am," he wrote, "perhaps chiefly because of both, I am going to say no to your coming to join me in America. The responsibility of bringing you with your family to a strange country is too great for me to assume on the slender basis of hope here. The leader, he continued, "should, I am now sure, be an American."

In his thousands of surviving letters, Wright is almost never contrite. Sometimes, as now, he tried to avert confrontation with a lie. "We have many applications for fellowships," the letter went on "although I have done nothing at all even with the prospectus." By now, he had been sending out both printed application forms and the printed prospectus for weeks.

Wijdeveld should really head his own school, Wright suggested, being "too far developed" to succeed in someone else's enterprise. But he didn't close the door completely. Instead he offered up the possibility of a demotion. "You would make an ideal associate if I could have you in the capacity. Perhaps when things are established and running you would be willing to take over or perhaps then I could offer you the leadership I am not willing to offer you now."

THE MONTH OF March brought another milestone: the official release of what became the Fellowship's most effective promotional tool, the first edition of Wright's autobiography. "F. L. Wright Tells of His Stormy Life. Individualistic Architect Sets Down Story of Long Struggle to Keep His 'Freedom' . . . . Predicts Death of Cities, Assails Skyscrapers," read the *New York Times* headline announcing the publication of *An Autobiography*.

In its pages Wright described Taliesin as the man-making refuge of his youth, and as the site where he was now fashioning an "organic architecture." It also called young men to war—a culture war that would bring America's dependence on the styles of dead civilizations to an end, and initiate a new culture for this new world. "I have longed for and still long for enlightened comradeship and the good will of my kind," Wright lamented. By coming to Taliesin, budding architects could join his solitary fight for beauty, and, in the process, make America right once more.

Wright sent a prospectus to his old friend Charles Ashbee, a man who made "comradeship" a core element of his own belief system. Ashbee's own English Arts and Crafts colony had long since disbanded, and Wright sent him a heartfelt entreaty: "I wish you might join." Ashbee declined. As Wright awaited the first apprentices' arrival, he sent his old friend a note of regret: "I think of you with gratitude and affection."

WRIGHT'S BELATED LETTER telling Wijdeveld not to come had ended with a curious closing: "Meanwhile—far more faithfully yours than were I to feel I had you on my conscience."

Dutchy *was* on Wright's conscience. The very idea for the Fellowship, after all, was Wijdeveld's. Nonetheless, when Wright wrote his account of its founding for the 1943 edition of his autobiography, the Dutchman's role was completely expunged.

But it wasn't just Wijdeveld's contribution that never found its way into the book. The entire founding of the Fellowship was reduced to one sentence: "After talking the 'idea' over, pro and con, we, a son of Wisconsin Welsh pioneers and a daughter of Montenegrin dignitaries aiming to be educators, composed and sent out during the summer of 1932 the following circular letter to a small list of friends." The text of the inserted letter was really a description of Dutchy's dream of a "work fellowship," modified here and there, of course, to color it with some of Wright's pet concerns.

After her husband's death, Olgivanna published her own version of these events. While she at least mentioned Wijdeveld, he might have wished that she'd kept her silence. The Dutchy she portrayed was a spineless figure indeed. After taking one look at the decayed Hillside building, she wrote, Wijdeveld told her and Frank that the restoration task was "insurmountable." When the Wrights were unable to persuade him otherwise, he turned down the leader position and returned to Holland. "We both were disappointed," she wrote, "not to have Mr. Wijdeveld at Taliesin."

Wijdeveld's true role was thus concealed from the public record, and until recently from history. To acknowledge that the very ideas underlying his Fellowship were crafted by a European would have compromised Wright's vision of an organically American community. But perhaps as important, Wright's updated autobiography would have had to explain just why Dutchy, who would likely read the new edition, never assumed the helm of the Fellowship.

In at least one respect, however, Wright did give Dutchy his due, though in a way few would ever recognize. The name Wijdeveld, as Wright had learned from one of the Dutchman's letters, meant "wide field" or "broad acres." So it could hardly have been a coincidence that, when the time came for Wright to name his utopian settlement, he called it Broadacre City—a phrase that became a talisman for the rest of his life.

PART III

THE FELLOWSHIP

Sunday evening at Taliesin, 1938. Wright and Olgivanna are at left, with Svetlana behind her mother and Iovanna at her feet. At top center is a music stand Wright designed.

EVERYTHING TO DREAM

"WHENEVER ARCHITECT FRANK LLOYD WRIGHT has a good idea," *Time* magazine wrote on September 5, 1932, "he does something about it. The best idea he ever had was Frank Lloyd Wright. He has been doing things about that for 63 years. His latest idea is to found a practical architect's school to educate architects in Frank Lloyd Wright's image."

The publicity following the announcement of the new Taliesin Fellowship, coupled with the release of Wright's extraordinarily intimate autobiography, put the man, his mission, and the possibility of joining it, before young imaginations across the country.

On September 14, 1932, a month before the Fellowship's announced opening, James Gehr of Shawano, Wisconsin, wrote a letter he hoped would change his life. "Dear Mr. Wright," it opened, "I hope you will not take this letter lightly—it means so much to me. I seem to know you. I read so much about you and your home Taliesin. And recently I read that you are going to found a 'Taliesin Fellowship' and do the things that I have always wanted to do but never had the opportunity to." Gehr confessed that he lacked the money for the tuition. "We would do anything—any kind of work—in fact mortgage our souls if the devil would take a second mortgage."

The following Sunday, in Milwaukee, 120 miles away, Grace Mundt sat down to pen a similar letter. "I have read so much about you," she began in her neat, back-slanted script, "and the great things you are doing that when I read about 'The Taliesin Fellowship' I longed to be one of the apprentices. I also think this is going to be a great fellowship. My desire to be one of the apprentices is so great that I would almost slave to be included."

The post office in Spring Green was swamped with letters. Karl Jensen answered them all. James Gehr's dream would have to be put off; exemptions from tuition could not be considered, Wright's secretary wrote him, until "the Fellowship is well underway." Those with the money were, for the most part, encouraged to come. And come they did.

SIX-FEET-FOUR and full of muscle, William Wesley Peters was so big that the ROTC was initially unable to find him a military uniform. Peters was an SAE fraternity boy studying architecture the Beaux Arts way at the Massachusetts Institute of Technology. And he felt sure he was just where he belonged. Wes, as he was called, was passionate about his studies; he excelled at engineering and architectural history, writing papers that addressed such topics as a "Comparison of Assyrian and Egyptian Architecture with Relation to Their Structural Materials."

Still, Peters was ripe for the Fellowship. He had enthusiastically entered the debate over whether Yale University's Gothic style was really the kind of architecture that should represent the American college. He didn't think so. Nor did he think much of America's classical monuments, including the Lincoln Memorial, dedicated a decade before. "With all due respects to its designers," he wrote his family, "I think it is out of place with Lincoln and with this country. . . . I think all those big buildings in Washington . . . are merely excellently designed barns with a bunch of orders varnished over their faces, and having no organic appearance or existence."

Wes Peters was the son of a legendary Indiana newspaper publisher who had helped push the Ku Klux Klan out of the state. His father, who had accumulated considerable wealth, feared that his son knew only how to spend it. "I doubt if you realize how much money you have been spending since you went to Boston," he wrote Wes at the end of his first semester. One year into the Depression, father reminded son that those without resources were about to spend a cold and hungry winter.

Wes saw the evidence all around him. Students were forced to leave school. "All the streets are full of beggars and prostitutes," he wrote home, "and every other day someone commits suicide in the neighborhood." If only he could have a budget, the young student pleaded, he could keep things in bounds.

Enthralled with the prospect of becoming an architect, Peters listened eagerly as his instructor on "Office Practice" told his students that they should expect to be head draftsmen of a medium-sized office five years after graduation. Two years after that, they could think about starting their own offices. If they knew what was good for them, though, they would all wait to marry until that five-year mark had passed.

Wes was the kind of guy who liked taking things to the limit, including practical jokes. At MIT, he got a bunch of buddies to haul a telephone pole to their dormitory. After opening windows on both sides, they inserted it through one window and pulled it through the window on the building's other side.

But one day Peters and some of his fraternity brothers went too far. Sometime in the fall of 1931, they blindfolded a young pledge and tied him next to the railroad tracks. A train soon came barreling down; the young man screamed for his life. When Wes and the others returned, they found the boy dead—of a heart attack.

This tragedy undoubtedly had something to do with Peters's decision to leave MIT, where he had been thriving in both the classroom and the studio. Not long after the pledge's death, Peters saw an announcement on a campus bulletin board that Frank Lloyd Wright was opening a school. Already taken with Wright's Princeton lectures and his autobiography, Peters was intrigued. The aspiring engineer asked several professors what they thought about him joining the Fellowship. "Oh, don't touch that stuff," one said. "Wright is just a joker," another warned. But one old professor disagreed. "Well, you've always been a bit of a rebellious type, I think you might find something there."

In July 1932, after finishing out his second year at MIT, Wes Peters got a ride from his parents to Madison under the pretext that he intended to transfer to the University of Wisconsin in the fall. Left off at Madison, Wes boarded a bus to Spring Green. From there he headed out on foot for Taliesin. After crossing the river and entering the valley, he spotted a farm family sitting in shirtsleeves on their porch. Where could he find Frank Lloyd Wright's place? He had already passed it, they told him. It was that place with all the "No Trespassing" signs.

Wes Peters

But the signs? "Oh, don't pay any attention to those keep-off signs," they advised. "Just go right on up." He did, and a long-haired Dane Karl Jensen greeted him. Jensen told Wes that Mr. Wright wouldn't be available until later.

Wes killed time walking around the neighboring farms. When he returned, he was sent into the drafting room, where he first laid eyes on the master.

As they faced each other across a drafting table, Wright told Peters of his grand plans for the Fellowship, of how the dilapidated Hillside School building would be repaired and expanded, of the "new kind of fellowship for architects" he planned.

"I made up my mind right there, that very minute," Wes remembered. "I wasn't going back to MIT."

Wright wanted to know if the young man could pay the whole tuition, six hundred dollars, right away. Peters, who had spent the summer doing construction on state roads, had the cash, even without going to his parents. Certainly, Wes replied. Wright was so chuffed that he took Wes down to the boiler room and cobbled together a complete copy of his 1911 Wasmuth portfolio for him as a gift. "I loved and admired him from the first moment I met him," Wes remembered.

The Fellowship had its first apprentice.

Eager to start, Peters moved into Taliesin in early October, a few weeks before its official opening. His father had grudgingly consented to Wes's plan—but only for a one-year stint.

His mother was more enthusiastic. "Dad and I are awfully eager to hear your impressions of Taliesin," she wrote him soon after he started. "There will be one thing that you will miss, I imagine, and that will be *arguments*. You live and breathe to argue." At the Fellowship, she warned, "you will all be of one mind about architecture at least. But surely, you bunch of eccentrics will find something to wrangle about."

EDGAR TAFEL WAS doing poorly in his first year as an architecture student at New York University. The son of successful Russian-Jewish immigrants, Tafel had grown up in a progressive utopian colony in New Jersey founded by garment workers; his mother was a fashion designer. As a teenager he had attended Olgivanna's friend Margaret Naumburg's Walden School. In the summer of 1932, the handsome, curly-haired twenty-year-old picked up Wright's newly published autobiography. Already primed by the books of Louis Sullivan, Edgar was hooked. He searched in vain for other books on Wright at the NYU library, and even saw Wright's model of the House on the Mesa at the Museum of Modern Art's International Style show.

"I was talking Frank Lloyd Wright all the time," he remembered. One day, as he was sitting with his aunt, she looked up from her *New York Herald Tribune* and announced, "Your hero is starting a school." Edgar took a look. "I read this thing and I went wild."

Tafel wrote immediately requesting Wright's brochure, which arrived at the summer camp where he was working. Captivated by what he saw as Wright's "glorious plan" to foster an authentic American culture, he wrote asking if the annual tuition could be reduced a few hundred dollars to $450—the price of his NYU tuition, and all that he could afford. The response, the first telegram the young man had ever received, was authored by Frank Lloyd Wright himself. "Believe we can manage a fellowship for you if you pay all." Edgar relented. He might be paying $200 a year more than at NYU, but he would be getting more than a college education. "I was going off," he thought, "to a way of life."

ABE DOMBAR WAS so enthralled by Wright's designs that his fellow architecture students at the University of Cincinnati nicknamed him "Frank." Dombar drew with consummate skill, so much so that he had been inducted

Edgar Tafel

into L'Atelier, the honorary architectural fraternity. The prize: Wright's autobiography, which cost the then-considerable sum of five dollars. Dubious about university instruction, Dombar was considering leaving the university to find a job with a local contractor so that he could learn to design from the actual practice of construction. Instead he found work designing the windows for Shillitos, a local department store. His windows quickly became a local attraction.

In June 1932, a small notice in the local newspaper caught his eye. Frank Lloyd Wright was going to speak to a real estate convention that very morning at the Netherland Plaza in downtown Cincinnati. Telling no one, Abe dressed in his best gray suit and skipped his morning classes. When he got to the hotel, the doorman blocked the way—delegates only. Inside the meeting room, Dombar spied a "handsome man with flowing white hair" standing on the speaker's platform, "watching the commotion below." To Abe, Mr. Wright looked sad, even bereft.

As the young man stood there, wondering what to do next, Wright came out of the hotel's meeting room to go to the bathroom. On his way back in, Dombar plucked up his courage and approached.

"Pardon me, Mr. Wright. I came down to hear you talk, and they won't let me in."

Wright impassively eyed him up and down.

"Architectural student?"

"Yes, sir; University of Cincinnati, finishing my second year."

As they approached the entrance, Wright put his arm on Dombar's shoulder. "I am taking this boy in," he said to the doorman.

"We sat in the back and talked, instead of him going back on the platform to wait to be called," Dombar recalled. "We talked and talked. . . . He was using me as an example to demonstrate how 'starved' the American youth was for real Architectural education. . . . This was more like the Wright I had expected to meet, in contrast to the sad looking man I had seen on the platform twenty minutes before."

Finally it was Wright's turn to speak to the realtors. For Marxists, profit was capitalism's macabre engine of doom. For Wright, that engine was rent. "Rent," he had just written in his autobiography, "is the fetish of an artificial economic system that now owns the city." The architect hated the transformation of land into real estate, the making of what he saw as the "unearned increment" from strategic location, the obscene urban densities enforced by high land prices, the speculative marketing of historicist styles. Wright was fond of comparing urban developers of this "anachronistic bosh" to "the money-changers in the temple."

Given what Wright was capable of, the real estate agents who were paying his fee got off easy. The worst was being labeled a bunch of "groundhogs." By the end of the talk, Wright had somehow managed to convince the crowd that it had been their privilege to listen to his gospel truth. The realtors rose as one in thunderous applause.

Taking no questions, Wright left the hall and returned to his room.

Abe Dombar slowly walked outside. "[A]lready Race Street felt like a strange world so different from the world that Wright had just painted. . . . This is not where the story ends," Abe said to himself. He went back inside. At the front desk he asked the number of Wright's room. They gave it to him. When he knocked on the door, Wright looked as if he had been expecting him.

"Come in, Abe."

After they talked a while about the architecture in Cincinnati, Wright interjected, "You haven't had lunch, have you?"

Abe hadn't.

"Come on."

Abe remembered every moment of that epiphanous afternoon. "He took me to the Netherland Plaza . . . and ordered lunch for the two of us. Even the waiter didn't know who he was. He kept calling him senator." Wright, who was wearing a white suit with a cane and a Panama hat attached by a cord to his lapel so it wouldn't blow away in the wind, criticized the design of every element in the dining room.

Ambling about town after lunch, Wright invited Abe to join the Fellowship. The young architectural student had never heard of it.

"What's it cost?"

"Six hundred and seventy-five dollars a year."

"That is about all the money I've got in the world, and with that money I could easily finish my three years at the university. If I come to you after the first year I'll be cleaned out. I won't be able to go back to school, won't be able to stay here. What will I do?"

"You bring your six hundred seventy five; if you make good, why, you can forget about paying after that."

"Well, I'll make good."

Abe's enthusiasm wasn't enough to convince his parents, who had heard lurid stories about Wright's "scandal of the wives."

The young man was undaunted. "I wanted to be an apprentice of this great genius." Abe brought in reinforcements—Arthur Kelsey, a Beaux-Arts Rome Prize winner, part-time instructor at the university, and friend of Wright's. At a dinner at his parents' house, Kelsey explained to the Dombars that the Fellowship "was a wonderful opportunity."

It worked. Though Abe's mother still believed her son "had been possessed by the Devil himself," she let him go. His father bought him a new trunk.

Abe immediately sent a letter to Wright formally requesting admission into the Fellowship. "Thursday was the most important day in my life," he wrote, reminding him of their day together in Cincinnati, "for then you made me realize that I had been following the wrong road. I have often dreamed of working for you, so the fact that I ate with you seems like a dream too." He signed it, "Your sincere friend and apostle, Abe."

The "apostle" faced one hitch: Abe Dombar was an observant Jew, and the food at the Fellowship wouldn't be kosher. Dombar went to his rabbi. After describing Wright's mission and the importance of the work of the Fellowship, the Cincinnati rabbi found an answer within Jewish law. "It is like war," he told his young congregant. Under such circumstances, the Torah allowed exemption from the dietary laws of *kashrut*.

YEN LIANG WAS no college dropout. A well-to-do Chinese mandarin, the young man had already earned a degree in Beijing and gone on to America for an advanced architectural education, hoping to return to China as a highly skilled architect. Yen completed Yale's five-year architecture program in only three years; from there he moved on to graduate studies at Harvard, where he began to question the value of what he was learning. He felt, he recalled, "no closer to understanding architecture." What good was all the time he had spent learning the classical orders? How, he wondered, "could [he] force Roman orders and the like" back home?

Wright was "taboo" at the university. Like so many others, Yen discovered Wright's memoir by "pure luck." "My awakening from reading *An Autobiog-*

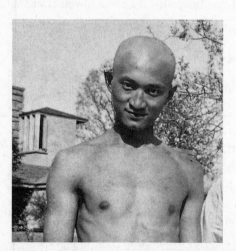

raphy was ecstatic," he recalled. He took special note of Wright's intense admiration for the art and culture of Asia. In Wright, Yen thought he discovered a sensibility that was modern yet somehow fitting for his native land. During the middle of his spring term at Harvard, he sent a note to Wright asking for work. He received instead an offer to join the Fellowship. "Come

Yen Liang

along," Wright urged. The twenty-three-year-old quit Harvard, bought a second-hand two-seater black Stutz, and set out for Spring Green. He was among the first apprentices who actually moved in.

Yen Liang's intuition about Wright must have been immediately confirmed when he arrived at Taliesin and was greeted by the "serene Buddha," a statue Wright had placed at the top of the grand stairway leading to the entrance of the house. Wright was in Chicago when Yen arrived and Karl Jensen directed him to a basement guestroom below Mr. Wright's room. On his way down, he saw a woman doing laundry by a fountain just outside the kitchen. Ignoring her, he made his way to his room. The washerwoman was Olgivanna. When she next saw him, she upbraided him for being so "arrogant and ill-mannered" as to ignore her. She never let him forget it.

BY THE TIME Edgar Tafel arrived in October 1932, Wright was back from Chicago. Herb Fritz Jr., son of the draftsman who was among the few survivors of Taliesin's 1914 fire and murders, picked him up in front of the hotel in Spring Green and dropped him off at the former Hillside School gym, now being converted into a theater. Tafel heard the sounds of a Beethoven symphony as he opened the door. There was a stage at the far end of the room, empty but for a grand piano, Frank Lloyd Wright, and a phonograph. Wright was using a record to test the theater's acoustics. Tafel was surprised at how short and stocky Wright was. But his stature didn't detract from the impression he made. "It was like coming into a presence . . . he shot out electricity everywhere." Just before walking up to the stage, Tafel whispered to himself, "you've made it."

"Mr. Wright," he announced, "I'm Edgar Tafel. From New York." Wright offered up a handshake. "Young man, help me move this piano." It was a fitting first task for the new apprentice, who became one of the Fellowship's best pianists. Wright kept a grand piano on a small balcony overlooking the drafting room. Every once in a while he would say, "Edgar, go up and play some Bach for us."

After moving the piano, they got into a car and an apprentice drove them along the narrow road that followed the contours around the hill separating the Hillside complex from Wright's house at Taliesin. Wright led the way into the living room. "It was breathtaking—I had never imagined such beauty and harmony." An "impressively regal" woman entered the room. Unlike poor Yen Liang, Tafel had the benefit of an introduction. "Mother," Wright said to his wife, "this is Edgar Tafel. From New York."

Edgar was in. Like the others, he was never asked to show his drawing work—or, for that matter, any evidence whatsoever of a talent for architecture.

Jack Howe, one of Wright's most talented draftsmen

The aspiring apprentices never knew why any of them was accepted or rejected. All Frank said to Olgivanna was, "That young man is very good-looking, isn't he? Like a curly-headed cherub."

JACK HOWE WENT from Evanston to nearby Chicago to hear Charles Morgan, a friend and former draftsman of Wright's, give a lecture promoting the Taliesin Fellowship. Once everyone was seated, Morgan cartwheeled on to the stage. Jack Howe didn't need the gimmick. A high-school senior in Evanston, Howe had been building things ever since he was a little kid and had long been enamored of Wright. What's more, his mother had been a student at the Hillside Home School. He desperately wanted to meet Mr. Wright and join the Fellowship. Morgan agreed to take the youngster for a visit to Taliesin. Howe was admitted, and he and Morgan passed that night in Taliesin's loggia.

There was a small problem. Jack had only $300, money earned from setting up pins at the Evanston Country Club bowling alley. While it was less than half of the tuition, Wright offered him a deal—keep the fireplaces and the hot water boilers going, and he could come for the $300. Howe agreed. His fellow apprentices later joked that Wright couldn't pass a fireplace without calling for Jack Howe.

WHEN THE FELLOWSHIP officially opened on October 25, 1932, it had been three years since the stock market crash. The month before, the Nazis had cut financial support for the German Bauhaus. And until they arrived, Edgar, Wes, Yen, Abe, Jack, and the other new apprentices had no idea that America's most famous architect, like his ordinary brethren, had no work. Earlier in the year he had done some studies for a planned development—a roadside market, an overhead service station, a prefabricated house, and a steel farm building—but the projects never went beyond the conceptual stage. The only real project was a small house, something easily handled in a few weeks by his remaining professional staff—Karl Jensen, Henry Klumb, Rudolph Mock, George Steckmesser, Juan Hsi Kuo, and Yvonne Renalier.

All but one of them came from abroad. Wright had originally recruited these highly cultured assistants, most of them Europeans, because he knew they expected to dedicate themselves to their master and were willing to live in the beautiful but socially dull isolation of his small compound. He had previously spurned young American men because he didn't think they would do that. Most of the foreigners were listed as charter members of the Fellowship. Now, however, Wright intended to get rid of them as soon as possible.

The neophytes, most of them American-born, had read the Taliesin Fellowship brochure and imagined themselves working alongside the great man at the drawing board on his projects. At first, the young arrivals had little need for their pencils—but they were instructed to bring hammers and saws, and these were enlisted immediately. Among the tasks at hand was the reconstruction of the old Hillside Home School into a residence and work space for themselves: Its carpenter shop was to be remade into a dining room, its classrooms into residences. A new drafting room was still to be constructed. The other major project, a seemingly odd priority, was the remodeling of a portion of the same building for use as a theater. Wright rode his horse over from Taliesin to supervise.

When it came to construction, the apprentices were mostly amateurs or worse. So Wright supplemented their labor by hiring four dozen skilled workers, all otherwise unable to find employment during the Depression. These men were given food and lodging in exchange for their labor, with a promise of wages when the good times arrived. The tradesmen taught the apprentices how to cut stone, lay pipes, make plaster, and mix cement. "We had to learn quickly from the plumbers and electricians," recalled Edgar Tafel, "so we could do piping and wiring ourselves. If the toilet got stopped up, we knew how to fix it. We had to know."

When the "good times" didn't come, the unpaid tradesmen began to leave, their jobs taken over by what seemed to be an unending stream of incoming apprentices. Pretty soon, only a few skilled artisans—the stone masons among them—remained.

ALTHOUGH HIS THIRTY or so apprentices were living in improvised housing—with Wisconsin's vicious winter just around the corner—the architect was hellbent on converting the old gymnasium into a theater. If Taliesin was to serve as a nucleus for his Broadacre City, he would need a theater as the requisite cultural venue for his rural complex. Wright also expected to earn income from selling tickets to the public.

But the theater also had a personal significance. Wright had wanted a stage of his own since he was fourteen, when he read Goethe's *Wilhelm Meister's Apprenticeship* with his mother. The novel told of a boy who was given a puppet theater by his mother, a gift that launched him as an "enchanter" on the pathway to being an actor, playwright, and director. Like Wright, Goethe's Wilhelm Meister was the son of a bourgeois aesthete; from childhood on he chose beauty over commerce, girdling himself in silk sash and meticulously designing his room "like a small kingdom." He was a creature of "self-satisfied modesty," Goethe wrote, who saw himself as a great actor and the founder of a future National Theater that would glorify both God and nature. Wright told his apprentices that it was his favorite book.

The theater had also served as Wright's portal into his own artistic and creative career, when Louis Sullivan made Chicago's Auditorium Theater Wright's first project—his induction into a relationship with Sullivan that Wright always remembered as his first taste of true "fellowship."

Wright had long dreamed of having his own intimate theater, where he could host performances by his own chamber orchestra and major guest artists. Olgivanna was also pleased with the idea. Ever since she was a teenager, she too had fantasized about having her own theater where she could "listen to music without having to isolate myself from crinkling papers and chattering tongues." Indeed, soon after marrying Valdemar Hinzenberg, she discovered love while performing with her childhood friend Luigi in the little cabaret theater designed by her husband. And of course public performance was the chief venue used by Gurdjieff to recruit new members for his movement.

What became known as the Taliesin Playhouse was not an ad hoc affair. Karl Jensen wrote to theater supply companies looking for deals on sixty-five chairs for permanent seating and two hundred portable chairs for the main floor. On the plaster wall next to the stage, Wright had a Whitman poem displayed in gold leaf: "Here is the test of wisdom . . . wisdom is not finally tested in schools . . . wisdom cannot be passed from one having it to another not having it . . . wisdom is of the soul."

For Wright, the Fellowship itself was a theater for testing and refining wisdom, with architecture as a vehicle for knowledge and the creative spirit.

"Here it was," Wright declared of his new playhouse, "far beyond Wilhelm Meister's or any Goethe himself could have designed. This surely counted us *one*?"

ASIDE FROM THE theater, the renovation of the Hillside building went slowly. Wright was forced to put some of the apprentices up in the main house, others in neighboring farmhouses.

A few apprentices took things into their own hands. One day Olgivanna looked out and saw a young man carrying a door he had unhinged from Taliesin's guest wing. "Wait a minute, wait a minute," she called out. "What are you doing with that door?"

"I have no door in my room, Mrs. Wright," Wes Peters replied. "I have taken this one from the guest wing below. I will pay for it."

"You take that door right back, and hang it where you took it from. It won't hurt you to be without a door for one day."

* * *

ABE DOMBAR HAD paid $135 down on his tuition. Like the others, he was told by Mr. Wright that he wouldn't know whether he would be accepted as a regular member until the end of a month-long "trial" period. Dombar hadn't even been there that long when Wright's secretary asked him for the remainder of his tuition. Dombar was taken aback. He wouldn't pay a penny more, he said, until he knew he had passed his trial period. Abe was informed that *he* was on trial, not the Fellowship. "[S]ince I had a check-book," Dombar noted wryly, "my month trial period was waived and I was allowed to pay in advance."

Debt-ridden, and now suddenly saddled with the need to purchase all the food his apprentices couldn't farm for themselves—not to mention building materials—Wright was desperate for cash. He was not, of course, unique. The Depression had only worsened. Crop prices had hit bottom; cotton was being left to rot in the fields. Farmers were losing their land. Industrial plants were idle. A quarter of American workers couldn't find a job. Shanty-towns were growing at the edge of every American city. Banks failed as customers took their deposits out, demanding they be converted into gold.

Under pressure, Wright's creativity turned in a surprising direction. Back in 1924, Dione Neutra noted on her arrival that on Sundays large crowds spontaneously showed up at Taliesin curious to the see the strange architect's strange estate. "Long caravans of cars" formed along the road, she recalled, while a lucky few found parking in the courtyard. The strangers would then "go through all the rooms, sniff around everywhere," and "leave this famous house astonished." As for the master of the house, Neutra reported, "According to his mood . . . Wright serves as guide, or is angered by them."

Now, eight years later, Wright saw the curious as a business opportunity. Three apprentices were put on tour duty each Sunday, one standing at the gate selling tickets stamped "Frank Lloyd Wright" (price fifty cents), the other two acting as guides. In the spring and summer, there were so many tourists that they got in the way. Rather than limiting the program, though, Wright expanded it with a deluxe tour. For one dollar, a brochure advertised, "in addition to going about the buildings they are given a detailed account of the drawings and models here at work by one of the apprentices." Tourists could also buy Wright's books. Even the Fellowship's prospectus was available—for the price of twenty-five cents.

On any given Sunday, the tourist business could bring in twenty dollars. With the cash in their hands, remembered one apprentice, "we'd rush to town and buy flour. I mean, it was just that close." The grocer was always threatening to cut off their food supplies. When the tour and tuition income ran short, as it often did, the Wrights borrowed money from friends and former clients.

But Wright's notorious history of stiffing his friends—Darwin Martin was still owed the $40,000 he had lent for the 1911 purchase of Taliesin—must have limited that source of funds. The Wrights never had enough. At one point, as some of Wright's frustrated former tradesmen began filing liens on Wright's land in hopes of collecting long-promised payments, even a shipment of blankets from Marshall Field's was held for failure to pay.

Undaunted, Wright never stopped renovating his estate. He convinced Pittsburgh Plate Glass to donate glass. American Radiator provided radiators and boilers. Labor, of course, was free. He had the apprentices, including the young women, quarry stone for the walls, cutting blocks of sandstone for Hillside and limestone for Taliesin itself. A girl, he joked, "is a fellow here."

With no money for lumber, Wright had the apprentices fell neighboring farmers' trees and trim their branches. He set up a saw mill, run by his steam tractor, where they dressed the logs into beams, boards, and planks, and then hauled the heavy oak slabs wherever they were needed. The Fellowship manufactured its own cement, refurbishing an old cairn of stones as a lime kiln. Workers and apprentices quarried and hauled the limestone, then tended the fire at the kiln for five or six days without a break, dozing off in sleeping bags and waking when other apprentices brought them food. The apprentices used the tons of cement they produced to rebuild Taliesin's dam, and even installed a turbine to generate electricity.

THE FELLOWSHIP SPENT its first year constructing itself, developing a system for allocating work, building the premises, preparing the fields for planting and harvesting corn, potatoes, and oats, feeding and heating the household.

There was a boisterous camaraderie among these sons and daughters of mostly affluent families, most of whom had no idea what it took to work a farm. Asked to slaughter a pig, one apprentice retrieved his revolver. Many found a kind of giddy satisfaction in building this new world together. But with so little architecture work Taliesin was really just a farm, the apprentices merely farmhands and construction workers. The "shining brow" was misted with the sweat of hard labor. Even Wright himself pitched in, getting on his hands and knees to weed the strawberry patch, running the thresher, driving the road grader.

The first bell rang at six-thirty in the morning. Breakfast was finished by seven-thirty, and the apprentices all set off to work the fields, tend the chickens and pigs, grade the roads, and repair and expand the buildings. They all returned to the house at four for a tea break, then back to work until it was time to clean up for dinner, which was served at seven. The lights went out at ten.

It was an exacting regimen. Wright conveyed a sense of urgency to all their work. His time, he worried, was short. For a while, to increase apprentice productivity, he even ended the lunch break at Hillside. Instead he had young women apprentices dress in milkmaid outfits and deliver store-bought bread and milk to his workers wherever they happened to be on the estate.

THE MANURE PIT had to be maintained. Standing barefoot, his pants rolled up, slicing into its rank goo, one apprentice who had just come from Yale thought to himself, "My God! This is the way I'm going to start being trained as an architect!" Just then Wright came by, beautifully dressed. "Don't give it a thought, young man, to the farmer it's worth its weight in gold."

Abe Dombar decided to celebrate manure in "At Taliesin" a newspaper column the Fellowship was accorded in the Madison *Capital Times*. Hundreds of these columns were written on rotation by apprentices, as a way for them to learn literary expression, and some by Wright himself. Not only was the ammonia given off by manure a "tonic to the lungs," Dombar mused (in a sentiment he obviously picked up from Olgivanna's Gurdjieffian lore), but it also was a privilege to be spreading it on the fields, to feed the "hungry ground," to "help the grain-germs find life." "This new life is born of the decay that is death. . . . This is immortality."

Work was initially allocated by a "senior boss," a post that rotated among the apprentices. Some apprentices made themselves scarce, even hiding in the closets, to avoid especially onerous jobs. When the shirking became obvious, Olgivanna took charge. Just as she had for Gurdjieff at the Prieuré a dozen years before, she began making up the weekly work list. And just as at the Prieuré, jobs were rotated to keep body and mind on edge in the face of ever-new tasks. Wes Peters, the engineering student from MIT, found himself behind a walking plow pulled by a team of horses. Harvesting was a collective affair, with both men and women threshing oats and picking corn.

Almost from the start, there was a chorus. And the Fellowship even had its own song: Bach's "Jesu, Joy of Man's Desiring," with new words by Wright himself, to be sung at public gatherings and at Sunday morning chapel as the bell stopped ringing:

> *Joy in work is man's desiring,*
> *Holy wisdom. Love most bright;*
> *Drawn by hope our souls aspiring,*
> *Soar to uncreated light . . .*

Drinks to joy from deathless springs,
Ours is beauty's fairest pleasure,
Ours is wisdom's greatest treasure,
Nature ever leads her own,
In the love of Joys unknown.

Sunday morning chapel was compulsory, something that did not go down easily with the atheists and agnostics among the apprentices. And then there were the Jews. Edgar Tafel felt a decided "mental strain" attending the Christian services, but decided to accommodate the Wrights nonetheless. It was not so bad, he recalled, "if you get yourself in the proper state of mind."

Others, however, did register their opposition to the religious services. With the workload and all the other mandatory events, the apprentices already had almost no time for themselves. Wright didn't care. "He published an announcement," Yen Liang reported, "declaring himself the 'master' whose opinion in all matters is sublime. Copies were distributed to the apprentices signed by the old man." As usual, Yen noted, "Mr. Wright with his childish obstinacy, tramped all opposition down; and so the 'chapel' becomes another item of '*culture.*' "

TWO MONTHS AFTER its opening, the Fellowship faced its first Wisconsin winter. Taliesin was not well insulated. Gangs of apprentices trudged out into the woods with their saws, often well before dawn, to harvest wood to keep the three steam boilers and the kitchen stove going. It would take a day to haul back two or three loads on the Caterpillar. Taliesin's sixty-five-year-old master often accompanied the work crews out to do the cutting.

Women, too, joined this detail. One female apprentice got so exhausted that she'd go off into the forest and cry. The apprentice assigned to boiler detail had to rise at around four in the morning, bundle up, and make his or her way to the dark cavernous area a story and a half below the living room. Others were assigned to heat big laundry tubs of water on the kitchen stove and then carry them steaming through the freezing air to the place where the apprentices took their weekly baths.

Feeding everyone was another major operation. During the Fellowship's first months, the Wrights paid for the full-time services of two paid cooks, Emma and Mabel, aunts of one of his pre-Fellowship draftsmen, Herb Fritz. But the expense was something they couldn't really afford, so Olgivanna soon persuaded her skeptical husband that the apprentices could handle most of the cooking. Food preparation was presented as an experience essential to becoming an architect—how else, after all, to understand kitchen design?

In the dark, frozen mornings of that first winter, the breakfast cookers had to get up even earlier than those assigned to farm. There were two big wood-burning ranges in the Taliesin kitchen. Two apprentices rose at three in the morning to chop enough wood to keep the ranges burning and the boilers hot. Others had to wash dishes for the more than fifty residents at each meal.

Many of the apprentices knew nothing about cooking; some even had grown up with live-in chefs, and it showed. Wright took his meals with the apprentices—it was said that he ate like a pig—and he often complained loudly when the apprentice-cooks' efforts fell short. If a dish was egregiously bad, he would even throw his plate out the window. Embarrassed, Olgivanna arranged to have a small private dining room constructed, where the family could eat out of sight and earshot of all but the apprentice assigned to serve them.

The valley was superb farmland, and the Fellowship did, as Wright had calculated, more or less feed itself. The apprentices canned tomatoes, put up rhubarb and blackberry preserves, made and bottled chokecherry, dandelion, and eventually grape wine. What was neither cooked nor canned was sold. Wright sometimes personally drove his Cord, loaded with baskets of peas and tomatoes, to Madison.

The kitchen was the one place where Olgivanna had undisputed control. Just as Gurdjieff had done for her, she systematically attempted to teach the apprentices to cook. She used simple stew-like recipes, many of which she had translated from Yugoslavian and Russian cookbooks. When it came to the culinary arts, at least, the goal of a unique native culture fell by the wayside. The Americans learned to make *golupsti*, *tiftilki*, *pirogi*, *blini*, *obertuk*, and Czar's bread. And the recipes had to be followed scrupulously. Olgivanna always seemed to know when a spice had been added or left out.

UNDER THE CIRCUMSTANCES, Wright seemed content having his charges' exposure to architecture limited to restoring and expanding his own buildings. Nonetheless, some educational opportunities did go to waste. Instead of seizing the chance to teach architectural drawing, for example, Wright generally did drawings himself, merely passing out the quick sketches to the workers when he finished.

At Taliesin, the neophytes witnessed an approach to architecture that would have shocked their future employers, if they should ever dare bring it with them into the world. Wright moved through the ongoing construction designing on the fly, lifting his walking stick as he surveyed a site, giving verbal instruction to apprentices who would scramble to execute his vision. "No more drawing-board architects at Taliesin!" he pledged, "Not if I can help it."

It was all a far cry from what apprentices like Wes Peters and Yen Liang had just learned at Yale or MIT. If anything, Wright's Fellowship was much closer in its emphases to the Prieuré, where hard physical work was one of the keys to correlating the body and mind. Any skepticism was met with the claim that everything you did at Taliesin was part of becoming an architect. While Wright kept promising the apprentices that they soon would learn to design buildings, the routine remained the same: digging, hammering, cooking, and plowing.

Abe Dombar was nonetheless enthralled. "I hope you are planning to come up this summer," he wrote his brothers and sisters. "[After] a day up here, a new world would open before your mind. Already our name has gone around the world; the greatest minds of the country have written us of their mental support (never financial)." Very few of the apprentices' parents, he realized, could understand what their children were doing at Taliesin. "They, by

Apprentices and paid workers doing construction.

force of habit, still think of us in terms of college . . . but can one describe true love." Like many of the apprentices in these early years, Dombar took on a rhapsodic tone that echoed Wright's own: "Ah! Taliesin!—the source of my newly found inspiration and clearer, noble outlook upon life."

Dombar was sold on Frank Lloyd Wright, and Wright on him. When it came time to memorialize the Fellowship's new home at the Hillside School, the master sought a volunteer to carve a sign into one of the stones to be placed in the wall that stretched across the building's north facade. Charley Curtis, a paid mason, prepared a large flat stone. Dombar, who had done lettering for display windows in Cincinnati, offered to do the carving. "I've cut letters into wood but never into stone, but I think I can do it." Wright, who claimed he could recognize the cut of each of his masons, gave him the go-ahead. It was freezing out, and Abe wanted to cut out of the large stone a block big enough for the lettering but small enough to bring indoors. Wright would have none of it. Working hours and hours in the chill Wisconsin gusts, Abe Dombar cut the letters:

THE TALIESIN FELLOWSHIP

HILLSIDE HOME SCHOOL

1886

As the months of construction work went on, however—and no architectural commissions appeared—even Dombar began having his doubts. Wright "didn't have any classes at all," he recalled. "[T]he brochure talked about classes. He had got this French girl there that was supposed to teach drawing, but she never did."

Abe made the best of it. He and the French girl, Yvonne Bannelier, became friends. They hiked together into the countryside, singing as they went. And he visited her room at night—something the Wrights had forbidden. Not that anything inappropriate took place: It was enough when he was swimming in the river one warm day, and Yvonne stripped naked and swam in after him. The shocked apprentice carefully kept his distance.

But such "revelations" could not compensate for the lack of architectural training. "We would spend all our time working till noon," Dombar recalled, "and then we'd come in for lunch. . . . When the farmers left because they weren't being paid, then we had to take over. When the carpenter left, we had to take over." After long days in the fields and doing construction, the frustrated apprentice made late-night incursions into Wright's drawing archives, where he studied the plans and perspectives, gleaning what he could.

Before long the grumbling reached critical mass, and Wright finally realized that he needed to provide at least a semblance of architectural training.

Gathering the apprentices into his Taliesin studio, he pulled out his ten-year-old drawings of the Imperial Hotel and had them trace them. As they worked, he paced about and reminisced about his years in Japan working with his first apprentices, explaining how he had designed the hotel to float on Tokyo's liquefiable soil as though it were held up by fingers the way a waiter supports a tray moving through the crowd. Sometimes, to make a point, he drew right on the original tracings. This was far from a serious educational program: "In a sense," Edgar Tafel recalled, "it was a make-work program."

This token classwork did little to quell the apprentices' rising frustration. With so little drafting to do, they turned their talents to literary jest, writing *the front page*, a newsletter tacked up in the drafting room for their common amusement. Under the banner "Taliesin's nose knows," it was full of items presumably mocking the outside world, where students wasted their lives accumulating useless academic knowledge:

> Fourteen thousand years ago Confucius said this and it is just as true today. What do we know of the Hanseatic League? Who do we know of incomplete metabolism of glucose? Of ontogeny recapitulating phylogeny? Of the libido of the condemned felon who may find himself willy nilly in jail? This country is all wong [sic].

In the Fellowship's first year, a visit from a pair of well-dressed gentlemen from Manhattan made quite a stir among the apprentices. The young, always elegant Philip Johnson, with his handsome, finely modeled face, and the older, more portly and less couth architectural historian and curator, Henry-Russell Hitchcock, came fresh from the success of their International Style show to see Wright's new enterprise. Johnson "wore lavender trousers, white shoes and a pale green shirt," announced the in-house organ posted in the drafting room in 1932. Hitchcock "wore light blue shoes, white trousers, and a pink shirt."

Hitchcock, in return, was impressed with Wright's clothing. "I don't know where they all came from, but those very strange hats were specially produced by a French hatter in the Place Vendome." Johnson, in contrast, was struck by how poor the Wrights were. The room he stayed in had a failing roof beam, he recalled. Without the money to fix it, Wright had propped it up with a two by four. And his approach to architecture seemed just as earthy and unpremeditated. When Johnson asked Wright how he composed his spaces, Wright replied: "I do it like a cow shits."

Johnson saw Wright as "so cruel to the kids who worked there"; Olgivanna struck him as "a horror." Hitchcock concurred, at least about Olgivanna.

* * *

WRIGHT'S SMALL PERSONAL studio at Taliesin itself was a room intended for a few paid draftsmen, not dozens of apprentices. While the plans
for a large drafting room at the Hillside complex had been completed before
the first apprentices arrived, its construction had been postponed. The lack of
a proper drafting studio only compounded the apprentices' discouragement
and frustration.

When the word came down that work on the studio would finally begin,
it was a clear signal that serious architecture training lay ahead, and the
apprentices were thrilled. When the assignments for digging the foundation
were announced, seventeen-year-old apprentice Herb Fritz Jr. was disappointed to discover that he had been assigned instead to cultivate corn. After
a few days in the fields, he trekked up to the house, where he encountered
Svetlana, now fifteen. Could he join the ditch diggers, he asked her? She left
and soon returned with her mother's approval.

The new drafting room was to be attached by a breezeway to the old Hillside building. Once the foundation was in, the apprentices began constructing huge roof trusses from lumber they had hewn themselves. The trusses,
Wright explained, were conceived as a kind of "abstract forest" through
which the light from the clerestory windows would bathe the drafting tables
below, a daylighting scheme reminiscent of his Oak Park studio. Unfortunately, the oak timbers they labored over were still green; over time they
shrunk and twisted so badly that they had to be replaced.

When the apprentices and workmen finally raised the roof, a party was in
order. Some of the apprentices put on little green freshmen beanies and clustered together. The room went quiet, a banjo started to play, and the boys
began to sing:

> *Taliesin, Taliesin, good old shining brow.*
> *Push the pencil round the paper*
> *Try to please Jack Howe*
> *Ra, ra, ra.*

> *We love Mozart, hate Beaux Arts*
> *And Ralph Adams Cram.*
> *Fight, freshmen, fight*
> *I'll live as I work as I am.*

> *We love fresh air, long hair, the red square*
> *To thee ever true*
> *Fight, freshmen, fight*
> *The studio is not for you!*

Wright had sat expressionless throughout the entire performance. Now all eyes turned to him. The curves of a smile rose on his face. And then he began to laugh.

The drafting room at Taliesin was not completed until the fall of 1939, seven years after the first apprentices arrived.

ALTHOUGH THEY HAD almost no clients, Frank and Olgivanna still seemed to live a pretty good life. For the moment Taliesin was no longer at risk of repossession, and the tuition income, supplemented by book royalties and speaking fees, even helped pay for fancy dinners on Sunday nights. Musically talented apprentices put on concerts. A number of them had brought along fine, well-functioning automobiles. Ranks of young people from good families farmed Taliesin's fields, cooked and cleaned, served the Wrights their meals, and restored and expanded Wright's greatest love, Taliesin itself. The apprentices stood whenever the Wrights walked into the room, their entrance silencing everyone. Conversation only resumed once they themselves began to talk. Frank was always called "Mr. Wright," Olgivanna "Mrs. Wright."

In the midst of the Depression, Wright's lifestyle must have been the envy of his colleagues. Many big-city architecture firms had been closed down. In others the drafting rooms were empty, the principals sitting alone in their private offices drafting up their own details for the first time since they were kids. Yet there was Frank Lloyd Wright, up on his shining brow, the country gentleman in his custom-made suits—clientless, but thriving.

Wright, nonetheless, behaved as though the Taliesin Fellowship were an exercise in self-sacrifice, often reminding his charges of what a burden they were. He insisted to them that he personally gained nothing from their tuition fees. Whatever surpluses remained after feeding them, he let them know, were poured into converting the dilapidated Hillside Home School into housing and a drafting room. "I felt in duty bound," he wrote, "to use what money they paid me (in the usual installments, of course) for that purpose only." He had no choice, he claimed, because "the still small voice of Conscience that is my misfortune—steadily carried on."

Wherever the tuition money went, little found its way into the hands of the skilled workers hired to renovate Hillside. Eventually many of them laid down their tools and marched on Taliesin in protest. "We are desperate here," Wright wrote, decrying their action as an "insurrection" he could barely hold in check. Somehow, with the help of long-term credit, he managed to keep going.

And even in this time of renewed income, Taliesin's record of correspondence, property liens, and other legal actions suggests that Wright still wasn't conscientious about paying his bills. Just three months after the Fellowship opened, Harry Roberts filed a lien of $111.60 against the Hillside property. Westinghouse Electric Supply Company eventually won a $313.44 judgment against Wright for nonpayment. The company that installed Taliesin's steam heat system got stiffed for $2,613.81, a small fortune in those days.

One former workman exacted his own justice. C. E. Secrest, accompanied by his sons, accosted Wright as he was getting out of his car and began to beat him. During the scuffle, Secrest landed a kick on Wright's nose, breaking it.

When their bloodied master returned to Taliesin, the apprentices were outraged. That evening, five of them, including Wes Peters, drove to Madison and barged into Secrest's house as he was having dinner with his wife. Karl Jensen struck him with a whip. Wes Peters socked him in the eye. Secrest rushed to the kitchen, returning with a knife as he held his wife in front of him as a shield.

The apprentices hid in a quarry a mile from Taliesin. When the police arrested them, Svetlana jumped in the car and drove to the jail with a food basket. Wes Peters was charged with inciting a riot and fined $175 and Secrest was expelled from town. Olgivanna and Frank were delighted with the boys' revenge.

WHEN IT CAME to loyalty, the apprentice "posse" was not entirely representative. In the first few years of the Fellowship many apprentices left over the lack of architecture training, and soon the project was at risk of failure. Wright, having feared from the start that he was not cut out to run a school, realized that he was out of his depth.

In the spring of 1933, as if nothing had happened, he wrote Hendrik Wijdeveld asking him once again to come on board. "I have not been able to find anyone I consider of the right quality for director of the Fellowship in America and now realize I must go to Europe for anyone sufficiently familiar with the crafts to carry on here successfully. I would prefer you to anyone I know if I could get you."

The scheme, he wrote, had moved "so rapidly towards realization— buildings and all—that there is no longer the uncertainty there was when you were over here." And money was not a problem. "I feel sure, now, the venture can be made a success and that there will be sufficient living for you and your family . . . a fair share of what was earned by the Fellowship could well go to the Wijdevelds. In short," he claimed, "I could support you all now without the uneasiness I felt about that when you were here and the contract for your coming was written for you to sign." Wright's optimism was running away with him again: With his mounting debts to everyone in town, plus Darwin Martin's forty thousand dollars, and past-due bills on his mortgage and taxes, it's unclear how he intended to pay Dutchy.

This time Wijdeveld didn't reply. Wright had his draftsman Henry Klumb write a second letter. Writing in German, Klumb was candid. "We miss the man who animates the thing," he wrote. "The Taliesin Fellowship exists at the moment only nominally. Nothing of importance has been undertaken. First the buildings, then the productive work was the motto (my ideas on that are different ones). On this basis everything has been going on until now. Often we have been close to despair." The apprentices, he went on, "want to create according to how it is described in the pamphlet. They do not want only to dig trenches, or run after the workman, and clean up, and saw wood to stay warm. They want to create. This Mr. Wright finally realizes." The Taliesin Fellowship was in need of a "leader," Klumb advised; Wijdeveld was that man.

But Hendrik Wijdeveld was busy once again trying to create a school of his own, this time in southern France. Though he agonized over the offer, he never replied. For Frank Lloyd Wright, salvation would have to come from elsewhere.

Svetlana Wright as a young woman

8.

₣LIGHT

SMART, ATTRACTIVE, AND CHARMING, OLGIVANNA'S elder daughter was fifteen when her mother and stepfather brought the thirty or so young people into their home. With a strong handshake and a big, infectious laugh, Svetlana Wright—Frank had by now adopted her—played the piano and milked goats with equal aplomb. Braving wind-chill temperatures as low as thirty below, she worked alongside the boys during the Fellowship's first winter, cutting cords of wood to keep the boilers going.

By the end of the Fellowship's first six months, many, if not most, of those boys were smitten with her. But Wes Peters, the burly prankster, was the first to get close. Together, Wes and Svetlana hauled five to six tons of wood across the frozen ground in a one-ton self-dumping truck. The two snuck into Jack Howe's room and stole his pants. Wes sent her joke letters:

> To Svet, from B. F. Howl, Master of th'ounds, K-9 Kennels, 497 Splutterworth Rd., Ipsdich, Pitchwock. . . . We understand that you are in the market for a dog and thought that you might like to view our stock before purchasing. We have some of the very finest specimens of practically all breeds, including the rarely known under-dog and the beautiful Mexican Sooner Dog (Sooner eat than sleep). Where you wish your canine friend for work or play, for field or lap, we can fill your every need. Our dogs are pals!

That first spring, the two spent their days together laboring in the fields, their evenings discussing the likes of D. H. Lawrence and Goethe. Svetlana was always straying from the roads, preferring to walk through the wildflowers in the fields. Still, Wes had to screw up all his courage to visit her in her basement room and ask her on a walk. He needn't have worried. He was, she confessed, her best friend.

Peters was elated, but he wanted more than that.

When Easter came, he was assigned to work on Olgivanna's Baba, a special bread. Waiting for it to bake, he discovered Svetlana in front of the fire in the little dining room, reading. "I was afraid again—But then—on the night before Easter—with the glow of the fire—red dark—and the glow of the candles—yellow dark—and the glow about Svet—fiery white and pure—and night fell—oh so happily!—and the Baba was made!"

The two pledged that someday they would marry.

OLGIVANNA DIDN'T JUST love Svetlana; she needed the young girl. Having once abandoned her young daughter, she was now desperate to keep her close by. Svetlana linked Olgivanna to her past, to Gurdjieff, to the risks of her journeys far from home. The two had shared hardships in Tiflis and Constantinople, when they knew that there might soon be nothing to eat, that the soldiers could strike at any moment, that bandits plundered on the unknown roads ahead. While Svetlana understood the gravity of survival, she leavened her understanding with a tender gaiety that Olgivanna lacked.

Frank also deeply loved "Kitani," as he called her. Tough yet delicate, the girl had a way of cajoling him that few others in the household could muster. And by now such cajoling was a much-needed skill in Taliesin. Stresses were building between the Wrights. Olgivanna understood herself to be a partner in the conception and management of the Fellowship. But her husband proved unwilling to grant her any real creative role—beyond, that is, teaching the apprentices to make a decent meal.

But Olgivanna, unbeknownst to Frank, was teaching more than cooking. In the vast expanse that was Taliesin, she found places where she could surreptitiously gather some of the Fellowship's women together and instruct them in the Gurdjieff philosophy and the sacred dances. The clique became known by the more skeptical among the apprentices as the "Know Nothing Party." She got away with it—for a while. "Mr. Wright came upon them one time," one of the women recalled, "and he was jealous because Mrs. Wright was taking part." Frank made a scene that left Olgivanna infuriated.

Svetlana had a way of calming the roiling waters. When her parents argued, as they did often now, she would "smooth it out," as Wes Peters recalled. "She was the only one who could kind of tease Mr. Wright, tell him, 'Well, you're being very silly, Daddy Frank.' And that would kind of tickle him."

It didn't always work. One night, at the age of seven, Iovanna was drawn down the hallway by shouting from her parents' bedroom. "Don't, Daddy

Frank, don't!" Svetlana was pleading. Iovanna arrived at the open doorway just in time to witness her father and mother in a scene heretofore unimaginable. "He threw her flat on her back," she recalled. "If it had been concrete, she would be dead." Olgivanna, whose head had hit the floor, was alternatively screaming and sobbing. To protect her mother from further harm, a horrified Svetlana grabbed "Daddy Frank" and muscled him into the hallway.

Iovanna watched as her father, his face near white with rage, grabbed her stepsister by the throat. Over and over he beat her head against the wooden closet doors until she managed to squirm free of his grip.

Olgivanna was finally able to drag herself into bed. "Frank, how could you have done this to me?" she sobbed.

Frank mutely went into his study and shut the door.

Iovanna was sent back to bed. "I understood nothing of what I had seen," she recalled. "But the horror of it stayed with me for the rest of my life. Next day mother and father were pale but amiable."

"INITIALLY," WES PETERS remembered, "Mrs. Wright had encouraged me to take her daughter along [hauling wood] in the truck. She had made a point of getting us together." But things took a downward turn when Wes decided to confide in Wright about their relationship and their plans to marry someday. "Mr. Wright had been so friendly with me," Wes thought, "I felt it was only right to be honest with him."

Wright instantly assumed that Wes had seduced Svetlana and that she was pregnant. He accused him of having betrayed him. Nothing Wes said could persuade him otherwise. He shot a vicious letter off to his apprentice's father. "I do not know you," Wes's father replied, "but you've written me things about my son that I simply cannot accept. My son has his faults, but they are not the faults of dishonesty or deceit." While Wright later wrote an apology to Mr. Peters, he never backed off when it came to the young couple.

Eight months after the Fellowship's opening, in the summer of 1933, sixteen-year-old Svetlana fled Taliesin with Wes. Too young by law to marry without her parents' permission, she made her way to the Chicago suburb of Wilmette, and moved into the home of a Dr. Geisse. She traded housekeeping and cooking for room and board, and enrolled in the local high school. Wes went home, to Evansville, Indiana, to live with his parents.

OCTOBER 26, 1933, marked the first anniversary of the opening of the Fellowship. The Wrights planned back-to-back events for that week: a Halloween costume party, followed the next day by an anniversary celebration.

The second event was open to the public, and Wright used it, according to apprentice Bob Bishop, as a way of saying "I told you so" to the locals, many of whom had been skeptical of their eccentric neighbor's scheme. The apprentices paid a big price for their victory party: Wright insisted that they finish construction on the playhouse on a crash basis. It "took the life out of us so thoroughly, what with a night, day, and Sunday schedule," Bishop reported, "that we were too tired to enjoy the parties." When Bishop complained of the workload, suggesting that the apprentices needed a little more time of their own, he was asked to leave.

But the place looked good, and the guests—a few hundred of them, most in evening gowns and tuxedos—were impressed. The just-completed playhouse was a prime attraction, a good thing given Wright's hope that ticket sales would help float the Fellowship for years to come.

A NEW APPRENTICE arrived just in time for the party; soon this young man took charge of Taliesin's film program, though ultimately this would be the least of his contributions. Gene Masselink became the master's personal secretary—his eyes and ears, his second voice, the one who could anticipate his desires, the agent through whom Wright's thoughts were translated into written directives and his work turned into money.

The son of a dentist, Masselink grew up in Grand Rapids, Michigan, only a few blocks from a house Wright had designed before he was born. During the summer of his junior year at Ohio State, he too became hooked on Wright after reading his autobiography. A week before the Fellowship was to open, Masselink, the newly elected president of Tau Sigma Delta, a national honorary fraternity for architecture and the allied arts, convinced Frank Lloyd Wright to come to the campus as a guest speaker.

Masselink knew Wright's appearance at the university would be controversial. Ohio State was, to put it mildly, no bastion of modernism. In his letter to Wright, he made it clear where he stood. Other guest speakers, he wrote, were not doing "true creative work." Then, in a sentence that surely warmed Wright's heart, Gene noted that he "could be expelled for saying even less than that."

Wright was always on the lookout for paid speaking engagements. On the day he responded to Masselink, he also dashed off a letter to one of his many creditors: "I haven't responded to your admirable contribution of shoes sooner because I hope to send some money with the acknowledgement. . . . I'll send you the balance as soon as I can send anybody any money at all. . . . Meantime—in your shoes—Sincerely yours, Frank Lloyd Wright."

His reply to Masselink wasn't quite as cavalier. "The usual fee for 'occasions' ($250) I don't think you boys would want to pay. So—if you pay to cover traveling expenses and all—say $125.—I should consider the insult sufficiently large in the circumstances." In fact, his typical fee for a lecture was twenty dollars, thirty for a long one. At the time, a good hotel room near Ohio State cost twelve.

Gene's invitation to the architect started a war between the university and the fraternity. And it wasn't just about Wright's architecture: The school's administration refused to allow Masselink to bring such an "immoral man" on campus.

Gene's solution was simple: He would hold the event off campus. But there was another sticking point. Wright had a contract with a lecture bureau that required him to pay them a percentage of all his lecture fees. Karl Jensen wrote to Masselink explaining the issue and Wright's insistence that the event be called a "banquet," not a "lecture." Gene went along with the gambit, and the deal was done.

When Wright drove to Columbus and finally met Gene, he was taken with the lean, good-looking, and polished blond aesthete, who carried himself with extraordinary poise. The young man was more a student of art than architecture, Wright learned; in fact, he was an already accomplished painter,

Gene Masselink, Wright's trusted secretary

with one-man shows to his credit in Grand Rapids, Michigan, and Columbus, Ohio. "More customary and nobler terms fall short of doing justice to
his sweeping paint and sudden color," wrote Barnarda Brysin, an art critic
in Columbus. Gene had also worked in California with Hans Hofmann, the
famed German exile expressionist painter. Influenced by Hofmann's bright
colors and bold forms, Gene's painting *The Bathers,* of four naked men posed
around a washtub, won first prize at an art show at the Corcoran, Washington, D.C.'s premier art museum.

Before the event, Gene took Wright to his fraternity house to see some of
his paintings. No fan of easel painting, Wright nonetheless liked what he saw.
"You have talent, young man, great talent. Work it, develop it. . . . An artist
must train himself not to look at nature, a tree, a landscape, a mountain, but
rather to look into it, to abstract the essential character and quality of it and
then create his own work on that foundation. Your place is with me—you
should join the Taliesin Fellowship and work with me."

Gene Masselink was in some of kind of ecstasy.

The "banquet" was a big success. Soon afterward, the Taliesin Fellowship
brochure arrived in Gene's mailbox. His excitement was tempered by the discovery of the substantial tuition. He wrote Jensen explaining that he would
need financial assistance from Taliesin in order to join.

Jensen's response to the all-too-common request was atypical. "Mr.
Wright wants to do something for you with respect to your coming here as
soon as he is able to do so," he wrote. "We don't know yet how soon this will be
as it will depend entirely on our economic ability. But we have put aside your
case among a very few others as deserving help as soon as we can do it. I hope
you will be able to carry on in the meanwhile until the situation eases up."

Wright knew that Gene Masselink was special.

Of all those who were tempted by the Fellowship, Gene, who was already
on the path to artistic success, had the most to lose. He had just been invited
to paint one of the large murals for the 1933 Chicago Century of Progress exposition, a huge world's fair to be held on the shores of Lake Michigan, an
event slated to draw millions of visitors. He would be in extraordinary company: Among the others invited to participate was Thomas Hart Benton, then
one of America's most renowned artists.

But Frank Lloyd Wright, who had himself been spurned by the Chicago
fair organizers and denied any architectural role, had captured his future.
Drawn by Wright's magnetic personality, the opportunity to work with a
mentor whom he believed would push his work forward, the chance to live
his art as well as produce it, Masselink turned down the Chicago fair. He
wanted to be ready for Taliesin when Taliesin was ready for him.

After graduating, Gene took a job teaching drawing at a farm camp in

Michigan, visiting the Century of Progress fair during a break. He also made his way to the Oak Park suburb to see Wright's early projects. "The next thing to heaven," he told a friend from school who had accompanied him, "would be a Taliesin Fellowship." Soon after, he wrote to Wright reminding him that he was still interested in coming.

And then it came. In late August, back at the camp, he was standing looking at the lake, the air dense with humidity, when the farmer walked up the hill and handed him a letter. "My dear Masselink," it began, "Ever since making your acquaintance I've waited to make a place for you here at the Fellowship and believe I can do it now. Won't you write me of your circumstances and plans?"

"My circumstances and plans for this coming winter," Gene wrote back, "are beautifully void."

THE APPRENTICES HAD been waiting for more than a year when Jack Howe and Abe Dombar got a big surprise. Mr. Wright needed them—in the drafting studio. At last, there was some architectural work to be done.

Nancy Willey, a Minneapolis housewife, and her husband, Malcolm, a sociology professor, had bought some land near the Mississippi River. Initially she wanted to build their house from a catalog given to her by her hairdresser. Then her husband happened to bring home a copy of Wright's autobiography. "And, gosh, it just sent me sky high!" she wrote to Wright back in June 1932, before the Fellowship opened. "I have little hope [that] you would take on anything so trivial that was also not near you."

"Nothing is trivial because it is not big," Wright replied. (Failing to mention, of course, that as his only current project, the Willey house would also be his largest.)

With Henry Klumb serving as the project's draftsman, Wright designed a two-story structure, complete with servants' quarters and an enclosed garage. When the bids came in way over their $10,000 maximum, the Willeys pulled the plug.

Now, in November 1933, Nancy Willey wrote to try again. "I do not want a seventeen thousand dollar house even at twelve or ten thousand dollars. I want an eight to ten thousand dollar house at eight to ten thousand dollars. Can I have it?"

"Mr. Wright called me in from the field to be a draftsman to work on the thing," Dombar recalled. "He had to call about three times. I was so used to be[ing] on the farm that I wouldn't even know what to do in the drafting room."

Fortunately for Abe, the highly competent Klumb was in charge. He and

Howe were only to assist. Guided by Wright, the trio rendered a single story, light-feeling structure of cypress and brick. The new design included no quarters for a live-in housekeeper; the kitchen was prominently located next to the compact living room-dining room. There was no pantry. It was a revolutionary form, anticipating, if not giving birth to, the suburban tract home that emerged decades later.

Wright would later call it a Usonian house.

SVETLANA'S FLIGHT FROM Taliesin left seven-year-old Iovanna facing her parents' battles alone. Olgivanna was stymied by Frank's refusal to let her teach Gurdjieff; Frank, the self-proclaimed source of all modern architecture, had been reduced to designing one small house. The frustration between them was palpable.

And it was audible. Sometimes at night Iovanna heard her father pounding his pillow with his fist, assailing his critics. "Damn fools! Damn fools," he cried. "He always yearned for praise," Iovanna recalled, "praise, praise, praise! It was only later that he realized how appreciated he was. It came too late for the family."

The Wrights' relationship was also burdened by sexual jealousy. Olgivanna, after all, was thirty years younger than Frank, much closer in age to the apprentices than her husband. And she was a sensuous woman, whose erotic allure was an instrument she used to provoke her husband's jealousy and thereby control him. A number of apprentices were attracted to Olgivanna, and believed that she gave off subtle signals of desire. Wright's fear of other men's attentions was nothing short of pathological. When he called and Olgivanna did not respond, he often assumed she was with another man. The thought of her unaccompanied in the world made him anxious. She had to use subterfuge to be allowed to drive alone into Madison.

One November night in 1933, the still-green lawn dusted with snow, Iovanna was awakened by another nighttime fight between her parents. This time, as she rushed to her mother's room, she would be left to her own resources. "I am leaving him," Olgivanna exclaimed as she shook with rage. "I cannot take this abuse any longer." Her father, dressed in overcoat, hat, and cane, passed her in the hallway carrying a small suitcase. "Stop him, Iovanna—quickly," Olgivanna implored. "For the love of God, stop him."

Iovanna ran barefoot into the frigid night. Catching up with her father, she grabbed his sleeve and pleaded with him to go back inside. "Please come back, Daddy. We love you—we need you."

Wright stopped, silent. "Daddy, it's cold—the snow pains my feet—come back." At this, her father turned and together they returned to the house. Iovanna went back to bed.

Perhaps it was no coincidence that Iovanna, who had just turned eight, was moved out of her parents' suite a few months later. Working from a sketch Mr. Wright drew on a shingle, the apprentices built two new rooms for her above Taliesin's loggia. Wright called the suite "Scherzo," probably because of the speed of its construction. "Until now," Abe Dombar joked upon its completion, "she was the only apprentice who didn't have his or her own room."

After the boys built in the furniture and the girls sewed and hung the curtains, the apprentices threw a "room-warming" party. Seated in a semicircle around the fireplace, each apprentice told her his or her own fairy story. Iovanna, who wanted to be a writer when she grew up, already made up her own ghost stories. She told them well, but couldn't put them to paper. Seeking to closet her from the world, her parents kept her out of school, and though they assigned apprentices like Abe to teach her, the strikingly bright child remained completely illiterate. The Wrights had the apprentices read to her. And when, for the room-warming party, she made up a poem in which her parents clothed themselves in gold and silver, she had to dictate it.

Now that Iovanna had a room of her own, Dombar wrote, "The rest is up to her." He envisioned a Fellowship-style education through hard labor: "She will carry the wood for her fireplace and keep the room in order. This will develop her sense of responsibility, a valuable trait that few grown-ups seem to have."

But responsibility would not come easily for Iovanna, who was treated with a level of deference befitting the member of a royal house. When she got angry, she was known to go into an apprentice's room, knock over chairs, and break things—and her hapless victims were expected to play along. Her parents denied her very little. The only thing they forbade her was popular culture: Wright burned the funny papers the child so adored. Absorbed with running the Fellowship, her parents made little time to supervise her. The apprentices assigned to oversee Iovanna rarely had the courage to discipline her, fearing her parents' disapproval.

Iovanna was the princess of the place, and she knew it. She sat on her father's lap, stroking his hair down over his forehead. "Spider man, spider man," she called him as he laughed. "Come birdie, come, and live with me," Wright chanted to her, "You shall be happy, gay and free. You shall mean all the world to me. Come birdie come, and live with me. And you never will forget it, if you come, where the bells are ringing and the girls are singing." On winter nights, when dry snow squeaks beneath one's feet, Wright would build a fire and he and Olgivanna took turns reading stories aloud, starting with fairy tales for Iovanna.

But all this attention could not erase the parental violence their daughter witnessed. While her older sister had been able to escape the troubled family, Iovanna, still a child, could only flee into her copious imagination. "I loved our flawless home," she remembers in her autobiography, "our castle made of trees and stone and low cliffs of crystal. In the surrounding azure-green, I watched Pegasus, the winged horse, go flying."

MEANWHILE, FROM THEIR perch in exile, Wes and Svetlana only grew angrier at Taliesin's flaws. But they were far from unique. Two other escapees—Betty Weber, now living with Svetlana at the Geisses' in Wilmette, and Louise Dees-Porch, Betty's close friend—had plenty to crab about. Before the Fellowship, Weber had worked with Henry Klumb setting up Wright's European show. And Dees-Porch, who aspired to be an architect, never really made it into the drafting room. Instead both had been assigned to household tasks, working on the curtains, in the gardens, and in the kitchen. "I don't think Mr. Wright planned on any of them becoming architects," Abe Dombar recalled.

Betty and Louise had encouraged Svetlana to leave. Dees-Porch, a Wellesley girl who considered herself a communist and once jokingly derided Svetlana as a "spineless jellyfish," now wrote to cheer her on. "Is there any thought in your head away off—of returning to Taliesin. Yahweh, I hope not."

To conceal her connection to Frank Lloyd Wright, Svetlana lived under the assumed name of Sargon Wilde, after a Persian king who shared her initials. She feared that her true identity might jeopardize her standing with her hosts, a family who at least seemed to know how to get along. "That is a thing which Svet has always been withheld," Betty Weber reported to Wes, "—always there has been strife."

To survive, Svetlana and Betty made and sold dozens of dollhouses and sets of miniature furniture. (Of course their toy business never brought her the success of her half-brother John Lloyd Wright, the inventor of Lincoln Logs.) Svetlana did get some sustenance from her mother—not money, but packages containing cakes and roasted chickens.

She also received considerable support from the friends she left behind at Taliesin: letters from apprentices, even visits when they passed through Chicago. Jack Howe wrote her: "I just found out you had something to do with stealing my trousers, and I am writing to you that I don't think that's playing the game. I think you know something about my pussy willows, too, so there."

Though she and Wes must have feared that they might become Fellowship pariahs, soon even Wright was being conciliatory. "I am sorry you are leaving the Fellowship," he wrote Peters three months later. "You have kept up your end and more. . . . If I had anything you really needed or wanted you should have it at this crucial time in your life." Wes did not respond.

But there was something that Wes wanted, something Wright himself didn't have: an architecture license. "I have resolved to drag—slug—push— until I get my examinations past," he wrote Svetlana, "and then—I'm going to make fur fly in a different way." He had already found in Evansville several clients for houses.

Wright had nothing but disdain for the licensing of architects. In 1897, early in his career, Illinois had become the first state to adopt licensing in an effort to regulate the practice of architecture. By the time the Fellowship opened, two-thirds of the states required a series of lengthy and difficult exams before one could call oneself an architect. In addition to passing the exams, applicants were required to apprentice to a licensed architect for seven years, or attend an accredited architecture school, followed by a lesser period of apprenticeship, before earning a license.

Peters understood that he needed a license to succeed in the profession. On its own, an apprenticeship with Wright would get him nowhere. Not only was the Taliesin Fellowship not an accredited school, but since Wright at that point had no license himself, studio time under his supervision would not count. No matter how long they had apprenticed at Taliesin, those who left were, in effect, starting their architecture careers from scratch.

Wes's mother cheered him on. "We're proud of you Billie!" she wrote him once while he was away. "We know it wasn't easy to decide to leave Taliesin now and that it took 'guts' to reach the conclusion you did. But with you, we think it will be best for all concerned. No matter how friendly Mr. and Mrs. Wright try to be, they will be suspicious of your every move and it will be devilish for Svetlana. And how long would you, my tempestuous giant, endure quietly suspicious observation. You'd break out some day and then the fat would be in the fire."

Svetlana and Wes traveled back and forth from Illinois to Indiana to see each other. Neither of them had much money. During one of her long stays with the Peters family, the two made Wright-inspired doll houses, with their own chairs, furniture, and fireplaces. She sold them for fifty dollars, a princely sum. When they were apart, they counted the days till they would reunite. They wrote furiously, sharing bits of poetry, musings on Beethoven and Bach, favorite passages from D. H. Lawrence. Wes identified with the stallion in Lawrence's novella *St. Mawr*, whose sex, he wrote her, was "craved" by America's wild spirit. Peters thought that Lawrence, like Beethoven, was "inwardly torn between love and hate. . . . Did you know that symphonies oppressed Lawrence?"

Svetlana around 1938

"He loved folk songs," Svetlana offered.

Apprentice Yen Liang tried to assuage his friend Wes's fury at Wright. "You prefer arguing 'inch by inch' but you also know too well that The God himself is not going to let his ego down to listen to a person half his age and to admit that he has been wrong."

However great Wes considered Mr. Wright's architecture, though—"the flowing genius that lies at the fingertips of that strange devil"—he now saw the man as pathetic. Taliesin, he believed, had betrayed its ideals just as Mr. Wright had betrayed him. And Wright would likewise betray all his vassals—young people who now, from the outside, looked similarly pitiable to him. "God damn it—Svet," he wrote, "what a bunch of below-the-average people there were at Taliesin."

SVETLANA MADE NO effort to return, and soon Olgivanna was beside herself. First she sent her daughter a "hysterical letter": Svetlana must either return to Taliesin, she demanded, or move to Paris and work with Gurdjieff. Svetlana refused both. Then came a more reasonable one: Olgivanna now understood, she reassured her daughter, that both options were out of the question.

Finally Svetlana agreed to spend Christmas at Taliesin, though only for three days. Wes was dismayed. "Oh! Don't go!" he pleaded. "Find something to keep you—say some big job has come up. I don't see why you 'practically have to go.' They can't force you to go. . . . Don't make us go thru all that again! Please! Please! It's bad—I know it's bad—I feel instinctively it's bad. The thing is a trap. . . . Never trust their type unless you have a gun trained on them."

Svetlana would not be dissuaded. This was a test, she told a friend, a proof of her own inner strength. "I guess," she informed her anxious fiancée, "I'm just tough!"

Her mother, by contrast, had allowed herself to be "stepped on," she wrote Wes—until the creation of the Fellowship, that is, where she had been "trying to grab for herself a little of the world . . . that was being *taken* away from her as a result of [Wright's] jealousy, ego." Svetlana knew what had been promised—that the Gurdjieff work would be a core part of the Fellowship. But her mother didn't know how to get her agenda off the ground, and was once again, she told Wes, "more or less a prisoner of Taliesin."

"After all, my mother brought me into this topsy-turvy world," she lamented. "It's been topsy-turvy for her. . . . I feel so miserably sorry for her because of her lack of strength as regards him."

Svetlana knew what her mother was capable of. Before leaving she arranged a secret code with Betty Weber, an SOS sign for her housemate to come quickly and get her out of there. She was confident that they couldn't keep her by force—if only for fear of bad publicity.

With Svetlana at Taliesin, Wes waited anxiously for word. When she didn't write, he became fearful that she was being sucked back in. "Don't you feel a certain sense of cheapening by lingering around that manure house?" he wrote her. "Can it be that you've amicably made up with that skunk Wright? I don't really see how with him—Oh God! How I hate him and his filthy brood!"

When Svetlana didn't come home as planned, Wes descended into rages and nightmares. "Are we—are you—on good terms with the Wrights—or what—you been persuaded—or what—oh God! Why don't you let a fellow know—Svet? . . . I still regard Frank Lloyd Wright as one of the scaliest rascals yet unhung and his wife as one of the craziest and dirtiest feminine demons I've ever heard of! The sooner they both curl up and die—the better I'll like it."

BUT SVETLANA HAD her distractions: She was wowing the boys at Taliesin. The sixteen-year-old had matured dramatically during her six months away. "Gee, it's good to have a real *girl* around," she was being told. "In evening dress," Yen Liang wrote Wes, "she makes the rest of the girls look pale and worn."

"Thank God! I'm not here for good," Svetlana whispered to herself, laughing at the goings-on. Yet despite all her misgivings, she found she enjoyed the morning arguments about Laotse and Gurdjieff with her mother and father and their guests, the long walks in the frozen hills, skating and spending time with the animals, whose innocent mien she found reassuring.

Olgivanna kept her promise not to press her daughter to stay. Instead she tried to use the apprentices, among them Wes and Svetlana's mutual friend Yen Liang. But he wouldn't go along. By now Liang himself could no longer tolerate Wright's officiousness, his interventions in the social life of the apprentices, trying to keep men and women from what Wright considered salacious encounters after dark. Happening on an evening party, Mr. Wright had accused them of gathering only for sex. "I tell you, Wes, it used to be unbearable," Yen wrote. "Now it is, to me, only a big joke. I have tr[ied] to talk, but I gave that up too, as wasting energy. . . . 'Listen to him and chuckle to yourself' is the only way to make staying at Taliesin bearable."

Svetlana finally left after the New Year. On the morning of her last day, Wright assaulted her—accusing her, as Liang put it, "of luring the boys." Her stepfather's tirade was "an awful blow," she told Wes. For Louise Dees-Porch, it was proof that Wright was "becoming psychopathic." Yen found it an execrable display. "Mr. Wright must be old," he suggested to Wes. "He is probably now just going into naturally [sic] impotency in sexual life, and that makes him jealous of all the youngsters. . . . He has fallen down the scale of my list of so-called great men, and he was not so very high in ranking before that."

Taliesin, Wes conceded, seemed somehow "too attractive—too colorful, almost to escape! There lies the evil! No! Taliesin is utterly inorganic!—and can only breed evil—No real good can come from its fundamentally rotten core." He was relieved that Svetlana had escaped "from that gangrenous place." "[A]re there any hopeful signs of the breakup of the Fellowship?" he asked. "That is a thing that has to come. The place has become a canker that really threatens the future growth of any real art in this country."

For Peters, Taliesin was a sham poisoned by Wright's egotism. Even America's money-making centers, he thought, were more natural, more clean. "Frank Lloyd Wright has switched camps. As the Arch-Fiend—nay—worse—the arch Ego in disguise—he is far more dangerous than the evils of the city—the evils of the mob—simply from the fact that he wears the armor of the Archangel still and surrounds himself with his halos."

Wes was impressed with Svetlana, and grateful—and not a little proud—that she had returned from Taliesin unscathed. "I more and more realize that you have done an extremely strong thing in facing the old cur in his cage. You now are free from them—They know now that they can have no hold on you—no way to force you back—that you could really come and go as you please."

Svetlana thought her fiancé a bit silly. "Honestly, Wes, aren't you ashamed for letting F.L.W. get your goat, like that?" she replied. "The idea of giving him the absolute power over your emotional being—causing you to go through agonies—You're constantly saying he is a worm and why don't you let it go at that? I hate to talk about worms, they are so damnably slimy."

ALTHOUGH THE COUPLE found the idea of returning to Taliesin unthinkable, they had both begun to fear that they might not be capable of realizing their artistic ideals, at least not on their own. Wes worried that he would never be one of "the mighty—outstanding prophets," those men who created the only culture that really mattered. Svetlana had started studying the violin, but what with her housework, giving music lessons, and taking care of children, she had little time to pursue her own musical goals. Instead she was thinking of dropping music and disappearing into the wilderness with her love.

While Wes still wanted to struggle for a clean, beautiful life in the midst of the machine city, he felt unable to communicate with the local architects. "I am getting to shrink from any contact at all—They could never understand or wouldn't try to—anything I would have to say to them—so why try—and that's the way everyone is."

Peters did, however, communicate well enough to get clients. After completing his first house design, he arranged for Jack Wilson, one of the workers Wright had cheated out of back pay, to come down and help him build it. When Wilson arrived in Evansville, he reported that the Wrights still had their "spy system" in place. All the "old regulars" were involved: "Jack Howe—known here and there as 'Pussyfoot' Jack—alias—'Keyhole Howe'— playing a leading part—with poor Iovanna being utilized more and more consistently." Iovanna was now just nine years old.

WHEN THE NEW Taliesin prospectus made its way to Peters, he creased himself laughing. It actually listed himself and Svetlana among its graduates. "Also all the bushwa which composes the text—particularly the two lines on the beautiful relationship of sex at Taliesin—these things panicked me—and when I read further and mentally noted the discrepancies between what that bunkum claims the places is—and what it really is—I didn't know whether to cry or to break down in an uproarious fit of laughter—so I did the latter." Likewise, he found the Fellowship's newspaper column in the *Capital Times*—and a series of Taliesin radio broadcasts—pathetic. "That column is making Taliesin the laughing stock of Madison I am afraid. Oh—I wish they would stop that," he griped. "The next step will be to start endorsing shaving cream and stuff like that."

BUT THERE WAS good news: The Taliesin Fellowship had finally done some architecture. In March 1934, the Willeys arrived at Taliesin to review the new design for their home. Unbeknownst to Wright, someone pinned a sign on the studio bulletin board: "Lo! On the Horizon a Customer Appeareth. By God, He shall not Perish on this Earth." Wright was furious with his boys. But the Willeys were happy, Nancy Willey in particular. "Wright was very responsive to women," she recalled. They approved the new design, and this time the bids came in on budget. When they had their approval to break ground and the digging began, Edgar Tafel and Yen Liang were assigned to monitor things at the site. The house was finished before the first snowfall of 1934.

*   *   *

MR. WRIGHT'S PREOCCUPATION with reshaping his apprentices—body, mind, and spirit—continued. As Yen Liang wrote Wes in March 1934, Wright was now demanding the Fellowship's "unquestioning" loyalty. Wright laid it all out in a three-page "dissertation" defining the relation between a master and his apprentices. "He believes," Yen continued, "that the apprentices should follow him not only in his ideals in Architecture and its allied Arts, but they should also follow him in his ideals of life." Apprenticeship, Liang added, meant "a complete worship of its Master"; refusal would indicate to Wright that the apprentice was unfit to remain. "Such," Yen concluded, "are the latest light (or darkness) on the status of the Fellows."

"Something is certain to burst soon," Wes wrote to Svetlana. "Mr. Wright's insane (it can be nothing less than that) ego is going to drink blood yet. . . . we could not—could not—have remained there and remained sane."

That month Olgivanna sent a one-foot-square yellow cake to her daughter. "You know," Svetlana wrote Wes, "it looks so like all the Fellowship that I couldn't taste it and feel sort of sick when I think it is in my room." The letter accompanying the cake only made it worse. "[W]hen I read her words I feel that a witch sits behind them! And I feel all sort of creepy and unclean!"

Yen Liang was now planning his own exit. When fall came, he got into his Model A Ford and drove off. Wright thought he was going to China to get married, and that he would surely be back. Instead Yen remained in China, where he went on to become a major architect and eventually a chief designer of the United Nations buildings in New York.

WHEN SVETLANA GOT an opportunity to trade cooking dinners for room, board, and music lessons in the home of Chicago symphony violinist Winifred Cree, in the nearby suburb of Winnetka, she jumped at it. This time, though, she didn't let her mother know where she was going. At the Crees', she improved on the violin and learned the viola, both very quickly. Soon she was playing Haydn quartets with the family. She performed in recitals and joined the community orchestra as a violist. But she wasn't interested in performance as a career; her true goal was to become a composer.

Olgivanna somehow tracked her daughter down, and soon she was at her doorstep again, pleading for her to return to Taliesin. Though this visit, like the others, was unsettling, Svetlana held firm.

But Olgivanna was not to be denied. Edgar Tafel, too, disliked the way Wes Peters had taken the adolescent Svetlana away; now, with Olgivanna's help, he began his own campaign to get her back. He wrote letters to both Svetlana and Wes, complaining that Wes had committed an "injustice," that "could ruin a life that wasn't made to be ruined." If Svetlana returned to

Taliesin, he offered—surely with Olgivanna's authorization—she would be afforded the time to work exclusively on her music.

Tafel wrote Svetlana that her mother "cannot understand your happiness in being free." She was making a mistake, he advised her—stunting her personal development, her music, all to satisfy Wes Peters's willful possessiveness. If "there is any true love between you two," he warned, Wes wouldn't "stand in the way of your doing anything to better yourself mentally."

Tafel also confessed that he had a romantic interest of his own in Svetlana. Regardless, he insisted, the road to betterment passed through Taliesin.

Wes vituperated to Svetlana about Tafel's "unasked—and unwanted" advice. How on earth Tafel "got the germ of the idea" that anyone wanted his opinion, Peters could not fathom. "I guess it's just his poor breeding in the New York slums or wherever he was hatched."

"Why get so wrought up," Svetlana replied, "over a small kike from New York?"

WITH THE GROUND softened by Tafel, Olgivanna came calling again. "Mother just left—and oh—God, Wes—I'm sorry—but I feel goddamned miserable in this horrible city—oh—and honest—I'm awful homesick for the country, Wes—what'll I do?"

Olgivanna's scheming was beginning to pay off. Within days, Svetlana did something unexpected and extravagant: She sent Tafel some caviar. "I guess that very devil was in me when I did that," she wrote Wes, "—oh gosh! Damn—oh, what did I did?" Yet she confessed that she was no longer angered by Edgar's letter. There was something romantic beneath his irksome qualities. And, she added, she had something to learn from him—his superb musicianship. She would overlook his defects.

Wes understood. He too doubted his own powers, his ability to make a beautiful life and design great architecture. And he too missed Taliesin, he finally conceded, "the growing things—real work outside." But he also remembered the "the hates—the jealousies—the intrigues—the commercialization of Nature which is being developed there." If they returned, he warned her, neither of them "would ever gain the treasures" that they once had there. "Those days are gone. . . . [T]he golden glory of the place itself—that—Svet—is lost—gone!"

Encouraged by the caviar—and no doubt by Olgivanna—Tafel sent Svetlana another letter. He began with some innocent encouragement, advising her to practice preludes and fugues. But he also suggested that when next she visited Taliesin the two of them could borrow a car and go out and get drunk.

At this, Peters lost all restraint. "Oh Svet, Grrrrr," Peters exploded. "Now you go on about Edgar. Grrrrr and I certainly am aroused. Just as we now get ourselves free once and for all from that filthy Jew. This is not anti-semitism. . . . Grrr. I can't see it Svet. If you do weaken and write him, I really think that will be awful. . . . I regard Edgar as an enemy—a dirty little useless thing. . . . Svet—Svet! What in the world has come over you!!"

Svetlana wouldn't stand down. She suggested to Wes that racial hatred might be affecting his evaluation of the man.

"I honor the Jews as a race—very much indeed," he replied. "It hurts—Svet—to have you think that—that I would take advantage in that way." The trouble with Tafel, he explained, is that "whenever any of his race shows in him—it is the New York 'kike'—a disgrace to a great race—rather than the Hebrew. . . . All of Tafel's actions are pushed—prompted—run by the would-be cleverness of the kike—and I can see nothing else—and I believe in nothing else! . . .

"[W]hat I mean to say—is—the 'kike' is the essential part of *Edgar*—not the Jew—the kike—!!—the little—dirty—clawing—snooping—clever—one. . . . I can't—Svet—can't see how you could yet like him—I nearly choke when I think of his filthy face—his terrible curly kike hair—his awful awful—rotten face—Why—oh why could I never see it before!! I should have at Taliesin—when night after night Tafel went into the house and sold himself completely."

As angry as he was, Wes was clear-eyed enough to see Tafel's meddling as "the filthy work of Mrs. Wright. . . . Obviously she brings in all that bunch of whelps for the purpose of getting you all worked up for Taliesin again."

IN THE MEANTIME, another Jewish apprentice, Abe Dombar, had become the master's favorite at the Fellowship. Wright had made him supervisor of the carpenters and masons reconstructing Taliesin. Abe had learned much from Taliesin's master stonemason, and now was cutting his own fine walls of pinkish sandstone. Under Henry Klumb's guidance, his drafting skills were now considerable. Wright appreciated Abe's physicality, the ease with which he directed a horse-drawn plow in the field and made fantastic birds out of corn husks. He even installed Abe in a room in Taliesin itself, below the living room. In the morning Abe could hear through the floor as Mr. Wright im-provised on the piano. Wright took Abe along to buy supplies in Richland Center and helped out when it was Dombar's turn for kitchen duty. In the summertime, Wright took Abe walking with him in the countryside after all the other apprentices went home. The young man was so skilled at imitating birdsong that sometimes he actually fooled Wright.

And although Olgivanna was always telling the nineteen-year-old Jewish boy that he looked "oriental," and worked to break him of the habit of talking with his hands, it was Abe whom she selected to instruct Iovanna, and who was always chosen to drive in the Wrights' car to picnics.

At Christmas, with rouged cheeks and homemade whiskers, Dombar was Taliesin's Santa Claus, standing on a balcony and sending down individual presents on a wire to delighted recipients below. One Halloween, Abe attached pieces of punk to each finger, lit all ten, and performed a dance of fingered light. Wright told him that if he wanted, Abe could become a dancer.

But Dombar had learned from Olgivanna that he could be much more. "Mr. Wright thinks a great deal of you," she told him. When everybody else had left the Fellowship, the master would count on Dombar to carry it on. Abe, however, was not sure he wanted to be the chosen one. Taliesin was not a place for family men. One by one, he had watched couples leave the Fellowship; the three who came in with him that first year had quickly departed. Staying at Taliesin, Dombar realized, would mean forgoing not only professional independence, but probably a family as well.

If he should leave, however, he was told it would "break the Master's heart."

Then a Taliesin visitor appeared to tip the balance. Dombar, who was raised an ardent Zionist, had another dream as well, one whose realization made marrying a Jewish girl an easy and celebrated thing. Rabbi Kadushin's wife had just spoken at Taliesin about the movement back to the land. "She made us all feel the new quality of thought awakening among the Jews." Dombar felt "such a strong urge to return to Palestine," he told his sister, that he just couldn't stay on. He went so far as to make contact with Dan Ben Dor, an architect in Palestine, who offered him a job if he would come. Dombar felt he could help build a Jewish state by introducing organic architecture there.

Being an observant Jew at Taliesin was not easy. Abe resented having to walk ten miles just to get to where he could hitchhike to Madison for Jewish High Holiday services. Once he found no ride and ended up spending the night in the crook of a sand dune.

One day, Abe made the mistake of sharing his dream of Palestine with another apprentice. "I was down at the river swimming," he recalled, "when one of the fellows said, 'Mr. Wright wants to talk to you[;] I told him that you were going to Israel and he wants to talk to you.' "

Dombar went with trepidation. "I'm sorry you had to hear it from somebody else," he told him.

"You know there never will be a Jewish state," the master replied. "The Jews were created to give their expertise to the whole world."

Wright then offered Dombar a place in his personal studio at Taliesin, a drafting space right next to his own. Abe would no longer be just one of the apprentices in the big drafting room: He would have a place at the master's side.

Abe felt flattered, but his mind was made up. "I began to feel that he looked upon me as a sponge absorbing 'Wright' for two years and now he wanted to squeeze me for a few years." He didn't turn down Wright's offer outright, but he didn't say yes either. To Wright, leaving Taliesin was both an act of disloyalty and a great risk for those who dared try. The "outside world," he warned those contemplating departure, was a "bad world." As Dombar recalled, his words left more than a few apprentices "afraid they'd be contaminated."

The possibility of flight, however, was in the air.

COMINGS AND GOINGS

TALIESIN AS A COLLECTIVE HAD miraculously survived its first year in Depression-plagued America. But Frank Lloyd Wright was constantly looking for new young people to keep his voracious little organism alive. Apprentices were leaving as fast they were coming; by the second year, half of the original group had left.

A look at the names in the roster reveals another ominous pattern. Of the nine women who arrived that first October—making up a remarkable one quarter of those seeking entry into an essentially all-male field—only one remained: Marybud Roberts, who had married fellow apprentice John Lautner. The struggles of women like Betty Weber and Louise Dees-Porch, sent to cover windows with curtains instead of drawing them, was typical.

That Wright affectionately referred to the apprentices as "my boys" was no accident. If the Taliesin Fellowship were ever to fulfill Wright's vision of a self-contained model community, however—at least a heterosexual one—it had a long way to go.

GENDER WAS NOT the only shift. By the end of 1933, all the paid professionals were gone. With the exception of himself, Frank Lloyd Wright's architecture practice was now an entirely amateur operation.

Henry Klumb was among the last to leave. He had arrived at Taliesin idealizing Wright, even writing poems about him. In his five-year tenure there, he had created a stunning black-and-white cover for the 1926 edition of Wright's Wasmuth portfolio, and worked on redesigning Taliesin and Hillside to house the Fellowship. He had been the point man on the Willey residence, the germ of Wright's new vision for middle-class houses. He had also played a central role in the design of San Marcos in the Desert, one of the projects featured in the Museum of Modern Art's show.

But when the paying apprentices arrived, the twenty-eight-year-old architect had found himself being sent out to do carpentry, and even menial tasks like chopping wood and fetching water, with the other draftsmen. The new, unpaid apprentices, on the other hand, were suddenly being granted open access to the master. Klumb found their "backstage gossip" particularly noxious, especially when it turned against him. With so little work, Klumb was left with almost no opportunity to do any designing.

In September 1933, Henry Klumb left Taliesin for a trip with his wife, fully expecting to return. But while they were vacationing in Brainerd, Minnesota, he had an epiphany. The outside world may have been bad, he realized, but professionally Taliesin was worse. It was clear to him that the International Style was winning in America, and he saw that it might be easier to join 'em than to beat 'em. "I decided," he recalled, "to face the cold reality of the world and its empty promises. Mimicking the past was still adhered to, but mimicking the imported style assured success and instant acknowledgement of status."

The opportunity to work trumped all, even his commitment to Wright's organic architecture. The Klumbs weren't alone in Brainerd: Another of Wright's paid draftsmen, Steven Arneson, decided to defect at around the same time, and the two friends soon found architectural work in the town. If Wright knew the real reason for their departure, he was in denial about it. He told Abe Dombar that the Klumbs had left because Elsa was pregnant, and they wanted to start their own household.

FORTUNATELY FOR THE Wrights, there seemed to be no shortage of eager recruits to replace the disenchanted. And Henry Klumb had left behind a legacy greater than any single design: Under his tutelage, Jack Howe had developed into an exceptionally capable draftsman. Howe was eager, well organized, and always there. On his own initiative, he brought order to Wright's disorganized drawing archive. "I knew where the drawings were, thanks to my filing system," he remembered, "and . . . I somehow managed to be there whenever Mr. Wright would come in." With his talent and devotion, Howe quickly emerged as the head of Wright's drafting studio after Klumb's departure.

Often, as day broke, Jack was the only one in the small studio—only eight drafting tables for twenty-three apprentices—when Mr. Wright entered. "Where is everybody?" Wright asked, forgetting "that he had sent them out to build the dams, work on the construction of Hillside, or bring in the corn crop," Howe recalled. "He would then ask me why I wasn't out there helping them with these emergencies."

Wright was always in a good mood when he arrived there, often humming a tune. He was forever repeating one of his favorite jokes—some of them "'darky' stories," Howe recalled, "in the days before you didn't talk down to blacks." Howe remembered how Wright "would mount the stairs leading to the area above the vault in which the Japanese prints were kept, sit at the old Steinway piano that was there, and roll out a few bars of his Bach-Beethoven-type improvisations" before going to work on a drawing.

Wright told the apprentices that he heard Beethoven in his head as he designed. "When you listen to Beethoven," he told them, "you are listening to a builder. You are seeing him take a theme, a motif, and building with it. . . . Building is the same thing." And indeed there are clear parallels between the music his father had taught him to appreciate and the architecture he created as an adult. Beethoven composed in modular fashion, particularly his later works, building up from small units known as *motives*, rather than from a longer melodic or lyrical line. Similarly, Wright drafted up his architecture on a grid, using simple, modular forms he repeated and varied throughout the entire edifice, achieving what he called a "symphonic" unity. From his use of what Wright considered "integral ornament," to his rejection of the symmetrical balance of the symphony in favor of codas that were often rich in thematic content, Beethoven offered a rich vein of inspiration to an architect eager to transcend the old symmetries of classical architecture.

GENE MASSELINK HAD no architectural aspirations. When he received the invitation to join the Fellowship from Wright's secretary, Karl Jensen, he didn't know that the young Dane had decided to resign, nor that this would matter to him in the least. Just three days later, Jensen turned in a two-page resignation letter. In it he assured Wright that he wasn't leaving because of the "little dissensions here that often place me 'between the devil and the deep sea.'" No, it was his own "temperament" that wasn't "suitable to the Fellowship experiment." He claimed he could no longer bear the "humiliation" of being in poverty. "Even the rich experience and great privilege of associating with a man like yourself does not alleviate this," he wrote. "I can no longer borrow anything so I have to go out to make enough to meet the obligations I have incurred and provide myself with those necessities I must have to keep my self-respect."

In reality, it was the other apprentices who humiliated Jensen. And no wonder: He made something of a spectacle of himself. The young Dane had a habit of appropriating Wright's gestures and ways of speaking, walking about with a cane, wearing his hair long. Jensen read from Friedrich Nietzsche's *Thus Spake Zarathustra* at Taliesin's own Sunday services. Fancying himself a ladies' man, he powdered his face with talc before going out on dates in town, and quoted Wrightisms to the young women he entertained in his private room. In the eyes of the more plainspoken American lads, he was fawning and arrogantly continental. He was also an anti-Semite who disapproved of the influx of Jewish apprentices—and let others know it. He became an irresistible target.

Wes Peters, who considered Karl Jensen a "dutiful buffoon who goes around snooping," had once circulated a poem he wrote about the man:

> *Karl Jensen came from far away*
> *He crossed the broad Atlantic*
> *He learned to quote what Frank Wright wrote*
> *But quoth it inorganic.*

Jensen had also become the butt of practical jokes. After Jensen affected a Wrightian walking cane, Peters and Edgar Tafel nailed it into the brush of a push broom. Another time, when the pranksters discovered that Jensen was in his room courting several female apprentices in a cozy cocktail gathering by the fire, they climbed up to the roof and smoked them out by covering the flue.

Wright himself seemed to relish tales of Jensen's torment. He even approved a column lampooning the man that ran in the Madison *Capital Times*'s "At Taliesin" space after Jensen decided to resign. A brewing revolution, the piece began, had been unearthed. "From an authentic manuscript of the revolutionary forces the general setup of the new liberal government officials was to be as follows: Chief Commander, Karl E. Jensen; Secretary to Commander, K. Edward Jensen; Dean of Work. E. K. Jensen; Dean of Women, Edward Jensen; Architect General, Jeans E. Jensen; Mulch Expert, Jensen Jensen; Chief Secret Police, Oscar Jensen. . . . The existing government suspects Karl Jensen as one culprit in this revolutionary force. Jensen has a long criminal record and was involved in the well-known Jensen Affair and the Jensen Putsch. Jensen refuses to talk."

Olgivanna was just as vexing to Jensen. "The woman," the young Dane reportedly told an apprentice, "was a foreigner, didn't understand America— had no place here and was 'no good.' "

Jensen had ended his resignation letter with an effort, no doubt sincere, to stay in Wright's good graces. "You are," he wrote, "one of the few truly great and loveable human beings of our time." But it was to no avail. His remarks about Olgivanna had gotten back to Wright. "For that," Wright wrote, "I

The Taliesin Chorus, 1938. Gene Masselink (in glasses) is standing next to piano; the shorter man to his left is Jack Howe, and Wes Peters is seated in front of Howe. Curtis Besinger is at left, directing.

should promptly kick you out. . . . Whatever your private opinion of Olgi-vanna may be she is my right hand man in this effort and whatever her short-comings she is of ultimate value to me as next of kin. Had you some of her quality of faithfulness and a self development comparable to hers in any way you would not be leaving Taliesin on any account."

Jensen, Wright sneered, had a "servant mind." "What made you weak here," he wrote, "will make you weak everywhere you go and you will walk out of one thing into another until you walk into an insane asylum or into the poor house."

AS THE DEPARTING paid staff were slowly but surely being replaced by ap-prentices, it was Olgivanna who decided that Gene Masselink should sup-plant Jensen. Like Wright, she had taken a shine to him. Lanky, wearing wire-rimmed glasses, Gene was a talented listener with what Fellowship client Nancy Willey called a "quiet, silky, silky way." He would gently tweak an ear as his signature good-bye. He loved to sing, his brother recalled, "dragg[ing] his voice up from the floor between his shoes." As a kid he and his mother started singing Christmas carols before Halloween. At Taliesin his baritone became a mainstay in the Taliesin Chorus, a group he later led. When Yen Liang composed a song, Gene learned to sing it in Chinese, with Yen accompanying on the violin.

Under Wright's influence, Gene now sought in his paintings to convert the fields, birds, and flowers into an abstract language. There was about him, apprentice Kay (Schneider) Rattenbury remembered, "a radiance, a heavenly radiance, of lightness and love and devotion that you could see . . . the mo-ment you saw him." Writer, painter, musician, bookkeeper, he seemed to do it all—except architecture.

SOON GENE WAS writing letters under the title of "Secretary to Mr. Wright." Picking up where Jensen left off, he tackled the piles of eager letters from Fellowship applicants and angry ones from creditors. Pecking away with two fingers, Gene did everything: took dictation, deciphered and tran-scribed Wright's scrawling handwritten notes, made up construction lists, as-signed rooms to incoming apprentices. He kept the books, paid the bills, and ordered all supplies. Masselink had a way of singing as he worked that charmed Wright. "Gene was the only one," Iovanna recalled, "who could make a strong effect on my father." Now that Svetlana was gone, it fell to Wright's young secretary to calm him in his rages and vituperations.

Forbidden by his father from seeing a movie starring Clara Bow because she was divorced, Masselink found himself living in the house of a man and his third wife who had been his former mistress. Wright had Masselink moved to a room at the foot of the stairs just below his bedroom, where he could call the young man in the middle of the night. As a smoker, Gene was forced to sneak outside and hide behind a distant wall to indulge the habit, which Wright forbade. At least he didn't have to worry about being discovered by Olgivanna, who taught him to hold his cigarette in the Russian manner, between the index finger and thumb, pinkie aloft. Mrs. Wright proved a valuable friend to Gene Masselink: When his room turned out to be too damp, it was she who had him moved to drier quarters.

The job was all-consuming. During the day, Gene worked in a small office next to Wright's. When Wright hosted clients in his office, he had his secretary hide behind a Japanese screen to take notes in secret. Even at night, when Wright liked to work in his bedroom, Gene would be there, working at a little desk set up next to the master's.

"Lists," Gene wrote, "lists everywhere and lists for everything. Large important Madison lists on large white paper. Spring Green lists on any old paper. Dodgeville grocery and butcher lists on ruled notepads from the kitchen. Lists typewritten and list handwritten in every kind of pen and or pencil within reach. Lists lost and half remembered—they flutter about me dominating my kingdom of letters and articles and filing cards and endless odds and ends of what is bravely called 'business.' "

Gene was always running, racing to town to get pig feed, casing nails, litharge for the roof, or bread for tea, tracking down one apprentice or another, hunting down Mr. or Mrs. Wright or both. Wright enlisted him as chauffeur, always pushing him to drive faster. And Gene handled Taliesin's incoming calls, which was no small thing. Whenever an outside call came in, he was forced to stop what he was doing and traipse all over the grounds till he'd tracked down the recipient.

For years, the Fellowship made do with a single wooden box telephone on Mr. Wright's office wall, loaned by the Farmer's Cooperative. The farmers' wives often listened in to Taliesin calls on the local party line, making it impossible for Wright to conduct his affairs without everyone knowing. Because he didn't pay his bills, Wright was not allowed to make long-distance calls; Gene had to be dispatched to Madison to send telegrams instead.

Keeping Taliesin's accounts was near impossible. Indeed, Wright was opposed to cost-accounting on general principle: "We don't need any records," he told Masselink. "We're never going to make any money." Yet it fell to Gene to judge how much to pay out to creditors based on what was coming in, and he worked frantically to keep up, routinely missing meals and sleep. Visits to Spring Green were an ordeal, as merchants ran out of their shops shouting "Pay me! Pay me!" when they saw him. He would soothe the loudest with a promise to send five dollars toward the account. Noting the strain Masselink was under, Olgivanna tried her best to shield him from her husband's demands.

On top of it all, Gene was still burdened with the usual apprentice chores. He would wake up in the pitch dark so that he could hike by flashlight and arrive at Taliesin's small dam by 5:30 A.M. to regulate the dynamo, which provided electricity for the buildings. At lights out, 10:00 P.M., he trekked back out to direct the water away from the dynamo, shutting off the compound's electric supply; he returned to find the apprentices reading by candlelight.

At the end of her son's first year, Gene's mother sent Wright a note thanking him for bringing Gene to Taliesin. "You have been most kind to my precious son and he has had a very happy year with you. We are indeed, very grateful." Gene, too, felt grateful to have entered a world where life was considered an art and art a way of living. When he took a brief break to visit a farm where he'd been working when he was accepted into the Fellowship, he stood on a hill and looked down at the buildings dotting the low hills that rolled down to Lake Michigan. In that moment, he wrote, "I saw clearer than I had ever seen before how the parts of my thinking and working and dreaming were . . . as separated from the whole of my life as the buildings of that small farm below are separated from each other. Just as meaningless a pattern as that barn, pigsty, chickenhouse, silo, and farmhouse make in scattered confusion on the hill slope, so meaningless were my painting and drawing." In Taliesin he had found "another country with greater hills—in a life which was as completely one creative unit as the buildings of Taliesin are themselves." He was in the midst of a "great movement toward the flowering of a great purpose and ideal . . . working hard within it.

"I stood upon the hill with all the blue of the world in my eyes and longed to immediately rejoin that endless work for organic creative life at Taliesin."

BEFORE TAKING OVER as Wright's personal secretary, Gene had been assigned as the projectionist for the just-opened Taliesin Playhouse. Overburdened as he was, he kept that job, too. As with everything else in Wright's self-contained world, the master insisted on adding his own twist to the moviegoing experience, modifying the projector to allow the film's oscillating soundtrack to be projected on a red border he'd had mounted at the left side of the screen. Watching this direct visual analog to the voices and music—of necessity slightly out of sync with the movie—must have been distracting. Gene's responsibilities soon grew to booking films, often foreign ones, from the distributors. Running a movie theater in those days was not without risk: On at least two occasions the films they rented caught fire, and in Taliesin's precarious financial state even the loss of a six-dollar projector bulb was a minor financial crisis.

Sunday had become Taliesin's culture day. Beyond the church service, Wright gave small chats and longer talks to the apprentices, usually after breakfast. "The common man," he told them, "is interested only in ham and eggs, fornication, and a good snore." The apprentices and Wright roared at this one. "That is what the acres and acres of little boxes he lives in are for."

The Sunday afternoon movie shows, which included the *Pathé News*, a Disney cartoon and a feature film, were open to the public; they gave the Fellowship a chance to show off, build local understanding and support, and—it was hoped—eventually make money. Before the feature, the apprentices offered a short interpretive introduction; afterward, they provided classical music. The fifty-cent admission included coffee and cookies served around the fireplace. Wright's favorite films included Rene Clair's *Liberty for Us*, which he showed a dozen times over the years, and John Ford's *The Informer*.

Some apprentices thought the Taliesin Playhouse a crazy indulgence. "The Theater is the biggest foolish affair we have yet to try to do in the history of the Fellowship," Yen Liang had complained. "Mr. Wright, every week, pays from $15 to $25 for a picture. And the audience would often be only two or three people. They pay 50 cents. That amounts to from $1.00 to $1.50—while we have no money to buy coal and other necessities."

In addition to movies, the Playhouse hosted a constant stream of guest lecturers and performers, among them Carl Sandburg, artist Rockwell Kent, and concert pianist Anton Rovinsky. Sometimes the lights went out in the middle of a concert. That usually meant that a turtle had gotten into the dynamo: Taliesin was still relying on the hydroelectric generator Wright had installed. An apprentice would be sent down the hill to extract the intruder.

In November 1935, Paul Robeson came at the invitation of Edgar Tafel, who had seen the celebrated African American singer while attending Margaret Naumberg's Walden School in New York. Mr. Wright was away, but Olgivanna gave her blessing. Naumberg wasn't the only Gurdjieffian in Robeson's circle: Alfred Orage had attempted to entice the singer—apparently, without success—into the work. Robeson, whose triumphs on the London stage included *Othello* and *The Emperor Jones*, had also traveled to the Soviet Union and sung in its factories, where for the first time he felt like a human being, not a racial type. "You cannot imagine what that means to me as a Negro," he declared.

On Wright's return, the excited apprentices raved about Robeson's appearance at the playhouse. His only reaction was fury at Olgivanna for having invited a black man to Taliesin, perhaps in reaction to the murder of Cheney.

* * *

THE APPRENTICES ALSO organized musical performances and plays of their own. One of them was staged by a young apprentice named Nicholas Ray, who later became famous as the director of *Rebel Without a Cause* and *Johnny Guitar*. In 1934, the strapping Wisconsin boy had just dropped out of the architectural program at the University of Chicago and come to study architecture at Taliesin at the urging of Wright's friend Thornton Wilder, the Pulitzer Prize-winning playwright.

Ray directed one of the Fellowship's first productions, a musical farce called *Piranese Calico* written and composed by the apprentices. As Ray wrote, the piece was their first attempt to "establish drama as architecture, where it belongs, and do it [as] indigenously as possible." Wright's theater was, he thought, "neither temple nor brothel, but a place where stage and audience architecturally melt rhythmically into one, and the performance—the play of the senses—and the audience blend together into an entity because of the construction of the whole."

But it was the dramatic arts, not architecture, that truly moved Ray: After only five months he left the Fellowship for New York, where he began directing plays and joined the radical Workers Laboratory Theater. For the

Paul Robeson's visit to Taliesin

rest of his life, he would credit Wright as a major influence on his film work—especially his taste for Cinemascope, with its strong horizontal line.

NICHOLAS RAY LEFT to pursue a theater career; Fred Langhorst left over his dog. After a year and a half at Taliesin, Langhorst's faithful companion, Rogue, made a fatal misstep: He ate a chicken. It wasn't the first time one of the Wrights' farm animals was lost to a dog. Olgivanna's hound, who sat proudly with the Wrights during the Sunday night "formals," had already consumed several chicks and even killed a sheep. But Rogue was just an apprentice dog, and Olgivanna demanded that he be killed for his infraction. Though still committed to Wright and architecture, Langhorst up and left the Fellowship at once.

"I went to look for you," Wright wrote him soon after, "and found you gone. . . . Of course I realize what a blow the loss of Rogue means to you. It was because I realized what a dog might mean in your life that I made an exception and allowed you to have one here. So perhaps I am to blame for your affliction."

Wright's self-recrimination lasted barely a sentence. "Some day," he continued, "you will lose your Father and your Mother and nearest and dearest of kin as I have and probably this trial was given to you to gain fortitude to meet such losses." Wright, who hadn't attended either of his parents' funerals, then gave Fred some advice on mourning. "I didn't want to sympathize over much with you because I have found sympathy debilitating and of little help. Courage and action are best." He went on to list Langhorst's weaknesses: his inability to "command" himself in the morning, his habit of starting things and not finishing them, his tendency to be impatient. In sum, Wright concluded, he lacked "the guts to stay put—hell or no."

Yet Wright gave Langhorst another chance to do just that, informing him that he was welcome to return to Taliesin. He did.

SOME CAME; MOST eventually went. Others were never allowed in.

"Why do you want to be an architect, boy?" Wright asked Antonio Rudolfo Oaxaca Quinn, a six-foot-tall Irish-Mexican fresh out of Los Angeles High School.

"I want to build cities, sir," Quinn replied, transfixed by Wright's penetrating eyes.

"Whole cities?" Wright asked.

"Yes, sir," Quinn replied. "Cities with room for a man to grow, and breathe."

Quinn recalled years later how Wright glanced without comment at some school drawings he had brought along and then turned his eyes back up at the young man.

"What's the matter with your speech, boy?"

"I don't know sir," Quinn replied. "What seems to be the problem?"

"You're stammering. That seems to be the problem. Why are you stammering?"

He was a little nervous, he explained.

"There's no reason to be tongue-tied around me. Open your mouth."

As Quinn stood there agape, Wright came over and peered inside. Frank had Antonio lift up his tongue.

"There's the problem," Wright announced, with Quinn's tongue still high in the air. "Your frenum's too thick. You should have it cut."

Quinn had never even heard of a frenum, so Wright opened his own mouth, pulled his tongue aside, and showed him the piece of tissue that connects the tongue to the floor of the mouth.

"If you want to be an architect you have to be able to communicate your ideas. Your clients won't listen to you if you stammer." He then sent the hopeful young man away with the name of a doctor, and invited him to return once he had had it fixed. The young man walked outside, tore up the note with the doctor's name, and threw the pieces into the breeze. He wasn't convinced that he needed the operation and couldn't afford it even if he did.

But Taliesin still beckoned, and Quinn was not the quitting type. A year later he returned, assuming that Wright wouldn't remember his frenum. Wright took one look at him and asked him to repeat, "Peter Piper picked a peck of pickled peppers."

Quinn stammered his way through it.

"Damn it, boy," Wright exclaimed, "That frenum's still there. What kind of student are you going to be if you can't follow simple instructions?"

"But I can't afford the operation, sir," Quinn replied.

"Then you can't afford to be an architect."

Wright sent him away again, telling him not to return until he'd had the surgery.

This time Quinn went to see a specialist who confirmed Wright's diagnosis. The surgery would cost $150. After telling the doctor about his meeting with Frank Lloyd Wright and his desire to join the Fellowship, the doctor allowed Quinn to pay him whenever he could.

Unfortunately, the surgery only exacerbated the young man's condition.

"My tongue," Quinn recalled, "was not used to flapping around unfastened, and I could not get it to do what I wanted." Still hoping to join Taliesin, he spotted an ad for a drama school that emphasized elocution and speech, run by former actress Katherine Hamil.

Anthony Quinn mastered his flapping tongue, but he never returned to Taliesin.

IT WASN'T JUST frenum-induced mumbling; the Wrights had no tolerance for aesthetic imperfection. For Frank Lloyd Wright, ugliness was a sin. He strove to make life's every aspect beautiful, a compulsion he imbibed during his four years in Japan. The importance the Japanese put on beautiful form was to him a "song of heaven." He was thrilled by the way they made mundane life beautiful, converted profane daily tasks into ceremonial rite. Every human practice, including an individual's posture, held a possibility for pleasurable form.

At Taliesin, the way apprentices looked, stood, walked, dressed, spoke, and kept their rooms were all subject to scrutiny. "Let your hair grow behind the ears," he advised them. "Join the long-haired tribe." Applicants like Quinn whom the Wrights considered physically defective, uncomely, or noticeably overweight, were usually rejected. Jewish apprentices, like Abe Dombar, who spoke too loudly and gesticulated with their hands were instructed to lower their voices and to develop an economy of gesture. A Chinese female apprentice was finally cleansed of her offensive giggle. When the apprentice Yen Liang shaved his head for the fun of it, Wright was appalled. "You know very well," Olgivanna scolded him, "Mr. Wright does not like hair cut short. Why do you do it?"

From the time of his first trip to Japan, Wright embraced the Shinto ideal of fashioning heaven in life's design on earth, which he found superior to the Christian way of denying earthly existence to prepare for heaven. As far as he was concerned, heaven's primal feature was its beauty. He was enthralled by the Japanese art of flower arranging, which resonated with Louis Sullivan's teachings on the orders and energies of flowers, as contained in their complex axes. At Taliesin he expected all his apprentices to learn the practice, advising his American boys never to pick up an upturned branch, only those curving down. While building the Imperial Hotel, he also became fascinated by the tea ceremony, which the Japanese first developed in their monasteries. Although the body position required was too hard on his knees, and its repetitiveness eventually bored him, the "philosophy of tea" always remained for Wright a template for a mindful way of living. He encouraged incoming apprentices to read Okakura Kakuzo's 1906 *Book of Tea*, even sitting them down and reading it aloud to them.

* * *

FOR THE WRIGHTS, work itself was an art. Olgivanna, too, saw ordinary tasks as pathways toward a more self-aware engagement with the world. Much of "the work" she had practiced with Gurdjieff, of course, involved manual labor of all sorts, above all the preparation of food. Work was part of a discipline designed to make each disciple feel present to himself by being one with his work. Like the Japanese tea service, the Wrights informed their apprentices, all work, no matter how menial, was important and should be marked by beauty both in its performance and its result. Table decoration and the pouring of mortar were treated equally as high art. There was a right way to hammer a nail, to stand, to serve the soup, to dress. And the act of serving should bring out the utmost grace in the servant. An ungainly table setting, a poorly cooked meal, a fireplace inadequately stoked—all became stains on one's record.

Jim de Long, an apprentice who arrived in later years, recalled one such "stain." While preparing breakfast in the Wrights' personal dining room, de Long had carefully ladled out Wright's piping hot, steel-cut oatmeal in a bowl, then set it aside so that he could clear the table before bringing it in. Returning to the kitchen, he discovered to his horror that someone had absconded with the bowl. There was nothing to do but scrape the remnants from the bottom of the pot, and serve them to Wright. Olgivanna chased de Long into the kitchen, furious. "You have ruined your master's oatmeal!" she screamed, completely out of control.

Beauty often trumped utility. Bill Michels, who lived all his life on one of Taliesin's neighboring farms, quietly recalled Wright the farmer. Wright did some strange things, the wizened old farmer recalled; among other things, he demanded that the apprentices spend days arranging bales of hay into a design he particularly liked—and then either threw it away or left it to rot.

And then there were the cows. One day the Wrights were gazing across their fields when Olgivanna mentioned to Frank that the color of their Holstein cows, "black and white like crumpled newspapers," didn't look as good on the landscape as would Guernseys. The Guernsey was nowhere near as productive a dairy cow, but no matter; Frank replaced the Holsteins.

Among the habits Wright found particularly ugly were smoking and drunkenness, the latter perhaps because he had watched Sullivan's alcoholic decline. Nonetheless, during the Fellowship's first year, Olgivanna convinced him to allow the apprentices to make wine from the grapes they harvested. One day the American painter Rockwell Kent came to visit, and the wine was served at dinner—in coffee cups. Many apprentices drank their fill, and after dinner they made a ruckus, singing loudly, hooting and hollering.

Some were seen running across the rooftops. Robert Bishop went over to Wright's Cord convertible, removed the radiator cap, and urinated into the opening—"to save alcohol," he told Edgar Tafel. (Alcohol was an essential ingredient of antifreeze.)

After breakfast the next morning, Wright summoned all the apprentices to a meeting in the drafting room, and asked everyone who consumed more than one cup of wine the night before to step forward. Nearly everyone did. When he upped the amount to more than two, four confessed. After giving them all a talk on alcoholism and how it wasn't acceptable at the Fellowship, Wright told the four worst offenders to follow him to his office—where he "invited" them to "pack up and leave."

"Sir, were any of your clients alcoholics?"one of the four asked Wright. Then another chimed in with a question about a certain house. Before long, Wright was regaling the four with stories about his clients. When he finished he said, "Boys, go back to work, and don't do it again."

10.

SORCERERS' APPRENTICES

"TALIESIN WAS MUCH HONORED LAST Sunday," trumpeted the July 26, 1934, edition of "At Taliesin," "by the visit of Georgi Gurdjieff, the noted philosopher and leader of the famous work at the Prieuré Fontainebleau."

It was her master's first visit, and Olgivanna was thrilled. Having lost the Prieuré, Gurdjieff was living in a Paris hotel room over the Café de la Paix, and looking for a new home for the Institute. If things went well, she knew, it could be Taliesin. Frank respected the man's philosophy, had learned the movements, and had even issued the invitation for the visit. Just how far would he be willing to go?

Olgivanna used her authority over the Fellowship's daily routine to create a place her special guest would find familiar. Just like Gurdjieff's charges at the Prieuré, the Taliesin apprentices were learning the deep truths by doing, not through book learning. They were routinely instructed in self-observation and encouraged to strive toward a high standard of comportment. Through the kitchen, the fields, the chorus, and the drafting room, they were taught to correlate their faculties (as Taliesin's original prospectus promised), and to work toward the refashioning of their fragmented selves into a unified "I." Even the Fellowship's hours and weekly rhythms matched those of the Prieuré—except that here the day-long discipline of hard physical labor was followed not by dance, but by work at the drawing board.

Olgivanna cast the Taliesin Fellowship as a kind of esoteric brotherhood, in which her husband possessed a secret knowledge about the deep structure of the natural world. Even though some, like Jack Howe, poked fun at the philosophical fancies of the master's wife, Wright understood how similar they were to his own understanding of the world. Wright believed that the universe is suffused with correspondences between the world below and the world above; throughout his life he sought to use the beauty of organic architecture to reveal those relations. Architecture was a way not just to build buildings, but also to gain spiritual knowledge—a kind of Gnostic exercise. In his view, it was a spiritual regimen that could not be taught; its secrets could only be gleaned through constant practice at his side.

The Taliesin Fellowship and the Institute for the Harmonious Development of Man had much in common.

OLGIVANNA KNEW THE risks of this first face-to-face meeting between Wright and Gurdjieff. Her husband was thin-skinned, her master an outrageous provocateur.

The Gurdjieff who arrived at Taliesin was not the same man who had been the rage in New York ten years before. "He had grown fat," Claude Bragdon recalled after seeing him in New York. "[H]e looked untidy; time had turned his long, black ringmaster's moustache to gray." Nonetheless, in Gurdjieff's eyes Bragdon still spotted that "old, arrogant, undaunted" look.

Gurdjieff's search for money, supporters, and an American home was nothing new. What was new was his desperation. He came to Taliesin from Chicago, where he was trying to shore up the groups Jean Toomer had abandoned. Toomer, now living in New Mexico, refused his call. Gurdjieff doubted Olgivanna's capacity to lead, but he needed someone to run things, and he had his eye on Taliesin. And she appears to have led him to believe such a thing was possible; when Gurdjieff arrived, he acted almost as if he already had the deal.

On July 22, 1934, the apprentices finally met the great man about whom Olgivanna talked so reverently. Olgivanna lured Svetlana back to Taliesin for the occasion, in the apparent hope that Gurdjieff might convince her to return permanently. After that first formal Sunday night dinner, Edgar Tafel played some of Gurdjieff and de Hartmann's compositions. Then the group listened as someone read from one of Gurdjieff's manuscripts, likely *Beelzebub's Tales to His Grandson*.

Gurdjieff immediately took charge. After requesting that the apprentices search out the toughest fowl they had, he took little bags of spices out of his pockets and made a wonderful repast. He taught the apprentices a recipe for sauerkraut so spicy that Gene Masselink thought it "would knock the roof off Corrells Drug Store if ignited."

Svetlana was appalled. "The last two days," she wrote Wes, had been "horrible—most of the time spent with Gurdjieff. A strange, kindly at times, ferocious, and violent at others times, man—O—I can't explain to you what it was like to see him treat us all like guinea pigs in his laboratory experimenting to see reactions set in."

Gurdjieff at least confirmed her appraisal of her stepfather. "You will get angry," the mystic told her privately, "but I want to tell you something. I have traveled much, seen millions of people—idiots. Not idiots *physically*, but *idiots*—but I've never seen such a big idiot as Mr. Wright is!" He also provided her with a kind of succor. She was "a poor girl," he said. A child should at least have one parent to whom she could turn in times of need. She had none, and had a right to expect more.

Gurdjieff completely dominated Wright in his own home. "He yelled at him," Svetlana wrote Wes, "told him to get up off the couch and sleep in his *bed*, called him down for things—and—o—it was a bit pitiful." Gurdjieff treated Wright like one of his followers, she reported. And Wright behaved as if he was "absolutely cowed." Her mother's faith in Gurdjieff was "so great that I know, she wishes with all her heart that she were free and could follow him."

The tension between the masters simmered for days; Taliesin had never seen anything like it. Finally, as Gurdjieff's teachings dominated yet another after-dinner session, Wright tossed a spark in his guest's direction. "Well, Mr. Gurdjieff, this is very interesting," Wright interjected. "I think I'll send some of my young people to you in Paris. Then they can come back to me and I'll finish them off."

"*You* finish! You are idiot," Gurdjieff retorted angrily. "*You* finish! No. *You* begin. I finish!"

Olgivanna did not hesitate to take sides. "You know, Frank," she said, "Mr. Gurdjieff is right."

Humiliated by both Gurdjieff and his wife, in front of his apprentices no less: It was too much for Wright. A handful of apprentices rose to their master's defense, as was gingerly reported in "At Taliesin." "The conversation turned on him," an apprentice wrote, "a difference of opinion quickens the tempo and we hear of the relation of the disciple to the master, of Orage to Gurdjieff, Saint Paul to Jesus."

But then, all at once, "lights go on in the house. It is still early, and yet tomorrow starts early too. The group gathers itself up and slowly disperses."

The evening had come to a sudden end.

And now all hell broke loose between Frank and Olgivanna. Back in their private quarters, they argued so long and loud that the apprentices couldn't help but overhear their screaming. Wright knew he couldn't displace Gurdjieff as the primary object of her devotion. He himself had felt Gurdjieff's power firsthand. But her renewed pressure to transform Taliesin into a site for the penniless Gurdjieff—this was going too far. His wife would have to decide which man she was going to serve.

Gurdjieff left Taliesin soon after, his need for an American home more desperate than ever. Through Jean Toomer, he sent out "urgent overtures" asking Mabel Dodge Luhan to reconsider making her Taos ranch available for the Institute. Luhan let it be known that Gurdjieff wasn't even welcome in her house.

Gurdjieff returned to Taliesin in mid-August, only to leave again shortly thereafter. With the Prieuré gone and Taliesin and Taos escaping his grasp, his future looked grim. Apprentice Jimmy Drought joked that he might end up selling "apples and bananas at the corner of Broadway and 42nd St."

AND YET WRIGHT still had the capacity to surprise. His refusal to share Taliesin, or Olgivanna, with Gurdjieff, didn't stop him from celebrating the man or his philosophy in the press. In a piece he wrote for the *Capital Times* after Gurdjieff left, Wright noted Gurdjieff's "massive sense of his own individual worth"—in this context, at least, a good thing. "A man able to reject most of the so-called culture of our period and set up more simple and organic standards of personal worth and courageously, outrageously, live up to them," he wrote, "George Gurdjeef [sic] seems to have the stuff in him of which our genuine prophets have been made." Gurdjieff was a philosopher who not only made Eastern wisdom intelligible to the West, Wright offered, but also devised a system to help Western man employ it in everyday life. He was, Wright declared, an "Organic Man."

His cordial air even extended to his private correspondence with Gurdjieff. "Olgivanna and I enjoyed our visit with you more than I can say," Wright wrote the master, now living in a supporter's apartment back in New York. "I have no doubt we were both greatly befitted."

By the end of Gurdjieff's stay, the rumor that he might be setting up shop at Taliesin had become so widespread that Wright was forced to address it. In the September 12, 1934, edition of the *Capital Times*, he set the record straight: There would be no Gurdjieff center at Taliesin.

EXHAUSTED FROM THE tension-filled visit, Svetlana nearly vomited on the train ride back from Taliesin to Chicago. Gurdjieff "had my thoughts all in a horrible conflict," she later wrote Wes, "and then he fed us horrible Turkish dishes."

Peters found it hard to believe that Wright had fallen for "a fakester." "I can't understand Mr. Wright," he wrote Svetlana, "Gosh he certainly must be getting old—God! I pity him with all my heart. Certainly, certainly that is it—that really could account for very much of Wright's actions of recent years—. A burnt-out life—lived at too terrific a pace—on a set-up that—apparently unlike this Gurdjieff guy's—was unable to stand the inroads of advancing age. By God—I forgive Mr. Wright all he ever did to us."

Back in Evansville, Wes and Svetlana were finally arranging to get their marriage license. And after having passed the difficult architectural licensing exams, he was now designing his second house. But with his architectural practice came frustrations: In spite of his best efforts, his designs inevitably came out looking like Wright's. His former master's work hung over him, he confessed to Svetlana, like a "black shadow."

And there was another shadow: Gurdjieff had gotten to Svetlana. "The whole business," she wrote Wes, "makes me weak—unsteady on my feet, and shaky in my hands—Gurdjieff—God—I wonder what type of man he is. . . . Gurdjieff's music—it *is* lovely—very mystic and oriental but very lovely—o—I wish I could crawl away in a corner and die."

Olgivanna must have sensed an opening. At her request, Gurdjieff visited Svetlana in Chicago after leaving Taliesin.

Wes wasn't particularly worried that his love might fall back under the spell of the man whose cooking had turned her stomach, the man he called "Good Chief—Gurdjieff." But he did confess to her that he harbored a lasting bias against the man—if only because her mother thought so highly of him.

"Don't let him try to hypnotize you," he warned. "What is his first name? Could it be Hank? Hankejeef—you know."

Gurdjieff's visit, however, brought Wes's lighthearted banter to a halt. In the course of their meeting, Gurdjieff actually proposed that Svetlana and her mother return with him to Europe. Olgivanna, incredibly, let her daughter know that she was prepared to abandon her husband and Taliesin—now out of the running as a Gurdjieff center—for the chance of reclaiming her first-born. Alternatively, Gurdjieff suggested, Svetlana could return alone to France with him. "I refused," Svetlana wrote Wes, "which hurt Mother dreadfully." For her refusal, Gurdjieff labeled her a "hopeless idiot." Maybe he is right, she wrote Wes. "I know what he means and maybe he is right, but he really was very fine to me."

"The inflated pig!" Wes replied. Gurdjieff, he complained, was probably nothing more than "a loud and extremely personally impressive bag of wind." If Gurdjieff had been a younger man, Wes would have knocked his lights out. "I hope you laughed in his face when he made you his offer—!!—I know I should have—The conceited divine!" Svetlana should have told him to go back to Turkey and peddle his "Skizzkabob."

"Mrs. Wright is a goddamned fool," Wes wrote Svetlana. "Why in the hell does she want to leave one mess, which she has arranged for herself with FLW to have this Greek gazebo kick her around in Slavokstok?"

Olgivanna was profoundly disappointed in Svetlana's refusal. Gurdjieff may have done some noxious, if not disgusting, things in front of her, she wrote her daughter, but they were of no significance—an outer show, a technique, not the essence of the man. "How I wish," she wrote, "that you had the chance to be with him longer. . . . And how I wish you [would] do as he asked you. . . . If you give all of your life to him—to do with it as he pleases—you will derive infinite and almost immortal (meaning indestructible values) that will stay and strengthen with you all your life time."

It was still not too late. Olgivanna sent her daughter Gurdjieff's New York address, in case she cared to make contact with her magus. With it came a telling request: Would Svetlana please destroy this and all their other recent letters?

Wright himself was oblivious to all of this. "We are rather tired of the Bache [sic] Chorale we are singing now," he had written Gurdjieff just three days earlier, "and something fresh and strong would serve us as a sort of rallying cry besides being beautiful in itself here where we practice the gospel of work." Would Gurdjieff do him a "great favor" and write the melody he had promised to accompany the lyrics that Wright had written and given to him? "[W]e can all sing the song together as a march or a hymn or whatever you feel would be appropriate. A work song!"

Wright signed the letter "our best love and loyalty to your own great work."

UNDER PRESSURE FROM her mother, Svetlana's position only hardened. Not only was she rejecting Gurdjieff, she was also going through with her marriage to Wes. And there was one more thing, something she didn't tell her mother and that would hurt Daddy Frank: She was planning to wed under the name of Svetlana Hinzenberg, not Wright.

Olgivanna and Frank were aghast at their wedding plans, as Iovanna heard in their living-room shouting matches. Bowing to the inevitable, Olgivanna proposed that the wedding be at Taliesin. Svetlana declined; all her friends, she claimed, had left the place.

For Olgivanna, Gurdjieff's long-anticipated first visit to Taliesin seemed to have made everything worse. Her hopes that he would lure Svetlana away from Wes, that Frank would agree to hosting Gurdjieff at Taliesin—all had come to naught.

Having seen her husband and her master side by side at last, too, Olgivanna saw that there was no comparison. After Gurdjieff, she confessed in a letter to Svetlana, "anybody appears light as a feather,—silly, with no genuine power." She reminded her daughter how "Daddy Frank" made a fool of himself chattering on and on in front of Gurdjieff. He could not "for the life of him stop it," she told Svetlana. "God if you knew how I felt before G."

"I feel very lonesome here now," Olgivanna concluded. "I had again a glimpse of the Reality that belongs to him—and life here is hard for me."

For Svetlana it seemed just the opposite. "I feel entirely cured tonite of the Gurdjieff business," she wrote Wes, "and feel much stronger for having gone thru it."

But she was not. Though Svetlana had declined Gurdjieff's offer, now her decision to stay away from Taliesin was wavering. Perhaps her decision to escape from Taliesin had been a "girlish whim." Wasn't the objective to develop "our control over ourselves," she wondered to Wes? Perhaps her actions had been too passionate, too precipitant, a slipping back into "primitive man's way of living."

This was Gurdjieff-speak—and Peters was beside himself. "I know the powerful effect of a strong evil mind like G's," he replied. "I know you don't believe any of it. I see in it the subtle ugly forces which have been troubling you—I think it is all . . . the worst kind of junk proceeding from a foul personal being."

True power, Wes reassured her, involved neither will nor passion. It was a function of being in contact with the cosmos, especially the brightest star in the constellation Taurus. "Look now—tonight on the eastern sky—Aldebaran is rising now—now—fairly early—a bright red yellow star just below the Pleiades! Look there—Svet—and feel its light . . . Aldebaran! A wonderful name! Its very sound a wonderful name!"

It was a curious point to stress. "Aldebaran" is Arabic for "the follower."

LONESOME AMID THE apprentices and her husband, desperate that she was going to lose Svetlana for good, Olgivanna wrote Gurdjieff in Manhattan begging him to come back once more. She knew her master couldn't even afford a hotel room, but she promised to find patients who would pay him to "cure" them.

"It is strange," Gurdjieff replied, "to read such a letter on my most desperate day in America in terms of finances and loneliness." Her letter, he told her, was "an outrage of providence." He was himself "totally helpless."

"I relied on you," he continued, "and counted that in case of my staying in America . . . I will have the needed help, because you, among all the millions, are the only one close to my internal world. And according to my logical comparison . . . you would have to be able to do this." She was, he told her, "the only person I completely relied on; I hoped here in America to receive the proper help from this person, and now the same person needs help."

Frank Lloyd Wright's rejection of the center clearly devastated Gurdjieff. And he laid the responsibility squarely on Olgivanna.

Gurdjieff telegrammed Svetlana that he was coming back to Chicago and wanted to see her again. "I am so weak now, so afraid," she wrote Wes, "I'll be caught in this moment." Desperate for his strength, she asked him to reply by special delivery.

"Brace up and give G my regards plus swift kick," Wes telegrammed back. "Why the hell doesn't he take Olgivanna and get the hell back to Greece or wherever?? O don't fall for any of their rat-like stuff."

Gurdjieff came to Chicago, but apparently saw Svetlana only once. The next time he telephoned, she refused to see him. To her stupefaction, she had just discovered that her father, Valdemar Hinzenberg, had become a Gurdjieffian. She thought him a weakling.

With her daughter once again mustering the will to resist Gurdjieff, Olgivanna seemed to give up. "I am not going to urge you any more," Olgivanna wrote her daughter a week or so after Gurdjieff's Chicago visit. "It was more the attempt of one who can see further in the future than you can." She reminded Svetlana that only a few in the "herd" learned how to really live. "I wanted you," she wrote, "to join those few—should they even number in 1 or 2—only. For this life of ours, very soon you shall find, ridiculously short."

BUT OLGIVANNA'S ASSIDUOUS campaign had begun to work. The following month, Svet admitted to Wes that she was thinking of returning to Taliesin. "I *could* go back, I mean, it would not be too terrible—and I think I *could* learn much." She could do something with her music there, she said, "and probably *only* there."

Wes read the letter in agony, pacing the floor like a caged bear. "I think you have been lured partially by Mr. Wright's deceptively big manner," he wrote back, "—partially by the glorious beauty of Taliesin. . . . I think submission to Mr. Wright fruitless—Although he promulgates the feudal system . . . he cannot practice it. . . . He always has failed—he always will fail." The feudal system, he reminded her, was based on a relationship between lords and "underlords." The apprentices were rather "slaves who perform the symbolic act of homage hourly for the master's pleasure." As for her music, he didn't think it had "the slightest chance at Taliesin," though if she really believed it did, he would support her. "Don't for a second—think dear Svet— that if you go to Taliesin—I shall desert you in thought—love—! . . . No! No!" They would just belong "to different lords."

But the next day he wrote that he would rather die than go to Taliesin himself. "The whole is fundamentally stinkingly rotten." Nothing, not even "the ideal of an organic architecture," was "half enough to begin to make up for the evil befouling of human relations . . . Not half enough to make up for the human perversion of Mr. Wright—perversion that *does*—does I tell you—destroy the life in humanity that he creates in his work!"

Unable to bear living apart from him much longer, Svetlana deferred to her fiancé. But she begged him to escape with her to someplace else, away from Chicago's cold grit—Florida, perhaps. "I dunno if I can stand it."

Florida was rank with "exploiters," Peters replied. The countryside was out. "We must outface the city and defeat it first—not merely turn back on it and flee."

GURDJIEFF'S STAY AT Taliesin produced at least one unambiguous result: He convinced the Wrights that their nine-year-old daughter needed to start school. "I couldn't read or write," Iovanna recalled, "and had no knowledge of numbers." Wright had forbidden her to have a formal education, Iovanna remembered, because of his "unedifying university experience in Madison."

Gurdjieff "took my small face in his hands and looked deeply into my eyes. The man, swarthy and commanding, announced his diagnosis to my mother, his deep voice cloaked in an inscrutable Greek-Armenian accent: 'Iovanna should be in school,' he declared, 'in company of other children.'"

"In one fell stroke," Iovanna recalled, "my father's misgivings were rendered impertinent." As an adult looking back, she savored the victory. "Only one man," she observed of Gurdjieff, "enjoyed that degree of influence over mother. . . . I started school the next day."

The transition would not be easy. As Iovanna was ignorant of even the alphabet, the principal put her in a grade with children who were several years her junior. The benefits of being in the "company of other children" may have come too late. Barbara Fritz, her closest friend at the time, remembered Iovanna as a strange playmate. "She really liked Ronald Colman, and I really liked Gary Cooper, and we were making scrapbooks about them. And you'd be very busy doing something, and she would decide to go off to get something or do something, and she wouldn't return."

After getting a horse, named Fleet, Iovanna forced Barbara to learn to ride so that she would have someone to ride with. Although she was forbidden by her mother to ride across the Wisconsin River, in whose dangerous currents more than a few had died, one day she rode to the riverbank with her friend. After surveying the river's "silvery flames," she plunged in with Fleet, rising and falling as on a merry-go-round as the horse swam to the

Gurdjieff in the 1930s

other side. On the return trip, Fleet caught its hind legs in quicksand and just barely escaped being sucked down into the riverbank.

Iovanna acted like a princess, Barbara remembered, but not because she was treated like one. "I always had the feeling that Mrs. Wright loved Svetlana a lot more than Iovanna." Barbara never saw Olgivanna being affectionate with Iovanna the way she was with Svetlana.

As to her father, if there was love, Barbara remembered it as "more of a cold love." She couldn't recall them ever touching. When she and Iovanna built a set in the Taliesin living room, planning to make their own Ronald Colman movie, Wright was furious. "My boys'll just have to clean this up," he rebuked her. Iovanna felt her second-class citizenship keenly, a friend of the Wrights remembered. "[T]he boys and the Fellowship came first, came before she was even considered. . . . The Fellowship guys are really just going to squeeze you right out if they can, and they do."

Iovanna's enrollment in school wasn't the only change Gurdjieff brought to Taliesin. When he left, the tensions between her parents abated. Gurdjieff had made a surprising discovery at Taliesin: After spending time alone with drawings and photographs of Wright's work, he emerged from the room and exclaimed, "Ah, now I understand." If Wright was an "idiot," in the ordinary sense of the word, Gurdjieff saw that he was one who had an extraordinary understanding of nature's inner structures. He instructed Olgivanna to bend to Frank, indeed to treat him as her teacher.

He also provided her with the tools to work with this difficult husband. He counseled her to be less confrontational, indeed to use stealth. One way or another, he assured her, she would get what she wanted . . . and what *he* wanted.

Georgi Gurdjieff was still dreaming of Taliesin.

A Taliesin picnic, 1940. Wright is just right of center, in striped jacket; Olgivanna is at his left.

PART IV
CULT OF GENIUS

11.

SOMETHING TO DO

FOR TWO YEARS, FRANK AND Olgivanna had struggled against the odds to get their Fellowship off the ground. Now, in the Depression's fifth year, there was still little hope for real architecture work, and therefore real apprenticeship. Whenever the fate of Taliesin seemed most desperate, Gurdjieff or his agents were there to tempt him. Each time Wright seemed intrigued; each time he stepped back. And each time fortune bailed him out.

He didn't have long to wait. Within days of Gurdjieff's departure from Taliesin, three new apprentices appeared. "Cornelia Brierly arrived fresh from the halls of Carnegie Tech," the next "At Taliesin" announced, "to learn with the rest of us the meaning of organic architecture." The twenty-two-year-old was assigned to work in the kitchen doing pots and pans, white-washing the guest rooms (there was no money for paint), and making curtains out of rough monk's cloth, the same cheap fabric Olgivanna was forced to use for her daughter's dresses.

"The boy," an apprentice observed of one of the other new arrivals, "appears to be quite nice even tho Jewish." Like Brierly, Edgar Kaufmann Jr. was from Pittsburgh. After reading about the Fellowship, he decided—out of curiosity—to pay a visit, and then, impulsively, signed up. That, at least, was what the apprentices believed. Wright knew better. In reality, Kaufmann had been sent to Taliesin as an advance man for his father.

When the young Kaufmann arrived at Taliesin in mid-October 1934, he left little doubt that he came from money. He not only paid the tuition out of his allowance—a fund that also allowed him to purchase a Rembrandt etching at the age of sixteen—but donated money for a scholarship. It was awarded to Fred Langhorst—reparations, one might imagine, for the death of his dog as ordered by Olgivanna.

If there was such a thing as a typical Wright apprentice, Edgar Kaufmann Jr.—or "Junior," as he was affectionately known—was not it. Others might have had rich families, but only Junior was so worldly. The twenty-four-year-old Theosophist had studied painting in Florence and Vienna before Hitler's rise drove him home. After his return, he later wrote, he felt "disconnected from the thoughts and ways of America." Frank Lloyd Wright seemed the perfect antidote. The architect's autobiography flowed into his mind "like the first trickle of irrigation in a desert land."

Junior's father, Edgar Kaufmann Sr., was an American department store pioneer, a Jewish "merchant prince." The Kaufmann Department Store in Pittsburgh, thirteen stories high, covered a full city block and employed twenty-five hundred workers. The store thrived on publicity. It had managed to fit the enormous girth of President Taft with trousers off the rack. When Charles Lindbergh flew solo across the Atlantic, Kaufmann placed the very first Pittsburgh-to-Paris telephone call to offer congratulations. He even reconstructed the airplane on the ground floor of his store.

The elder Kaufmann aspired to the grandeur of the American bourgeois. He built major buildings—including his own estate, a Norman-style monster with eighteen fireplaces—and bought Old Masters paintings. As one apprentice noted, his wife Liliane's taste could be summed up in two words: "Marie Antoinette." The Pittsburgh socialite liked to dress in a dirndl gown and enter her dogs in shows.

But Kaufmann, like his women customers, was now turning to the modern. And like many of the largest players in the retail merchant class, with their dependence on local economic growth, he saw the wisdom of investing his time and money in civic projects in the city where his customers lived. When his son started encouraging him to consider Frank Lloyd Wright to design his future projects, Kaufmann wrote to entice the architect to meet with him in Pittsburgh. Short on traveling money, Wright sent a tepid reply: "Could I do anything for you by correspondence."

Yet somehow Wright found the cash to send his former secretary Karl Jensen on a spying mission to Pittsburgh. Jensen reported back that Kaufmann "is jewish, about 50, a very charming and very intelligent. . . . He has one son (25, dabbling with painting), intelligent but not the father's strong character." Kaufmann, Jensen reported, wanted to build a planetarium across the street from his store as well as a new parking garage.

A series of phone calls and cables followed. Kaufmann wanted his son to go to Taliesin; Wright saw his recruitment as a way to land his father's business. In the third week of September, Edgar Jr. arrived for an interview with Wright. It was pro forma; days before, Wright had already revealed to a former apprentice that the young heir had joined.

A little more than a week after the interview, the elder Kaufmann assured Wright that the planetarium project was his. "I was interested long ago in the planetarium as an architect's problem," Wright wrote in response to the offer, a reference to his unbuilt 1924 Gordon Strong project, "and would like to do one to your satisfaction. Your son is a fine chap and we look forward to him here with us. I hope you and Mrs. Kaufmann can come here to visit us someday."

ON FRIDAY, NOVEMBER 16, 1934, the Kaufmanns took him up on his offer, visiting Taliesin to see how their son was faring and to take Wright's measure. "They are very, very jewish looking people," Svetlana reported to Wes four days later.

Pioneers in their respective fields, Wright and Kaufmann liked each other immediately. Wright was attracted to the outgoing Kaufmann's handsome virility. The Kaufmanns joined the apprentices in a misty Sunday morning picnic, and stood with them as they sang their Bach-based work song before Sunday dinner. They were enchanted. After a dinner that included homemade wine followed by apprentice performances on piano, violin, and both solo and choral singing—everyone of course in formal wear—the elder Kaufmann gave a short talk to the Fellowship describing his efforts to get his fellow store-owners to pressure manufacturers to make better products. Quick on the up-take, Kaufmann assured the group, in markedly Wrightian terms, that every article he sold had a form, a color, and a quality appropriate to its nature.

Then it was Wright's turn to talk. "Something interesting has happened," he announced to the assembled Fellowship. He had received an invitation from the Industrial Arts Exposition to build and exhibit his plan for an alternative American landscape—Broadacre City—at Rockefeller Center. It was too bad he didn't have the money. Broadacre City on display at Radio City— that would have been terrific.

Wright went on to describe his ambitious proposal to remake America into a network of small, decentralized communities. The apprentices had heard it all many times—the evils of the city, the liberating potential of the automobile. The proposal called for a new kind of retail shopping center to be built out in the countryside next to gasoline stations. The high-density downtowns where men like Kaufmann located their department stores would be obsolete.

"Well," Kaufmann interjected, "it sounds pretty good to me. You'd do big business with these department stores, you know, in the country."

Wright's book on the scheme, *The Disappearing City*, had not sold well. People would only get behind the idea, he now believed, if they could actually

Wright with Edgar Kaufmann Sr. (right) and Jr.

see its physical form. If he only had the money, Wright told the group, he could build a scale model of it and take it on the road, sending the message all across the country.

How much did Wright need, Kaufmann wanted to know?

"E. J., pretty good!" Wright instantly replied. "Let's start out with a thousand bucks."

"Mr. Wright, you can start tomorrow."

THE FELLOWSHIP WAS in business. Like Junior's joining, however, the event was not as spontaneous as it appeared. Wright had arranged for Karl Jensen to solicit the Broadacre City funding from Kaufmann even before he arrived at Taliesin. The retail magnate had been playing a part that Wright scripted for him. Before leaving, Kaufmann handed Wright a folded check for $500. "Let me know when you need the rest," he said.

Wright personally wrote an "At Taliesin" column documenting the weekend. Kaufmann, he noted, "showed that romance has not dropped out of merchandising just because Marco Polo is gone." Instead he "gave us the most encouraging view we have had of the hand the enlightened merchant is taking in improving the product he sells." Kaufmann, he declared, was part of "the great impulse that will build a new and better way of American life for the American people."

From the time of his aborted Hillside Home School of the Allied Arts, Wright had worked—without success—to ally his school schemes with the manufacturing sector. Now fate had brought him another breed of businessman: the large retailer. This was nothing new: In both America and Europe, Jewish businessmen had been among the earliest and biggest supporters of modern architecture. Schlesinger and Mayer gave a commission to Louis Sullivan, Schoken hired Erich Mendelsohn for his Stuttgart emporium, and the Goldman and Salatch department store in Vienna was designed by Adolph Loos. Jews were outsiders to whom history had been unkind. In developing a new organizational form, it was only natural that they would be receptive to a new, nonhistoricist architecture as well. (Indeed, just a few weeks after the Kaufmanns left, Stanley Marcus, the Jewish American leader of the Dallas retailer Neiman Marcus, arrived at Taliesin to look into commissioning a Wright house.)

Although Wright harbored a measure of anti-Semitism, which expressed itself when he felt threatened, he trusted the talent and depended on the progressive tastes of Jews. His years with Adler and Sullivan showed him the way. Architects, like other professionals, tend to cull their clients from within their own social circle, and the brilliant engineer Dankmar Adler, a Jew, brought in a predominantly Jewish clientele. After two nearly barren years, clients were beginning to flow into the Fellowship. And for quite some time they would be overwhelmingly Jewish. Even at Taliesin one quarter of the apprentices were Jewish; if the pattern continued, Wright wisecracked, he would have to rename the place "Talestine."

KAUFMANN'S LARGESSE MADE a huge and immediate change at the Fellowship. The Rockefeller Center exhibition would open in five months. Before, only two apprentices had been needed for the architecture work; now all hands were enlisted. The Broadacre City model was to be large, twelve feet by twelve feet. There was a landscape to invent—one based, some say, on the topography of Taliesin itself. They needed able hands to craft every aspect of Wright's imagined world: tiny cars for the broad boulevards he envisioned for his automobile-centered urban form, hundreds of tiny buildings carefully crafted in wood. For some of their designs, Wright dug back into his old drawings and resurrected projects his foolish patrons never saw fit to build; for the architect, it must have been a kind of sweet comeuppance.

As large as the model was, Wright wrote Kaufmann fearing that it would be swamped in the Rockefeller exposition hall. Could he show it at his department store as well? Kaufmann agreed, and invited Wright to Pittsburgh to talk about building the planetarium.

All around Taliesin, the excitement was palpable. Even the jaundiced apprentice Robert Bishop was upbeat, excitedly sending his fiancée a letter announcing that Kaufmann "has a son here, and he is sold on Wright and the boys." "[T]his Pittsburgh trip of Mr. Wright's is very promising."

Indeed it was. Once in Pittsburgh, the elder Kaufmann asked Frank to design him a new office inside his department store. Then he drove his architect south of the city to the 1600 acres of rugged forest he owned there. The property included a simple cabin, once a resort for the store's employees; now the Kaufmanns used it as a summer residence. Junior suggested that Mr. Wright would be the man to make it into a year-round country house. The elder Kaufmann then took Wright on a hike down to a rock expanse at the edge of a mountain stream, Bear Run. As they stood before the waterfall there, Kaufmann regaled Wright with stories of family picnics on the spot, with Junior sunbathing nude on the rocks before diving into the icy water.

"You love this waterfall, don't you?" Frank asked E. J. "Then why build your house miles away, so you will have to walk to it?"

* * *

WITH THIS WINDFALL of work—and a host of largely untested apprentices—Wright yearned to lure his old draftsman Henry Klumb back to the fold. But Klumb and another of Wright's former paid draftsmen, Steve Arneson, recently landed a hospital project in Staples, Minnesota. When the two moved there to start work they wrote the Wrights asking them to send on their things. Wright wrote back warning the men that they weren't ready to design anything on their own, no doubt hoping to make them feel insecure enough to return—even perhaps bringing the project with them.

He succeeded, in part. Designing a hospital on one's own was a big responsibility, and Klumb became uncertain whether they could do it. After the two Taliesin "alumni" put their ideas to paper, they sent a copy of the drawings to Wright and asked his advice. For Wright, it was a vexing request. As he busied himself with a theoretical city, his defecting apprentices had an authentic big job. And to make matters worse, their design strayed from his principles. Wright responded with an even nastier letter permanently expelling the two men.

With such tension between them, it wouldn't be easy for Wright to recruit Klumb back to Taliesin. Beyond the hospital, the German architect now had his own exhibition to design in Washington. "It would be difficult to give up what I have begun to establish," he replied to Wright. But the door was not shut. Klumb assured Wright that there was "nothing more foremost in my mind than the chance of doing actual work with you." Having more work than his potential employer, though, he was in a position to make a demand. He no longer wanted to be an ordinary apprentice. He would not come, he declared, "if I would not feel assured that I would have your entire confidence and that any 'back stage gossip' would not undermine our relations as I felt often in reactions shown to me."

In the end, Wright declined to invite Klumb back as a full-fledged architect with his own projects. The jobs would have to be his, Wright insisted, with Klumb relegated to the status of supervisor. "Chasing rainbows, ergo jobs," he told Klumb, "is a fascinating but eventually a heartbreaking past time like hunting and fishing. . . . But to me now building steadily, if slowly, is much better. I have had the other."

It was a loss: Klumb would go on to collaborate with Louis Kahn, designing International Style cooperative Greenbelt communities and developing the idea of a prefabricated life core around which a building could be customized. In the 1940s, he made his way to Puerto Rico, where he developed an extraordinarily open tropical modernism. It wouldn't be the last time the

Wrights allowed someone who could have been a great asset to the Fellowship to slip away.

BACK AT TALIESIN, the apprentices were working feverishly on the Broadacre model.

Robert Bishop's optimism didn't last. At twenty-four, with an architecture degree from Swarthmore, he was older and better-trained than most. He wrote again to his fiancée, now telling her he felt stupid for joining the Fellowship. "So many irresponsibles," he wrote, referring to his fellow apprentices, "that I will have to finish the model myself, and I am sorry to say I think the model itself is a rather stupid idea." It wasn't Broadacre's design that Bishop found troubling. "I object only to Mr. Wright's claims about it," he wrote. "I wish he would stick to architecture instead of going off half-cocked into economics." As a "social savior," Bishop concluded, Wright was out of his league.

Bishop wouldn't have known that a good deal of Mr. Wright's "half-cocked" economics—also known as social credit theory—had come via Olgivanna from Gurdjieff's American agent Alfred Orage. The Englishman had long promoted the idea that there was a divide between the banks' ability to create credit, to generate money, and the ability of the economy to produce saleable goods. Under the current system, money and production were out of sync. The results—low levels of production, high levels of unemployment—were still hampering the American economy.

Orage's ideas had impressed Wright when they first met in Manhattan at his wife's urging, and now he made them a core element of his Broadacre City plans. Socializing credit would allow production, money, and consumption to be properly correlated. Orage saw the solution as a sociological exemplar of Gurdjieff's "law of three." And his ideas were getting a serious hearing. On November 5, 1934, just a few weeks after Junior joined the Fellowship, he gave a widely discussed talk on the BBC World Service. Ultimately, he told listeners, steam, electricity, and even atomic energy would "transfer work from the backs of Men to the broader backs of Nature's other forces." The state would then be able to generate an enormous increase in income, which it could distribute as a dividend to all its citizens. This dividend would ultimately replace the wage. The day after that broadcast, Orage died of an aneurism.

"Poor Orage," Gurdjieff told a follower on hearing the news, "why did he have to spend so much time and energy on monetary reform?" "What a disaster for so many of us," wrote Muriel Draper, in whose apartment Orage's groups met for so many years. "What a strong ghost he has left!" George

Bernard Shaw and T. S. Eliot wrote tributes. But the ultimate tribute would be if someone put his ideas into practice. Broadacre City, Wright hoped, would do just that.

WRIGHT'S ECONOMIC THEORIES—borrowed or not—were only part of what bothered Robert Bishop. "I have been writing as if a couple of commissions would make Taliesin a fine place to stay indefinitely," he informed Lydia, "but I think now that there is something in the nature of the Wrights that makes this place impossible for mature people. . . . One day this place seems just perfect (if we could be here together). And the next, it is full of petty personalities and Mr. Wright's god complex. . . . It would be the worst place I can think of to start out our common life."

Bishop was not alone in his assessment. "To overidealize a hero is to depreciate his real personality—Chang Po-Ling," read a note anonymously posted on the bulletin board by Fred Langhorst, the recipient of the Edgar Kaufmann-funded scholarship.

The next day there was another posting. "To live in fear of the overideal is to miss one's youth. Men thrive by their enthusiasms, though they overshoot the mark. Frank Lloyd Wright."

But Bishop had spied something even more disturbing in Mr. Wright than a god complex: He saw hypocrisy. "In spite of his best lines about the good old soil in one's hands," he wrote Lydia, "the maestro is at his best in Park Avenue apartments. . . . He has been urging us all to give up these silly conventional clothes and to design and have made more sensible all-around suits, with shorter, jacket-like coats and trousers fitting tight around the ankles. And now after many of the boys have spent all their funds on such effects and made themselves, with the help of a ham dressmaker in Spring Green, more or less ridiculous, the boss comes back from his southern trip clad in the smartest suit, overcoat, shoes, and beret you ever saw. All perfectly tailored by his special Chicago tailor, and as beautiful as can be. And terrifically expensive. I could dare guess high enough." Some of Kaufmann's cash outlay for Broadacre City—for beautifying America—had been diverted, it seems, to beautifying Frank himself.

Still, with all his critical reserve, Bishop was ultimately vulnerable to the seductions of the master. "I have decided," he soon wrote Lydia, "that Mr. Wright and I will never have any more arguments. If he is wrong, I shan't mind, because I am more sure than ever of his genius. . . ." There was little danger in "apprenticing oneself to such a person," he concluded, if "one is big enough to absorb the principles, instead of just copying the forms."

Wright clearly saw something special in Bishop. To the apprentice's great pleasure, the two often spent time together alone. When he shared a Christmas card in which the sender had written, "To hell with Christmas but good luck to you," Bishop suggested Wright reply, "To hell with you and a merry Christmas."

"Gad but Mr. Wright is a grand man when one gets him more or less alone," Bishop wrote his fiancée. "It makes me resent the Fellowship in a way. He takes so much time giving out sermons and identifying himself with the creative spirit of our times when he feels himself the guiding light of our colony, that it is swell to be with him when he lets down and gets human. . . . We discussed at length his inability to have close friends, and he 'confessed' that his worst weakness, and the most conscience-pricking, was his unconcern for others as people in their own right, to be cherished, remembered, and befriended."

Although flattered by Wright's attention, Bishop was still able to see clearly. "He knows his limitations, abilities, and acknowledges his good luck," he wrote Lydia. "But to see him as official master of these thirty apprentices you would think he was Jehovah himself. Or think that he thought he was. And so I wish he didn't have a Fellowship. If there was only a few of us here—only those truly and deeply interested in his work—he would be much more of a perpetual inspiration. Instead he is playing schoolmaster to a bunch of immatures who are having a nice life—are scared of him, but do not really appreciate him."

WHEN WRIGHT RETURNED from Pittsburgh at the end of December 1934, the long, gloomy Wisconsin winter was upon them. Half the apprentices, cracked one, worked to keep the other half warm. It wasn't far from the truth. Wright was talking about transporting the entire Fellowship in a caravan of cars and trucks out to the desert. In the fall, he had written his old client Dr. Chandler in Arizona asking to bring the Fellowship to winter there on a regular basis. Chandler offered the architect space at his ranch; Wright made a brief trip there on his own, returning with tales of grapefruits and oranges there for the eating, of swimming pools and cactus gardens.

The caravan was on. With the Rockefeller Center opening just four months away, it was a crazy idea. When word of the Taliesin migration reached the exhibition officials, they actually assumed Wright had abandoned the idea of showing the Broadacre City model. He hadn't, of course. Yet neither had Wright gotten very far with the project; though he had worked out the concept, there was still no specific plan for Broadacre City. By the time they pulled up stakes for Arizona, the apprentices had built only the four three-foot square sections that would form the model's base and a few individual houses.

The migration to the desert would take a lot of time and money. Wright had his excuses: He claimed there was no room at Taliesin to build the twelve-foot square model, a strange claim given Taliesin's hundreds of acres. He also later suggested that he couldn't afford the $3,500 per winter it cost to heat the place. At any rate, he had probably already decided to go when there wasn't any work, and he wasn't going to let losing weeks on the Broadacre City project get in the way. They could work on it when they arrived in Arizona—faster than ever, of course.

ABE DOMBAR GAVE the last sermon in the Lloyd Jones chapel before the Fellowship took flight. His task, he told his audience, reminded him of his *bar mitzvah*, when a "Hebrew boy . . . is admitted into the tribe." Abe and his younger brother, Bennie, now also an apprentice, together sang the words recited in the synagogue service when the Torah is taken out of the ark. Dombar compared the Taliesin Fellowship to the "Hebrew Race," with Frank Lloyd Wright an architectural Moses who, "in spite of the discouragements of the past two years . . . has managed to keep the Vision foremost in his mind."

The logistics of the journey to Arizona were considerable. The apprentices drained Taliesin's radiators and shut down the boilers. They assembled a traveling larder, a stake truck loaded with home-cured hams, hundreds of jars of garden vegetables, barrels of sauerkraut (Gurdjieff's fiery recipe), and eggs covered in salt to preserve them. Half the canned fruit and vegetables, the bedding, drafting tables, and materials were stacked up in the new red truck, with the four plywood sections for the Broadacre City model at the top, all covered with canvas. Before they left, each apprentice bought a ten-dollar sleeping bag at Sears for the trip.

Their much-anticipated departure was set for January 23, 1935, a Wednesday. At 4:30 A.M., they were still struggling to get ready. The wind chill was thirty below zero as they started Wright's Cord up the icy hill where the caravan was to form behind it. It stalled. They finally made it, but one thing must have been recorded for future reference: Future winter migrations should commence before January.

"To start 30 people in one direction—all at once—and keep them going for 2,296 miles over ice and through mountains was the problem," Gene Masselink reported in "At Taliesin." They had planned to leave at dawn, but Wright wasn't feeling well. He had gotten a bad chill driving into Madison with Masselink to fix the Cord and was drinking hot lemonade, hot milk, and cognac to prepare himself.

It wasn't until noon that the cars finally began lining up on Taliesin's hill. "Mrs. Wright," Gene wrote, "had become the very proud owner of a new Ford sedan." Marybud and John Lautner pulled up in their red and grey Graham Paige convertible. Edgar Tafel sat in his freshly waxed and recently repaired Ford cabriolet. Fred Langhorst had commandeered his family's Ford. Frank Lloyd Wright's long gray Cord had been freshly painted for the occasion, adding a red square on the right side of the hood near the radiator that, Gene observed, "made it sing." A giant new red truck had been decorated with a very large red swastika, the ancient symbol of life and good luck not yet polluted by its association with Hitler. Gene called it "a family Fellowship of cars." Between Olgivanna's new Ford, the giant truck, and Frank's new wardrobe, Edgar Kaufmann's grant for Broadacre City must have been more than spent.

"It will probably be hard to write en route," Bishop warned Lydia, "as Mr. Wright has it all planned caravan-style and every meal will be a public picnic, and we will have to stop at tourist camps. . . . Good bye sweetheart."

Wright had decided that all the girls were to travel in his station wagon. Abe Dombar, thinking it would be nice to share the female company, suggested to Wright that the girls should ride one in each car. "Mr. Wright," he said wryly, "you shouldn't put all your eggs into one basket." Wright blushed, but kept the girls where they were.

By the time the caravan departed, at 1:40 P.M., the sun was shining bright and the Cord—with Gene behind the wheel and Wright at his side—had warmed up enough to roar out of the gate and onto two-lane Highway 23, heading south over the hill to Dodgeville. The Fords, Plymouths, and Nashes, the Graham Paige and the big red truck, all followed in line. Those lucky enough to have the recently available car radios likely tuned in for the big hits of the day: "I Get a Kick Out of You," "Blue Moon," or perhaps "I Only Have Eyes for You."

It must have been glorious.

At Dodgeville, half an hour from Taliesin by car, Wright's friends at Etta Hocking's market served lunch for the group. By the time they pulled into Cedar Rapids, only 120 miles away, the Cord again needed repairs. While the rest went on to Lawrence, Kansas, Wright and a few of the boys stayed behind, waiting for the mechanic to finish. Gene considered himself one of the lucky ones, the small group that traveled with Mr. Wright, wolfing down steaks and beers at midnight, then checking into the Mecca, a rundown hotel.

The next day they picked up the Cord and joined up with rest of the caravan in Lawrence, where the main party—more than twenty strong—spent the night with George and Helen Beal, former apprentices. The route to Arizona was dotted with such stops, where they could prevail on the good graces of friends and former clients.

From Lawrence, the roads now free of ice and snow, the Taliesin Fellowship caravan rolled on. "Quite a centipede to drag 2400 miles," Wright remarked to his boys. In Tulsa, they stayed with Wright's straight-talking, racist cousin, Richard Lloyd Jones. Frank had designed Richard's house using concrete block, his material of choice during the twenties. "Pictures of the house," Gene noted, "had given no suggestion nor any idea of the atmosphere it really creates. It is the color of soft mother-of-pearl. It glows in fading sunlight. . . . I fell asleep in my sleeping bag on the floor of the tall dining room—30 of us slept like that that night, all over the house."

From Oklahoma they crossed the Texas panhandle, approaching the foothills of the Rocky Mountains at dusk. "The sun," Gene remembered, "sank behind the mountains as the Cord wound its way into them. It was very quiet and night fell as sharper curves and a hot motor made us realize that we were in new country." They pulled over for the night. Their food was running out; they were reduced to eating peanut butter and jelly sandwiches for dinner.

On the final day of the trip Wright's Cord led the caravan, as it had at the start. As they were about to negotiate the narrow and dangerous curves of Devil's Canyon, with its "gigantic rock surfaces flung upwards," Mr. Wright took the wheel from Gene. The tension turned to ecstasy as they emerged from the canyon and descended the western slope.

"Magically we came out from the mountains as the sun was nearing the horizon," Gene recalled, "and we rode out upon the Arizona desert. Tall ancient saguaro and gracefully waving ocatillo and the vivid green on the floor of the desert and the purple mountains beyond. A garden like none I had ever seen. A desert like something I had never dreamed."

They had been on the road for a week.

It was night by the time the caravan pulled into La Hacienda, a shabby polo stable Chandler had converted into housing for fruit laborers. The tiny cowtown of Chandler, Arizona, was populated largely by such workers, many of them Mexicans, who toiled in the orchards, the ranches and the hotels.

"I bet you are ready to kill me for not writing during the trip," Bob Bishop wrote Lydia, "It seems months ago that we left Spring Green, tho' it has been just a week, and so much happened that I won't be able to remember it all."

IN THE MORNING the apprentices woke to the warm Arizona sun. After breakfast—at first they lived on oranges and grapefruit—they set up the Broadacre City model in the stable's courtyard and got right to work. Working at drafting boards set up in its courtyard, the apprentices, many of whom wore short jackets and pants tucked in at the ankle that Wright had designed especially for them, worked feverishly on the model.

Each of the four plywood sections represented a square mile. A quarter the size of Manhattan, Broadacre City was intended to house ten thousand inhabitants. Apprentices were assigned different plots to work on. Working from earlier Wright plans for different building types—service stations, farms, small inexpensive houses—they slowly laid out the city and built its tiny models. There were many new things to design—suspension bridges, the highway interchange, a stadium—and larger models, such as St. Mark's on the Bowerie, that would accompany the exhibit. Everyone worked on every part of the job.

It got so warm that the boys shed their shirts and worked on the model bare-chested. "It's an exciting experience," Cornelia Brierly wrote while there, "to create a landscape to determine its orchards, fields of blooming clover, tennis courts, swimming pools, its reservoirs, its forests. We live in this future city."

One afternoon, the apprentices spied Wright walking down the mountain, carrying over his shoulder the fifteen-foot dried stalk and flowers of a century plant. He placed it in the courtyard, next to the Broadacre City model. "Something told me," he told the apprentices, "that if we get it home, I'll live a hundred years."

"But his apprentices know," Cornelia Brierly remarked at the time, "that he will live forever—even as the desert."

Working on the Broadacre City model at La Hacienda

Wright chose Brierly's idea for the model's color scheme. At Taliesin she had never been able to work in the studio; this was her first chance to show Wright what she could do. Olgivanna, she recalled, was "extremely jealous" of her as a woman with architectural talent, which explains why it took years for her to make it into the studio. Wright himself had no problem working with women. At Oak Park, he was particularly close with his female principal draftsperson, Marion Mahony. But that didn't mean that he was particularly supportive of women. Wright never believed that women were likely to produce great architecture or music—the arts he called "objective expression"—as opposed to painting or writing. Architecture was a manly calling.

Olgivanna actively worked to keep women out of the drafting room. She didn't trust them, and she knew her husband could be flirtatious. Indeed, she suspected that Cornelia had designs on her husband. As a result, women rarely stayed more than a year, if that long. The ones who truly settled in did so only when Olgivanna embraced them. Although Cornelia Brierly had obvious architecture talent, she was no different. As a woman, she spent much of her time sewing for Mrs. Wright, arranging children's parties, and canning hundreds of jars of tomatoes and pickles. Her organizational skills, which

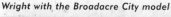

Wright with the Broadacre City model

could have been a boon in the studio, were directed instead to the purchasing of Taliesin's building supplies, produce, groceries, and decorating items. She also became one of the Wrights' favorite cooks, sometimes serving as chef for months on end.

ABE DOMBAR PUT in his time chiseling hills and rivers into the model, but his mind was elsewhere. Looking out at the San Tan mountain range, the desert's vastness, he forgot about everything—"family and friends and Taliesin and about race and religion and government." The fact was, he was cracking. Pulled away from everything he knew, he was forced to concentrate on this imaginary world in the courtyard of an old stable. "Broadacre City—what does it mean?" he wrote in his diary. His hand was no longer steady on the chisel. He had, he admitted, lost his ambition. And Wright was looking to him to take the initiative for the new designs.

But all Abe Dombar wanted to do was to follow a woman—a farmer's daughter, no less. The Mexican farmer next door, where Abe went to buy turnips for the apprentices, had a good-looking daughter who tipped him off that she liked to swim in the irrigation ditch at night. Whenever Wright left La Hacienda to sleep in his hotel room or to go for dinner and cocktails with potential clients in Phoenix, Dombar would wander down to the canal, lined with tall white cottonwoods. The tension between his desire and his "super civilized veneer" made him want to cry. In fact he tried to, but just couldn't.

SOON AFTER ARRIVING in Chandler, the apprentices made pilgrimage to nearby Ocatillo to see what was left of the encampment Mr. Wright had built there in 1928 while working on San Marcos in the Desert. Wright's return, of course, marked the realization of the enduring vision he first experienced here, a community of apprentices gathered loyally in the desert about their master. The apprentices had read about the encampment in his autobiography, had seen the pictures of the canvas-topped cabins that once stood here like a group of huge butterflies poised briefly amidst the rock outcroppings. On the cabin gables, Wright had painted scarlet triangles to match the Ocatillo bloom. "Ocatillo"—the camp—is ephemera," he wrote. "To drop a seed or two, itself? Who knows?"

Now, as the apprentices arrived at the site, they were disappointed to find virtually nothing left. Everything worth stealing had been carted away by the Indians.

* * *

ON SATURDAYS, THE apprentices would take a break from the model to explore the nearby mountains. "We pile ourselves and our sleeping bags into the gorgeous new truck," Cornelia Brierly recalled, "and as we speed toward the desert the wind beats at our foreheads and whips through our hair." They became friendly with some of the Mexicans who panned the mountain washes for gold, sharing their strong coffee and beans.

Dr. Chandler had the apprentices frequently to his San Marcos Resort Hotel, where the Fellowship's musicians entertained the guests. At one point Wright's other benefactors, the senior Edgar Kaufmann and his wife, Liliane, showed up to visit their philanthropic and biological progeny—the Broadacre model and their son. The Kaufmanns, who joined the boys to watch the Mexican cock fights, also hosted the Fellowship in their rooms at Chandler's hotel.

"Last night," Bob Bishop wrote his fiancée, "the whole gang went out. We were invited to the San Marcos Hotel to hear a piano concert. The evening was saved early by the senior Kaufmanns who invited the whole Fellowship in to have highballs before the music." The group gathered in the Kaufmanns' cottage at the hotel, where they were plied with Irish and Scotch whiskies. "It was swell," Bishop reported. "Mr. and Mrs. Wright were in a tough spot. They couldn't say a thing, as their flock tried to get quite cockeyed under their very noses. There were three quarts of whiskey there when we arrived and we soon ran out and Mrs. Kaufmann insisted that her husband send for more."

WRIGHT SERVED AS La Hacienda's early-morning bugler. The "bugle," in this case, was a new radio, a Christmas present he used to blast everybody awake. If that didn't work, he resorted to throwing oranges at the sleeping figures.

For Fred Langhorst, neither the radio nor the oranges were enough. He had lagged behind the Taliesin caravan to Arizona enjoying ambling conversations with Indians, cowboys, and gas station attendants. By the time he pulled into La Hacienda he was wearing a ten-gallon hat and silver-studded boots, carting a collection of yarns and Indians rugs, baskets, and jewelry. He had also acquired a new dog to replace the one Olgivanna had ordered killed. Entranced by the big-sky west, he stayed up late reading all he could find about it, finally crawling out when the sun was high and the apprentices had already been working for three or four hours.

Wright finally called him into the office.

"Fred, you're wasting your time here."

"For Christ's sake, Mr. Wright," Langhorst angrily replied, "why didn't you tell me that months ago?"

Now a former apprentice, Fred left for San Francisco, where he found a
real architecture job with William Wurster, a respected California modernist.

A MONTH BEFORE the still-unfinished Broadacre model needed to be installed in New York, Wright took some of the apprentices on a break. "At exactly midnight—Thursday, March 14th," Gene Masselink wrote a friend,
"just two hours after we got permission—and just two hours and fifteen
minutes after Mr. Wright heard he had to go to L.A., eighteen of us piled onto
the famous truck—fifteen in back, the canvas cover over the top—mattresses
piled on the floor and with sleeping bags and blankets made into a real Pull-
man coach. We slept like sardines and when it came daylight we took off the
canvas cover and watched the mountains go by. . . . We made the 470 miles in
just 12 hours arriving in Pasadena at noon Friday."

Wright took them on an architectural tour of his concrete block houses,
the apprentices standing in the back of the truck as they traveled from one to
another. After bedding down in Beverly Hills at the home of the family of a
former apprentice, the next morning they met Mr. Wright at one of his 1920s
projects: the Millard house, or "La Miniatura," as he had dubbed the concrete
block gem. "It seems so precious—so small," Gene observed, "as if you could
cup it in your hand."

Then they drove east to apprentice Betty Barnsdall's mother's place,
Wright's Hollyhock House. Her mother was the eccentric oil heiress Aline
Barnsdall—"socialist and socialite," as the newspapers were fond of saying.
Betty, who had driven her own new La Salle on the caravan to Arizona, was
nearing the end of her second year at the Fellowship. After touring the
house, the elder Barnsdall took them all out to lunch at Sardi's. "Food was
magnificent," Gene recalled, "and Hollywood galore: actresses, stars, and
everything."

The surrounding architecture, however, appalled the apprentices. "Hollywood is the center of superficialities and the caché of Hollywood culture depends on how many more fake towers and artificial balconies and how high
on the mountain side the Hollywooder can build above his neighbor," noted
one of them. "The picture-artist seems to have run dry, he can't hold up
much longer to the whims and fancies for the exotic nor can the hills forever
supply the sites."

The apprentices had abandoned places like MIT and Yale for this other
education, seeing the country, meeting pioneers of modernism, ogling Hollywood stars, being by Wright's side at the creation of a new, new world, Broadacre City. The promise of the Fellowship seemed finally to have arrived. After
spending a night sleeping on the sand at Huntington Beach, they drove to a

morning mass at the Mission San Juan Capistrano, and then headed east back to Arizona to finish the model.

RETURNING TO LA Hacienda, the apprentices worked day and night to ensure that the Broadacre exhibit would be ready for its April 15, 1935, debut at the Industrial Arts Exposition at Radio City. Gene Masselink worked overtime lettering and drawing the plans. "It is the swellest and biggest job since I've been at Taliesin," he wrote to a friend.

"The magnum opus, Broadacres," Wright wrote former apprentice Alden Dow, "grows into something very beautiful and we all hope and believe, something useful. You'll see it at Radio City which it is capable of blowing up into thin air." After two months in the desert, Wright was able to write the elder Edgar Kaufmann that the "model is now emerging from chaos. I am sure it is going to do us all proud."

EDGAR JR. WAS another story. Junior no longer saw any significance in becoming a painter, and it was clear to all that he would never be an architect either. "Junior is sagging a little," Wright wrote the senior Kaufmann. "He feels his end here with us is near, for which I am deeply sorry. Just as we were getting attached to him he is off somewhere, but if it is to you it is not too bad. His time here has not been wasted. He has been a fine spirit and a good worker."

In truth, Wright was contemptuous of the magnate's son, nicknaming him "whippoorwill" after the reclusive night bird whom nobody sees, but everybody hears. And Junior's homosexuality was just too public—enough that the two quarreled about it. Even though Edgar was the son of his only solid client, Wright told him that he had to leave. He did, however, allow the son of its bankroller to accompany the Broadacre City model to New York. Junior was irate, but he was still committed to Wright and joined the others preparing to drive east.

On April 1, 1935, the apprentices carefully packed the big model into the truck, sending his revolutionary vision from the desert into the city it sought to replace. To the apprentices, it felt as though the future of the Fellowship hung in the balance: Writing in "At Taliesin," Gene Masselink referred to the model lying in the truck bed as "all our eggs in its basket."

As Edgar Tafel and Bob Mosher drove the truck, Edgar Kaufmann Jr. and Robert Bishop, both of whom were leaving the Fellowship, followed in Kaufmann's car. After helping to set up the model, they would be returning to their private lives. Abe Dombar was forbidden from riding in Junior's car. "Wright," he recalled, "was afraid that Edgar would talk me into leaving also."

On the eve of Edgar Jr.'s departure, Wright apparently gave him one last lecture about his future path. "I have not forgotten what you told me the night before I left," Junior later wrote to Wright, "and realize its truth. Still, out of myself, I know that I can only improve by my own unaided powers, if at all. I am not good material for your real needs; but I hope always to fulfill the less enviable role of sincere, and I trust a little useful, propagandist." He became just that: As an architectural curator at the Museum of Modern Art and a professor at Columbia University, Kaufmann promoted Wright's architecture tirelessly. To his gay colleagues, such as Philip Johnson, he claimed that Wright never knew about his homosexuality. And to the public, he kept it quite discreet.

A THOUSAND PEOPLE streamed through the Broadacre City exhibit at Rockefeller Center each day, listening to the apprentices explain the principles of this alternative American landscape. In the houses perched within the model, middle-class visitors saw homes they might be able to afford. Many showed interest; some returned to the exhibit several times. Wright told the apprentices to be on the lookout for potential clients. Edgar Jr. did his part: "I cannot help thinking how very many small houses of your design must be really wanted ALL over the country," he reported to Wright, "if out of 5000 people, I alone had 5 requests."

When a group of Yale students came to the exhibition and discovered that Bob Bishop was a Yale man, they invited him to the campus to give a talk on the Fellowship. Bishop didn't want to do it, but Robert Mosher offered to go if Yale would take care of the expenses.

Bob Mosher—who dumped his real first name, Byron, to end schoolmate harassment—was a short, boyish-looking yellowy blond with full lips and a prematurely receding hairline. He had also come to Taliesin with an architecture degree. When he first showed up at Taliesin, Wright suggested that he forget everything the professors had taught him. "Mr. Wright," Mosher replied, "that won't be difficult at all because I was the worst—you could say the lousiest—student in the whole university."

"Bobby, that counts you one," Wright replied.

When Mosher returned to New York from the Yale talk, honorarium in his pocket, Mr. Wright was at the exhibition hall.

"Where have you been, Bobby?" Wright asked with irritation. "I knew I shouldn't have left you alone in this evil city."

The young man explained. Yale University? Wright didn't believe him.

Mosher pulled out the twenty dollar bill to prove it.

Mr. Wright brightened. "Now let's you and I take a stroll up Fifth Avenue."

Going into Saks Fifth Avenue, Mosher remarked that Mr. Wright had left his beret behind at the exhibit.

The architect directed them to the men's counter. Did they have any French berets, Wright inquired?

No berets, but they did have some nice caps from Scotland.

"Well, they won't do, really. I've got to have a beret."

Mr. Wright tried on the most expensive hat at the counter, then took it off and ripped off the visor. The clerk was apoplectic.

Placing the altered cap on his head, he blithely announced, "All right, now we can go for a stroll along the avenue."

Mr. Wright had no money to pay for the ruined hat. Mosher had to surrender his honorarium before they could leave the store.

WITH THE COMING of spring, it was time for the apprentices who'd stayed behind in Arizona to make their way back to Taliesin. This time there was no orderly caravan; the cars just dribbled into Taliesin over the course of six days. On April 18, Gene Masselink used an "At Taliesin" column to pass on the word about Wright's Radio City exhibit: "News of Broadacre City's triumph comes to us from New York." Masselink thought Broadacre was perhaps Wright's "greatest edifice."

There was also news from Indiana: Wes Peters had married Svetlana, now nineteen years old, in a private ceremony conducted by a Methodist minister in Evansville. Not even Wes's parents were invited. Svetlana had written her mother and got her blessing, but the couple had not asked Mr. Wright. Olgivanna shared the unhappy news with her older sister, Julia. "I feel so sorry Svetlana got married so early," Julia commiserated.

Svetlana and Wes spent the summer on the Peters's family farm, 160 acres of apple and peach orchards and woodlands; on the Ohio River below, you could hear the steamboat leadsmen call out, "Mark Twain!"

Although Wes had built a house in Evansville for them, he was afraid that it would be too small, that his wife's music would suffer there, that their life would not measure up to the high aesthetic standards they had experienced at Taliesin. We must work, he told Svetlana, "to make our life beautiful in all the little mechanical ways. Beautiful in our cooking—our eating, in the washing of dishes—the making of the beds! All we must conquer—not by eliminating them—but by creatively making them into a beautiful and simple part of our living! And that is where we are going to run into our trouble—this house and all its appurtenances . . . are designed by and large for an old un-beautiful—complicated way of living not ours!—the very rooms—the knives—the dishes—the glasses—all—all crush us in their implications."

But truly beautiful things would require money they didn't have. Now a licensed architect, Wes was lining up clients; soon he was at work designing an addition for his father's newspaper building. Olgivanna began to fear that she was losing Svetlana forever.

IF OLGIVANNA WAS missing a daughter, the Swiss-born Kornelia Schneider desperately needed a mother. Kornelia had been just twelve years old when she first decided she wanted to be an architect. The following year, 1931, she attended a lecture by Frank Lloyd Wright and was smitten. Now in 1935, the seventeen-year-old prevailed upon her father and his new wife, a woman from Richland Center whose father had been a Wright client, to take her to visit Taliesin.

No one, it seemed, had ever spent much time on Kornelia. During her childhood in Switzerland she had been ignored and verbally abused by her ill-tempered but mystically inclined mother, who spent her time traveling around Europe. As a teenager, Kornelia studied Buddhism and believed in reincarnation. After her family came to the United States, her parents divorced; she was left in the care of her engineer father, who was as distracted as he was brilliant. By the mid-1930s it was apparent to many that war was coming, and he was preoccupied with the design of a new submarine engine at Annapolis. At first he thought of shipping Kornelia out to a finishing school on the East Coast, one of those starched places with gravel paths and clipped lawns where girls learned French and tennis and prepared themselves to be mates for wealthy husbands.

When they arrived at Taliesin, however, the young girl didn't even have to get out of the car. "The minute I saw it, I felt," Kornelia recalled, "this is home. This is where I belong."

When Wright asked the teenager what she wanted to do with her life, she recounted the dreary prospect that awaited her. "Well," he said, "if you go to a finishing school that will finish you."

That wasn't what she wanted, Kornelia insisted. She wanted to become an architect.

Something about the young girl caught Wright's eye. Turning to his wife, he asked, "Doesn't she remind you of Svet?" Olgivanna agreed. And then Wright offered his words of deliverance: "Why don't you join the Fellowship?"

Two weeks later, in June 1935, Kornelia returned with her father. Heinrich Schneider got on famously with Wright. He had invented an automatic transmission back in Switzerland, and now the two agreed to design a new car together, body by Frank Lloyd Wright, engine by Heinrich Schneider.

Kornelia was admitted to Taliesin, but there was a hitch: The Fellowship already boasted one "Kornelia," Cornelia Brierly. So they renamed the new girl "Kay," a change that was publicly announced in the Fellowship's newspaper column—by Cornelia Brierly, naturally.

Architecture may have been Kay Schneider's dream, but it wasn't exactly what the Wrights had in mind for her. Olgivanna set out to redesign the young girl. "Mrs. Wright took me into the House," Schneider recalled, "and she started teaching me how to clean house, how to do things. Because I had no practical knowledge of anything. All I had done before was draw, paint." Gene taught her to arrange flowers. Kay Schneider would go on to run the Taliesin household, becoming an ersatz daughter, and agent, for Olgivanna. Moonstruck by her mistress, she would do anything she was asked. "My impression of Mrs. Wright," she recalled of her early days at Taliesin, "was that she was the wisest, most beautiful woman I had ever met, or would ever meet in my life."

IT HAD BEEN nine months since Edgar Kaufmann Sr. had brought Wright to Bear Run and asked him to design a summer getaway to replace the "simple cabin" on his property there. Since then Wright had been to Pittsburgh four times, but had not yet put pencil to paper. Given the stakes, it was an awesome dawdle—at least according to official lore.

On the morning of Sunday, September 22, 1935, the phone rang at Taliesin. Kaufmann was in Milwaukee on business and wanted to drive over to Taliesin and see the preliminary drawings. "Come along, E. J.," Frank answered, "We're ready for you."

"I looked across my drafting table at the apprentice in front of me, Bob Mosher," Edgar Tafel recalled; Mosher's back had "stiffened at the words." Not one line had been drawn. From Milwaukee to Spring Green was roughly 140 miles; Kaufmann would arrive in a little more than two hours.

Kay Schnieder, who became Olgivanna's confidante

"Get me that topographical plan of Bear Run out," Wright told Mosher, "and color the water in blue and the big boulders brown. I guess we'll have to get to work!"

Wright then went for a stroll in the garden. By the time he returned, Mosher had finished the coloring. He took the apprentice's place at the drawing board and started to work. Mosher stood to his right, handing him freshly sharpened colored pencils like a golf caddy. "Every line he drew," he recalled, "vertically and especially horizontally, I watched with complete fascination."

About two hours later, so the story goes, it was over—floor plans, cross sections, and exterior elevations. The design was extraordinary, even for the master. It was a virtuoso display, Mosher recalled—Paganini played at double time. Either Wright had synthesized the building on the spot, or he had been composing and storing elements of the complex three-dimensional design in his head for months, awaiting this moment—a feat perhaps more astounding still. It was, he told the apprentices, "thought-built."

Like a religious miracle, the birth of Fallingwater was remembered differently by different apostles. In early accounts, Mosher himself placed the event not on his drawing board, but at Wright's. Jack Howe also remembers it that way, but in his telling it was he, not Mosher, who handed Wright his sharpened colored pencils. Cornelia Brierly recalled that Wright's drawings were already done when the apprentices arrived in the studio at six-thirty in the morning. Another apprentice, Blaine Drake, thought the drawings had been made months before, after Wright visited the site early that summer; though

(From left) Jack Howe, Edgar Tafel, and Bob Mosher

he usually enjoyed working before an audience, Drake remembered him saying, "Boys, I would like to work on this alone," then settling down to complete the design.

Whatever the truth, when Kaufmann arrived around noon on September 22, Wright greeted him at the top of the steps: "E. J., we've been waiting for you."

Sporting a Brooks Brothers suit and hat, Kaufmann accompanied Wright to the studio, where the apprentices were waiting. "Come over here," Frank reportedly said, "I'm going to show you your Fallingwater."

Kaufmann stared at the drawings, taken aback. "You don't mean to tell me you're putting it over the waterfall instead of the other side?"

"Yes, E. J. I want you and your family to become such an intimate part of what the great nature has given you. I give you this."

Wright had designed the house in the image of the waterfall itself, or at least the jutting stones that underlay it—its series of concrete terraces reaching out from the rocks and over the stream with no apparent support. The drawings were stunning, the building almost unprecedented. The design recalled Wright's 1904 design for Zona's aunt, Laura Gale, in Oak Park, but the resemblances are mostly superficial. This new house was audacious in concept, in execution—and, most surprising, in its near-total flouting of every sermon on organic architecture Wright had ever preached. The architect had set his own house, Taliesin, on the brow of a hill, in modest deference to nature. Now he went one step further: Kaufmann's house would be set right atop a waterfall, its broad decks jutting out impossibly from their precarious perch high above the stream.

For all its extraordinary art, however, the structure looked as if it would surely collapse, or at least cost a fortune to build. Bob Mosher was convinced that Kaufmann would balk.

"Okay," E. J. said after studying the drawings. "When do we start?"

ꟼHE ꟼEST

THE EDGAR KAUFMANN–FUNDED BROADACRE City was a provocative fantasy, but, like an architecture school exercise, it stood little chance of ever being built. Fallingwater, a project for E. J. and his family, was another story. If Wright actually did throw it together in a few hours, he may not have realized just what he had gotten himself into. The engineering and construction problems were formidable. And he had no professional staff left to pull it off. If the apprentices were indeed a bunch of incompetents, as Wes Peters had charged, the stage was set for disaster.

Wright assigned Bob Mosher, Edgar Tafel, and Blaine Drake to work with him on turning the idea into something that could be built. Bear Run wasn't their only project. The visit from Dallas retailer Stanley Marcus had led to a commission, and there was a professor's house to be built in Palo Alto, California. But Fallingwater was the priority. Three months after Kaufmann gave the go-ahead, the team finished a set of more detailed drawings—without yet addressing the design's structural challenges—and sent them off to him in Pittsburgh.

In January 1936, Wright and the Fellowship fled the Wisconsin winter once more to work on Bear Run and their other jobs in the relative warmth of Chandler.

Thirty-year-old Stanley Marcus, son of the founder of Neiman Marcus ("the poshest place on the prairie"), had chosen Wright over two other modernists, William Lescaze and Wright's old nemesis Richard Neutra, to design his Dallas house. Wright had prevailed, in part, by promising that the house would cost no more than ten thousand dollars.

Wright's initial design—doubtless influenced by his own eccentric approach to living in the Southwest—had no bedrooms, on the premise that his wealthy client and his family would sleep outside. Nor had he included closets for this clothier's home. "[C]losets are rotten," he told Marcus. "They just accumulate junk."

Wright had convinced Edgar Kaufmann to go along with an equally outrageous idea—covering his beloved waterfall—but Stanley and Mary Marcus balked. After all, they made their living *filling* closets. But when Wright came up with a new design, with both closets and bedrooms, the couple agreed to travel to Arizona to see a scale model. Wright phoned his former client, the Biltmore Hotel, to reserve them a room. At one point in the conversation there was a pause. Wright was heard to say, "He is, but she isn't." Stanley and Mary got a room in spite of the hotel's policy of restricting Jews.

The meeting went well and the couple approved the new design. But when Marcus sent the plans out to bid the lowest estimate was $150,000, fifteen times his architect's promised price.

Contractors can't read plans, Wright responded.

"Whose fault is that—yours or theirs?" Marcus retorted. Wright was terminated, a local architect hired in his place. When construction was completed, Marcus sent Wright a newspaper article that featured a photograph of his new house.

"I didn't know you would be satisfied with so little," came the reply.

IN APRIL, WITH spring coming to Wisconsin, a line of Fellowship vehicles headed out of Chandler for the return trip. They had finished the architectural drawings for Fallingwater and made some progress on the structural design, even though Wright had no real engineering experts with him in Arizona.

For a time, it looked as though the drawings Wright saw as containing the future of American architecture might never make it back to Spring Green. The culprit was a dot on the Wrights' map marked "Tuweep."

About three hundred miles out of Chandler, the Wrights got curious about Tuweep, off the main road in the middle of nowhere. Turning off the road to look for the route, they soon encountered a group of Indians. How do you get to Tuweep? they asked. The Indians just laughed and shook their heads. The road, they said, was impassible. But Tuweep had become an idée fixe, something they just had to do. They managed to find a ranger who sketched them a map.

While the rest of the group looked for a place to make camp, five of the cars started off in search of Tuweep. The dirt road gently rose through low desert scrub through stacks of red-brown boulders that dwarfed their cars. At Short Creek, a Mormon settlement, they stopped for food and gas. The local store had nothing to eat, so Gene Masselink and Cornelia Brierly went looking for a home where they might get sandwiches. In the process, they lost the rest of the caravan. Their faces became so chapped from the cold that they put Cornelia's lipstick on to protect them. Finally they spotted a single cabin light in the distance. When the old lady who lived there opened the door, she was greeted by a lipstick-smeared Gene Masselink.

The road beyond Short Creek was uncertain and rutted; there were no signs of human habitation. Night was rapidly coming, and for some— including Betty Barnsdall, a redheaded Marlene Dietrich look-alike—the adventure was getting out of hand. After pulling over in one barren area, the oil heiress's daughter left her LaSalle and ran stumbling over to Mr. and Mrs. Wright's car, furious about what the unpaved roads were doing to her luxury car.

"Goddamn you," she yelled at Wright, "I'm not going any further."

"Let someone else drive your car for you," Olgivanna told her. "You are foolish about your car. I told you that at the beginning. Don't be so over-possessive. . . . If I can take it, you can." Betty returned to her vehicle crying.

Pushing on, they ran into an old couple who told them that Tuweep was ahead another fifty miles, through "unknown desert."

"It was then," Olgivanna recalled, "that my own spirit began to weaken, and I asked to go back, but no matter how reasonably I pleaded, my husband was relentless."

It would have been hard for her not to remember that day in Constantinople when Gurdjieff took her on a similarly grueling excursion. Then she had begged for it to end; both times her pleadings were ignored. Her husband's eyes, she saw, were "brilliant with challenge."

"Never you mind," he told her, "get back into the cars. We're going on."

"Sometimes octopus-like bypaths started out in every direction," Gene recalled, "and we would get down on all fours searching for the trail—the trail our cars had left behind." They would follow the freshest trail only to discover that it ended at the side of a mountain.

Retracing their route miles back to a place where they had seen a light, they found two tiny crude houses and a stockade. A young woman opened the door.

How do we get to Tuweep? somebody asked.

"I am the Postmistress of Tuweep," she replied, "and this is Tuweep."

AFTER AN "AGREEABLE" short visit and coffee, the troupe left the post-mistress; it was two in the morning before they found their way back to the Taliesin camp. "There we were," Kay Schneider recalled, "with no water, no gas, mountain lions roaring, coyotes howling, it was pitch black—and Jack

Howe, as we were eating, complained, 'Where's the mustard, Mabel?'"
Mabel was Taliesin's last remaining paid cook from the pre-Fellowship
days.

But Wright was chipper as they sat around the campfire. "This is the only
way to see our country," he announced. The apprentices seemed perplexed.
"People looked at him sadly," Olgivanna recalled, "because they hadn't seen
anything for the last two hours."

He persisted. "This is the only way to travel. One must go through hardships to enjoy leisure. People are getting too soft from too much soft living."

Betty Barnsdall sat there sniffling, blowing her nose. "Yes," Wright went
on, exhilarated, "this is what will make men and women out of you. Take a
deep breath," he said, taking one himself. "Enjoy this pure air. A human foot
has probably not stepped on this ground for years." He then asked that the
fire be kept alive going through the night. "[W]e are in the country of mountain lions," he warned.

The apprentices' faces looked "dark and pale with the shadows of the
flickering fire," Olgivanna recalled.

"Did you bring a gun?" one whispered to another.

"Thank God," came the reply. "I did."

Mountain lions, it turned out, were the least of their worries. In the light
of morning, they discovered that Mr. and Mrs. Wright had rolled out their
sleeping bags just a few feet from the edge of the Grand Canyon. "[A] sheer
rock cliff," Gene recalled, "dropped three thousand feet to where the Colorado distantly roared below."

"Providence," Olgivanna remarked, "does take care of those whom it has
blessed with courage."

TRAVELING IN EUROPE, Edgar Kaufmann may have never learned just
how close the Fallingwater vellums, not to mention their creator, had come to
falling into the abyss. When he unrolled the copies Wright had sent on to
Pittsburgh, he was thrilled, but anxious. Those decks shooting out into space
seemed almost impossible to support.

Wright's jutting decks were not completely original, as Kaufmann himself may have known. It was he who had suggested early on that Wright look
for structural inspiration to his former draftsman Richard Neutra's 1929
Lovell House near Los Angeles, which had been featured in the MoMA
show. With its dramatic floors projecting out toward the street, the Lovell
house had made a stir in modernist circles. Wright's son Lloyd, who was living in Los Angeles when the landmark house was built, surely knew the
project in detail; his father did too. But the senior Wright could of course

claim precedence with his even earlier house completed in 1909 for Zona Gale's aunt.

The staggered horizontal concrete projections of Fallingwater, its massive, undecorated painted surfaces, the way it hovered in the air—all these suggested that Wright was playing off not just Neutra but also the whole aesthetic thrust of his European enemies. But Wright intended Fallingwater as critique, not homage. He had told apprentice Cornelia Brierly as much: With this house, he said, they would beat "the Internationalists at their own game." Among his targets was the master of the airborne building, the Swiss architect Le Corbusier, whose centralized urban planning theories he was hoping to replace with Broadacre City.

Fallingwater was much more boldly three-dimensional than anything coming from Europe; its composition referred to forms and forces of nature, not the machine. Wright left space for trees to grow right through the bedroom terrace. He specificed locally quarried flagstone for the walls and the floors, not just to blend with the site, but also to suggest the stratified outcroppings through which the water coursed below. And the horizontal concrete decks were sustained and penetrated by vertical stacks of Taliesin-like masonry stone.

The message of Fallingwater was clear: The European avant-garde stood on his foundations, their branches had grown from his trunk.

THERE WAS ONE aspect of the forest retreat that was strikingly at odds with the natural context: Its horizontal concrete bands were originally to be coated with gold leaf, like the Japanese screens Wright so loved. Associating gold with the successful Jewish merchant, according to an apprentice working on the project, Wright proposed it to Kaufmann, who approved the idea. A gilder was brought down from Pittsburgh to give it a go. After a few hours, he quit. "You people are crazy," he declared as he left.

In its bold defiance of gravity, there was also something dangerous about the design—something with roots deep in Wright's psychic past. As a sixteen-year-old, Wright had been close enough to hear the roar of whole floors tumbling down to the basement when shoddily built piers caused an addition to the Wisconsin State Capitol building to collapse. One of the cornices crushed a workman against the sill; with horror, young Frank watched him hanging upside down, a line of his blood streaked against the white wall. Other bodies were strewn across the lawn, caked white with calcium dust.

"The youth," Wright wrote, referring to himself, "stayed for hours clinging to the iron fence that surrounded the park, too heartsick to go away. . . . Then he went home—ill. Dreamed of it all that night and the next and the next. The horror of the scene has never entirely left his consciousness and remains to prompt him to this day."

But prompt him to what? Not toward designs that ensured and communicated safety, but to one that dared to thrust half a building's mass off into the air as the land and water fell away below it. Just as those who suffer trauma often feel the need to return to it, the horror Wright witnessed as a youth had apparently given him a perverse desire to tempt fate.

There is a visceral thrill to Fallingwater, something even Wright's drawings convey. Like a gymnast on the high bars who freezes his body horizontally at the top of his arc, the house appears to defy gravity with an impossible muscularity. In magic, the technique is called "misdirection." Looking beneath the building's projections to find adequate support, we are mystified to find only air. The magician-architect knows where the observer will look for support—in the logical, but wrong, place. Instead, he extends his hidden support beams from the front edge of the "floating" deck back through and beyond the house deep into the hill beyond.

The engineering principle behind such a structure is that of the cantilever—a beam or floor slab that is rigid enough to extend into space without support from below. Cantilevers are not inherently unsafe; in fact they are commonly found in nature, in tree branches and rock outcroppings like the one that created the waterfall over which Wright wanted to build the house. "Nature," he told his initially doubtful client, "cantilevered those boulders out over the fall. . . . I can cantilever the house over the boulders."

But the cantilevers shown in the Fallingwater drawings appeared to defy the engineer's basic rule of thumb: For every foot of cantilever, at least two feet of the structural member must be contained entirely within the building. Wright knew this; indeed, he cleverly concealed some of what is called the "back span" in a concrete trellis behind the house. Even another architect might have, at first glance, been fooled into thinking the decks would eventually collapse. This was a far cry from the form-follows-function mantra of the age, or even from the structural "honesty" of the Gothic cathedral. It was a trick, albeit a wonderful one.

Wright nonetheless saw himself as the successor to the great Gothic builders; he understood the importance of engineering to great architecture. He loved regaling listeners with tales of how the Romeo and Juliet windmill and the Imperial Hotel had survived apparently impossible circumstances—stories intended to bolster his reputation for genius in both architecture and engineering, to put him in the company of the Gothic masters and Michelangelo. Like Michelangelo's dome for St. Peter's Basilica, Fallingwater was a bravado test of engineering genius. If things went well, it would remind the world that the man who had defied nature in Tokyo was still in possession of his powers.

Of course, Michelangelo's structural genius was largely intuitive. The structural engineering Wright studied at the university, and that Dankmar Adler brought to his partnership with Louis Sullivan, was based on mathematical models, formulas used to predict structural strength. And although he claimed otherwise, engineering had never been Wright's strong suit—especially, it appears, when it came to calculation. Many of his early houses, projects executed just after leaving Adler and Sullivan, had in fact suffered from his mediocre structural skills.

Wright apparently understood his limitations. After his string of Oak Park houses, when he began landing larger projects that involved real engineering challenges, he brought in a German immigrant named Paul Mueller, who had been Dankmar Adler's protégé during Wright's tenure with Adler and Sullivan. Mueller made important contributions to all of Wright's major concrete buildings before Fallingwater, including the Unity Temple, the Larkin Building, and San Marcos in the Desert; the engineer even accompanied Wright to Tokyo to oversee the construction of the Imperial Hotel. And it was a good thing: While it was Wright who thought of using a floating foundation for the earthquake-prone city, Mueller had actually designed one—a raft foundation of crisscrossed railroad ties for the Auditorium Building, built in Chicago's soft blue clay.

But Paul Mueller had died before Wright could enlist him to help solve the structural challenges of Fallingwater. Instead he turned to an engineer named Mendel Glickman. The irreligious son of religious Jews, Glickman had worked as an engineer for International Harvester until 1929, when he left for a two-year stint in the Soviet Union directing the construction of Stalingrad's immense tractor factory. Just before the Fellowship began, Glickman contacted Wright hoping to trade his engineering skills for architectural training.

Glickman had moved into Taliesin in 1931 with his wife and two children—but they left shortly after, when Glickman's mother, and presumably his wife, protested what she called "Mrs. Wright's queenly behavior." Now, five years later, with his masterpiece on the line, Wright prevailed on him to return.

Glickman clearly understood his employer. "Wright did not show anti-Semitism," the engineer remarked, "when he needed people." Wright was always sensitive about his dependence on others' engineering talents; it was a reminder of the limits of his genius. Now he fell back into his old pattern at Adler and Sullivan where the divide between the art of architecture and the science of engineering became the difference between a Christian and a Jew.

Though Wright trusted in Glickman's skill, the engineer himself was a Taliesin outsider, a former comrade who had cut and run. And he wasn't the only such figure to rejoin the fold. Soon Taliesin would welcome back a more beloved prodigal son—a former MIT engineering student, and a Christian to boot.

"I'VE BOUGHT THE nails to renail Romeo and Juliet," Wright wrote Svetlana the first week of July 1936. "[T]hey are waiting for Wes."

Wright was referring to the old windmill, but the symbolism would not have been lost on any of them: Wes and Svetlana were Taliesin's forbidden lovers, who, rather than killing themselves, had run away and married. And now they were coming home.

Their return had taken some doing. "I frankly didn't want to come back," Wes recalled. "Neither did Svet." But Olgivanna had taken the long view, patiently spinning images of the nest awaiting them and the great work her son-in-law could accomplish at Taliesin. She knew Svetlana wanted time to work on her music, which would be difficult on a starting architect's income. Frank promised to hire a first-class cellist and violinist with whom Svetlana could perform as a trio. Olgivanna even promised to exempt her daughter from kitchen duty.

Svetlana had always been more inclined to give Taliesin another chance, and not just because of her mother and stepfather's lures. Svetlana had come to identify again with Wright's mission: "struggling, fighting, impoverishing himself to carry thru another great ideal," she declared to Wes, "—to bring a *slight grain* of sense of those young fools. I do admire him and I feel bitterly sorry that he has such fickle material to work with. . . ." Mr. Wright needs help, she told Wes. And this time she knew she would have her husband to protect her from her parents' all-consuming demands.

Wes was the harder nut. But Wright had been sending him what Peters described as "beautiful letters." And Olgivanna arranged for him to visit Taliesin, where Wright looked approvingly at his son-in-law's recent drawings for clients, including an underground house on a small city lot. For someone who feared that he lacked the talent to do great work, Peters must have welcomed the affirmation.

Not long after, Peters's father suddenly died of a stroke. It was then that Wright took the extraordinary step of formally inviting Wes to return to Taliesin. But the timing wasn't exactly selfless: Wes's engineering skills were sorely needed at Taliesin, and so was his substantial inheritance. The Bank of Wisconsin was again threatening foreclosure.

By now, Svetlana was so eager to get back that she wasn't even willing to wait for her husband to finish the houses he had designed in Evansville. The new bride left Wes behind and moved into Taliesin by herself, sharing a room with Kay Schneider in the guest wing.

When Wes finally joined Svetlana at Taliesin, they were immediately established as regents and heirs. Wright made Peters his number two, the permanent "Boss," a job that had previously rotated among the apprentices. Wes now made up the daily and weekly assignment lists, showing them to Wright for approval before hanging them in Gene Masselink's office. Svetlana was soon directing the Taliesin chorus, and entertaining the apprentices with her violin; Wright loved to hear her play Beethoven's Sonata in A Major.

Though the lovers' return was a victory for Olgivanna, she was still furious at her daughter for abandoning her. Underlying her anger, she confessed to Svetlana, "was such despair and truly longing to have you. . . . Such things happen to me however, even towards Daddy Frank. Evidently everyone is doomed by some peculiarity of their inner structure."

Still, Svetlana was quickly reabsorbed into the household. Among other things, her mother put her in charge of Iovanna; Svetlana found herself cleaning the child's room, packing for her when they went on trips, and shouting the little girl down. For the apprentices, it was a relief to have an ally in the household who could come to their aid if Iovanna should report their supposed misdeeds to her mother.

Svetlana also pitched in to help Olgivanna train her putative replacement, the doe-eyed Kay Schneider, showing her how to clean the house and to make tea. Together they waxed the cypress floors, vacuumed the stones. "Kay," Svetlana instructed, "it's not what you do; it's the way that you do it." What was important was the purity of one's intent, the banishment of negative emotion, feelings that would inevitably be projected into one's work.

WRIGHT SAW PETERS as a growing engineering talent, and assigned him to be Glickman's assistant on Fallingwater. Wes really learned his trade under the engineer, whom he came to respect for both his talent and his ethics. Though Glickman was the son of a rabbi, Wes felt that he "exercised more Christian virtues than anybody else I ever saw." It was a far cry from how he generally described Wright.

By all accounts, Wright's studio operated in a remarkably casual way. The layers of error-checking found in more businesslike firms did not exist. In fact, even with a project as challenging as Fallingwater, Wright paid little attention to the engineering drawings until they were done. And when he finally did, he felt free to change them casually, leaving Wes and Glickman to pick up the pieces.

One of Wright's changes risked disaster. The cantilevered decks were to be made of reinforced concrete, which uses a grid of steel rods within the concrete to help the otherwise brittle material resist sagging. After careful calculations, Glickman and Peters had specified rods of a full inch in diameter, along with others of smaller size. Wright summarily changed them all to a measly half inch, hopelessly inadequate for a cantilever of this size. Glickman and Peters were aghast. Rather than confront Wright, though, they clandestinely made up a duplicate set of structural drawings showing the one-inch rods and sent them off to Kaufmann. Wright evidently discovered this, for the half-inch rods had returned when he later met with Kaufmann at the site. At that meeting, Wright agreed to split the difference and the bars were upgraded to three quarters of an inch—engineering by barter, not calculation.

Without informing Wright, Kaufmann forwarded these drawings to his own engineers in Pittsburgh for checking. The rods didn't seem to bother them, but almost everything else did. They questioned the long-term stability of the rock on which the house was to sit. They thought that insufficient attention had been paid to the effects of the stream at flood levels. They did independent calculations that indicated that the stone foundation walls should be one third thicker. The plans, they pointed out, "do not show dimensions of principal supporting members of the building, nor structural details such as the arrangement of steel reinforcement." And, in a devastating indictment, they complained that the drawings didn't have enough information for them to confirm, one way or the other, whether the structure was safe.

When E. J. sent the document to Taliesin, Wright exploded. He demanded the return of his plans; Kaufmann didn't deserve the house. Kaufmann apologized and later buried the report in one of the walls. This would prove to be a mistake.

WITH KAUFMANN'S DE facto approval of the dubious engineering, Wright and the apprentices were free to complete a set of working drawings. Sometimes referred to as "the blueprints," working drawings are much like a composer's score, a set of instructions for producing what will hopefully be a work of art. Well before construction begins, the builder needs these drawings to estimate the cost of a project. Construction is invariably burdened with uncertainty. How much will the lumber cost? How long will it take the carpenters to frame the structure? How much, in the end, to charge the owner? The builder knows only what's in the working drawings and what he gleans from visiting the site.

With an unprecedented design like Fallingwater, where virtually nothing is conventional, a contractor would need exceptionally precise and detailed drawings. But Wright's approach to drawings was as eccentric as his designs.

Working drawings are generally dotted with hundreds of dimensions; the builders who opened the Fallingwater drawings found almost none. Influenced by the Japanese tatami mat system of sizing buildings, Wright designed using standard modules, such as a four-foot-square grid; his drawings showed only the grid and the position of elements upon it. The contractors were left to convert the drawings into more conventional terms, using what are known as "string dimensions." The sparseness of precise dimensions had the perhaps intentional effect of passing the responsibility for arithmetic errors from Wright to the contractor. Not a few builders, when confronted with Wright's drawings, either refused to bid or bid high in order to protect themselves.

Those who took such jobs often regretted it. Wright's drawings were not only unorthodox, but also often incomplete. To make matters worse, Wright loved to come to the construction site, using his cane to point out things he didn't like and ordering them changed on the spot, regardless of whether his original plans had been followed. Of the thousands of letters in Wright's archives, the belligerent exchanges between Wright and his builders are rivaled in number only by those with his creditors.

AFTER FORTY YEARS of practicing architecture, Wright surely knew that the construction of Fallingwater would be a high-wire act, one in which critical decisions would routinely be required at the job site. Instead of handling the task himself, he made the astonishing move of giving the site supervisor job to Abe Dombar—a seriously inexperienced young man who had quit the Fellowship seven months before.

Wright viewed his apprentices as his "boys," and those he was especially fond of, like Dombar, as his "sons." Dombar had wanted a real paying job, a wife and a family, maybe even a pilgrimage to Palestine. But Wright expected his apprentices to devote their full energies to Taliesin, leaving them with very little free time of their own. Family events like holidays, birthdays and anniversaries, even funerals were generally to be ignored. There were no vacations, and parents who sent their sons and daughters off to become apprentices had to travel to Wisconsin or Arizona to see them.

By the same token, apprentices who married and had children had to make a willful choice to shield their families from the gravitational pull of Taliesin, to draw their children away from their peers at mealtime, to make a separate intimate circle into which they alone had access. And their efforts were almost always unsuccessful: Parents at Taliesin often neglected their children, letting them wander around the premises unsupervised. Children were injured by passing cars or falls from high, unprotected places. Over the years, some older children would attempt suicide. Most apprentices who wanted children left.

Taliesin was a clan of unrelated men and women pledging fealty to a man they called their master. Although the vast majority of apprentices stayed for no more than a year, the ideal was to stay forever. Frank Lloyd Wright, the product of a broken home who had abandoned his own children to run off with a client's wife, had little patience for the family ties of his apprentices.

Nor did he react well when one of his "sons" announced his decision to leave. Many never mustered the courage to confront him directly. Some fled in the night. When Abe Dombar made up his mind to leave Taliesin, he did what apprentices before him had done—he lied. His father was ailing, he claimed; he would have to return home to help the family financially.

"Go home and bury your father and then come back to me," Wright had told him.

"I will bury you first," Dombar thought to himself.

When Dombar did not return, Wright wrote chiding the twenty-two-year-old for putting his "neck into the money-yoke." Unless his family was near starving, he said, it was "very stupid" for Abe's mother to let money stand in the way of his promising future. "Taliesin's sons," he added, "should belong to Taliesin for their own sake and the sake of a greater cause than merely family relationships which are everywhere pretty much the same . . ."

The young man was unmoved. At Taliesin, Dombar had become close friends with Edgar Kaufmann Jr. and had gotten to know Junior's father when the Broadacre exhibition traveled from Rockefeller Center to his department store. Having worked on store window displays before joining Wright, Abe called the Kaufmanns before leaving Taliesin to ask for a job doing the same for them. Junior gave him the job.

In April 1936, the elder Kaufmann alerted Dombar that Wright was coming east to take another look at the Fallingwater site. Dombar was away when Wright dropped by the store's art department, but they met that evening when Kaufmann asked Abe to drive them all to Bear Run. "Abe," Wright warned the nervous driver, "you hold within your hands the future of modern architecture in America . . . drive carefully."

Along the way, Kaufmann mentioned that Dombar would be designing a summer house for his cousin at Bear Run and "a couple of houses for Junior who's going to build some houses for the market."

"Why are you having Abe do this?" Wright replied angrily, reminding Kaufmann that Abe had no experience. "I'd be glad to do it." Kaufmann didn't bite.

At Bear Run, while Wright napped, Kaufmann reassured Dombar. "Abe," he said, "don't pay attention to what Mr. Wright said, you are going to do those houses."

The next day Kaufmann asked Wright if he planned to have somebody supervise the Bear Run site. When Wright said yes, Kaufmann suggested that Abe should do it. "He understands the plans and the work," he added, "and he is already here."

Wright agreed, and Dombar, assuming he would be paid to supervise, resigned his position at the store.

Wright promised that instructions would come soon after Abe started work at Bear Run, but nothing arrived. The contractor carried on as best he could, pouring the foundation for a bridge over the stream. Two or three weeks later, as they were preparing to start on the house itself, Wright still hadn't sent Dombar the promised instructions.

AND ABE HADN'T received a paycheck. When Dombar phoned Wright, the master replied that Abe was still his apprentice, and shouldn't expect to be paid. Dombar couldn't get Wright to change his mind. "If I could find someone that I could learn something from," Wright chided Dombar, "I would crawl on my hands and knees to them."

Abe was willing to carry on, but he needed to eat. Wright asked Kaufmann to pay Dombar. "Hell, no. I already paid you two percent of the cost for supervision," Edgar replied, "so you pay him." Ultimately, though, Kaufmann agreed to cover his room and board.

Back at Taliesin, the apprentices groused that Dombar, a traitor who had left the Fellowship just months before, had been awarded the prize of supervising their greatest project. The discontent struck a chord with the master. One morning toward the end of May, Edgar Tafel came to fetch Bob Mosher from the kitchen, where he was scraping vegetables. "Mr. Wright says we're going to Pittsburgh right away. Be sure to take enough clothing—you're going to stay at Bear Run." Mosher snuck out of the kitchen, elated. That wasn't unusual; Mosher's cheerful disposition had led the master to nickname him "little sunshine."

His cheerfulness would soon be tested.

WRIGHT, MOSHER, TAFEL, and Manuel Sandoval, an apprentice skilled at carpentry, climbed into Wright's red Ford convertible and headed for Pittsburgh. After dropping Sandoval off to begin the cabinet work on Kaufmann's private office, the other three continued on the winding sixty-mile road to Bear Run.

"We hiked," Mosher recalled, "through the heavy woods along the torrential stream, Bear Run, to the spot where it formed a roaring waterfall below a huge boulder jutting out from the north bank of the stream. We stood on a bridge spanning the stream, facing the top of the waterfall. The maestro said, 'I'm leaving you here. Do you have any questions?' "

Mosher had one. "Can you tell me how to locate the exact datum of the first floor?" Mosher had familiarized himself with the project on paper, but being confronted with the complexity of the actual site was a different thing altogether. Even veteran architects are sometimes bewildered when they first unroll their drawings at a job site and try to figure out how they relate to the real world.

Precisely how high off the ground should the floor of the house be set? Mosher asked.

"That's a good question, Bobby." Wright replied. "Now go across the stream and climb up on that boulder."

Easier said than done: Wright was pointing to a boulder that towered more than eighteen feet above the streambed. Mosher struggled to the top by grabbing small saplings that had grown out of the crevices in the rock. When he reached the top, the master yelled up at him over the roar of the stream, "All right, Bobby, you've answered your own question."

"Mr. Wright," Mosher yelled back, looking down at his feet, "is this it?"

"That's it. Now goodbye and good luck and don't pull too many mistakes."

Wright hiked off, leaving "little sunshine" alone with his thoughts and a roll of drawings for what was, for its size, easily the most challenging house anyone had ever built.

EDGAR KAUFMANN SR. rehired Abe Dombar at the store after his blowup with Wright. The promise of designing houses for Junior apparently never came through, but Dombar's interest in architecture persisted; on weekends he went up to Bear Run to watch the construction. Kaufmann saw real talent in his window dresser and happily became his patron, offering Abe the chance to design a line of furniture for the store after watching him work with Manuel Sandoval on the furniture for his Wright-designed private office. He even offered Abe an acre of his own in Bear Run if he would only stay.

But Abe still dreamed of becoming an architect, and he decided to return to Cincinnati and try to make it there. Before leaving he made a brief visit to Taliesin, where his brother Benjamin was still an apprentice. He got a frosty reception. "Wright had warned them against the bad world outside," he recalled, "and they were afraid they'd be contaminated. . . . Mrs. Wright preached to me about deserting the cause and what damage I had done to my 'soul.' " When Abe later asked Wright for a letter of recommendation to use in applying for his architect's license, Wright refused. The butcher in Spring Green had known him longer, the master replied curtly.

*   *   *

LOCATING THE FLOOR levels of Fallingwater turned out to be the least of Bob Mosher's problems. As "clerk of the works" of the project, he found himself trying to mediate among Edgar Kaufmann Sr., the client; Walter Hall, the contractor; and Frank Lloyd Wright, the architect. It was nearly impossible.

By August, the wooden formwork for the first-floor concrete slab was going up. Of course, the first floor of this house was hardly at ground level. The slab would hover high in the air over the stream, cantilevering fifteen feet beyond the stone piers below. Spooked anew by the sight, Kaufmann brought the latest drawings back to his own engineers. They recommended both extending forward the supporting piers, which Wright wanted to be inconspicuous, and doubling the amount of steel rebar to stiffen the concrete beams. This was rebar that Peters and Glickman had already increased, surreptitiously, beyond what Wright had thought necessary. Mosher took it on himself to agree to both changes.

On a visit to the site, after the slab had been poured, Kaufmann confessed that he'd called for the changes. "If you've not noticed it in these last two hours of inspection," Kaufmann suggested, apparently in sarcasm, "there can't be anything very bad about it, architecturally."

"E. J.," Wright replied, "come with me." Mosher accompanied the men down below the cantilevered slab, where Wright had a surprise of his own: He'd already ordered Mosher to remove the top four inches of the wall extension Kaufmann's engineers had recommended. What remained was no longer supporting the tons of concrete hanging over their heads.

"Now the terrace has shown no signs of falling," Wright admonished. "Shall we take down the extra four feet of wall?" They did.

The second change agreed to by Bob Mosher—doubling the steel—caused a furor. "If you are paying to have the concrete engineering done down there," Wright later wrote Kaufmann, "there is no use whatever in our doing it here. I am willing you should take it over but I am not willing to be insulted. . . . I am unaccustomed to such treatment where I have built buildings and do not intend to put up with it now so I am calling Bob back until we can work out something or nothing. . . . I don't know what kind of architect you are familiar with but it apparently isn't the kind I think I am. You seem not to know how to treat a decent one. I have put so much more into this house than you or any other client has a right to expect that if I haven't your confidence—to hell with the whole thing."

Kaufmann turned Wright's words back on him. "I am," he wrote back, "unaccustomed to such treatment where I have been building before and I do not intend to put up with it now so I am calling upon you to come down here, which I hoped you could have done during the past few weeks, to inspect the work under Mr. Hall's direction who is an unknown foreman to you, instead of allowing the entire responsibility of his craftsmanship to rest upon us here. . . . I don't know what kind of clients you are familiar with but apparently they are not the kind I think I am. You seem not know how to treat a decent one. I have put so much confidence and enthusiasm behind this whole project in my limited way, to help the fulfillment of your efforts that if I do not have your confidence in the matter—to hell with the whole thing.

"It is difficult," he closed, "for me to conceive that a man of your magnitude and understanding could write such a letter. In deference to our past association I must naturally put it aside as if it had never been written as it certainly does not conform to the facts."

Wright called "little sunshine" back to Taliesin. "I was in disgrace," Mosher remembered. Kaufmann was chagrined to lose this second apprentice supervisor. Mosher, he wrote Wright, "seems entirely wrapped up in his work and in its progress but this is beyond my control and you must use your own judgment."

". . . Bob should come back here for a cinch in his belt," Wright replied. "He needs a little seasoning perhaps. He'll get it. Perhaps I need it too. I'll get it."

In a later edition of his autobiography, Wright not only blamed Mosher for the ill-considered changes, but claimed that it was Kaufmann who took the apprentice off the job. "Take him away," E. J. supposedly told Wright. "His blunders will cost me money. Take him away!"

MOSHER, IN FACT, had probably saved the project. When they removed the wooden formwork after pouring the concrete cantilever, the slab immediately sagged two inches. Some sag is to be expected when forms are pulled, but no more than a half an inch, according to sound engineering practice. If Mosher hadn't approved the extra steel, the slab might have collapsed altogether. Yet his inexperience, coupled with minimal direction from Wright and the contractor's inexperience with this kind of construction, also contributed to the structure's essential instability. Any experienced builder would have adjusted for the weight of the concrete by tilting the forms slightly up so that the expected sag would bring everything back to level when the forms were removed. Hall's men had built the forms level, and when the structure sagged, it sagged visibly.

But there was plenty of blame to go around. When Mendel Glickman learned of the two-inch sag, he was stunned. "Oh my God," he gasped, "we left out the negative reinforcement." It was an astounding mistake: In a cantilever, negative reinforcement bars must be placed toward the top of a slab or beam

Fallingwater during construction. Fearing a collapse, the workmen refused to remove the wood braces. (Note the precariously placed construction shed atop the cantilevered terrace.)

to prevent the upper portion from stretching, allowing it to bow downward under its own weight. For Glickman to leave out something as critical as the negative reinforcement was bad enough; that no one else caught the error suggests a startling inattention to detail, to say the least. The drawings reviewed by Kaufmann's engineers may have been so incomplete, and the need for the reinforcement so obvious, that they just assumed it would be addressed. Wes Peters may have been too inexperienced to catch it. And while Wright had designed plenty of cantilevers, none had been built of reinforced concrete.

Completely ignoring the negative reinforcement issue, Wright blamed the problem on the one thing that certainly *wasn't* an issue: the weight of the extra steel recommended by Kaufmann's engineers and snuck in by his own renegade apprentice, Mosher. Steel does weigh about three times as much as concrete, but the amount of extra steel installed was so tiny, the extra rebar was such a small proportion of the total, that its impact would have been inconsequential.

WRIGHT REPLACED MOSHER with Edgar Tafel, who was immediately confronted with more structural problems. The upper floor deck, constructed much like the troubled one below, had originally been engineered to hold itself up without bearing on the lower one. But Wright had decided to beef up the spindly vertical mullions in the windows that rose from the lower deck to the underside of the master bedroom deck above. The lighter mullions, he realized, would have buckled when the upper deck inevitably sagged a little. But the stronger replacements created a more severe problem: They transferred the extra weight onto the already troubled lower cantilever.

The workmen were so worried about the structure that they balked at removing the temporary supports below when the forms were removed, afraid that the whole affair would collapse on top of them. The contractor had to do it himself.

Fallingwater would prove to be the most spectacular house that Wright would ever design. As a unique solution to a unique site, however, it was arguably not the most important. A few months after the apparently miraculous, nearly instantaneous design for Bear Run, the architect received a letter from a considerably less well-heeled prospective client. "This may be an obsession," began Robert Lusk, the managing editor of *The Evening Huronite*, "this desire on my part to get a sample of your work in South Dakota . . . It would have to be small—very small." The location was not exciting, he conceded. "But maybe that presents a problem just as interesting and important as the designing of a home in a beautiful setting."

Wright accepted the challenge, and after the usual months of procrastination he produced preliminary sketches. He and the apprentices had been working on an economical house for the everyman for Broadacre City, so he felt well prepared for the assignment. "They may shock you," he wrote in the letter accompanying the drawings, "and even offend you at first. Although they embody your requirements they go by the two story house as an unnecessary tax upon comfort and spread you out comfortably on your own piece of ground to live your own life on the level. Upstairs for upstarts. The ground for nobler humans."

This simple, one-story house, Wright claimed, would be most economical. It would be built on a concrete slab, except for a small basement for the heater, laundry, and storage. The garage would not be "shut in—as I see little reason for it with cars as they are now and increasingly will be." Despite Wright's reputation as someone who insisted on having his way, he closed his letter in a collaborative spirit: "[N]othing is final. Let us have your reactions and we'll cooperate." The architect tended to be accommodating and generous with little people, clients who had little money, no pull, yet enough daring to solicit a design from him. It was with the wealthy and the powerful that he chose to act the prima donna.

Lusk didn't see anything shocking in the design, but he probably should have. Contained in Wright's plans were many ideas, not yet commonplace, that would eventually shape the future of American mass housing. There was Wright's new kind of housing for the automobile, the carport. Wood-framed floors were, for the first time, replaced by a concrete slab. And the kitchen, rather then being shunted aside as servant territory, was positioned as the heart of the household.

The Lusk home was one of the first in a series of modular designs that Wright called Usonians, after the name he had invented for the United States in the glow of his first months with Olgivanna. Wright filled them with standardized details, allowing him to reuse them in his later houses. He was sure that his Usonian design would allow architects to "bring the factory to the job," as he put it, prefabricating flexible units that could be reassembled in different patterns and arrangements depending on the circumstances. Some of Wright's later Usonians were built almost entirely in the mill and brought to the site as large roof and wall panels. Wright's prefabricated houses were fifty years ahead of the prefab housing industry.

Not long after the Lusk design, later in 1936, an ambitious New York developer named Robert Levitt made regular visits to a construction site in Great Neck, New York, to watch another of Wright's Usonian designs under construction. He was impressed by the potential economies: no basement, no deep foundation, an easily standardized modular structure. Years later he would recall Wright's innovations as he planned Levittown, a Long Island potato field that became the first mass-produced suburb.

Neither the Lusks nor the Hoults, clients for a similar house, ever got their Usonian houses built. The Lusks were denied an FHA mortgage because of Wright's unconventional design; then a devastating June drought killed the project. The Hoults' $5,500 dream house met with a more familiar fate. "We have had an estimate made from the plans we have," Mrs. Hoult wrote Wright in April 1936. "To my surprise and great disappointment it was $10,000."

Wright replied that he had erred in not alerting them to the expanding budget. He then offered to try for a less expensive scheme. "But if you are disillusioned," he wrote in closing, "kindly return the sketches for which there will be no charge in the circumstances." Disillusioned they must have been, for the correspondence ends there.

MR. WRIGHT USUALLY opened the mail as the apprentices milled around his office, keeping up a running commentary as he did. One day, sitting at his desk next to the drafting studio, he opened an envelope and pulled out a check from the Johnson Wax company for one thousand dollars. "It's all right boys," he announced, waving the check in the air, "we got the job!" *We got the opportunity* would have been more like it—the money was only for a preliminary proposal—but it was good news nonetheless.

What made it all possible was a substance called Glo-Coat. Four years earlier, Johnson Wax was the first to come up with a new product idea—self-polishing floor wax. Fighting for survival during the Depression, the company's president, Herbert Johnson, decided on a daring marketing scheme. Without any orders, he sent a carton of Glo-Coat to each of his 90,000 dealers. It worked. By 1936, with the new wax a nationwide success, the company hired a local Racine architect, J. Mandor Matson, to design a new building. Matson's plans included a modernist entrance flanked by bas-reliefs of a woman waxing a floor, a boy waxing a table, and a man painting some mechanical object. Johnson didn't like the bas-reliefs and went looking for a sculptor. When his manager showed the drawings to their public relations firm in Chicago, its art director told them they needed an architect, not a sculptor. He took them to meet Frank Lloyd Wright.

Johnson traveled to Taliesin to meet the man. Whenever Mr. Wright talked to current or potential clients, Jack Howe recalled, he never wanted any of the apprentices around. The apprentices missed quite a show. During his lunch with the Wrights, Johnson spread out the drawings prepared by Matson. "He insulted me about everything," Johnson recalled, "and I insulted him, but he did a better job." Matson's design, Wright didn't hesitate to say, "was awful." One of the few things they could agree on was cars. "He had a Lincoln-Zephyr," Johnson remembered, "and I had one."

And they agreed on something else: Wright would get the chance to come up with a design. If the company liked it, he would get the job. "If that guy can talk like that," Johnson told his associates on his return to Racine, "he must have something." Not all of Wright's arguments were convincing: He also tried, unsuccessfully, to talk Johnson into relocating his building to the countryside to form the basis for a Broadacre City. But no matter: In the Johnson Wax building, the Fellowship had its first big project.

Wright hadn't worked on anything larger than a house in ten years. Now he called on all the best apprentices to pitch in, including Jack Howe, Wes Peters, and Edgar Tafel. Bob Mosher, who had been spelling Tafel at Fallingwater, returned to join them. Wright had agreed to bring his design to Racine in only ten days. By comparison, the claimed two- or three-hour miracle birth of Fallingwater would seem easy.

SWEATY FROM THE fields, the chaff still sticking to his skin, Gene Masselink's brother, Ben, had stopped by his brother's office to chat. Ben was visiting Taliesin, working the fields and the kitchen, hanging out with the boys. Only a few days had passed since they had started on Johnson Wax.

Suddenly, Mr. Wright appeared from behind the Japanese screen separating the two offices. Ben was terrified. "He wore a tweed suit and scarf and hat and shoes so tiny and perfect; they were the kind Ratty wore in the *Wind in the Willows*. He saw me and fixed me . . . I froze."

"Who's that?" Wright asked.

"That's my brother," Gene replied.

"How long has he been with us?"

"Two months."

Ben grinned nervously. Wright grunted and tossed a scrap of paper on his brother's desk. "What do you think of that, Gene?" he asked. Unnerved by Wright's commanding presence, Ben fled the room. On the scrap, he later learned, was Wright's first sketch of the now-famous columns for the Johnson Wax building, an element he had lifted from his unbuilt design for a newspaper plant in Salem, Oregon.

Wright worked with his boys day and night on the design of Johnson Wax, moving quickly from drawing board to drawing board, commenting and making changes. Occasionally he would go over to a bench near the fireplace and take a fifteen- or twenty-minute nap. The apprentices would arrive in the drafting room early in the morning only to find that their master had been there since dawn, marking up changes on the previous day's drawings.

One morning, Edgar Tafel arrived to find that a light bulb in his drafting lamp had started a small fire, ruining a drawing he had labored over for days.

"Something always happens in the country," Wright told his apprentice. With precious little time left, Tafel spent two days recreating the drawing.

At some point during the blitz, Frank's sister Maginel was in the "little dining room" having lunch with Olgivanna and eleven-year-old Iovanna when Wright came in humming. He sat down at the table and, as was his habit, pushed all of his silver off to one side.

"I think I've just done something pretty good," he told the group, who had already begun eating. "I'll show you later."

After lunch, everybody trooped down with Mr. Wright to the drafting room. "On his table," Maginel remembered, "beautifully drawn, was the first rendering of a plan for a building. . . . It was very stirring to see this bold conception fresh from his mind and hand." A forest of lily-pad columns rose from the large open space where the secretaries would type their reports and letters, the natural light filtering in from the glass openings between the pads above. Just as Wright saw Fallingwater as a way to beat the International Style architects at their own game, these drawings were his attempt to one-up the Streamline Moderne style that was currently in vogue.

"Frank," Olgivanna exclaimed, "it is wonderful."

"Well, we haven't got it yet," he reminded her. "So keep your fingers crossed."

As the tenth day approached, Wright declared the drawings done. "What a release of pent-up creative energy—the making of those plans!" he wrote in his autobiography. At about ten o'clock in the evening, he left the studio and returned with four Japanese prints, which he placed on each of the assisting apprentices' drafting boards. He appreciated their effort, he told them. "He then walked out the door," Tafel recalled, "and turned around as he always did, and warmly said, 'Good night.' We all looked at each other, collected our prints, and turned off the lights as we went to our rooms."

On August 9, 1936, Wright and Tafel bundled up the drawings, got into Wright's car, and headed for Racine to make the presentation. They brought no alternatives to the radical design. If the company's executives didn't go for it, it was probably all over.

When they got out of the car, Tafel put the roll under his arm. Wright took it from him. "The architect," he told the apprentice, "carries his own plans."

Hours later, the telephone rang at Taliesin. The news spread quickly. " 'We got it! We got it!' cried one apprentice to another." The word went out in a wave. "It spread," Maginel recalled, "to the courts, to the gardens, to the far fields. Self-appointed couriers ran over the hills to tell those who were working in the farthest gardens and others who were working on the new buildings at Hillside."

* * *

AROUND THIS TIME, Herbert Jacobs, a newspaperman from Madison, visited Taliesin with his wife, hoping to convince Wright to design a "decent" five-thousand-dollar house for them.

"Would you really be satisfied with a five-thousand-dollar house?" Wright asked. Then, no doubt thinking of the poor Hoults, he told Jacobs that what most people really want is a ten-thousand-dollar house for five thousand dollars.

Wright laid down the conditions. The house would have no tile in the bathroom, no expensive interior cabinetry. He would use radiant heat, putting hot water pipes right into the concrete to heat the rooms. There would be an open carport: "A car is not a horse, and it doesn't need a barn," he told them. The bathroom would be clustered next to the kitchen, allowing a cheaper plumbing core. There would be no gutters or downspouts; the water would run right off the roof, just as it did at Taliesin. The walls would be a "sandwich" of raw wooden boards held in place by battens, with building paper between them for waterproofing, thus eliminating wood studs, plaster, and paint.

At Wright's direction Jacobs found a cheap site in the countryside, and on November 15, 1936, Wright signed his first and only agreement to design a house to be built for a guaranteed price: $5,500.

"The average builder of the small house doesn't know how to build [an economical house] anymore than the average family knows how to live in one," Wright lectured the apprentices as they worked on the evolving Jacobs design. This house, he boasted, would be "a direct answer that makes one wonder why it has never appeared before."

BEN MASSELINK WAS serving the last night in a week's worth of "little dining room" duty when Mr. and Mrs. Johnson came in from Racine for dinner. Serving the Wrights for a full week exempted one from all other duties. "You were the King and Queen's servant," Ben recalled. "No one could ask you to do anything." The Johnson dinner was a big event, and he was anxious to get it right.

As waiter for the Wrights, Ben was responsible for every aspect of the presentation. One night, Olgivanna requested squab for the next night's dinner. There were no squab, so he and Wes Peters went out to the barn with flashlights, shined them into the eyes of the pigeons roosting there, and slipped them into burlap bags. They spent the evening plucking the birds clean—and Olgivanna got her "squab."

Waiters were also expected to prepare a new floral centerpiece for each meal, three different displays per day for seven days. For the big dinner with the Johnsons, Ben went all out: He took a glass domed cover for cakes and converted it to a terrarium, arranging stones, pebbles, and twigs around a small pool of water. Beneath some leaves, he placed a small frog he had caught in a creek. "He blended right in," Ben remembered. "You couldn't see him unless you were looking for him."

When the Wrights and the Johnsons showed up in the dining room, they were entranced by the terrarium. But then, Ben recalled, "As I was serving the soup Mr. Wright lifted the dome to make the stones better and the frog jumped out and landed in Mr. Johnson's split pea soup. Mrs. Wright gasped. I was ready to run."

But Wright just laughed. Then, turning to Ben, he winked.

JOHNSON GAVE THE Wrights an expensive Capehart phonograph, a cutting-edge player that automatically changed and flipped the heavy 78 RPM records of the day. While the apprentices worked, Mr. Wright kept the hills flooded with sound. He would put a stack of records on the changer— Beethoven, Bach, Vivaldi, Mozart, and Brahms. Yen Liang had shown Wright that Vivaldi had paved the way to Bach, much as Wright believed that Sullivan had paved the way for him. Fauré's *Requiem* was a particular favorite, as were Dvorak's Slavonic Dances. He arranged for extra speakers to pump the music throughout the compound, even out into the fields. When the winds were right, you could hear it miles away.

One day Ben Masselink snuck into the Wrights' quarters and slipped a few of his own 78s into the stack before rushing out to the fields to work. A few minutes later, he and the other apprentices chortled with glee as Count Basie's "One O'Clock Jump" resounded across the hills. Wright, the son of a church organist and semiclassical composer, hated jazz; its status as a truly American art form—a musical analog of what he hoped to accomplish in architecture—was lost upon him.

Olgivanna eventually put a stop to her husband's relentless roster of classical records; hearing random shards of different composers, she complained, was destroying her knowledge of the individual compositions. "Music across the hills" was discontinued. Besides, whenever the Capehart was out of alignment, which was often, it would break the records when it flipped them over.

BETWEEN JOHNSON WAX and Fallingwater, substantial fees were finally pouring in. Wright, of course, used none of it to retire his substantial debt; the Johnson Wax fee bought another farm next to Taliesin.

Darwin Martin, his biggest creditor, had died the previous year, but not before informing his heirs that Wright still owed him the $43,000 he had lent him to first purchase Taliesin and later save it from foreclosure. Now Martin's widow and son were doing what Darwin may not have had the heart to do: They were suing Wright to get the money back.

The Martins had no chance of getting that kind of cash out of Wright. But he did have assets—his land. On September 14, 1936, the First Wisconsin National Bank reissued the Taliesin mortgage in the name of "Olga Lloyd Wright." Then, twelve days later, Olgivanna assigned the deed to none other than William Wesley Peters.

"While overcoming a practical bankruptcy," Wright later wrote Peters, "I turned over a 650 acre farm to you . . . ." It wasn't, of course, just "turned over" to Wes. Peters had used some of his recent inheritance to buy out the Martins' interest in the property, almost certainly in an effort to shield it from the lawsuit. In so doing, he became the owner of Taliesin—a secret guarded so closely that, even late in life, Frank's own daughter Iovanna didn't know it.

Wes and Svetlana's return had been timely indeed.

AROUND THIS TIME, Wright applied for his first recorded architecture license; he received it on January 29, 1937. Doubtless he was prompted by the need to secure a building permit for Johnson Wax, but the apprentices would benefit as well: now that their employer was officially an architect, their time at Taliesin could finally be credited toward the internship period for their own licenses.

WES PETERS WAS a very fast driver, but probably never so fast as on one bitterly cold day in December 1936. That day, when the roads were littered with unsalted ice sheets, he drove Wright's Lincoln Zephyr at what seemed like a hundred miles an hour on an urgent errand.

Frank Lloyd Wright had been stricken with pneumonia, and there wasn't a doctor in Madison who would drive all the way out to Spring Green to see him. Though he was running a dangerously high fever, Wright insisted that he was only going to a hospital if it were time to die. It was up to Peters to fetch the doctor.

Olgivanna was beside herself. She assigned Bob Mosher to stay in his room to watch him and to keep the fire going. Wright was delirious in those first days, jabbering in a fever. "Too heavy," Mosher heard him say at one point. "Not enough steel." Excoriated for adding steel at Fallingwater, Mosher felt vindicated, even if it came through the master's subconscious.

Every morning Peters drove to Spring Green to pick up Dr. Wahl, the local doctor. Olgivanna showed Mosher where they kept the Haig and Haig scotch to provide the doctor with his morning "tipper."

In their worry, the Fellowship had almost forgotten that Wright's old friend Carl Sandburg had been invited to spend the weekend. The poet, dressed in a black suit, entered Wright's room, knelt down by the bed, and kissed him on the brow.

Olgivanna took the poet aside. "Please help me," she said. "I have to make a decision whether to send Mr. Wright to a hospital or keep him here. He doesn't want to go to a hospital, and I'm afraid we can't take care of him well enough at Taliesin."

Sandburg paced back and forth in the Taliesin living room. "When Abraham Lincoln before the Battle of Gettysburg," he said, "thought defeat was facing him every place he said, 'We must take action!'" What kind of action? Sandburg didn't say; he just left the room. Olgivanna was furious over his useless patter.

Next she reached out to Gurdjieff. The mystic responded to her urgent telegram with concrete advice: calf's head soup. Svetlana and Kay carefully followed the recipe Gurdjieff wired back, cleaning the animal's head, putting in the vegetables and herbs, cooking it for hours. They prepared a tureen every day and served Wright just the liquid, as per Gurdjieff's instructions. He also prescribed a diet of milk, orange juice, and raw cabbage for Olgivanna, to help her deal with the stress.

"How is father progressing?" Wright's son Lloyd cabled from California on New Year's Day 1937. "I want to come to Taliesin as soon as he is strong enough to see me. Will you wire my expense?"

"Your father," Olgivanna replied tersely, "expecting you all day to day. Greatly disappointed to see your telegram instead. Believe you should see him as soon as possible if you care for him." There was no response to Lloyd's request for money, and no record that he ever came.

Finally, after days and days of calf's head soup, Wright asked for speckled trout and champagne. He had made it through. To signal his gratitude, he had Olgivanna's name spelled out in electric lights, hung on the oak tree in the tea circle.

THE CRISIS HAD put Wright out of commission—and much of the studio along with him, as Peters and the others nursed him back to health. The Johnson Wax working drawings were still not complete. To make things worse, Wright bowed to pressure from his client and allowed the contractor to start excavating the foundation before the winter freeze without complete architectural and engineering drawings. Incomplete drawings were still haunting Fallingwater, and that was just a house, albeit a complicated one. The Racine project was much larger than Bear Run, and it would prove every bit as challenging.

PARADISE VALLEY

EDGAR TAFEL GOT THE WORD on the blackboard on the Racine site office wall. "Mr. Wright," read the chalk message from Herbert "Hib" Johnson, "authorizes Edgar Tafel to carry on first and Wes Peters second during his stay in Arizona." Still in his mid-twenties, having supervised the construction of only half a house, Edgar Tafel was Wright's new clerk of the works for Johnson Wax.

The timing of Wright's departure could not have been worse. The Fellowship was not only still playing catch-up on the drawings for Racine, and struggling with the construction of Fallingwater, but also had just been hired to design a large house for Hib Johnson and a number of small ones, his Usonians, for ordinary folks.

With all this on the line, the Wrights left for an extraordinary three-month tour to New York, California, and Arizona. And just six weeks after their return in April they were off again, this time for Moscow. With two of his most visionary projects—Johnson Wax and Fallingwater—on the line, Wright was leaving the apprentices to fend for themselves.

FOR THE FIRST time, Edgar Tafel, Wes Peters, and the others would be on their own. Even the most senior among them were still relatively untested. By this time, the spring of 1937, Tafel and Peters each had five years of apprenticeship behind them, but most of that had been spent farming and maintaining Taliesin. Bob Mosher, a self-described architecture school failure, who would again be in charge at Fallingwater, was still learning on the job. And while the drafting room had by now produced quite a few drawings under Jack Howe's supervision, not many had been successfully tested by actual construction.

Just before leaving, Wright had marked up the drawings for the newer commissions, and had Gene Masselink reassure his clients that he would be checking "the boys'" work upon his return, to ensure that any rookie mistakes were rectified before construction began. But Johnson Wax and Fallingwater were another matter. With construction well under way, workers would need fast answers. The apprentices would not always have the time to track down their wandering master for guidance. And Wright made no special effort to be available. "Have Edgar and Wes take good care of the Johnson job," he wrote Gene after arriving in California. That was about it.

Tafel and Peters had their hands full. After six months of construction, Johnson Wax was way behind schedule; even the pouring of the foundation was delayed by still-incomplete drawings and other problems. As construction costs mounted, the company's impatience was starting to show. "[W]e can all blame any past delays on to that pneumonia germ," the company's general manager wrote Wright at the end of February, ". . . but how about action now?"

While errors of omission were delaying Johnson Wax, errors of commission continued to threaten Fallingwater. Only weeks before Wright planned to leave, he had received a report that the huge living room balcony cantilever had unexpectedly drooped one full inch, and the roof of the guest balcony was doing much the same. Ominous cracks were appearing all over the building. Wright understood what he had dumped on his boys. "We are on the spot at Pittsburg," he had written Mendel Glickman just before leaving, "and way behind with Racine, holding up the building."

ON FEBRUARY 12, 1937, the end of the Wrights' second week in New York, the contractor at Johnson Wax pulled his men off the job. Tafel, Peters, and the others had been unable to provide them the missing drawings fast enough. When Wright made a brief return to Wisconsin, he discovered that the drawings were not the only problem. The Racine Industrial Commission, which had allowed the project to go forward pending approval of several of Wright's controversial ideas, was still refusing to issue the building permit. Yet Wright returned to complete his stay in New York without resolving the issues, and then headed west with his family for the three-thousand-mile trip to Los Angeles. From there it was north to Palo Alto to check on the construction of the Hanna house, the first Usonian laid out on a hexagonal, as opposed to a rectangular, grid.

Just before leaving Taliesin, Wright had received a letter from Jean Hanna. Concerned about his slow recovery from the pneumonia, she suggested that "a bit of desert air" might be good for his lungs. She must have repeated her advice during the visit, for instead of returning home as planned, Frank, Olgivanna, and Iovanna now decided to head for Arizona.

ON MARCH 18, Wright wrote Gene, "Have Edgar and Wes take good care of the Johnson job . . . as to general fellowship matters you are in charge and I hope you will exercise your very best judgment." The letter was followed the next day by a telegram. "Everything should proceed," he instructed Gene, "as though we were present." Svetlana and Wes were to be in charge of the house, Mabel the kitchen. There was no mention of when they expected to return. Ten days later, Gene still didn't know. The twenty-six-year-old, it appeared, would be accountable for running the Fellowship indefinitely.

THE WRIGHTS TOOK lodging at the Jokake Inn just outside of Phoenix. The desert air probably wasn't quite what they had expected; it was one of the coldest winters on record.

The desert held a special place in Wright's imagination, beginning with his childhood fascination with the stories of *The Thousand and One Nights* and their boy hero, Aladdin, the pure-hearted commoner who outfoxes an evil sorcerer who sends him to retrieve a wish-granting oil lamp from a dangerous cave. It is not hard to imagine the appeal that such a lamp—and the romance of the desert nomadic life—would have had for a boy hiding out from his bickering parents in his attic bedroom in the freezing Midwest.

The Arizona desert, of course, was also where he and his draftsmen had built the tent camp dubbed Ocatillo, where Wright had been inspired to design not just the unbuilt San Marcos in the Desert but also the Fellowship itself. And just two years before, in 1935, this desert landscape had also been the happy site where he had fabricated his most ambitious creation, Broadacre City. "[T]here could be nothing more inspiring to an architect on this earth," he would say, "than that spot of pure desert in Arizona."

In the past, Wright had been frustrated in his efforts to build there for clients. But in 1935, while working on the Broadacre model, he had attempted to buy property of his own in the Santan Mountains just southwest of Chandler. On that trip he was unable to strike a deal with the owner, but he retained his dream of building a place of his own there.

Olgivanna, too, was ecstatic in Arizona. "I love every stone," she wrote to Svetlana. "I love everything my eyes fall on—the contours of the mountains, the sahuras, ocatillas—I can weep from mere exaltation." When Olgivanna, Frank, and Iovanna walked up to Camelback to sit on the rocks there, Olgivanna felt they were breathing "the purest air that the earth has to offer to a mortal. And beautiful and eternal and centuries marked stones formed different levels all around us. . . . So at last I found what I was looking for—God knows I needed it."

It was little wonder that Olgivanna preferred Arizona. For her, Wright's Wisconsin estate remained suffused with memories of another woman— Mamah Cheney—for whom it had been built and who was buried across the road. The valley's Lloyd Jones family didn't much cotton to Olgivanna; and she had never won the affections of the locals as Mamah had. And Spring Green's landscape never resonated with her like the expansive desert, its fierce and subtle light. In 1927, when she had accompanied her husband to work on the Arizona Biltmore, she had pleaded with him that they should one day live here. And he had promised they would.

Now, as Wright regained his strength in the desert air, she prodded him to resume the search for a southwestern home. She appears to have enlisted some help: Wright was taken to a Dr. Matanovich who urged him to stay in the desert for at least a month and then gave him a surprisingly specific prescription. "Get land," he suggested, "and spend winters in Arizona." Dr. Matanovich, it turns out, was Olgivanna's cousin.

WITH HIS TROUBLED real-world projects thousands of miles away, Wright used his stay at the Jokake Inn to escape into his urban theories. With his friend Baker Brownell, a professor at Northwestern University, he was working on a manuscript that would be published later in the year as *Architecture and Modern Life*. In this book he renewed his condemnation of America's cities and advocated a cultured country life—the very same approach he was experimenting with at the Fellowship.

"With Christianity for tenant today," Wright wrote, "architecture is a parasite, content with an imitation of an imitation like the spurious St. John the Divine in New York City. To go along with the imported cathedral are such inversions as the Lincoln Memorial, such aberrations as our capitols, such morgues as our museums, monuments, and such grandomania as our city halls. Abortions of sentiment, like the 'Great White Whale' at Princeton. . . . Corpses encumber the ground. As for religion or art, a pig may live in a palace: any cat can scratch the face of a king." Wright's alternative, presented in both words and pictures, was of course Broadacre City.

Wright saved his venom for America's young modern architects. In a magazine article he wrote alone and published while he was still recuperating in Arizona, he condemned the typical young American modern architect as so ambitious and selfish "that he would not hesitate to kill his own grandmother with an axe" if necessary. These young upstarts, he wrote, had achieved premature recognition—acclaim that had taken him fifteen years to earn.

The title of that article was "What the Cause of Architecture Needs Most," and given its hostile tone the answer he gave was startling: The cause of architecture, he said, needed love. Always sensitive to his age, particularly given his recent brush with death, he turned the tables on his younger colleagues, labeling their behavior as "aged," his own as youthful. While they hungered for fame and material success—drives, he implied, of the elderly—he operated out the spirit of youth, "the spirit of love."

BACK AT TALIESIN, youth was struggling to hold the fort. At noon on Saturday, March 13, Madison's WIBA broadcast a news flash: Wright's ownership of Taliesin was threatened by his failure to pay $15,000 in delinquent back property taxes. Before leaving on his extended trip, Wright had paid one long past-due bill—dating back to 1931, the year before the Fellowship started. For the six subsequent years, however, he claimed to the authorities that he shouldn't have to pay anything. Taliesin, he asserted, should be exempted as an educational institution.

Not surprisingly, the belated claim had not impressed the Wyoming County tax committee. For one thing, Wright had never even applied for tax exempt status. If the matter was not settled immediately, the radio newscaster announced, the county was threatening to take the deed.

With Wright away, the burden fell on Gene Masselink to manage the crisis. Four days after the news report, Masselink wrote to the *Capital Times*, the owner of the radio station, complaining that they had taken an issue that was "merely pending" and blown it up into a "threat." Implying that the failure to incorporate was a technical legal matter that would soon be resolved, Masselink asked the station to retract their statement.

Gene worked desperately with Wright's attorney, James Hill, to prepare an appeal. The day before the discomfiting radio announcement, Hill had asked Gene to send him the original Fellowship papers so that he could "revamp" them for resubmission to the county. When he received the document he made the unhappy discovery that, content aside, the Fellowship's articles of incorporation had never been signed. "There isn't much we can do," he wrote Gene, "until Mr. Wright returns." Even then, he added, not much could be done until the title to Taliesin passed to an educational corporation. Since Wright was no longer the property's legal owner, he had no standing to make the transfer; Wes Peters would have to do it. Nonetheless, the attorney put together his best case and submitted an appeal.

Not surprisingly the "re-vamped" Fellowship documents did not work. Hill was informed by the tax committee that the title to the land must be held by a legally incorporated educational institution to qualify for the exemption. "I am concerned," he wrote Gene, that "neither Mr. or Mrs. Wright can afford to risk a conveyance of the title to any institution." Neither, he noted, could they "afford to gamble with the title to the property for the sake of the taxes." The Wrights were caught in a bind—either pay the taxes, which they could not afford, or transfer their land to a new educational corporation, which would make the property legally vulnerable to seizure in lieu of back taxes, perhaps even to the still-unresolved claims of the Darwin Martin heirs. Gene Masselink faced an unhappy prospect: alerting Wright that the game appeared to be over.

And there was trouble for Wright on another front. Bob Mosher wired him to say that the largest of Fallingwater's cantilevered decks had more than doubled its deflection. It was now sagging more than two inches—an ominous sign.

THE WRIGHTS RETURNED home to even more bad news, this time concerning Gene Masselink. Running from Taliesin to the Hillside drafting room to finish a drawing before bedtime, the perennially overburdened Gene had caught his foot in a cow grate. Found lying on the road by other apprentices, his pelvis fractured, Gene was taken to St. Joseph's Hospital in nearby Dodgeville; he lay there for three months, his leg in a plaster cast, subjected to traction with twenty-five pound weights. As a get-well present, Wright gave Gene his greatest gift: a Hiroshige print.

"It was a fairly good hip as hips go," Masselink wrote cheerily in an "At Taliesin" column, "and as hips go this hip went." But it was a devastating blow: The long break in his pelvis never healed properly. For the rest of his life, Gene Masselink tried painfully to mask his injury, walking as though his legs were of equal length, but often faltered and sometimes even fell. For years after, he could be heard groaning in the night.

On his return from the hospital Gene faced a backlog of paperwork—client documents to be typed, orders for equipment, creditors to be paid or kept at bay, and letters from aspiring organic architects. "I feel as though I already belong to the Fellowship," one young man from Colorado pleaded. The Wrights lost four apprentices that year, but accepted ten more; the population of Taliesin, including the family, now hovered around forty-five, up slightly from previous years.

WRIGHT WAS STILL unable to resist promoting himself as an engineering genius. Usually he restricted his boasts to the triumphs of the past: the

Imperial Hotel, the Romeo and Juliet windmill. But it was quite another thing to stage a dramatic test of an unproven structure—as he did on a June day in 1937, when he put his image on the line before the public eye.

Or so it seemed.

On that Friday, Frank, Olgivanna, and a smattering of apprentices joined Johnson Wax executives and the press at the Racine construction site for a test of the slim columns that were to support the roof of Wright's radical new design. Wright had gone out of his way to design columns that appeared incapable of withstanding even their own weight. The archetype of structural stability is the pyramid, a mass that widens at its base. Wright's columns, perversely, narrowed as they approached the bottom. At the point where they would transfer all their weight—and that of the roof high above—to the floor, they were only nine inches in diameter, not unlike a ballet dancer on point. To make matters worse, some of the columns were weakened by being hollowed out to make room for concealed downspouts from the roof.

With Fallingwater, Wright had sought to amaze onlookers with a display of apparently impossible-to-support horizontal weight. Now he was doing the same thing on a vertical plane.

Wright's gee-whiz engineering was not mere self-promotion. He was transforming what could have been a utilitarian office building for a wax manufacturer into an instance of his "ideal," a "dream of heaven." "Somber, forest-abstract made in stone," he wrote as the Johnson Wax columns were being engineered, "the architecture we call Gothic is much nearer to us and has taken itself a long course of time in which to die." With Johnson Wax, Wright was resurrecting and reinterpreting, albeit very subtly, the Gothic cathedral with its columns and vaults—much as Sullivan had done with Notre Dame in the Auditorium Building, the first building on which young Frank had worked. Wright had attempted the same thing, to a much more modest effect, with some of his Prairie houses at the turn of the century. Just as the Gothic rose with the power of the new merchants, he viewed progressive entrepreneurs like Herbert Johnson and Edgar Kaufmann as patrons who would enable his architecture, its modern successor, to flourish.

Not everyone, however, was so eager to sponsor Wright's vision. Among the skeptical were the members of the Industrial Commission of the State of Wisconsin, the agency that issued building permits. Their engineers had never seen such a thing.

Building inspectors, schooled in engineering, reviewed the calculations Peters and Glickman supplied. But they couldn't accept that the tree-shaped columns, "dendriform" as Wright called them, were strong enough. In fact, many aspects of the design—from the building's foundations and concrete screen walls to its radiant heating and "breather" ventilation system of tubes, which circulated fresh air from the outside—defied local building codes. So did its emergency exits. Wright agreed to some changes, but was able to convince the officials to accept the substandard exits, on the premise that the all-brick building would never catch fire.

On the columns, though, the officials wouldn't budge. The inspectors' own calculations suggested that they needed to be thirty inches thick at their base, not the nine specified in Taliesin's drawings. Peters and Glickman insisted that the design was sound, even efficient. After all, they likely argued, anybody can design something that won't break. The highest goal of engineering is efficiency—achieving the needed strength with the minimum materials.

The authorities finally allowed "non-structural" construction to proceed pending a test of a sample column. Yet Wright had spent much of his life in confrontation with powers that deigned to assert authority over him, and he made it clear what he would do if the city attempted to halt the work. "We will construct," Wright decreed, "until they call out the militia."

The moment of truth came on June 4, 1937, four days before his seventieth birthday.

The interested parties gathered at the dusty construction site dressed to the nines—suit, tie, and hat for Wright, Hib Johnson, and contractor Ben Wiltschek. Olgivanna stood in the dirt decked out as if she had stopped off on the way to a fancy affair. Svetlana, surrounded by construction debris, looked elegant in her hat. Her husband had been responsible for much of the building's engineering; this would be his big moment too.

Before them was a single concrete lily pad, tapering down gracefully into a slender column. The whole affair was propped up by wood timbers to prevent it from tipping sideways. One by one, sandbags were hauled up and set on top of the pad. As a crowd gathered to view the spectacle, Wright went around with pencil and pad in hand, explaining the structural theory to anyone who cared to listen.

When they reached the required weight—twelve tons—Wright insisted that they go on. At 4:00 P.M., after eighteen tons had been loaded, they took a break. All the observers were invited to the Johnson Wax recreation room, where they were treated to beer and pretzels and a short talk by Wright. The architect explained why he had used steel mesh instead of conventional reinforcing rods to strengthen the columns. "Iron rods in concrete represent the bones of the foot," he told the crowd. "The steel mesh, however, plays the role of muscles and sinews. Muscles and sinews are stronger than bones."

The workmen continued to add weight to the column. At thirty tons Wright declared, "Keep piling." When they ran out of sandbags they dumped loose sand and then pig iron on top. His bravado unchecked by the failing structure at Fallingwater, Wright periodically walked right under the column,

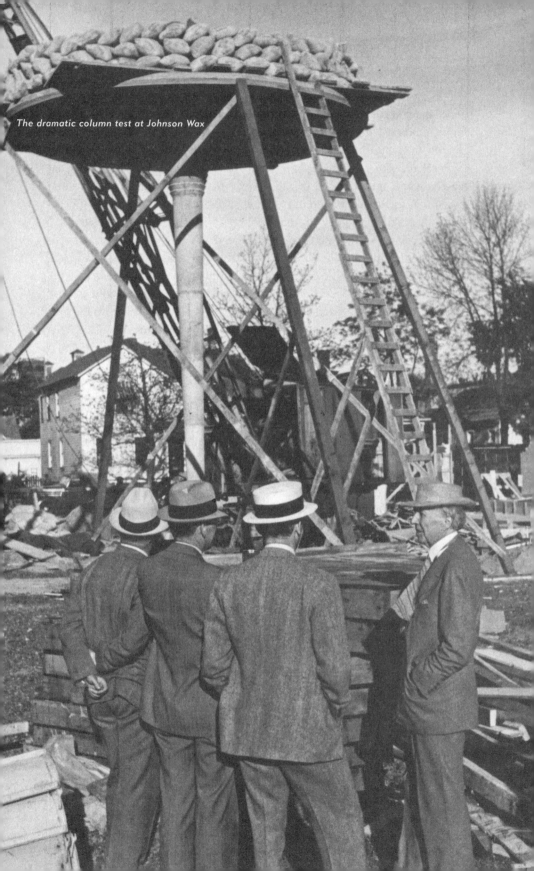

The dramatic column test at Johnson Wax

kicking it and hitting it with his cane. Olgivanna later scolded him for gloating at the expense of the board.

At sixty tons—five times the required weight—slight cracks began to appear. "Well I guess that's enough," Wright said as the sun began to set. "Pull the column down." A crane yanked away one of the timber braces and the column snapped at the top. The impact of the weight falling was so great that it caused a drainpipe ten feet underground to break; relieved of its cap, the thin column remained intact.

The city of Racine issued the permit. Yet Wright's demonstration, it turns out, was something of a sham. There were three sizes of column in the Johnson Wax building, and the column they mocked up was, at a little more than twenty-one feet, one of the shorter ones. The only real way to test the structure's stability would have been to test the tallest ones. They were not only a third taller than the one mocked up, but also would have to support both the roof and the weight of the intermediate floors. Their additional height would make the tallest columns more prone to buckle—yet in Wright's design they would have to bear the heaviest loads, not to mention the additional twisting stresses created by the balcony whose weight they would carry.

Were those tallest columns properly engineered? Hindsight confirms it: They stand to this day. Wright, Peters, and Glickman must have had confidence in their design; otherwise it's hard to imagine that they would ever have allowed Mr. Wright to stroll beneath the shorter column, with its extra load of sandbags and pig iron. Their little spectacle was far less dangerous than it seemed, but it was quite a birthday present for Wright—and quite a show.

WRIGHT HAD RECENTLY received another, perhaps bigger, present. *Architectural Forum*, America's most eminent architectural magazine, had decided to dedicate its entire January 1938 issue to his work. Moreover, it was breaking all precedent and giving Wright himself free rein over the magazine, from laying out its pages to writing its copy. The project would occupy many of the apprentices for the next six months.

America's renewed interest in the great architect was also being felt overseas. In May, just before the column test, he had received an invitation from Moscow to speak to the First All-Union Congress of Soviet Architects. Wright was fascinated by the Soviet experiment. He showed Russian movies at Taliesin and tried to recruit Soviet students to the Fellowship. The Russians, he was sure, had an opportunity to create a great new architecture to accompany the new social order they were fashioning. And they returned his interest: The Soviets had followed his Broadacre City ideas, noting his denunciations of the capitalist city and his calls for a "Russian art for Russian life."

Immediately after the test in Racine, Wright took Olgivanna and Iovanna, now eleven, on a trip to Russia. They sailed first to France aboard Cunard's *Queen Mary*, and then on to Moscow by train; the Soviets picked up
the entire tab. For Olgivanna, who had fled the Russian revolution twenty
years before, the prospect of going to Moscow made her so anxious that she
hyperventilated.

The trip had an inauspicious start. When her trunk failed to appear at the
train station in New York, she had to board the ship without it. "[I]magine
what that meant to her!" Wright wrote Svetlana, ". . . she went out of her
mind." This was no figure of speech: Olgivanna was completely incapacitated. Finally, once at sea, they received a radio message that the trunk was located and would be on the next ship. "Then only," Wright reported, "could
she eat or anything."

The apprentices were back on their own, their master more incommuni-
cado than ever. And this time Gene Masselink, the Fellowship's anchor, was
immobilized by his slowly recovering broken hip. "Give my love to Wes,"
Wright wrote Svetlana from the *Queen Mary*. "I depend on him a lot—you
know."

After a stop at Southhampton, England, they crossed the channel to Le
Havre and on to Paris, where Olgivanna briefly saw Gurdjieff. He sensed an
ominous perturbance in her future. "We've got to work together," he said,
pressing her to remain with him in Paris. Gurdjieff became ashen when Olgivanna told him what had recently happened to Svetlana: She had been in
an auto accident while driving with Wes Peters and Gene Masselink. The
car had rolled over, her slashed and bruised face needing plastic surgery.
To Gurdjieff, it was an omen of impending death. "We've got to work together," he repeated. "You've got to stay." But Frank would not leave Olgivanna alone in Paris with her spiritual master, not to mention her former
lover.

The Wrights left Paris on a train to Moscow. As they approached the
Russian border, Olgivanna gave her husband a warning: "You had better be
careful in what you say or else we both may land in prison." When the train
stopped just across the border, Wright refused an official's request to open
the package he was carrying with him. "I will not have you pawing through
my drawings," he announced. Asked to show how much money he was carrying, he became livid. "What kind of people are you? Do you always look
through your guests' pockets when you invite them to your country?"

Wright stormed down the platform, only to return a few minutes later at
the point of a soldier's rifle. It took a number of calls to Moscow before the
Wrights were allowed to continue their trip. When they boarded the next
train, they discovered that they were its only passengers. Nonetheless, they

were ordered to keep their hot sleeping compartment closed and locked with a safety chain.

Frank Lloyd Wright arrived in Moscow just as Joseph Stalin's purges, in which millions would lose their lives, were reaching their barbarous heights. The Congress to which Wright had been invited to speak was part of the Communist Party's drive to assert complete artistic control over the architectural profession.

It was a strange alliance, but Wright and the Soviet Party shared a common enemy. The party rejected European modernism for what they considered its "formalism"—rooted as it was in neither the Russian nation nor the international proletariat. Instead they called for architecture to create a synthesis of the great civilizations of the past, particularly that of the Greeks, whom Karl Marx had so admired. And the stakes were far higher than the simple matter of who got the plum government contracts. Russian architects were being imprisoned for their aesthetics. Once welcomed in the Soviet Union, European modernists were fleeing in droves. Even the Russian constructivists, who sought to make engineering into poetry, were being denounced.

The purpose of the All-Union Congress was to destroy, once and for all, what the party denounced as architectural "formalism"—in other words, buildings that were said to sacrifice function for aesthetic effect. "Formalist" was an imprecise and elastic term; aimed primarily at European modernists like Le Corbusier, it served effectively as an all-purpose political club. Stalin, who did not like the European modernists, personally wrote the opening welcome for the delegates. A Ukrainian delegate praised "the great architect Comrade Stalin." *Pravda* reported that the architects in attendance included a number of enemies of the people, a contingent of bourgeois leftists following the European modernists. Some constructivist architects at the Congress got up and recanted their past errors. Some did not. A number would be purged from the profession.

When Wright spoke on the last day, he sounded every bit the Marxist aesthetician "The fact that our buildings excel in top-quality workmanship," he told the Congress, "is a poor consolation for us architects. Our highly acclaimed architectural achievement is the skyscraper. But what does it really represent? The skyscraper is no more and no less than a victory for engineering and the defeat of architecture. This rising, steel framework of a skyscraper is generally hidden behind a thin facing of stone blocks imitating the masonry of feudal towers. Skyscrapers are stunning, but they are false and artificial, like the economic structures that gave rise to their emergence in dull congested urban areas."

The Soviet Union, he urged, should spurn its palatial past and develop a new architecture to match its new society—something, he added, the United States had yet to learn. "America is far behind from correct town planning. Its economic system interferes with this. Private property ownership makes correct planning impossible. Soviet Russia, however, came to the realization of the value of correct planning ideas. Organized architecture will not only express such ideas of a new free life but also ensure, in the USSR, the possibility of living one's life better than anywhere else."

WRIGHT'S COMMENTS ATTRACTED international attention, and upon his return to the States he faced a hostile homecoming. In response, he pugnaciously defended the Soviets. "If Comrade Stalin, as disconcerted outsiders are saying, is betraying the revolution, then, in the light of what I have seen in Moscow, I say he is betraying it into the hands of the Russian people." For an architect who was finally making some headway securing major corporate commissions, this was quite a stand. As the Johnson Wax building began to take shape, the local *Racine Journal Times* went after him: "We wonder if Mr. Wright doesn't realize that his statements (concerning Russia) are likely to have this country's leading 'red hunters' down around his neck. Men have been called hired hands and accused of plotting the overthrow of American government for saying less."

Wright struck back. "This 'red' menace," he replied, "I see as a special

Wright at the Congress of Soviet Architects, 1937

creation of a very bad social consequence in our country and just about as valid as the 'yellow peril' started echoing down the columns of the press by the late Kaiser. . . . The big newspaper, the big interests, big institutions of every kind—they are now the real menace to candor and veracity of every sort not favorable to the profit-motive. 'Bigs' have given the truth concerning the Russian spirit and what it is doing, a bad slant."

The Soviet Union's American defenders sought him out, particularly organizations lobbying for U.S.–Soviet friendship. Courted by the American Russian Institute in New York, he agreed to let them use his name if it would be "of any use to your cause . . ." Alexander Portnoff of the Philadelphia chapter sent him an invitation to meet the Russian ambassador. Unable just then to leave Taliesin, Wright declined, suggesting instead that the ambassador come to Taliesin and see his Fellowship. "I think he would enjoy the little America within America."

BACK AT TALIESIN, Wright found his major new projects much as he had left them: Johnson Wax slowly coming together, Fallingwater slowly coming apart. Cracks that had recently been filled at Bear Run were now open again. Again Kaufmann asked his own engineering firm to assess the problem; the structure, they reported back, was overstressed and less than secure. They recommended installing additional walls for strength, but once again Wright managed to persuade his anxious client that the cantilevers would hold, without any extra walls.

AT THE BEGINNING of November, Wright received a letter from his old friend Franz Aust, the Wisconsin professor who had tried so hard to help him start the Hillside School a decade before. Aust was hoping to arrange for Gropius finally to meet Wright and see Taliesin. Gropius, who had recently fled Nazi Germany, was visiting the University of Wisconsin before joining Harvard as the head of its architecture school. Wright must have known that Gropius would use that prestigious platform to spread his European brand of modernism in America. "I have no curiosity concerning Herr Gropius," Wright shot back to Aust. "It is my privilege to invite him to Taliesin. I have not done so . . . And please pass this on to your Madison and University friends. If hereafter they would roast their chestnuts by my fireside . . . they will be badly burned."

For a moment, it seemed as though these two titans of modernism would never meet face-to-face. But Wright was in for a surprise. When Edgar Tafel drove him to Madison to check on the progress of construction at the Jacobs residence—the first Usonian to be completed—the two men pulled up to the site in Wright's Lincoln Zephyr . . . and there was Gropius.

Ever the proper German, Gropius came over to the car and leaned down to the window. "Mr. Wright, it's a pleasure to meet you."

Wright turned ever so slightly toward his European counterpart. "Herr Gropius, you're a guest of the university here. I just want to tell you that they're as snobbish here as they are at Harvard, only they don't have a New England accent."

"Well," he then said, turning to Tafel, "we have to get on, Edgar." They drove off, never even getting out of the car to examine the construction.

A few days later, Gropius gave a public lecture at the university. Wright sent a contingent from the Fellowship. Apprentice Charles Samson, who may very well have been sent specifically to report on the lecture for "At Taliesin," claimed in his piece that Gropius left his audience bored, bewildered, and indifferent. He and the other apprentices "were left equally at sea," he conceded, "but our disgust was aroused by the whole performance." The spirit of Gropius's work was "one of negation and self-evident impotence," he charged, in a phrase that mimicked the master. And, of course, it was inorganic.

To Wright, the difference between himself and European modernists like Gropius and Le Corbusier was the difference between a musical composer and a painter. When Le Corbusier got a new project, Wright told his apprentices, he "shuts himself up in a studio to brush paint on canvas. When I get a project to study, I go to the piano and play it—much more precise."

ON CHRISTMAS OF 1937, Edgar and Liliane Kaufmann decided it was time to move into Fallingwater. It was one of the happiest weekends of their lives, Liliane reported to Wright. Her exuberant letter reached him in Arizona. With the snows returning to Taliesin, he and Olgivanna had once more left for the desert for what would now be their third lengthy absence from Taliesin within the year.

By now, Wright's desire to live and build in this desert had turned into an obsession. It was not about his physical health, or about saving on electricity. He was looking for "refreshment"—that is, for circumstances that would inspire him to design something unprecedented, as his visit to Japan at the turn of the century had led to his revolutionary 1905 design for the Unity Temple in Oak Park. While Unity's plan bears a remarkable resemblance to that of a seventeenth-century mausoleum he had just seen in Nikko, a mountain resort north of Tokyo, with the Oak Park building Wright managed to transcend the overt trappings of Japanese influence. When Wright went looking for "refreshment," he was never interested in mere appropriation. He was in search of new catalysts for his imagination.

Fallingwater and Johnson Wax were beautiful and brilliant. But Wright would have understood that as statements—rooted as they were in one-upmanship of his modernist contemporaries—they were not as revolutionary as some of his early buildings. To Wright, the greatest sources of "refreshment" were not contemporary trends in architecture, but the principles of civilizations far from the modern West—and, above all, nature itself, unspoiled and untraveled by denizens of the metropolis.

With its savage beauty and the remnants of a highly spiritual native culture, the Arizona desert had both those elements. And Wright believed that regular sojourns here would lead him to fresh architectural visions that would counter the degeneracy he saw around him—on the one side the architectural submission to the machine, on the other the modernist artists glorying in an animalistic primitivism. "Now," he told a friend about the Arizona camp, "mankind needs the refreshment afforded by the conscious return to the verities of being—returning to Nature not only in that early obvious sense but with more prophetic understanding and appreciation."

In the Arizona desert, Wright hoped to develop a new set of forms, one that would push architecture beyond the European modernists. All he needed was a chance to build something here—an opportunity he had been awaiting for decades.

WITH THE FELLOWSHIP standing by as free labor, the only obstacles were finding land and the cash to buy it. Dr. Chandler had recently sent a letter seeking to partner with him to resurrect the Santan Mountains deal. Olgivanna didn't like that property, Wright replied; it was quite remote, and she wanted to be closer to Phoenix. Chandler pressed on, suggesting that he had potential investors for a new project. "I am banking," he wrote Wright, "on your ability to work out something more attractive in the desert than has ever been produced before." Something, he added, that would not only offset Olgivanna's resistance but also "completely change that place and make it nationally and internationally famous." The appeal to Wright's ego apparently didn't work; nothing came of the Santan site.

As the Wrights combed the desert for land, back at Taliesin the apprentices prepared their caravan and awaited word of their destination. If a property were found, they would have to move quickly if they were to start building that winter. And if no property turned up, Olgivanna wrote Mendel Glickman's wife, the Fellowship would simply become a tribe of nomads bearing sleeping bags and tents, "ever-moving in caravan for 3 months."

The Wrights began to focus their search on an area they knew well from their first winter 1935 *hegira*, as Wright called it, referring to the Prophet Mohammed's escape to Medina from his enemies in Mecca. Paradise Valley, now a town, was then the name of an area of rugged high desert near Scottsdale, and much closer to Phoenix than the Santan site.

One Sunday in late December 1937, Frank and Olgivanna finally found a parcel of land there that they could agree on. The land was generously covered with that most architectural of all plants—cactus in all its varieties, including saguaro, prickly pear, cholla, and staghorn. "On a mesa just below McDowell Peak," he wrote of that moment, "we stopped, turned, and looked around. The top of the world!" Olgivanna was more prosaic: "I always liked Phoenix," she recalled, "and was able to convince my husband to buy property some twenty miles away from town."

ON NEW YEARS' Eve Wright sent a telegram to Gene Masselink back in Wisconsin: "Weather warm. Beautiful site in hand. Come Jokake Inn soon you are ready." To make sure that his boys would arrive prepared for construction, Wright told Gene to bring with them shovels, rakes, hoes, a hose, a wheelbarrow, a concrete mixer, and a small Kohler electricity generator. To put together a studio, they should pack eighteen drafting boards, and to set up housekeeping in the desert, he told Masselink to bring a water heater, oil stoves, and rugs. And because the Fellowship without music would be unthinkable, they should also have with them their melodeon (a variant of the accordion), a viola, and a cello.

The Wrights had found their land, but they hadn't figured out how to pay for it. Hib Johnson, who had advanced Wright money for previous urgencies, was a potential lender. But there was now considerable tension between the two. The delays in completing the drawings for Johnson Wax, irksome for the client, were becoming a windfall for his architect. Wright's contract called for him to be paid 10 percent of the construction cost. Now, due largely to the architect's own failures, costs were running well beyond the original estimate—and Wright was lining his pockets on the overruns.

Never short on nerve, Wright decided to hit up Johnson anyway. The day before he summoned the apprentices to Arizona, he wrote a letter to Johnson that began with a defense of his fees and ended with an appeal: It wouldn't hurt Johnson Wax, or their friendship, if Johnson were to send "quite a check" to help him get started in the desert.

Johnson pointedly replied that all the delays and cost overruns had been "embarrassing for me, to say the least." He accused his architect of lowballing the original estimates to "sell the job" and further his art. But Wright hadn't yet found the limits of Johnson's patience, or his pocketbook. "Now Frankie," he continued, "this letter is no complaint as it would do no good to complain. You have us hooked and we can't get away."

Hib Johnson, it seemed, believed in this scoundrel genius. But there was more to it than that: His own fortunes were now married to the architect's well-being. Wright was building both Johnson's corporate building and his house; Johnson needed him healthy and happy. And so, in spite of his irritation, he proposed a solution that would facilitate Wright's personal desert project. Wright's fees for Johnson Wax were to be paid at the end of each of specific project phases. The next payment was not due until the end of construction—an uncertain date, to say the least. To help Wright finance his new Arizona camp, Johnson offered to pay at the end of each month for the portion of the work completed to date. He enclosed the first installment, a check for $3,100.

The Fellowship's desert home was a go.

WHEN THE APPRENTICES joined the Wrights several weeks later, shovels and violas in hand, they faced the same challenges as countless desert pioneers before them. There was "no water, no building, nothing," Kay Schneider recalled, "just open range with cattle and wild horses in large herds and sheepherders with sheep." They had eight hundred acres of desert scrub— some purchased, some leased—gently sloping northward to the foot of the McDowell range, a low rocky outcrop. From the base of the hill, looking southward, the wide basin spread out in an unobstructed panorama from east to west. It was, Wright noted, "a look over the rim of the world."

Phoenix, twenty-six miles southwest, could be reached in about an hour over dusty, rutted dirt roads. With a population of more than fifty thousand, this farming center was growing quickly into a regional hub. Nearby Scottsdale took less than half that time to reach, but it was just a dirt road with a few houses, a gas station that doubled as the sheriff's office, and two bars. Chandler, where the Fellowship briefly stayed again at La Hacienda before moving on to their site, was about a twenty-mile trip from the new property.

The land was cheap, $3.50 an acre, and for a good reason. "No water on that side of the valley," a local had warned Wright, "waste of money to try." Wright eagerly set out to prove him wrong—and he did, but only after paying a well digger ten thousand dollars, more than three times the price of the land, to find water 486 feet underground.

That, however, took a long time. For three years the Fellowship had no water. "We had to carry it," Kay Schneider remembered. "We took the big truck, filled it with empty fifty gallon cans, went down to the ranch—the man was kind enough to fill it up for us, and the one truckload would last about a week. We had to do the washing, and we had to do the cooking, dish-washing, and we each got one gallon a week for washing ourselves—for brushing our teeth and washing our faces. Once a week all the women went to the YWCA and all the men went to the YMCA for a shower." By then, the apprentices often smelled pretty ripe.

Wright laid out the plans for the camp on brown wrapping paper. The ap-prentices cleared the site and began to dig footings in the rocky soil. The nighttime accommodations—a sleeping bag inside a sheep herder's tent—were no better than the sanitation. Kay Schneider remembered scorpions nesting beneath their bedclothes and biting the apprentices; there were rat-tlesnakes, too, which they would capture and keep in cages beneath their drafting tables. The Wrights had it a little better. The apprentices built a con-crete platform on to which they built small canvas-covered "sleeping boxes" with a fireplace in the corner. Olgivanna loved it.

With a steady stream of client fees and apprentice tuitions, Wright's in-come had probably never been better. But the added cost of purchasing and developing a second estate—coupled with his tax liabilities on the first—more than offset their burgeoning receipts. The Wrights might have been sol-vent had the apprentices been able to devote more of their time to outside commissions instead of Wright's own properties. As it was, though, the situ-ation was so bad that the Fellowship often lacked cash for food. The appren-tices often went to a neighboring orchard with a truck and paid two dollars to pick a load of grapefruit. Some days they lived on grapefruits and cottage cheese. Meat was rationed out once a week. When the New York playwright Mark Connelly arrived with a wooden crate filled with T-bone steaks, the ap-prentices rejoiced, and grilled them in the fireplace.

It was left to Gene Masselink to manage this financial nightmare. He re-lied on the same system Wright had found effective over the years: Almost everything was bought on credit, and bills were ignored. Pleading letters from Depression-plagued vendors arrived almost daily, some with heartrend-ing details of their struggles to remain afloat.

Staving off local businessmen proved easy; the large credit firms were harder to ignore. Two years earlier, Wright had financed the two cars he'd purchased for his first caravan to Arizona. The automobiles were purchased in Olgivanna's name, likely a way around his notorious credit history. That account was now delinquent to the tune of $176. Gene Masselink wrote to the Universal Credit Company claiming that the correct amount was only $147—no doubt a stall. The creditor demanded the full amount and threatened to send a representative to collect it. Wright's secretary sent the money. Now current, he went right back to ignoring the monthly payments.

After six months, the Universal representative showed up at Taliesin. He returned empty-handed; the company added a six-dollar service charge to Wright's tab.

It was one thing to have Gene discreetly stiffing creditors, another to suffer the embarrassment of a bill collector at Taliesin's door. The next letter to Universal was from Wright himself. "There must be some limit," he wrote, "to the petty impositions you seem to practice with impunity." Wright blustered for a face-saving victory: He enclosed a check for the balance due, less the six dollars for the visit, and concluded the letter with a threat: "If you don't care to accept this we will make a test case of the matter. It's time somebody called you and did so. I am willing to be the goat."

Then there was the long-delinquent account for the two Bechstein pianos Wright had bought on credit from Wanamaker's in New York. The $1,400 account—another in Olgivanna's name—was now in the hands of the store's lawyers. After a series of increasingly hostile letters from the lawyer, Gene wrote to offer Wanamaker's a fraction of the balance as "full settlement." When the offer was rejected, Wright sent another angry response, characterizing the interest charges as an effort "to defeat us" and the lawyer's words as "threats of violence." Nonetheless he agreed to pay—just not now. "[T]he work," the busier-than-ever architect claimed, "goes slowly."

IN THE FIRST year of the Fellowship, Henry Klumb had been appalled to see the apprentices spending so much of their time maintaining and enlarging Wright's estate instead of developing their architectural skills. That was nothing. Now they were building an entire complex from scratch, on land that would have challenged even seasoned builders. Unlike Wisconsin, where centuries of plant decay and high rainfall had left rich, aerated farming soil, in Arizona there was nothing but dry, unyielding desert floor. The apprentices struggled with the shovels they hauled from Wisconsin to clear a long winding dirt road up to a mesa not far from the foot of the mountain, where Wright had decided to locate the buildings. Then they excavated for their foundations. In his autobiography, Wright made light of the arduous work. "A major rule in the Fellowship," he wrote, "had always been 'do something while resting.' So we preferred to build something while on vacation."

Not all the apprentices took this "vacation." Edgar Tafel, for one, had remained behind in Racine. The curly-headed New Yorker had risen to the extraordinary challenges of coordinating the complex design work for the ongoing construction of Johnson Wax. "Building progresses well," Herbert Johnson had cabled Wright when he had been in Moscow, "Tafel making minor decisions like a master . . ."

But those changes were hardly minor; many resulted in what are known as "field changes." Though occasionally just benign clarifications of the architect's intentions, field changes are typically corrections or additions to drawings that prove inadequate once construction has begun. In either case they involve considerable risk. They can introduce new problems to a design, since it can be difficult to trace all the implications of a last-minute change through a complex set of drawings. Those new problems usually create construction delays. And such changes, problems, and delays inevitably snowball into extra charges to the client. Johnson Wax was becoming a case study in the dangers of designing through field changes rather then providing accurate and complete drawings in the first place.

While some of these problems at Johnson Wax can be attributed to Wright's recent illness, coupled perhaps with the inexperience of the apprentices, the truth was that Wright saw designing during construction as an essential part of his approach, an aspect of a genius at work. After all, his beloved Gothic cathedrals had been built the same way.

Medieval serfs and lords may have taken such changes in stride; American corporations and builders were another story. As the work dragged on, the Johnson Wax executives and their contractor, Jack Ramsey, came to suspect that the incomplete drawings simply meant shoddy work. When Ramsey told Wright as much in a letter, Wright responded with a typical mix of self-pity and organic metaphor. "Your 'crab' received—don't be too hard on the boys, and me! Will you? They do pretty damned well with a pretty difficult task—you would say if you knew all. You see the building grows as it is built and not too easy, therefore, to keep up with always."

Wright's constant design changes caused problems among the apprentices as well. And when their frustration bubbled over, Wright had his stock rejoinders ready. "Every change is for the betterment," he repeated ad infinitum. If an apprentice got up the nerve to remind him that he'd previously issued contradictory instructions, he would reply: "That was all right yesterday, but it's not right today." And those who suggested that it was too late to introduce a new idea were reminded that the "last change is made when the boom comes down."

With Johnson Wax, the boom never seemed to come down. A year into construction, masonry workers waited as Wright drafted up revisions to the design of the theater, cafeteria, and squash court. Another major change came even later, after the Fellowship had returned to Wisconsin. The day before concrete was to be poured for the second floor, site supervisor Edgar Tafel learned that Wright—operating from Taliesin—had decided to add a new row of short columns to support the roof over the boardroom. The other columns on each floor were spaced twenty feet apart, each column directly over the column on the floor below. But Wright's new columns would land instead in the middle of a floor whose reinforcing steel would be woefully inadequate to support them. "The builders were ready to pour the floor," Wes Peters recalled, "and there was nothing to hold these new columns up."

Peters called the contractor in a panic. *Hold the pour!* "I rushed down to Racine, and we did some, very, very fast engineering on the job; threw some big reinforcements in right and left over that area where these columns were going to come, and they went ahead with the pour that afternoon and poured on into the night."

"Very fast engineering," reinforcements "thrown in" on the fly: This was astonishingly risky business, especially given the flaws in the far more deliberate work Peters and Mendel Glickman had done on Fallingwater. The safety of all who entered Johnson Wax would rest on the hurried calculations Wes Peters had made on site that day. They got away with it; the building is still in use. But it is hard to imagine any structural engineer not thinking that Peters had been fortunate indeed.

EDGAR TAFEL'S FATHER was concerned about his son. "Would it be too much of you," he wrote Wright, "to express your opinion of Edgar?" Was he, in fact, being prepared to work on his own?

Wright's reply smacked at the father's very right to ask. In the "process of becoming an architect," he wrote back, Edgar "has not drawn on his blood parents very heavily and has acquired another kind of parent. A kind of spiritual fatherhood seldom rewarded in our 'system.' . . . I can't go on forever breaking in colts to pull the plough or pull chestnuts out of the fire for the system or just for themselves or for 'parents'. . . . If Edgar is as good as I think he is, he is now a son of Taliesin with affection for his New York parents but no obligation to them."

IF WRIGHT SEEMED more self-important than ever, he wasn't the only one so impressed. In January 1938, *Time* magazine featured the handsome, leonine seventy-year-old on its cover, anointing him "the greatest architect of the 20th Century." With the design of Fallingwater and Johnson Wax, "his most amazing work," Wright was said to have redeemed himself at last from the "scandalous episodes ground from the inhuman interest mill of the tabloid newspapers."

In a coup any professional publicist would have envied, the new *Time* appeared simultaneously with the extraordinary edition of *Architectural Forum* that Wright had written and designed himself. Abe Dombar's brother Bennie drew the entire Taliesin floor plan for the issue. Calling the drafting feat the "fifth symphony," Wright allowed that it was the first time Taliesin's plan had ever been committed to paper. To make the press deadline, he and a group of apprentices had had to travel to the journal's New York offices for a series of all-night sessions. The result was well worth their trouble. Filled with images of the architect working with his apprentices, as well as photographs and drawings of their work, the special edition was as much a recruiting device for the Fellowship as a demonstration of Wright's still-vital design genius.

With his simultaneous cover appearances in two national magazines, Wright had captured—at least for the moment—the high ground from the European modernists.

AS THE MAGAZINES hit the stands, Johnson cabled Wright in Arizona letting him know that he wouldn't be needed in Racine for the next two months. Between Edgar Tafel's competent work—assisted by a new drafts-man hired by the company—and the slow progress due to winter weather, they would get along without him. It was just as well; having graded their Arizona land the previous winter, Wright and the apprentices were hoping to start work on the buildings themselves.

What Johnson didn't tell Wright, or perhaps didn't know, was just how much Tafel had to struggle to make it all work. Like Robert Mosher before him at Fallingwater, Tafel was walking a tightrope between the conflicting de-mands of his master and the client. Kaufmann and Johnson, Wright's two wealthy clients, were both remarkably successful men who had gotten there by employing proactive problem-solving skills. And both had been frus-trated to find that their architect had little concern for time, money, or the limitations of building contractors. Wright's clerks-of-the-works spent much of their time acting as go-betweens, trying to further their respective projects without unnecessary derailments.

Somehow, in the midst of it all, Tafel was able to squeeze in a side project. His easygoing charm won him friends in town, especially within Racine's small Jewish community, and one family, the Alberts, hired him to design a house for them. Wright's policy in such situations—perhaps inspired by his own memories of how Sullivan had fired him for moonlighting—was to al-low apprentices to take on projects of their own as long as they were formally brought into the Fellowship and Wright got a generous share of the fees. To this Tafel happily agreed.

Tafel's work on the Albert residence was good—too good. The design meshed well with Wright's idiom and Tafel had carefully supervised its con-struction while still managing to oversee things at Johnson Wax. Sometime after the Alberts moved in, Wright and Wes Peters drove in to inspect the office building. While they stood talking, a friend of the Albert family walked over and shared with them "how nice the house was that Edgar Tafel designed." It was beautiful, functional—and, he added, "it didn't leak."

It was a sore point: Leaking roofs had become almost a signature for Wright. Wright turned to Wes and announced, "We are needed back at Taliesin." They left immediately. Back in Spring Green, he called a meeting of the entire Fellowship and announced that apprentices would no longer be allowed to take on their own projects. "From now on," he announced, "there will be one prima donna in our organization. And that is me."

EVERYBODY BUT WRIGHT seemed to know that the skylights designed for Johnson Wax were going to leak. Hib Johnson certainly thought so. The skylights were unusual in many respects. The building's roof wasn't really a roof at all, in the traditional sense: As the columns spread out at their apex into their elegant circular caps, like checkers pushed together, the space between them was to be filled by four-pointed skylights.

The shape of these skylights would certainly be unusual, but that wasn't the problem. Instead of specifying standard skylight construction—typically flat sheets of glass sealed into metal frames—Wright intended to use a system of glass rods lined up side by side. He had used the same detail for some of the windows in the building with little problem. But this was a skylight; in a pounding rain, even the most careful arrangement of glass rods would inevitably leak. Wright thought he could solve the problem by caulking the rods where they met. But the merest sloppiness in installation, or the expansion or contraction of the rods, or the slightest vibration or settling of the building, would be certain to open up gaps and let water in. And caulking—especially the caulking of Wright's day—inevitably shrinks with age. Leaks were guaranteed.

Both Tafel and Peters knew the rods wouldn't work, and, on several occasions tried to convince Wright to change the design. But he kept insisting that if it worked on the windows it would work on the skylights. Then Tafel actually had the temerity to share his concerns with the contractor, which resulted in a skylight company in Chicago preparing manufacturing drawings for conventional glass units. When Tafel drove back to Taliesin and tried to show them to Wright, the master was so furious at Tafel's insubordination that he refused even to look at the new idea.

Tafel carried the bad news back to Racine, but Hib Johnson instructed the contractor to order the standard skylights anyway. Tafel waited for Johnson to leave the room before calling Wright to alert him to the change. Wright was enraged. Shortly thereafter, Johnson barged in. "You snitched!" he yelled at Edgar. "Get off the premises. You're fired!"

Tafel packed his things and drove to a nearby pay telephone to call Wright. "If he fires you," the voice in the receiver declared, "he's fired me." On Wright's orders, Tafel returned to the job. Johnson threw up his hands, and took back not only Edgar Tafel but also Wright's glass-rod skylights.

They leaked.

Yet the sunlight filtering down through the glass tubes was glorious. Before leaving for Los Angeles to supervise a small Usonian Wright had designed for a steep hillside lot there, apprentice John Lautner took his mother to see what Wright had created at Racine. What they found there was sublime. Flowing around the caps of the fluted lily-pad columns and down their delicate tapering lines, the soft light spread across the office floor below, creating within the voluminous room a feeling of vast yet intimate silence. Lautner's mother cast her eyes upward and wept.

A FEW DAYS before Lautner and his apprentice wife, Mary Bud, left Taliesin for Los Angeles, Wright received his friend Alexander Woollcott. Eager to show his rotund buddy Johnson Wax, he enlisted Edgar Tafel to drive them east. When the three arrived in Racine, the police stopped them for speeding on Main Street and failing to signal a turn. To make matters worse, Tafel had left his license in his workpants and the car appeared to have no registration.

"Officer," Wright said, "this is Alex Woollcott, the great *New Yorker* writer."

"And Officer," Woollcott chimed in, "this is Wisconsin's Frank Lloyd Wright, America's foremost architect—no, the world's best architect." The writer's fame may have bypassed Racine, but the architect's surely hadn't. The policeman let them go.

When they arrived at the building, Wright raced ahead. The portly Woollcott finally caught up with him inside the grand atrium. After craning his head up for a long look, the writer began to wave his arms about. "Frank, I want to dance! I want to dance!"

"Alex," Wright proclaimed, "*this* is education! This is culture."

An odd way to describe a building, perhaps, but Woollcott had read Wright's autobiography, and likely knew of his friend's obsession with Victor Hugo's architectural theories. They were certainly on Wright's mind in that extraordinary year: Just before construction on Johnson Wax began, Wright had predicted in a press statement that the building would be "in no way inferior in harmony to the ancient cathedral." Wright was seizing the mantle of Hugo's prophesied genius, the man who would recapture architecture's place at the top of the cultural hierarchy. Whether or not corporate capitalism was becoming America's new civil religion, few who have experienced the building's columned atrium would deny that Frank Lloyd Wright had built a kind of modern-day Gothic cathedral.

When Philip Johnson saw the building, he realized that he had been wrong to dismiss Wright as "the greatest architect of the nineteenth century." Johnson Wax's illuminated, rhythmic space astounded him, divided as it was "into small enough units so that you don't feel silly at a typewriter. See you can't go into Grand Central Station and start typing a letter." He might want to see that nasty man from the MoMA show once again after all.

When Woollcott returned to his home in Vermont, he received a memento of his visit with Wright, a photograph of the two of them taken by Edgar Tafel. "Any photograph which showed me as benign and him as spiritual," Woollcott wrote, thanking Tafel, "would be regarded as a collector's item."

Woollcott, for his part, sent Wright new talent: Victor Cusack, a penniless Yale architecture student who had been doing renderings of classical orders at Yale when he was captivated by Wright's lecture there in 1935. He wrote to inquire about joining the Fellowship, but there was no room. But Cusack knew of Mr. Wright's friendship with Woollcott, and perceived that the writer "was one man who could make Wright shut up and listen without any interruption . . ."

Wright with Alexander Woollcott

As it happened, Woollcott was in tryouts for his play at New Haven's Shubert Theater. After some prompting, Woollcott invited Cusack to join him for a midnight dinner. Over raw oysters and Welsh rarebit, the playwright promised the young man that he would write on his behalf. But that alone would not suffice, he counseled.

"Young man, beard the lion in his den! Go! Go there!"

Woollcott wrote to Wright explaining that he had urged Cusack to "hitchhike his way to Wisconsin, lurk in the shrubbery, and spring out at you some day to try his strength in what is known, I believe, as the direct appeal. If you are thus assaulted by a young man named Cusack, you can blame me."

IN APRIL 1938, a cryptic message from a doctor with the unlikely name of Ludd Spivey presented Wright with an opportunity to design buildings that would unmistakably fall under the rubric of "education" and "culture." "Desire conference with you," the telegram read, "concerning plans for great education temple in Florida." That was all.

Dr. Spivey was the president of Florida Southern, a Methodist liberal arts college. Though the college itself was small, the project—a master plan and buildings for an entire new campus—would be far and away the largest of Wright's career. There was only one hitch: Spivey had no money to build it. "[I]f you'll design the buildings," he told Wright when they met soon thereafter at Taliesin, "I'll work night and day to raise the means." Taking a page from his own playbook, Wright suggested that Spivey could save money by using his students as labor.

A short time later Wright took a train to Florida; when he returned, he announced to the Fellowship that he had got the job. Wright moved fast. Only about a month later, the college had a groundbreaking ceremony for the chapel, the first of eighteen buildings. Wes Peters was sent down to supervise. "I don't know what to do about this job down here," he wrote home to Svetlana. "They apparently don't have enough money to go ahead with the job in decent fashion." Then, without any apparent irony, he added, "They keep trying to run things with these damn college boys. . . . I don't know what the whole thing is coming to." Spivey had taken Wright's advice: The first three structures at Florida Southern were in fact built by students—though, unlike Wright's apprentices, at least they received a tuition credit for their labor.

Everything about Florida bothered Peters. The locals, he complained to his wife, weren't "living with this place, they just live on it." As a result, he concluded, they had "made it reek of squalor and decay." By now, Wes Peters had come full circle in his regard for Wright's power—so much so that he believed the master's new college campus might change all that. The Florida

Southern master plan would take twenty years to build. The verdict is out on the project's effect on the state's "squalor and decay."

Peters stayed on the job for only a matter of months. When he returned to Taliesin, he began work on something that would have been impossible for a normal apprentice—one, that is, who was neither married into the Wright family nor the owner of "their" land. He and Svetlana had decided to relocate to a farm of their own, a plot just outside Taliesin they called Aldebaran. They wanted a family; she wanted to cook her own meals. Now Wes began to build them a house. He even purchased an eighteenth-century violin for his wife, costing close to a thousand dollars.

IN EARLY SUMMER Gene Masselink's only brother, Ben, drove up Taliesin's gravel driveway with a new recruit, John deKoven Hill Jr. A teenager fresh out of high school, "Johnny" Hill would soon make his way into the Wrights' inner circle; he would go on to serve the Fellowship for almost sixty years.

If not for the publicity surrounding Johnson Wax, Johnny Hill would never have dreamed that working with Frank Lloyd Wright was even a possibility. Hill's father was head of advertising for Curtis Publications, the publishers of the *Saturday Evening Post*, and one of the magazine's advertisers was Johnson Wax. That was how Johnny learned that Frank Lloyd Wright was conducting student tours through the construction site—even, much to his surprise, that the legendary architect was still alive.

Johnny's interest in design had blossomed from boyhood, when the family lived in a Georgian style house in Evanston, a Chicago suburb. His mother was a writer and musician—a style-conscious woman said to be the first in her native Cleveland to have bobbed hair. Young Johnny entertained himself by rearranging the period furniture and paintings in his house. If his father had had his way, he would have become a football player. But he dreamed of becoming an architect. At thirteen, a visit to Chicago's Century of Progress Exposition refined his aspirations: Now he wanted to be a *modern* architect.

Johnny had heard about Taliesin from a favorite high school geometry teacher in Evanston, whose previous students included Jack Howe. By the time he finished high school in 1936, after reading Wright's books, Johnny knew that he wanted to be an *organic* modern architect. Hoping to gain admission to the Fellowship, he wrote to Taliesin, but didn't get an answer. A short time later, his father, John Hill Sr., was staying at a dude ranch in Tucson when he learned that the Wrights were nearby at the Jokake Inn and decided to pay a visit. Lunching with the Wrights, the senior Hill found Frank charming and handsome—looking "like a million dollars." Wright must have been seeing dollar signs too: Somehow he got the impression (mistaken) that the boy's father actually owned the company he merely worked for, the Curtis Publishing Corporation.

Late that night, back in Chicago, the phone rang at the Hills' luxury apartment. "Well, I don't know whether this is going to advance your career as an architect or not," Johnny Hill's father told him, "but a year or two with those people would be good for anybody, and I've enrolled you."

Despite his enthusiasm for Wright, Johnny was apprehensive. "I knew so little about him that I was expecting to just learn to love white Formica and stainless steel and all these . . . things. And I gritted my teeth." When he arrived with his parents at Spring Green in May 1938, though, Johnny looked around and did something he had never done before: He cried. "I had never let go and cried in my life," he said. "But it was so beautiful and answered every kind of thing that I loved. . . . I felt as if I had arrived home."

Unable to wait a moment longer, Johnny skipped his high school graduation. When Ben Masselink drove to Chicago to pick up the teenager, Johnny's parents invited him for dinner. Afterward the boys went out on the town, ending up at the Blackhawk, a club where jazz trombonist Jack Teagarden was playing. After the show, they were handed a bill for five dollars. They had almost no money. "We had no idea there was a cover charge," Ben recalled. He suggested that they run.

"We can't run," Johnny replied.

"Well, then, let's wash dishes—or how are we gonna get out of here?"

Johnny Hill in his room
at Taliesin

Teagarden's singer, a young woman named Kitty Callen, overheard them and asked if they were having a problem. When Ben explained, Callen told them not to worry; she would take care of it. (As Kitty Kallen, she would later have a big hit with a song called "Little Things Mean a Lot.")

The next morning Johnny loaded his stuff into Ben Masselink's Ford, dropped off his five dollars at the Blackhawk, and headed north for Taliesin. Along the way they talked mostly about jazz and where they would get their next beer.

At one point, Hill opened up. "Do you notice anything funny about my dad?"

Ben hadn't.

"Of course you wouldn't, but I don't really know my dad. He quit drinking two weeks ago." The elder Hill had been drinking all Johnny's life; now that he was sobered up, he was a different person. "He doesn't talk the same way, and we don't have the same interests."

Hours later, Ben pulled the car up by the stables behind Taliesin, where his brother had his room. Ben yelled for Gene, who limped out to greet them. Gene took Johnny to his room. "Those rooms," Ben remembered, "were small, beautiful rooms but then there was a big competition about [them], and no one ever said anything but *How we are going to make this room look better than the rest?* . . . So they all did Wright stuff—bring[ing] in branches, you know, had them hanging over the bed. . . . And Johnny of course fit right in."

The Wrights weren't there when Johnny arrived; two weeks later, Frank and Olgivanna finally returned on the midnight train. "No theatrical entrance I have ever seen matched their entrance into the Taliesin studio," Johnny remembered. "Stylish, handsome, electric—they moved rather quickly through the room."

The next morning, Hill was sent to work hoeing corn by himself in the hot sun. Johnny was bent over and sweating in his bathing suit when Gene Masselink suddenly drove up and announced that Mr. Wright wanted to see him. There was no time to change or to shower. When Wright finished writing a letter, he looked up to see the perspiring, shirtless, dirty seventeen-year-old in front of him. "Well, you've got a nice flat belly," Wright exclaimed.

And then Mr. Wright did something unexpected, something that forged a bond that would last forever: He had Gene drive him and Johnny back over to the distant corn fields. The two of them hoed corn together, Johnny half-naked and Frank in his tweed suit and hat. "We both hoed and he explained the principle of a hoe—you don't just hack, you slice them . . . And right there the fear stopped."

Well-mannered and musically skilled, Johnny Hill became one of those rare young men like Gene Masselink to whom both Mr. and Mrs. Wright took a shine. He was often invited to dine with the Wrights; the architect assigned him to take care of his clothes in his bedroom, and to pick and arrange fresh flowers there. Olgivanna took him out with her to weed her large flower gardens. Johnny was a natural: He could discern family resemblances in the structure of flowers just as he could with furniture and china.

Johnny learned interior decoration from the master. "One of the things that he did for relaxation," Johnny recalled, "was putter around with the objets d'art in the house and rearrange them. . . . And I would do that with him, sort of like a shadow." "We must make little rhythms," Wright told him, "so each looks better because of its neighbors. Making pleasing assemblies can be vitamins for your soul."

Wright used Johnny's room to show visitors how his apprentices lived. When special guests were expected, he would send Johnny to fix up the guest-room, make sure the furniture in the living room was just right, and provide an elegant arrangement of fresh-cut flowers. Mr. Wright came to rely on Johnny to do the interior design of his buildings—not just their color schemes, but also the design and layout of the furniture, from the preliminary plans to the working drawings. It was Johnny Hill who was, by his own account at least, actually responsible for shaping the interior spaces of some of the most memorable rooms of Wright's later career.

JOHNNY HILL WAS also assigned to help Iovanna, who at thirteen had become exceedingly difficult to handle. "She was so used to being treated so specially," Hill recalled, "that she couldn't think of it as being otherwise." Her mother, who had studied techniques for altering behavior at the Prieuré, was at a loss. "I was getting out of control even in her hands," Iovanna recalled. Olgivanna was beginning to contemplate sending her off to Gurdjieff himself.

Wes Peters suggested a solution: Why not send Iovanna an alligator for Christmas? "They will ship them up specially wrapped," he mused to Svetlana, "and guarantee a live, healthy delivery." Johnny Hill tried earnestly to help Iovanna "get through being thirteen." It wasn't easy. She had a "wonderful mind," he recalled, "[w]e just couldn't stand each other. . . . Whatever one did the other hated." Yet he persevered, teaching her dance and Latin.

Around this time Iovanna Lloyd Wright started getting migraine headaches. "I remember," she recalled, "I was riding horseback and this severe pain came over me." Migraines would plague her into her adult life, and their treatment would lead to debilitating drug addiction.

* * *

TWO DAYS AFTER the new year of 1939, the Fellowship caravan left Wisconsin for Arizona to continue work on their winter home. They endured the usual cheap hotels with straw mattresses, six in a room at thirty-five cents per night. Sometimes they just pulled over to the side of the road and slept in the open. At one point they ran out of water, forcing the apprentices to go from rock to rock searching for hollows where rainwater had accumulated.

Two years after Wright bought the mesa below McDowell Peak, the roads had been graded, the foundations excavated, and they were ready to start raising the actual buildings. Wright had had plenty of time to think it all out. "Arizona character seems to cry out for a space-loving architecture of its own," he observed. "The straight line and flat plane must come here—of all places—but they should become the dotted line, the broad, low, extended plane textured because in all this astounding desert there is not one hard undotted line to be seen."

The "dotted line" is an architect's drawing convention for an edge that's unseen within a building—either because it's behind the imaginary position of the viewer, the "picture plane," or because it's concealed behind a wall or another object. A "hard line," in contrast, is a visible edge, like a roof against the sky. Wright may have been exaggerating, but his observation rings true. Exactly where does the desert floor end and the foothills begin? It happens so gradually that one can never point to the spot. Wright's organic theory had always advocated this kind of ambiguity. And his buildings, with occasional dramatic exceptions, celebrated the blurring of boundaries. The column caps at Johnson Wax, are they of the column or of the roof? Where does the column stop and the roof start?

For his winter retreat, Wright set out to demonstrate that a man-made structure could grow almost imperceptibly out of the desert. The mesa he chose as his building site, at the base of the McDowell range, was like Taliesin the "brow" of a hill. Wright laid out the main structure, a drafting room connected to a kitchen and dining room, to capture the desert vistas—Black Mountain to the east and the broad valley and distant mountains to the south. His design echoed the canvas-roofed ephemera of his first desert camp, Ocatillo, but it was also a durable structure built to protect against the desert's brutality. "[O]ut there," he explained, "everything was sharp, hard, clean, and savage. Everything in the desert was armed . . ." His desert structures should be the same. The result was a structure built along primeval lines— one as original as those of the ancient Maya, he boasted, but "far beyond it."

Like the walls of the Maya, Wright designed his to last thousands of years. Building them was back-breaking work for his apprentices. Wright had developed a construction system he called "desert rubble masonry wall." Nearly all the materials were scavenged from the site; the only thing they purchased was cement, which they mixed with the desert sand to make concrete. The apprentices began by erecting temporary wooden formwork, tracing angles that followed the nearby mountain. Then they trudged up the hill behind the site to select rocks to place inside. And not just any would do: Unlike the limestone used at Taliesin, Wright's desert rocks were quartzite, a much denser stone not suitable for splitting with a chisel to create a flat face. The apprentices had to find ones that were already flat, at least on one side.

Formed under different geological conditions, the mineral-rich local stone came in a striking variety of colors, from rusty reds to cool blue-grays. The sizes of the rocks, the distribution of their colors in the finished walls— Wright wanted to control every aspect of how the stones were used, and tracking their placement inside the wooden forms was not easy. Far worse, though, was handling them: The heaviest stones weighed hundreds of pounds, and muscling them into place was grueling work for the apprentices.

Wright's desert-rubble masonry system forced the apprentices to operate blind: Not until the concrete was dry and the forms removed would they really know what they had. No matter how it looked, though, they knew that this concrete structure—which was wider at the bottom and tapered as it rose—would be as eternally stable as the pyramids. And they would echo other, even more ancient forms. Just before the concrete was poured, Wright was boating nearby when he noticed horizontal serrations on the exposed rock faces around the lake. Eager to evoke these geological scars, he had the apprentices affix narrow horizontal strips of wood inside the forms. When the wood was pulled away, they left horizontal grooves every few feet up the wall.

"And how our boys worked!" Wright wrote of that winter of 1939, which ended with Hitler's armies violating the Munich Pact. "Talk about hardening up for a soldier. Why, that bunch of lads could make any soldier look like a stick! They weren't killing anything either, except a rattlesnake, a tarantula, or a scorpion now and then as the season grew warmer. . . . [S]tripped to a pair of shorts they were just getting something born, that's all, but as excited about the birth as the soldier is in his V's when they come through. More so if my observation counts."

Once the camp's rock walls were in place, the apprentices laid a series of wooden beams overhead and stretched themselves a canvas roof, which could be rolled back to allow in warmth and light, or pulled down to shield the rooms from heat, glare, or rain. "The canvas overhead being translucent,"

Wright bragged shortly thereafter as he narrated a silent movie of the construction before a meeting of the Royal Institute of British Architects, "there is a very beautiful light to live and work in; I have experienced nothing like it elsewhere except in Japan somewhat, in their houses with sliding paper walls or 'shoji.'"

On occasion, the desert's torrential winter downpours impeded their progress. Gene Masselink's parents were expected for a visit when one storm erupted, sending flash floods rushing down the ravines and washing the roads up to the Fellowship's camp in five or six feet of muddy water. When his parents didn't appear, Gene got stranded in a wash himself before he found them. It wasn't the only such incident: "Frequently visitors trying to see us," Wright wrote, "were nearly drowned in the desert."

The canvas roofs, like the glass tube skylights at Johnson Wax, came up short. In the years that followed, Wright and the apprentices would experiment with ways to stop the leaking, but nothing worked. Finally, after World War II, Olgivanna insisted that the canvas be replaced by glass. But the leaks continued.

Then, when the desert sun finally dried things out, there was the dust. On their way to Phoenix, down "sheepherder trails" to Camelback Road, the main artery, their old Ford station wagon would fill up with dust. "We'd go have a shower, wash our hair," Kay Schneider recalled, "and the dirt would pour down on us from the dust and from the week's accumulation."

THE ARRIVAL OF spring once again drew the Fellowship back to Wisconsin.

Frank Lloyd Wright had begun looking toward death, and beyond. He elicited tears from more than one apprentice by sharing his hope that the Taliesin Fellowship would survive him. Of course, he continued, when he died "there will be a drop, sudden and precipitous, but I want it to climb and grow up again that we may establish a new way of life—that the thousand acres of the 'Frank Lloyd Wright Foundation' may develop into an ideal valley"—Broadacre City—"where there is no rent where man can be free to work and create."

On June 8, 1939, his seventy-second birthday, Wright opened a special wooden box and lifted out a handsome colored pencil-and-gold paint abstract sketch of the desert called "Desert May" by apprentice Blaine Drake. Next he pulled out Johnny Hill's, a picture of a desert house made of canvas and adobe. Johnny had had to be dragged into the drafting room to learn to draw, but under Jack Howe he had made quick progress. Kevin Lynch, an apprentice in his second year, wasn't so fortunate: His contribution, "A Flower Stand and Some Flower Pots," was unimaginative and poorly drawn.

Shortly thereafter, Lynch would leave Taliesin and begin a major career in urban planning.

The offering of drawings in honor of Wright's birthday had become a ritual event. Olgivanna had instituted the practice a few years before as a way for the apprentices to give Mr. Wright a Christmas present. Now, each year, one apprentice would also design what was known as the "birthday box," each more elegant or fanciful than the last, with special hinges, fabrics, stained glass, and gold leaf. Then the residents of Taliesin—apprentices, spouses, children—all contributed a piece of their own work to the trove: architectural drawings from most of the apprentices, poems, music, fabrics, or pressed flowers from the others. The apprentices would gather around to see the box opened, and Wright would pull them out one by one, making his opinion known to one and all.

For some this was a pleasant and relaxed affair, a chance for the apprentices to express their creativity. Sometimes the drawings were touched with whimsy. When one apprentice drew a structure floating in the sky, Wright asked how it would be moored. "Why by helium balloons, of course, Mr. Wright!" the apprentice replied, and Wright laughed.

For others, though, the birthday box was a daunting prospect. As one apprentice remembered, Wright didn't "mince words in his criticism." The apprentices took the affair very seriously, jockeying for pride of place in the presentation order. The ceremony was the only time when an apprentice's own creative work might be subjected to the master's public judgment; in that instant when Wright lifted a new item from the box, the fortunes of any given apprentice might hang in the balance. One apprentice was so frightened of Wright's disfavor that he never put a single offering in the box.

For most apprentices, though, "the box" was an expected part of their training in both design and public presentation. Mimicry was *verboten*—mimickry, at least, of historicist or European modernist styles. On the other hand, Wright did expect his apprentices to work within the precepts of his vision of organic architecture. The problem was that many apprentices didn't really know what "organic architecture" was—other than that it looked like Frank Lloyd Wright's buildings.

Still, the master didn't like it when they imitated him too slavishly. "Well, there is nothing new in this one," he told one. "I wonder what you could do on your own." Another time, his reaction was more acerbic: "God, I do not want to look at my own regurgitation."

THE SUMMER OF 1939 had brought in a strong worker, another young man who, like Johnny Hill, would end up spending his life serving Wright

TIME

The Weekly Newsmagazine

Color photograph for TIME by Valentino Sarra

FRANK LLOYD WRIGHT
His city would be everywhere and nowhere.
(See ART)

Volume XXXI

Number 3

Circulation Office, 330 East 22nd Street, Chicago.   (Reg. U. S. Pat. Off.)   Editorial and Advertising Offices, 135 East 42nd Street, New York

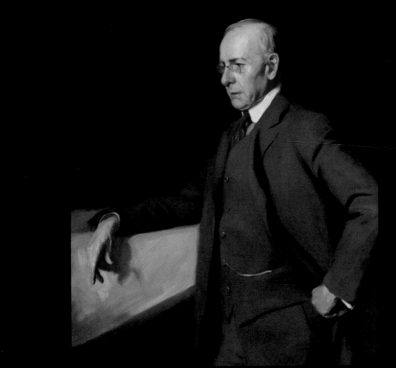

Louis Sullivan, Wright's *leiber meister*, in his later years, when he was reconnected with his protégé.

The house Wright designed for Zona Gale's aunt Laura, in Oak Park, Illinois. He would later cite it as a precursor to Fallingwater.

The Prieuré, home of Gurdjieff's Institute for the Harmonious Development of Man in the Fontainebleau region of France.

Taliesin, Spring Green, Wisconsin

The Hillside Home School building at Taliesin, which Wright transformed from a boarding school to the home of the Taliesin Fellowship in 1932.

One of the first pres
for Edgar and Lillia
Wright produced in

Fallingwater, Bear Run, Pennsylvania

The Johnson Wax Administration Building,
Racine, Wisconsin

THE AMERICAN QUALITY

By Frank Lloyd Wright

Three years after his coronation by *Time*, Wright made the cover of a very different magazine: the October 1941 edition of *Scribner's Commentator*, an isolationist magazine secretly funded by the German government.

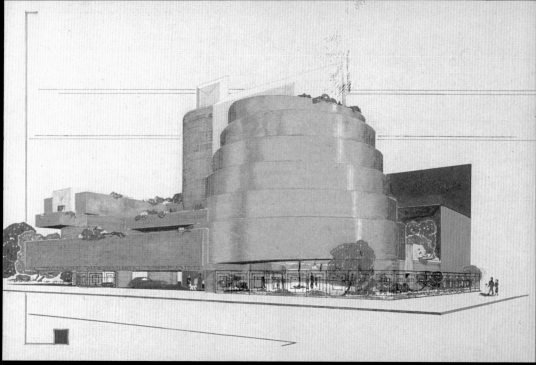

Early presentation drawings for the Guggenheim Museum in New York—a version based on his unbuilt Gordon Strong Automobile Object project of 1924 . . .

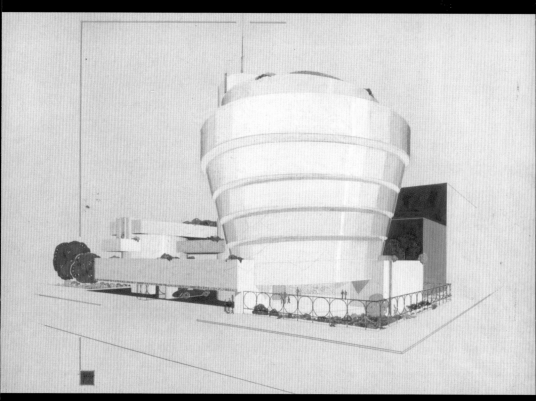

. . . and the inverted version that became the basis of Wright's final design.

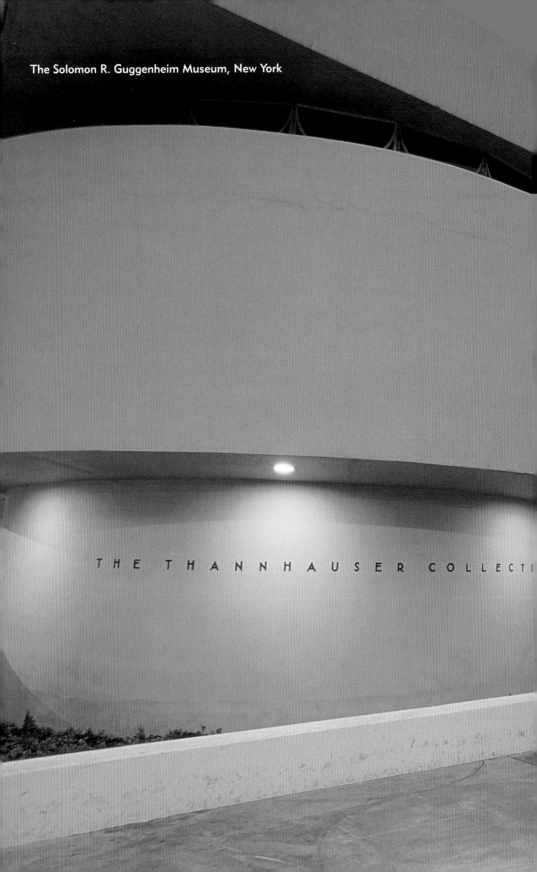

The Solomon R. Guggenheim Museum, New York

THE THANNHAUSER COLLECTI

With apprentices in the Taliesin drafting room, near the end

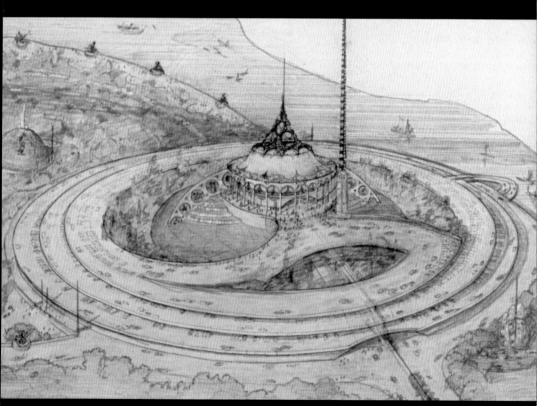

Wright's design for an opera house in Baghdad, rejected after the overthrow of the monarchy in 1958. After his death, it was reworked as an auditorium for Arizona State University (see opposite).

Taliesin West, Scottsdale, Arizona

Olgivanna Lloyd Wright, keeper of the flame, 1971

and the Fellowship. Kenneth Lockhart had taken a circuitous path to Taliesin. After almost two years of art school in Minneapolis, he had written to Wright about joining, only to discover that he needed about a thousand dollars for tuition. "I tried unsuccessfully to work on a freighter out of Los Angeles," he recalled, "and then I tried to go to Alaska via Seattle to work in the platinum mines." But his schemes were foiled by longshoremen's strikes, and after three years of struggle he wrote Wright again and offered to work off the tuition. "Come and see me," Wright replied.

Lockhart knew that Wright accepted some penniless apprentices who agreed to do extra work in lieu of tuition. Wright agreed to admit him on the "work/study" plan, but he warned him that the work would be onerous, and it would take him a long time to become an architect.

First, Lockhart was assigned to the always-busy kitchen. Only fifty apprentices or so usually showed up for breakfast, but the number swelled to about eighty for lunch, including the paid laborers Wright had once again hired. Lockhart's kitchen duty began at five in the morning and ended at nine at night. He learned little about architecture washing dishes, but after demonstrating considerable carpentry skills doing work on his own room, Wright moved him up to construction. It would be another three years before he was assigned to the drafting room.

The following winter, Lockhart joined the others for his first migration to the desert. There were buildings there now, but none for sleeping; the apprentices were still living in tents. "You ask how we keep warm," apprentice Bob May wrote his mother. "When it isn't so warm as right now, we wear heavier clothes and more of them and hover around the fireplace when not working, and even then get cold sometimes." On this trip, they hoped to start building sleeping quarters and showers. Only the kitchen had hot running water.

As May revealed to his mother, however, there were other priorities. "Construction of Wright's living wing went ahead like fire under the impetus of a drive all week in a competition between concrete pourers and carpenters making the wood forming. The idea was that the 'wood monkeys' keep ahead of the concrete crew. I am on the pouring gang. Wes Peters, who is great for bets, was responsible for the competition. Work always goes well with Wes around, as he is a good worker himself, and knows his stuff, as well as being a capital fellow. Then if we run out of material (which we always do), he takes the authority to order it from Phoenix. With Mr. Wright away we can get more done, too, because he would have boys scattered all over the place getting yucca and cacti to plant, repairing etc. We can finish the work in another two days, at the rate we've been going, then start on the apprentice dormitory wing."

Between Taliesin and the desert camp, the members of the Fellowship had been building intensely since the day the Fellowship first opened it doors. Even Wright , a workhorse himself, was beginning to feel the strain. "Hardships toward the latter end of the great experiment," he recalled of this period, "were almost more than flesh and blood could bear. Olgivanna and I, living in the midst of a rushing building operation for seven years, began to wear down."

THE TALIESIN FELLOWSHIP was not the first group to build in Paradise Valley. At the end of the fourteenth century, just as Gothic cathedral-building waned in Europe, a remarkable Native American tribe had mysteriously disappeared from this very ground. They were called Hohokan, "vanished ones," by the inhabitants who followed. As the apprentices dug into the desert floor, they discovered evidence of these ancient people, who had first migrated into the region around the time of the birth of Christ. In the boulders they surveyed for use in the building, the apprentices found petroglyphs, some consisting of mysterious circular patterns, etched there by the Hohokans centuries before.

Wright had the apprentices relocate the carvings to carefully selected locations around the emerging compound. He made sure that the petroglyphs were placed in the same compass orientations as those in which they had been found. "When the Indians come back 2000 years from now to claim their land," he told the Fellowship, "they will note we had respect for their orientation." The entire complex, in fact, paid respect to the ancient culture, aligned along an axis pointing to distant landmarks that the Wrights understood held spiritual power for its first inhabitants.

More than desert ecology and the ghosts of native civilization shaped Wright's imagination as he built on the foothills of the McDowell range. There was also romance. Wright had originally wanted to name the new complex "Aladdin." Unlike Taliesin—a house first built as a nest for Wright and Mamah Cheney—the desert complex was specifically created for a group primarily composed of young men. What could be more apt than to name this real-world manly desert escape after the boy in *The Thousand and One Nights*? "What a romantic of the race was this Persian, what mystic romance this Persia!" Wright and Brownell had written during Wright's earlier recuperation at the Jokake Inn. "Aladdin with that wonderful lamp? The wonderful lamp was Persian imagination."

Wright soon changed his mind, though, and chose simply "Taliesin, Paradise Valley" as the name for his new western headquarters. As Wright scholar Neil Levine has conjectured, "Aladdin" may have been just too personal. The name did find a place on some of the drawings for the camp, among them the large living room, which was labeled the "Aladdin Garden Room." The room, with its roof of canvas stretched between sloping timber frames arrayed like the rib cage of a huge prehistoric beast, recalled the words Wright and Brownell had used to describe the shelters of the Persians: It was a "splendid, gorgeous" tent.

Over those three winters, from 1937 to 1939, a remarkable and mysterious collection of buildings emerged in the desert foothills. The architecture was without precedent. In the Paradise Valley compound, Wright was drawing on a kind of galactic awareness of the earth. "All materials," he wrote as the camp was being built, "lie piled in masses or float as gases in the landscape of this planet much as the cataclysms of creation left them." And "the cosmic elements"—the forces of the glaciers, of wind and water—sculpted these elements over time, altering their shape in a "ceaseless procession of change." This "nobler" process of evolution and change, he now understood, governed manmade structures as well as the earth's own contours.

For Wright the desert camp was more than a metaphor, more than mere artifice; it would be a living, changing part of nature's cosmic process. And the apprentices' backbreaking work—guided by a master tuned, or so many believed, to the forces of the infinite—was only the beginning.

Frank Lloyd Wright had been refreshed.

PART V

BEHIND THE LINES

ḶITTLE ᴀMERICᴀ ꟻIRST

TWICE A YEAR NOW, WRIGHT'S streamlined Zephyr sped back and forth between the Wisconsin countryside and the Arizona high desert, followed by a line of ordinary cars packed with apprentices committed to remaking the passing landscape into a new land. Wright hoped that his Fellowship—"little America," as he sometimes called it—and its two enchanted principalities might help give rise to this new land he called Usonia. But if Americans were falling back in love with Wright's buildings, it wasn't so certain that they were prepared to see themselves as Usonians, if they even understood what that meant. Wright might have been better off if they didn't. With Europe facing war with totalitarian Germany, and American involvement already on the horizon, the architect was proposing that enormous political power be put in the hands of organic architects—effectively a class of one. Already suspect over his flirtation with the Soviets, his idiosyncratic politics would become an even bigger liability in the face of Hitler's Reich.

WRIGHT'S USONIAN HOUSE, a moderately priced, modernist residence for the everyman, was taking off. In January 1938, Wright's Jacobs residence, the first Usonian house to be completed, was featured in Henry Luce's *Time*. The magazine was deluged with inquiries. So many visitors came to see the house that the Jacobses were able to charge a fifty-cent admission, ultimately recouping their entire architectural fee.

Hoping to stimulate a housing boom by convincing American renters to build their own homes, Edgar Kaufmann backed Luce's new magazine, *Life*, in asking a select group of American architects to come up with "dream houses" for families with more modest incomes. Wright was chosen to design one for the Blackbourns, a family with an annual income of five thousand dollars. *Life* published his design that September, putting the Usonian back in the public eye. The apprentices were helping the cause, spreading the word and bringing in clients. By 1940, there were scads of houses on the boards. Wright was finally able to finish the Hillside drafting room, giving the Fellowship the desperately needed room to execute all this work. At last, everything seemed to be going their way.

There were a few glitches. As commissions for the Usonians poured in, the apprentices scurried to draw them up and get them built. The more experienced, such as Peters and Tafel, had learned a painful lesson from Fallingwater and Johnson Wax: The master had serious shortcomings as a structural engineer. They had also learned the fine art of saving his designs by slipping in steel beams and columns after Wright signed off. Failing that, plan B was to do the deed at the construction site, as with Fallingwater. When an apprentice was sent out to supervise one of the Usonians, Wes and Edgar would pull him aside for a lesson in "the facts of structural life," as Tafel put it. Yet not every apprentice was willing to go against Wright; in one such case the roof collapsed during construction.

GENE MASSELINK'S JOB included finding sites for the regular Sunday picnic, a task complicated by the skepticism of local farmers. "I know the farmers thought we were crazy to want to sit around with a mess of cow pies," Gene's brother Ben remembered. "Some thought we were Commies with our long hair and funny shoes. Others were sure we were gypsies, and they hid their children." One summer Sunday in 1938, Ben joined an advance party at a glen his brother had chosen on the banks of the Wisconsin River. They lugged over a hundred ears of sweet corn picked the previous night and laid it all in a shallow pit, covering it with river clay. They built a fire over the pit and hoped for the best. Later a group of waiters and cooks arrived with baskets of bread, big cans of milk, and sheepskins, which they laid out along the bank. Others brought chairs, footstools, and large Japanese pillows.

"A fine spot, a fine spot," Wright declared when he emerged from their 1935 Cord. "Thoreau would approve." The Wrights were served wine in crystal glasses. The cooks broke open the baked clay to get to the corn, as the apprentices hopped from foot to foot on the hot river mud. Wright lounged in the summer sun. By the end of the meal, he was reading Walt Whitman aloud to the apprentices.

As soon as Wright stood up, it was understood that the picnic was over. Everyone jumped to their feet too. "Good feed, boys," he declared, waving his cane, and he and Olgivanna disappeared in their red Cherokee convertible.

* * *

IN EUROPE, MANY of Wright's modernist enemies were on the run—not from organic architecture, but from the Nazis. Among them was Mies van der Rohe, the German architect and former Bauhaus director whose cool, minimalist glass-and-metal compositions had so beguiled Philip Johnson during the 1932 MoMA show. Of course, the idea of architectural enemies had come entirely from Wright's side. When Mies arrived in the United States, he took pains to make a pilgrimage to Taliesin. He wanted, he cracked, to give Wright a chance to tell him how bad he thought Mies's architecture was. Visiting Chicago, an American colleague called Wright to let him know that Mies wanted to see Taliesin. "I should think he would," Wright replied.

As it happened, the two men got on famously. Each got what they wanted from the visit: Wright got his respect, Mies his lecture on his architectural shortcomings. Unexpectedly invited to spend the night, Mies had to borrow clothes. They also got an eyeful when a beautiful Taliesin girl passed barefoot, the laundry in her arms. "Now there, boys," Wright remarked, "goes a pair of breasts." The German's reaction went undocumented. Later, Wright showed his guest his collection of Japanese prints, inviting him to choose whichever one he wanted as a gift. When Mies chose one of the best, Wright wouldn't give it to him.

On October 18, 1938, Wright and nine apprentices, including Wes Peters and Jack Howe, drove to Chicago's grand Palmer House hotel to attend an event welcoming Mies van der Rohe to the faculty of the city's Armour Institute. In his opening remarks, Wright was both gracious and self-promoting. "Ladies and gentleman," he told the audience of more than four hundred, "I give you Mies van der Rohe. But for me there would have been no Mies— certainly none here tonight. I admire him as an architect, respect and love him as a man. You treat him well and love him as I do. He will reward you."

Wright's homage to the Internationalist master was more than reciprocated when none other than the Museum of Modern Art—the very institution that had marginalized Wright while celebrating the European modernists— decided to make amends with a Frank Lloyd Wright show in 1940. The show, which would fill the entire museum, would feature a Usonian house that would be built right in the museum's courtyard. Wright's huge Broadacre City model would be on display too; his passion for the scheme had only grown in the three years since it was first exhibited in New York.

After the show closed, Henry-Russell Hitchcock, the International Style show's curator, had even agreed to write a book on Wright at the architect's suggestion. "Since you choose to write on the topic," Wright had written him, "why do you not devote some years of your life to learning something of architecture? Your knowledge is so superficial. . . . We will take you as an apprentice at Taliesin for a year and see if we can't put some fundamental understanding of the great art you only serve to abuse and confuse into the empty hole that seems to be where super knowledge should be."

Hitchcock started making regular visits to Taliesin to study Wright's drawings. The resulting book, *In the Nature of Materials*, was—incredibly—the first book on Wright's work ever published in the United States.

While Hitchcock was reviewing Wright's archive, he penciled "HRH" in the corner of a number of Wright's drawings, to note the ones he'd seen. At one point he came across a striking drawing of a house hanging cantilevered over a canyon—not Wright's work but a birthday box design by Robert Mosher, who happened to be in the drafting room with Wright at the time.

"Oh, Frank, I want to show you something," Hitchcock said. "It doesn't have a date on."

"Oh yes, Hitch," Wright replied, "it must have been around the turn of the century."

"Bobby," he said, turning to Mosher, "bring me my red pencil." Frank sharpened the pencil, blocked out a red Taliesin square on the drawing, and added the initials "FLLW."

"I think I won't put the date on it, because I don't remember it," Wright told Hitchcock, winking at Mosher.

"THE LANDS OF my dreams—Japan and Germany," the architect had written in 1932. He had celebrated the first for its architecture, sculpture, and printmaking, the second for its composers and philosophers. Indeed, he was inspired by the same German romantic antiliberalism that was now drawing so many sophisticated Germans to Hitler.

By the late 1930s, American was heading toward war with these two authoritarian states. Japan invaded China in July 1937; Germany seized Austria in March 1938. The September 1938 issue of *Life* that displayed Wright's Usonian house also carried a huge story on British prime minister Neville Chamberlain's surprise visit to Adolf Hitler's mountain retreat in Berchtesgaden. Chamberlain was trying to avoid Britain's entry into the war by appeasing the dictator. "Boldest stroke of diplomacy in 20 years," *Life* opined. "It dramatically convinced the peoples of the West that Englishmen are not standing on their dignity in their efforts to avoid war." Within months the Nazis had taken Czechoslovakia.

Wright's most admired countries were about to be declared enemies of America, but the prophet of Usonia thought otherwise. In a May 1939 address at London's Royal Institute of British Architects, Wright made his position on the German threat clear. Having already alienated some in the huge audience by suggesting that all but London's central core be razed and converted to parkland, its population decentralized, he began chiding his host country for its needless concern over the Nazis.

"When I got here," he told the crowd, "I was immensely disappointed to see the fear that exists among you. Where is the great old England, standing up, afraid of nothing, magnanimous, splendid, not afraid of life, because she was living? If she still lives why be afraid of anything today, even of a great idea? Certainly not afraid of an aeroplane carrying bombs."

The "great ideas" the English feared included not just Nazism, it seemed, but Wright's own vision of Broadacre City, which threatened to level much of London as surely as Hitler's bombs; the irony would not have his escaped his audience. Then, as if his rant weren't narcissistic enough, he proposed a new solution to the struggle between British democracy and German fascism: Putting power in the hands of a new breed of politicians, imbued with an organic sense of structure—say, in the hands of an architect like himself. What other choice was there? After all, he teased, "the more you analyze communism, the more you analyze fascism and democracy, the less you will be able to see any substantial differences between them in practice after the theory has evaporated."

Astoundingly, Wright's British hosts seemed to take it all in stride. Only the younger architects took umbrage. "Like Marie Antoinette," snorted one critic, "he offered us cake." Perhaps some saw Wright's indifference and his wild proposals for London as less than serious. Perhaps they could not yet imagine what lie ahead.

ONE WHO RECOGNIZED the coming threat was Georgi Gurdjieff. "Horrors on an enormous scale . . . were about to take place," he had told British follower Stanley Nott. After the London lectures, Wright headed to Paris with Olgivanna and Iovanna to see Georgivanich. The Wrights had met up with him not long before, in New York. Gurdjieff's friends there had begged him not to return to Europe; probably without consulting Frank, Olgivanna had suggested once again that he relocate to Taliesin. But Gurdjieff, who had secured a German passport in 1934, refused to abandon France. He resolved to wait out the coming storm. "Half the world is Christian, yet steals old Jewish God," he mused. "Like the Germans, all people begin now to hate Jews. Yet they carry old Jewish God in heart."

Gurdjieff's rooms in Paris were packed, figurines crowded on various chests, their walls covered with Eastern art and bad pictures by refugees. When the Wrights arrived for dinner, it was also crowded with women, most of whom were lesbians. Olgivanna's onetime lover Jane Heap had formed a Gurdjieff group in Paris made up entirely of lesbians. Margaret Anderson, her former soul mate and Wright's old friend, was one. The writer Kathryn Hulme, who would later become famous for *A Nun's Story*, was another. "The Rope," as the group was called, also included expatriate American writers Gertrude Stein and Solita Solano and French actress Georgette LeBlanc.

Heap was no longer in Paris when the Wrights arrived, having been sent by Gurdjieff to teach in England. But the rest of the group gathered with the Wrights around the table for dinner that night, positioned per Gurdjieff's instructions. Each diner was referred to by an "inner animal" name given them by the mystic. At Gurdjieff's right sat *egout* and *poubelle* ("sewer" and "garbage pail" respectively), two followers assigned to eat the food he left behind. At such meals Gurdjieff often served roasted calf's brains, served bubbling inside the calf's sawed-off head. During the meal he would pluck out one eye and then the other and offer it to one of his honored guests.

It didn't take long for Frank and Georgivanich to pick up where they had left off during Gurdjieff's contentious visit to Taliesin four years before. The dinner ritual began when "the Director," sitting on Gurdjieff's left, led the requisite toasts to several of the "idiots." Wright announced that he had invented some "idiots" himself. When Gurdjieff remained silent, the architect added, "You know, you are a very good cook. You could earn a lot of money cooking."

"Not so much as I could shearing sheep," Gurdjieff replied. ("Shearing sheep" was his term for collecting money from naive enthusiasts.)

"I've raised sheep," Wright said, taking him literally, "[b]ut I don't know anything about shearing." Gurdjieff assured Wright that it was a difficult skill to learn.

After dinner, Gurdjieff brought out a chapter he had written about his wanderings in the east for *Tales of Remarkable Men*. Would somebody read it? "I read very well," Wright offered. When Gurdjieff briefly left the room, Wright confided to the gathering, "I don't want to hurt the old man's feelings."

After reading a bit, Wright said to Gurdjieff, "You know, Mr. G., this is interesting and it's a pity it's not well written. You know you talk English very well; too bad you can't dictate. Now if I had time you could dictate to me and I could write this for you in good English."

Gurdjieff said nothing; Wright continued reading. After a while he put down the book. "Now I must go and take my little daughter home," he told Gurdjieff. "She's sleepy and so is her father."

"Yes, for her sake, stop," Gurdjieff said. "She is young. You, of course, are old man now and life finish. But she only begin."

The architect's face flushed. "My life is NOT finished," he snarled. "I could right now make six more like her. . . ."

Olgivanna had tears in her eyes as she led her thirteen-year-old daughter to the door.

Wright's boasting may have been defensive. Olgivanna would later claim that around this time he lost his sex drive for a period of several years, before it returned with a vengeance. In the meantime he apparently channeled his romantic feelings in another direction, exchanging a series of torrid love letters with his old friend Robert La Follette's daugther Mary, forty years his junior.

"He never touched me," she claimed.

BY SEPTEMBER 1939—just four months after Wright had browbeaten his London audience for their fears—Hitler had seized Poland, and Britain and France had declared war on Germany. As Jews were being walled into the Warsaw ghetto, women and children were being evacuated from London and other British cities. Though the American public overwhelmingly opposed joining the combat—and some, like publisher Henry Luce, had even embraced fascism—Franklin Roosevelt was straining to prepare America for war. The president pushed legislation through a hesitant Congress allowing for arms to be sold to Europe's democracies, and initiated a program to rearm America, particularly its air force.

As the clouds gathered, Wright wrote articles, one after the other, claiming that America didn't know how to build the military machinery necessary to defeat the Nazis—and that, in any case, the United States should let Europe fight its own battles. For Wright, it was a familiar debate: His uncle Jenkin Lloyd Jones had opposed America's entry into World War I so strongly that he was charged with sedition. American isolationism wasn't just another quirk of Wright's clan. Many American liberals—and Wisconsin had more than its share—were convinced that Britain was trying to drag its former colony into the war to save the imperialist system. To Wright, though, the best defense against foreign threats was a strong democratic America . . . and the best way to ensure that was to transform the nation into a coast-to-coast network of Broadacre Cities.

IN MAY 1940, as the Luftwaffe made its way into Holland and Belgium, French armed forces fell back to Paris, and the British to Dunkirk, aviation pioneer Charles Lindbergh took to the radio invoking America to accept the inevitable victory of Germany's air force. Lindbergh knew well the capacity of the German military: Hitler's air marshal, Hermann Goering, had presented him the Service Cross of the German Eagle. The Fuhrer himself had signed the proclamation accompanying the white medal, with its four small red swastikas. Lindbergh inveighed upon his countrymen to ignore "this hysterical chatter of calamity and invasion."

Lindbergh was an American hero, but he was also an anti-Semite; he saw the coming war in racial terms, as a bloodletting among white brothers, in which the strong would vanquish the weak. A long war, he argued, would "reduce the strength and destroy the treasures of the White race." Better for America to be herself militarily impregnable, he wrote in *Reader's Digest*, "so that it might be part of a 'Western Wall' of race and arms which can hold back either a Genghis Khan or the infiltration of inferior blood."

Wright took notice and cheered. "We all knew you could fly straight," he wrote Lindbergh. "Now we know you can think straight and when talk is quite generally cheap and unreliable—you are brave enough to talk straight. I respect your integrity."

By the end of the following month, Hitler's forces had seized most of Europe, the swastika flew from the Eiffel Tower, and Heinrich Himmler had ordered the construction of Auschwitz. Britain was now the only remaining European power still resisting the Nazis. July brought the Battle of Britain, and the Nazi blitz of London and other English cities.

As her husband continued to dismiss the Nazi threat, Olgivanna offered Taliesin as a summer safe haven for the Englishman and Gurdjieff follower Stanley Nott. When Nott arrived with his wife, Rosemary, and their two children, he understood right away how Olgivanna had integrated Gurdjieff's techniques of correlating mind, emotion, and body into the daily life of the Fellowship. And he made his own contribution: a precious typescript of *Beelzebub's Tales*, which he gave to Olgivanna to copy for her own study. Rosemary Nott, a gifted pianist and movements teacher, brought some of Gurdjieff's music in manuscript to Taliesin, but her performances rankled Wright. The architect reminded Nott of a small boy; in Gurdjieffian terms, he seemed to have developed his personality, but not his essence, "so that his inner life was strangely empty. . . ." Geniuses, he believed, were often that way.

Taliesin enchanted the Notts. The apprentices roasted a whole sheep for a picnic, drank homemade wine, sang Bach and Negro spirituals in their talented choir. And the Notts' children blossomed there. Adam and Jimmy joined the "Taliesin Junior Fellowship," a scheme Olgivanna and Svetlana had dreamed up to make a little money and get some new playmates for Iovanna. For two hundred and fifty dollars, a child could join the summer program, coming to Taliesin to study plants and Wright's Japanese prints, perform pieces of drama, and weed the vegetable garden. "In the evening," the brochure read, "the Juniors will join the Fellowship as the guests of Mr. and Mrs. Wright in the living room at Taliesin. Everyone wears best clothes with such manners as they have." The children received German lessons from Kay

Kay Schneider (second from right) and Svetlana (center) in a picnic food line.

Schneider. They sang in the Taliesin chorus under the direction of Gene Masselink; the girls could tell that he was "half in love" with Svetlana, who sang with them.

The Junior Fellowship failed in at least one respect: Iovanna didn't seem very interested in making new friends. She remained aloof, eating with her parents in the little dining room instead of joining the other kids and the apprentices. The "junior fellows" didn't envy her status as the daughter of Frank Lloyd Wright. When she dressed up one night in a pretty new dress, putting on jewelry and doing her hair, her father just sniffed. "You look like a Christmas tree," he said as the other children looked on.

Still, the visitors were unfazed. Taliesin represented "the highest culture that could be found in America," Stanley Nott declared—second only to Gurdjieff's Prieuré.

TALIESIN, HOWEVER, WAS at risk of suffering the same fate as the Prieuré, and for the same reason—money. The Fellowship had been collecting a substantial income from tuition and fees, but Wright had been using it to expand his personal empire; he still had not even begun to retire his debts. There were back taxes and back mortgage payments, unpaid bills from virtually every local merchant, and the large loan still owed to Darwin Martin's heirs.

Wright consulted a new attorney, who suggested what previous counsel had been reluctant to recommend—creating a nonprofit educational corporation. Unlike the old Wright, Inc., the new Frank Lloyd Wright Foundation would include no conventional architecture practice, at least as far as tax authorities were concerned. All its activities would be presented as part of an education program. "The business and purpose of such corporation," the articles of incorporation read, "shall be: To encourage the fine arts by the education and teaching of the arts of architecture and collateral crafts."

On November 29, 1940, the Frank Lloyd Wright Foundation came into being. Frank was the new corporation's president, Olgivanna its vice president, Wes Peters its secretary.

Nobody, Wright believed, could touch him now. All the personal assets the Martins hoped to attach were now owned by the Foundation; all future earnings would now be claimed as tax exempt. But Wright made two huge miscalculations: For several years to come, the Frank Lloyd Wright Foundation would file no federal tax returns, and when they finally did, the returns were full of red flags.

"WHY DO THE English have to fight Germany?" Wright had asked Stanley Nott that summer. "They are the same race and ought to be friends." But fight they did, and increasingly it appeared that Wright's own countrymen would too. Wright believed that America's entry into the war would be disastrous for the future of both America and his own "little America." A nation at war would have few resources available to devote to organic architecture, or to the remaking of the country into an architect-governed Usonia. Private commissions would dry up; materiel would be reserved for military purposes; a military draft would take his apprentices.

On September 4, 1940, the America First Committee—formed by Yale law students anxious to keep the United States out of war—went public with its agenda. Three days later, Hitler's bombs began to ravage London. The new organization subsequently mushroomed into a national movement 800,000 members strong, headed by Robert Wood, former chair of Sears, Roebuck. Charles Lindbergh called on Kingman Brewster—then student head of the *Yale Daily News*, later president of the university itself—to be its public face. America First even included two future presidents of the United States, John F. Kennedy and Gerald Ford. It also included Frank Lloyd Wright. The architect might have even been recruited to its board—except that, as one staff member sniffed, he had "quite a reputation for immorality."

Wright raved about America First to his apprentices, pointing to Lindbergh's involvement as evidence of its righteousness and the courageous support it deserved. Henry Ford, another anti-Semite admired by Wright, was also a big supporter, although by the 1940s his Jew-hating was so public that even America First refused to have him on its board.

Ford and Wright had been mutual admirers since the carmaker had invited Wright to design his estate in 1909. In 1940, when Ford developed an exclusive Lincoln Continental Cabriolet V-12, he had a rendering of the vehicle sent to Wright. As a promotion, the Ford Motor Company had offered to give away a number of new models to prominent Americans, including Wright. When the architect appeared at the Chicago showroom, however, he demanded two—one for each of his estates—and insisted that they be delivered to Taliesin repainted in his signature Cherokee red. Ford complied.

The founding of America First coincided with America's first peacetime draft, intended to create an army of nearly a million men. In the summer and fall of 1940, before conscription became law, young men all over the United States were signing up to fight. But none from the Fellowship volunteered, and their decision wasn't lost on outsiders: Before long, Taliesin's normally congenial movie nights and formal dinners were being interrupted by violent arguments between the apprentices and angry visitors.

Their resistance to the war came from the top down. "Wake up America," Wright warned in an article in *Christian Century*; only an enlightened minority of the nation's "most creative minds" could save the country from war and the ruin of the American "way of life." The "make-shift money-system," he was sure, was at the base of the whole thing. And the Jews, Wright was suggesting, were among the monied interests pushing the United States into this conflict.

> But, if as a people we are going on to ultimate victory over selfish or vengeful interests that infect us because those interests are unable to feel outside their own pockets, see beyond their own factory floors, or rise above their murdered European relatives, it will go on alive only because the country can see with the help of its own free minority the murderous character of 'power-politics' as now played in unison by the two parties. . . .

Wright's anti-Semitism was political and proverbial. He believed that big Jewish money was manipulating his country into war. He was hardly alone in his thinking: anti-Semitism ran deep in the grain of rural Wisconsin, as in much of American life. To Wright, one apprentice recalled, to bargain over prices was to "Jew him down." Of course, Wright also depended on Jews ("good" Jews, in Lindbergh's term); they were among his most important clients and best apprentices. When they crossed him, he often resorted to anti-Semitic invective.

But he liked them as long as they served his purposes, and they generally liked him. Long after his death, Jewish apprentices with whom he was on good terms would swear that Frank Lloyd Wright was absolutely free of hatred toward Jews.

THE U.S. ARMY was about to start coming for Wright's boys. The draft, he declared in the *Christian Century*, was symptomatic of America's own slide into dictatorship. A real democracy would fight only with volunteers.

Wright's views on conscription were well known within the Fellowship. His apprentices would go to war "over his dead body," he declared. And by and large the apprentices agreed; they believed that their work at Taliesin, creating a "true" American culture, was infinitely more important. "True defense for us," Wright wrote in November 1940, as Britain entered its third month of bombing, "must be a matter of putting better ideas than Hitler's total-state and total-war-among-states in practical effect here and now."

After enduring four months of Nazi devastation, a desperate Winston Churchill turned to America, and on December 17, 1940, Franklin D. Roosevelt told the nation that America would help the British directly with military matériel. America was now in the war, even if its soldiers were not yet fighting.

FROM ITS VERY start, Wright had seen the Fellowship as a "seed" for his vision of Usonia and Broadacre City. But there was never any clear sense of how the seed was supposed to grow. It had been almost ten years now since he had conceived the idea, yet after a book, numerous articles, a traveling exhibit of the model, and countless lectures around the world, Wright's ideas had garnered little support, and no financial backing. It was time for him to take matters into his own hands. He would build the first Broadacre City himself, in the valley of the God-almighty Joneses.

The key to Wright's plan was the acquisition of large amounts of land adjacent to Taliesin—land to be controlled, if not owned, by the Frank Lloyd Wright Foundation. And much of the money would come from the apprentices. After tapping Wes Peters's inheritance to save Taliesin, Frank now looked to other apprentices to expand it. In 1928, Wright had owned only seventy acres. By the time Peters agreed to assume the title in 1936, the estate had grown to six hundred and fifty. Now, in 1941, Wright began to cajole other apprentices into buying farms, with the understanding that the land would become part of the first Broadacre City. Gene Masselink, Herb and Eloise Fritz, Frances and Cary Caraway, and Henning and Carolyn Watterston all complied, some of them at huge personal cost. Kay Schneider and Davy Davison, who were soon to marry, also ended up with nearby acreage.

And by now Wes's holdings included two of the old Lloyd Jones farms, three hundred fifty acres in total. "Wes coveted it and I egged him on to buy it," Wright recalled with remarkable frankness. "He seemed the kind of lad who could use ground. And I wanted to see Taliesin expand. . . ."

Wright dubbed the operation "cooperative farmsteads." Under Wes's co-ordination, the farms harvested hay, corn, oats, and small grains, and raised sheep and hogs. The proceeds were distributed back to the apprentice-farmers according to each farm's acreage. The for-profit venture was put un-der the aegis of Wright's educational foundation, an illegality that would eventually catch up with him. For the moment, though, Wright was in clover: Between the apprentice farms, Taliesin, and Peters's own holdings, the Frank Lloyd Wright Foundation potentially controlled well over a thousand acres in the valley—an area larger than nearby Spring Green. The first Broadacre City was taking shape before his eyes.

AT ALDEBARAN, THE farm Wes Peters had named for the follower star in the Taurus constellation, Wright's senior apprentice had built a house for the family he and his wife hoped to have. For Svetlana, it meant a life apart from her over-bearing mother; for him it meant a house with beams, ceilings, and doorways high enough that he wouldn't crack his head on them, as he often did at Taliesin, both east and west. Wright called Aldebaran "Taliesin's first real extension—collateral human growth," clearly viewing it as part of his plans for the valley.

With Svetlana out of the household, Olgivanna enlisted Kay Schneider as her most trusted insider. It was Kay who delivered Mrs. Wright's summary judgments to the apprentices, as when she denounced one apprentice for dec-orating the dining room badly. Unlike Svetlana, Schneider had few qualms about serving as Olgivanna's spy and chief collector of gossip.

At least once, though, Kay surely cursed her new status. One Saturday, she found herself the hostess for one Mr. Maron, a Jewish refugee from Germany who had purchased the cheese factory in Spring Green and wanted Wright to rebuild it. At dinner, sitting between Wright and Maron, the prospective client began to flirt with her. Rather than putting a stop to it, Wright joined in.

"And I just scrunched up," Kay recalled. "I absolutely felt terrible, as though my father was flirting with me, you know. So I couldn't eat. I just froze."

That night, she told Olgivanna all about it. "I just wanted to throw up," she confided. "I couldn't stand Mr. Wright flirting with me."

Olgivanna was not surprised. Not long before, Frank had had the dubi-ous judgment to mention to her "what a stride Cornelia had, what a beautiful girl," and how "Hulda looked so wonderful in her playsuit." Indeed, Wright raved about all the girls at Taliesin.

"Can I tell Mr. Wright what you just told me?" Olgivanna asked Kay. She agreed.

The next morning, Wright called in his accuser. "Mr. Wright gave me the 'beating' of his life," Kay recalled. "How could I insult him? How could I dream that he would flirt with me! . . . He called me every name under the sun."

Hovering within earshot, Olgivanna interrupted and called Kay into her room. "Tell him you respect him and love him like your father," she whispered.

"And it was true," Kay recalled. "So I stood up to him, I said, 'Mr. Wright, I love and respect you like my own father! I couldn't love anybody more than that! But I wouldn't feel right if my father flirted with me!'"

Wright would not be mollified. "[T]he 'beating' went on for over an hour," Kay continued. "Finally Mr. Wright said, 'Well, I guess I told you! You can go now.' So I went out of the room, shaking—absolutely. It was like a tsunami and a hurricane and a volcano all at once. He never flirted with another girl at Taliesin after that. Never. That was it. And before that he'd flirted with every girl."

In this case, Kay Schneider was clearly a victim of unwanted advances. But Svetlana regarded her mother's confidante as a fawning seductress. In a fury brought on by her long history of abandonment—Olgivanna had of course twice left her as a child, first for Gurdjieff, then for Wright—Svetlana wrote her mother a long, detailed letter laying out the case against her rival. Kay had just married Davy Davison a month after getting pregnant; Svetlana found her loose in her morals, not to mention loud and insecure. She charged Kay with seducing another handsome young apprentice, painstakingly recounting how Kay had invited him to teach her horseback riding by night. The child Kay was carrying, she claimed, belonged not to Davison but to the other apprentice. "If it were anyone else," Svetlana raged at her mother, "you would talk with me as you always did and that little gutter snipe should hold the identically same position with you that I *held* (and I use the *past* tense)."

Svetlana seemed to know precisely why her mother and stepfather had taken to Kay. "She isn't worth it—not even with the Westinghouse backdrop," she scolded, referring to the estate Olgivanna believed Kay would inherit. "Perhaps," she added, Daddy Frank "is right in saying that he can build the Broadacre City with people like Kay and Davy—mere puppets, whom you can pull around—You both seem to like people like that but I thought you saw them for what they are not what they may represent financially. . . ."

BY FEBRUARY 1941, the Luftwaffe's relentless terror bombing of London—intended to frighten Britain into surrender—had been going for six months, burning large sections of the city and killing tens of thousands. In London to receive the Royal Gold Medal for Architecture from King George, Wright was asked by a newspaper to write a piece on how he would rebuild the city. He wrote blithely that the destruction was paving the way for the decentralization of the population and the realization of Broadacre City. "Human congestion," he added, "is murder; murder if not of the carcass, then murder of the most desirable human sensibilities." As for the ongoing murder of the mere "carcass," he had nothing to offer.

That same month, Wright began circulating a regular broadsheet he called the "Taliesin Square-Paper" to his friends, clients, and supporters. The title referred to the red-square symbol Wright had made his signature, but also to the notion of a "square" deal; Wright billed the publication "A Nonpolitical Voice From Our Democratic Minority."

The first "Square-Paper" expanded on Wright's ideas for Britain's defense and London's reconstruction, in addition to his architectural vision of Broadacre City. If the beleaguered people of Britain would only put a stop to their speculation in money, land, and ideas—eliminating the gold standard, unused private property, and patents—he believed they could render their nation impregnable, inhospitable to dictators, averse to war. Perhaps architecture could only "live again . . . because of bombs in irresponsible hands," he mused. "Who knows?" Things might still turn out all right; Hitler might even be doing them a favor.

IN MARCH 1941, twenty-six Taliesin apprentices signed a joint statement to their draft board in nearby Dodgeville, a copy of which they sent to Charles Lindbergh. Like the government, they claimed, they too were pursuing a "national objective" by establishing a "convincing example of indigenous American culture" and designing "buildings more truly expressive of the land we live in and of the people of our great Democracy." The work of Taliesin was "a true form of self-defense." And their principles rendered them "unfit for destruction and the mass murder called war." After the years they had spent building a cohesive group to carry out their mission, they were finally ready. To draft their best men, they declared, would be "to render us impotent."

One by one, the draft board interviewed the apprentices. The military code held that conscientious objectors could be exempted only on religious grounds. The apprentices, it seemed, put their faith elsewhere. "Each member claimed to be possessed of the ability of a genius insofar as being an architect was concerned," one draft board member recalled.

Their requests were all refused.

* * *

IN 1941, WRIGHT conducted a military invasion of his own. He had designed a house in Southern California's Malibu mountains for radio writer Arch Oboler and his family. The clients had been accommodating throughout the process, agreeing to spend twice the amount they had intended. When the architect had dropped by to say that the Fellowship couldn't afford groceries, Arch Oboler even agreed to advance him five hundred dollars on the job. Only later did he discover that Wright had used the money to buy ancient Egyptian vases from an antique dealer in Beverly Hills.

When the plans were completed, Wright gave the Obolers a piece of advice: "During the actual building of your house, get out of town!" Nonetheless, after only a section of the main house had been completed, the family moved in. But the Obolers would commit an even worse transgression when they had the builders make changes to Wright's design—raising the ceiling, substituting narrow redwood siding for wider pine, building a redwood fence behind the house, and relocating the guest house.

One afternoon when the family was having friends over for a barbecue, a long caravan of imported cars came up the mountain road and, as Arch Oboler put it, "curved into our driveway and stopped in a draftsman's precise line."

Out stepped Frank Lloyd Wright, Malacca cane in hand, and instructed one of the twenty apprentices to take out a crowbar. Pointing his cane at the redwood fence, he roared, "Rip it out!"

"Mr. Wright, that wall cost me five hundred dollars!" Oboler complained as "twenty sets of eager muscles leaped and shoved."

When the fence was gone, Oboler had to admit that things looked better.

"Then we are in complete agreement," Wright said as he removed his cape and gestured to the apprentices to join the Oboler's guests in eating the barbecue. After lunch, Wright left four apprentices behind to reverse his client's other changes.

BETWEEN THE DRAFT and the always-present seductions of the outside world, Wright was starting to face a real battle to hold onto his apprentices. Jack Howe was one. For nine years Howe had been responsible for the critically important construction drawings, and the stress was taking its toll. Wright saw him as "quite indispensable in the studio," but Howe had been itching to try his hand as a site supervisor, or even to quit altogether. Wright finally relented, sending Howe to oversee construction on a brick Usonian in Kansas City, Missouri. Jack was satisfied, at least for the moment.

* * *

WRIGHT KEPT UP his drumbeat against the war. America, he wrote in late May 1941, could not expect to win if it should enter the war; nor did she have the military material to save Britain. There was a better way. "The best defense," he offered, was to build a true democracy based on a "natural capitalist economy"—one whose design he and the boys had already worked out in the form of Broadacre City. The solution of our world problems "in the face of Germany, Russia, France, Italy, and Japan, slave-empire," he wrote, lay "in the green hills of the Taliesins of our great nation and will be found there if ever found at all."

That same week, in a "Taliesin Square-Paper," he attacked Roosevelt for being willing to sacrifice American lives to shore up the British Empire, a move that would make America complicit in Britain's imperialism. In the end, Wright charged, it was all about money. America was militarily weak, its industrial plant decrepit and outmoded, because the financial institutions were hoarding their money; millions were still unemployed because of the artificial scarcity produced by the hoarding; and Roosevelt wanted to go to war in the interest of big business.

There was an enemy within, and Wright knew just where to find him—on the East Coast, which he saw as "an out-and-out pseudo fascist empire reflecting the great disappearing British empire." If America went forward with the war, he warned, there would be "a great upsurge of resentment" against our home-grown "pseudo fascists," and the results would be "disastrous." The plutocrats and their ilk would get theirs in the end.

Even some of Wright's loyal supporters thought the old man had crossed the line. His old East Coast (and half-Jewish) friend Lewis Mumford had already sent Wright a letter warning him that "Period politics are as bad as period architecture." Now he was enraged.

> What a spectacle! You shrink into your selfish ego and urge America to follow you; you are willing to abandon to their terrible fate the conquered, the helpless, the humiliated, the suffering: you carefully refrain from offending ... those Nazi overlords to whom in your heart you, like Lindbergh, have already given the fruits of victory. In short: you have become a living corpse: a spreader of active corruption.

Wright replied in kind.

> Time will discover you a deserter. A traitor on a battle-field that did you honor only to discover in you a vengeful, conceited writer. . . . Is meeting force with force the only way you see now? Then I am sorry for you—you amateur essayist on culture. . . . Goodbye, Lewis, I shall read your 'brief' in

the *New Yorker* with shame. I shall read it knowing your real opinion is worthless whatever you may write.

The two would not communicate again for a decade.

WRIGHT'S "LITTLE AMERICA" was not faring much better than the big one. Taliesin was starting to take its toll on those senior apprentices who actually aspired to become independent architects. After Edgar Tafel's all-too-successful house in Racine attracted Wright's wrath, the seniors were no longer allowed direct access to clients, or granted the equal share of the fees Wright had previously allowed. Now the seniors were expected to supervise jobs in exchange for a third of the fee and none of the credit.

The apprentices' frustration almost came to a head when Tafel brought another new client to Wright, only to find himself relegated to handling the details. And, then, somehow, his cut of the fee never materialized. As always, Wright had a little philosophy at the ready. The architectural marketplace, he clucked, was a place where "all work is more or less prostitute to wages"; it would simply "kill [Tafel's] new effort."

When Tafel eventually mustered the nerve to complain to Wright about the new policy, Wright cavalierly pulled out of his pocket a hundred-dollar bill—a month's income for an architect on the outside—and gave it to him. Tafel took the money, but he and Taliesin's other experienced hands weren't buying the philosophy. Wright was improvising the rules as he went along, and the seniors were growing restless. And, for some reason, so was Wright.

By the summer of 1941, the situation was tense enough that Wright gathered the eight senior apprentices for a private meeting. They had all been there too long, he told them. He was going to abolish the whole system of senior apprentices. They would no longer be able to bring their work into the Fellowship; instead, Wright urged them to leave and set up their own practices. He even offered to help them do it.

"I can't stay. I'm leaving," Edgar Tafel told a group of like-minded apprentices. Clearly there would never be any opportunity to do independent work at Taliesin. Seven of eight seniors decided to leave, but they agreed to slip away one by one, to avoid the embarrassing impression of a collective protest.

Tafel told Wright of his decision. "Since you know what you want to do," came the reply, "the sooner the better. Tell Mrs. Wright your decision." After Tafel and his wife left, he received a letter from Wright. "I hope you and Sally are finding wage-slavery a better choice than fellowship-Cooperation," he wrote. "But, I have my doubts. A pity you should allow the place you made for yourself with us to grow cold. A mink coat for Sally wouldn't make up for it. As a matter of fact all mink coats are for some kind of prostitution, I believe?"

Tafel's wife was named Jean, not Sally. Wright had renamed her because Jean sounded like Gene.

IN JUNE 1941 Hitler attacked Stalin in Operation Barbarossa, and the Fuhrer's Einsatzgruppen began their mass murder of Jews. President Roosevelt was readying for war.

Wright's next move was astonishing: He decapitated Washington, D.C.—at least on paper. In his August 1941 "Taliesin Square-Paper," the architect proposed to reorganize what he called the forty-eight states of Usonia—formerly America—into just three. Wright's master plan effectively cut away the power centers of America's "Eastern establishment," dividing most of the country into two new states, Usonia and Usonia South, while quarantining the pro-war centers of New York and Washington, D.C., into a much smaller state he called simply "New England," in a sly nod to their complicity with English imperialism.

The State of Usonia, the largest of the three, would be the heartland of a new America, housing the new national capital and all the "former" Midwest and Western states. Not coincidentally, it also contained both Taliesins. Just eight months before, as apprentices were buying up farms at the master's urging, Wright began referring to his Wisconsin property as "Taliesin East" and his Arizona estate "Taliesin West." Taliesin East was already on course to become the first Broadacre City; the eight-hundred-acre Taliesin West estate, surrounded by nothing but more cheap land, was likely next in line. On Wright's new national map, Wright's compounds were positioned as the eastern and western centers of the central state of Usonia.

Having devoted more than a decade to creating these twin centers of culture, Frank Lloyd Wright was trying to gerrymander his way into making them the nerve centers of this new State of Usonia. If things went his way, the "real" America would be his.

Scornful of others whose ideas were overblown, Wright had even coined a term for the disease: "grandomania." Now, as he dreamed away in his isolated Taliesins, bolstered by loyal apprentices and a wife who believed in his genius, Wright's grandiosity—his grandomania—was running away with him.

AMERICA FIRST COMMITTEES were proliferating across the country, and Wright's friend Charles Lindbergh was stumping before huge crowds nationwide. On September 4, 1941, America came closer to entering the war when a German sub attacked an American destroyer en route from Newfoundland.

A week later, addressing a crowd in Des Moines, Iowa, Lindbergh finally showed all his cards. There were three forces, he announced, pushing America toward war: Roosevelt, the British, and the Jews.

Instead of agitating for war, he went on, Jews "should be opposing it in every possible way, for they will be among the first to feel its consequences. Tolerance is a virtue that depends upon peace and strength. . . . A few far-sighted Jewish people realize this, and stand opposed to intervention. But the majority still do not. Their greatest danger to this country lies in their large ownership and influence in our motion pictures, our press, our radio, and our Government."

The following month, Wright made the cover of *Scribner's Commentator*, an isolationist organ founded by a Lindbergh enthusiast and secretly financed by the German government. Inside was an article by the architect accompanied by photographs of Fallingwater, Johnson Wax, and several of the Usonians. Wright's article, however, was not about architecture, at least not directly. Instead the piece targeted not only conscription and the bankers of New York and London—likely also a code for the international Jewish conspiracy—but also the universities, which he wanted to close in order to put "the innumerable four year loafers back to work at their place of origin." The essay ended with a remarkable leap of logic: If America were reconfigured as he suggested, who would want to fight it? "Certainly not Hitler."

WHILE WRIGHT WAS mulling over his plans for national insurrection, his senior apprentices continued one of their own. Jack Howe, for one, was still thinking of leaving. A few months before, not for the first time, he had requested permission to go home for his birthday. Wright told Howe to stay and finish some drawings and some furniture he was making for Olgivanna.

Howe began to plan his exit. Having supervised construction on one of Wright's Usonian houses, he now felt confident setting out to design and build small houses on his own. In the fall of 1941, he sent home his books and some invaluable Japanese prints for safekeeping. Soon, he resolved, he would leave and look for a drafting job in Chicago.

By early October, though, half of the seniors had left, and the Wrights began working the remaining four more selectively in an effort to keep them from leaving. Howe noticed the difference: The Wrights had been awfully nice to him lately, he wrote home, and he was reluctant to desert them like the others had. Nevertheless, the following month he went to Wright and announced that he was leaving.

Wright's response stunned the apprentice. He told Howe that he had decided to let him in on a closely guarded secret: After his death, he wanted Howe to play a key role in ensuring the survival of Taliesin. "He pointed out it would be a great mistake to leave now," Jack wrote to his mother, "as this is a crucial time for the Fellowship and, with all the other 'seniors' gone he is setting up the Fellowship for after he is gone as an endowed corporation with Mrs. Wright and then Iovanna as President." And he was to be part of the inner circle, one of its four "stockholders," along with Wes and Svetlana Peters and Gene Masselink. "Keep all this under your hat," he told his mother, "and don't even mention it to me."

WITH HIS ATTENTIONS focused on Taliesin East's collateral farms scheme and his crusade against the war, Wright decided to forgo the Fellowship's costly and time-consuming winter migration to Arizona. The hiatus would last three years, leaving the vacant "camp" vulnerable to the elements, vandalism, and locals who used it as a picnic site. At one point, apprentice Kenn Lockhart, who seemed able to fix anything, offered to go to Arizona to guard the place and work on repairs. A few days later, Wright took him to a motorcycle shop in Madison. "I bought you this motorcycle to go to Arizona," Wright told Lockhart, presenting him with a 1932 Harley Davidson with a sidecar. "[Y]ou can drive one can't you?" Kenn never had, but the salesman took him for a ride to demonstrate. That afternoon, he packed up his things and roared west. The trip took two weeks.

ON DECEMBER 7, 1941, Howe and other apprentices were working in the Taliesin West drafting room when the news came that Japanese Zero warplanes had sunk or damaged twelve American warships in Hawaii. Japan, that other land of Wright's dreams, had finally forced America into the war.

Though the architect would suspend his campaign of isolationist screeds, Japan's surprise attack did nothing to change Wright's opposition to American involvement in the war. And most of the apprentices followed suit: Though Pedro Guerrero was persuaded by his father that loyalty to his country trumped loyalty to Wright, most still stood by the master. At first, only a handful decided to serve. Bob Mosher left within weeks to join the Office of Strategic Services, America's espionage network, which would become the CIA after the war. And three months later the laconic Jim Charlton, so lean the apprentices called him "lightbody," left to join the Air Force. Charlton's father had flown military missions in World War I, and died in a crash as a postal pilot. Jim would fly twenty-six combat missions over enemy territory in a P-51 Mustang. He prized a photo of himself sitting in the cockpit, lighting a cigarette and sporting what he called his "fuck you" smile.

Ten days after Pearl Harbor, the Fellowship gained a new member—

Svetlana and Wes's first child, a son. They named the husky boy Brandoch after Lord Brandoch Daha, a heroic character in the 1926 fantasy novel *The
Worm Ouroboros*, the book Svetlana was reading when Wes first kissed her.
"Taliesin had a son, a daughter, and a grandson," Wright crowed in the
manuscript for the second edition of his autobiography. "Taliesin has other
faithful competent sons—many of them an asset to Fellowship, but the
young man Olgivanna and I drove away years ago with the unkind assumption that he was stealing away a daughter. . . . Wes . . . is a right bower, the
best example of What-Taliesin-Can-Do for-a-Young-Apprentice (his wife
thrown in) and what a young apprentice can do for Taliesin."

"A FOOLISH CONSISTENCY is the hobgoblin of little minds," said one of
Wright's great heroes, the American Transcendentalist Ralph Waldo Emerson.
Now, just months after Wright issued his final antiwar diatribe, the Taliesin
Fellowship was doing war work. Preserving Taliesin was more important
than moral purity. Wright not only rented Taliesin West to the army, but also
took a contract to build a hundred houses for defense workers near Pittsfield,
Massachusetts. Wright was hoping to strike a deal: If the government would
defer his apprentices from conscription, he would move the entire Fellowship
to the construction site.

Wright created a series of ingenious designs for the project, using walls of
thin pre-cast concrete panels. The plans had been approved by the government
and were ready to go when local lawmakers passed legislation requiring that the
job go instead to a nearby Massachusetts firm. A short time later, Wright got a
commission to do preliminary drawings for demountable houses to be used
around Washington, D.C., but that project never went into construction either.

The Fellowship's fledgling attempts at war work failed to impress the local
draft board. In the fall of 1942, Marcus Weston became the first apprentice to
refuse to report for induction. At his trial he was repeatedly pressed on whether
Wright had unduly influenced him. "I think you boys are living under a bad influence with that man Wright," the judge declared in his summation. "I am
afraid he is poisoning your minds." Weston was furious. "To accuse Frank Lloyd
Wright or any one person of responsibility of my convictions," he declared to
the press, "is ridiculous and insulting both to me and to him." Patrick Stone, the
federal judge, delayed sentencing and urged the twenty-seven-year-old Weston
to leave Taliesin and "stay away from that man Wright." Weston did not comply.

When the time for sentencing came, Justice Stone not only sent Marcus
Weston to jail, but also demanded that Wright be investigated for obstructing
the war effort. Wright publicly attacked the judge. By now, he noted, nineteen
of his apprentices were in uniform; he hadn't stood in their way. It was the

judge who was being obstructive, he charged, by standing in the way of those apprentices who wanted to serve their country at Taliesin. "I have occasion to know well," he wrote the judge, "the arrogant prejudice raised against any man who refuses to run with the pack."

By this time, Wright's behavior had made him the target of an FBI investigation. J. Edgar Hoover, who had long been suspicious of him, smelled sedition. The FBI interviewed the apprentices, looking for evidence that Wright had encouraged their draft resistance. In a confidential memo to Hoover, the investigating agent reported that Wright "was regarded by members of the fellowship as somewhat of an idol, a tin god, or a master, who could do no wrong."

The apprentices stonewalled the agents.

The truth would have been very damning. "He told us we didn't have to register," recalled Pedro Guerrero years later. "And then if we were registered, we didn't have to go. And if we were arrested and sent to prison that we always had a place to come back to when we were out."

Although one had already been jailed, neither Wright nor the apprentices seemed to fear the agency. When agents later showed up at Taliesin on another matter—Wright was stockpiling tires in case of wartime shortages, and the Feds suspected him of trafficking them on the black market—Wes Peters drove them off with a shotgun.

The war was thinning Taliesin's ranks. One day, Wright asked the remaining apprentices a rhetorical question: Who are the real heroes? "The boys who shoot down planes [and] kill Germans?" No, he told them, the real heroes are "the Conscientious Objectors, the boys who have the courage to refuse to go out and kill." And to emphasize the point, Taliesin's teatime now had a new feature: the reading aloud of Marcus Weston's letters from prison.

THERE WAS STILL the occasional new apprentice. In the fall of 1942, a married Jewish couple, Priscilla and David Henken, arrived from New York. Priscilla had been a schoolteacher in Manhattan, David an industrial engineer working at the frontiers of mass-production packaging. But everything had changed when David visited Wright's 1940 MoMA show. With its model of Broadacre City and its plan for a cooperative housing project in Michigan, the show had seemed like a divine message. Standing before the exhibits, Henken decided on the spot that he wanted to start an ideal community of his own, and that he would someday apprentice to Wright, gain the skills to organize it, and convince the master to design it.

"In this day of destruction," Henken finally wrote Wright in July 1942, "it does not seem to me out of place to think of building for the good life." Proclaiming his belief in the "brotherhood of man" and the "cooperative commonwealth as a means of achieving it," he told Wright that he had already refused to use his skills for war and offered himself as an apprentice.

Wright wrote back welcoming the couple in, but when the Henkens arrived not everyone was so pleased. Within the hermetic circles around the Wrights they were seen as pushy, and the reactions of some apprentices were flatly anti-Semitic. Olgivanna, for her part, was suspicious. With his all-too-convenient 4-F medical draft exemption, she worried aloud that David was a government agent sent in to gather evidence against her husband.

THERE WAS TROUBLE brewing among the founding citizens of Broadacre City. "Whether we like it or not," Wright had written Svetlana, "we are building up the valley for the Fritzes—the Hennings—the Dick and Mary Jones et al. . . . But we don't want to plant the valley to nourish the weeds (so to speak) and starve the crop."

"The Hennings" was a reference to Henning Watterston, one of the apprentices who had bought an adjacent farm at Wright's urging. After a year on the former Richard and Mary Lloyd Jones farm, however, Watterston and his wife had become "weeds": They had the temerity to leave the Fellowship without relinquishing the property to the Foundation. It was a setback for Broadacre City and Wright was incensed. That farm "once belong[ed] to my own people," he reminded Waterston in a blistering letter. "Instead of turning the farm . . . back to us and quitting the neighborhood as any real man in the circumstances would have done you chose to play the role of a spiteful old woman, hanging around where you knew you were not wanted." Things became so bad between the two that Watterston had to sue to retrieve his personal belongings from Taliesin. But when he later offered to sell Wright the farm, Wright—no doubt lacking the requisite funds—exploded. "You belong in 'the valley' about as much as some vicious stray dog," he replied. "I hope never to buy it. . . ."

Unlike Watterston, Herb Fritz had old and deep ties to the valley; his relatives the Fritz sisters had been Wright's longtime cooks at Taliesin, and his draftsman father had been one of the few survivors of the 1914 fire and murder at Taliesin. An apprentice since 1937, Herb Jr. had borrowed eight thousand dollars to buy a farm that once belonged to Wright's aunt Mary Lloyd Jones, understanding that it "was to eventually become a part of Broadacre City. . . . We were to live on the land but be centered at Taliesin."

Wright's Broadacre City was based on the idea that each family would have its own farm as a secondary business, just as he did. Likewise, the master expected apprentices who bought farms to remain at their Fellowship posts. Fritz's farm, known as "Hilltop," had twenty head of cattle and some pigs. Fritz hired two Swiss brothers to work the land, but when they disappeared Fritz was left to cover the mortgage on his own. With no other income, he suddenly had to learn to farm himself, harvesting the grain and milking the cows, all while still apprenticing at Taliesin. "There's no way I can milk the cows and [attend] rehearsal," Fritz complained. When the Fellowship next migrated to Arizona, he stayed behind. Wright could not forgive him; the two didn't really talk again until well after the war.

WRIGHT'S FAILURE TO land serious war work was critical. Only five new projects, none of them large, found their way to Taliesin during 1942, compared with twenty-six the year before. Most of the work was now farming and maintenance, just as it had been during the Fellowship's first struggling years. In the first year of the war, the apprentices who remained at Taliesin, unwilling or unable to be drafted, often had nothing to do. Wes Peters sometimes filled the time playing raconteur, telling stories about medieval knights or cowboys and bandits. One boring afternoon he entertained the Fellowship by demonstrating his skill hypnotizing chickens.

Jack Howe applied for conscientious objector status, but he was turned down. The decision had Wright in a frenzy, contacting generals and senators in Arizona and Wisconsin. Wright even talked of approaching the president personally over the matter.

Hoping to make extra cash, Wright devoted his spare time to preparing a new edition of his autobiography. The updated version paid a good deal of attention to the Fellowship. It also contained a paean to his isolationist allies Charles Lindbergh and Henry Ford. Although America was officially at war with Germany, both had still refused to return their Nazi medals. "To the American Eagle," it began, referring to Lindbergh. "If you must have a skyscraper—he is a flyer. . . . Honor, too, to the true American who put him into the service of his country for better or for worse. A staunch man, Henry Ford." Roosevelt wouldn't let Lindbergh into the air force, so Henry Ford had given him a job working at his Willow Run A-24 air bomber factory. When the new version of *An Autobiography* came out the following year, Wright sent each man a copy.

With German U-boats now harassing America's eastern seaboard and the American air attack under way in Europe, Jack Howe's number finally came up. Like Marcus Weston he had decided not to go, and he wrote his mother to inform her of his decision. At first she hid it from her husband, a traveling clothing salesman. When she finally admitted what their son intended, he couldn't really believe Jack was one of those "that are so 'queer' that they think they are 'C.O.'s.'" His son's decision was not only cowardly, but also would get him ostracized from American society for the rest of his life.

Howe did not back down. Following Wright's line, he told his father that the war was being engineered by the monied interests. America's allies were not democracies; the whole thing was engineered in order to build up a corporate dictatorship at home. What the country needed is "one of those people whom you refer to as 'queer,' who would be strong enough to lead the country back to Democracy." If America were lucky enough to survive this war, he wrote, before long it would surely find itself engaged in another war, this time against the inside forces who had lured it into this one.

Soon enough his mother was on the phone to Taliesin, crying hysterically. The FBI had come calling. He would not go to jail, he reassured her; if anything, he would get himself declared a conscientious objector and serve as a noncombatant. He had been fortunate, he wrote to his parents, to have availed himself of Wright's "cosmic mind." Wright would one day be recognized as one of the few who had seen clearly.

Howe's brother Bill, already in the military, thought otherwise. The problem, he believed, was the Fellowship. Jack had been railroaded by a "mutual fanning of enthusiasm and emotions in a group—*that* is mob spirit, as at a lynching party, not convictions."

With more than Howe's future at stake, Wright hired a lawyer to try to get all his male apprentices a deferment by having Taliesin declared a "work of national importance." The attempt failed.

Six months after declaring himself a conscientious objector, Howe made the short drive from Taliesin to Dodgeville to make his case in person before the draft board. Once again, the argument that working for Frank Lloyd Wright was equivalent to a religious conviction failed to carry the day. Howe's request was denied, and the hearing officer scolded Wright for having coerced his young apprentice into resisting.

Jack came away believing that the board's decision—and the resulting jail sentence—had less to do with him personally than with a plot to close down Taliesin altogether. " 'Architecture' is to them a peace-time occupation along with needle-point and painting china. . . . The very principles of an organic architecture and life demand this kind of action. Culture is not a matter of Women's Clubs and Art Institutes. It is the basic feeling of a people." To the truly committed apprentices like Jack Howe, organic architecture was the real religion, a religion that came "from within, organic, not a matter of hanging on the fringe of some sect."

The "sect" Howe had in mind was Christianity—a useless panacea, he believed, a "mere refuge." Like Wright himself, Jack Howe had begun to see the war as a kind of racial fratricide. A new "*organic* way of thinking must come in," he declared, "if we as a race are not to decline as quickly as we have come into supremacy." And the war, he felt, was hastening that decline. If it continued, it would lead to the "destruction of the white race."

To Jack Howe, saving Taliesin and saving the white race had become a single struggle. Once anxious to make it as an architect on his own, Howe now saw himself as belonging to the inner circle of a secret brotherhood. Having listened carefully to the master, he would do his duty and proudly so. "All I ask of you both," he told his parents, "is to believe in me and any decisions I may make and be willing to back me up. . . . I hope, and will do my best, to avert any unhappiness on your part for seeming to have given birth to an ugly duckling. . . . Thank God that I'm not standing alone on this for I wouldn't have the strength to buck."

HAVING TAKEN SUCH pains to keep Jack at Taliesin, now Wright was losing him anyway. Desperate to find a way to prevent other apprentices from ending up in the clink or the trenches, he sent a letter to William Joseph "Wild Bill" Donovan, recently tapped by Roosevelt to create what would become the CIA. Addressing him as "Joe," Wright asked Donovan's help in persuading the government to let him keep twenty-four apprentices—"good young engineering-architects but poor soldiers"—to develop Broadacre City as a "post-war asset." "My god, dear man, this country is a neglected backyard coast to coast!" Wright also asked Donovan to help convince Washington to give him thirty thousand dollars to house and feed the two dozen apprentices. "You . . . are now a national hero and an official favorite while I sit and bite my nails in outer darkness. Where and when could I talk to you about it where the F.B.I. couldn't hear," he asked.

There is no record of Donovan's reply.

Wright followed up with a direct appeal to the Roosevelt administration to fund the Broadacre scheme—"a true capitalistic society," as he put it to them. He managed to secure the support of an impressive list of signatories, including John Dewey, Charles Beard, Robert Moses, MoMA director Alfred Barr, and Nelson Rockefeller, whose affiliation was listed as "Capitalist, Washington and New York." Wright even got his old Bauhaus rival Walter Gropius to add his name. The petition, not surprisingly, went nowhere. In Roosevelt's eleventh year running a White House that embodied centralized political power, the president was hardly likely to sign on to decentralizing the country, not to mention putting it in the hands of a bunch of organic architects.

ON FEBRUARY 24, 1943, Jack Howe was arrested for failing to present himself for induction and freed on bond until his court hearing. Wright went to Washington on a dual mission—to pursue more government contracts, and to visit the Justice Department to explore how he might save his remaining apprentices. Howe wasn't the only apprentice risking a trip to prison. Another would-be objector was Davy Davison, the relatively new apprentice who had married Kay Schneider. Having failed to convince the draft board, and FDR himself, of the national importance of Broadacre City, Wright was now trying to have his apprentices exempted from conscription as agriculture workers, a legitimate basis for a deferment. Wes Peters, who owned his own farm, had managed one. Wright calculated that Taliesin had enough agricultural "units"—a unit was six cows and ten acres of crops—to defer eight young men. As Wright worked that angle, Peters ferried back and forth to Washington hoping to find other ways for Jack to avoid a trial.

The agricultural deferment was Jack and Davy's last hope, and when it was denied Howe was ordered to stand trial in Superior, Wisconsin. If convicted, he would join Marcus Weston at Sandstone Prison in Minnesota. Jack somehow held out hope that Wright might still save him. "I feel a little like Brunhilde waiting to be snatched from the flames," he wrote. But he prepared for the worst, arranging for Johnny Hill to take over his job tending the flower gardens at Hillside.

Howe and Davison were both convicted and sentenced to five years in prison. Kay visited them in the county jail, bringing ice cream and fresh strawberries and radishes from the Taliesin garden.

As Howe and Davison awaited transfer to Sandstone, Olgivanna took it on herself to deal with Taliesin's other big problem: New construction had ground to a halt after Pearl Harbor, and Taliesin was desperate for work. She wrote a letter to her husband's good friend Alexander Woollcott, a big Roosevelt supporter, asking him to try to arrange a meeting between Frank and the president, presumably hoping for another shot at war work. One of America's own sons, she wrote, "is laid aside by his own government. . . . Here is Frank now, like a lion in the cage, pacing the floor of Taliesin. Full of force, full of fire, will to work—and nothing to do."

AND THEN IT happened again. Just when things seemed as bleak as they could be, and in spite of Wright's very public callousness toward the fate of German Jews, another one appeared just in time. This time it was not Edgar Kaufmann, but Solomon Guggenheim, who came forward to save him.

Soon after he arrived at Sandstone, Jack Howe learned that Wright was en route to New York to negotiate a contract to design an art museum in New York. "I should hate to miss out on drawing any museum," he wrote his mother.

SPACE LOVERS

COPPER MAGNATE SOLOMON GUGGENHEIM HAD been in no hurry.
For eight years, he had housed his collection of modern paintings in a suite at
the Plaza Hotel. In 1939, it was moved into a gallery space on East 54th
Street. But Guggenheim was in his eighties, and he wanted to give his collection a permanent home. And so the job of finding an architect fell to the
gallery's curator, Hilla Rebay.

A redheaded German of Alsatian birth, Baroness Hilla Rebay von Ehren-
wiesen, who liked to be called Contessa v. Rebay, was an artist and a mystic.
She had first come in contact with Solomon Guggenheim in the late 1920s,
when his wife, Irene, bought several of her paintings; the Guggenheims soon
became like second parents to her. In 1928, the avant-garde artist grudgingly
agreed to paint a very traditional portrait of Solomon, a collector of Old
Masters and French primitives. But the voluble Rebay exposed the sixty-
eight-year-old man to a new aesthetic—to the mystical ecstasies, as she saw
them, of modern art. Guggenheim found himself identifying with Rebay's
beloved renegade artists. The son of a mining magnate, Solomon had pioneered a new way of extracting copper, only to have his own renegade idea
rejected by his more conservative father.

Rebay's passion for modern art was coupled with a devotion to Theosophy. To her, the two were not unrelated. She considered the painter Wassily
Kandinsky the greatest practitioner of what she called non-objective art.
Non-objective painters shunned the portrayal of recognizable objects—or
even abstractions of them—in favor of rhythmic gestures of pure form and
color. And for Kandinsky, at least, those gestures were based on Theosophical
theory. His paintings, he suggested, were capable of inducing mental vibrations that related to cosmic occurrences. Rebay believed that such art could
connect one to God, not as a divine figure, but as an energized pattern, a

rhythm, a moving force. Non-objectivity, she wrote in one of her earliest catalogs, "will be the religion of the future. Very soon the nations on earth will turn to it in thought and feeling and develop such intuitive powers which lead them to harmony."

On a trip with Rebay to Europe, Guggenheim saw an exhibition of non-objective works. "Ah," he told Rebay, "that's what I want to collect."

"Mr. Guggenheim," she replied, "you're much too old for that . . . you'll only make yourself look ridiculous."

THE CONTESSA FOUND most of American architecture monotonous and "inorganic." For the new museum, she wanted to find an architect capable of something spiritual. And just as non-objective art did away with the artist's illusion of three dimensions in favor of another kind of space, Rebay wanted a museum whose interior limitlessness would accord with the paintings she had collected. When a friend, the Bauhaus designer László Moholy-Nagy, suggested a series of European modernists, she replied that they "would never do for the work I have in mind."

What would do? The answer struck her one day—literally—while she was at home lying on the couch. Suddenly, one of Wright's books fell off an over-head shelf and hit her on the head. It landed open to a page with his picture. He was certainly handsome, she thought. Rebay took the event as a sign; she had known of Wright, but thought he was dead. She left an inquiry with the book's editor, but for a long time it brought no reply. And then one day the phone rang at her office. "This is Frank Lloyd Wright," said the man on the line. "I hear you want to meet me. Shall I bring my wife and some people along?"

HAVING NEVER SEEN one of Wright's buildings in person, Rebay began to study them in books. She was particularly impressed by Johnson Wax. As someone who saw space as the spiritual "third dimension," she recognized and appreciated that it was space, not surface or mass, that was at the core of Wright's architecture. "Organic architecture," she read in Wright's newly re-vised autobiography, "designed this great building to be as inspiring a place to work in as any cathedral ever was in which to worship." Wright, she hoped, could build the kind of space she had in mind.

The architect had another thing in his favor: He was American. Baroness Rebay's collection for Guggenheim had already been criticized as too Euro-pean, specifically too German. That she was an enemy alien, and one recently accused of sending signals from her Connecticut home to a German submarine offshore, didn't make things any easier. That charge was dropped, but another—that she had hoarded food for her big dinner parties—had landed her in jail. Guggenheim had been able to spring her, but only after going to President Roosevelt.

Rebay was convinced that Wright was her man, but there was reason for concern: Wright had little respect for the painter's craft, which he dismissed as "easel painting." "I do not think these paintings are easel paintings," Rebay countered. "They are order, creating order and are sensitive . . . to space . . . I need a fighter, a lover of space, an originator, a tester and a wise man. Your three books . . . gave me the feeling that no one else would do."

Having first offered to come to New York, Wright now tried to get Guggenheim and Rebay to visit Taliesin. She declined. "Mr Guggenheim is 82 years old and we have no time to lose. . . . Please come to New York. You have to see the collection to realize the great work done and greater to come. I know what is needed. Nothing that is heavy, but organic, refined, sensitive to space most of all."

Within days Wright was on the train to New York, the city he saw as a huge prison block, the very first city that would be leveled if he could ever get the country to implement Broadacre City. New York was also home to the Museum of Modern Art, where his European enemies, the International Style, had first been beatified. Yet this was the big top, and he was determined to make his way in.

Rebay had not yet visited a single Wright building, and Guggenheim thought some of Wright's designs "crazy." Nonetheless they were prepared to sign with him. Guggenheim trusted his curator's choice of architect as surely as he did her taste in artists. For his part, Wright promised to design a museum that could be completed, land and all, for less than a million dollars. On June 29, 1943, Guggenheim signed a contract with Wright to begin preliminary studies on the general nature of the museum. No actual design work was to start until a site had been found. If that didn't happen within a year, the contract would expire. All the design requirements, according to the agreement, were to be determined by Rebay. Where that would lead, Wright could have never guessed.

JACK HOWE HAD been in prison for a year when the master wrote him with the news. The museum was a thrilling development, Howe replied, "though I must say that the prospect of not participating gives me a strange feeling in my chest." In prison Howe had found only pedestrian uses for his talent—drawing up a chuck wagon to carry food out to prison farmworkers, sketching a new layout for the prison's electric power grid. In a letter a few weeks later, Wright counseled Howe to "cheer up." "We've got the Guggenheim Gallery to build, sketches and plans to make soon—to be ready for 'Peace' and action in the field. . . . I have the idea in mind that you will be making marks alongside me on this project . . . ."

On his way back from New York, Wright had stopped in Washington to ask whether Jack might be paroled into Taliesin's care. But nothing came of it—no surprise, since the presiding judge had labeled Wright himself the real culprit.

When Wright later heard that Howe had another prison job, teaching inmates mechanical drawing, he wrote again. Jack was now in a position where his "tendencies to over-boss the job" would have free rein, he counseled. "You are a son of Taliesin and Taliesin has a right to expect great things of Jack Howe's inner-man. . . . So suck away at the teats of humility and kindness, Jack. Make those boys love you because you are learning to love them."

By the time Wright read Jack's letter to the remaining apprentices at the afternoon tea circle, they were down another member. Curtis Besinger, the fourth to be convicted, had just left to serve time in a work camp for conscientious objectors—a "concentration camp," as Wright called it in his next letter to Jack. "This episode in your life is one," he wrote Howe, "that you will look back upon with pride. . . . standing for principle is not common nor ever mean. . . . The hero business is changing." Jack was so elated by the letter that he read it aloud to his fellow prisoners. Gene Masselink also wrote Jack, filling his letters with gossip and cartoons.

As busy as he was, Wright occasionally found time to make the seven-hundred-mile round trip to see Jack and Davy at Sandstone. The architect even arranged to deliver a lecture to the inmates. Their "inviolate inner strength," he told them, would safeguard the future of American democracy. But there was another way, he announced, a world with free distribution of land and no speculators, a world without reason for war: Broadacre City. This was no mere fantasy, he assured the prisoners; it had all been worked out at Taliesin. The only thing standing in the way was that the government was wasting billions on war.

The prisoners, many of them war resistors, were electrified. Jack beamed with pride. "Several fellows claim," he wrote his parents, it was the "biggest event in their lives."

Wright was more anxious then ever to have his gifted chief draftsman back. Not necessarily because of the museum—until they had a site, there was little for anyone to do in the drafting room—but because other projects had begun to roll in. Two big ones, in fact: Ludd Spivey had authorized another addition, a music building, for his Florida Southern campus. And Hib Johnson—apparently recovered from the struggle over his administration

building—had set Wright loose on another Johnson Wax structure, a technically challenging tower to house laboratory facilities.

WRIGHT MUST HAVE been relieved to be back in business with clients
who ultimately deferred to his genius, no matter their differences. Hilla Rebay was another story. She was not just a high-born woman who had made
her career as the gatekeeper between a huge fortune and artists looking for
patronage. She was—in what may have been a first for Wright—a client
whose aesthetic philosophy was self-conscious, crystalline, and demanding.
She showed him little deference, even on architectural matters. In fact, she
saw herself as something of an expert on architecture's relationship to the
mystical—an interest that dated back as early as 1904, when the precocious
teenager attended a series of lectures by Rudolph Steiner, the architect,
Theosophist, and author of scholarly works on Wright's beloved Nietzsche
and Goethe. Rebay believed she had much to teach the self-proclaimed
world's greatest architect, and she pursued her mission through a torrent of
letters, shared writings, and long conversations when he visited New York.
Over the course of several months she laid down for him a specific program,
grounded in Theosophy, and challenged him to convert it into a building the
likes of which he had never built before.

Of course, Wright had heard all this before. His Unity Temple in Oak
Park, completed the year after young Hilla Rebay attended her first Steiner
lecture, was just such a conversion of Unitarian cosmology into built form.
And Madame Blavatsky's Theosophy itself was familiar ground to him: It
had been the rage during his early years as an architect, and inspired the architecture of close colleagues Hendrik Wijdeveld and Claude Bragdon, who
wrote extensively on the subject. Bragdon's *The Frozen Fountain* was primarily devoted to the relationship of Theosophy and ornament; Louis Sullivan's 1924 book on the same subject overtly connected mysticism with
architecture.

And Frank also had an intimate connection to Hilla Rebay's occult world,
through Olgivanna, who had read both Steiner and Blavatsky. Small groups
at Taliesin often sat for hours openly discussing Blavatsky's work. And there
were other links: Theosophical theories had been the starting point for Georgi
Gurdjieff's mystical journey, and Thomas de Hartmann, his composer, was a
lifelong friend of Rebay's mentor, Kandinsky.

In her mystical pursuits, Rebay had also become seriously involved with
something called Mentalphysics, a fusion of Buddhist cosmology and Yogic
breathing. Even here Wright had a way in: His son Lloyd had been hired to
design a Mentalphysics center for a site in the California desert, and the

center's founder had hoped that Wright himself would eventually design his grand scheme, the City of Mentalphysics. It was really a very small cosmos.

HILLA REBAY'S CAMPAIGN to educate Wright in the occult, then, fell on knowing ears. But there was still the matter of his unshakable bias toward architecture as infinitely superior to painting. Rebay tried to show Wright that great painters could deliver cosmic vibrations directly, but her insistence that architects were too "bound to earth, bound to gravitation, to weight, to practicality, to material," rankled him.

"My dear Hilla," he replied, "great art is never jealous of great art. Architecture (there is none in New York City) is the mother-art of arts where she really *is* she is not likely to murder her infants or frustrate her sons and daughters. The trouble is sometimes her upstarts do not know their own mother—the brats."

Rebay was determined to control the architect she had chosen. He was designing not just a museum, she reminded him, but a temple for "spiritual enfoldment." "Enfoldment" is a Theosophical concept that refers to containing and making manifest higher powers that are otherwise invisible to us. "The divine force that organizes everything to perfection," she wrote him, "I feel confident, will inspire you to do what I so earnestly feel only you can do. . . ."

Rebay did not limit her advice to the museum. Wright was just then updating his 1932 book *The Disappearing City*, retitled *When Democracy Builds* as an apparent nod to postwar opportunities. In the new edition he pledged that Broadacre City would not only end urban congestion, but usher in a "new and higher Spiritual Order of all things and living persons." But Wright's fundamental prediction— that the automobile would allow the American population to disperse back to the countryside— struck Rebay as prosaic. "Very likely," she wrote him, "as races become more spiritual, they will not need to move physically."

Hilla Rebay, Wright's intellectual sparring partner in conceiving the design of the Guggenheim Museum

The prospect of a huge contract, and the opportunity to show New Yorkers how to build, were enough to keep Wright listening carefully to Rebay, even in her wackier moments. Nonetheless he must have been alarmed to realize that she also considered herself something of an expert on architecture—indeed, of *museum* architecture. She had long dreamed of designing what she called "The Temple of Non-Objectivity." She had even tried her hand designing a pavilion for Guggenheim, a grouping of twelve galleries around a circular garden intended as a setting for his collection at the 1939 New York World's Fair. Rebay's design, which was never built, was inspired by Kandinsky, who had declared the circle "a link with [the] cosmic." Now she would have another chance to realize her vision. There was only one hitch: She would have to channel her ideas through Frank Lloyd Wright.

And a highly developed vision it was. Visitors would enter the museum through a room with blue ceiling lights, "like Napoleon's Tomb," where they would be cleansed of the psychic slag accumulated in the Manhattan streets. Once in the main gallery, they would experience the art while the music of Bach was played by live musicians. The museum, she wrote a friend, must become "the standard for greatness for all nations, truly the Temple of Peace in the universe."

FRANK WAS NOT the only family member trying to make it in New York. He and Olgivanna had sent Iovanna to Manhattan to study harp with a master teacher, Marcel Gradjany. Music was an obligation in the Wright household, and Iovanna had chosen the harp after seeing angels playing them in picture books. (It didn't hurt that the harp was also the instrument of the Welsh bard Taliesin.) Iovanna had practiced hard and showed promise. Wright sent her to Manhattan hoping that his daughter would blossom into a great talent there.

But Iovanna was now seventeen, beautiful and womanly; she would be on her own in the big city, and the prospect made Wright anxious. Just how anxious became clear when, some time before she left, a number of guests gathered in the living room. Iovanna entered resplendent in an off-the-shoulder Grecian evening dress her mother had bought her. Johnny Hill thought she looked lovely, and he could tell she thought so, too. In front of everybody, her father spat out at her, "You are not going to dress like a prostitute in my house." He was afraid he might lose her. "Cheekie," he told her before she left Taliesin. "I don't want you to get married until you are forty years old."

Iovanna saw Manhattan as a test. She wanted her own "accomplishment," she wrote her father. She knew he would never accept mediocrity, and the pressure was enormous. Wright had praised her half-sister, Svetlana, for her "innate sense of music," but Iovanna had also seen her mother reduced to playing piano in private after Wright insulted her playing. Iovanna desperately wanted to return from New York a more polished performer, polished enough to earn her father's regard. "Taliesin is a great place and a great hope," he wrote her shortly after her arrival in New York. "So are you. We all look forward to what you are going to get out of this experience. It ought to add much to Taliesin's charm and usefulness."

WHATEVER HIS FEELINGS about Hilla Rebay's metaphysical approach to architecture, Wright was impatient to start on a real design for the Guggenheim museum. Without the land he could not do any real design, or at least be paid to do it, and, if they didn't close a deal over the next ten months, his agreement would terminate. Rebay tried to calm him by explaining that the birth of this building would necessarily be a slow process. Perhaps, she ventured, her discipline of Mentalphysics might help. Stop coffee and meat, practice breath control. He needed to "learn about the holy breath to be really the greatest architect."

There is no record of Wright's reaction to the suggestion that he was not *already* the greatest architect. Nor, for that matter, to her attempts to dictate the core ideas behind the design. The museum, she now informed him, should be an expression of "om," the sound miming creation, the cosmic breath itself.

In an intimate, disjointed, associative prose, she wrote him a series of letters trying to push beyond the words themselves to suggest directly the desired rhythm and breath. "You are far advanced to what you say," she wrote in one, "and so you still lovingly think you must say because you love it still; so-so-so-so-so-so-so-so-s-o-s-0 . . . s!o! S.O. the: non—but s.o . . . Frank loves s.o. his kimono!!!" it is such a charming one, one, one, one non, on and on, and finally (it almost is) 'om' only 'om'."

Wright did love the Japanese kimono, and Rebay was using that fact to press him to integrate the spiritual ideas associated with it in the design for her museum. The "om" she pushed upon him is a sound without the partitions of consonants, a sound that to her evoked the boundless, continuous infinite cosmic space inside one's body, inside everything—the ever-evolving oneness.

Wright found the spirit of God, as he would always say, in "nature with a capital 'N'." And nature had inspired his architecture for half a century, as recently as the stalklike columns of Johnson Wax. But Rebay wanted him to reach beyond nature's perceptible forms. "Let us forget the 'forest,' the trees," she wrote him, "as we want no abstraction of any existing growth." Wright must learn to see past his love of nature, indeed of materials themselves, in order to "enfold" the cosmic energy in between, "the one of Rhythm itself."

What Wright actually made of this it is hard to say. But he reassured her that her aesthetic intuitions were already his own. Although he worried that her cosmology was lacking in "humanity," it was close enough that he could call it "our" message.

Three days later, Rebay sent a remarkably condescending response. She could intuit the inside of the museum, she told him. If he would only compose the space she imagined, the outside would follow. The interior space, she advised, should transport its inhabitants so they would feel no need of walls. And it all could be realized, if only Wright would open himself up to the experience of non-objective art. "Go and find out, and we find it always—o my dear little Frank," she wrote, "you are making a nice nice big jump already and you don't know it—the inbetween is already magnificent and you know that, but where you will land, this will be the surprise!" To a man who wore elevator shoes, being called "little Frank" could not have gone down easily.

Less than a week later Rebay received a letter from Wright assuring her that he understood the deeper meaning of his kimonos, along with one of his two remaining copies of his 1912 booklet *The Japanese Print—An Interpretation*. There Hilla would read of how the structural, asymmetric aesthetics of these prints had inspired his architecture, and how the Japanese artist's grammar of form, subdued and even hidden, had allowed him to reveal in his architecture the "secret of getting to the hidden core of reality." "Way back there in the tall grass of the prairie architecture," he wrote in his accompanying letter, he had been on the road to what she now called non-objective art.

Ultimately, Wright may not have needed to play quite so hard on Rebay's turf. Though she had tried to steer the architect away from the forms of nature, there was one image in which each of them might have found common ground. In the Sanskrit tradition from which Theosophy derives, that which contains the breath of life is sometimes likened to a shell.

ROUNDS OF OFFERINGS, both material and spiritual, shuttled back and forth between Taliesin and Manhattan. Wright sent Rebay presents, including a proof set of rare Hokusai prints, favorite books, and hams and apples from the Taliesin farm. She sent him films to screen for the Fellowship.

Hilla and Olgivanna shared their respective mystical philosophies. Rebay started reading Ouspensky and listening to the Gurdjieff music of Kandinsky's friend de Hartmann. As they grew to know each other better, Rebay became convinced that Olgivanna was a psychic.

Guggenheim's curator was eager to control more than Wright's architecture.

Indeed, on their visits to Manhattan, Frank and Olgivanna gave their very bodies up to her reworking. Hilla Rebay believed that the couple's old, infected teeth were emitting toxins that could lead to emotional instability. The treatment was obvious: Soon thereafter, Frank and Olgivanna went to Gene Masselink's father, a dentist, to have their teeth removed. Frank had them all taken in one sitting, never flinching. A few months later, when the swelling had finally come down, he returned and was fitted for dentures. "I've had a hard time getting adjusted to new dentures," he wrote Hilla. Olgivanna, on the other hand, bounced right back. "She was most in need of help," Hilla observed, "and will realize the miracle cure, when she lives in youth, from now on."

But Rebay wasn't done with the Wrights. She also believed in the curative power of leeching, and subjected herself and even Guggenheim to dozens of treatments. Leeching was "just plain common sense," she believed, and she urged Frank and Olgivanna to see her German doctor in Manhattan. Dr. Meyer applied large black leeches—only the Hungarian variety would do—to their throats. They sucked until they were sated, then fell off to die. "Don't call me a physician," the doctor jibed. "Just call me a plumber."

Wright actually believed in the regimen. It was an "ancient treatment but scientifically applied for latent phlebitis," he wrote Jack Howe in prison. Howe was bemused. "The remodeling job on the family's teeth and veins sounds interesting," he replied, "and I trust the result is not merely psychological."

Later, Olgivanna would joke that the Guggenheim was one building for which they had literally given their blood.

IOVANNA WAS LIVING in a French *pension* on the east side of Manhattan, its rooms done up in gold, white, and rose, stuffed with furniture from the proprietor's chateau, her only view a light shaft. She practiced the harp diligently and seriously. "I cannot tell you how grateful I am that you have made it possible for me to study with a great artist," she wrote her father. When her right hand was injured after being caught between two doors, she continued practicing with her left.

Iovanna also studied harmony with her mother's close friend and roommate at the Prieuré, the pianist Carol Robinson. "She should be competent," her father wrote his daughter. "How inspiring I do not know. Women seldom inspire women. But Carol is stronger than most women."

Iovanna also had family in Manhattan. Living nearby were her uncle Vlado and aunt Sophie, who had raised Svetlana after Olgivanna sent her away from the Prieuré. Now they watched out for Iovanna, warning her not to stand face-to-face with passengers on the subway (to avoid getting colds) and never to daydream while crossing the street. They invited Iovanna for meals, and Edgar Tafel's mother did the same.

Nonetheless, the young girl longed for home. Wasn't it too bad that her teacher had to live in "such an ugly city," she wrote her father in her scrawling, sloppy hand. "Living in it all their lives, I should think they would eventually go crazy." The "poor and scrubby" trees in Central Park did not match up to those at Taliesin. She tried to control her line of vision while walking through the park, blocking out the skyscrapers to help preserve the illusion that she was in the countryside. The bridle path reminded her of the tracks she had cut through the woods of Wisconsin on her horse.

Her letters to "Dearest Daddy" were forlorn and full of appeals to her father's sensibility: "It's too bad that the place I live in now has to be this old fashioned French business." Most of all she wanted him to write. "If you have any time, I wish you would write me a letter! I miss you and Taliesin so much."

Wright was relying on his usual financial tricks to float Iovanna's Manhattan adventure. Her concert grand harp was purchased on credit. He told her landlady and her music teacher that they needn't bill him, that he would send them regular checks. One by one, they asked Iovanna to get her father to pay. She knew he couldn't cope with money and told him so. When she got a dunning letter for the unpaid bill on her harp, she forwarded it to her father, pleading that they would soon repossess it if he didn't pay quickly.

Despite her commitment to practicing, Iovanna wasn't measuring up to her harp teacher's expectations. Often she broke into tears after leaving his apartment, finding a favorite tree in Central Park to sob against before going back to her rooms. "Please don't expect too much of me when I come home," she cautioned her father. "I can't play and sing with the harp yet."

But there were also positive things to report. She was swept away at a performance of Debussy's impressionist opera *Pelleas and Melisande.* "I was practically an emotional wreck when it was finished," she wrote her father afterward. Wright had once admired the French composer, but now found him much too emotional, and identified him as a musical fellow-traveler with Picasso and Le Corbusier. Wright wanted his daughter to fall in love with his own favorites, Bach and Beethoven. When Iovanna reported that her music teacher had taught her to appreciate Bach's beautiful structures, Wright was delighted. "You have convinced her," he wrote her teacher, "something I tried, in vain, to do. Debussy was her idol; I could not convert her to Bach. But the master has succeeded where 'le pere' failed." Wright invited the musician and his family to spend the following summer in Taliesin.

Wright also asked Hilla Rebay to take Iovanna under her wing. "You could do her a lot of good," he wrote her. Olgivanna instructed her daughter to be most gracious with Hilla because of her sway over Solomon Guggenheim. The future of the museum, she told the teenager, was in her hands.

IF THE MUSEUM had to be in the city, Wright hoped that at least it might be somewhere on the outskirts, where it could be surrounded by some semblance of nature. The Cloisters—a museum based on the architecture of French monasteries, completed five years earlier on land provided by John D. Rockefeller Jr.—was just such a setting. There was a smaller but similarly picturesque wooded site available just north of the Cloisters at Spuyten Duyvil, and Wright lobbied for it. "The sidewalk crowd means less than nothing to our enterprise," he had written to Guggenheim. "We are neither a cigar store nor any business."

But Rebay and Guggenheim both found the Spuyten Duyvil site too remote; it would preclude poor people without cars from visiting. And the site would always be too far uptown, Hilla remarked, given that "negro dangerous Harlem prevents New York from moving further up." Besides, she noted, the 57th Street art dealers—and the press they controlled—would consider it "a triumph to see us in the cold." For a new museum in New York City, it was important to be at the center of things.

Wright's preference for a wooded site reflected another issue. He was hoping to design a horizontal building, something that hugged the earth in the spirit of Taliesin. But Rebay envisioned something more vertical, a gesture to the cosmos. Hoping to inspire his client to look for a less congested location, Wright wrote suggesting that Guggenheim come to Taliesin. Rebay nixed the idea. "Frankly," she wrote him in August 1943, "I doubt if Taliesin would be just what he should see." The museum was a "new task, which will inspire you to a sensitiveness, that will not only spread horizontally, but also vertically, up to the infinite infinity of space and delicacy of the most spiritual enfoldment." She wanted the museum to embrace both the sky and the ground. It should have no heavy roof to stand between the heavens above and the spiritual "inner uplift" of the space below.

Site after site fell through, however, and Wright grew increasingly worried. Guggenheim was an old man; he could die or lose interest. Wright knew that real estate prices were likely to soar after the war, eating into the funds for the building itself. That fall, he began designing the museum in his head. "I hope we can get a plot," he wrote Rebay, "as I am so full of ideas for our museum that I am likely to blow up or commit suicide unless I can let them out on paper."

* * *

WHEN THE TIME finally came for Hilla Rebay to meet Iovanna, Wright's patron saw it as an opportunity to work on her third member of the family. Hilla, who wore big hats with ostrich feathers, surveyed the girl. "Vell," she said, "you are certainly badly dressed." She instructed Iovanna to get better shoes, to wear stockings and a different dress. Iovanna obeyed. Another time, Iovanna showed up wearing her favorite hat, a felt bonnet topped with a row of felt flowers. Hilla sat Iovanna down on her bed, and with three quick scissors snips the flowers dropped to the floor. "Better now," Hilla said, "otherwise you look like leetle girl." Afraid of jeopardizing her father's project, the holy terror of Taliesin contained her temper.

For Iovanna, Christmas at Taliesin had always been a joyful time. But this year she would have to miss it. Her parents, she was told, couldn't afford the train ticket. Stuck in Manhattan, she would miss the moment when her father led the entourage to pick the perfect tree—always a red cedar, never a pine, which he felt ruined the proportions of his living room. Wright felled the tree himself; the apprentices dragged it back. And she would miss Christmas night, a huge formal feast with apprentices and important guests, her mother dressed in an evening gown, her father in a white suit.

Iovanna's train fare was a pittance compared with the money Wright was spending on other things around this time. Expecting Guggenheim and Rebay to visit Taliesin eventually, he was redoing the living room, the loggia, the porch, and the main entrance. Iovanna's room, ironically, was being expanded into a large suite for Hilla's use. Still expanding his estate, he had even purchased a new piece of land nearby, offering to give Jack Howe a portion of it after his release from prison. No doubt unaware of all this spending, Iovanna sent her father an understanding letter. "I realize very well," she wrote, "how hard it is with money and I wouldn't dream of throwing that extra load on you, dearest Daddy, even if it were partly possible."

WRIGHT DID BUY Iovanna a white evening gown to wear at the Christmas eve dinner at her French-speaking *pension*. Later the Baroness took her to see Noel Coward's *The Scoundrel*. Wright also sent her two presents, a heart-shaped pearl ring with a stone at the center, and a poem, dated December 25, 1943, that he had written out in his own hand.

> *IOVANNA IN NEW YORK*
> . . . *Christmas and Christmas and Christmas*
> *with no daughter at all . . .*
> . . . *Daughter with a dollar perhaps*
> *Daughter with fifty cents with ten cents*

> *Daughter perhaps with no cents at all. . . .*
> *Where and how and for what*
> *Is my daughter for whom if not for me?*
> *Daddy at Taliesin.*

"Taliesin missed you so much at Christmas," Wright wrote Iovanna just after the new year, "that I am sure your harp must have sighed and sighed. Your heart too must have ached." As for the harp, at least, she was now doing well enough that Wright arranged for her to become a "special" student at Julliard. Despite her obvious talent, though, there was no real talk of her becoming a professional. "Don't ever worry about my getting submerged in a career," she assured him, "that could never happen." Her music would instead find a home at Taliesin, Wright promised. No "ordinary place for any ordinary daughter," he wrote, but a place that "no one but IOVANNA can fill."

Wright also remembered Jack Howe at Christmas. "It must be pretty tough at times," he wrote him the day before, "and a sob in the pillow not so far away. But at least this 'station of the cross' you are doing binds us closer together and the haven of refuge here that we are trying to beautifully build seems all the more desirable to us all. . . . Take it easy—you are 'doing time' now but you are safe so long as we are here at work in a greater and greater work."

With special permission from the warden, Howe and Davy Davison had prepared drawings for Wright's Christmas box. When Wright lifted Jack's offering from the box, he was surprised. Howe's previous designs had always looked just like Wright's own buildings, but now, far from the Taliesin drafting room, Howe had done his most imaginative and nonderivative work. "The fantasy called the Airport," the master wrote back, "is the best and a beautiful rendering I thought. But two of the collection of Usonians were daisies. I could build them just as they are—almost. Time at Taliesin made good by time at Sandstone." He sent both Howe and Davison his congratulations. "Thank you sons," he wrote. "Your work vindicates both yourselves and me." Wright never had trouble praising an apprentice's renderings of his own work, his grandson Eric remembered, but this was something different: "it was very difficult for him to praise their own creative work in a box project. . . ."

All that Jack wanted for Christmas that year was the section on Broadacre City Wright had written for the revised edition of his autobiography. His body may have been locked in Sandstone, but his mind was still living at Taliesin, following every project. When Jack received a copy of Hitchcock's new book on Wright, *In the Nature of Materials*, he went through it in a way almost no one else could. Just by reading and looking at the illustrations, he was able to take himself on mental tours of the houses. He pestered his parents to send him photographs of Taliesin—Hillside, the Wisconsin valley, the desert camp.

That winter, after a three-year hiatus, the Fellowship drew on its Guggenheim windfall and headed back to Arizona.

FIVE DAYS AFTER Christmas, in a rare change of heart, Wright cabled Rebay to suggest that "our" idea of the building should be vertical after all. The change, he suggested cryptically, would allow them to "go where we please" with the design. He asked her to present the new direction to Guggenheim for approval.

Rebay surprised him. "Don't like perpendicular museum," she cabled back on January 3, worried that he was leaning toward a more conventional Manhattan-style building.

It was not what she was imagining, he replied at once. He was envisioning a "spacious horizontality going upward on wings." Perhaps anxious that Rebay's confidence was shaken, he wrote again the next day to stress that their sympathies were in complete alignment. "My enthusiasm for your project has held," he told Rebay, "because I see it as a move forward to free painting from all the clichés and let it go forward into the great realm of imagination."

Wright also contacted Guggenheim directly with his more vertical idea, suggesting that he take an option on one of the likely properties and allow Wright to demonstrate the idea with preliminary sketches. If nothing else, Wright suggested, this would help give him a sense of "the ideal building." But Guggenheim was expecting real estate prices to come down after the war, and he demurred. Afraid that the project might stall, Rebay pressed Wright to go ahead with the sketches, using a lot next to the Morgan Library as a theoretical site.

Wright had once again become intrigued by the idea of incorporating a circle into his design. Both Monona Terrace and his new music building for Florida Southern had been based on circles. But the "spacious horizontality" that began to emerge in the Guggenheim drawings was only circular in plan view; its true shape was actually a spiral, a three-dimensional form. In one early sketch, he toyed with the idea of a spiraling tower, a miniature version of the old "automobile objective" he had once designed for Sugarloaf Mountain in Maryland. That had been a ziggurat, stepping inward as it rose, coming almost to a point at its apex, the form artists had for centuries assumed for the ancient Tower of Babylon.

Then, in another sketch, Wright turned the ziggurat upside down, so that it grew wider as it rose. It was an outrageous idea. In a city laid out on a compact rectangular grid, with every building driven by economics to fill its rectangular lot, the museum would be just as eccentric as the sight of Wright himself standing on a Manhattan sidewalk in his porkpie hat and cape.

But the spiral ziggurat was much more than just a statement of Wright's individuality. As a Theosophist, Rebay understood the spiral as a spiritual pathway, as a model of the evolution of all "monads," energized systems from atoms up to galaxies. Theosophy taught that the universe's original divine energies are contained in seven rays—a concept derived from Babylonian religion. Madame Blavatsky had celebrated Babylon's great seven-layered ziggurat, from whose summit one approached the solar divinity. Wright not only labeled his presentation drawing "Ziggurat," but also designed a spiral that turned six times, giving the museum seven levels.

With his inverted ziggurat, Wright had found a way to address Rebay's agenda while pursuing his own. She had asked for a building that expressed the nature of non-objective painting, while capturing, as she put it, "the cosmic wave." Wright's corkscrewing gallery was just that; he compared the parapets of the spiral ramp to a "curving wave that never breaks." Wright had undoubtedly also found inspiration in his beloved Japanese woodblock prints—especially the work of Hokusai, whose prints he had given to Rebay. In one of his most celebrated works, *In the Hollow of a Wave off the Coast at Kanagawa*, Hokusai had captured a great curling wave about to engulf a group of fishermen's boats. Rebay was welcome to view the building as a non-objective, cosmic enfoldment; for Wright it remained an abstraction of an ocean wave, the very kind of natural inspiration Rebay had warned him against, but that had animated many of his greatest projects.

He even included an abstraction of seed pods, the source of Theosophy's divine sparks, in the base of the building—a mischievous gesture that must have delighted him.

WRIGHT HADN'T YET shown Rebay his finished design, but he updated her regularly on his progress, and the Baroness passed the excited word on to Iovanna. "I hear you are doing a great deal of work in the studio now!" she wrote her father on January 12. Two weeks later, Wright wrote to Rebay with a tease: "I find the antique Ziggurat has great possibilities for our building. You will see."

As the design evolved, three circular schemes emerged. In this respect, they recalled Hilla's own design for the World's Fair pavilion. But there was one critical difference: In Rebay's design, the gallery walls projected straight out like spokes from the center of the circle. In Wright's design the gallery walls themselves were curved—raising the question of how to hang flat paintings on a curved wall. With Rebay and Guggenheim both expressing concern about the idea, Wright added hexagonal interior walls inside the exterior spiral, with flat wall segments that would be more practical for hanging art.

Rebay had another objection. In one letter Wright mentioned that one of the schemes, based on a Babylonian red-brick ziggurat, was to be constructed of red marble. "But for heaven's *sake*," Hilla shot back, "*not red never red never never*. . . ." Red was a Wright signature—the color of the Taliesin logo and all of his vehicles—but to Theosophists it was a carnal, materialistic color, associated with the most primitive generative forces. She proposed blue and yellow instead.

"The Sun is the soul of Red," Wright wrote back. "I see nothing carnal in the color, Hilla." And besides, she was thinking like a painter, not an architect. Color, he chided, was insignificant compared with architectural form.

WHEN WRIGHT AND the apprentices finally finished their drawings, they mounted four museum proposals in the space outside the studio door: three round designs and a hexagonal plan that, unique among the schemes, sported a level floor. Rebay had long hated interior staircases, which she believed disturbed the "unity" of a house. Wright had planned to assuage her concern by having visitors ascend into the tall atrium gallery by a ramp. In the round versions he took her idea one step further, making the gallery floor itself into one long spiral ramp. A visitor viewing a given painting would thus always be standing with one foot slightly further uphill than the other, a constant reminder of the building's ascending physical space.

It was an outrageous plan and he knew it. When he told Olgivanna he planned to show Rebay all four schemes, she told him not to give her a choice. "Give them what they should have," she advised him. Still, Wright instructed Johnny Hill, who had taken Howe's place running the drafting room, to prepare presentation drawings for all four schemes. He was no doubt afraid that a gallery with sloping floors and curved walls would be rejected when he brought his work to New York in February; without a more conventional backup, he might lose the job altogether. The hexagonal version was apparently his safety net.

The day before Wright left, the apprentices had to work all night finishing the drawings. Working in the corner of the studio lettering the titles on each sheet, Kenn Lockhart shouted "Bang!" each time he reached the final task— filling in Taliesin's emblematic red square.

HILLA HAD HEARD a great deal from Wright in the preceding months, but she had seen nothing. "You may be shocked," Wright wrote her. "A museum should be one extended expansive well proportioned floor space from bottom to top—a wheel chair going around and up and down, *throughout*. No stops anywhere. . . . The whole thing will either throw you off your guard entirely or be just about what you have been dreaming about."

Wright arrived in New York in the third week of February 1944. He had had the drawings mounted on a redwood board and covered with Cherokee red leather. Rebay recalled him "trembling with nervousness." "What a great man," she thought, in earnest.

Hilla looked at the plans. "I was carried away," she recalled years later. "Oh God, it was so beautiful."

Wright, she observed, "was so relieved."

And Rebay had felt "enfolded by some wonderful . . . physical contact which made me" she gushed, "feel a part of mine is to be explored, *au naturel!*"

The architecture had seduced the curator.

OLGIVANNA FEARED THAT the architect had been seduced as well. With her regimen of breathing exercises, bloodsucking therapy, radical dental surgery, and Mentalphysics, Rebay was a new high priestess of occult healing in the Wrights' circle, and her influence on the architect threatened to eclipse Gurdjieff's. It was time to put the curator in her place. "I have boundless respect for my teacher," she finally wrote Rebay, "and I am happy to say—so does Frank."

SPACE WARRIORS

HAD IT BEEN ANOTHER ARCHITECT'S book that fell on Hilla Rebay's head that day, it's unlikely that things would have worked out as well. She had stumbled on a mystically inclined architect with a renewed passion for circles, the geometric form she thought most appropriate for the spiritual contemplation of her non-objective art. Somehow, this unlikely pair had talked their way into a design that satisfied both their highly personal sensibilities.

Yet there was still a long way to go. Solomon Guggenheim himself had not yet seen the designs. And they weren't even based on an actual site—much less one that he owned.

All of that was about to change. In March 1944, just three months before Wright's contract would expire, Guggenheim bought a property at Fifth Avenue and 89th Street, across from Central Park and a few blocks north of the Metropolitan Museum. Wright's theoretical exercise would now have to be adapted to an actual plot of land, and then sold to its owner.

Wright was scheduled to visit Guggenheim and Rebay during their vacation in New Hampshire in July of that year; that gave Wright and the apprentices four months to prepare revised drawings. Rebay, who had seen all four designs, had left it to him to choose which ones he would present. Guggenheim was not like her, she warned; once he made up his mind he rarely changed course. This left Wright in a rare moment of architectural indecision. He had a great deal at stake: the Guggenheim, he saw, might well become the culmination of his life's work. If his patron favored his more conservative fallback design, he could be stuck with it.

For practical purposes, he would have preferred the hexagon. It would certainly be the easiest to draw, engineer, and build. Having struggled with the building authorities in Racine, Wright must have known that the straight-wall scheme would also be easier to get approved by the city of

New York, perhaps the most contentious building bureaucracy in the country.

In face of his insecurity, he asked Olgivanna what she would do. She picked the circular spiral. While she was likely encouraging her husband to follow his intution, as she often did, it was probably also her personal preference. The natural form of a seashell, to which Wright likened his spiral, was a shape much loved by Gurdjieff.

As Solomon Guggenheim stood by in a " 'nervous' state of apprehension," Wright finally settled on the spiral design, and set to work adapting it to the real site. He felt both Howe's and Davison's absence acutely in the drafting studio. "I need you two fellows terribly," he wrote Howe. "And the more I need you," he added, with more than a hint of paranoia, "the more bureaucrats are going to keep you."

With two years left in his sentence, Jack requested an early parole back to the Fellowship, telling the board that Taliesin needed his help with farming and postwar building. A parole was approved, but only if he agreed to accept a job at a medical or mental hospital instead. He refused. The job would be mere "slave labor," he explained to his parents. In a letter to Wright, though, Howe let down his bravado. "I may sound cool headed and brimming over with contentment," he wrote, "but to give it straight, I think I'd go nuts under two more years confinement."

WES AND SVETLANA Peters were now ensconced at Aldebaran with their three-year-old son, Brandoch, and a second child on the way. Wright was in Peters's debt. Having paid off Wright's mortgage to the core of Taliesin's land, Wes was spending the rest of his inheritance acquiring more and more property. Aldebaran was on its way to being bigger than Taliesin and the apprentice farms combined, soon reaching nearly fifteen hundred acres. Taking into account Taliesin, Aldebaran, and the land owned by the other apprentices, the Fellowship now controlled almost precisely the four square miles represented in the Broadacre City model.

Wright saw Aldebaran as an operational center for his embryonic Broadacre experiment, a hub from which all the farms would be managed. And any deviation from that plan drove him to fits of jealousy. When he came across a piece of gilt-edged stationery for a cattle-raising side business Wes Peters was operating with Ben Graves, a former Taliesin farm manager, Wright was enraged. This was his ancestral land, after all, and Peters was putting it to an alien purpose.

"I suggest if you have a boy," Wright wrote the pregnant Svetlana, "you two name him after Ben."

Svetlana was furious, and Olgivanna wrote her daughter that her own relationship with Frank had become "abominable" over the issue. She and Frank had repaired to Arizona without the usual caravan, and from time to time she would flee into the desert, lying in the sun on a rug on the site where Svetlana and Wes normally kept their tent. "It is hard to feel so thoroughly alone," she wrote Svetlana. "It is hard to always try to spread the wings, when there is so little energy to open them, fly up high and have that good old birds' eye view of things." Kay, she added, was a "poor substitute for you."

At war with "Daddy Frank," Svetlana turned to her biological father. After years of silence, she wrote to Valdemar Hinzenberg, who was thrilled to learn that he was already a grandfather, and about to be once more. Having left architecture behind, Hinzenberg was working as an assistant production manager of a company that made deluxe perfume boxes. He sent Svetlana candies and begged her to send word—even a postcard—when the second baby came.

Wright, meanwhile, found the whole mess distressing. "The time is coming near when we will have to work out something," Wright wrote Wes. "I cannot bear to share my home, my everyday effort and my life with anyone who feels toward me as Svetlana has now declared that she does." On the back of the letter Wright drew clothesline posts, with the cryptic instruction: "Take out the white lilacs and move them down the hill below the cesspool or around it."

Wes had been aghast at Wright's reaction to his cattle venture. "It is a very great sorrow to me, Mr. Wright, after having, as I believe, served you with love and faith," he replied, "to know that in any question of misunderstanding your inevitable reaction is one of distrust, enmity and reproach." His arrangement with Graves was no partnership, he promised—and, besides, it was Wright himself who had encouraged him to hire the former manager so that Wes would have more time for engineering and architecture.

Wes's letter elicited an extraordinary confession from his father-in-law. It also laid out an obligation that Peters would struggle to fulfill for the remainder of his life. Wright admitted that he didn't like feeling dependent on his son-in-law for the financial support he had offered—clearing Taliesin of debt, shielding it from creditors, assuming the mortgage, buying machinery and farm animals. "I allow you were sharing with me in carrying on the domestic establishment of our families—and what I want an accounting for now to establish in my own mind how much I should pay back to you when money comes my way again as it soon will, I trust. I like to be on good terms with myself and soon resent being under obligation to anybody and apt to grow to dislike . . . the people who put [me] there—under."

Cash was tight again that winter. Wright had stopped hiring outside construction workers, and the Arizona contingent was forced to subsist on beans and eggs because they couldn't afford meat. Under the circumstances, Wright couldn't believe that his son-in-law would invest personal funds in an outside business venture, instead of putting them back into Taliesin. Wright expected Wes to fold all his property and livestock into Wright's "cooperative farmsteads," not to be conducting independent business on his own estate. "How callow to imagine you could make any investment to compare with the production into which the Foundation is going. For what? . . . If you don't focus on that you may be handsome and strong but actually dumb." His money woes were clearly affected by his assessment of the Fellowship's physical plant. "Taliesin is still a wreck," he complained. "It is time something happened to stop its downward course. It is a dependent, badly kept place above an ugly ditch with an unfinished barn—no machinery and no independence."

Wright was highly sensitive about the fact that he'd been forced to create the Frank Lloyd Wright Foundation to operate the Fellowship and his farmstead operation. And he had an enormous personal investment in Wes Peters, whom he had knighted as his one and only spiritual son. With Svetlana, Wes was expected to sustain the Wright lineage in spirit, deed, and territory under the aegis of the Foundation. All of this eventually conspired to quell his anger toward his most valued apprentice. "I have no son but you who has stood by me in my work or in my life," he wrote Wes. "When you came to me back there in 1932 I recognized something in you that belonged to me. I can't say just what it is, though I think I know."

"NO MORE WAGES!" Wright added at the bottom. He had decided to pay Peters a salary for his future Guggenheim work, which he likely saw as a way to return borrowed monies to his son-in-law. Wright instructed Gene Masselink to prepare an accounting of his financial relationship with Wes. "The affair has drifted long enough with Wes and with me. I have no idea how much Wes contributes—except that he is probably going broke himself—with it all. . . . Put it in simples—with necessary details."

Wright eventually wrote Svetlana a fatherly love letter. "I am awfully sorry that I hurt you," she replied. The constant flow of guests at Taliesin, she conceded, had made her feel that her parents had "deserted" her. "Daddy Frank" had picked on her at the wrong time. "I am so worried that I have spoiled things between you and mother. You have no idea how different the atmosphere is when there is harmony between you two." Svetlana was looking forward to the summer when the Fellowship would return from Arizona, and "we will be a complete family again."

The royal family, it appeared, had found its equilibrium. "By this time," Wright wrote Svetlana in April 1944, "I think [the baby] must be a girl and you are more able to see with the sense of proportion called humour for lack of a better word. I was sarcastic but thoughtless because the whole episode didn't go very deep with me—just scratchy. . . . I am sorry, as always when I hurt your feelings—especially at this time—Both you and Wes are good soldiers—nevertheless and not withstanding and I mean to be one myself. So cheer up. I tease those I love most.

"Remember when I stole a little girl—(looked something like you)— about twenty years ago and shared what I had with her ever since except when she walked out on me hand in hand with a big-boy for a year or two? Hell, I am sorry, but that little girl now doesn't think I am so much. And she has lost perspective of these years and says—I'm no good. Just an arrogant old egotist who'll be left all alone in my old age because he is so mean. Ah well—better to be alone independent than dependent on unappreciative, un- sympathetic people? But I am in no such danger. Neither is the little girl and all the little boys and (or girls) she's making."

Wright again insisted that only her investment with Wes in Taliesin would ever pay "in coin." He signed his letter "AS I AM—with love—The man who stole you and everything else he has. Daddy Frank—'Vitriolist.' "

Daddy Frank had guessed wrong about the baby: In early May 1944, Svet- lana gave birth to a nine-pound boy they named Daniel. Wes celebrated by bringing cigars to Taliesin and baking a terrible pie. "I hope Wes is bearing up and trying to look proud and walking around chesty," Wright teased Svetlana. "Really manly like."

According to Kay, the baby looked just like Olgivanna's brother, Vlado. "He was a Lazovich," she observed.

The following month, Vlado himself moved into Taliesin with his wife, Sophie. The childless couple had been Svetlana's de facto parents when Olgi- vanna had abandoned her daughter; perhaps now, with the arrival of their new "grandchild," they felt an urge to once again be close.

Within days of arriving, Vlado received a carbon copy of a letter stamped SECRET. Dated June 15, just nine days after D-Day, the unsigned letter was addressed to a Lt. Col. Mann and a David Williamson. "I have assigned Mr. Lazovich the duty of formulating a plan for penetrating Austria and Hungary from Yugoslav bases and for recommending competent personnel for this task," it read. "Mr. Lazovich's contribution to this assignment should be ac- complished by July 1 . . ." Vlado's native Montenegro was by now part of Yugoslavia, and Marshal Tito's forces were on the brink of driving the Nazis from the country. Lazovich, clearly, was performing secret work for the resis- tance effort—and now he was doing it at Taliesin, the estate of a man now nearly as famous for his isolationism as for his architecture.

* * *

JOHNNY HILL HAD to shepherd the Guggenheim design through the studio. Jack Howe was still trying for an early release, but his latest strategy—naming Gene Masselink, not Wright, as his parole supervisor—got him nowhere. Near the end of July, drawings in hand, Wright left to meet with Guggenheim and Rebay at Pecketts-on-Sugar Hill, a New Hampshire resort.

At first, leafing through the drawings of the spiral scheme, Guggenheim said nothing. Then tears welled in his eyes.

"Mr. Wright, I knew you would do it. This is it."

On July 27, 1944, Guggenheim approved the preliminary drawing and authorized Wright to make detailed plans and a model.

Wright assigned Johnny Hill and Kenn Lockhart to make a model, which required its very own set of drawings. The huge skylight crowning the museum's atrium was modeled out of Plexiglas; to the consternation of the apprentices on kitchen duty, their oven was used to mold the shape. Wright went to Madison to buy colored macaroni and vials of colored beads, which Johnny would use to simulate exterior foliage. "I couldn't imagine anybody would like it but me," Hill recalled. Wright was delighted with the result. Drawings are a poor tool for visualizing such a complex, three-dimensional idea, and Wright learned a lot from the model—enough to know that he wanted changes. Hill and Lockhart would go on to make many models of the museum, even as Taliesin's mice kept eating the macaroni off their previous efforts.

Wes Peters was struck by just how hard it was for Wright to come to closure on the shape. "Mr. Wright had more difficulty with the Guggenheim Museum," he remembered, "than finally any other building that I know of that he ever worked on." One reason was that Wright hadn't followed his usual strategy of designing from the inside out, letting the functional demands determine the interior, which in turn dictated the exterior form. Instead he started with the spiral form, and then was forced to create an interior space to work within it. The Guggenheim's shape may have had a cosmic "function," but it was a strikingly challenging venue to use in viewing art—the building's very reason for being.

No wonder he was struggling.

BESIDES THE MUSEUM, Wright was still juggling the new Johnson Wax building, a complex tower scheme, and the unfolding Florida Southern project. He wrote to Howe complaining that between farming and studio work the Fellowship was "way beyond our present capacity while you capables . . . are kept there under the 'corrective lash' so to speak, a kind of social debris." A day later he wrote Howe again. "I've never needed my own 'Fellows' so much as I need them now," he told him. "And I know how much you Fellows need your Fellowship. My impotence in connection with your imprisonment is hard to bear."

Jack, no doubt, returned the sentiment. Wright's daughter Iovanna, in contrast, had lost all interest in being at Taliesin. In the closing weeks of 1944, when she attended her landlady's Christmas party, she met a young naval lieutenant on leave from the war. Tall, good-looking, a great dancer, Waring Howe wanted to make the most of his hiatus from danger. He and Iovanna spent the next weeks together, drunk on love. Waring was Iovanna's first lover. "How honorable to get in bed and feel his long root in me," she recalled. "When he finished I felt as though I were covered with flowers." After Howe shipped out, the Taliesin holidays Iovanna had once pined for seemed to lose their allure.

COSMIC OBJECTIVES AND structural imperatives were not an easy mix. Wright had decided early on to build his seven-tier spiral with reinforced concrete—the same structural system he had engineered, with such precarious results, at Fallingwater. And, as with that project, he was planning once again to create the illusion of an almost miraculous levitation. The huge continuously twisting ramp, nearly the entire floor area of the building, was to be cantilevered off the walls.

Wright also chose his Fallingwater engineers, Mendel Glickman and Wes Peters, to handle the project. Wright had given Wes his "cactus lecture" many times: how the structure of the saguaro depended on vertical "reinforcing bars," how the staghorn and the chola derived their strength from fibers arrayed in a diagonal mesh. For his new spiral ramp, Wright had decided that such a mesh system would work. Heavy steel wires welded into a square grid mesh were a standard method of reinforcing concrete, a system Glickman and Peters had already incorporated at Johnson Wax. Wright would later discover that New York City's plan check engineers were less than convinced by his cactus theory.

Reinforcing the ramp was relatively simple compared with supporting it as it spiraled up seven tiers. Glickman and Peters had hoped they could cantilever the enormously heavy ramp off the building's exterior walls and elevator shaft, but their calculations indicated otherwise. The structure would require concrete columns and steel struts for support. To Wright, these struts looked like toothpicks holding up a fish's mouth; he found them repellent, and tried repeatedly—and unsuccessfully—to get rid of them. Rebay's Theosophy held that there was no inherent conflict between the spiritual and the scientific, but here the laws of physics shouldered aside the ideals of philosophy. Throughout his career, Wright had espoused a belief in the honest expression of structure, the hallmark of his beloved Gothic cathedrals. Yet in the past he had been willing to ignore such limitations when they became inconvenient, and now he decided to part with his "Ideal" and conceal the unwelcome structure.

What had begun as an attempt to use a cantilever to create the illusion of a floating spiral had been reduced to an attempt to create the illusion of a cantilever. Ultimately, though, Wright was proud of the compromise. He boasted that the spiral "basket" was "virtually indestructible by natural forces." And after the war he added unnatural forces: In the event of an atomic bomb, he promised, the spiral would act like a spring, the whole thing popping up into the air and then bouncing on the ground until it came to rest unharmed.

REBAY AND WRIGHT had reached accord on the museum's design, but one thing remained unresolved—how the paintings were to be displayed. With the hexagonal plan now discarded in favor of Wright's sinuous spiral, the architect turned his attention to the challenge of displaying flat paintings on curved walls. In fact, the curve wasn't the only problem: these walls would actually angle outward from the floor to the ceiling, not unlike a giant painter's easel. Wright proposed that the canvases be installed along the lower portion of the walls—frameless. They would be lit by diffused sunlight, filtering down from a continuous spiraling skylight mounted above the pitched wall. Setting the paintings low and angling them upward, he told Rebay, would put them perpendicular to the viewer's line of vision, not to the horizon, as paintings were traditionally hung.

It was a dubious claim at best; after all, paintings hung vertically are perpendicular as long as the viewer is looking straight ahead. But it isn't hard to divine Wright's real agenda. Installing the paintings close to the floor would make them less likely to distract from the thing he really cared about: his building. In effect, the paintings would be sitting down—something he often asked of visitors at Taliesin, complaining that by standing they were "ruining the architecture."

But Rebay was on to him. Frameless paintings mounted low on an angle would "look awful," she told him. The building should complement the art, not dominate it. Even worse, she feared that Wright's idea would prevent her paintings from unleashing their spiritual powers. She countered with an equally unorthodox proposal—that the paintings be installed at normal height and built permanently into the walls.

Their battle between painting and architecture quickly escalated, with the project itself hanging in the balance. Rebay was terrified that Wright would disregard her specifications and subordinate the exhibition of non-objective art to his architecture. Over the next four months, she asked him repeatedly to create a full-size sample of his proposed display wall. He promised, but never did. Finally, Rebay did the unthinkable: She suggested that Mies van der Rohe, one of the "international boys," be brought in to consult. Wright went ballistic. Dismissing her "fickle fears and unstable suspicions," he told her that nothing in his design could be "interjected or interfered with without marring the peace and quiet of the whole Concept. You could take this in, in a Painting. Why then are you unable to take this in, in Architecture—the *Mother-Art* of which *Painting* is but a daughter."

Olgivanna joined in with her own imperious letters, but Hilla would not be cowed. "Olgivanna, I love you very much, but my darling, do not tell people to be humble before your dear husband or you make yourself just a bit ridiculous. . . . I listen to no one but my own intuition and for this excellent gift I am most humbly grateful to God and not to Frank." Her paintings, she declared, were more important to her than architecture was to Frank Lloyd Wright—a man "surrounded all the time," she sniped, "by doting ladies and disciples."

Rebay wrote Wright the same day, demanding to know why he hadn't constructed the sample wall. It would be so easy, she said. "But, no, I am told, none of your business; when the omelette is baked, you eat it. Results, evasion, and all that was promised me, forgotten, ignored." She called Wright an "idiot"—in the common, not the Gurdjieff meaning—and charged that he must be under the influence of a "black wolf." "All I ask you to do is serve my paintings as best you can, because I love my paintings. . . . They are," she told Wright, "the utter perfection of the spiritual suns." They come "from the heart of God."

"You have a sense of cosmic values," Wright countered, "but only as you glimpse them through your little painter keyhole."

IN EARLY JANUARY 1945, a few weeks after Allied bombers set off a firestorm that leveled Dresden, a letter from Holland arrived at Taliesin. "An unconscious feeling of the fall of our old-world made me once search for a new beginning in the U.S.A.," it began. The writer was Hendrik Wijdeveld, and he was at pains to remind Wright how they had planned the Taliesin Fellowship together more than fifteen years before.

The Nazi occupation had laid the Dutchman waste. Initially he had not been hostile to Nazi ideals; he had even written naive articles praising Hitler's opening of a *Deutscher Kunst*, or House of German Art in Munich. Nor had he resigned from the Nazi-controlled architectural association when the

Germans took Holland. Now, however, he had neither work nor students, and had just been forced to sell his building. Most of his Jewish wife's family had been exterminated, and the couple had been reduced to near-starvation. To top it all, his countrymen shunned him as a collaborator.

"Sometimes," Dutchy concluded his letter, "I try to reconstruct my stay at 'Taliesin,' for it lingers in me like a dream." And he hoped to make the dream a reality. "Let us come," he now urged, "we two, to start the collaboration which broke off. . . . May 1931 become 1946!"

Wright did not reply.

Their mutual friend, the Jewish architect Eric Mendelsohn, wrote to implore Wright—on practical, humane, and professional grounds—to bring Wijdeveld on board.

Again, Wright did not reply.

After the Fellowship returned to Wisconsin, Mendelsohn paid a visit, again imploring Wright to help Dutchy.

Wright said no.

THAT SUMMER, WRIGHT received a birthday-box package from someone he saw more clearly as a war victim: Jack Howe, with his last such contribution from prison. "Yours was a swell exhibit," Wright congratulated him. "The Birthday Box overflowed with it and shows you have digested the 'Ausgefurthe Bauten und Entwurte' "—his famous German portfolio—"skin and all, but don't spit out the seeds—so to speak. How helpful you could be here now!"

"I fear," Jack replied, "you are coming to expect some kind of prize package where I am concerned. . . . I feel it is my duty to here warn you against that inevitable day of disillusionment; that I am not as whole. . . . as may seem at such distance."

IOVANNA HAD ANNOUNCED that she was going to marry Waring Howe, her naval lieutenant, but Wright blanched at the idea. Though he grudgingly gave his assent for the ceremony, set for March 20, 1945, in Miami, neither he nor Olgivanna attended. After a two-day honeymoon in Key West, Howe shipped out aboard a mine sweeper and Iovanna made her way back to New York.

A little more than a month after the wedding, Adolf Hitler committed suicide, and a week later Germany surrendered. Iovanna wrote Waring begging him to secure shore leave, but he wasn't able to arrange it. By year's end, she had had enough of both Waring Howe and New York. When she told her father that she wanted to return to Taliesin, he relented—after a fashion. "Of course I have no daughter to be sure of," he replied, "but I am going to get a harpist—and I ought to be grateful for that—mother says."

FOR A WHILE it looked like the conflict over how to display Guggenheim's paintings would explode. Ultimately, though, neither the architect nor the curator could afford to let the dispute scuttle the museum. Wright told Rebay to wait for the scale model, which he promised would be far better than any full-size wall sample in making his case for installing the art his way.

Rebay, in turn, took the sting out of her worst insult. She had not actually asked Mies van der Rohe to consult on the building, she told Wright—only to lend his Kandinsky to the collection. And she made sure to report the flattering response: Mies had told her he would agree to the loan because she'd chosen the right architect. "He expects perfection," Mies had written Rebay, "so do I." Wright concurred with Mies. As an architect, he told her, he was inspired by "the Good Spirit"—that is, God. "Sometimes I am 'him' and sometimes he is me."

With Rebay and Solomon Guggenheim at the public unveiling of the museum design

* * *

ON JULY 9, 1945, with the new model completed, Guggenheim and Rebay went public with the design, holding a luncheon for the press at New York's Plaza Hotel. Two months later the working drawings were complete; soon thereafter, Guggenheim personally signed off on the plans.

The story was picked up by nearly all the major magazines. "The daring dean of modern architects," *Time* reported, "announced last week that he had completed plans, and secured backing (a million dollars), for the long-contemplated Solomon R. Guggenheim Museum of Non-Objective Painting. It sounded like a jumping-off-place for Buck Rogers, the man from the 25th century." Wright made some peculiar pronouncements—that the museum would be "self-cleaning," that visitors would be suction-cleaned as they passed through the entry vestibule. ("There will be no drooling down the surface," he promised.) Films would be projected on to the museum's ceiling, watched by audiences lying in deck chairs. There would be an observatory for "the study of the cosmic order."

Once the publicity campaign was over, the model was packed up and shipped back to Taliesin. Somewhere in transit it was destroyed.

Johnny Hill was charged with its reconstruction. As he stood in the drafting room with Mr. and Mrs. Wright admiring the new one, Wright placed a marble Greek male nude right next to it. Look how similar they were, he said—the torso's twist and the spiral's turn, the monomaterial, the articulation of the forms. Wright then went to the vault and took out the sketches of the floral ornament and the finely modeled male nudes Louis Sullivan had given him just before he died. Sullivan had also designed his urban buildings to have the qualities of male bodies, handsome in their muscularity—"comely in the nude," as he put it. In the Guggenheim, Wright had produced his own, stripped-down male torso. Wright's *lieber meister* would have understood; Hilla Rebay would never suspect a thing.

With the project more or less under control, Frank and Olgivanna made what would be their last trip to Sandstone, and Wright treated the inmates to another lecture. "How you did let in the fresh air!" Jack Howe wrote Wright afterward. "For many the Bible had been the sole source of concurrence and inspiration, and I believe you took your place alongside the saints."

NOT EVERYONE AGREED. Published photographs of the Guggenheim model stirred ridicule as well as praise, evoking comparisons to washing machines and inverted Jell-O molds. One irreverent New York newsman said it looked like a "big, white ice cream freezer." Jack Howe saw one headline that called it the "Museum That Drycleans."

Then, to Rebay's dismay, Wright began to insult reporters and their photographers. Especially hurtful was one interview he gave to an art editor, in which he mentioned Rebay only once, to complain about her request for a gray interior. "Knowing how much a kind word could have helped me before that crowd," she later complained, "this was a very heartless thing to do." Wright seemed bent on undercutting her in public and in Guggenheim's eyes. Was he thinking of jettisoning her at a time when her application for citizenship was up for consideration? "Dear Frank," she pleaded. "I don't think it would help you if someone else would be curator if I was thrown out of this country."

Rebay convinced Guggenheim that they should spend a weekend at Taliesin to "see in whose hands we really are." When they arrived on a Saturday morning all the apprentices were hard at work at their drawing boards, as per Wright's instruction. Guggenheim and Rebay made quite an entrance. Hilla had become so rotund that she could not button her jacket; she was wearing an oversize hat that slipped down over her eyes, topped with a long pheasant plume that plunged forward like a feathered antenna. Accompanied by his manservant, Solomon entered all in black—jacket, jodhpurs, boots, and hat, brandishing a riding crop as though he were in the Lake District awaiting the release of a fox.

Before long, they were enchanted. Seeing Wright relaxed and charming at home was both disarming and reassuring. At one point Wright procured some matted Japanese prints from his study and carried them into his small family kitchen in his residence, a dark room lit by skylights over the sinks. He set up the prints on a table positioned against the wall, leaning them back at an angle. Then he called his patron to join him in the kitchen.

"Absolutely marvelous, Mr. Wright," Guggenheim declared when he saw the prints bathed in the light pouring down from the skylight—just as his paintings would be in Wright's vision of the museum. "I see what you mean. We need not deliberate any further. Go ahead with your plan."

"Passing clouds, the lowering sun," Wright replied, "will all have a charming effect on the display. It is wrong to plan lighting that remains constant. No artist ever saw his work as he was painting it under the same light the same way twice."

Solomon Guggenheim was convinced. Hilla Rebay was not.

NEITHER REBAY NOR Guggenheim had ever seen Johnson Wax, the building whose photographs had convinced her to hire Wright. Frank arranged for Wes Peters to take them out to Racine the next day, a Sunday. From there they would head south to Chicago to catch a train east. It was an ambitious agenda. Wes Peters was doing sixty miles per hour, trying to make time on their way to Racine, when Hilla piped up from the rear, "You can't. Mr. Guggenheim doesn't drive faster than forty miles per hour."

They arrived late, well after lunch. Rather than go directly to Johnson Wax, Hilla roped them into a leisurely supper at the Racine Hotel. By the time they made it to the building, Guggenheim was sure they'd never make it to Chicago on time.

"Well," Wes admitted, "it's going to be a miracle if we can get that train."

Rebay had just stepped into Wright's intimate entry when Solomon declared, "Hilla, I must make the train!"

Bitterly disappointed, Rebay wheeled around and returned to the car without truly seeing the building she had come so far to witness.

"Mr. Guggenheim," Wes announced, "if you want to make that train, I'm going to have to drive very, very fast." They streaked down the lake shore toward Chicago on the old trunk roads, doing close to ninety miles an hour, with Hilla offering a constant stream of tactical advice from the back. The manservant's face was green.

Peters shot through red lights in Chicago, pulling up to Union Station just as the train was scheduled to depart. He raced the car to a side entrance, bolted down to the train room, and convinced the conductor to hold the train five minutes for the magnate.

Guggenheim rushed on to the platform—but where was Rebay? Wes looked up and spied her at the top of a steep flight of stairs, trailing her voluminous feather boa, her purse stuffed with a lifetime's collection of postcards.

Then, as Wes watched, Hilla Rebay tripped and her large body began rolling down the staircase step by step, like a Turkish carpet, feathers drifting off in the sooty air, postcards scattering everywhere.

"Don't touch me," Hilla whimpered when Wes and Guggenheim reached her. "My back is broken."

"Get her up," Guggenheim commanded Wes.

"Well she might be injured," Wes interjected.

"She's not injured. She couldn't be making all that sound that she's making. Get her up." Wes gently ushered his limping charge onto the train.

He later received a letter from Guggenheim praising his driving.

WRIGHT'S REFUSAL TO bend to Hilla Rebay's demands—even at the risk of losing the commission—was reminiscent of Howard Roark, the lead character in Ayn Rand's novel *The Fountainhead*, published just two years earlier. Although she would deny it, Rand had apparently modeled Roark on Wright.

She reveled in her character's legendary courage, his supreme commitment to individuality.

Both Frank and Olgivanna read it. Mrs. Wright was not impressed. "My goodness, what slush," she wrote Svetlana. Frank, on the other hand, loved it. The couple even argued about it.

Rand had never met Wright himself. While working on the novel, the Russian Jewish émigré had requested an interview with the architect—though not to gather facts, she reassured him. "It is only the inspiration of seeing before me a living miracle—because the man I am writing about is a miracle whom I want to make alive."

At the time, Wright had declined her request. Now, however, Wright was happy to welcome her to Taliesin. Rand looked forward to comparing the reality with her ideal, but in the end both novelist and architect were disappointed. "It was like a feudal establishment," she declared. "They [the apprentices] were like medieval serfs. The most horrible thing was that the menu for his table, where his guests also ate, was different than the menu for his students. We sat on a raised platform, high above the others, we ate fancy delicacies and they got fried eggs; it was a real caste system. The idea for all of it was his wife's. He was the deity of the place, its spirit, and she was the practical manager." That the apprentices paid for such privileges simply stunned her. When she and Wright argued, apprentices nearby "bared their teeth that I was disagreeing with the master." And she was distressed to see that their work "was badly imitative of Wright."

If Wright played the part of Roark on the outside, in his private life she found him insecure and dependent on what others thought of him, using deceit and flattery to win a people whom he deemed beneath him. Indeed, when she really thought about it, it seemed that Wright "wants other men to live up to his buildings. . . . [H]is version of the beautiful, dramatic life becomes a show to impress those he despises. . . ." Wright's honesty was confined to his materials.

Wright, for his part, couldn't bear Rand's chain-smoking. At one point he grabbed the cigarette out of her mouth and threw it in the fireplace.

Despite Rand's disillusionment, Wright was asked to design the fictitious architect's buildings for the movie version of *The Fountainhead*. He agreed, but on condition that he be given the right to approve both the script and the actors. The studio refused. Perhaps as an act of retribution, Roark's signature design, the Enright Building, came straight out of the International Style.

IT HAD BEEN two years since Solomon Guggenheim had entered into contract with Wright. Given his advanced age, Rebay warned the architect that getting the museum built was an urgent matter. Once the drawings were done, however, Guggenheim seemed in no hurry whatsoever. Having originally agreed to a budget of less than a million dollars for both land and construction, Wright now informed Guggenheim that the building alone would cost a million. And the figure kept rising.

Solomon's fondness for art had not completely sapped his business sense; he was still hoping to hold off long enough for the war-related inflation in construction materials to recede. Before long, there was another cause for delay: Guggenheim decided to buy an adjacent lot, forcing Wright to revise his plans to account for the larger site.

Jack Howe might get his chance after all.

In one of his last letters from prison, though, Howe's burgeoning doubt surfaced again. "My one hope for the future is that I can be a comfort to you rather than a friction," he wrote. "Is it in the cards? Is it in me?"

Iovanna (center) and her fellow dancers in a Gurdjieff-inspired dance performance

PART VI
THE STRUGGLE WITHIN

A FRESH START

ON A WARM SATURDAY EVENING in March 1946, Wes Peters stood among the cactus in front of Taliesin West firing his rifle—round after round—into the vast black sky, as the entire Fellowship watched a car approaching them up the narrow dirt road. After almost three years in prison, Jack Howe and Davy Davison were finally "Free! Free! Free! Free! Free! Free! Free!" as Howe wrote Gene Masselink en route. The two of them looked "like two traveling morticians," he warned, "decked out in government issue black suits."

They looked "pretty bad," new apprentice Carter Manny recorded in his diary that day. "They haven't indicated that they were mistreated physically too much," he wrote, "but surely they couldn't have looked as bad when they left. . . . Was Wright correct in leading these fellows so? I don't know, but I certainly wonder."

To welcome the prisoners home, Wright held a special dinner in the theater, with roast beef and chocolate éclairs. After the best meal he'd had in years, Jack repaired to his old room, whose current occupant had been sent to a tent.

Wright considered his apprentices who had chosen jail over military service the real heroes. "Why didn't you go to jail like an honorable man," he queried his former apprentice photographer Pedro Guerrero, who had served in the army air corps. In the immediate aftermath of the war, many apprentices who had left to serve in America's armed forces would get a frosty reception upon their return to Taliesin.

THE "WAR PRISONERS" were not the only returnees. After following in her half-sister's footsteps, leaving Taliesin as a teenager to study music and getting married while away, Iovanna also came back in the months after the war. But unlike Svetlana, who had returned with her wealthy and brilliant husband,

Iovanna arrived alone, bringing back only the stigma of a failed marriage. At least Wright's extended family was reunited—if only physically. Iovanna had developed strong independent tastes in her time away from her father, exploring a broad range of composers, including the French Impressionists. After her return, Wright renewed his ban on Claude Debussy and Maurice Ravel, her favorites.

She was not the only one who had trouble reintegrating into Taliesin. Within weeks of returning, draft resister Marcus Weston did something he long must have dreamed of in prison: He got married. But Olgivanna was indifferent to his four years of suffering; his bride didn't fit into her "image of what a woman at Taliesin should be AT ALL," according to fellow apprentice-prisoner Curtis Besinger, and Mrs. Wright made it known that Weston would have to choose between Frank Lloyd Wright and his new wife. Within a few months Weston was gone.

There were many waiting to take his place. Wright had cursed the prospect of his boys joining the military, but he was more than happy to have returning soldiers join his crusade. Wright even managed to have the Taliesin Fellowship approved for government tuition payments under the G.I. Bill. He must have chuckled at the idea of the federal government funding an enterprise that was dedicated to its destruction through Broadacre City decentralization.

Jim Dresser had become enthralled by Frank Lloyd Wright while reading the autobiography in his Quonset hut in the Aleutian Islands. Trying to decide between being a surgeon or an architect after the war, Dresser was also struggling to figure out, as he put it, "what this thing God is." In Wright's organic philosophy, he saw a way to study architecture and apply the principles of His work at the same time. Dresser sent some sketches to Taliesin; Wright sent back an invitation to come along.

There were many others like Dresser. Aided by the influx of veterans, Taliesin's population was now more than sixty, well exceeding its prewar heights. But these new recruits were hardly "boys" in quite the same way as earlier apprentices. Hardened by combat, Dresser and his cohorts had seen more of life than they might ever have wished.

Of all the new more worldly recruits, Carter Manny was likely the least cowed by the presence of Frank Lloyd Wright. Not only had he graduated magna cum laude from Harvard; his classmate there was none other than Philip Johnson. Manny was dismayed to discover the lack of democracy under the man who had just published *When Democracy Builds*. Anyone who dared to praise architecture other than Wright's, he noted, was considered guilty of "heresy or breach of loyalty." And the master's historical views seemed loony. One minute Wright berated President Lincoln for going to war, the next he explained that the Japanese had gone to war to protect their culture against "Anglosaxon commercialization." At one of the Fellowship's mountain picnics, furs spread among the boulders, Manny took in the spectacle of Wright, with his coat worn like a cape, his flowing white hair, and his Charlie Chaplin cane. "Hitler in his mountain top," he remarked in his diary, "never had anything to surpass this, I am sure. It must have been quite close to the imaginings of Wagner."

Along with the new manpower had come a good deal of client work, both commercial and residential. Jack was back at his post as head of the drafting room, and he drew on his experience teaching drafting in prison to start a series of classes to get the new apprentices up to speed. They worked on both modest Usonians and grander abodes—including one for none other than Ayn Rand.

AFTER A DECADE of marriage and two children, all was not well between Wes and Svetlana. He loved hanging out with the other apprentices—more so now, it seemed, than with his wife at their home at Aldebaran. Every evening she would lay out clothes for him to wear to dinner after coming in dirty from the fields or Taliesin construction. Sometimes he would show up, sometimes not. "Sometimes," Kay recalled, "he'd spend the whole evening with [some] friends, and forget about coming home."

And when he did come home, Svetlana sometimes regretted it. Wes could become so enraged with her that he would start to shake her violently. With Kay and her other spies on the lookout, it wasn't long before Olgivanna heard about Wes's behavior, which must have been an unwelcome reminder of her own violent marital history. "You don't do that here," Olgivanna warned Wes. "If you don't stop, you will kill the thing you love."

Yet Frank chose not to intervene. Iovanna believed that this was because her father needed Wes as the apprentice who "had more design talent than the others." She didn't know that he also needed Peters's money. Given his own tendencies, though, it's likely that Wright also identified with Wes.

Her father swung "between extremes," Iovanna recalled. All it took was a bad review of a building or the loss of a client to trigger his violent streak. One morning around this time she watched her pajama-clad parents get into a shouting match in the living room. "My father was insulting and angry, accusing mother unjustly," Iovanna recalled.

When she saw him come after her mother menacingly, backing her up against a table, Iovanna knew what was next. "I couldn't take it anymore," she remembered. She jumped out of her seat, rushed over, hauled back, and socked her father in the face. "I stood absolutely silent after that. There was no reproach in his eyes, no anger. Not one of us said anything. I left the room and went to my bedroom."

She never apologized, and her father, she claims, never attacked her mother again. "I think I saved my mother."

WES AND SVETLANA were part of a foursome at Taliesin that included Johnny Hill and Gene Masselink. The quartet could often be found eating lunch together, or, when their other responsibilities allowed, just hanging around. Their friendship was formed in part around music. With Johnny providing accompaniment on the piano, Gene would sing or Svetlana play the violin. Hill had musical promise, and Olgivanna arranged for Carol Robinson, her dear friend from the Institute, to tutor him during her regular summer visits.

Within the foursome, Wes and Gene were good buddies—an inconvenience, it would turn out. Olgivanna's doubts about her son-in-law contrasted sharply with her feeling for the gentle, elegant Gene. And, according to Iovanna, Gene Masselink had fallen in love with Olgivanna. Their age difference was not all that great—fourteen years, much less than that between her and her husband. The two spent a good deal of the day together, often alone, usually working, but not always. Olgivanna periodically took time away from her Fellowship duties to allow Gene to paint her in a series of portraits.

If any apprentice understood the frailties of the Wrights' marriage, and the possibilities for an affair, it was Gene. His room was within calling distance of Wright's, close enough to hear the arguments, and even the violence, that Olgivanna had to endure. And what he didn't overhear, she may well have told him. He was the one man inside Taliesin in whom she confided. And her confidences were safe with him; in a community rife with gossip, there is not a single story that can be traced to Gene.

When Gene finally revealed his feelings for Mrs. Wright, Olgivanna made it clear that she would not, could not, respond to his advances. Her heart, she told him, "was completely with her husband."

"I wouldn't have him," Olgivanna later told Iovanna, recalling the conversation. Instead she suggested an alternative: "[M]y daughter looks a lot like me. Why don't you flirt with her?" It wasn't the recently divorced Iovanna she meant, but the very married Svetlana. The idea didn't come out of the blue: Olgivanna had a matchmaking streak, and by this point, Iovanna recalls, she was very unhappy with Svetlana's marriage, which of course she had opposed from the start. But this was risky business. Wes was money; Svetlana was blood. Together they represented the future of the Fellowship.

But the idea took hold. By all accounts Gene fell in love with his best friend's wife, and she, it is said, with him. The two were frequently seen walking together around Taliesin or strolling through the fields. And often they joined Olgivanna in the evening for a cocktail, without Wes. Gene became a kind of second father to Brandoch and Daniel. "It was like *Jules and Jim*," Gene's brother recalled years later, referring to the classic French film about two men in love with the same woman.

ON SEPTEMBER 30, 1946, apprentice Jim de Long stood by the road watching as Svetlana packed Brandoch, his kitten, and Daniel into her Jeep and drove off to Spring Green for some groceries. It was a day that would change everything.

Svetlana had never wanted the soft-top war-issue Jeep. Having been in an accident a decade before, she had asked Wes to buy a closed, conventional car. And Jim had warned him against it too. One of the new crop of veterans, he knew all about Jeeps, how their short wheelbase required hair-trigger reflexes to steer straight.

But Wes would hear none of it.

After collecting the deposits on some pop bottles at the service station, Svetlana and the boys finished their errands and headed back to Taliesin. As they approached a narrow bridge that crossed over a slough off the Wisconsin River, Brandoch's kitten climbed up on Svetlana's neck. Startled, she lost control. The Jeep swerved, clipped the edge of an abutment, and flipped over into four feet of water.

The service station owner was driving by in a tow truck when he saw Brandoch running down the road. "Won't you please help me!" the boy cried. "My mommy went in the water." The boy led him down to the scene, where Svetlana and Daniel were trapped in the water and mud beneath the overturned Jeep. Svetlana's neck had snapped.

Wes was working in the drafting room when he got the news. Driving madly down the dirt road to the bridge, spinning his car at the site, he lifted Svetlana in his arms and wept. Kay Davison fainted when she got to the scene. Jack Howe had to call Mr. and Mrs. Wright, who were in Chicago. "It can't be that bad," Wright said. "It can't be worse," Jack replied. Wright cried.

Brandoch was the only survivor.

The Wrights returned immediately. That night, after a disconsolate Olgivanna retreated to the house, Jim de Long happened to pass through the Hillside drafting studio. For once the big room was empty, except for Frank Lloyd Wright, sitting at a far-off drawing board, lost in a design. Jim left quietly before he was noticed.

The funeral was set for five o'clock the next evening at the little Unity Chapel across the road. Wes Peters and Gene Masselink dug the grave together,

Olgivanna soon after the death of Svetlana

filling it with fall leaves and wild asters. As Johnny Hill made a path of red maple leaves from the chapel gate to the grave, Wes and Gene placed Daniel in Svetlana's arms, their bodies facing back toward Taliesin.

It's uncertain whether either man knew it, but Svetlana was pregnant when she died. The father, she had confided to Kay, was Gene Masselink.

"The weeks move by endlessly—the sun is a continuous benediction and there is work to do," Gene later wrote to a friend informing him of the tragedy. "Otherwise there is nothing I can feel to say now." It was nearly three weeks after the accident when Gene finally wrote Valdemar Hinzenberg. "She never knew what happened," the letter read. This was Svetlana's father's formal notification of his daughter's death; he had not been invited to the funeral.

Each morning, for days and days after the burial, Wes's pillow was found drenched with tears.

OLGIVANNA HAD CABLED Gurdjieff immediately after the accident. Years before, he had foretold the deadly event. "He was the only person," she recalled, from whom she felt "steady, permanent support."

Gurdjieff called back immediately.

"Is she, is she . . . ?" Olgivanna could not finish her sentence; she began to cry. "Is she existing now?"

"Yes, she is," Gurdjieff replied. "She was already highly developed spirit. That immortal. I cannot guarantee other cosmoses, but in this cosmos in which we are, she is living."

"She must always live," Olgivanna told Gene, relieved. "We will make her live and nourish her with our love and our prayer, our thoughts, so she goes on and does not fall asleep there as we too may fall asleep here. So we must keep living aware in our inner world that she may stay awake in hers."

Yet Gurdjieff's reassurances were not enough. Olgivanna was not herself. She stopped wearing jewelry and makeup, gave up meat, alcohol, and coffee. Always thin, she began to look emaciated. She sought solace from both friends and strangers. Carol Robinson, always close by at critical moments, was there. And when Mansinh Rana, a young Indian man, joined the Fellowship, Olgivanna took him aside: Could he help her make contact with Svetlana? He couldn't. Despite Gurdjieff's advice that she not try to contact her dead daughter, Olgivanna traveled to Chicago, where she had found a medium willing to try. She returned with a message for Wes: "Your wife says that you are walking in darkness."

Peters needed no reminder of his culpability. Iovanna, cleaning his room just after the accident, found a note pinned to her dead sister's pillow: "Oh Svetlana, how could I have failed you so."

A USONIAN IN PARIS

WITH SO MANY PROJECTS TO be drawn and built, Taliesin's apprentices could not afford to grieve for too long, especially the widower. Within a few weeks of the accident, Wes was back supervising construction at widely dispersed sites. With his wife gone, his surviving son, Brandoch, became the ward of his grandmother. "I am so glad to have complete responsibility of him," Olgivanna wrote Wes two months after Svetlana's death, "because now I know everything he needs and how he needs it." Svetlana had just started Brandoch on the cello when she died, so Olgivanna got Johnny Hill to study the instrument with him. One thing she apparently thought Brandoch needed was periodic reminders of how he had caused his mother's death by bringing his kitten along that day.

Svetlana's mother was inconsolable. In the winter the Fellowship returned to Arizona, where the apprentices made a totem pole for her. Finding little comfort in her husband, Olgivanna moved into a tent to grieve on her own. Almost anything could set her back: At one point she became so enraged by a cat that an apprentice had to chase it down and remove it. Whenever she saw an expectant mother, or a young woman holding a child's hand, she confided in Gene, "I grow numb with pain, a cloud comes over my eyes, which do not want to see."

IOVANNA COULD BARELY compete with her half-sister when alive; in death it was impossible. In her grief, Olgivanna paid little or no attention to her. Iovanna's relationship with her father had become openly hostile. One day, while sitting around the living room with her parents and her Aunt Maginel, Iovanna did "something disrespectful" to him and they argued. Wright finally slapped her and stormed out of the room, declaring that there was "no more filial piety left in this world."

Desperate for attention, doubtful that she would ever measure up to her father's standards and dubious that it was worth trying, Iovanna turned to the appreciating eyes of the men at Taliesin. Roland Rebay, recently sent to Taliesin by his aunt Hilla, was one of many young men who climbed an outside wall and crawled in through Iovanna's bedroom window at night. Entry through the window was mandatory; well aware of the temptation posed by his daughter, Wright had her room wired so that his alarm clock would ring the moment her door opened. Once he grew wise to his apprentices' window tricks, he started running spot checks on Iovanna's room. Whenever Iovanna or one of the apprentices heard Wright's footfall, the young man would scramble out the window to the ground below. Wright would peer out into the dark night through the window screen trying to discern the culprit. He rarely yelled at her, leaving her mother to engage her in regular shouting matches in the morning. But he did give her a piece of advice: "There is no conscience in a stiff prick."

Iovanna was not without discernment, but her fusion of authority and lust was a dangerous mix. Very late one night, a smitten apprentice—who had earlier followed her around the kitchen declaring his love—sneaked into her room. "You rat," she yelled at him as she pummeled his head with her fists. The next day she informed her parents, and the love-struck young man was called into a meeting. "What are you going to do about it?" Olgivanna asked. "I guess I'd better leave," he replied nervously. It was the right answer.

THE WRIGHTS' DAUGHTER understood how the apprentices felt. It was difficult to be perfect. When her parents were both absent, even for a night, the apprentices experienced an exhilarating sense of liberation. It was usually an occasion for forbidden acts—for heavy drinking, smoking, dancing, for irreverent jest, the grotesque and the extravagant. Jim de Long, the last apprentice to see Svetlana alive, had sought refuge during one of these reveries in his usual quiet way, playing the piano in the Hillside living room. Turning the lights off, he read the sheet music from the full moon's light as the other apprentices whooped it up in the distance.

Before long, a drunken Iovanna staggered in and began swaying to his music. Would Jim play some Debussy, she asked? De Long began to play a piece by the forbidden composer. A few measures into "Clare de Lune," Iovanna leaned against the piano, thrust her head under its upright lid, and vomited on the strings and soundboard. Iovanna fled, leaving Jim to clean up the terrible mess.

When Wright returned the next day, the wretched smell still wafted from his piano. He assembled the Fellowship. "Who is responsible for this?" he growled.

No one spoke; Jim's gesture across the room to Iovanna, a signal that he would not betray her, was almost imperceptible.

ON SEPTEMBER 3, 1947, just weeks before the first anniversary of Svetlana's death, the Wrights received what could be seen as an act of expiation. On that day, a deed was recorded with the county transferring the title to Taliesin from Wes Peters to the Frank Lloyd Wright Foundation for the token sum of one dollar.

The document had been drawn up in 1944, at the height of Wright's effort to get the apprentices to buy nearby farms as part of building Broadacre City. If Peters could now be persuaded to throw in Aldebaran as well, the bold project might have a real shot. But for the Foundation to develop an experimental town, it needed someone with a head for business. Years before, Wright's cousin Richard Lloyd Jones had recognized Olgivanna as such a person, and by all accounts she was the only one who had been paying attention to the Fellowship's income. A kind of proof came in the year after Svetlana's death, 1947, when Olgivanna was largely incapacitated by grief: It was

Iovanna with her parents. "What is the matter with me?" she wrote of this rare photo from her personal album. "My father is laughing at me."

the first year that the Foundation actually lost money. The shortfall came despite a surfeit of work, including the planning of a community of fifty houses Wright called Usonia II, a civic project in Pittsburgh spearheaded by Edgar Kaufmann, new buildings at Florida Southern College, and more than thirty houses.

Just as his wife was at her lowest ebb, Wright was finally picking up where he had left off before the war, when the press had greeted Fallingwater and Johnson Wax as his second coming. In January 1948, exactly ten years after *Architectural Forum*'s first all-Wright issue, the magazine published another special edition entirely devoted to him. And all the publicity brought the architect yet another windfall of applications for apprenticeship.

Among the many letters asking for a place at Taliesin, none compared in boldness to the one Wright received from Holland. "[F]ind a form for my joining you as an education-worker at Taliesin or Arizona. INVITE ME!!" It was from Mr. Broadacre himself, Hendrik Wijdeveld, a man now scratching to survive in postwar Europe.

Apparently taken aback, Wright wrote multiple draft letters in response. The first few dismissed Dutchy as just another left-wing modernist wanting to come to an America already overrun with them. But the one he finally sent bore a tone rare among his thousands of letters: contrition. "You are one of the occasions," it began, "that weigh on my conscience." Still, Wright's feelings of guilt were insufficient to persuade him to offer Wijdeveld, the man who first envisioned the Taliesin Fellowship, a place there. "Two rams in one small sheep pasture," he wrote, "are certainly one too many."

"I DID A lot of things they didn't know about," Iovanna recalled of her distracted parents. One thing she did was pursue a career in writing. The same month that the *Architectural Forum* came out, she secretly enrolled in a journalism class at nearby Arizona State University. But she soon felt that her professor was harassing her because he "detested" her father. When other students received what she saw as less arduous first assignments, she was told to find a fire to cover. Arriving at the small Phoenix fire station in a pretty pink dress, she naively asked, "Where is the fire?"

"Miss," a fireman replied, "we don't just order fire. They have a way of suddenly showing up." And then the man complimented her on her dress. If they did get a call, he warned her, a dress like that could easily catch fire; why not take it off? Though she found him attractive, and he offered her his fireman's jacket, she managed to decline.

The experience confirmed her fear that the Wright-hating professor was out to get her, putting an end to her fledgling journalism career. But it was "just as well," she recalled—for soon "plans were made for me to go and study with my mother's teacher, the doctor philosopher G. I. Gurdjieff."

THOSE PLANS WERE not made by her mother and father. They were Gurdjieff's idea. Sitting in his Paris flat, the eighty-year-old master, now sickly and obese, was worried over the future of his beliefs after his death. But he had renewed his interest in the movements, and now he sent a telegram summoning Olgivanna and Iovanna to meet him in New York, where he planned to recruit the next generation of dancers and relaunch his network. Iovanna, he thought, could join his preparatory movements class and then sail back to Paris with her new master.

Olgivanna was thrilled. Unable to control Iovanna herself, she was happy to turn her over to Gurdjieff's discipline. She hoped that Gurdjieff's personal guidance might help her daughter find the self-knowledge necessary not just to live as an adult, but to function on a high spiritual plane. And Iovanna might also provide a vehicle to help her bring the movements into the Fellowship, something her husband had forbidden years before. Frank, after all, denied Iovanna nothing.

There was reason for Olgivanna to be optimistic. After Svetlana's death, Wright had apparently tamped down his resistance to her Gurdjieff teachings at Taliesin. His grieving wife's very frailty had become her strength. One female apprentice, Elizabeth Kassler, sensed it immediately: After a stint in the Fellowship before the war, she returned in 1948 to find that Gurdjieff's influence, once almost invisible, was now "very evident."

Olgivanna renewed her intention to make Taliesin, once and for all, an American center for the "work." She thought the apprentices needed a lot of it—work, that is. "Were I to judge the young people in the Fellowship by the standard I have created in my vision," she confessed to her brother Vlado, "there would not be any Fellowship at all." But she had lowered her standard, and "with hope, tolerance and patience most of the young people become valid, contributing, constructive members of our life. For some it takes longer than others . . ."

NEARING EIGHTY, FRANK Lloyd Wright was feeling his own mortality. While designing a mortuary in San Francisco for Nicholas Daphne, the architect wondered aloud "if I felt as well as I should. But Nick had a way of referring to the deceased, always, as 'the merchandise,' and that would cheer me up. I pulled through. . . ."

* * *

AT LONG LAST, Gurdjieff had finally completed his two-thousand-page manuscript of *Beelzebub's Tales to His Grandson*. In the novel, effectively a work of science fiction, Beelzebub arrives from outer space for a visit to Earth. Like his fictional Beelzebub, who made America his last stop on earth, Gurdjieff saw the United States as a final platform for his teachings. There he would supplement the teaching of the movements with public readings of *Beelzebub's Tales*. Gurdjieff even appointed an official *Beelzebub* reader for his American audiences, instructing his lieutenants that it should be read across the land in huge auditoriums. "My words will be heard in churches," he told his followers.

The American crowds were in for an edifying evening. Gurdjieff's Beelzebub discovers a land populated by a fallen people, chasing after money and easy pleasures, a country with lazy women made worse by women's rights movements, a people who were killing themselves by sealing food in tins, their toilet seats so comfortable that they weakened man's musculature and his ability to expel gases. Though they were gullible, superficial, and affable to a fault, Beelzebub also saw Americans as a pragmatic bunch, able to respond to new possibilities—including, of course, Gurdjieff.

In the fall of 1948, the master sent a young Frenchman to New York to teach a preparatory class in the movements at Carnegie Hall. Gurdjieff intended to select six young American women—"calves"—to return with him to Paris to lead his new movements demonstrations, and later to function as teachers. Fresh from her stay with Olgivanna, Carol Robinson accompanied the classes, performing new pieces Thomas de Hartmann had written for the new movements.

Around the beginning of September, Robinson sent the sheet music to Olgivanna. Once again, contact with Gurdjieff's world brought Olgivanna out of a deep depression. Just as contact with the spirit of Gurdjieff's dead wife had lifted her spirits after Iovanna's birth, the new music—and the prospect that her remaining daughter might help her keep Gurdjieff's work alive—suddenly awakened Olgivanna from her years of mourning Svetlana. The compositions transported her "into another dimension," she wrote Robinson, and "filled [her] with Hope, Faith, with sacred passion for greater achievement of life Divine."

Gurdjieff agreed to include Iovanna as part of his select group. But there was a hitch. Wright, who had once declared Gurdjieff a "curious mixture of God and the devil," was building Iovanna her own place at Taliesin West, and was not happy about his daughter moving away to become one of these calves. Unlike Olgivanna, Frank feared that time with Gurdjieff might further corrupt his daughter, not cure her. He knew of Gurdjieff's past sexual relationships with his pupils, including, he suspected, his wife. Wright had never forgotten Gurdjieff's boast when he visited Taliesin in 1934 that he had "104 sons of his own" as well as twenty-seven daughters. The rumor was that only those women followers who had sex with him had "*really* been initiated into his work." Wright even raised the question with his wife, only to receive a less-than-reassuring answer. "But Frank," Olgivanna replied, "he was my teacher. It was completely different from two lovers."

In the end, Olgivanna prevailed: Wright allowed Iovanna to attend Gurdjieff's New York classes. Wright "turned pale and was shaking" when she left, Iovanna recalled. "He was certain that I would never come back."

GURDJIEFF WAS SO determined to get to America that even a major accident wasn't enough to stop him. In August 1948 he fractured his skull, broke several ribs, and opened his sternum in a car crash, suffering severe internal bleeding. Yet somehow his lungs drained of blood quickly—by his own powers, it was understood—and he was restored to wholeness in time to make the trip.

Four months later, on December 17, he landed in New York and moved into the Wellington Hotel, ready to gather the children of his oldest and closest followers as his "calves." A number of these were, in fact, children he had sired with his followers—a fact they discovered only now. One was dancer Jessmin Howarth's twenty-four-year-old daughter, Dushka. When Howarth brought her daughter to the Wellington, she introduced Gurdjieff with the words, "This is your father." The young woman was stunned. Another follower, Edith Taylor, brought her daughter, twenty-year-old Eve, to New York to be greeted with the same news.

The Wrights soon arrived in the city, taking a room at the Plaza, just a few blocks from Gurdjieff's hotel. When Iovanna met Eve Taylor, she brought her fellow calf back to the Plaza to meet her mother. Olgivanna nearly had a nervous breakdown when she laid eyes on the girl. "How could you do this to me?" Olgivanna cried bitterly. "Get her out of here." Iovanna, who immediately suspected the source of her mother's hysteria, escorted her new friend down into the lobby. As the two huddled over tea, she retrieved a photo of her dead half-sister, Svetlana, from her purse and showed it to the shaken young woman. The resemblance between the two was unmistakable.

Many in the movement believed that Eve Taylor and Svetlana Hinzenberg Peters shared a father—Georgi Gurdjieff. And Gurdjieff claimed to believe it, too. But Valdemar Hinzenberg never doubted that he was Svetlana's father, and Gurdjieff was a notorious prevaricator. For his paternity even to have been feasible, he would have to have known Olgivanna before she married Valdemar. While that is not impossible—both had lived in Moscow earlier, perhaps at the same time—there is no direct evidence for it. Olgivanna's re-action to Eve could easily have been triggered by her innocent passing resem-blance to her dead daughter.

Olgivanna evidently reconciled herself to Eve's presence; a short time later she joined her husband, daughter, and the others for dinner in Gurdji-eff's suite. Although the Wellington forbid cooking in its rooms, Gurdjieff had converted his bathroom into a makeshift kitchen. The lavatory doubled as a kitchen sink, food scraps were flushed down the toilet, and a board was laid across the bathtub as a platform for a little grill.

As the other guests sat on windowsills, side chairs, and the floor, Frank, Olgivanna, and Iovanna squeezed around a tightly packed table. Gurdjieff was sporting a suit of ivory-colored silk and a red fez with a black tassel. To Iovanna, his hands seemed to radiate some unearthly power. "Mr. Gurdjieff," she recalled, "seemed deeply pleased that Mother wanted me to go and study with him. Yet another 'calf' returning to the fold."

The following month, January 1949, the Wrights took a second trip to New York to bid Iovanna farewell. In two nights she would accompany Gur-djieff on his return voyage to France. This time, Gurdjieff placed Olgivanna next to him at his ritual dinner at the Wellington. They spoke in Russian to-gether the entire evening; the things he said sometimes made her cry.

Gurdjieff began his meals with the command, "Tell, Mr. Director, tell, tell!" Whoever was serving as the "Director" would respond by toasting the "ordinary idiots" at the table. Everyone—every man, at least—was then ex-pected to drain a glass of Armagnac.

When Wright was asked to say what kind of idiot he was, he replied that he was an "idiotic idiot." But that was his own invention, and Gurdjieff re-fused to accept it. "In that case," Wright declared, "I'm an arch idiot," the only category that had any architectural resonance. Wright had chosen a re-spected category of idiot.

On a strict diet for an aggravated gall bladder, Wright tried to refrain from drinking. But Gurdjieff insisted that he drink the full toasts, and with peppered Armagnac. More than a decade before, he claimed to have cured Wright of his gall bladder complaints by serving him spicy food on a visit to Taliesin. Fight fire with fire, his theory went. But this time Gurdjieff also goaded the architect into eating a full plate of fresh dill as a palliative. When Wright objected that his doctor had him on a different regimen, Gurdjieff told him to ignore it. "I, seven times doctor," he said. Wright complied.

The next day, Wright told Gurdjieff that his gall bladder hadn't bothered him in the least. In fact, he had spent most of the night vomiting.

* * *

WRIGHT HAD CONSENTED to Iovanna's trip with Gurdjieff, but he was far from happy about it. When Gurdjieff asked him to float her $500 first-class fare on the Queen Mary, in fact, Wright was openly surly. The next day Gurdjieff handed the cash to Iovanna without telling her where he got it, telling her to spend it however she liked. She went to Bergdorf Goodman and bought her mother a beautiful suit as a good-bye present. Realizing what had happened—that Gurdjieff was trying to teach her husband a lesson—Olgivanna commanded Iovanna to return the suit. She would not risk Iovanna's trip over a blowup between her husband and her master.

That evening, at their last dinner before sailing, a chastised Wright again handed Gurdjieff the $500. Even after paying his daughter's fare twice, he wasn't ready to let her go. He implored Gurdjieff to delay her departure until after his eightieth birthday celebration in June—in reality, of course, Wright's eighty-second. "No, has to be now," Gurdjieff replied, aware no doubt of his own rapidly failing health. He was still coughing from the injuries to his lungs.

"I accept," Wright relented, "and leave a humbled man."

The next day, Olgivanna sent her daughter off with a piece of hard-earned advice: "Do everything he tells you to do."

IN PARIS, IOVANNA entered Gurdjieff's world, and got a taste of her mother's past. Gurdjieff was based in a small, dark apartment on the Rue des Colonels-Renard, whose mirrored salon, lined with glass cases full of figurines—Nubians on camels, ballerinas, sheiks on horseback—could not have felt more different from Taliesin. Gurdjieff's place was inundated with requests to found new groups, and with a constant stream of followers from all over Europe and America.

Whatever their paternity, Gurdjieff called all his young dancers his "daughters," and Iovanna took the designation quite seriously. In a letter to Olgivanna, Madame de Salzmann wrote that Iovanna "was like a little child, without defense, and so naive." Ashamed by the contrast between her silk stockings and designer pumps and the cotton stockings and heavy shoes of her fellow dancers, she began dressing more modestly. She was also more earnest about Gurdjieff's teachings than the other calves, trying desperately to "remember herself" and awaken from the slumber Gurdjieff claimed most people mistook for life. Her new master was elliptical and playfully enigmatic, but she took his every word literally, a trait he thought peculiarly American. When he joked one day that she might as well sleep on the floor, she started doing just that. As a result she was always tired, missing important readings, sometimes falling asleep before the dinners were finished.

Gurdjieff made it clear that much was at stake. Convinced that her mother was Gurdjieff's greatest student—an "idiot" one category below Moses—Iovanna felt tremendous pressure to perform. "I had a lot to live up to," she recalled. When the other girls went out exploring Paris, she stayed behind to demonstrate her dedication. "She took it all so seriously," Eve Taylor recalled, "whereas we didn't."

At every meal, Iovanna heard the toast to the "all hopeless idiots." Was she one of the class Gurdjieff called "subjectively hopeless"—those who are aware of their nullity—or one of the "objectively hopeless," whose obliviousness rendered them unable to repent, and thus destined "to perish like dogs"? Grown men had been known to break down and cry at the suggestion of this verdict; some were even checked into mental hospitals. Iovanna had to struggle to stay afloat.

And she witnessed what appeared to be Gurdjieff's sometimes frightening powers. One evening, she listened as an obnoxious guest complained about the taste of the food and the ugliness of the apartment. Suddenly the visitor informed the table that he was feeling a strange and unexpected surge of sexual desire. Gurdjieff said nothing. The man couldn't get up from the table because of his obvious erection. "I think that as well as believing in God," Iovanna remarked of Gurdjieff, "he was friends with the devil."

Gurdjieff's new movements demanded far more precision and quickness than those her mother had performed. So Iovanna rented her own practice room, where she often spent the whole morning working. In the afternoons, after long lunches at Gurdjieff's apartment, she participated in hours of movement practice in an upstairs rehearsal room at the Salle Pleyel, a new concert hall near the Arc de Triomphe. With Jeanne de Salzmann improvising on the piano, Gurdjieff personally instructed the select group. Though his stomach was grossly distended from gas, he would demonstrate the positions himself. The calves practiced them for weeks, struggling to align their inner vision and their bodily postures.

One day, while they were working on the "Alleluia," an up-and-down movement, Gurdjieff decided to have the girls accompany by singing the movement's name with each shift in position up and down the scale. Suddenly he motioned them to stop and walked over to Iovanna.

"You like to sing, huh?" he asked her.

"Oh yes, yes," she replied eagerly.

"All right, tomorrow you come apartment. I give you special singing exercise only for you."

The other dancers recognized that Gurdjieff wasn't singling Iovanna out for praise; as he left, he was overheard muttering in Russian that her voice was "spoiling everything." But Iovanna, who didn't know Russian, took his gesture as approval. From that day on she sang, at least softly to herself, wherever she went.

At one point, Iovanna and the other calves were joined by fifty followers to prepare for a public performance. The group was struggling through a dress rehearsal of a very difficult movement called the "automatons," in which the dancers simulate human machines, when Iovanna made a misstep that threw off her entire row.

"STOP!" Gurdjieff yelled, walking over to her. "You destroy line, you prostitute! You oblige descend into street and you walk street rest of life. You not bother me again. You never destroy line again."

In photographs from the time, the self-assured radiance of Iovanna's childhood seems to have disappeared from Iovanna's face. She appears anxious, even desperate. She was often homesick. She sent liqueur-filled French chocolates to her mother, asking for Hershey bars in return. Boxes of them arrived.

One winter day, in her chilly room looking out on a leafless Bois de Boulogne, Iovanna pored over a letter from Arizona. In characteristically colorful prose, Gene Masselink described her parents' "joyous faces" as they returned to Taliesin from a long recent journey, how they walked through the studio, the pergola, and the house, praising all the good work that had been done in their absence. He described the "sudden peace" he felt on their return, the feeling of radiance and light "as life once more begins to go forward into another fascinating, familiar (and yet completely unknown) maze of light and shade."

Once she had wanted to escape Taliesin. Now she longed to return.

ȻHE SEX ȻLUBS

IOVANNA'S ABSENCE FROM TALIESIN HAD made at least one problem worse. From the Fellowship's very inception, there were never enough women to go around. Wright had assumed that his architectural mission and the solidarity of comradeship would absorb all his boys' energies, but Olgivanna knew better. One way or another, the lusts of so many young men were a force that could not be ignored. She would try everything she could to address them. Yet her solutions would create perverse problems of their own.

THE FELLOWSHIP HAD barely opened when the excursions began. Apprentices would push their cars into the night, turning on the ignition only when they thought they were out of earshot. With their headlights off, they drove off to meet up with local farm girls or to visit a house just outside Spring Green where some enterprising prostitutes had set up shop.

In doing so, of course, they were risking expulsion. "Members of the Fellowship," the 1934 regulations read, "are requested not to seek the town for relaxation. If relaxation of this sort is necessary some quality that should be present in work and fellowship is missing. . . . Either the life at Taliesin will be for the purpose of membership here, complete, or the member 'town-relaxed' will be invited to return to the life of the town where, manifestly he belongs."

Taliesin's reputation for licentiousness dated back to the 1910s, when Wright moved there with Mamah Cheney and pronounced himself an avatar of a new and more honest sexual morality. The neighboring farmers and their wives clucked over the spectacle of the dissolute architect and his blithe attitude toward marriage and divorce, at his habit of bedding women without the blessing of matrimony. And the whiff of moral turpitude never quite disappeared: After the Fellowship was formed, locals used to hide in the

Apprentices building Taliesin West, 1940

bushes and take photographs of the apprentices swimming nude in the river. But Wright recognized that his stance as an educator made him answerable to his students' respectable families—and that his whole enterprise was dependent on the good graces of local merchants. As the apprentices' nighttime excursions inevitably led to local scandals, and then a pregnancy or two, he saw that something had to be done.

Olgivanna Wright had her own unorthodox views on sexuality. A true student of Gurdjieff, she considered it an expression of one's essence, a path to spiritual development. And she took an intense interest in the sex lives of the apprentices, both male and female—not only in who was doing what to whom, but in the very mechanics of their relations, in who was a good lover and who was not. She knew "every position, every way and every problem of intercourse," one former resident claimed. Many an apprentice was shocked when out of nowhere she brought up the importance of orgasms and how they benefited creativity. And not just any orgasm: Gurdjieff taught that masturbation made it impossible for one to develop a soul.

Olgivanna was keenly aware that the shortage of Taliesin women put the boys in a bind. And, not long after the Fellowship began, she came up with a bold solution. With no women nearby to satisfy them, she advised, they should "seek each other out rather than creating all this problem in Spring Green."

It was an extraordinary suggestion. Even Gurdjieff had taught her that homosexuality—Athenianism, he called it—prevented spiritual progress. But apparently Mrs. Wright saw no other way to keep the apprentices from looking for satisfaction off campus.

Olgivanna went well beyond just recommending that the male apprentices start tending to one anothers' needs. As Jack Howe later told apprentice Jim de Long, she called a secret meeting of a number of the unattached male apprentices to teach them how to do it. But she wasn't content with that bit of instruction. Proud of her ability to sense whether two people would make a good couple, Olgivanna ended the gathering with a dramatic flourish: She had the selected apprentices—straight and gay alike—stand in two lines facing one another, paired the incredulous young men off, and sent them away to try it on their own.

What she was suggesting, of course, was hardly foreign to her. Though her own youthful affair with Jane Heap was brief, her closeness to lesbians hadn't ended there. Her next Prieuré roommate—and lifelong friend—Carol Robinson was almost certainly gay. Olgivanna was comfortable with homosexuality, and over the years she would counsel the apprentices that it was in no way a perversion.

*   *   *

WHILE OLGIVANNA'S "SOLUTION" may have served to contain some amount of sexual activity within the Fellowship, for many it was also redundant. For gay men had been thriving at Taliesin, at least discreetly, from the very beginning. Just as many Wright's oldest and closest personal friends were homosexual—Charles Ashbee, Alexander Woollcott, Charles Laughton, and probably Louis Sullivan—the core group of apprentices with whom he surrounded himself, and upon whom he most depended, was disproportionately gay. The master always knew instantly which new apprentices he wanted in his inner sanctum. Many, if not most, were homosexual.

Indeed, without the talents and devotion of this core group, Frank Lloyd Wright's career might not have flourished as it did. They brought in some of his most important clients, photographed his buildings, and worked to promote him in magazines and museum shows. Many were profoundly grateful for this safe haven, where they could contribute to the design and construction of some of America's most handsome architecture. Wright, in turn, depended on their loyalty and basked in their admiration. A few of them even fell in love with him.

That gay men were central to this community, which produced some of America's greatest architecture, may come as no surprise. The differential attraction to beauty among gay men is a commonplace. But Taliesin, where the beautiful was prized in every aspect of life, was special. Along the river, in the fields, at the various construction projects around the estate, dozens of shirtless men could be found working together at any given time, lean and tanned from their long hours pouring concrete, shoveling, and hammering in the sun. For a gay man, a place like Taliesin—like the navy or the seminary—could be a kind of heaven.

NEVERTHELESS, IT WAS a heaven that all concerned were desperate to hide from public view. Any revelation of homosexuality at Taliesin would have been disastrous for both recruitment and Wright's architectural practice. The Wrights expected the apprentices to conduct their sexual adventures with discretion—out of their sight and everyone else's.

But over the years things got out of hand, especially with the apprentice Wright most depended on, chief draftsman Jack Howe. A participant in Olgivanna's "lineup," Howe became so forward in pursuing other apprentices that they started refusing to room with him. Howe was especially notorious for seducing the new "boys," inviting attractive young apprentices down to the river for a naked swim and a sun-dry on the rocks.

Howe may have been the most aggressive, but he was hardly the only one. After World War II homosexual activity at the Fellowship became profligate, perhaps fed by the energies of young soldiers who had spent years sequestered with their own kind. With Jack Howe leading the way, Taliesin soon gave rise to an informal node for homosexual couplings and orgies that became known as "the sex club."

The apprentices weren't the only ones who fell under Howe's spell. Another was Philip Johnson, who visited Taliesin often at Wright's invitation. Frank often referred to Johnson's architecture department at MoMA as the "Pansy Patch of the Museum of Foreign Art," once even presenting Johnson with printed stationery bearing that letterhead. But Johnson's manner also brought out Wright's own softer side. "I always enjoy your intelligent, quiet company so much," Wright wrote him in September 1946. "Seems to quiet me." When Johnson told Wright he would visit the following month, Wright cabled back: "Not fast enough Philip. Our landscape is most beautiful now. Break your chains, choose a traveling companion and come and stay awhile with the good ground."

Johnson loved visiting Taliesin, not just for the architecture or his friendship with Wright, but also for the lovers he found there. One apprentice made a pass at him; another took him on a naked erotic voyage into the desert. When asked about his visits more than fifty years later, Johnson had

Jack Howe, whose increasingly aggressive advances toward fellow apprentices came to a head in the 1940s.

forgotten all the names but one—Jack Howe. "I fell in love with Jack," he remembered.

THOUGH SHE HAD supported it at first, Taliesin's increasingly rambunctious homosexuality—and its potential for scandal—eventually troubled Olgivanna. But kicking out Taliesin's gay apprentices was not an option. Nor could she allow the ranks of young homosexual men to grow indefinitely. If she wanted to stem the homosexual tide at Taliesin, she would have to call in reinforcements.

Her directives were not subtle. More than a few women felt "forced" by Olgivanna to have a relationship with the male apprentices, although some dove into the project enthusiastically. One married woman—Kay Davison, a mother of two—was well known for rotating through the ranks at her mistress's behest. "I had them all," she once boasted. Later, when Olgivanna brought in outsiders to study Gurdjieff with her, they understood that part of their function was to "help keep the boys of Taliesin happy and content."

This was Taliesin's other "sex club," the heterosexual one. Olgivanna worked tirelessly to make sex with women easily available. She hoped to keep some straight men from going over, and experimented with converting homosexuals to the other side.

Getting women to turn tricks for Taliesin wasn't always easy. Barbara Fritz, Iovanna's closest Spring Green friend (and draftsman Herb Fritz Sr.'s daughter), lived just outside of Taliesin East until after the war, when she married Jim Dresser, one of the new breed of war veteran apprentices. Olgivanna gave the union her blessing; the ceremony was held at Taliesin, and after the wedding Barbara joined her husband as a resident.

Things began well enough. Jim Dresser, who was devoted to Wright, enjoyed learning architecture from the master and contributing to the Fellowship. But when his bride was asked to make her own contribution, they left Taliesin abruptly, without ever telling their fellow apprentices why. In fact, it would be fifty years before they revealed the reason. "We were in the desert," Jim recalled, as Barbara listened quietly, "and Mrs. Wright called her in for a private meeting, at which time she strongly urged her to have sexual intercourse with some of the other senior apprentices. They had no mates and they had needs that should be satisfied, and pass yourself around. Barbara came back and told me that."

"I was not to become another Kay," Barbara declared defiantly all those years later, still anxious to distance herself from Kay Davison's activities.

"She had no morals as I use the word morals," Jim Dresser said of Olgivanna, "none whatsoever."

Despite Olgivanna's best efforts, she was never able to reverse what she had unleashed during the early years of the Fellowship. At end of 1948, more than a year after the Dressers' departure, a new apprentice named Don Erickson arrived. One afternoon, on his way to a swim, the nineteen-year-old apprentice stopped in the drafting room to see Jack Howe. Erickson loved watching Howe draw; Howe found the new apprentice, in his bathing suit, fascinating for different reasons. "Jack grew very inquisitive about a certain part of my anatomy," Erickson recalled, "and made some suggestions which I denied." The teenage Erickson barely even knew that homosexuality existed. And then Howe suddenly "reached across the table and grabbed me." Erickson jumped back in horror. Thereafter he tried to steer clear of Howe, not always successfully.

Taliesin was a hot house, "a love colony," as apprentice Betty Bauer called it. The apprentices lived in close quarters in thin-walled rooms, and the air was full of sexual gossip. Arguments and intimacies of all sorts became common property. Lois Davidson, who had come to Taliesin with Erickson, found out about Howe's hyperactive sex life because she "happened to know somebody whose bedroom was right next to one of their bedrooms." Although Davidson would deny it, a number of apprentices claimed—and Wright believed—that it was she who told Olgivanna that Jack Howe was a predatory homosexual.

"THE RUMOR HAD already buzzed, just shot through," remembered Wright's recently arrived grandson, Eric, of that early spring day in Arizona in 1949 when the bell rang in the night calling everybody to an extraordinary midweek meeting.

The apprentices filed into the living room, sitting on the heavy chairs, the cushioned seats, and the floor. As Mr. and Mrs. Wright sat somberly, Jack Howe was brought into the room and seated next to Mr. Wright. And so began the event that would come to be known as "the trial."

There had been accusations of Jack Howe's homosexuality, Wright gravely announced. If the rumors were true, Jack would have to leave. If they were not, the rumors would have to stop. "Now is the time for anyone that has any information about this to step forward and present it."

There was absolute silence. Every body was taut and motionless, as if to avoid disturbing the very air in the room. You could hear the friction of a rubber heel turning on the living room floor.

"Well, since there aren't any accusers, then this rumor is going to stop."

The senior apprentices all knew what was happening: No one wanted to betray Wright's chief draftsman.

Then, two words: "Mr. Wright." It was Don Erickson who finally broke the painful silence. It was terribly embarrassing and he was sure it would mean his ejection, but he had no choice. Standing up, he described to the Wrights and the breathless apprentices that day he spent watching Howe at the drawing board. "[I]t was just a miracle for me to watch him draw and I could learn by watching. . . ." As the apprentices sat frozen in horror, he went on to describe Howe's advances.

He sat down. There was another long silence. And then, one by one, other young men stood up and told similar stories.

It was all too much for Olgivanna. Howe had lied to her about his homosexual activity, she started screaming; he should be expelled. She had never liked him anyway. He was too edgy, too bossy, too independent. Howe must have been seething; after all, it was she who had first sent him down the path. A few brave apprentices stood up and protested that Mrs. Wright's tirade expressed an unwarranted prejudice.

And then Wright spoke again. At one point he even broke down and started crying. "We've got this reputation we've got to uphold," he told the apprentices. "We should not be recognized as this kind of a place." As he warned the apprentices about the perils of a homosexual reputation, his mind wandered in a highly suggestive direction—to memories of his old master, Louis Sullivan, on whose biography *Genius and Mobocracy* he was just then working. His eyes swelling with tears, he told the apprentices how he had clutched Sullivan's dying body, his heart beating through his wasted body as their chests touched.

The message was clear: Dignity *could* be found in the love of another man, as long as it was properly expressed.

Wright's association with Louis Sullivan had begun in devotion and grown into a fierce and fearful identification. More than one writer has noted something sensual and romantic in their relationship. Wright had found the older man's glance uncanny, penetrating; he loved to hear Sullivan say his name aloud. "I always loved the way the word came from him." In the 1930s, he had found a place at Taliesin for a muscular sailor who sang beautifully, but had no interest in architecture, simply because his eyes reminded him of those of his *lieber meister*.

But there was more. Sullivan felt that his own architectural cre-

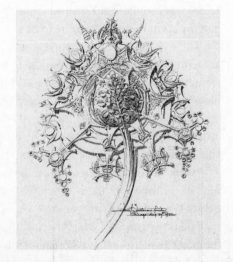

One of Sullivan's exuberant floral
sketches, from his last book

ativity emanated from the feminine forces, a "seed-germ," within himself. Identifying that creativity with the procreation of plant life, he filled his last book with fantastic flowers—not delicate blooms, but thrusting, aggressive, orgasmic structures that seemed to explode on the page, taking efflorescence to its limit. Wright's mentor viewed the vines and flowers with which he covered his building's surfaces—the ornamentation work for which he had first recruited young Wright—as feminine forces latent within his masculine self. In his design explorations, Sullivan had derived the feminine flower from the masculine, rational square, the shape that Wright later made his own emblem. For Wright, who grappled all his life with issues of masculinity, this architectural sexual ambiguity was a source of deep discomfort. He understood Sullivan's artistic creativity as a means of "erotic expression." From the start of his career, he worked to overlay masculine geometries onto the efflorescent floral patterns he understood as expressions of Sullivan's love. And he spent the rest of his life finding ways to incorporate plant forms directly into the most masculine aspect of a building—its structural support. Where Sullivan had used floral imagery for delicate decoration, Wright's imagination led him to images like the lily pad columns at Johnson Wax, delicate forms employed to carry crushing weight. For anyone attuned to his mindset, the implication was unmistakable. A man, like a building, could be powerful even when drawing on the feminine within.

Wright also recognized that pursuing the feminine ideal too far could be career suicide. Sullivan had fallen into oblivion when his work grew too ornamental. Wright was determined not to follow him along that path. "It is better to die of Ornaphobia by the wayside," he wrote, with his *lieber meister* surely in mind, "than it is to build any more 'ornamental' buildings, as such, and die any more ignoble deaths of 'Ornamentia.'" He understood that he had to guard against the erotic dangers in organic architecture, in himself, and in his own Fellowship.

DESPITE HIS WIFE'S protests, Wright declined to eject Jack Howe. He depended too much on Jack, who had been responsible for drawing his most celebrated buildings, including Fallingwater and Johnson Wax. That dependency had been painfully obvious during Jack's incarceration; Wright's act of loyalty could only have further bonded the architect and his chief draftsman.

In fact, Jack hadn't been accused of doing anything he hadn't been doing for years, and that most everybody apparently tolerated. Only the complaint was new. And perhaps that was why Jack Howe's trial eventually turned from the accused to the woman Wright saw as the chief accuser. "You are trying to destroy my Fellowship," Wright told a stunned Lois Davidson. The words would be seared so deeply in her memory that years later she could recall little else about that day. Within months she would leave the Fellowship, though she claimed it had nothing to do with Wright's accusation. Davidson says she could no longer suffer Olgivanna, who accused her—among other things—of trying to poison the Fellowship one Easter weekend by using a lead pencil to trace a mold for a loaf of Pasch bread.

Don Erickson was also spared from expulsion. But those who had revealed Taliesin's public secret were shamed, and those who had complained about Mrs. Wright's apparent prejudice were summarily ejected.

The senior apprentices were horrified by the Wrights' sexual show trial. A number of the new recruits dropped out in horror. Even those closest to the Wrights were disgusted. Kay Davison, Olgivanna's aide-de-camp, had stomped out of the room in anger. Gene Masselink felt that Don Erickson should have been thrown out. Wright's grandson Eric called it "just the worst thing in the world."

For Olgivanna, though, the whole spectacle was pure Gurdjieff: humiliation as a technique of personal growth. Abusers "should be shamed and made to feel embarrassed for their conduct," she would write, "so that their conscience may remain alive."

Howe's abasement did not end with his trial. Afterward he was ordered, probably by Olgivanna, to meet with each member of the Fellowship and apologize. He dutifully carried out the sentence, wearing dark glasses. He was not a homosexual, he told Don Erickson; he was bisexual. Erickson accepted the apology, and stopped avoiding him.

The Wrights, too, made it clear that in their magnanimity they had forgiven him. Mrs. Wright even resolved to try to reform him. It was time for Jack Howe to start looking for a wife.

JUST WEEKS LATER, in early April, Frank Lloyd Wright would tell the world where he stood on homosexuality. The forum was the Western Round Table on Modern Art, a three-day panel discussion in San Francisco. "Ok," Wright had replied to the invitation, "you asked for it."

Wright was joined at the table by a host of modernist luminaries: artists Marcel Duchamp and Mark Tobey, composers Darius Milhaud and Arnold Schoenberg, along with Gregory Bateson, the anthropologist and husband of Margaret Mead. In a private session before the forum began, Duchamp—an art provocateur who occasionally assumed the persona (and wardrobe) of an upper-class woman, Rose Sélavy—was asked by Wright about the relation between homosexuality and modern art. "I think I'll bring it up at the opening meeting tonight," Wright had told him. If he did, Duchamp replied, he would "make a great hit."

Duchamp had misread the architect's intentions.

To a standing-room-only audience, Wright set the tone for the public session that evening by insulting Duchamp's nearly forty-year-old landmark painting *Nude Descending a Staircase*, which was on display in the hall that night. The painting, he charged, was "degenerate." For that matter, so was all modern art.

"We heard that term not so many years ago," Milhaud interjected incredulously, "from another artist called Adolf Hitler."

Wright tried to clarify what he meant by degeneracy, but in doing so he began to sound even more like a Nazi aesthetician. "We instinctively hark back to the primitive," he replied. "We find it in Negro sculpture, we find it in these things Picasso presents to us, which could hang on the wall of any of the primitive African performances." He went on to describe Picasso as "in absolute collapse, spiritually speaking," by reducing himself to imitating primitive forms. "I regard him," he concluded, "as a clown and a slanderer."

Wright was not speaking from ignorance; after all, he had held his own in his interminable discussions on modern painting with Hilla Rebay. His problem was not with the entire genre, only with those artists who seemed to him to have returned to the origin of species—to the Dark Continent, to the world the white man had left behind.

Wright was slowly coming around to his main point, to the issue that had obviously lingered on his mind since the Howe trial. Wright asked Duchamp if he thought that homosexuality—he called it "intersexuality"—was degenerate.

"No, it is not," Duchamp replied. "It's very essential. The Greeks had it."

Wright pushed on. "You would say that this movement which we call modern art and painting has been greatly in debt to homosexualism?"

"I admit it," the artist replied. "The homosexual world has more . . . interest or more curiosity, are more interested in a new movement like modern art. . . . Maybe it's a physiological difference."

"But no man," Wright countered, "in his confusion, in his inability to conduct his life and himself on a plane of more or less of manhood as we understand it—maybe it's a mistake—feels the need of this refreshment, and goes to the darkie, goes to the primitive, wherever he can find it, and feeling strengthened by it and begins to copy it, begins to imitate it . . . this thing that belonged like a property of childhood to the early days of the race. . . ."

Duchamp was speechless.

Homosexuality, in Wright's view, was a forbidden and dangerous refreshment, a degenerative snack that could be fatal to one's manhood. And modern art, at least Picasso's and Duchamp's branch of it, was a regression to primitive forms—of same-sex desire and childlike bodily abstraction. Real

modernism—*his* modernism, otherwise known as organic architecture—
was an aesthetic for real men.

FRANK LLOYD WRIGHT cast himself as an image of American manhood—
as a man who fought his way from nothing to become America's master
builder, a tough man who said and did what he wanted and fought with his
fists and his tongue to defend his position. Wright was an architect who
wielded the saws and chisels, the graders and cement mixers, himself. He
was also a notorious womanizer. Women hung on his dry wit, his mannered
jocularity; they repeatedly made passes at this small gray-haired man in elevator shoes, who always seemed far larger and more robust than he actually
was.

And yet how to reconcile this willfully manly posture with Wright the
aesthete, the one who loved flowers so much that he made them his emblem
and took exquisite pains with their arrangement, the man who designed his
wife's clothing, the dandy who affected a wardrobe so fussy and prettified
that he recalled Oscar Wilde, that most public of homosexuals? Wright loved
women, and they him. But he also admired, and wanted others to admire, his
own beauty. When apprentice Bob Bishop encountered Wright dressed up in
a new set of tailored formal wear, he described him as "strutting around—
like a little girl in a Shirley Temple dress."

Wright was not a homosexual. But there was reason enough for anyone
acquainted with his persona to wonder about his orientation. Every apprentice knew from his autobiography that his mother had worried that he was
listing in that direction. And for some reason, around the time of Howe's
trial, Wright had felt compelled to tell his apprentices that he had never
encountered homosexuality during his early years. But the apprentices, or
anyone who had read Wright's autobiography, could easily have thought
otherwise—especially those who paid attention to the story of his friendship
with Cecil Corwin.

During Wright's early years in Chicago, before he met Louis Sullivan,
Frank and Cecil had begun a relationship that Wright himself described in
romantic terms. When *An Autobiography* was first published, Corwin—who
had since married and built a career in "the decorative field"—wrote Wright
to compliment him. Wright's reply, written during the second month of the
Fellowship, would have done little to squelch speculation.

"It is not so long since we were Damon and Pythias," he wrote Corwin,
"and those old days were romance. . . . I haven't changed much since 'our
time', haven't learned very much—battered up somewhat but as young as
ever where foolishness is concerned." Damon and Pythias were Greek lovers,

young men whose mutual love was so great that when one was condemned to death the other risked his own life to serve as a bondsman so that he could leave to get his affairs in order.

Love between men, an eroticized friendship that need not entail physical sex, was a late nineteenth-century ideal among a certain caste of aesthetic and political radicals of Europe and America, of which Wright was one. That love was not incidental to their vision, nor was it effeminate. Ever since Walt Whitman published his first edition of *Leaves of Grass* in 1860, with its "Calamus" poems celebrating his own homosexuality, these men had embraced his vision of a love among men that involved a muscular valor, the highest form of solidarity. And Whitman's vision informed both Charles Ashbee's Guild and Wright's Fellowship. "Old Walt," Wright wrote in the very year he founded the Fellowship, "is much more with me now." Like Sullivan, Wright revered the poet. "I became one of Walt Whitman's lovers," he wrote.

At the San Francisco event, Wright could have used the then-fashionable language of disease to describe homosexuality. Instead, he labeled it a form of degeneracy. For Wright the problem lay not in the nature of the desire, but in its physical expression—a behavior that represented a weakness of character, a backsliding toward the primitive. Nonetheless, he understood, even sympathized with, the sexual liabilities of the artistic temperament. For an artist, he once told the sister of harpsichordist Ralph Kirkpatrick, "it is so easy to become a dear boy . . . Don't worry about brother." It wasn't that homosexual desires were an aberration; it was that real men had the ability to resist them.

Whether or not Wright had to fight to sustain his own heterosexuality, there is no evidence whatsoever that Wright was lying when he told the apprentices that he had never had a gay relationship. But he was undeniably drawn to gay men, and felt comfortable with them.

He even attempted to recruit known homosexuals to the Fellowship. Though he publicly called Bruce Goff one of the "pansies," the very effeminate architect claimed that Wright repeatedly "tried with all his might" to get him to come to Taliesin. But Goff, an unschooled design prodigy who created eccentric and fantastic houses embedded with dime-store ashtrays and turkey feathers, always resisted. Wright quipped to the Oklahoman that the difference between their architecture was that his was organic and Goff's was "orgasmic." But he saw, too, that they had much in common. Once, in an evident reference to the younger man's homosexuality, he mused to Goff, "There but for the grace of God go I."

Wright was aware of his own effeminate tendencies. So was Olgivanna. When she became his wife, she convinced him to cut his hair shorter and to stop wearing the flowing artist ties he favored. He would later come to regret a frontispiece photo the publishers used on one of his books because his long hair made him look effeminate. Spying the book, he would take it down from friends' shelves and black out the long hairline with a pencil.

His heterosexual strut never ended. On Saturday nights he made sure there were good-looking women on hand to serve cocktails, and then positioned them around the dinner table to give himself the best possible view of them. On movie nights, he made loud bawdy comments—about Sophia Loren's ample breasts, for example. "Frahnk, Frahnk, please," Olgivanna hissed in her Montenegrin accent. The apprentices laughed.

"Sex," Olgivanna once told apprentice John Geiger, was "no more than blowing your nose." She had learned from Gurdjieff that sexuality was important only because a person's sex "center," one of seven such "centers," was the source of most thought. This explained why his techniques were so sexually oriented. Men without proper consciousness would lose their sexual energy to other centers, particularly the emotional one. Given what she obviously considered the infantile state of her husband's emotions, she must have thought this a serious problem. Only if one's sex center got a certain form of hydrogen, the theory went, could it play its proper role and feed the development of the higher intellectual and emotional centers.

Whatever else she actually did to help her husband satisfy his hydrogen needs, Olgivanna dedicated a fair amount of carbon and oxygen to her husband's sex life—even making sure his virile reputation outlasted his life and hers. In extracts from her memoirs published by Taliesin after her death, she relayed how Frank made up his own erotic stories and drew hundreds of pornographic scenes, some featuring trees like human bodies—drawings she subsequently burned. When he was aroused, she claimed, he could not be deterred. She also claimed that he made passionate love to her twice and even three times a day when he was in his eighties, continuing until the very week he died at nearly ninety-two.

Olgivanna didn't confine these revelations to her private writings. She delighted in bringing up her husband's virility out of the blue, even with the apprentices. One morning around the time of the Howe trial, Jim de Long was serving breakfast to her when she suddenly told him that her husband's sexual stamina rivaled that of the legendary Indian yogis. Sometimes, she complained, the eighty-year-old's sexual demands were beyond her. Fearing that something was wrong with him, she even consulted a physician.

No one knows what the doctor may have said, but Olgivanna did have at least one theory of her own, one that she had shared with Iovanna: "Geniuses are oversexed."

The genius-virility connection would have certainly appealed to Frank, who flaunted both qualities in himself—even at age ninety, when some apprentices recall him bragging, as one put it, that he "fucked his wife every night." A few years earlier, in conversation with *House Beautiful* editor Elizabeth Gordon—who was purportedly in love with him—he had tempered his boasting, at least somewhat. "I can do everything I ever did, better than I ever did it before," he told her when he was in his eighties, "but I can't do it so long or so often."

If even half of the claims of Wright's profligate sexuality are true, one thing is clear: When it came to sexual activity, he did not practice what he preached to the apprentices. A few years before the Howe trial, suspicious that his married apprentices' sexual activities were draining their spirits, he assembled Taliesin's husbands together, lecturing them that even sleeping next to a woman's body would drain the energy from a man's body and erode his capacity for creative work. Of course his theory flew in the face of Olgivanna's beliefs about the benefits of orgasm, but no matter: That very night some of them returned to their rooms and literally sawed their matrimonial beds in half.

WRIGHT'S HETEROSEXUAL BOASTING went hand in hand with a pattern of homophobic banter, as if even late in life he felt the need to prove something. Two years after the Round Table, for instance, he dropped by the Manhattan editorial offices of the *Architectural Forum*, where he liked to hang around and wait to be invited out to lunch. While there he ran into Peter Blake, later the architectural curator at MoMA, who enthusiastically showed him photos of a glass dome designed by two former Taliesin apprentices.

"Look at what we just got out of a house two of your 'boys' built in the desert," Blake told him.

"Oh, yeah," Wright replied, glancing at the photos, "it's by those two faggots, Soleri and Mills. I had to kick them out." Reaching for a reason to condemn their disloyalty, Wright fell into his old habit of charging his enemies with homosexuality. Blake was taken aback by the spew of obscenities that followed from Wright's lips.

It was all a lie. In fact, Paolo Soleri, who went on to found his own apprentice community in the Arizona desert, was reputed to be a lothario with women. When Wright kicked Soleri and Mark Mills out of the Fellowship, six months before the Howe trial, it had nothing to do with homosexuality: Wright accused them of using Olgivanna's brother Vlado's car without permission, and of working nearly naked one summer while maintaining Taliesin West after the others had left for Wisconsin.

TO THE OUTSIDE world, then, Wright was on the record as a gay-baiter. For the most part, though, his Fellowship would remain a safe haven for ho-

Halloween at Taliesin, 1940. Apprentice Jim Charlton is standing, in harem costume.

mosexual men who were willing to remain discreet. "You couldn't swish, no flaming, no wearing dresses," one resident recalled.

Olgivanna may have had no shame about openly managing gay life at the Fellowship, but more than one apprentice believed that Wright was naive and prudish, not just about gays at Taliesin, but about homosexuality itself. "You always have to realize," Lois Davidson recalled, "that he was a man left over from the Victorian era. His values and everything were [of the] Victorian age, even though he was architecturally and artistically thinking way ahead." She felt sure that it was through the Howe trial that he first discovered the gay subculture under his nose.

Davidson was wrong. In fact, Wright had always had a ribald familiarity with—even a grudging acceptance of—Taliesin's homosexual world. Photographer Edmund Teske, an openly gay apprentice whom Wright had recruited in 1936, had first been attracted to Wright because of his open expression of youthful homoeroticism in his autobiography, and throughout his time at Taliesin he never found anything homophobic about him. The Fellowship loved a costume party, and Halloween was inevitably a time for cross-dressing. One year, Teske attended Taliesin's Halloween ball with his lover, an apprentice dressed in a cream-colored gown of Spanish lace. "He made a more beautiful woman than he did a man," Teske remembered. The two men were dancing in the Taliesin living room when Wright tapped Teske's shoulder. "I stepped aside and turned the Spanish prima donna over to him, and he danced with her."

A few years later, when the lithe, nineteen-year-old Jim Charlton arrived at Spring Green, he was already an active gay man. "Here's a playmate for you, Jack," Wright told Howe archly. Though Wright counseled apprentices that homosexuality was "inorganic," Charlton never took his comments seriously. Even Wright's tirades against smoking seemed more heartfelt. A man whose sexual partners would later include Christopher Isherwood and Tennessee Williams, Charlton had four lovers during his three-year apprenticeship with Wright, once even taking advantage of the Wrights' departure from Taliesin West to make love in their bed.

Most of the apprentices were more cautious. Gene Masselink, Wright's personal secretary, was a very model of decorum. Gene was attracted to both women and men, as his crush on Svetlana demonstrated, but Olgivanna concluded that at heart he was homosexual. Though Mrs. Wright tried repeatedly to marry him off, Masselink's only serious documented romantic relationship was with Johnny Hill. "Your letters are a delight," Hill wrote him from the field. "I watch the mailbox which palpitated visibly when there is word from camp." Hill, of course, was also part of the Wrights' inner circle of gay men. "Adonis," Olgivanna called him.

When Richard Carney, a gay World War II veteran, arrived at Taliesin in 1948, Wright immediately enlisted him to arrange his room, keep his clothes, and drive him to his appointments. He later became Masselink's assistant and would eventually succeed him as secretary. As the years went by, homosexual men came to assume nearly every critical responsibility at Taliesin.

IF WRIGHT SERVED as a father figure for the gay men who came to work with him, Olgivanna could be a doting mother. She pressed many of the gay apprentices into marriages, almost all of which failed miserably. The one notable exception was Jack Howe, an avowed bisexual who understood what she expected and was not displeased by the idea. Soon after his trial, he began dating women in earnest. One of them was Lu Sparks, a stylish girl of modest means from rural Missouri. They had actually met two years before at a private girls' school dance in Scottsdale, after the school asked Taliesin to send down some men for the dance. Howe and Sparks dated until Lu moved away. After Jack's trial, Lu moved back to work as the school secretary; the two soon fell in love.

When Jack first brought Lu to Taliesin, she remembers, she was "sort of speechless." When he asked her to be his bride, he made it clear that he wanted Taliesin to be their home. Lu was in awe of the place; she felt culturally unprepared for the artistic universe its denizens seemed to maneuver with ease. Mrs. Wright had struck Lu as a beautiful woman. Up close and personal, however, Olgivanna was not so pretty. Her "demeaning" interview with the bride-to-be nearly scotched the romance. Lu was so put off that she cut off relations with Jack for a time. When Jack and Lu finally did marry, Mrs. Wright put her to work as a secretary. Their marriage lasted until Jack's death in 1997. He kept his homosexual past—an adaptation to circumstances, he would tearfully claim to a fellow ex-apprentice—from his wife. Although Howe had a number of gay friends, there is no evidence that he had any homosexual activity during his marriage.

THERE WERE MANY reasons gay men were so central at Wright's Taliesin Fellowship. They made loyal sons. They didn't marry. They found mates within. They had no children. In a place where leaving was traitorous, and most apprentices lasted no more than a year, their devotion was prized.

For another, they posed no sexual threat to their master. While no apprentice has come forward claiming an actual sexual relationship with Olgivanna, it was not for lack of interest among the straight men, particularly in the early years. She could be very seductive. "Mrs. Wright had sex appeal," remembered Gene Masselink's brother, Ben. She "had every guy hung up on her. She looked rather like Dorothy Lamour, black hair and red lips." Once, when Jim de Long was called to Olgivanna's room, he found her sitting with her back to the door, combing her hair. She stood and turned, allowing her robe to fall open, revealing her naked body. "We all wanted to fuck her," Masselink recalled.

In this light, it may be clear why gay men were preferred at Taliesin's core—in the same way that homosexual men have traditionally gained entry to women's intimacies as hairdressers and interior decorators. If Wright's relatively youthful wife was going to be hanging around a lot of young, attractive men, her "cosmically jealous" husband would have given her ample reason to make sure they were gay.

IN THE SAME year as Howe's public outing, a slender, sensitive young gay man named Bruce Pfeiffer came to Taliesin as a new apprentice. Pfeiffer's wealthy father, who allegedly contributed handsomely to Taliesin, hoped the Wrights would transform him. Olgivanna became Bruce's protector and confessor, trying to muscle him up by sending him out to mix concrete with the boys.

It didn't work. Not long afterward, twenty-year-old Louis Wiehle arrived at Taliesin. Olgivanna saw something in the new apprentice that he didn't expect. "She was the first person who told me I was gay," he recalled. Wiehle became Bruce Pfeiffer's first lover at Taliesin—and one of many in the years to come.

When Wright discovered that Pfeiffer was gay, he goaded him: "Bruce, why don't you cut your dinky dick off?" Homosexuality was something he felt compelled to resist when confronted with it directly. Even Olgivanna never found a way to make him comfortable with the subject. *Just look at Michelangelo*, she chided him, *or Da Vinci. Look at your own beloved Walt Whitman.* "All right, Mother," he replied compliantly.

With the Howe affair, however, open homosexuality had become a serious liability at Taliesin. Olgivanna tried "a little bit of conversion" on Louis Wiehle, setting him up with a female mate. When he refused to marry her, he was asked to leave the Fellowship—with the understanding that he would be allowed back if he could bring himself to stop having sex with men. He spent the next two years away from Taliesin living a celibate life, and then asked Olgivanna for reinstatement, reporting honestly that he'd had no homosexual relationships. His wish was granted: Welcomed back to Taliesin, Wiehle would spend the next fourteen years there as a very discreet gay apprentice. He had learned to work the system to perfection.

A NEW CALF AT TALIESIN

TOILING AWAY IN PARIS, HOMESICK for Taliesin, Iovanna wanted desperately to measure up to her mother's expectations. She still labored under the illusion that her mother had been Gurdjieff's perfect acolyte; if Olgivanna had shared the truth of her own struggle to please him in the early years, it might have reassured her. Iovanna did have reason to be hopeful: Madame de Salzmann, who had taken Iovanna under her wing in Paris, reported back to Olgivanna that her daughter was making "astonishing progress" in the movements. Gurdjieff was impressed. "It seems to me," de Salzmann wrote Olgivanna, "that I see you."

Even for the hyper-serious Iovanna, life with Gurdjieff had its pleasures. Gurdjieff enjoyed driving a caravan of his good-looking "calves" into the French countryside for a relaxing afternoon. On occasion, Iovanna was even invited to ride with the master in the lead vehicle, his fifteen-horsepower black Citroën. Along the way they would stop to picnic, dining on cucumber salad, pâté, roast chickens, herring, wine for the adults, and lemonade for the children. Gurdjieff often brought a windup gramophone to provide music while they ate.

But Iovanna had a habit of going off by herself to meditate on nature under a tree, leaving Gurdjieff to scurry about trying to find her when it was time to leave. She was like a dog running from one piece of greenery to another, he chided, raising its leg to pee. No, he snarled, she was worse—like a dog with a red pepper up its behind.

Now and then the caravan would stop at a cathedral, usually Gothic, and Iovanna and the others would leave Gurdjieff in the car while they went to look around. When they returned to describe what they had seen and felt, he would explain the building's deeper, esoteric meanings. Here, at least, Iovanna was on familiar ground: Gurdjieff and her father shared a reverence for Gothic cathedrals. Some years before, when one of his followers was pregnant with his child, Gurdjieff even instructed her to travel to Rouen so to give birth in sight of its great cathedral.

In the late spring of 1949, Iovanna joined what would be Gurdjieff's last caravan, a long haul to the Paleolithic caves at Lascaux. Though his legs were now swelling, he made his way down the steep passage to see the beautifully rendered, polychromatic wall paintings, with their elaborately antlered stags, Chinese horses, ibexes, black bulls, even a unicorn. He pointed to an unusual composite animal—an emblem of an esoteric society that allowed its members to recognize one another, he claimed, much like the enneagram.

When the group emerged from the darkness, Gurdjieff bought pictures for everybody. For Iovanna, he purchased a special album to be given to her father. "Tell him that such place exist," he told her, and that the first sacred representations were of nature, not of man.

Gurdjieff saw Iovanna as an emissary to the organic architect. He was clearly trying to understand her father, and was pleased to learn that Wright was returning the favor, reading *Beelzebub's Tales*. After so many years of rejected overtures, perhaps the moment had come for Wright to incorporate "the work" into Taliesin. A cryptic sentence in a letter from Madame de Salzmann to Olgivanna suggested that at least something was up. Reporting on Iovanna's extraordinary new command of the movements, de Salzmann had asked Olgivanna to tell Frank that his daughter "is improving in such a way that she really will help him well when she comes back."

IN MARCH, AFTER nearly a lifetime poking his finger into the eye of the organization, Wright received the American Institute of Architects' Gold Medal, its highest honor. The award is given not for a building, but for lifetime achievement; after Wright's extraordinary fifty-year career, it was overdue. But the award had been a controversial decision; some in the old guard were still outraged by Wright's moral transgressions, though they were ultimately outvoted by a new generation of AIA leaders.

When Wright appeared at the presentation dinner in Houston to accept, he received an enormous ovation. And when he began speaking, the architects got a dose of vintage Wright. Warning them that he had come prepared to "look you in the face and insult you," he lambasted the AIA members for the state of American cities—in which, he told them, nothing of value had been built.

A few members actually walked out during the presentation of the medal. Still, even his worst detractors would have been hard-pressed to deny the master his due. Over the course of his career, Wright had re-envisioned architecture, especially the single family dwelling. His open-plan prairie houses had inspired architects both at home and in Europe; his Usonians were already influencing the character of American mass housing. And the AIA itself would later name Fallingwater the greatest building of the twentieth century.

Wright had a special box made for the medal, and kept it in his bedroom.

IN SEPTEMBER 1949, Iovanna returned home and proudly informed her mother that Gurdjieff had instructed her to start a movements group at Taliesin. No more than twenty-four students, he had insisted.

The anxiety Iovanna saw in her mother's face reflected not displeasure at the news—which she both expected and relished—but fear about her husband's reaction. Olgivanna had been on this cusp before, more than once. And each time, after being tempted, Frank had backed away. He was simply unwilling to share the attention at Taliesin.

Gurdjieff in Paris, 1949

Right now, Olgivanna warned her daughter, he required extraordinary love.

THE GUGGENHEIM PROJECT had been in the studio for six years. Construction had yet to begin. Now there were rumors that Solomon intended to pull the plug. As Iovanna was nearing the end of her stay in Paris, her father had written to Hilla Rebay desperate for word. "For years, I have waited and I am still waiting for knowledge from S.R.G. [Solomon R. Guggenheim] whether to proceed or not or if ever. . . . I am loath to spend more money making useless plans and details until I know what to expect and when to proceed to build." When Olgivanna worried aloud over the fate of the building, Solomon was affronted. "The House of Guggenheim never goes back on its word," he told her. "The museum will be built. You should pay no attention to what people say."

The issue for Guggenheim had always been the same—money. Dismayed by the projected building costs, he was still hoping for a recession to bring prices down. Yet instead they continued to rise, so much that even Guggenheim's new $2 million cap on building costs was soon cast in doubt.

Solomon Guggenheim was an old man when the project began; now he was a sick old man. And, to make matters worse for Wright, he and his client were still operating on the original contract, which called only for a preliminary design. If Guggenheim were to die, there was no legal guarantee that his heirs would continue the project—or even that Wright would remain the architect if they did.

In mid-October, at a dinner with Guggenheim, Wright promised that he would build the museum for the $2 million. But to do so he had to rethink its construction. Like Fallingwater, the museum had been designed for reinforced concrete. The formwork alone would take months to erect. But now he had a new cost-saving measure in mind: The construction time could be slashed by switching to prefabricated steel, the system that had allowed the Empire State Building to be completed in just one year. Steel structural components could be made in an efficient shop environment, lessening the risk of lost time from bad weather. Though Wright told Rebay he was "loath" to make more potentially useless plans, he ordered Wes Peters to revise the engineering completely.

THE APPRENTICES HAD already drawn and redrawn the museum many times. This time, the redesign put a real strain on the studio. The backlog of other projects was so large that Jack Howe was cranking out designs with no input from Wright whatsoever. "Occasionally one of these gets out," Howe joked, "without the benefit of clergy."

OLGIVANNA HAD TAKEN it on herself to bring her husband the "good news" about Gurdjieff's directive that Iovanna should start a group at Taliesin. That night, Iovanna heard the rage barking from her parents' room. "That old, vague nausea rolled in my gut again," she remembered. Yet the morning brought a surprise: Wright had given permission. Iovanna could teach a movements class in the evening—and in the drafting room no less. The feat was not accomplished, however, without some deception. Gurdjieff had given Iovanna one of his prized harmoniums, a musical instrument Wright had long admired. During their argument, Olgivanna had told Wright that the mystic had actually sent it as a gift for him. All puffed up, Wright announced to the Fellowship that he would be starting a series of readings from Gurdjieff's writings, each Thursday at teatime. And he did, although it lasted for only two Thursdays.

The day chosen to launch the Gurdjieff work at Taliesin was charged with meaning—September 27, 1949, which would have been Svetlana's thirty-second birthday. That evening, after pushing back the drafting tables, Iovanna stood on the low platform where by day her father kept the model for the Guggenheim Museum. "The movements you will learn," she proudly told the two dozen apprentices standing before her, "are what you might call documentary fragments of ancient ritual exercises, ones Mr. Gurdjieff memorized in his travels to the monasteries and schools of the East."

Olgivanna had struggled twenty-five years for this moment.

WHEN GURDJIEFF SAILED from Manhattan to Paris with Iovanna the previous year, he had assured his American followers that he would return. Now he began planning a November trip to America with two members of "The Rope," his Paris lesbian group. He wanted to mount a new series of public demonstrations in the United States, to help attract new followers and build a new base. One of the stops on his itinerary was Taliesin; Iovanna's activities there were big news. "We know all about the events you have organized," Gurdjieff's personal secretary, Olga de Hartmann, wrote Olgivanna shortly before the scheduled departure.

Iovanna was excited that Gurdjieff was coming to see the work center she and her mother had started. But it was not to be. On October 14, 1949, the master collapsed in front of his movements class and was taken to the American hospital at Neuilly, where he was diagnosed with cancer. Soon, followers were streaming in to visit the ailing magus. Every detail of his deteriorating condition spread through the community—the changing color of his skin, a fear of intestinal bleeding that turned out to be only hemorrhoids. Despite great suffering, though, Gurdjieff always looked at peace. At one point he asked a close follower to bend down so the others could not hear. "Very, very bad pain," he whispered. At the hospital, his beatific manner made the doctors and the nurses cry.

Two weeks later he was dead. "Bravo America," was the last thing he was heard to say.

OLGIVANNA CAME INTO Iovanna's room, a telegram crumpled in her hand. "Mr. Gurdjieff is dead," she said softly. They embraced, but just for a moment.

Iovanna heard a roar growing in her ears. "How could you?" Olgivanna raged.

Iovanna didn't understand.

"How could you have left him like that?" her mother continued, her body trembling. "You should have stayed with him, through all the hell that came later."

The two ultimately embraced again, sobbing. Iovanna left the room, sat down at the piano, and played a piece Gurdjieff had taught her, the Great Prayer of the Dervishes of Kadgar.

Mother and daughter scheduled a memorial at the Hillside Theater. As Frank, Iovanna, and the apprentices waited in their seats, apprentice John Geiger drove Olgivanna over. Geiger had never been fond of Mrs. Wright, but as they sat side by side in the car, he found himself suddenly struck by her presence. She "looked lovely," he recalled, "and for the first time in my life I saw her as a vulnerable, very gentle, loving person." "You are all my children," she told him, stroking his cheek.

Wright delivered the eulogy. "Real men who are real forces for an organic culture of the individual today are rare. I venture to say one might count them on the fingers of one hand with thumb to spare—unless the thumb were to go to Georgi Gurdjieff of the Prieuré . . . and spare the little finger." Gurdjieff, he continued, had not only written "nine fat volumes," but had also composed eight thousand unpublished pieces of music "of such quality that undoubtedly when he presents their publication he will be known as the author of a new school of 'objective' music . . . music so crystal clear and simply related to human feeling that all men will weep or smile or dance as the music itself does."

Recalling Gurdjieff's visits to Taliesin, Wright noted that the man "affected us strangely as though some oriental Buddha had come alive in our midst." He estimated that the mystic had left about forty thousand followers behind, as well as "104 sons of his own and 27 daughters for whose education he has made provision. . . ."

Wright even reached back to put his own spin on an image to which Gurdjieff had introduced him decades before. "Not caring at all for America or Americans," he told the mourners, Gurdjieff had come west, "as he frankly puts it, 'to shear sheep.' He will turn the wool into some kind of good work for humanity . . . American food he finds unfit to eat—likes only our tomato juice and our dollars. But eats enormously just the same. The style of our money he affirms. But the shearing I imagine is not so good. The wool is now so short. Notwithstanding the abundance of personal idiosyncrasy Georgi Gurdjieff seems to have the stuff in him of which our genuine prophets have been made."

GURDJIEFF'S FUNERAL WAS held on November 3, 1949, not far from the Prieuré. Followers came from around the world to be with their teacher as he was buried in a suit he had bought for his trip to America. "He looked as handsome as before," Olga de Hartmann wrote Olgivanna. "I got the feeling . . . he was even smiling." The Russian Orthodox priest's closing words were written by her husband, Thomas: "God and all his angels keep us from doing evil by helping us always and everywhere to remember ourselves."

Olga wrote Olgivanna that they were both now "alone without him in the physical meaning." Even before Gurdjieff died Olgivanna had tried convincing them to move to Taliesin to be with her. Having Gurdjieff's longtime confidantes there would certainly bolster the claim that Taliesin was a legitimate heir to the Prieuré. And Iovanna had grown close to the couple in Paris: Thomas had taught Iovanna harmony, and she even accompanied him on radio broadcasts. Frightened that another Communist revolution might soon erupt in Western Europe, and already concerned that Olgivanna was still practicing a mourner's austerities three years after Svetlana's death, the couple soon took up her offer.

SOLOMON GUGGENHEIM DIED the very same day as Gurdjieff. His will was silent on the matter of whether Wright should carry on as architect of the museum—an especially precarious omission, since Wright's relationship with Hilla Rebay was more strained than ever. They were still fighting over how to display the paintings, but that was the least of it: Though Guggenheim had approved Wright's design, Rebay had recently suggested that it be fundamentally reworked. Wright again accused her of taking a painterly view of architecture. "So may I suggest," he wrote her, "you just sit down and make a painting of the building you want and we will see if S.R.G. wants it constructed." Before he died Solomon had rejected Rebay's proposed changes, before she'd had a chance to commit them to canvas.

With the patron's death, though, it wasn't clear that the two were arguing over anything more than paper. Having heard that Wright's buildings almost always cost more than his projections, the Guggenheim trustees were wary about going forward with him. Wright responded with a frontal assault, notifying the foundation's president that Guggenheim had trusted and employed him, and that he did not consider himself to be working for the trustees. "No carping, doubting building-committee is going to hamper the effort." The outburst could only have discomfited the trustees even more, but any final decision on the architect would have to wait for the estate to be settled. That, as it turned out, would take months.

WRIGHT PLANNED TO put Wes Peters in charge of the museum's construction. In an unprecedented gesture, he had even offered Wes money for the effort—an annual salary of five thousand dollars. What appeared as an uncharacteristically generous gesture represented only a fraction of what Wes felt he was due for his past investments in Taliesin. Having exhausted his inheritance bailing out Wright's property, footing the bills for farm machinery and other equipment for Taliesin, and buying his own land, Peters now needed the money.

Wright knew Peters was in trouble. But he wasn't above subjecting his son-in-law to the same techniques he used to keep creditors at bay. When Wes started bandying about various dollar amounts he believed he was owed, Wright asked him for a reckoning. Wes calculated that he was owed $65,000—the sum he claimed he had personally invested in Taliesin.

In response, Wes got a nasty dose of classic Frank Lloyd Wright. "I want to look that extraordinary ghost-horse in the mouth to see what I was doing meantime," Wright began his long, detailed, but loosely reasoned letter challenging the figure. Wright did acknowledge that Wes had saved Taliesin, but he reminded Wes of what he had given in return. "While overcoming a practical bankruptcy, I turned over a 650 acre farm to you—kept you alongside me as a promising young engineer to train you in my work—while I maintained your growing family alongside my own—sharing all I had with you and yours."

He also conceded that Peters had bought machinery, hired laborers to work, and purchased materials to restore the barns at Taliesin, to the tune of eight thousand dollars. Everything else—including, presumably, covering Taliesin's mortgage—was both unauthorized and unwanted. "Your generosity outside that sum," he wrote Wes, outrageously, "was as uncalled for as it was embarrassing, fantastic and unfair."

Wright then cataloged the monies he believed Wes owed him. Since Wes had operated Taliesin's farm as part of his own, Wright now claimed he should have paid rent for the privilege. Moreover, for the seven years Peters and his wife had lived at Taliesin itself, Wright had provided him exquisite food, beautiful shelter, and a cultural life without parallel. This too had monetary value. "You owed me your Fellowships," he wrote. Wes had received valuable architectural and engineering training without tuition—ignoring the fact that in return Peters had given him fourteen years of essentially uncompensated architecture and engineering work. After adding it all up, Wright offered a reckoning of his own: Peters owed him $131,000.

In his tirade, Wright channeled his frustration at the failure of his dream of "collateral farms"—his plan to use apprentice money to buy up the valley for Broadacre City. "Every time I've counted on you to help me in my scheme for the Foundation," he told Wes, "I've found you involved in your own private property affairs." Of course, this wasn't Wes's fault: With the exception of Gene Masselink's and Davy Davison's farms, the other apprentices' properties had since fallen into the hands of outsiders. But Wes's private schemes, and his farming failures, made things worse. "Every G-damn effort I've made here to expand the prestige and power of the Foundation in this valley has gone haywire," Wright had earlier complained to Peters.

For Wes Peters, the letter was a crushing blow. This most valuable apprentice, a man who had more than once saved Taliesin from foreclosure, who had made invaluable engineering contributions to Fallingwater and Johnson Wax, had been declared a traitor to the cause. According to Peters's son, the rift between the two would never quite be repaired.

A LITTLE MORE than a month after Gurdjieff's death, Madame de Salzmann arrived from Paris to start rebuilding the American network. In his last days, the master had entrusted her to build a "nucleus," with Olgivanna at its center. Indeed, Olgivanna was one of the only women to whom de Salzmann felt she could turn. "My dear dear Olga I wish to come to you," she had written right after his death. "I will come."

The future of Gurdjieff's "work" was on de Salzmann's shoulders. Her close friend Peter Brook, the British film director and a member of Jane Heap's English Gurdjieff group, described her dilemma. "All over the world there were groups of students left rudderless, in a state of confusion that seemed destined to splinter, distort, and degrade the material that they had been given."

Taliesin would be a priority for de Salzmann, who planned to bring one of the other "calves" with her to help Iovanna. "I am so happy you took your people in your hands again, your burden on your shoulders," Madame de Salzmann wrote Olgivanna. "I take you in my arms."

Olgivanna was elated. And even Wright himself seemed to be on board. After Gurdjieff's death, he had sent money to de Salzmann to help her establish a new foundation in Gurdjieff's flat, and to the de Hartmanns to help with their transcription and recording of the master's music. De Hartmann was finalizing the compositions for Gurdjieff's later movements, many of which the master had improvised in the years before his death. Wright even paid for de Hartmann's new grand piano, and supported his and his wife's passport applications to the United States by inviting them to Taliesin.

Jeanne de Salzmann arrived at Taliesin West in January 1950. With her was Lise Tracol, the nineteen-year-old "calf" assigned to help Iovanna. Iovanna's evening movements classes had attracted a fair amount of attention among the apprentices; even the lumbering Wes Peters had come that first day. Some found Gurdjieff's demanding exercises transformative and energizing, but others found them beyond their grasp, or even just plain silly. Still others found it just too irksome to submit to the authority of the Wrights' spoiled daughter—or suspected that the whole affair was Olgivanna's way of trying to wrest control of the Fellowship away from her husband.

Some of these more hostile apprentices let their feelings be known. When Madame de Salzmann arrived, she gathered all the senior apprentices to ask if they were interested in the Gurdjieff work. When one of them said no, Olgivanna let him know she was not amused. Another time, an angry apprentice drove up behind Olgivanna and de Salzmann on the dirt road back from Phoenix and gleefully sped past their Lincoln Continental, engulfing it in a cloud of dust.

Still, de Salzmann was enthralled by the Wrights and their world. "Tell your husband Taliesin makes impossible the return to life," she wrote Olgivanna after she left. "Olga we must work. G. I. has given us something sacred, a germ of being that we are responsible for and we cannot let perish. We owe him that, otherwise all his efforts will have been in vain." Determined to prevent any distortion of the canon of thirty-nine movements that Gurdjieff had developed before he died, she resolved to make Taliesin a center for their preservation and dissemination. Soon she was making plans to return to Taliesin with Thomas de Hartmann to work with Olgivanna.

Yet Frank's beneficence toward the Gurdjieffians didn't hold; at length he became vituperative about Olgivanna's project. His wife and daughter were getting just too much attention. He forbade his wife to do the movements with Iovanna because men were also doing them. Despondent, Olgivanna wrote de Salzmann for support. "I wish I could be near you and bring you the help of my affection," her friend replied. Life "is difficult, so difficult because it is empty without Him." The only way to bring Frank back to Gurdjieff, she counseled, was to work on herself.

In reality, the success of the Gurdjieff enterprise at Taliesin depended on Iovanna. As jealous as he was, Wright now saw before him an intensely dedicated and focused young woman, a vast improvement over the undisciplined girl she had been before leaving for Paris. With his daughter's equilibrium at stake, he could not bring himself to pull the plug.

THE GUGGENHEIM MODEL wasn't the only thing Iovanna pushed aside in her father's studio. Another was Roland Rebay, Hilla's son, one of the apprentices who'd sneaked in her window before her trip to Paris. Roland had been eager to pick up where he'd left off with Iovanna. "You have a sexuality I have never known," he pleaded. But he had lost his allure to Iovanna. To prove his love, Roland spent one night walking barefoot through the rocky hills until his feet bled—a stunt inspired by the story of Olgivanna's exhausting trek through the wilderness with Gurdjieff. But Iovanna was repulsed by the comparison with her mother's actions, which she considered a "true sign of devotion." The relationship was over.

BY THE TIME of the spring migration back to Wisconsin, many apprentices had become openly derisive of what they considered the woo-woo mysticism being foisted on them by the master's wife and daughter. Resentment within the core group grew steadily as apprentices were pulled away from the drafting room despite their crushing architectural workload.

If they expected support from Mr. Wright, however, they misjudged the man—and his wife. One Sunday in June 1950, Wright gave one of his regular weekly after-breakfast talks. Calling Gurdjieff's ideas "just another phase of organic architecture," he reminded them that the tenets of organic architecture required members of the Fellowship to "work upon ourselves[;] that's really what we're here for." Architecture was more than a science, he said; it was a "sense of what is beyond." And for that reason he was "very happy" to have at Taliesin this "grip of the mind on the body" that was "exemplified so beautifully by Gurdjieff, who now has passed away and is dead."

Wright chided those who mocked his daughter's classes. The apprentices who were trying hardest to get out of them, he said, were the ones who needed them most. Attending his daughter's movements class would help them obtain the self-knowledge necessary to become good architects. "That's what these exercises we're doing mean. That's why I'm for them. That's why I think they're a great benefit in the direction we're going." To understand the inner principles of a building, one had to understand oneself. The Gurdjieff philosophy, he declared unequivocally, "could do more for modern life and modern civilization than almost anything that could happen."

"Well," he concluded, "I've said all I have to say, how about you boys? Am I right about this thing? Have I spoken truly? Is what I have said in line with what you feel about where you are and why you're here[?] And if it is, well, play ball!"

No one said a word.

Olgivanna had clearly scored a victory. By now, though, she knew better than to gloat. If she were to sustain her extraordinary progress, she understood, her husband would have to see this as *his* Gurdjieff program. When she instituted her own lecture series, she scheduled it during her husband's naptime.

For Iovanna, too, this was a shining hour. After a lifetime as the lesser sister, she had revived a project her mother had dreamed of for decades—one that carried the personal imprimatur of both Georgi Ivanovich Gurdjieff and Frank Lloyd Wright. Flush with excitement, she proved an imperious and demanding taskmaster at her classes. As Frank and Olgivanna's sole heir, she also had reason to believe what her father had told Jack Howe, that the Fellowship would someday be hers.

"THIS IS OUR day of celebration," Wright told the apprentices after breakfast on October 29, 1950, the first anniversary of Gurdjieff's death. "We are celebrating the passing away of a great constructive philosopher, Asiatic in origin—Gurdjieff. Gurgivanich we who know him lovingly call him." Gurdjieff saw "that we were on the road along the line that he himself was endeavoring to blaze," Wright said, "and we had his complete confidence and sympathy." With that, Wright urged them to go out and fast for the day.

That evening, the apprentices and a host of locals gathered for a special presentation of the movements at Hillside. Also in attendance were Olga de Hartmann and her husband, Thomas, the composer of the accompanying music.

The evening was a triumph, a kind of coming-out party for Taliesin's new status as a center for the Gurdjieff program. By all accounts the audience was impressed, and Iovanna and Olgivanna were thrilled. By now they had won over a large group within the Fellowship; indeed, of the twenty-two new arrivals that year, five had come specifically for the Gurdjieff program. There seemed to be no limit to how far they could go.

Public Gurdjieff demonstrations at Taliesin became a staple each Easter. (In Gurdjieff's spiritual landscape, Christ was understood as the "completed enneagram.") In 1950, the audience at Taliesin West included birth-control advocate Margaret Sanger, Kamala Nehru, the wife of the prime minister of India (himself a student of Theosophy), and the renowned conductor Serge Koussevitzky.

Koussevitzky was effusive. "I've never seen anything like it," he declared. He called for the movements to be performed on a public stage, not just at Taliesin. When Wright countered that the demonstrations would be misunderstood in a more public context, Koussevitzky stood him down. "No, this work *will* be performed for the public. You have no right to keep this art from the people!"

This was not what Wright had imagined when he endorsed Iovanna's class a year before. He saw the movements as a technique to further the cause of organic architecture, not as an independent art form—and certainly not as an occasion to link Taliesin with Gurdjieff in the public eye. He could accept Gurdjieff's work as an inside discipline for apprentices, and perhaps as something to share with neighbors on an occasional basis. Making them into an official Taliesin production—that was taking things too far.

Encouraged by people like Koussevitsky, though, Iovanna and Olgivanna set their sights on the outside world. They started holding movement training two nights per week. To them, the Taliesin Fellowship was more than architecture; it was a way of life into which all the arts should be integrated. If they needed to make that case to Frank, they had only to cite the very first Fellowship prospectus, which he had penned himself. Architecture, music, dance, religion, it was to encompass them all.

THE INCREASING PREVALENCE of Gurdjieff's ideas at Taliesin, and the attention his wife was garnering, inevitably stirred Wright's jealousy. As a Unitarian, Wright would have seen Gurdjieff's as one of many paths toward the single truth; he was not, however, about to concede that the mystic's esoteric practices were, in any sense, "the" way. When Gurdjieff's book *All and Everything* appeared in 1950, mother and daughter urged all the apprentices to go out and buy a copy. Wright countered by buying an entire carton of his own American philosopher-sage Ralph Waldo Emerson's writings and giving them out to the apprentices for free.

In August 1951, speaking at the dedication of his First Unitarian Society Meeting House in Madison, Wright used the occasion to trumpet his own, uniquely American sources. Mindful that the Fellowship would soon be staging a Gurdjieffian demonstration in the same church, Wright told the congregation that Emerson, himself a former Unitarian minister, was the "strongest, purest, finest mind this country has ever produced and everybody should read him daily." Gurdjieff, by implication, was something less: a teacher who studied the secret wisdom of the past, not an artistic genius who created anew, who had the power—as Emerson described it—"to detect and watch that gleam of light which flashes across his mind from within." From now on, he announced to the congregation, Emerson would be "obligatory" reading at the Fellowship.

YET WRIGHT KEPT his hand in with the Gurdjieffians. In November, coordinated with other Gurdjieff groups in London, Paris, and New York, Taliesin's dancers marked the master's death at the Unitarian meeting house. In a column he wrote for the local newspaper Wright announced that the performance would be given by "my daughter and the Taliesin Fellowship." Making no mention of Olgivanna, Wright touted Gurdjieff the "philosopher," a "builder" of character, who had converted the ancient wisdom of the East into a "way of WORK." "That is why the training-methods of Georgevanitch [sic] fit so well into our work here at Taliesin."

When the day came, Wright stood before two hundred and fifty guests to introduce the performance, explaining Gurdjieff's movements—exercises that even he was doing privately at home. His grandson Eric delivered the opening rite of prayer. (Eric's father, Lloyd Wright, was outraged at Olgivanna for "thinking of Taliesin as a place to promote the Gurdjieff dances"— and for draining resources from his father's architecture in the process.)

The local reviews of this first outside display of Taliesin's Gurdjieff program were good. But even though he had blessed the event, they roused Wright's ire: "For the first time," Iovanna recalled, "father had something to be jealous of in our work on the movements. . . . Father never liked to share the limelight."

For Olgivanna, though, the only important result was the encouragement she received from within the movement. "The young people you 'created' around you are so great," Olga de Hartmann wrote Olgivanna. "[T]his is something very big you did. . . . It is very important your husband knows that, even when he sometimes snarls." Thomas de Hartmann sent his own words of support, words that confirmed the sense that Olgivanna was carrying out Gurdjieff's instructions. "Do whatever you want to do," he said, "but you have to complete your assignment."

Many big names in the movement now increased their support for Olgivanna's efforts at Taliesin. The de Hartmanns came for extended stays in the years that followed, lecturing to the apprentices and providing Olgivanna and Iovanna with music for their dances and movements. Countess Maria Andreevna, a child of the Tolstoy family and onetime mistress of Maxim Gorki, paid a long visit. So did Elizabeta Stjernvall, the physician's wife who had borne a child by Gurdjieff in Tiflis. "I think you amazingly managed to organize your life connecting your husband's work with Georgi Ivanovitch's ideological life," she wrote Olgivanna in 1954.

Gurdjieff's chosen successor, Jeanne de Salzmann, was also enthusiastic about lending her knowledge and prestige to ensure success at Taliesin. When she told the Wrights she planned to return, Frank and Olgivanna offered to pay her expenses and even a salary. At first she welcomed the invitation: "I wish to stay a long time," she wrote Olgivanna, "in order to spend as much as I wish near you." She was still struggling to codify and preserve Gurdjieff's music and movements, including "the 39," the last movements that he had completed just days before his death. Not as knowledgeable about the later movements as Iovanna, and lacking Olgivanna's experience with the early ones, she wanted their help notating the choreography. Eventually, however, she changed her mind about coming back. "I really am more and more sure," she wrote Olgivanna, "that in the near future we will be together, but we have first to work for a time each one alone until we feel the time has come to unite our efforts."

For now de Salzmann remained at her new home in London, summoning Iovanna to assist her in the filming of Gurdjieff's more abstract, mathematical movements "before they will be distorted all over the world." "I will take good care of her," de Salzmann wrote to Wright. "You know she will be like my daughter." She invited Olgivanna to come as well.

The Wrights had already scheduled a trip to Italy in the early summer of 1951; Olgivanna could have made London a quick stop on her way. Instead, she sent only Iovanna.

De Salzmann was hurt and disappointed.

Olgivanna, it appears, had grown wary of joining forces with her European colleague. After more than twenty-five years of maneuvering, she was finally realizing her dream of having her own center; she was in no hurry to subordinate herself to someone who actually outranked her. At the very least, Madame de Salzmann would expect to share control in America, and she might well get in the way. Olgivanna didn't want to be beholden to anybody.

IN JUNE, DURING their travels in northern Italy, Wright received the Italian state's Star of Solidarity at the Ducal palace in Venice; then he was awarded the Medici medal at the Florentine Palazzo Strozzi. The Medici medal apparently took Wright back to where it all started, with Hugo's *Notre-Dame de Paris* and the author's hope that another Dante might someday emerge to save architecture. "Dante wanted [the medal] and never got it," Wright told the press soon after receiving it. "Then they go ahead and give it to an American from the tall grass of the western prairies."

OLGIVANNA WAS CERTAIN that the Fellowship had enjoyed a past life. She had learned from Gurdjieff that history was a palimpsest; beneath the bloody rumble of warriors and potentates there was a hidden, fragile chain of esoteric schools, small groups nourishing their secret knowledge of the soul. There was no way that the Taliesin Fellowship could simply "have just started in Wisconsin one day," one longtime apprentice recalls her saying, "without having been a long term experience which started to gather momentum over the period of many lives."

Olgivanna was fond of showing the apprentices the film adaptation of Lerner and Lowe's musical *Brigadoon*, where two Americans, hunting grouse in the misty Scottish moors, chance upon the enchanted village of Brigadoon. Brigadoon is a place outside history that reappears every century for a day, experienced by its inhabitants as though it were a hundred years. Taliesin, she was convinced, was just such a parallel universe, a home for the spirits that had animated the greatest Gothic and—in her mind, if not Wright's—Renaissance builders. She told more than a few confidantes that the apprentices around her husband had been together before, during the Renaissance, when they built a cathedral in northern Italy. Though she knew her husband didn't much like the cathedral's architecture, she maintained that Wright had been its master-builder.

Olgivanna had long felt certain that her husband was the reincarnation of Michelangelo, whose earliest architectural masterpieces were in Florence, where Wright was getting the prize. She wasn't alone in sensing a kinship between the two men: "To his followers," *Time* had reported, "the old master is a modern Michelangelo whose sculptures can be lived in." The Italian master had been held up as an exemplar by no less than Louis Sullivan, who celebrated him as the "first mighty Craftsman . . . the man of super-power, the glorified man."

To Wright, however, Michelangelo's genius lay not in his architecture, but in his work as a painter. The problem was that he took a painterly approach to building. As he told the apprentices, "I never could see that the dome on stilts of Michelangelo was anything but a painter's theatrical effort to produce an effect." Just as Michelangelo had struggled with the structural design of St. Peter's dome at the end of his life, in his own final years Wright was striving to build a domed shrine in the Guggenheim. And his struggles with the Guggenheim family must have reminded him of Michelangelo's face-offs with the Medicis.

During their stay in Florence, Olgivanna experienced an uncanny, unsettling intimation of the immortality that had long been her obsession. While standing on the exact spot where the radical fifteenth-century Dominican priest Savonarola had been burned, she began gasping, overcome with a sudden feeling that she was suffocating. She was sure she was going to die. On hearing her tell the story later, at least one friend was convinced that Olgivanna had been Savonarola in a past life. Michelangelo had fallen under the influence of Savonarola, who briefly instituted a "dictatorship of God" in the city and convinced his Florentine followers to burn their Renaissance treasures in the "bonfires of the vanities"—including Botticelli, who threw his own nonreligious paintings into the flames.

BACK IN THE United States, Olgivanna continued to expand her Gurdjieff program. In 1952 she sought help from Dushka Howarth, one of Iovanna's fellow "calves" and the daughter of the woman chosen by Gurdjieff to promote the movements in America. Though her mother was wary of Olgivanna's tendencies toward experimentation and self-aggrandizement, she agreed to let Dushka go, certain that Olgivanna needed the help.

According to Dushka, though, Olgivanna had other plans for her. After two weeks at Taliesin, the young woman hadn't even observed a movements class, much less taught one. Rather, she had been assigned to letter the linoleum specifications for the Guggenheim museum. Her perch in the drafting room put her in proximity to Wes Peters, and Dushka was convinced that Olgivanna was hoping to arrange a marriage between them, one that would tie Taliesin to Gurdjieff's bloodline. But the pairing didn't take. After Dushka jibed that she wanted the roller skate concession at the top of the Guggenheim, Wright cold-shouldered her for the remainder of her stay.

No doubt encouraged by her mother, Iovanna now demanded her own space to perform the movements, threatening to leave Taliesin if her father didn't oblige. Wright called her bluff. "I lose the heaviest and (as I once thought) most important investment in this affair of life with my daughter—the care of life at Taliesin," he wrote her. "So, make up your mind what you want to do and I'll try my best to help—lose my own daughter."

When a trash fire got out of control in the spring of 1952, destroying the Hillside Theater, some gossiped that Iovanna had started it. The smoke had barely cleared before Wright was sketching a new Hillside in the air with his cane. In the new layout, Wright met his daughter's demand and included a larger stage, incorporating both the stairwell and the entrance foyer into the stage. As apprentice Curtis Besinger saw it, "at the insistence of St. Olga and her little priestess," Wright had seriously compromised his architecture.

On the new stage, Iovanna pushed her dancers—many of them inexperienced—to master Gurdjieff's movements, insisting on a rigor that went beyond what some of their bodies could bear. Those who faltered were subject to her rage.

David Dodge was one of the rare architecture apprentices who had come to Taliesin interested in dance. Soon after arriving in 1951, the grandson of the founder of Dodge Motors had crept along the upstairs balcony at the Hillside Theater, where he could watch unobserved as Wright's daughter conducted her class. He was transfixed by Iovanna's rendition of Gurdjieff's old "Stop!" technique, in which dancers were commanded to freeze in position. "They just have to freeze exactly there, and . . . some people fall on the floor because they're in the middle of a movement, and you know, it's crazy and a brutal thing to be doing." Dodge found Iovanna's discipline admirable. "She was skilled almost to the point of genius," he observed. "With considerable agony, she could make very first class dancers out of very un-first class material." Yet he found Iovanna's treatment of the dancers too cruel to bear. "The character of it was so bad I was not going to be part of the movements."

Dodge wasn't the only one concerned by Iovanna's behavior. "She looked so pale and her expression was so anxious," Jeanne de Salzmann wrote Olgivanna after a visit from Iovanna in New York. Her daughter had made "incredible progress," de Salzmann wrote, but she is "still a child and does not see how difficult the work on unity is. . . . She is not alone she must know."

For Iovanna the challenge was not "unity," but separation. Olgivanna was the real guru; Iovanna was expected to remain a subordinate technician, a dancer, an emissary. Her mother had had a similar struggle with Gurdjieff, though Iovanna didn't know that. The two began to jostle for control.

There was one place, however, where her powers were untrammeled—the bedroom. As she herself admits, "I was pairing off with the apprentices as never before." Some nights they would take her sequentially. Some male apprentices summoned to perform a minor task in her room feared that they would be pressed into her sexual service.

APPRENTICE JOHN GEIGER was serving breakfast in the cove at Taliesin West when he happened on the Wrights in battle. "You are not going to turn this into a Gurdjieff Institute," Wright hissed at his wife. "Not while I am alive."

"Frahnk," she pleaded. "Frahnk, be reasonable."

Frank had long since signed off on movements instruction at Taliesin, but it was becoming apparent that his wife wanted much more. She had begun forming outside Gurdjieff groups, first in Chicago, then in Ohio, Arizona, New York, and Pennsylvania. When Iovanna went to launch the Chicago group, she told her father she was going on a shopping trip. Olgivanna sent out such emissaries to organize and run the groups; when they could, the dispersed adepts would make weekend pilgrimages to the central shrine, Taliesin, where the guru herself would instruct, guide, and restore their energy.

When Wright discovered all this, he forbade the Chicagoans from coming to Taliesin. For a while, Olgivanna made do with a change of venue to her husband's famous Chicago masterpiece, the Robie House. She gave her students reading assignments—Ouspensky, Gurdjieff, some writings of her own—and tapped one member to read aloud and then lead a discussion. Sometimes Iovanna slipped out to instruct the groups, always insisting that her mother was the "real teacher," and she a mere "guide."

Wright eventually relented and allowed the Gurdjieff groups to return for retreats at Taliesin, where Olgivanna would lecture them while Iovanna conducted movements instruction. Almost all of them treated Olgivanna with awe; one even kissed her feet. She expected the wealthy ones to give her money in exchange for her ministrations.

Each Friday after work, members of the Chicago group would squeeze into cars and head for Taliesin. As they wound their way through the county roads, their singing and banter faded to silence as they approached Spring Green, usually well after midnight. A note tacked on the door told them where to sleep. While the weekenders focused their time on the Gurdjieff program, they were in many ways integrated into the regular Fellowship routine, performing maintenance functions, doing menial work in the studio, and joining the apprentices at formal Saturday dinners.

The groups were greeted with some resentment, particularly from apprentices who were told to vacate their rooms for them. Some apprentices were taken aback by the kind of people who sought help through Olgivanna. Many were friendless, depressed, or addicted. A number came directly from Alcoholics Anonymous. A few were profoundly debilitated. One weekend, when a particularly unstable woman became angry, Olgivanna hit her on the head with one of her husband's Chinese brass gongs. Almost fifty years later, the woman claimed that she had never fully recovered. (Olgivanna had once told an apprentice that Gurdjieff's "awakening" process made it necessary to "crack open a person's head to put something in it," though she couldn't have meant it this literally.)

More typically, Olgivanna tried to shock her students out of their complacency with words. "Oh, that mask," she exclaimed to one well-dressed and subtly made-up woman. "What can you see behind the mask?" The question was obviously intended metaphorically, but the woman evidently thought it a criticism of her makeup, and ran from the room devastated.

Olgivanna grew ever bolder; soon she was visiting her therapeutic interventions upon the apprentices, not just on outside adepts. Kay Davison would inform each apprentice that he or she was expected to appear for a session with Mrs. Wright, usually in either the family dining room or the old office at Hillside. In these encounters, which she concealed from her husband, Olgivanna would plumb their psyches for weaknesses and recommend correctives. In almost every instance the focus eventually came around to the apprentice's sex life, giving Olgivanna a chance to indulge her old matchmaking habits.

Between these counseling sessions, the movements classes, and her *sub rosa* lectures, Olgivanna was slowly but surely positioning herself as a power equal to her husband.

PERPETUALLY IN SEARCH of self-improvement strategies, Mary Stanton was ripe for Taliesin's new offerings. After the war, she had divorced her husband and moved with her two sons from San Diego to Arizona, where she joined an early Dianetics group and practiced L. Ron Hubbard's Scientology. It was at one of these meetings that she met Jack Stanton, her future husband. In 1952, Jack responded to an advertisement in the local newspaper announcing a meeting for a new Gurdjieff group. The next week he took Mary there on a date.

It was Olgivanna's Scottsdale group. During the Fellowship's winter migration, the members would spend weekends at Taliesin West. When they weren't washing windows, weeding the cactus garden, raking the gravel paths, or typing out architectural specifications, they would practice the movements on the concrete patio adjacent to Iovanna's cottage. The pavement "would be just burning," Mary Stanton remembered, the ground crawling with bugs. "It was an incredible experience," she recalled without irony. Iovanna choreographed elaborate costumed performances to be staged for the public. As they improved, the Scottsdale group was invited to join the apprentices as members of the troupe.

As with the apprentices, Olgivanna made it a policy to bring each member of her Gurdjieff groups in for a private talk. When Mary Stanton was summoned, she found to her surprise that Olgivanna had slated her for a fashion makeover. Rejecting her straight skirt and blouse and long, thin earrings, Olgivanna sent Kay Davison out to fetch Mary a golden squaw dress and blouse, with puffy off-the-shoulder sleeves, as well as a new set of chunky, jeweled earrings. "She put those on me," Stanton recalled. "Then she changed my hairdo. I walked out of that room a different person." Olgivanna reassured her that this new persona would help her "expand more" into herself.

Soon Mary's duties were "expanding." Olgivanna enlisted her as a personal seamstress, on call to fit her gowns and execute intricate embroidery. Mary felt privileged "just being with her and hearing what she had to say, and how she talked with other people. . . ." Olgivanna also recruited Mary's husband, Jack, a skilled jeweler, to design and construct headdresses for the dance costumes; he even built a huge nativity scene for Olgivanna, with foot-high figures outfitted in exquisite brocade he fashioned himself. Christmas required all of Jack's talents: He had to rush to finish countless pieces of ornate jewelry for Mrs. Wright to give as gifts, often staying up all night on Christmas Eve so that Mary could deliver a piece at dawn.

But there were things about Olgivanna that made Mary uneasy. She was disturbed more than once when she saw Olgivanna explode unexpectedly at someone for a misstep. "I think that made us even more afraid to be honest," she remembered, "because we'd feel her anger." Mary never felt she could really be herself at Taliesin, only what Olgivanna expected her to be. Increasingly, Mrs. Wright's behavior seemed to contradict her philosophy.

But it took a long time—a whole decade, in fact—before the Stantons were able to extricate themselves. And then, just as their union had coincided with their entry into Olgivanna's world, their separation coincided with their exit. After divorcing Jack in 1963, Mary moved to Scotland, where she lived for seven years in the Findhorn community, whose gardeners grew enormous vegetables as a result of their communication with the "elemental kingdom." Then it was on to Well Springs, another program for the transformation of human consciousness. By 1993 she had moved on again, joining Science of Mind, a religious organization based on the theory that there is "one infinite mind which of necessity includes all that is."

OLGIVANNA AND IOVANNA were moving forward. For the night of November 3, 1953, the fourth anniversary of Gurdjieff's funeral, they rented Chicago's Goodman Theatre, a major venue next to the Art Institute. They were planning to bring the public an elaborate costumed performance in the master's tradition, not as entertainment but as a means of attracting followers and donations. Iovanna hit up her father and his clients to finance the enormous show, which would feature twenty-four exercises and dances, all accompanied by a small orchestra with six harps. The apprentices were put to work sewing costumes; Gene Masselink and Wes Peters designed the sets, for which they got Wright's approval. It could not have pleased Wright to know that Gene Masselink was not only painting enneagrams for Olgivanna, but incorporating Gurdjieff's laws of three and seven into his own murals.

The timing could not have been worse. Solomon Guggenheim's estate had just been settled, and the fees to finish the plans for the museum had been transferred to the Foundation. The Guggenheim Foundation had forced Hilla Rebay's resignation, in part because they were fed up with her mystical mumbo jumbo. Wright now answered almost exclusively to Harry Guggenheim, Solomon's businesslike nephew. With the path finally cleared to build the museum, Wright could hardly afford to have his crew's time and energies siphoned off for Olgivanna's "extracurricular" projects.

Wes and the others had their hands full. Beyond the formidable process of getting a New York City building permit, there were major plan changes to be made. The trustees had augmented the original site with two adjacent properties on Fifth Avenue, giving Wright the entire city block between Eighty-eighth and Eighty-ninth streets, and enabling him to position the spiral gallery as he had originally intended. Jack Howe and Curtis Besinger now started on yet another massive revision of the drawings. By the spring of 1952, the vellum on which they were penciled had grown dangerously thin from erasing.

WRIGHT WAS IN perpetual limbo over his wife's and daughter's ambitions, alternately encouraging their efforts and becoming furious at the attention they received. As they prepared for the Chicago performance, the apprentices were torn between their drafting work and "the work." In the process, the dirty work—cleaning, food preparation, serving, building maintenance—was landing on a relatively small group of increasingly disgruntled apprentices.

Wright's discomfort mounted as the Goodman Theatre date drew near. He had always believed in a distinction between hosting Gurdjieff activities at Taliesin—things like his daughter's movements classes—and turning the place into a Gurdjieff "institute." And now his wife and daughter seemed determined to cross the line.

Wright's jealousy took many passive-aggressive, but obvious, forms. He would come to Iovanna's rehearsals and start moving things around just when she needed the space clear for her dancers. Chancing upon a practice session, he would spin about, miming a dervish, distracting the dancers from his daughter. Iovanna understood what was happening: "He had the emotions of a baby, my father."

The pressure of the upcoming performance, combined with her father's interference and her mother's competitive streak, drove Iovanna to sneak an occasional cigarette. One night, thinking he was asleep, she leaned over to kiss him good night. She was wrong.

"Have you been smoking?"

Just one cigarette, she pleaded.

"You know the rules here. I'll tell you what you do now. Go up to your room, pack your bags, carry them yourself. Walk to the railroad station and take a train anywhere you please. Get out of my house and get out now! Don't dare to try to come back!"

Iovanna fled to her room. Olgivanna stormed in moments later, terrified and enraged. How could her daughter have been so stupid? She had risked everything. Only by begging, Olgivanna told her, had she convinced her father that his daughter truly loved him after all. "So now, Iovanna, you may thank God and thank me that you are still here."

The twenty-seven-year-old woman hugged her mother. "I don't want to leave you and father and Taliesin ever," she said tearfully.

THE WRIGHTS KNEW well that, whatever its virtues, a life lived in organic architecture was no guarantee of perfect happiness. Still, they must have been

Iovanna rehearsing Fellowship members for their Goodman Theatre performance in Chicago

shocked in September 1952 when Liliane Kaufmann was found dead at Fallingwater. The cause of death was an overdose of sleeping pills. While some thought it was accidental, she had been chronically depressed over, among other things, her husband's philandering. "Your mother needs no sympathy," Wright wrote to Junior. "She shines brightly now that she no longer suffers."

The Guggenheim Museum under construction

PART VII

LOSING GROUND

ℒAWS OF ℬEAUTY

THERE WERE NOW TWO WARRING worlds at Taliesin—organic architecture and Gurdjieffian spiritualism. And both stood at the brink. As 1952
came to a close, the Gurdjieff program had staked its future on the upcoming
public performance in Chicago, and Wright's architecture studio was struggling to bring Wright's long-overdue New York architectural debut to
fruition. If he could not pull off the Guggenheim, the architect told his
daughter, his "entire career would be ruined."

The European modernists had gained the high ground on American
shores. As Wright drew and redrew his plans for the Guggenheim site, the
glass and steel Lever House opened just two miles away. Straight out of the International Style, but designed by the American firm of Skidmore, Owings
and Merrill, the soap company's headquarters quickly became corporate
America's new model office tower. Meanwhile, for a site not far from the Lever
House, Brazilian architect Oscar Niemeyer, a Communist and disciple of Le
Corbusier, was on the team designing the new United Nations building (as
was Wright's former apprentice Yen Liang, now practicing in China). "Niemeyer knows no more about architecture," Wright told his apprentices, "than
a bee knows about steel." Wright may have known far more, but his heroic
fight for the Guggenheim Museum had clearly become a rearguard action.

In April, after Harry Guggenheim approved Wright's latest revision, the
plans were submitted to the city for a building permit. After discovering
thirty-two code violations in the drawings, the Building Commission denied
the permit. Wright might have met the demands of cosmic law, but he had
ignored the city's profane building regulations.

The problems were not subtle. For one thing, as the building stepped up
and out, its diameter eventually reached beyond the property line. In a letter
to the Guggenheim trustees, without acknowledging what was clearly an

embarrassing error, Wright explained that he was asking the city, "in the interest of good proportion," to allow "a small extension on cornice rights in exchange for the wide openings which we leave at the corners of the block." City ordinances allowed for a building's decorative cornices to cross a streetside property line, if only for a few feet. But Wright despised cornices, and of course the Guggenheim had no such thing. What crossed onto the city's property was a portion of the building itself.

In his letter to the trustees, Wright characterized the balance of the thirty-two code violations as "minor points of conflict." They were anything but. For one thing, the museum—like Johnson Wax—lacked sufficient exit doors to meet the city's fire safety regulations. Its exit stairways were too few and too small, and the building's huge atrium posed its own fire hazard. Wright tried the same argument that had prevailed in Wisconsin—that the building was made of noncombustible concrete. But New York was not Racine, and the city insisted on strict code enforcement.

If Wright had had his way, New York would have been a Broadacre City in a coast-to-coast Usonia, plan checkers would have been sympathetic organic architects, and such battles would be long behind him. But New York was still New York, and capitulation was inevitable. Wright's "cornice rights" argument must have failed; in later drawings the walls at the building's highest level are more vertical than the ones below, reducing the diameter, and, presumably, keeping the building on its own property.

But not every problem could be so easily resolved. As far as the city officials were concerned, Wright and the apprentices had made a lot of mistakes. The thirty-two violations—coupled with problems even the city overlooked—would ultimately lead to a massive redesign.

EVEN AS NEW York building officials were holding Wright's feet to the fire, the federal government was hoping to put him out of business completely. With America's red scare in full swing, FBI director J. Edgar Hoover was compiling a Frank Lloyd Wright case file that would eventually reach two inches thick. Hoover's stack of reports cast the architect as a subversive, but the question of whether Wright was too pink or too blue remained unclear. He had both written for *Soviet Russia Today* and aligned himself with right-wing isolationists who accused Jewish financiers of maneuvering the country into war.

Whatever Wright's politics, he did not mince words. "Which is most dangerous to Our Democratic system of free men," Wright asked in the *Wisconsin Athenaean*, "a sociologic idiot like a Communist or a political pervert like a McCarthy?"

Joseph McCarthy, who received a constant stream of information from Hoover, was well into his infamous anti-Communist campaign, and Frank Lloyd Wright was one of the Wisconsin senator's most visible constituents. In the 1940s, Wright had screened so many Soviet films at Taliesin that the distributor, Artkino, gave him a discount rate. Inspired by Russian cartoons, he even tried to convince Walt Disney to make his films more beautiful. As early as 1948, California's "little" HUAC was listing Wright as a member of a Communist-front organization, the Citizens' Committee for Better Education, as well as the National Council Against Conscription, the American Committee for Protection of Foreign Born, and Russian War Relief. In 1950, Wright signed a plea for parole of eight of the Hollywood Ten, a group of movie actors, writers, and directors accused of Communist sympathies. And of course the architect's highly public prewar statements in defense of the Soviet Union, and his attempts to save his apprentices from the draft, only bolstered the case against him. The draft contretemps had even stirred Hoover to investigate Wright for sedition.

Wright understood the forces aligning against him. Speaking to the apprentices in 1951, he cried, "if you raise your voice against it and try to see the other side, why, you must be 'communistic,' there must be some 'communism' in your background somewhere, and you are suspect. And the first thing you know, you will shut up, too."

As the red scare gathered mass and gravity, Wright remained defiant. In January 1953, together with his friend Albert Einstein, he signed on as a sponsor of a conference to protect political, academic, and artistic freedom organized by the Civil Rights Congress, a group labeled as "subversive" by the U.S. Attorney General. Membership lists had long been the anti-Communist crusade's tool of choice; by now Wright's name graced an array of suspicious mastheads.

Inside Taliesin, however, a very different Frank Lloyd Wright held court— one who looked increasingly like his public nemesis McCarthy. At one Sunday morning talk to the apprentices at Taliesin West, he railed against his old bête noire, the International Style, complaining that it was killing the "romantic" impulse in America. "Romanticism in architecture is at a low ebb," he told them, "ever since the box came up on the scene again and they took off its clothes, stripped it and showed it to you naked." Lamenting this "very severe denial of the element of romance in architecture," he asked the apprentices if they could think of anything less romantic than a Le Corbusier box on stilts.

"Gropius' box on stilts," Wes Peters shot back, to the master's delight.

Wright saw his opening. Walter Gropius—the "gentle doctor at Harvard," Wright called him—"spreads the Communist principle completely where it is most harmful. Communism has found in architecture its exponent and shepherd. Quantity vanquishes quality. If any Harvard can thus indoctrinate the building of a free Democracy with what cannot be said, now is this emasculation of the individual?"

Warming to his subject, Wright told the apprentices that both organic architecture and American culture were at stake in the new cold war. "You must recognize," he warned, "that this rise of the Communist spirit is something not only novel, but extremely dangerous and very likely to prevail. But there must be some denial." That denial would come from places like the Taliesin Fellowship, which could serve as certain monastic orders had during the Middle Ages—as a small pocket of believers who would preserve the faith through the coming apocalypse, both a beacon and a bridge into a better future.

"Anybody can see," he told his followers, "that we don't have Democracy on this high plane in this country except in spots. Well now those spots are the salvation of the quality of human achievement in [the] future."

Olgivanna disagreed. "But must you put architecture dependent on any of those social forms?" she interjected. Hadn't he always insisted that organic architecture trumped every *ism*? Shouldn't architecture be above politics, above forms of government?

Wright tried to ignore the point, but his wife pressed on. Wasn't the architect's role to be a visionary leader, she parried, a man ahead of his time? That much Wright agreed with. "Then," she added, "you are out of any forms of government, if you are ahead of time and above . . ."

Wright cut her off. "So there is something in what Olgivanna says," he told the apprentices, "but you needn't pay any attention to it."

Surely thinking of the recent complaints from New York, Wright tried to sum up his argument. "Government is the enemy," he announced. Governments couldn't create anything, especially architecture. Still, the apprentices had a responsibility to learn the difference between a Communist form and a democratic form. "You must know those things. You must know that the box is a symbol of containment, and if you are going to build boxes, you can put them up on stilts," he added sarcastically.

"Well, that's what McCarthy thinks," Olgivanna shot back. "We cannot do that. It is such a horrible example because . . ."

"I run the risk of being identified with McCarthy I suppose because of accusing him [Gropius] of Communism," Wright conceded. "But this is on a little different plane. This doesn't accuse him of belonging to any Communist party. It doesn't accuse him of any Communist act. It accuses him of unconsciously spreading the Communist principle from on high, which is a different matter."

*   *   *

WRIGHT NEEDED HELP in his fight with the New York building authorities. He even appealed to his distant cousin Robert Moses, New York's legendary planning czar. He was gearing up for a long and costly slog.

Though Wright shuttled back and forth to the city many times throughout the process, the job of reconciling his concrete fantasy with the city's requirements fell to Wes Peters. Plan checkers never get in trouble for saying no, and Wright's unprecedented concrete spiral cried out for rejection. As Peters soon discovered, there wasn't a single city engineer in Manhattan capable of assessing the structural soundness of Wright's complex design. There was one in nearby Queens, however, and Wes managed to have the project transferred there.

If Wright wanted his permit, he would clearly have to entertain some serious concessions. The city had also declared the huge skylight that capped the museum's atrium unacceptable: If a fire started near the base, the smoke would billow right up to the top. And if the heat damaged the thin glass tubes proposed for the skylight, as it quickly would, the whole building would function like a chimney, drawing the flames upward.

Solving these problems was no small matter; the apprentices were forced to make serious revisions, reducing the size of the atrium, adding extra fire stairs and exit doors. But those were minor challenges compared with what Mendel Glickman and Wes Peters faced. After considering prestressed concrete and welded steel framing as structural systems, Wright had instructed the pair to engineer the building using concrete reinforced with steel mesh. But New York's building code had no provision for approving mesh reinforcing, so Glickman and Peters had to rework the entire design using steel bars—the same approach that, through carelessness, had led to such precarious results at Fallingwater. As the two ran their formulas, they must have thought more than once of those decks at Bear Run, sagging even further after fourteen years.

IN THE MIDST of all this, Wright suddenly found a new ally in his war against the "international boys" and their American followers. For the last twelve years, Elizabeth Gordon had been the editor of the Hearst-owned *House Beautiful*, the country's premier magazine catering to the burgeoning home furnishings market. Though the magazine strove to bring high-class taste to middle-class families, Gordon herself cared little for the socialites and celebrities who wanted their residences displayed in its pages.

Wright knew the magazine well. Back in 1896, when it was first launched, it had promoted architectural interiors that were beautiful, simple, and useful, as well as women's rights, democracy, and improved public health. It was also the first American magazine to feature one of his houses.

Gordon had something special planned for her April 1953 issue. "I have decided to speak up," she wrote in her lead editorial, "The Threat to the Next America." "What I want to tell you about has never been put into print by us or any other publication, to my knowledge. Your first reaction will be amazement, disbelief, and shock. You will say 'It can't happen here!'

"There is a well-established movement, in modern architecture, decorating, and furnishing," she continued, "which is promoting the mystical idea that 'less is more' . . . They are promoting unlivability, stripped-down emptiness, lack of storage space and therefore lack of possessions." That movement, of course, was the International Style, with its unshaded windows and "tricks like putting heavy buildings up on thin, delicate stilts—even though they cost more and instinctively worry the eye." It was an elitist movement, she complained, and one whose political implications were clear: With its lack of privacy, its refusal of ornamentation, its reduction of the palette to black and white, its application of industrial forms to the design of homes, its emphasis on two-dimensional appearances, the International Style was inimical to democracy.

The purveyors of this movement, Gordon claimed, were "dictators in matters of taste" who were preparing Americans to accept dictators in every

Wright with his champion and ally, Elizabeth Gordon

aspect of life. A willingness to tolerate an uncomfortable chair, she wrote, was a step toward accepting an "inhuman philosophy." These tastemakers, she charged, were subtly preparing the country for Communism. "Break people's confidence in reason and their own common sense," she warned, "and they are on the way to attaching themselves to a leader, a mass movement, or any sort of authority beyond themselves."

When Gordon's staff read her manifesto, many of them quit the magazine. Other reactions were more facetious. "Grandmother, what big teeth you have!" wrote George Howe, chairman of Yale's department of architecture. "The 'Party' had no idea it was doing so well . . . Until you disclosed the cheering facts I did not know how extensively the ideologies of our foreign agents, Mies, Gropius and Le Corbusier, had infiltrated the American consciousness."

Gordon had taken direct aim at MoMA by including pictures of Mies van der Rohe's and Le Corbusier's residences, both credited to the Museum of Modern Art. Mies van der Rohe's Farnsworth house was apparently the structure that provoked Gordon into action. Though she refrained from naming him in her article, Gordon knew that another MoMA "cultist," architectural curator Philip Johnson, had arranged Mies's entry into the United States. She also knew he was gay. "You know," she observed years later, "he was a homosexual. I'm not sure homosexual[s] can be true to anything."

From the museums and the American Institute for Architecture to the architectural and home furnishings magazines, Gordon's screed had an incendiary effect. Both Johnson and his fellow MoMA curator and *Architectural Forum* editor, Peter Blake, felt that Gordon's campaign damaged the reputation of modern architecture. It hurt the ability of modernist architects to get teaching positions and commissions alike. They were especially appalled by Gordon's casting of modern architecture as a stalking horse for Bolshevism, which they found both silly and potentially dangerous. As for Gordon herself, Johnson recognized that she was in a very powerful position. "We thought she was evil itself," he recalled.

When asked about Gordon's motives, Johnson replied, "When enemies hate you from various sides, [do] you worry about why? You worry about killing them."

FRANK LLOYD WRIGHT, on the other hand, was genuinely thrilled. "Surprised and delighted," he immediately cabled Gordon. "Did not know you had it in you. From now on at your service. Sending you the latest from my standpoint. Godfather."

When Gordon got the telegram, at first she didn't know who the "Godfather" was. Wright followed up with a note asking Gordon why she had "been describing the play of *Hamlet* with Hamlet left out?" Of course he meant himself, although Gordon had in fact credited Sullivan and Wright with developing the principles of good "organic" design. But that wasn't enough for Wright. If she really wanted to "throw a pretty brick through the plate glass window of the International," he suggested, she might consider reprinting one of the Italian reviews of his work that was published in conjunction with having received the gold medal in Florence. "Meantime my hat is in my hand and I greet you."

The Wisconsin architect agreed with all of Gordon's prejudices—not just that the Farnsworth house "was a streetcar stranded waiting for somebody to come a take a ride," he wrote her, but that MoMA curators foisting the anti-home International Style on America were "a lot of little Johnny-Jump Ups from a Pansy bed."

In the next issue of *House Beautiful*, Gordon decided to feature Wright. She sent the architect a draft of her introduction, and he returned it rewritten. Wright actually softened Gordon's invective against the International Style modernists. "If we are to succeed there must appear neither bitterness nor jealousy," he advised. "Most of them are my friends." Still, he made clear that the modernists would "betray the American people in the name of a style and so rob the nation of its birthright."

Gordon published the rewritten version. Within weeks, the architect ended his exclusive publishing arrangement with the International Style–leaning *Architectural Forum*. In *House Beautiful* he had found an ideological ally, and more: He was on his way to turning a magazine with 750,000 readers into his house organ.

"I HAVE A feeling that you want to get out and do things on your own," Olgivanna told apprentice Johnny Hill shortly after Frank's pact with Elizabeth Gordon, "and it's probably time for that." When James Marston Fitch, *House Beautiful*'s modernist architecture editor, quit the magazine, Gordon asked Wright to suggest a replacement. "I have something for you that money can't buy," he replied. "John Hill is born of Taliesin, but you can help him grow up." With Hill, Wright used a different sales pitch: "It would probably be very nice to have a regular paycheck," he said ruefully. Gordon offered him the job, and Hill accepted.

Hill's departure from Taliesin was unique. Nearly every apprentice who had left the Fellowship had been branded a traitor. Johnny Hill was being sent out as an agent.

*   *   *

ON DECEMBER 8, 1953, Wright wired Harry Guggenheim that he was with-drawing his permit application for the Guggenheim until his revisions were complete. But now there were pressures from other directions as well: Even Wright's increased budget, it was becoming clear, was completely unrealistic.

One issue alone made building the Guggenheim a financial nightmare. Usually, concrete structures were economical to build because the wooden formwork used to cast the walls could be moved from floor to floor and reused. But the Guggenheim's spiral design meant that each section of the formwork had to be unique; once used, the forms were worthless. In effect, the builders would be building the structure twice: first in the form of a huge wooden mold—one strong enough to bear the extra weight of wet concrete—and then again in the concrete itself.

In nature, the nautilus shell grows into its shape with breathtaking ele-gance and an economy of materials. Wright's concrete nautilus, on the other hand, was coaxed into being not through basic principles, but through sleight of hand. Wright had given up his plan to cantilever the ramp off the building's interior structure, grudgingly accepting the need for steel struts to support the ramp. But when the plan checkers reviewed the plans, they in-sisted that the supports be encased in concrete for fire protection. This would make them fat and conspicuous, revealing the cantilevered ramp to be what it was—an illusion, and a far more visible one than the similar braces beneath Fallingwater.

Wright was not at all pleased. Desperate for an alternative, he redesigned the ramp so that it would be supported instead by vertical walls, or "webs," as he called them. These webs, placed perpendicular to the curving outside wall, broke the ramp into distinct exhibition alcoves, and provided much-needed flat, vertical display space, much to the relief of the museum's new curator.

But each new solution only worsened the budget problem. The domed skylight over the atrium was another such case. After the building depart-ment rejected Wright's original glass tube design, the architect replaced it with a new design using concentric steel rings and conventional sheet glass. But the cost estimate soon killed the idea. Ultimately the solution came from Wright's engineers, Glickman and Peters; working with another apprentice, Peter Berndtson, they figured out how to carry the new vertical walls, which Wright had only reluctantly agreed to, right into the dome itself, simplifying its means of support. The idea satisfied the building department, and saved a hundred thousand dollars, but it came at a cost. What Wright had envisioned as a skylike dome floating ethereally overhead—evoking both the architect's natural inspirations and Hilla Rebay's Theosophy—was now earthbound, tied inexorably into the building's structure.

By this point the apprentices were in the studio around the clock, working in shifts to revise the museum plans. But there were other projects competing for their time—including a revolutionary nineteen-story office building, the Price tower for Bartlesville, Oklahoma, whose floors truly did cantilever into space. And there were dozens of houses to design and draw. With Wright's attention consumed by the big jobs, Jack Howe was increasingly left to handle the residences himself. Wright's input was often little more than very rough sketches and a quick review of the preliminary drawings. The clients almost certainly never knew.

IN THE MIDST of all this, Wright's good friend Charles Laughton came for a visit to Taliesin West. Laughton was the actor who gave life to Quasimodo, the deformed but sensitive foundling left at the Gothic cathedral door in the 1939 film of Victor Hugo's *The Hunchback of Notre Dame*. He was also a homosexual who loved surrounding himself with beautiful young men, and he arrived in Arizona at a time when he had become voracious in his sexual appetites, consuming chauffeurs, masseurs, and road men, assembling groups of lovers, barroom flotsam whom he paid for favors. Frank's "boys" must have stunned him, their tanned muscles rippling as they worked outside in the sun. In the years that followed he became one of Wright's most frequent, and favorite, guests.

Though rarely comfortable with powerful heterosexual men, Laughton was completely at ease with Wright. When Laughton came calling, Wright dropped everything to join him on long walks or to drive out into the desert. Once, losing track of time and distance, they ran out of gas and had to hitchhike home. The two men were quite physical with each other. One time, Wes Peters recalled, the portly Laughton lumbered toward Wright and embraced him. "Frank," he said sobbing, "we're the world's two biggest hams."

With his sonorous voice and his crisp elocution, Laughton graced the apprentices with readings from Genesis and selected poets. "He read it like he was playing a drum[s] making a tribal statement about the earth," recalled apprentice David Dodge. At the end of one of his readings Olgivanna stood up and left without saying a word—offended, she said, by his liberties with the Gospel and by his dramatic style.

On a subsequent visit, Laughton happened to mention that he had never been to Sedona. Wright turned to Dodge. "Make up a hundred hamburgers," he said. "We're leaving for Sedona."

"Do you want ketchup or mustard?"

"Never mind about that; we don't have time. We're leaving in two hours." With a huge backlog of work hanging over their heads, the Fellowship (minus Olgivanna) scrambled into a convoy of cars. That night by the campfire, they roasted a lamb and sang songs. While the apprentices dozed in sleeping bags, Frank and Charles retired to a Sedona motel, returning the next morning to a hamburger breakfast.

THE WRIGHTS PERSONALLY delivered Johnny Hill to Elizabeth Gordon in New York. "This is Johnny," he told the editor. "His father left him on my doorstep in a basket." Gordon invited them to an exquisite dinner party, where she served Chinese smoked squab. At first she was unsure of Hill, fearing that he might be too passive for the job. But Olgivanna reassured her that Hill would make his own way.

As soon as they began working together in earnest, Gordon was impressed. Johnny's saunter and dress sense gave him a sleek, streamlined look. He catered to his new employer, carrying her bag when the two of them walked together. At Taliesin, Johnny had learned everything there was to know about house design—not to mention plenty of cooking and food presentation skills picked up during his long years of kitchen duty. Wright had trained him well in interior design, and he had learned how to set up photographic shoots so that there were multiple layers of interest. And he was himself a talented designer. "All in all, I think you have given us a real person," Gordon wrote Wright. "I thank you and Mrs. Wright . . . for making what I am sure is a sacrifice to let him go. I will try to take good care of him and help him develop in new ways."

Indeed she did. Having convinced her publisher that editors should live the life they wrote about, Gordon invited Johnny to frequent dinners at her home at Dobbs Ferry, overlooking the Hudson River, where some of New York's great chefs cooked for them. She set out to make his tastes as refined as her own, taking him on his first trip to Europe, where Alice B. Toklas—by then a penniless cooking writer for the magazine—gave him a tour of Paris.

She also took the young gay man to bed. It was, he recalled, a serious affair. And though it soon ended, their working relationship remained intact. Gordon even chose Hill to design the interior of her own place. Gay men, she was convinced, had an eye for beauty that was denied to both heterosexual men and women. "I trusted him completely . . . well, as much as you could trust any homosexual," recalled Gordon.

If there was any camaraderie among the denizens of New York's art world, it wasn't extended to Johnny Hill, who got the cold shoulder. "They're mean, gossipy kind of young men for the most part," he recalled. A lot of them were gay, he noted, "which you'd think would have made them fun, but it didn't."

* * *

AS WRIGHT STRUGGLED under a mountain of work, Olgivanna and Iovanna's moment of truth at the Goodman Theatre in Chicago was drawing near. The problem was that both enterprises were dependent on the same labor pool—the increasingly stressed and polarized apprentices. By the summer of 1953, most of them were beginning to choose sides. To make matters worse, Iovanna was feeling such stress that she went into the hospital for tests and X-rays.

There were other distractions. At just the moment when the FBI was targeting Wright as a subversive, the State Department was sponsoring an international exhibition of Wright's work entitled *Sixty Years of Living Architecture*—as part of the agency's culture war against Communism, no less. It was a strange pairing: As early as 1947, Wright had called for the elimination of State. Yet after the show's premiere in Florence, the department toured it through other European cities.

When an opportunity arose to bring the show to New York, Olgivanna objected, concerned that the apprentices were already overworked. Frank ignored her. This was the largest one-man show the architect had ever been offered, an exhibition that would include original drawings, blueprints, photographs, sculptures, fabrics and furniture, and models of both the Guggenheim and Broadacre City. Shortly before Solomon Guggenheim died, Wright convinced him to pay to bring the show to New York, including one item not in the original show: a 1,700-square-foot full-size Usonian house. *House Beautiful* agreed to furnish, photograph, and run the exhibition house, to be erected on the future Guggenheim site. For Wright and Gordon, it was another part of their battle against the political-aesthetic threat from abroad.

The exhibition put apprentice Curtis Besinger at wit's end. It was then slated to open in late September 1953, eight weeks before the Chicago dance performance. As one of Wright's best men, Besinger was already slaving away at the Guggenheim revisions. But Olgivanna also had him serving as the pianist for the sacred dances—and sewing costumes. His drafting time was further limited by kitchen duty, chorus practice, and cello lessons for Brandoch Peters. Now Wright tapped him, along with John Geiger, to work on the Usonian house for the New York exhibition.

The dueling deadlines inevitably led to conflict. When Wright diverted half a dozen apprentices from Taliesin to Manhattan to work on the exhibition, Olgivanna protested that he couldn't take anyone who was working on her show. When Frank sent dancer-architects Kenneth Lockhart and Tom Casey to New York, the Wrights fought publicly.

As the apprentices' feverish work continued on-site, Wright sometimes accompanied their efforts on a concert grand piano provided especially by Steinway for the purpose. The exhibition's temporary pavilion structure was built to substantially lower standards than a "real" building, and Besinger worried constantly that the floor platform—made of lightweight asbestos-filled cement—would collapse under the piano's enormous weight. The piano was a loaner, but Besinger knew the master was hoping to cart it the back to Taliesin after the exhibition.

The task of building the exhibition's Usonian house fell to David Henken, the former apprentice, now living in New York. It would be the first Wright house most Manhattanites had ever seen. Having participated in the construction of four dozen Usonian-style houses just upstate in Pleasantville, Henken seemed an appropriate choice. He even convinced Wright to use his own construction company, aided by Taliesin apprentices. Working under crash conditions, he was forced to begin construction working from sketches Wright drew on the backs of envelopes, supplemented by the master's verbal instructions. Even the fully drafted plans and elevations that arrived later were so incomplete that he still had to improvise.

Just days before the *Sixty Years* show was to open, seven apprentices were still working overtime to finish the 9,000-square-foot pavilion and model Usonian house. When apprentice John Rattenbury arrived to work on the Usonian's interior cabinets, he found that neither the house nor the pavilion was even close to being finished. Backed against the wall, Wright pushed the show's opening back three more weeks—to October 23, eleven days before the Chicago dance performance.

Olgivanna called her two dancers—Lockhart and Casey—back to Taliesin to continue practicing the movements. Flying in the face of Frank's architectural deadlines, she cleared the studio of drafting tables to make way for rehearsals, waiting until just before her husband's return to push them back into place.

With the rescheduled opening day fast approaching, Wright kept importing apprentices to Manhattan. They worked day and night, even violating New York's blue laws by working on Sundays—a transgression that required David Henken to stroll out to the curb with an envelope for an officer sitting in a patrol car. As a finishing touch, a group of apprentices drove out to Guggenheim's estate on Long Island to ferry back trees and bushes, in an attempt to bring at least a touch of nature to the surroundings.

It was then that Curtis Besinger got a call from Olgivanna. She instructed him to tell her husband that he wanted to return to Wisconsin to accompany the movements rehearsals on piano—without, however, revealing that she had put him up to it. Besinger refused.

WHILE PUTTING TOGETHER the show, Wright managed to find time to create a little new material for his FBI case file. Appearing on Tex and Jinx

McCrary's nationally popular NBC radio and television show, he was asked to suggest a postscript to a letter he had just written to Mamie Eisenhower, the president's wife. "You have married a military man," he offered. "Kindly restrain him."

"And now, Mr. Wright," a shocked Jinx McCrary asked as a follow-up, "what have you to say about the future of New York in an atom bomb world?"

"The whole atom bomb business is just a 'commercial' to scare poor sheep," Wright replied. "We have nothing to fear from the Russians."

Counterattack, an anticommunist watchdog publication, reported his comments in their next issue, along with some advice to the media: "Wright is the Einstein of the architectural world, but, like Einstein, he doesn't understand Communism or Russia. Radio and TV stars who interview famous persons on their programs should look into the backgrounds of their prospective guests. The questions asked of Wright were innocent enough, but whether it was deliberate or not, he certainly used them to the advantage of the Kremlin."

DAVID HENKEN MANAGED to make the extended deadline, but the model house came in significantly over budget—not surprising, given that he was forced to bid it without plans. Having paid for the extras out of pocket, he now submitted the amount to Wright for reimbursement. The master was livid. "Let your beard grow back and go on being a rabbi," he snidely told Henken, who looked every bit the Eastern European Jew.

A FEW DAYS before the opening, Olgivanna summoned Curtis Besinger to a meeting at the Plaza Hotel. The dance performances were not going well, she confessed, and she needed him right away. Bruce Pfeiffer, the substitute pianist, was apparently unable to keep steady time. Again Besinger refused: He would not leave until the exhibition had opened.

On opening day, Wright personally escorted Lewis Mumford through the exhibits. The two had recently repaired their old friendship, which had been in shambles over Wright's opposition to the war. As they walked through the show, Mumford felt he was seeing the work not of a single individual, but of a century unfolding, of a whole culture displayed before him. Fallingwater, he thought, made Le Corbusier's work seem like "flat cardboard compositions."

Yet seeing Wright's life "spread before me, with his voice as a persistent undertone," Mumford confessed in his memoirs, wasn't an entirely positive experience. "I realized as never before how the insolence of his genius sometimes repelled me," he conceded. Wright seemed to heed neither the client nor the culture. In his *New Yorker* review, Mumford sneered at Wright's buildings as isolated monuments to his own greatness, built to satisfy nobody but himself.

Wright was furious, calling Mumford a "mere scribbler," an "ignoramus." Mumford stood his ground; he later disparaged the Guggenheim as an "overmassive pillbox." Their relationship never fully recovered.

ON THAT SAME opening day, Olgivanna and Curtis Besinger flew back to Madison, pulling into Taliesin at nine in the evening. Exhausted, Besinger went to sleep. The next morning, Olgivanna found him giving Brandoch Peters a cello lesson. What in heaven's name was he doing? Why hadn't he been up all night with the others preparing for the Chicago show?

Besinger, who usually kept his emotions in check, lost his temper completely. He had worked to the breaking point in New York, he told her. He needed at least a night's rest. And Gurdjieff's movements, he spat back, were not his concern.

Besinger was temporarily excommunicated. He found himself eating alone—until Wes and Gene convinced him to apologize, and he went back to work as the movements' pianist.

OLGIVANNA WAS ALSO headed for a falling-out with Jeanne de Salzmann, Gurdjieff's chosen heir. Concerned that the Chicago performance might deviate from Gurdjieff's teachings, de Salzmann got into a quarrel with Olgivanna over the phone. She later sent a conciliatory letter, to which Olgivanna replied that Gurdjieff had always intended the movements to evolve. "He too kept living and dying," she wrote, "and we now follow him the same way . . ."

Less than reassured, de Salzmann asked Olgivanna to get permission for the performance from the Janus Society, the publisher of Gurdjieff's music. The request came just weeks before the Chicago date; Olgivanna saw it as a jealous woman's last-minute play for control. "Why are you worried?" she wrote Jeanne. "My trust in you is complete. Is your trust in me not complete?"

Olgivanna was going all out for the Goodman Theatre event. Besinger's piano accompaniment was just for practice; for the actual performance she recruited Arthur Zak, the conductor of the Rockland Symphony Orchestra, along with some of his musicians. Zak arrived for his first run-through just two days before the event; his orchestra didn't lay eyes on the music until the morning thereof.

In one of their few rehearsals together, Iovanna was putting the dancers through the Ho-Ia Dervish when Zak asked her to stop. "Miss," he told Iovanna, "you're just ruining this piece. This music is wild and savage." He had the dancers add bloodcurdling screams.

"IN THE MOVING pageant of these dances you shall see the reflection of truth and knowledge since time began." So began the program notes for the Goodman Theatre performance—notes that included detailed descriptions of things like the enneagram and the laws of three and seven. "Man must consciously struggle," it read, "in order to achieve the free Trinity of immortal being within himself."

As the audience arrived at Chicago's oldest and largest theater, a white-suited Frank Lloyd Wright greeted them in the foyer. Once everyone was seated, he made the introduction. He was in an ebullient mood: his *Sixty Years* retrospective had been an immediate smash, with forty thousand visitors lining up during the first three weeks alone. More than once written off by the city's tastemakers, he was now the toast of the town.

"You know that old saying, 'He ain't got no rhythm?'" Wright now told the crowd. "Well, there's a lot of rhythm here tonight." With the stage lights turned up full at Olgivanna's request, the music and dancing began. The show was extraordinarily demanding: twenty-four different exercises, including the "Octave," which, according to the program notes, symbolized "the knowledge of the Law of Seven with two intervals between mi and fa and si and do, each containing a triad, thus always uniting with the Law of Three, the 'Sacred Trinity'." In an effort to make the music sound more "oriental," Zak had instructed his orchestra to detune their instruments.

"The dancing," wrote the *Chicago Sun-Times* reviewer, "was preceded by brief remarks from Taliesin's founder, the great Frank Lloyd Wright, whose daughter Iovanna heads the group. He assured us, among other things, that not many would understand what was going on. He was right."

"The reviews," apprentice David Dodge recalled, "were absolutely crushing." "The program notes reek of numerology," one critic opined, and "questionable metaphysics. . . . The same kind of cosmic nonsense was repeated on stage." The performers "danced with grim, awful solemnity," the *Sun-Times* noted, with some of the numbers stirring "painful memories of hours of close order drill."

A number of Gurdjieff's American followers were in the audience that night, and some of them were even more hostile, if for different reasons. Olgivanna, they felt, had shamed Gurdjieff's name; the whole affair was an unconscionable display of self-aggrandizement. Jessmin Howarth, who had coached Iovanna in the movements, was "sick at heart over it." Taliesin had ventured beyond its depth. Some of Gurdjieff's pupils had taken years and years of intensive practice to learn the master's intricate choreography. The Taliesin troupe had not had nearly enough practice.

Howarth complained bitterly to Ethel Merston, an English confidante of Gurdjieff's. "I am simply horrified at Olgivanna," Merston wrote back. "It is the evil spirit and it's always the way that sacred teaching gets debased and perverted until it's lost. . . . One can't blame Iovanna. She's the product of two spoiled parents who exploit her. Olgivanna was always a lazy, self-indulgent woman at the Prieuré and rather conceited. And now she's using the work towards her own end."

In the aftermath of the performance, Olgivanna had an attack of tachycardia, a draining and potentially dangerous rapid heartbeat; it lasted almost twelve days.

There was, however, one positive outcome—almost. Elizabeth Gordon and Johnny Hill had timed a business visit to Chicago in order to attend the Goodman Theatre show. Mesmerized by the exotic beauty of the costumes, Gordon arranged to have them shipped to New York so that she could show them to Schumacher, America's finest fabric maker, whom she had already sold on producing a line of Taliesin fabrics. Schumacher liked the designs— but when Wright learned of the idea, he insisted that only his designs be used. Apprentice Heloise Schweizer, who had designed them in collaboration with Olgivanna, was out of luck.

EVEN AFTER WRIGHT'S *Sixty Years* exhibition opened, David Henken was still out of pocket for his extra expenses building the Usonian house. When he persisted, Wright wrote him a letter that could have been cribbed from his response to Wes Peters in similar circumstances. He ripped into his former apprentice, claiming that the only reason for the extra costs was that Henken lacked the qualifications and equipment for the job. "Now why, David, does not some sense of failure get to you?" he chided. If he hadn't stepped in to "go into it all myself," there would have been no show. "The museum owes you nothing because I owe you nothing." If anything, Wright charged, Henken really owed him for the publicity his construction company had received. If only there were "any way to collect out of your hide," Wright sniped. Henken was devastated.

With huge crowds still lining up to see the show, though, the true beneficiary of *Sixty Years* was of course Wright himself. New York City loved Frank Lloyd Wright. And Wright was delighted. (Although he didn't get every last thing he wanted: When Steinway got wind of his plan to abscond with their piano, they sent a moving van for it a week before the show closed.)

Until the exhibition, New York City had been at the top of Wright's list of cities slated for total destruction. Now he saw it with new eyes, as a potential gold mine for organic architecture. Though he was in his mid-eighties, Wright had come to see the Guggenheim as a fresh start. "He felt so vindicated," Philip Johnson remembered, "so proud that at last he, too, could stand up with the Brahmins."

One key to Wright's hopes for New York was Johnny Hill, his mole at *House Beautiful*. Viewing Hill as a "socially presentable representative" who could help him build his New York practice, he installed the former apprentice in his Plaza suite, charging him $7.50 per night for the privilege. In the hotel's basement garage Wright kept a new Mercedes-Benz, a gift from his car dealer client Max Hoffman; this he apparently allowed Johnny to drive without charge.

The Wrights' periodic arrivals at the Plaza were royal events. "It cost a fortune to fill that place with bouquets every time they came," Hill recalled. "And you had to be in full attendance." Elizabeth Gordon would release Johnny from his duties to chauffeur the master around. And, despite the extra work, Hill was grateful to have Wright all to himself.

"You know, Johnny," he recalled Wright saying to him as they lunched at the Plaza's imposing Oak Room, "I sat here with Louis Sullivan just the way you're here with me now." Sullivan's greatness was in the plasticity of his ornament, he mused, the telltale symptom of the sentimental. "I went beyond him," he then added. "I've created new forms for architecture." The old man paused and looked directly at Johnny. "I don't think you'll ever create new forms. One day you might play Brahms to my Beethoven." Wright was the manly creator, something that the effeminate Johnny Hill would never be.

"FRANK LLOYD WRIGHT is a great architect and an indulgent father," the reviewer for the *Chicago American* wrote after the Goodman show. "He could not possibly take seriously the performance of his daughter, Iovanna Lloyd Wright, and her twenty-eight

Johnny Hill with House Beautiful writer Marva Shearer, at a party in Los Angeles

playmates who indulged themselves in ritual exercises and temple dances of the late Georgi Gurdjieff. . . ."

Iovanna was devastated by the reviews. "She was ready to kill somebody," recalled Kamal Amin, one of her dancers. Her rage landed on one dancer, then another. "It must have just about tore the soul out of her," thought David Dodge. It was around this time, he believes, that Iovanna's spirit began to crack.

Others were made of tougher stuff. "They didn't like it. So what?" recalled Heloise Schweizer, one of the dancers. Olgivanna herself was undeterred, eager for more public performances. "The young people had bad press reports," she wrote Lewis Mumford's wife, Sophie, "but the audience was completely with them." And it was the audience who mattered. "Many [of them] were moved to tears," Olgivanna wrote years later, "and sat entranced long after the curtain went down. And from many, Iovanna received letters pleading with her for repeat performances."

To the chagrin of the Gurdjieff establishment, Olgivanna and Iovanna began planning a demonstration in Arizona and a larger one in Los Angeles. Olgivanna was even planning a return to the Goodman—this time for five whole days—and a show in Manhattan, the center of the American Gurdjieff network. She hosted a group to practice the movements in their suite at the Plaza, and dreamed of mounting the kind of tour Gurdjieff once had, a small esoteric awakening with herself at its center.

Determined to lay down the law, Jeanne de Salzmann decided to pay a visit to Olgivanna. She accused her of composing her own music instead of using Gurdjieff's, a charge that may have stemmed from Arthur Zak's creative input before the Goodman Theatre show. Olgivanna denied it—but the accusation apparently gave her an idea. "Well," she told her movements group, "we'll write our own." She began composing one étude after another, most of them based on Slavic themes from the popular music around Tiflis. Just as Gurdjieff had done with de Hartmann, she would sing or hum her melodic lines, and apprentice Bruce Pfeiffer faithfully transcribed them. Even some of her detractors thought her musically gifted.

Iovanna followed her mother's heterodox approach to the movements, adapting Gurdjieffian flows and postures into "dance-dramas" that even contained spoken parts. She also started pushing her father to design her a theater, "a movements temple" complete with a stage, curtains, lighting, even a cyclorama. When Kamal Amin submitted a "Movement Pavilion for Egypt" as his Christmas box project, Wright met it with derision. "Give that to Iovanna," he said.

Still, Wright never found it easy to turn his daughter down. He dutifully sketched a performance space to seat two hundred, and before long the project was in construction. Using two of her most loyal apprentices, Olgivanna even arranged secretly to enlarge the design beyond what her husband had agreed to. Apprentice Jackson Wong, who was doing excavation for the project, was told to jump out of the ditch immediately if Mr. Wright happened along, so the young man's height wouldn't highlight the size of the excavation.

Wong disapproved of the pavilion's siting; it interfered with the exterior lines of Wright's cabaret theater and its visual extension to the mountains beyond. When he asked Mr. Wright about it, the architect replied, "I've been fighting an uphill battle all my life and now I am fighting it here at home." Wright certainly dragged his heels; the space he called the "music pavilion"— to be used for chamber music and chorus as well as Gurdjieffian dances— would not be completed for three years.

For Wright's wife and daughter, though, the pavilion was just the beginning. The Fellowship, Olgivanna told a skeptical Curtis Besinger, "was only a scaffolding for what it was to become after Mr. Wright's death."

IN JUNE 1954, a handful of sympathetic apprentices gathered with the Wrights at the Holy Trinity Cathedral in Chicago to witness Iovanna's second wedding. With Eric Lloyd Wright as best man and apprentice Heloise Schweizer as her matron of honor, Iovanna stood at the altar in a pearl-white lace gown, her wrists ritually tied to those of her fiancé . . . and her veil on fire. The priest snuffed out the burning lace—Iovanna had gotten too close to a candle—and continued the rite.

Having chosen her first husband herself, and badly, Iovanna allowed her mother to choose her second. The groom was Arthur Pieper, a tall, lean, and ever-smiling apprentice and recent divorcé. Though most in the inner circle found Pieper insubstantial—"evaporating," said Johnny Hill—Olgivanna felt he had promise as a future manager at Taliesin. She also felt her daughter could use the stability of a marriage relationship. Although the twenty-nine-year-old bride didn't like her younger groom all that much, she "trusted mother's wisdom."

Pieper's fortunes, it seemed, were on the rise; his first wife had been another apprentice, but now he was marrying the woman Frank Lloyd Wright expected to take over Taliesin. After their honeymoon in Europe, the couple planned to make their home at Taliesin. Almost immediately on their return, though, Frank got his new son-in-law an assignment in New York—not an architectural project, but a job writing for *House and Home,* a magazine for builders, designers, and real estate developers. The magazine was edited by Carl Norcross, Elizabeth Gordon's estranged husband, but it had yet to adopt the organic architecture dogma.

With his new son-in-law aboard, Wright must have expected to change all that. Arthur Pieper could now join Johnny Hill and infiltrate the cultural circles of New York. "The little Philly-Johnson pansy-bunch and apostates," Wright wrote his new son-in-law, "are all the enemy in sight," clinging to the "provincial notion that American culture comes from abroad. They are too damn near right—but for us."

Olgivanna had her own reasons for sending the couple away. Iovanna was overly dependent on her; she needed to be on her own. But Iovanna didn't care for the small, tawdry apartment Pieper was able to afford, even with his father's money. She thought it below his station, and more important, hers. For that matter, she still didn't much care for Pieper himself.

The relationship deteriorated into the kind of violence that Iovanna had witnessed with her parents—only this time the wife was the perpetrator. At one point she grabbed her six-foot-four-inch husband by the hair and threw him around the room. Iovanna finally persuaded her father to let the couple take over his suite at the Plaza Hotel, but even that couldn't make Iovanna happy, and the couple returned to Taliesin. Iovanna quickly took up with other men and a divorce followed.

"Arthur Pieper had a wife and couldn't keep her," Wright joked.

"OUR SURVIVAL LIES in the destruction of the false self," Olgivanna had lectured her apprentices. Franco D'Ayala Valva, a young Italian aristocrat who arrived in Wisconsin from Rome the month after Iovanna's wedding, got a taste of that destruction almost immediately. A recent architectural school graduate, D'Ayala was drawn to what he considered Wright's "principled" composition of space, which he preferred to what he saw as the European modernists' emphasis on material surfaces. But such high-minded matters would not be D'Ayala's initial focus at Taliesin. Pronouncing him overly intellectual, Olgivanna sent the young man to work in the stables, where he spent two months feeding the horses and shoveling manure.

Olgivanna, who considered herself heir to a noble Montenegrin bloodline, was impressed with wealthy, titled Europeans. Among the others at Taliesin with D'Ayala was the handsome painter Prince Giovanni del Drago, and the two Romans quickly joined the Wrights' circle of favorites. Olgivanna fretted over D'Ayala's physical strength, and sent an apprentice to his room every morning with a warm hard-boiled egg. He was always seated at the family dinner table, and after his stint in the stables he was exempted from hard labor. All of this brought resentment from Olgivanna's longtime intimates, so much so that D'Ayala eventually begged her to let him to do kitchen duty. She relented, but only once.

One thing that surprised D'Ayala was how little architectural discussion he encountered among the apprentices. He fell in with a small group of mostly foreign apprentices—two Swiss, a Japanese, and, as he put it, "a Jew, a real Jew"—who took walks in the desert to discuss architecture without anyone else listening in. They talked about what they were seeing on the boards in Wright's studio, about the training they were receiving, about the strange dances the apprentices were being encouraged to take up.

Late one night, D'Ayala was summoned to the house for a meeting with the Wrights. The group, it turned out, was being watched; Frank sensed subversion. Olgivanna asked whether he was a Communist. The Italian—who was actually a royalist at the time—was shocked. Of course not, he replied, and left the house perplexed.

"Well, gentlemen, good morning," Wright greeted the assembled apprentices the next day. "It is a good morning, isn't it? There are only a few of us left. . . . We've been throwing them out at a great rate here lately." D'Ayala's friends had been summarily expelled for complaining about being assigned manual labor when they had expected training in the drafting room. "These youngsters," he announced, were "what the Germans used to call the '*funfte column*'—we've always had a 'fifth column,' a little more or less. . . . So now, we've been weeding it out." The young Roman, who had seen real Communists firsthand, was stunned to hear the label applied to a few disgruntled apprentices.

If she had not asked whether D'Ayala, too, was a Communist, Olgivanna later confided, the master would have thrown him out as well.

LOOKING FORWARD TO the start of construction on the Guggenheim— and the other New York jobs he hoped would follow—Wright set up an office in a second-floor corner suite at the Plaza. Tapped to redecorate the interior, Johnny Hill had everything removed except two rose velvet chairs—arms capped with swan's heads—left there by the previous occupants, movie producer David Selznick and actress Jennifer Jones. Hill then bedecked the rooms with rich plum-colored velvet curtains, silk Japanese wallpaper, and Taliesin-made black lacquer furniture with red trim. Though Wright sometimes referred to the office as yet another Taliesin, he refused to have it photographed for *House Beautiful* because he didn't want to be identified in the public mind with its lavishness.

Still, the architect didn't mind holding court there. Georgia O'Keeffe arrived bearing gifts—her painting *Pelvis with Shadows and the Moon*, which Wright displayed on the wall next to drawings of one of his own buildings. Marilyn Monroe, newly married to Arthur Miller, came to ask him to design them a house in Roxbury, Connecticut, for what she hoped would be an expanding family. Wright chose Johnny Hill to take her through a house he had under construction upstate. As he helped her up a ladder, Hill remembered with exquisite clarity, Monroe turned and kissed him. Wright designed the house, its low circular pavilion capped with a Guggenheim-like oculus—but Monroe and Miller separated before the project could go into construction.

THE MUSEUM, HOWEVER, was moving forward. Now that the plans were finalized, the next big concern was the cost of construction. Former apprentice Edgar Tafel, now a practicing architect in New York, was working at the time with a small concrete firm he trusted. When he showed the owner Wright's plans, the man was wild to be on the bidding list. Tafel called his old master, but Wright said no dice. The big boys were bidding; he was sure they would come in under bid just for the honor of building the Guggenheim.

They didn't. The lowest estimate was more than twice the $2 million price cap. Six weeks later, early on a Saturday morning in the fall of 1954, Edgar picked up the phone to hear the distinctive throat-clearing he knew so well.

"Hello, Mr. Wright. How are you?"

"Battered, but still in the ring. Edgar, where's your concrete man? Get him here as soon as possible."

When George Cohen entered Wright's hotel suite, Wright greeted him at the door. "So you are the expert in concrete?"

"No, Mr. Wright. I have come to learn from you."

"You are my man," Wright replied, pulling him bodily into his suite.

He handed Cohen the plans. "Young man, here are the plans for the Archeseum," his neologism for the Guggenheim. "They represent twelve years of study. 'Arch' means 'great'. . . . We have two million dollars with which to build it. If your price is higher than that, then don't bother to come back."

In his medium—concrete—Cohen was brilliant. He first suggested saving money by changing the ramp from circular to a something more like a hexagon or octagon, a flat-sided shape that would still approximate a circle, an idea that harked back to Wright's fallback scheme. This would allow them to avoid constructing complicated curved formwork. Wright briefly entertained the idea, then recanted. Cohen's next recommendation fared better. With a slight adjustment in the shape of the cantilevered portion of the ramp, he realized, its formwork could be reused. Wright agreed to the change.

Then Cohen came up with an idea that must have saved hundreds of thousands of dollars. Instead of pouring the concrete into the cavity of a double-sided plywood form, he suggested installing forms on the outside only and spraying a material called Gunite against the plywood. A mixture of sand and cement that can be shot through a hose nozzle, Gunite is commonly used in creating walls for tunnels and swimming pools. After the plywood was removed, the exterior would be essentially done; the interior would merely need to be smoothed out with a trowel before the cement fully hardened.

It was an inspired stroke, eliminating about half the cost of formwork as well as hundreds of tons of concrete and tons of steel. There was only one downside: The engineers would have to rework the plans for a fifth time—and then have them rechecked by the city. But the change helped bring them within $335,000 of the magic $2 million mark.

The deal was on.

Wright sent Wes Peters back to do battle with the city, but he and Mendel Glickman didn't know exactly how to model it mathematically. Yet the engineers believed intuitively that the revised structure would work, so they did the only thing they could think of: They concocted reams of empty calculations, enough to impress and befuddle the plan checkers. It wasn't easy, but it worked.

The fate of Fallingwater hadn't robbed them of their bravado.

ᕼEᗩᗪIᑎG ᖴOᖇ ᖶᕼE ᑕOᔕᗰOᔕ

IN THE CLASH BETWEEN COSMIC and city laws, the Guggenheim Museum was falling prey to earthly interests. Hilla Rebay had predicted as much after the foundation's trustees sent her packing. "You must now be very happy to see your great benefactor's wishes sold down the river," she wrote Wright, "his coming museum just an ordinary salesplace of French dealer interests . . ."

Wright replied in kind. If it hadn't been for her insistence on building on Fifth Avenue "to be in the ring," Solomon Guggenheim would have lived to see the museum. She claimed he had never understood non-objective art; he retorted that her metaphysics were stupid. There was nothing "non" about God.

At least her motives were pure, Rebay shot back. All she wanted was to build the museum; he was obviously in it for the money. As a result, she told Wright, their "temple of God is now never to be built."

BEFORE THEIR BITTER break, Rebay and Wright had worked well together because of their common mystical sensibility. Her replacement offered Wright nothing of the kind. James Sweeney was a former curator at the Museum of Modern Art—the enemy camp Wright was still denouncing to the apprentices as a site of "utter degeneracy." Predictably, the thin-lipped and humorless new curator despised Wright's design. Like many New York artists, he was certain that everything about the museum—the curved and sloping interior walls, the cantilevered ramp, the ivory interior—would be terrible for showing paintings. He immediately set about trying to get the trustees to strip away the essence of Wright's building by eliminating all these elements.

Sweeney also fretted over how much useful square footage the museum would actually offer. It was a legitimate concern; an enormous portion of the building's volume was taken up not by art, offices, or storage, but by the towering atrium. Wright dismissed the curator's objections out of hand, telling Harry Guggenheim that Sweeney was like the Medicis giving Michelangelo specs for the statue of David: "required circumference of biceps, area of belly, number of inches around diameter of calf."

As for the collection itself, Sweeney intended to expand it to include non-non-objective works, including that old "degenerate" Picasso. In a gesture that would have gratified Hilla Rebay, Wright reminded the new curator that the building had been designed specifically for non-objective art. Anything else would defeat the whole point of the design.

Sweeney demanded that the interior walls be white. Wright told him it would make his museum look like the "toilets of the Racquet Club."

Finally, in what must have seemed the ultimate in ignorance, Sweeney insisted that the paintings be lit with artificial, not natural light. Wright had had his fill. "For an Irishman," he wired the curator, "you're small potatoes."

"You can say that sort of thing to us, Mr. Wright," Edgar Tafel advised him. "We love you. But Sweeney, he doesn't love you."

THERE WERE A lot of flies that spring at Taliesin. As his boys slaved away on the final building code corrections, Wright swatted them one after another. "That's Gropius," he called out. "And that's Corbusier."

Wright's campaign to win over New York was on the brink of a major victory in 1954 when those pesky International Style flies swarmed back in and ruined the party. In a generous gesture that revealed how one-sided their rivalry was, Philip Johnson had recommended Wright—along with Mies van der Rohe and Le Corbusier—to Seagram's, the liquor company, as candidates to design a skyscraper for the company's New York headquarters. The company's representatives soon eliminated Le Corbusier, who worked from Paris, as too difficult and too far away. That made Wright the front-runner—until the Seagrams officers met him at Taliesin and found him at least as cantankerous and narcissistic as the Frenchman. So the team selected the arthritic Mies, who in turn chose to collaborate on the project with none other than Philip Johnson. Newly licensed as an architect, Johnson was leaving MoMA to devote himself exclusively to architectural practice—at the urging of Frank Lloyd Wright.

*   *   *

J. EDGAR HOOVER, meanwhile, had been doing some serious digging on Wright—enough, he hoped, to prevent any more Taliesin apprentices from covering their tuition under the G.I. Bill. In a memo to the investigative director of the Veterans Administration, Hoover passed along the conclusions of his sources:

> [According to one informant,] the Wright Foundation appeared to be a religious cult that followed the teachings of one Georgi Gurdjieff, whom he describes as a metaphysician of possible oriental origin. He stated that the foundation held dances to the moon, told the students how to think and what to think and that if a student did not attend certain meetings which had nothing to do with the study of architecture, the student would be dismissed from the school. He also advised that he had heard there were homosexuals attending the school.

The reports from Hoover's field offices were damning enough not just to strip Taliesin of tuition support, but also to jeopardize the legal status of Wright's tax-exempt "educational" corporation. The Taliesin Fellowship, the field agents contended, was not a school at all. It was a place where strange rites were practiced, where the apprentices were "restricted in their movements" while their associations and attendance were constantly monitored. The "students" were largely undesirables, the agents reported—not just homosexuals, but draft-dodgers and conscientious objectors.

The Wrights, of course, would have quibbled with the FBI's portrait of their noble experiment. On a factual basis, however, there was little to dispute. The report's conclusion, that "the foundation was subversive in that it taught things contrary to the American way of life," could just as easily have come from Wright's own hand.

HOOVER SOMEHOW FAILED to stop the flow of G.I. benefits to the apprentices. But Taliesin's nonprofit tax status was in serious jeopardy. After the Wright Foundation was formed in 1940, Wright had assumed he no longer needed to file property tax returns. And for a while, he didn't. In 1952 Iowa County revisited the matter, declaring that the Fellowship was not an educational institution, and that the Foundation therefore deserved no property tax exemption. Now they were demanding thousands of dollars in back taxes. If Wright couldn't muster a convincing counterargument, he would have to pay the piper.

Even if Wright could prove that the Fellowship was educational, though, he was still in trouble. From the start, he had commingled funds from his

architecture practice, by any measure a for-profit business, with his apprentice program. And then there was Wright's so-called "collateral farms" project, where the apprentices bought land, at Wright's instruction, to jump start
Broadacre City. This was real estate development plain and simple, and it too
had been under the control of the nonprofit foundation.

Now, as the clouds gathered, the Wrights set out to prove they were running a bona fide school. Frank solicited testimonial letters from "alumni" like
Abe Dombar, describing how they had benefited from their Taliesin education. ("Now is the time for all good men to come to the aid of the party,"
Wright implored.) Olgivanna readied the place for a site inspection, goading
the apprentices into pretending that a variety of classes were being taught.
Heloise Schweizer became an art student sculpting a bust of Mr. Wright. Another apprentice, Joe Fabris, was told to set up looms and start weaving.

Gene Masselink found himself in court almost daily. In 1953, his request
for tax forgiveness based on nonprofit status was struck down. According to
the court, Wright was collecting an average of $80,000 to $100,000 per year
in architectural fees, $4,000 to $12,000 in farm income, and $18,000 to
$36,000 in tuition. Taliesin was a profitable architectural practice, easily net-
ting $20,000 to $40,000 annually. Architectural training, the court concluded, was incidental to this moneymaking enterprise.

A year later, Wisconsin's supreme court upheld the local court's ruling.
Some inside Taliesin blamed Masselink for the judgment. Wright was so en-
raged that he told Olgivanna that he was going to leave the state and burn
Taliesin to the ground.

"For God's sake, don't burn Taliesin," she pleaded. "It would not speak
well of you."

Fleeing the state, on the other hand, had its appeal. They could count their
friends in Wisconsin on one hand, Olgivanna said. Why not move to New
York? After all, they had a home away from home at the Plaza. They could
build a third Taliesin in the New York countryside, she said, a place where
they would be "reincarnated, reborn, different." She even enlisted a real estate
agent who showed them prospective properties.

"Well, boys," he told the apprentices on returning, "I guess we will have
to move to New York. I saw beautiful land there where we can build a new
Taliesin."

This was exciting news. "When do we start, Mr. Wright?" one of them
asked.

"We will do that by and by," he replied. "We will pull our roots out of here.
We will turn this into a museum. I am not happy here any longer."

The New York idea faded, but the Wrights still had one eye on the door.
Sometime later, Wright announced that he planned to live at the Plaza for

the next year and then relocate permanently to Arizona. It was another passing fancy.

Paying up the property taxes would be a trifle. The tougher task would be satisfying the state of Wisconsin and the federal government, which had launched parallel investigations of Wright's finances. The Internal Revenue Service alone sued Wright for $20 million in unpaid income and business taxes. But how much did Wright really owe? When the IRS inspector arrived at Taliesin, he discovered that the Fellowship had never kept decent records. Mindful of Wright's low opinion of cost accounting, Gene Masselink had relied instead on his own crude system, categorizing expenditures using colored slips of paper. Gene befriended the inspector, moving the man into his room to work; together they spent days poring over ledgers and little colored slips.

The work was nerve-racking, though, and Masselink seemed on the verge of a nervous breakdown when a young woman named Marian Kanouse saved the day. A sweetheart of some of the boys, Kanouse was also the main clerk at the Bank of Spring Green, and she had long been aware of Wright's casual approach to bookkeeping. For years, it turned out, she had been keeping copies of all Taliesin's records, just in case. Wright's tax problems would take years to resolve, but without Kanouse's files his case might have been hopeless.

No longer tempted to flee Wisconsin, Wright was suddenly bothered by how eager his apprentices had been to pull up stakes. Didn't they love Taliesin?

WITH HUGE NEW tax liabilities pending, Wright needed a major new commission. And now there was one on the horizon, from a surprising client—the United States Air Force, which was building a new academy near Colorado Springs, Colorado. His friend Charles Lindbergh had helped choose the site. "Your eye for a site is as good as your eye for a flight," Wright had cabled the aviator. Taliesin drew up a proposed design, and by 1955 he was one of two finalists. But the secretary of the air force opposed Wright after learning of his "Communist" leanings. The American Legion also threatened to make a stink over the architect's long-standing opposition to the use of American military force. And Wright did himself no favors, refusing to go to Washington to sell himself and his design. "I assume that an architect shouldn't be asked to plead his own case or tell who he is," he declared. "The world knows what I can do in architecture. If officials of the air force have missed this, I can do no more than feel sorry for what both have lost." Wright withdrew his name in frustration.

The approval process on the Guggenheim was dragging into its fourth year when Mies and Johnson were approved to start construction on the Seagram's building. Wright was incensed. Wes Peters marched off to confront officials at the building department. Why were big projects like the Mies/Johnson tower getting cleared so quickly, when his project had languished so long? They took Peters into a room 150 feet long, where plans were piled on a counter from end to end. The buildings department just didn't have enough staff to handle the backlog, they complained. However, they had a proposition: If Wright could come up with $3,000, they might be able to hire some extra personnel to expedite it. The architect knew a scam when he saw one, and he refused. But when Harry Guggenheim heard of it, he paid up.

JEANNE DE SALZMANN'S fears had been warranted. Olgivanna's ambition was running away with her. "This is not a Gurdjieff group," she now told her disciples. "This is my teachings, my work." Gurdjieff, she explained, had created an "alphabet," and she was using it to construct her own language.

With her teachings taking off, Olgivanna called in her brother Vlado to help run her groups. Vlado, who didn't even believe in the soul's immortality, was happy to help his sister's cause, but when she asked him to read passages from *Beelzebub's Tales* to the Scottsdale group, he was nonplussed. "From now on, you said, it's Olgivanna," he wrote his sister, "and now you're bringing G. I. in again."

Olgivanna's followers had one thing in common with Vlado: They didn't warm to Gurdjieff's text. Gurdjieff "calls the stories of Thousand-and-one Night sacred writing, which is very difficult to put over even to an ignorant group like this one here," Vlado complained. Gurdjieff knew neither philology nor philosophy, he groused; the master had considered one Mullah Nassr Eddin, "a witty clown well liked in the Arabic world," to be more important than Aristotle. It was too bad that Gurdjieff had ever written anything down, Vlado concluded. He should have remained a "mysterious traveler with a message to the world, and all kinds of marvelous sayings could be attributed to him. This way he spoiled everything." Vlado would help her maintain her authority over the group, he assured his sister, "but please, don't ask me to read to them this nonsense."

Against all odds, though, Vlado was a success. Charles Montooth, a Taliesin apprentice in the Scottsdale group, reported that "Uncle Vlado handles us extremely well. He lets each of us speak and even insists upon it but he brooks no nonsense from us."

FOR YEARS, WRIGHT had insisted that the only thing his wife was allowed to teach was cooking. Now that Olgivanna was going public as a guru in her own right, he could hardly stand it. His anger came to a head later that year, when she published a book of her lectures—a book in which Gurdjieff was never even mentioned. Frank had recommended the book for publication to his friend Ben Raeburn of the Horizon Press. But when Raeburn brought the first six copies to Taliesin, Wright picked one up and threw it back down on the table unopened. "What is this anyway? This is what my wife is doing! I no longer have a wife. I got me an author now."

Olgivanna reminded her husband that he was the one who had suggested its publication in the first place. He should read it.

"I don't have to read the book," he snipped. "I know what you did. You let people into our bedroom. You let us down into the street. . . . You wrote the book because you felt you didn't have a secure enough position as my wife." If he had read it, he would have discovered that he was right. Though their personal life is never mentioned explicitly, Olgivanna wrote that in relations between equals, one person, fearing subordination, will be likely to sense "a certain superiority" in the other and strive for supremacy. This, she noted, "often poisons friendship and marriage."

Not long afterward, the Wrights made one of their frequent trips to New York. As usual, streams of admirers showed up at their suite at the Plaza—but this time they were coming for Olgivanna, each carrying a book for her to sign. When the editor of *House and Home* asked for her autograph, in front of Frank, Olgivanna's entire body trembled. When the editor left, Wright went berserk, kicking chairs and shoving furniture around. She had become his enemy, he shouted.

His ire surfaced again on their way back to Arizona when they stopped to spend the night at the home of Harold Price, a client in Bartlesville, Oklahoma. Harold asked Olgivanna if she would like a drink.

"Yes," Wright said, "give a drink to my wife. Give as many drinks as she wants to drink. It doesn't matter any more. She now has written this funny book of hers. Go right ahead. Let her have another and another. It will make her feel better."

"Frank," she said as he undressed for bed, "I am not going to bed. I am leaving you. . . . We had thirty-one good years until now, but I have come to the end of my journey with you. I am going to take nothing from you. Nothing except the clothes I have on and that is because I can't go out naked."

Olgivanna put on her hat and coat, lifted her bag, and started to walk out. "You have destroyed every promise, every hope," she said in parting. "Take all my things. They are yours. I care for nothing from you. Goodbye, Frank."

According to Olgivanna, Wright leapt from the bed, held her tight, and pleaded with her, "Don't! Don't do that to me. I give you my word of honor. From now on I will only praise your book. Don't you understand, my love is so strong for you that I can't stand the admiration people have for you. I want to be the only one."

"That isn't true," she replied. "What you couldn't stand was your vanity that anybody could turn toward me and regard me as a person."

In Olgivanna's account, Wright fell to his knees and begged her to stay. "I cannot live without you. I can do nothing without you. You will destroy me if you leave."

Olgivanna relented. Her husband took off her hat and coat, unzipped her dress, and slipped a nightgown over her head.

"It was the first night in months," Olgivanna recalled, "that I slept in peace."

IN MARCH 1956, thirteen years after Hilla Rebay first contacted Wright, the Guggenheim plans were finally approved by the City of New York. They could start construction at last. The approved drawings bore the term Wright had coined: It was his "archeseum." "Arch," he told Harry Guggenheim, "means 'great' like in 'archduke,' 'archangel' or, as a matter of fact, in 'architect,' the great man, the designer, the boss." The term "museum," he informed Guggenheim, was too "shopworn." Harry, however, thought "museum" was just fine.

Just after the permit was approved, twenty-one artists, including Willem de Kooning and Robert Motherwell, wrote an open letter to the *New York Times* asking the Guggenheim trustees to reconsider the design. The museum "indicates a callous disregard for the fundamental rectilinear frame of reference necessary for the adequate visual contemplation of works of art," said the letter, a missive apparently inspired by Sweeney.

Wright took pains to defend his design. There was no "rectangular frame of reference" for a painting—except, he declared implausibly, "for the one raised by callous disregard for nature." Painters and curators, he added, "know too little of the nature of the mother art: architecture."

Ages ago, Hilla Rebay had begged Wright to build a full-scale "sample wall" to demonstrate how the paintings would look on the skewed and curving wall. Wright had promised but never followed up. Now Sweeney was making the same demand, but he insisted that the mock-up must demonstrate his artificial lighting scheme alongside Wright's natural light. Wright refused. "The Museum itself is a lighting project," he cabled Wes Peters—one that Solomon Guggenheim had already seen at Taliesin. "You see in this a duel between Uncle Sol's man, myself[,] and Harry's man, Sweeney. Uncle Sol's man has not much chance because Uncle Sol is dead."

Things finally got so bad that Guggenheim stopped talking to Wright. His wife, Alicia, suggested that Wright send Wes Peters, whom Harry liked, down to their Florida residence to try to smooth things over. Arriving at four in the morning, Peters had to wait two hours before being ushered into the house.

"Your boss is a son of a bitch," Harry said to him as he entered.

"Mr. Guggenheim, I can't be here and listen to things like that because I know that isn't true."

Guggenheim set about making omelets, raising his arms as his butler tied an apron around his waist, calling for utensils as though he were a surgeon. Harry made a very good omelet; Wes must have made a few promises; and by the end of the visit peace was restored, at least for a while.

THE START OF the museum's construction in May revealed just what a ragtag affair Taliesin was. The only telephone at Taliesin West was in Wright's private office, unavailable to the apprentices charged with fielding questions from the contractor. And if ever a project was likely to generate questions, the Guggenheim was it. Eventually, they worked out a system: When a problem arose, the contractor would notify Taliesin by telegram. After Western Union drove the message to Taliesin, a group of apprentices would roll up the drawings, drive to Scottsdale, park next to a phone booth, unroll the drawings on the hood of the car, drop in a handful of coins, and call New York with the answer.

There were many problems, however, that could be resolved only in person. One of the biggest was the basic challenge of laying out Wright's corkscrew design, with its tilting planes and spiraling tower, and placing it accurately within the site. Wes hit upon an ingenious strategy, planting a tall pipe at what would be the center of the museum's circular plan, locating it meticulously within a thirty-second of an inch. Using a string attached to a rotating collar on the pipe, Wes and the builder were able to pull accurate lines and transfer dimensions from the scale drawings to the full-sized building. Wes checked and rechecked the dimensions every step of the way, and the results were said to be perfect.

To no one's surprise—least of all the apprentices'—some of the construction issues involved Wright changing his mind. In a move recalling his last-minute revisions at Johnson Wax, Wright decided midstream to add a semicircular projection out of a corner of the horizontal band at the base of the building. He had been struggling all along with how to marry the vertical tower with this horizontal band, and felt sure this would resolve it.

At the Guggenheim site, near the end
of construction

By this time, however, the foundation had already been laid; changing it now was no small matter. The new design affected the main floor, and the steel reinforcements there had already been installed. Wes Peters objected—after all, it was he who'd been forced to re-engineer Johnson Wax the day before its foundation pour—but Wright insisted. The altercation escalated until Wright finally roared, "Who is the architect?" Peters and Glickman retreated to redo the engineering; the other apprentices produced yet another set of working drawings. A month later, the changes were complete—and Wright saved himself additional delays by never submitting the revised plans to the city.

OVER AT *HOUSE Beautiful*, Elizabeth Gordon had developed total trust in Johnny Hill's aesthetic judgment. "John could take three stones and some branches from a tree and make an exciting composition," she said. He changed the magazine's cover design, its photographic layouts, even its typeface. He featured former Taliesin apprentices like Fay Jones and Aaron Green. He even designed kitchens and houses himself, then featured them in articles. *House Beautiful* let it be known that Johnny Hill would gladly design a space at the magazine's own expense if the client would finance construction in return for a feature in the magazine. They offered the same thing to manufacturers, building sets to use in photographing their new products.

Elizabeth Gordon also asked Taliesin for designs for her own house at Dobbs Ferry—from a tile mural to dishes and a tablecloth, all of which appeared later in *House Beautiful*. Johnny brought his close friend and occasional lover, Gene Masselink, to New York to work on the project. With his hands full operating the business of Taliesin, Gene still somehow found time for his first passion, painting. Under Wright's influence, his colors had become more subdued over the years, his strokes less expressive and more abstract. Wright had allowed him to contribute his artistic vision to the buildings, executing abstract designs for wall murals, screens, and doors. "These works of art [are] designed to give life to the space they occupy," Gordon wrote in an article describing Gene's contribution to her own house. They "are like music: you can feel them differently at different times. Masselink's designs convey . . . subtle rhythms and the sense of underlying structure." As Gordon's description suggests, some of his work seemed to parallel non-objective painting.

When the article on Gene appeared, Wright's jealousy flared again. Why hadn't Gordon asked him to do the design? he seethed. Olgivanna tried to calm him. "Frank, that was her house and Gene was asked to do this for her because she liked his work," she said. "Everybody knows you occupy the place of master in his life."

Johnny Hill and Elizabeth Gordon eventually launched their own design studio together. They named it Joel Design Projects, a composite of John and Elizabeth. (The fact that "Joel" sounded Jewish, they thought, wouldn't hurt them in New York either.) They did interiors for several of Wright's Jewish clients, like Max Hoffman and Gerald Tonkens, and even redesigned the interior of Tavern on the Green.

Hill scored a major coup when the magazine convinced the Los Angeles County Fair to finance the construction of twenty-three rooms for an exhibit called "The Arts of Daily Living." The idea was to show ordinary readers how to introduce artistry into daily life by employing craftsmen and designers. Finding it difficult to locate architects that met his standards, Hill designed nearly all of them himself, in the Wrightian style.

Johnny wrote little vignettes describing each room's presumed occupant. "A Room to Be Alone In," featured on the cover of *House Beautiful*, was designed "as a retreat for a business man who sometimes brings his work home and who is interested in mineralogy." With its rough, layered concrete block wall and its gnarled woods, deeply shadowed and lit from below, the room was replete with diamond, chevron, and triangular shapes. Johnny also placed beautifully faceted rock specimens at the base of the fireplace and terrazzo cut into geometric shapes on the tabletops.

Wright may have fumed over Gene's artistic ventures, but he embraced Johnny Hill's work: Not only did he visit the exhibition, he gave it his blessing. He wasn't the only one who liked it: Each day, tens of thousands of people lined up in the smoggy sun to walk through the show, which outdrew even the local racetrack. A million people saw the show before it closed. It made great copy for several issues of *House Beautiful*. "Look carefully," one father told his son, hoisting him up for a better view. "You might never see something so beautiful again."

The success of Johnny Hill paved the way for other apprentices to join Gordon's magazine as writers and editors. *House Beautiful*'s status as Taliesin's house organ seemed secured. When the magazine devoted a third special issue to Wright in 1955, it sold out immediately. And even though the FBI was monitoring the architect at home, the United States Information Agency sent hundreds of copies abroad.

It was an ironic turn of events: In his battle to elevate the manly art of organic architecture, Wright had found his greatest allies in a women's magazine and the young gay man he had sent to help run it.

CURTIS BESINGER SAW his future, and he didn't like it. Not only was Taliesin tipping toward Gurdjieffianism, but Olgivanna was also starting to "intrude on the design end of things." She even wanted to redesign *him*. If he would just let her work on his personality, she pressed, she could make him more effective in the drafting room, just as she had for others. Besinger dodged her, but in the long term he knew she was planning to take control over work assignments in the studio, at which point he would become a mere draftsman pumping out work to fund her extraneous projects. Besinger had no intention of becoming her supplicant—as he felt had happened to John Rattenbury, whom he found lacking in design talent but who seemed to garner plum studio jobs because he was close to Mrs. Wright.

Among the apprentices, the Fellowship was sometimes referred to, only half-jokingly, as the "bad mothers club." If that applied to anybody, it was Rattenbury, whose mother was so notorious that she eventually became the subject of a book and a movie. John's father, Francis Rattenbury, born in 1867, was a preeminent Canadian architect in the Victorian style. But Francis Rattenbury shared more with Wright than just a profession and a birth year: His well-publicized adulterous affair with Alma Pakenham was as big a scandal as Wright's with Mamah Cheney. Where Cheney became a murder victim, though, Alma went one better, becoming an accused murderer. Six years after John's birth, Alma began an affair with her seventeen-year-old chauffeur, often sleeping with him when young John was asleep in the same room. When Francis Rattenbury was later found bludgeoned to death, Alma and the chauffeur were arrested. Only the chauffeur was convicted, but four days after the trial Alma Rattenbury took her own life.

For Curtis Besinger, John Rattenbury's success at Taliesin was the final insult. It was one of Rattenbury's derivative box projects that Wright had likened to his own "regurgitation." But that wasn't the only problem Besinger saw with his younger colleague's work. One of the studio elite, Besinger was asked by Jack Howe to check a set of Rattenbury's drawings. They were, he discovered, "a complete mess." Not only were there inconsistencies among the floor plans, cross sections, and elevations, but the stairs lacked sufficient headroom—a rookie mistake. Instead of concentrating on his work, Besinger felt Rattenbury spent too much time talking to Olgivanna in the "little kitchen" where she held court with her women. "So there I sat for a couple of weeks or so, erasing the drawings that Rattenbury was getting credit for having done," Besinger recalled. "I didn't want to spend the rest of my life doing that sort of thing."

By the summer of 1955, Besinger had had enough. He informed Mr. Wright and Wes that he intended to leave, but he didn't tell Olgivanna, and when she found out she gave him one of her tongue-lashings. For once, though, Frank wasn't angry at all. Curtis had done the right thing, he told one visitor. "For the first time, he realized that he was old and could not expect to live much longer and that he should not try to hold on to his boys."

*   *   *

EVEN AS THE eighty-eight-year-old architect was finally letting go of his followers, Olgivanna was reeling hers in. *The Struggle Within*, like her husband's autobiography, had served as a magnet for needy souls around the country. When newcomers arrived for their first weekend of spiritual guidance at Taliesin, she made it clear that this was not a Gurdjieff group. "What you will receive here," she announced, "will be my instructions to show you how to lead a worthy life." And as proof she invoked her most prominent success story—her husband. Frank Lloyd Wright's decades of late-in-life architectural achievement, she claimed, were the direct result of her efforts to introduce him to Gurdjieff's work.

She was quite serious. When Franco D'Ayala made the mistake of praising Wright's 1905 Unity Temple to Olgivanna, she was incensed. "Franco," Olgivanna chided, "you don't understand anything." Her husband's true greatness, she explained, had begun with her.

When apprentice Nick Devenney heard Olgivanna make the same claim during one of her spiritual groups, he couldn't hide the doubt on his face.

"I see we have somebody here who does not agree," the ever-vigilant Olgivanna announced to the others. For Devenney, that was his first and last exposure to Olgivanna's teachings. He had come to study Mr. Wright's architecture, he said, not Mrs. Wright's "bullshit."

MINDFUL OF HER husband's jealousy, Olgivanna struggled to make her enterprise appear more modest. She told her weekend students to slip in for dinner in ones and twos, to avoid revealing how many there were, and distracted Frank as they trickled in. She even assigned a beautiful young woman to turn his head, engaging Wright in conversation as Olgivanna's followers came into view. This beautiful woman was none other than the great-niece of Zona Gale, the woman he had always wanted but never won.

A dark-haired, milk-skinned Irish beauty, Jane Gale had found her way into Olgivanna's Chicago group when the bottom fell out in her own life. In 1955, while modeling for the Home Show at Chicago's Navy Pier, she found herself sitting offstage crying. Her marriage to a polo-playing inventor had ended badly; a beloved cousin had just died; she was tired of modeling. In Gurdjieff, she saw a way forward.

When Jane arrived for a weekend retreat at Taliesin, Wright stared at her for what seemed a very long time. "You belong here," he finally told her. He admitted that he liked Jane because she reminded him of Zona, and had her positioned in his line of sight at dinner. She was, she claimed, the only woman at Taliesin allowed to wear black, because on her Wright found it becoming. Gale never felt there was anything sexual about Mr. Wright's attentions. "He liked looking at pretty things," she explained.

Still, the whole thing made Olgivanna uncomfortable. "I bet you wished that Mr. Wright had married Zona," she remarked to Gale one day. Jane didn't dare reply.

AMID ALL THE hubbub over Olgivanna's project, Iovanna was forced to grapple with incursions from her mother and father alike. Her once-supportive father was increasingly meddlesome, once even pushing Iovanna and ten of her dancers right off the stage. And Olgivanna insisted on absolute control over the spiritual project at Taliesin, despite everything her daughter had done to help bring it there. In the last days before a performance, Olgivanna often stepped in to wrest the program away from her daughter and change the choreography to her own liking. Iovanna would relinquish the reins, sometimes even refusing to dance in the performance—a move that always upset her father.

Given all this, it was no wonder that Iovanna sought consolation in the arms of the apprentices. If it was not love, at least it made her feel worthy. Wright had nothing but contempt for his daughter's lusty behavior. "I cannot believe that she is the fruit of my loins," he remarked to one apprentice as she walked by.

Ten years after her death, the ghost of Svetlana still hung over Iovanna's head. Jane Gale noticed how often they talked about Svetlana—how wonderful she had been, how much she was missed. Wright's youngest daughter could never measure up to her sister, who was even more sublime in death than she had been in life.

Iovanna looked constantly to her mother for approval. But Olgivanna reserved her tenderness for the motherless Heloise Schweizer. And, like Svetlana before her, Iovanna was enraged by how much time and attention her mother lavished on her minion Kay Davison. Svetlana had reserved her anger for

Jane Gale with apprentice Prince Giovanni del Drago at Taliesin's Venetian Festival, 1955

her mother, but Iovanna took it out on Kay, twice beating her up, throwing her to the ground, and kicking her. Kay just curled up and waited for it to end. Instead of scolding her daughter, Olgivanna was upset with Kay for not fighting back.

Still, "the work" continued. The inaugural performance at Iovanna's two-hundred-seat pavilion at Taliesin West was scheduled for April 1957. Jane Gale, who had a big voice, was slated to sing "Deep in the Silent Earth," a beautiful dirge Iovanna had adapted from the Russian as a memorial to Gurdjieff. At first the dancers were to be clothed in simple white costumes, but soon they were replaced by hundreds of elaborate costumes embroidered with pearls, velvet ribbons, and gold trim. Elizabeth Gordon arranged to photograph the dancers' extraordinary headdresses, and later published the pictures in a trade magazine.

As the date approached, Olgivanna dragooned ever more men out of the drafting room to complete the structure in time. One of the "missing," Kamal Amin, had just finished working on a bit of last-minute welding when suddenly Wright appeared over his shoulder and smashed his cane in anger against the pipe Amin was working on. On opening day, in a fit of jealousy, Wright insisted that some of his drawings be placed in the back of the theater. Iovanna objected and Olgivanna dissuaded him. Just before the show, Wright stomped off to the parking lot. There was no reason for him to stay,

Iovanna teaching "the movements" at Taliesin West

he said. Olgivanna pursued him in tears. "I don't want you to go," she pleaded. "No, Frank, please, I don't want you to go."

She prevailed. Wright joined the apprentices, Gurdjieff students, and assembled guests to hear Olgivanna introduce the evening's program. The dances, she explained, would transform the pavilion into a temple for the pursuit of truth and the unification with divinity. In the first dance, the "Initiation of the Priestess," Iovanna had skillfully choreographed the movements of a golden-gowned woman who turns her back on life to dedicate herself to the temple. In a later piece, thirty men in purple robes did the veiled dance of the dervishes. Her head bedecked with a jeweled fan, Iovanna danced with beauty and grace and just a hint of haughtiness.

THAT NIGHT, WHILE dancing, Jane Gale had an extraordinary out-of-body experience. When the bewildered beauty asked Olgivanna to explain what had happened, though, she refused. "She wanted you to believe that she sat at the right hand of God," Jane recalled, "but she wanted to keep you in what she called the kindergarten years." At the same time, Olgivanna insisted that she already knew everything about Gale—especially about her sex life. "You must be a beautiful lover," Olgivanna ventured in one of her private audiences. "I understand you are beautiful in love." Jane remained obdurately silent; that was none of Mrs. Wright's business. "Why are you resisting me?" Olgivanna insisted. "I am not teaching Gurdjieff. I am teaching me."

Gale was convinced that Olgivanna wanted to "break" her. Most people are clay, Olgivanna told her. She had to mold them, and when she took her hands off they would soon return to their old shape. But Jane was different. "She said I was like a rock that had to be chipped away. But when it was done, it was permanent."

Gale found Olgivanna's tutelage increasingly disturbing. She knew that Gurdjieff had given "tasks" to his pupils to help them command their weaknesses—instructing the loquacious to remain silent, those with sweet tooths to swear off sugar, writers to stay away from their pens. Olgivanna told her followers she wouldn't employ such extreme "tasks" and "shocks." But Jane Gale found the tasks she did prescribe odd and usually self-serving. Nancy and Ed Simpson, two fellow members of the Chicago group, were given the "task" of buying Olgivanna a bathrobe for Christmas made of vicuna, a material more expensive than cashmere. The task would "expand them," Olgivanna claimed. According to Jane, Olgivanna even convinced

Dr. Joseph Rorke, a group member from Pittsburgh, that it would expand him to give up his medical practice and become her personal physician.

Gale's own assignment was to stop writing to her lover, Steve Oyakawa, a Japanese American apprentice from Hawaii. This "task" took her to the limits of her will, for she was so deeply in love and psychically connected with him that she felt she could sense when he entered a building without seeing or hearing him. Gale had expected Steve to propose, but Olgivanna had given him a task of his own—to cut off contact with Gale. To facilitate this, she instructed him to stay behind in Arizona when the rest of the Fellowship returned to Wisconsin.

By the time Oyakawa finally returned to Wisconsin, he was embroiled in an affair with Kay Davison, the still-married mother of two. Gale was heartbroken. "Mrs. Wright got me out of the way," she believed, expressly to pave the way for Kay.

When Kay later gave birth to a child with Japanese features, Wright took one look and said, "Well, Kay, you better leave." At first Olgivanna hoped to keep her by suggesting that they have the baby's eyes "fixed." But Kay's husband, Davy Davison, was so furious that Olgivanna feared he might leave. To avoid losing his valuable talent, she agreed that Steve Oyakawa and Kay should be banished.

Kay divorced Davy, married Steve, and the couple moved to Hawaii. But the marriage foundered and Kay eventually returned to the Fellowship.

Taliesin, Jane Gale recalled, "made Peyton Place look like Utah."

"THE MERRY WIVES of Taliesin," as one apprentice called them, were the women Olgivanna rotated among the much larger male population to keep the boys from straying off the reservation, or, sometimes, to help them "cure" their homosexuality. The next improbable apprentice to take a merry wife was Johnny Hill.

Heloise Fichter, a former UCLA art student and Iovanna's matron of honor, had come to Taliesin in 1949. A tall, attractive woman, she had married and then divorced another apprentice, Nils Schweizer. She had also been courted by Wes Peters, who showered her with gifts, television sets, and jewelry. An exquisite dancer and movements teacher, one of the stars of the Goodman Theatre show, Heloise had grown up in Japan, in a house filled with servants but lacking in love. In Olgivanna, Heloise found a guide, even a mother figure. "If you listen to that woman long enough," she mused after one of her personal interviews with Olgivanna, "you begin to actually believe what she says."

Encouraged by Olgivanna, Heloise fell in love with another apprentice, a much-sought-after certified heterosexual. In 1957, she became pregnant with his child. But her lover wasn't interested in marrying Heloise. No matter: Olgivanna had other plans for Heloise. She was about to become Heloise Fichter Schweizer Hill.

"Nothing will ever be the same," Heloise told a friend dejectedly as she announced her departure for New York to marry Johnny Hill. At least she would have a legitimate husband, and her baby a father.

"Heloise and I had been fond of each other on and off for some time," Hill recalled. "I don't know why I thought it would work. . . . It just suddenly seemed like the thing to do."

Elizabeth Gordon was astounded. So were Johnny's parents.

Olgivanna's scheme was short-lived. Even before giving birth, Heloise was ready to return to Taliesin. Not one to make friends easily, and not much for shopping or museum-going alone, she found herself trapped in Johnny's Manhattan apartment. And she missed Mrs. Wright. When Heloise returned to have the baby, Olgivanna was disturbed to find that the expectant mother hadn't bought any baby clothes. After giving birth to a boy named Christopher, Heloise remained at Taliesin.

Though Johnny occasionally visited Heloise and Christopher at Taliesin, he wasn't suited to fatherhood. "I do not like little children," he would admit, "even at their best." When the boy started to speak, he never called Hill "Dad" or "Father," always "Johnny." Once, when Christopher was five, the boy asked him: "Can you make decisions?"

WRIGHT WAS NOW approaching ninety and most of his friends were gone. Ferdinand Schevill, whom he considered his best friend, had died in 1954. Now, two years later, Wright received a letter from the University of Chicago seeking a donation to establish a fellowship in the historian's honor. Noting that Schevill was one of his dearest friends, he told the university that he wanted to be more than a "mere contributor to any memorial . . . I owe him a whole one."

The university was initially excited, but then a year passed with no donation. Having assumed that the "whole one" referred to a very large sum, they wrote Wright again, this time specifically suggesting that for $50,000 they would establish a Frank Lloyd Wright-Ferdinand Schevill Fellowship.

Wright's reply set them straight: By a "whole one," he had meant "a whole memorial not a fraction. We have established a whole Ferdinand Schevill Fellowship at Taliesin where Ferdinand loved to be and in which he believed beyond the Chicago University . . . Ferdinand's memory is more at home here."

There is no record of any such Schevill Fellowship at Taliesin.

"I FELT REALLY that my boyhood had come forward and captured me again," Wright recalled about what was indisputably his most bizarre commission. In May 1957, Wright left Taliesin with Olgivanna and Wes to meet with the architects and engineers of the city of Baghdad. Wright had been hired to design an opera house for the city on the Tigris River, whose ninth-century golden age was the setting for Wright's beloved *The Thousand and One Nights*.

The capital of Iraq, at this point a constitutional monarchy ruled by King Faisal II, Baghdad was rife with intrigue, teeming with Arab nationalists, Baath socialists, and army officers fuming about the country's dependence on imperial Britain. Olgivanna was sure she could sense Gurdjieff's presence in the city's haunting music and the "radiations" of the people on the street. Even as Wright was signing the opera house deal, a twenty-year-old Saddam Hussein was joining the Baath Party.

In a speech to the city's architects and engineers, Wright introduced himself as "one of the 'subjects' of Harun al-Rashid, the fifth caliph of the Abbasid dynasty and a great patron of the arts, by the way of the tales of *A Thousand and One Nights*." Wright was alerting the Iraqis that he would not impose Western culture on them, that he intended to root his design in local traditions. This was not just a rhetorical gesture: Wright saw Baghdad as yet another front in his battle with those who would homogenize the world's architecture into a single style. Walter Gropius had been commissioned to design the University of Baghdad, Mies van der Rohe its mosque, Le Corbusier an indoor sports hall. Once more, organic architecture would be going head to head against the International Style.

Inspired by Baghdad's rich architectural past, his own sympathies for Arabian romance, and a generous budget funded by Iraq's oil riches, Wright went on to design a building that would have surely amazed Harun al-Rashid. Working with the circular geometry that generated the Guggenheim, the architect created an enormous desert tent. The building's superstructure perched over a partially subterranean ziggurat, a buried variation of the same aborted 1925 "Automobile Objective" project on which he had based the museum. Wright arranged for cars to park down inside the structure, making them nearly invisible in the landscape. The opera house would be surrounded by a large verdant park, complete with a lake, which he called "the Garden of Eden." (The historic site of the fabled garden was thought to be just south of Baghdad.) Wright renamed the island Edena—an improvement over its original name, Pig Island.

Out of the top of the parking ziggurat, Wright designed a circular array of delicate concrete "tent poles," rising five stories into the air where they would engage a semicircular arch. Suspended within each arch, Wright proposed to hang a pair of huge semicircular fans, molded out of concrete, but evoking folds of cloth. The whole affair was crowned by a dome shaped like an inverted cupcake, evoking the form of some traditional mosque domes. A spire shot up from the roof, doubling the height of the building.

At first glance, all this suggested a kind of a huge Arabian merry-go-round. But Wright wasn't done. To the concrete tent he added a "Crescent Rainbow," a pair of ornate filigreed projections arching out over the landscape and touching down at a distance nearly equal to the diameter of the giant "tent" itself. These projections were to be encrusted with sculptural depictions of scenes from *A Thousand and One Nights*. Inside the theater, the Crescent Rainbow morphed into a proscenium derived from Sullivan's Auditorium Theatre. The building now owed a debt not just to his childhood fascination with *A Thousand and One Nights*, but to the first project he had worked on for his *lieber meister*. The final product was nothing less than a mosque to the arts, and an autobiographical summation of Wright's life and work.

OLGIVANNA HADN'T FINISHED meddling in Jane Gale's love life. Jane soon began an affair with an apprentice from a wealthy international family, whose parents had sent their son to America to get him out of a dangerously repressive regime at home. The apprentice had no interest in either architecture or Gurdjieff, but the Wrights agreed to take him in exchange for a substantial fee.

When Gale became pregnant, Olgivanna told her to have an abortion, sending her to Chicago with three hundred dollars to pay for it. Gale's lover joined her. Once in Chicago, though, Gale had a premonition that this might be her only chance in life to have a baby. And the apprentice decided that he too wanted the child. Instead of getting the abortion, the two were married in a ceremony on Chicago's south side.

When the pregnant bride and her groom returned to Taliesin, Olgivanna was enraged. She announced to her Gurdjieff group that Jane Gale would be leaving Taliesin, and asked a member of the group to drive Jane back to Chicago immediately. Jane left without her husband.

In Chicago, Jane taught movements classes and continued to attend Mrs. Wright's group meetings in the city despite her exile from Taliesin. When she was five months pregnant, Jane encountered her husband at the Gurdjieff group's Christmas party. Their conversation made it clear that their separation had irreparably damaged their relationship. Jane was convinced that Olgivanna had helped cause the rift.

Gale spent the money Olgivanna had given her for the abortion on the birth of her baby, and hired an attorney to sue Olgivanna for alienation of her husband's affections. And she wouldn't stop there. She knew everyone in Chicago—celebrities, mobsters, columnists at the *Chicago Sun-Times*. She was going to create a scandal. "I wanted to get back at that bitch."

When Olgivanna got Gale's letter threatening to sue, she became agitated. After trying to convince Jane to give the baby up for adoption, she sent Gale a contemptuous letter, lambasting her for starting her "reckless love affair" without consulting her.

Olgivanna did make one surprising suggestion: If she needed money, she might ask for help from the Chicago group. But then she sent a copy of her damning letter to a member of the group, instructing her to read it aloud at a meeting. After that, Olgivanna must have known, Jane would be lucky to be allowed to stay in the group, much less get their financial help.

In the end, Jane dropped her threat to sue. Just as she had foreseen, though, she was never able to have another child.

Meanwhile, with or without her mother's intervention, Iovanna took another husband. Apprentice Charles Gardner's tenure in the royal family came and went so quickly that few even remember it.

WHILE OLGIVANNA COULD be brutal in her control of her minions, her usual manner was far more subtle, and more effective. Anna Durco, another young Gurdjieffian in these years, understood this well. Olgivanna's capacity to understand people, to see and listen and zero in on their motivations, stunned Durco. "Mrs. Wright," she recalled, "was such a teacher that she could teach even with a glance or a gesture of her hand." Her lessons would strike her students like small blows. A glance from Mrs. Wright could be withering. Even a smile would make Anna Durco wonder, "Is that for me?" Once, when Anna received that glance, she had to leave the room. As painful as it could be, any look from Olgivanna was a mark of attention, a gesture to awaken the person—and something to be grateful for. Women in Mrs. Wright's groups would argue over who had received the severest blow, the hardest shock.

*   *   *

EVEN WITH THE support of Elizabeth Gordon and *House Beautiful*, Wright's campaign for organic architecture had done nothing to stem the influence of the European modernists. To the contrary, Wright's old nemesis Le Corbusier had just produced a stunning late-career masterpiece, the Notre Dame de Haut. Usually referred to as Ronchamp, after the French village where it is sited, the small chapel was a sensation, a building as iconic for the 1950s as Fallingwater had been for the 1930s.

But architecture is not a winner-take-all game, and despite his advanced age Wright kept attracting new clients—a remarkable thing given that building projects inevitably took years. Now, one of them provided the perfect opportunity for a response to Ronchamp.

What would become a five-year project started in 1956, the year after the completion of Le Corbusier's church, when a Greek Orthodox congregation from a Milwaukee suburb approached Wright. Soon after, apprentice Dick Carney was driving Wright through Madison. "He looked up at the state capital," Carney recalled, "with its imitation of the Michelangelo dome on St. Peter's Cathedral. He called it phony and said that all domes were phony, that all they were was an infinite arch." Carney daringly suggested that a reinforced concrete dome would be both interesting and original for the new church project.

"Mr. Wright pooh-poohed the idea and called it stupid," Carney recalled.

The next day, Wright entered the Hillside studio with three sketches he had prepared early that morning, each for a different project. He placed one on each of the senior apprentices' desks. The design for the Greek Orthodox church, David Dodge noted, sported a concrete dome.

In describing the church, Wright chose to emphasize the building's precedents in Byzantine church architecture, particularly the sixth-century Hagia Sophia, the Church of St. Sophia in Constantinople. "[T]his is your church," he told its parishioners, placing a saucer over a coffee cup. "We'll all be right here in the palm of His hand." The presentation drawings revealed that the church's shallow concrete dome was mirrored by another upright saucer below; the whole affair was lifted off the ground on a concrete pedestal based on the geometry of the Greek Orthodox cross.

Wright's "saucer" demonstration couldn't have been more apt: From Davy Davison's rendering to the finished building, the church evokes an extraterrestrial visitation. "It appears that aliens have landed at N. 92nd St. and Congress Ave. on Milwaukee's northwest side," reads one latter-day guide to the city's architecture, "but don't panic, it's simply Frank Lloyd Wright's Annunciation Greek Orthodox Church building."

When the congregation signed off on the design, Wes Peters and Mendel Glickman took on the engineering of the concrete dome. It would rest on a circular channel beam containing hundreds of thousands of greased steel ball bearings. The ball bearings were designed to reduce the horizontal stresses on the outside walls—and render it possible, theoretically at least, to spin the dome.

The domed roof bore no Greek crucifix. Instead the circled cross was integrated into the structure of the building, the four piers that held up the main floor of the church. This was another idea that originated not with Wright, but an outside contributor—in this case Olgivanna, who took a special interest in the project, inspired by childhood memories of attending Orthodox services with her father every Sunday.

When the building was completed in 1961, many critics were dumbfounded. In an age that had finally embraced modernism, some who recognized its Byzantine roots called it historicist. Others saw it as futuristic, something out of science fiction.

Almost no one thought it was good.

ON JULY 14, 1958, Iraq's King Faisal and Crown Prince Abdullah were assassinated in a military coup. The country's new strongman cancelled Wright's remarkable, if gaudy, Baghdad Opera House. The projects of Walter Gropius, Mies van der Rohe, and Le Corbusier were allowed to go forward.

That summer, at the age of ninety-one, Wright asked an apprentice to lay out a clean sheet of drafting paper. A few hours later, he got up from

Wright's Greek Annunciation Church, completed after his death.

the table. "This morning the architect designed his own tomb," he declared. But the drawings showed more than that. While the design was focused on his own imposing mausoleum across the road from the original Taliesin, Wright had also laid out a long row of ordinary graves for the apprentices.

SUCCESSION

HE WAS HUMAN AFTER ALL.

The months following the design of his own tomb were not kind to Frank Lloyd Wright. He suffered a small stroke. Cataracts began closing out the light. He beckoned Gene Masselink to stay at his side to read to him, and the two would talk for hours. Iovanna read him O. Henry stories most every night.

The Easter of 1959 would be his last. Death was already close by. Four days before, his son David arrived unexpectedly from Los Angeles with somber news. Catherine, the mother of six of Wright's children, had been cremated earlier that day.

"Why didn't you tell me?" Wright asked, tears in his eyes.

"You never showed any interest," David replied.

OLGIVANNA WENT EARLY to her husband's room to wish him a happy Easter. Both dressed in white, the couple walked out to greet their apprentices and their guests for what was still one of the most celebrated days at Taliesin. "Balloons flew everywhere," Olgivanna recalled. "Tables were spread with flowers, Babas rose from circles of multicolored eggs, the Pascha cheese shimmered white in garlands of blossoms and leaves." As the Wrights sat and listened to the Taliesin choir, the "voices rose, the music echoed in the vastness of the desert space and sky."

After the meal, the Wrights, their guests and the apprentices walked over to Taliesin's theater for a screening of *The Day of Triumph*, the first film of the life of Jesus in which the actor portraying Christ actually speaks. Then there was music—a Beethoven piano piece performed by Carol Robinson.

It was a long day. Olgivanna had kept Wright up until nearly midnight the last few nights, entertaining guests well beyond his usual seven o'clock bedtime. He was sitting under an umbrella when apprentice Robert Green saw him raise his hand several times and lower it to the table in a gesture of impatience and fatigue. "And then," Green recalled, "I heard him say to no one in particular, 'Let's get the show on the road; let's get the show on the road.'"

THE FOLLOWING SATURDAY night, the Fellowship was seated in the Taliesin West theater with a local paying audience waiting for one of Iovanna and Olgivanna's public dance performances to begin. The Wrights were late. The performers held the curtain for a while, then finally began without them.

Wright had been rushed to St. Joseph's Hospital in Phoenix with an intestinal blockage. "The pain," he complained to Olgivanna. "Can't bear it. Mother chop the old tree down." The doctors wouldn't increase his pain medication, fearing that, at his age, it could kill him.

On Monday, they performed surgery. Iovanna was with him when he

Frank and Olgivanna reading Aldous Huxley's Brave New World Revisited, *published the year before Wright's death*

awoke. Wright asked for a glass of milk, and told her he wanted to breathe some country air.

By Wednesday he was enveloped in an oxygen tent, his condition listed as "satisfactory." Gene, Iovanna, and Uncle Vlado kept constant watch. At about one o'clock the next morning, April 9, Olgivanna visited her husband, then returned to the makeshift bedroom the hospital had provided for her. Later in the day, with the surgeons and Taliesin's Dr. Joe Rorke present, Wright's heart stopped. They attempted resuscitation, but the great architect was no more. "There were no last words," Dr. Rorke reported.

Frank Lloyd Wright had died as Olgivanna slept, his death caused by complications from a burst gall bladder. Dr. Rorke would blame Gurdjieff, who back in 1934 had advised Olgivanna, "You have to show the gall bladder who is master. Feed it more grease." The Wrights would follow the prescription frequently over the years.

After hearing he had gone, Olgivanna entered the room and put her hand on her husband's forehead. "You will not be alone Frank. Svetlana has turned down your bed for you. Frank, from now on you can rest. How could you have left me?"

She was furious at herself for not having taken him home to die. "I would have brought him his glass of milk," she cried.

Olgivanna returned from the house wearing a shroud, but without tears. Then, overcome with emotion, she went for a walk alone. An apprentice was assigned to trail her in case she needed help.

"FRANK LLOYD WRIGHT, regarded by many as the greatest architect of the twentieth century, died early today in St. Joseph's Hospital," the *New York Times* reported in a huge obituary the next day.

At Taliesin West there was silence as apprentices built a coffin, gathered flowers, and readied the living room for the body. After the embalming, Wright's corpse, clothed in a white suit, was placed in the coffin, lined with quilted satin in Wright's signature Cherokee red.

The apprentices came to the living room to pay their respects. It was the only time Jack Howe's wife had ever seen him cry. Kamal Amin, who spent an entire night by the casket, couldn't stop crying for days. Without Wright, he feared he would never again know the difference between right and wrong in architecture. "I felt a terrible loss—more than I ever felt for my father or any people who had died, ever."

Despite Wright's age, many apprentices had apparently never considered the possibility of his death. It seemed he had another decade in him at least. Twenty-eight new students, remarkably, had arrived within the previous year.

Upon hearing the news of Wright's death, a few quit the Fellowship immediately, "with a roar of screeching tires and desert dust," one apprentice recalled.

THERE WAS NO doubt about what to do with the remains. After a short service at Taliesin West—Carol Robinson played a concert of Wright's favorite romantics, followed by Iovanna on the harp and Brandoch on the cello— Wright's body was loaded into the back of a Ford Ranchero station wagon bound for Wisconsin and the official funeral. To accompany the body Olgivanna chose Wes Peters and Gene Masselink, who would drive the station wagon for twenty-eight hours straight through the night. The apprentices who stayed behind watched the car until it disappeared behind the cactus-bearded hill.

The brief memorial at Taliesin West was the only service most of the apprentices would attend. The Fellowship had already been preparing for their regular trek back to Wisconsin, but now Olgivanna suddenly ordered them to unpack. Only she and her inner circle were going to Spring Green. Most of those left behind would have been willing to pay their own way to Wisconsin, if only they had had the money. Many of Wright's former apprentices, now scattered around the world, booked passage for Spring Green as soon as they heard.

Olgivanna and her entourage flew to Wisconsin on a client's corporate plane. When Wes and Gene arrived with the remains, the coffin was opened, filled with flowers, and set in front of the great stone fireplace of Taliesin's living room, next to the Bechstein piano he loved. As they paid their respects, the apprentices could see the green sprigs placed in his hands.

As the sun set the next day, April 12, the bell tolled at the Lloyd Jones Unity Chapel. The coffin was carried down to a horse-drawn wagon. With Wes and Gene at the reins, two black Percheron horses pulled the flower-covered wagon down the dirt road. Iovanna and Olgivanna walked behind. Trailed by ranks of ex-apprentices and friends, the caravan rolled slowly toward the old Lloyd Jones graveyard, next to the Unity Chapel. Frank Lloyd Wright would be buried with his mother's people.

Wright's design for his own mausoleum had never gone beyond drawings, but he had once made it known that he wanted to be buried next to Mamah Cheney. He got his wish, more or less. The hole awaiting him, surrounded by yellow chrysanthemums, pine boughs, and birds of paradise, was just yards away from Cheney's forty-five-year-old grave.

In a poem about that day, Iovanna wrote: *Was all nature of which he made a rebel's music sleeping now, dreaming the forever presence of the past?* When she broke down, Aunt Sophie came to her side and hugged her.

*   *   *

THE DAY AFTER the funeral, Olgivanna held a meeting of the Foundation's board of directors to announce that the Fellowship was to be reorganized. It had always been run as a triumvirate, with Wright as president, she as vice president, and Wes as secretary. Olgivanna would now assume the title of president and treasurer, Wes of vice president, and Gene Masselink of secretary.

All those of dubious personal loyalty to her were now cut away. Wright's will had named Jack and Lu Howe as directors. She excluded them. Wright had passed over his talented son Lloyd for the board, but he did name Lloyd's son Eric, a former apprentice. Olgivanna cut him out, too. Indeed, Lloyd and his son were even excluded from the meeting. Lloyd was heard shouting at Olgivanna, whom he blamed for his father's death. The surgery had been unnecessary, he told his stepmother, the anesthetic too much for Wright's heart. He left Taliesin and never returned.

Wright's funeral procession, April 12, 1959

*   *   *

A MONTH LATER, the directors discovered that reorganizing the Fellowship was the least of their problems. A threatening letter from the United States Treasury Department made it clear that the government was preparing to take action against the Frank Lloyd Wright Foundation. Although all Foundation records prior to 1946 "are alleged to have been destroyed by fire in a truck accident," the letter charged, "you maintained complete files relating to clients. . . ." The Treasury Department's implication was clear: The Foundation had been defrauding the government.

The investigators had done their homework. They knew about the huge loans Wes Peters had made to Wright, even though, as their letter stated, no "notes were given, not even a record was kept of such advances." Foundation funds had been used to pay off Wright's old personal debts, some of which were incurred before the Foundation came into existence. The Foundation had covered Wright's property taxes on land to which Wright personally held the title. It had even bought a "wedding gift [for] Iovanna Lloyd Wright."

Taliesin's farming component was singled out for an especially stinging accusation. Peters and other apprentices had obtained agricultural draft deferments based on the claim that their farming was substantial, yet in filing his income tax returns Wright had claimed that farming was incidental to architectural training. The inconsistency suggested to the government a convenient "manipulation of facts." The federal investigators also uncovered Wright's "collateral farms" scheme, in which some apprentices claimed that farms they purchased were later deeded to the Foundation without compensation.

The intent of all these transactions, the investigators concluded, was to "vest the life interests in the Wright family at no cost to themselves." In other words, the purpose of the Foundation was to support the Wrights' extravagant lifestyle. All of this was in stark contrast to the declared mission of the Foundation, the text of which the Treasury Department pointedly repeated: "To encourage the fine arts by the education and teaching of the art of architecture and the collateral crafts."

Despite the Wrights' intense efforts to conjure the appearance of a real school for the inspector's site visit, the feds were not taken in. The apprentices, the letter concluded, "work in the kitchen, garden, farm, or on plans, specifications and on construction work." There were no textbooks, no "conventional" classes. "Mr. Wright would give an occasional lecture at Sunday breakfast," they conceded. The Foundation didn't educate; it made money. From 1946 to 1954, 75 percent of its income had come from the architecture business and farming.

The seven single-spaced pages of charges and evidence culminated in a ruling: The Frank Lloyd Wright Foundation was organized to "take over the professional activities of Frank Lloyd Wright, including his business affairs as an architect, lecturer and farmer. He and his family were assured of all their needs. He also received the benefit of the services of his associates, at minimum cost, and the services of his apprentices for little or nothing."

Taliesin's educational tax exemption was being revoked; seventeen years of back taxes, interest, and penalties would now be assessed. The directors had thirty days to appeal.

THEY CERTAINLY COULDN'T solve their tax problems through tuition. The Wrights had already done all they could to tap the apprentices' wallets—even charging their spouses full tuition.

At least one couple, the Greens, couldn't afford it. A few days after the Treasury Department letter arrived, their friend Harold Long was summoned to see Gene Masselink at the main house. Green, who accompanied him, hadn't seen Masselink since Wright's death. "He looked like he had aged ten years, at least," he recalled.

Something was up. Wes Peters was there too.

"I am glad you came with him, Bob," Masselink told Green. "Mrs. Wright wanted me to ask the two of you where you were yesterday, her first Sunday home. She said that you should have been here for the Sunday meal . . ."

"We were in Madison. Looking at the houses of Mr. Wright," Green responded angrily.

Peters brightened. "Well, that should explain that to anybody's satisfaction!"

The real reason for the meeting, it turned out, wasn't attendance; it was money. Will your wife be joining you in Wisconsin? Gene asked Green. No, he answered, she was staying in Phoenix at her teaching job. They couldn't afford the double tuition.

"Well, in that case," Gene replied, "Mrs. Wright said that you would have to leave the Fellowship. She didn't want to take a chance of breaking up your marriage, she said."

Their marriage would be fine, Harold protested. In six months, when the Fellowship returned to Arizona, they would be back together.

"I'm sorry, but Mrs. Wright was adamant. Either you pay for both of you, or you'll both have to go."

"I can't afford to pay for both."

"Well," Gene replied, "I'm sorry."

Seething, Green announced he was quitting the Fellowship. "Wes Peters looked sad when I said I would be leaving, but he said nothing."

* * *

WRIGHT'S BIRTHDAY CAME a week later. Olgivanna, who had lost a lot of weight, invited about one hundred and fifty guests to a celebration and memorial. Former Democratic presidential candidate Adlai Stevenson showed up, as did Edgar Tafel and many other past apprentices. That whole evening, apprentice Richard Carney recalled, "you kept feeling that he was in the next room and that he was going to show up. There was no sense of his not being there." This sense of presence lingered a long time at Taliesin. For some it never faded away.

At the memorial dinner, a host of speakers remembered Wright and expressed confidence in his widow's ability to carry forward his ideas. Buckminster Fuller, a fledgling guru himself, spoke warmly of the visionary who, he noted, was already thirty-five years old when the airplane was invented. Frank Wright, as he called him, "represented the great closing of the round-the-world pattern that started millenniums ago, the pattern of western-bound man."

Wright had "built an immortal chapter into the continuity of western civilization," declared Adlai Stevenson. "And for that we have not only the members of the Fellowship to pay homage to, but most of all, to Olgivanna Wright." Under her inspiration, the future United Nations ambassador predicted, "this work will be continued."

THAT THE FELLOWSHIP would outlive Frank Lloyd Wright was not a foregone conclusion. At times even Wright himself had had second thoughts about continuing to minister to the endless flow of young people who appeared on his doorstep each year needing nourishment and guidance. "Oh, Katy," he told Kay Davison one day in his suite at the Plaza, "it's wonderful to be here and not have to be a teacher." But each time he suggested giving it up, Olgivanna convinced him to soldier on.

Even so, by the 1950s Wright seemed convinced that there was no reason for the Fellowship to survive him. At one point he even put that sentiment into a legal document. Taliesin, it stated, should be used personally by his wife and his daughter for as long as they lived—but once both passed away, the properties should be taken over by, of all things, the government. Some time before he died, Wright also wrote a will dividing his assets equally between Iovanna and Olgivanna, with no apparent provision for the Fellowship.

Olgivanna, of course, had her own reasons to preserve the Fellowship. But Wright himself saw little point in keeping a group of apprentices together after his death. And as for the Fellowship carrying on his architectural mission, on at least one occasion during his later years, in conversation with client Arch Oboler, he made it clear that he didn't believe the talent was there.

In 1956, while away in California, Wright penciled a personal letter to Olgivanna insisting that the Fellowship be closed down with his death. Surely, he told her, Wes Peters and Gene Masselink shouldn't be chained to the place after he died. He also shared his worries with Johnny Hill that Taliesin would become a "religious . . . kind of thing." That same year, in a letter to Elizabeth Gordon, he admitted that it would be selfish to want to see the Fellowship continue after his death. Wouldn't it better for his "boys" to leave the nest after he died, not merely continue his own work?

A year before his death, however, Wright changed his mind. In what would be his final will, he called for the Fellowship to survive him. And, despite his long-standing commitment to the apprenticeship system, he asked that it survive him as a "school." While Olgivanna must have influenced his reversal, the Wrights' ongoing battle with the local, state, and federal tax authorities was surely another factor. "Your views on the young college of Architecture my will is establishing would be especially welcome to me at this time," he wrote Lewis Mumford, clearly serious about the prospect.

Whatever the reason, Olgivanna got from the will what she wanted: The Fellowship would continue, hers to conduct as she saw fit. Others did not fare so well. To his children by his first wife, Catherine, Wright had bequeathed something that had always been in short supply: "his love." His son Llewellyn, an attorney, contested the will unsuccessfully.

IF MANY OF the apprentices were surprised by Wright's death, Olgivanna had clearly been planning for it. Her gradual assumption of control inside the Fellowship had been evident for some time. And it now became clear that she had been preparing, more subtly, to present herself to the outside world as her husband's successor.

Having garnered a certain public profile with her first book, *The Struggle Within*, Olgivanna published a second one just before Frank's death. Its title, *Our House*, left little doubt about its objective—to establish herself as an equal partner in Taliesin. The book opens in a fashionable Scottsdale restaurant where Frank tells her, "sooner or later I get bored with everyone I know. You are the only person in the world with whom I never get bored." The rest of the book is just as unabashedly self-promoting, often at the expense of her husband. In vignette after vignette, she portrays herself as the dutiful wife of an impossible husband whose arrogance, jealousy, and thoughtlessness can only be tolerated as by-products of his genius. At her most modest, she shows herself to be his muse; more often, she is his better.

The following year Olgivanna published *The Shining Brow*, an attempt to document her campaign to "be the perfect wife" to Frank Lloyd Wright. It is the wife, she claimed, who determines the success of any marriage. "If the wife is superior to her husband, she will raise him to her level; if she is inferior, she will pull him down to her level." The reader was left to conclude the obvious.

The day after the birthday memorial, as Edgar Tafel was saying good-bye to Mrs. Wright, she invited him to represent the former apprentices on Taliesin's board of directors. It was another remarkable reversal: The prodigal children, long considered traitors, were being welcomed back to the fold. But this was likely no sudden kindness. Coming just two weeks after the Treasury Department ruling, the idea of bringing in respected outside directors was likely a clever attempt to make the Foundation appear to be a legitimate nonprofit corporation—and to increase Olgivanna's chances of prevailing on appeal.

Tafel, who surely knew none of this, ran with it. The Fellowship could draw on the services of countless former apprentices now practicing Wright's organic architecture around the world, he proposed excitedly. A newly reorganized Taliesin could become a permanent center for the promotion of Wright's principles, conducting new architectural work and training alike.

Olgivanna did not respond.

WHEN SVETLANA DIED, Olgivanna was immobilized for months. After Frank's death, she hit the ground running. The very next day she began taking charge of Taliesin's accounts, changing the authorization signature at the bank from Frank's to hers.

Three days after the birthday party, Olgivanna did receive some good financial news. The city of Madison had approved Wright's preliminary plans for a huge project called Monona Terrace, releasing a $122,500 payment to the Foundation. The influx of operating cash must have been welcome, but the amount was insignificant in the face of the Treasury Department's findings: With penalties, the Foundation owed the government six million dollars.

The problem hung heavy over the ruling triumvirate of Olgivanna, Wes Peters, and Gene Masselink. If they failed to prevail on appeal, they would have to raise the money by selling off assets. These, of course, were considerable: hundreds of acres of land between the two estates, and a still-valuable collection of Asian art. And their ace in the hole was the collection of Wright's own architectural drawings, and even a few of Louis Sullivan's—all of considerable value to collectors.

Cash problems, of course, were hardly new to the Wrights. But there were two big differences this time. For one thing, Wes Peters was no longer able to save the day. Two weeks before Wright died, Wes had bounced a $150 check to his attorney. His years of fealty to Frank Lloyd Wright had finally drained his inheritance. The other difference was the absence of Wright himself. The Foundation's finances had always been buoyed by apprentice fees. How many new seekers could be expected to pay for a Fellowship absent Wright, and what would keep the remaining apprentices from leaving?

On top of these worries, some of those who had already left wanted their money back. After Edward Vogt Jr. quit Taliesin immediately after Wright's death, his financially strained family asked the Fellowship to refund the unused portion of his tuition. The policy of the Fellowship, Gene wrote back, was no refunds. The Vogts hired an attorney.

Georgia O'Keeffe didn't want any money back, just her valuable *Pelvis with Shadows and the Moon*, which she had given Frank for his Plaza suite. It belonged to the Foundation now, Olgivanna informed her.

Not for long: Olgivanna sold off O'Keeffe's painting in exchange for ready cash. As her financial concerns grew, she continued her plan to sell off art of all kinds. At first she envisioned creating a $10 million investment fund by selling her husband's drawings at $100,000 each. Whether she had overvalued them, or perhaps became concerned over the image of it, that idea was never executed. But she would sell off Sullivan's drawings as well as many of the art objects that Wright had collected over the years, including many of the Japanese prints he had proudly displayed thirty-five years before on her first visit to Taliesin.

WRIGHT LEFT BEHIND a large backlog of unfinished projects, more than thirty in all. The most important, the Guggenheim Museum, was still under construction. When he had last visited the site, three months before he died, he and curator Sweeney were still engaged in trench warfare over how the paintings would be displayed, among other matters. Wright had never fulfilled his promise to build two sample walls to demonstrate the difference between their strategies—one showing Sweeney's desired approach, with the paintings floated off the sloping walls so that they hung vertically, and Wright's, with the art laid flat against the sloping walls. The one sample he built showed only his own approach. Still, Sweeney got much of what he wanted. Wright's skylights were vetoed in favor of Sweeney's artificial lighting; a conservator's workshop at the top of the ramp, which Wright had rejected, was finally built; and the interior walls were painted white, something Wright had always believed would invite comparison with a urinal.

Wright missed the official opening of his final masterpiece by only six months. In his stead came Olgivanna and Iovanna, Gene Masselink, and Wes Peters. The "miracle on Fifth Avenue stood as a spirit from another world," Olgivanna thought as her car approached the building.

The opening was more notable for who didn't come than who did. One no-show was Hilla Rebay, who had helped spark it all. Still bitter, the former curator even held Solomon Guggenheim's paintings hostage, resisting nephew Harry's calls to relinquish them to the museum. "When I die perhaps then," she said. "Perhaps not. . . . Why should I strip the walls of my home for that pigsty?"

Harry Guggenheim chose the speakers for the museum's dedication ceremony, and Sweeney was not on the list. Neither was Olgivanna, although she was honored with a seat on the dais. Had her husband been alive, she later told reporters, he would have stayed away, rather than endure ratification of Sweeney's desecration of his interior.

Whatever Wright's dissatisfactions, he surely knew that with the Guggenheim he had achieved something like the dramatic flow of space he found in Notre Dame—in the exhilarating passage from the museum's narrow entry into the atrium, its quarter-mile-long continuous ramp ringing a space that thrust nearly one hundred feet into the air. Even some of his philosophical enemies found themselves in awe. The spiraling interior, Philip Johnson raved, was one of the greatest rooms of the twentieth century.

Within the year, almost a million people would visit.

TO MANY ON the outside, the Fellowship's long-term prospects seemed dubious. Wright's long-standing resolution that Taliesin should have only one "prima donna," himself, had condemned its most talented apprentices to obscurity. If the public knew any other Taliesin figure by name, it was Olgivanna Lloyd Wright—and whatever she was, Wright's widow was certainly not an architect.

Where would Taliesin find clients? Where would they find new apprentices?

Olgivanna immediately set out to address the problem, firing off letters to current and prospective clients. "The Frank Lloyd Wright Foundation," one began, "is ready and able to provide complete architectural services through the staff of The Taliesin Associated Architects." She signed the letter as "Mrs. Frank Lloyd Wright, President, The Frank Lloyd Wright Foundation."

Even with the loss of Wright, never in the history of the profession has a new architecture venture been better positioned to succeed than this new creation, the Taliesin Associated Architects. The prospect of carrying on as a school may have been dubious without Wright there to attract new apprentices, but an architectural practice was a different matter. The Taliesin Associated Architects would carry the imprimatur of a man celebrated at his death as America's, perhaps the world's, greatest architect. And there were countless other advantages: The new firm would be well-connected to wealth and power. It would have a staff more than forty strong, with no rent to pay and almost no payroll—indeed, many of its "employees" were paying to work there. The economics of the practice would have been the envy of any architect.

As its name revealed, this new Taliesin practice did involve one major change to the status quo. The men and women of the Fellowship had long accepted the label "apprentice," some of them for nearly thirty years. Now, at last, they were being granted the dignity of being considered architects. Perhaps intentionally, the name evoked an ordinary commercial firm; it communicated just the kind of professionalism Wright had always reviled.

The question was simple: Could the eccentric practice of a singular genius be successfully carried on by a firm of unknown architects?

The architects of TAA, as it was sometimes known, had some reason for optimism. Several of them—Jack Howe especially—had long ago mastered the art of designing houses that Wright would claim as his own, sometimes with few or no changes. And for years Wes Peters had ensured that things were built according to the plans. All of this occurred without outsiders having any knowledge of their contribution. And for a while TAA wouldn't even necessarily have to create new designs: Wright had long since established a tradition of resurrecting unbuilt projects when a new client came along.

But the transition from apprentices-for-life to architects-in-charge would not be easy. Their success hinged primarily on two things: the validity of the premise of Wright's organic architecture—that great buildings can reliably be derived from nature-based "principles"—and the creative talent of Wright's apprentices. Neither alone would be enough. It was a situation with some precedent in recent architectural history—indeed, in the annals of Wright's long-resented European modernists. In the hands of artists like Le Corbusier and Adolph Loos, the movement yielded flat-roofed, white-walled masterpieces. But the same elements, applied by lesser talents, generated only the deadly stucco boxes that later proliferated in suburbs around the country.

And there was one more ominous sign. In the years since the Fellowship began, the apprentices who left it behind were often the most promising—

those who knew they had talent of their own, and who felt there simply wasn't room at Taliesin for independent ideas.

BEYOND THE WALLS of the Fellowship, there was much speculation about who would take the architectural reins at Taliesin. There were even attempted interventions by interested outsiders. Immediately after Wright's death, his son John and his wife Frances sent an entreaty to the Fellowship's long-lost godfather, Hendrik Wijdeveld. "We hope you will return to America," they wrote. "We need you." Lewis Mumford also wrote Dutchy. "It is as if nature, having brought forth Wright, was a little anxious as to what might happen if some accident should stop him in mid-career, and so almost a generation later produced a second Wright." Mumford hoped that Olgivanna would turn to Wijdeveld, because "no-one else . . . could possibly carry on Wright's work in his own spirit—yet without his weaknesses and foibles." But he knew Olgivanna was unlikely to offer Wijdeveld the position Wright had denied him twenty-seven years before; she was "too tightly bound up in the memory of Wright to include anyone she sees as a rival." He was right.

If a talent for designing in the master's style was the determining factor in naming a new chief architect, Jack Howe was the obvious choice. But Howe had always been an inside man, and his edgy personality was problematic. More important, he didn't care for Mrs. Wright, and she clearly didn't cotton to him. If Taliesin had a public face—one with any real relationship to its architectural output, that is—it was Wes Peters.

The Wrights had long seen Wes as a worthy successor. In her book *Our House*, in a chapter titled "Our Fellowship," Olgivanna described Wes as an apprentice who "grew to the stature of a man with vision and understanding" under the Wrights' guidance, as "a natural leader with magnetic force and a strong personality." There was never any real doubt that he would be put in charge. Olgivanna marked Peters's succession by presenting him her husband's favorite black and white silk scarf.

At least in one respect, the choice was stupefying. Though Wes was a gifted engineer, there was no evidence that he had, or even believed he had, any talent for design. Indeed, he had spent relatively little time in the drafting room. On a personal level, though, Wes had much to recommend him. As Olgivanna perceived, he was a natural leader; his outsized will was complemented by an infectious exuberance. He was huge in everything he did. He sported an inch-high ring bearing the likeness of St. George astride his horse, holding a spear pointed down the dragon's open gullet. He was unsparingly generous, once giving away sixty Eames chairs, each worth hundreds of dollars.

Peters had another thing going for him: When he eloped with Svetlana, he had taken the trouble to obtain his own architectural license—making him the only candidate for heading the studio other than Jack Howe; he could, after Wright's death, legally call himself an architect and sign the drawings.

And there was one real trump card: Wes Peters was family. In running the modern-day feudal estate that was Taliesin, the Wrights had always valued kinship. As Olgivanna's son-in-law, and the father of her grandson Brandoch, Peters had long ago become indivisible from Taliesin. "His devotion to Mr. Wright and me," she wrote of Wes just before Wright's death, "is absolute."

TO ADVERTISE ITS presence, the new Taliesin called on some powerful outside help. Elizabeth Gordon and Johnny Hill dedicated the entire October 1959 issue of *House Beautiful* not just to memorializing Wright's architectural legacy, but to declaring that Wright's architectural principles would live on. "So infinite and intense are sparks cast off by this great mind," they wrote, "that an architect of today or tomorrow seizing any one of them, could fan it into an accomplishment worthy of a life's work."

Elizabeth Gordon's memorial salute to Wright

And the Taliesin Fellowship was there to make it so. The magazine featured a photograph of the apprentices at their drafting boards, decked out in coats and ties. "Work Continues in the Taliesin Studio," read the accompanying text. "The experienced organization of 19 key men—registered architects, engineers, and designers—who worked closely with Mr. Wright for from 20 to 27 years, are continuing the work already in progress in the studio and are accepting many new projects of all types."

House Beautiful presented Taliesin to the public as a temple storehouse filled with Wright's unbuilt projects. "All of this treasure, in safekeeping at Taliesin, lies waiting only for a present or a future generation who will realize the riches that might be theirs."

All of this, in other words, could be yours.

Olgivanna critiquing apprentice work after Wright's death. Wes Peters is seated at left, Gene Masselink and Jack Howe (with sunglasses) at right.

PART VIII
OLGIVANNA UNBOUND

GRANDOMANIA

"IN MY LIFE AT MR. Wright's side for thirty-five years," Olgivanna Lloyd Wright declared to the Phoenix Art Museum League, "I had to learn about architecture, because it was our morning, our day, our evening. . . . I saw the world of architecture through his eyes."

The widow's claim to share her husband's architectural vision was meant as more than a rhetorical gesture. Long before Wright's death, the apprentices had been hearing Olgivanna say that her husband's work had only really flourished after he married her, a claim she pursued with renewed vigor now, among those he left behind. Olgivanna believed it had fallen to her to carry on Wright's architectural mission. To a select few, she would even claim she still sought his advice telepathically, from the grave.

Whatever her powers of osmosis and telepathy, they would hardly be enough for Olgivanna Lloyd Wright to take the helm at an architectural practice. Hanging around the drawing boards and directing the work being done there were two very different things. She would need to ask for help—without, however, losing her control.

NOW THAT WES Peters was installed as her front man, Olgivanna set about remaking her old, rough-and-tumble son-in-law. She created not only a new role for him, but a new persona, one that played to his grandiosity. Internal Fellowship memos had always used the apprentices' nicknames, and Wes was no different. Within six months after Wright's death, the memos were referring to him as *William Wesley Peters*, a name that rolled off the tongue suspiciously like *Frank Lloyd Wright*.

Peters became both Olgivanna's chief architect and her prince consort. Having grown up enthralled by tales of King Arthur, he understood knightly service. He told his friends that he would transfer the loyalty he felt for the architect to his widow. The sixty-two-year-old Olgivanna had the forty-seven-year-old Wes escort her to Saturday night dinners and seated him in her husband's old place at the table.

Wes's transformation to William Wesley Peters was all too apparent to the apprentices. The seniors, who had assumed that they would collectively organize the studio, were irritated to discover that his name alone would appear on client contracts. They were also taken aback to see this lifelong engineer now presenting himself as a designer. And some were dismayed to see him step so eagerly into the role Mrs. Wright held out to him.

Some even doubted his leadership powers. "He was headstrong," Johnny Hill remembered, ". . . just like a great big boy." Wes may have spread around favors for all, but the seniors also sensed his arrogant streak, his tendency to view his colleagues as "plebians."

Peters had assured the senior apprentices that he would use his privileged position to protect the studio from outside interference—meaning Mrs. Wright. Even if he meant it, however, it was an impossible promise to fulfill. At first, Olgivanna did stay away from the studio. Though initially she took over her husband's office, she thought better of that too. But soon she was compelling the lead designers to bring their plans to her apartment for review—and making changes, ranging from color and details to basic concepts. Almost everything required her formal approval. Some architects had to cancel client presentations after Mrs. Wright rejected their designs and made them start from scratch. On the other hand, architects in Olgivanna's inner circle now had free ticket to design, even on major projects, regardless of their level of talent. Even Peters's role as chief architect did not carry complete autonomy, although Olgivanna deferred to him on many strictly architectural issues.

Jack Howe, much to his disappointment, remained chief draftsman under the new regime. For twenty-seven years he had executed the great majority of the Fellowship's drawings—and more than a few actual designs. But it wasn't just being passed over for a promotion that irked him; once the "pencil in Mr. Wright's hand," Howe would now be the pencil in Mrs. Wright's, a galling assignment given her lack of architectural skill or aesthetic judgment.

From the start, Olgivanna's architectural judgments grated on Howe, the one man who could divine Wright's intent from a few lines he sketched on a scrap of paper. Just after Wright died, she handed him a sketch for a private garden to be cut out of a meadow to the south of their Taliesin residence in Wisconsin. The drawing called for a set of ten-foot-high flagstone walls, with a huge circle cut in their center for a "moon gate." Mr. Wright, she said, had sketched this in his hospital bed at her request. Wright had indeed done a rough plan view of the garden, but apparently without elevations, and certainly without such a gate. Jack didn't like the design, which broke the feeling of continuity with the surrounding fields. Others suspected it was conceived by someone other than Wright. Certainly the master would never have countenanced such a garden the way Olgivanna eventually decorated it, with an almond-shaped swimming pool, garish yin-yang sunshades, even a kitschy statue of a dog poised by the side of the door.

FLANKED BY WES, Jack, and Gene, Olgivanna now presided over the apprentices' birthday box presentations. "When a drawing is presented to me," she noted, "and I see something remiss in it, I take the approach that I absorbed from him, trying to give the quality of judgment and criticism that will help the student evolve in a new direction . . ."

Many apprentices saw it differently. Olgivanna sometimes dismissed an entire project based on its color scheme alone. "Oh it's so ugly, it's so ugly, take it away, take it away!" she would declare histrionically, as the apprentice stood by mortified. The savvy apprentices learned to use her favorite colors—gold and pink. Olgivanna rarely had anything specific to say about building design, about floor plans or structure. She focused on the "whole presentation," as one apprentice put it—and that might even include an apprentice's demeanor, especially if she sensed any ego there. It was design critique *cum* Gurdjieffian therapy. "So many build beautiful buildings and yet live an ugly life," she explained. The apprentices should aim for both.

Wes and Jack tried to soften her blows, mindful of Mr. Wright's ability to criticize "constructively and with kindness," particularly with neophytes. But neither dared say anything in public. In the interest of kindness, the senior apprentices approached junior members privately with their critiques, but tensions mounted nonetheless. For many who had devoted their lives to Wright's work, it was too much to bear.

A few who couldn't stomach the present dedicated their energies to the past. Howe had always found time to catalog and store Wright's drawings. Now he threw himself into preserving them, enlisting apprentice David Wheatley to help him painstakingly renumber each drawing, and arranging for them to be stored in a climate-controlled Bekins vault in Phoenix. This was the beginning of Taliesin's archive, a treasure unmatched in American architecture.

"JUNE 8, 1869 will forever mark the beginning of a new epoch for the world," Olgivanna told the world in the first sentence of her book *The Shining*

Brow, written immediately after her husband's death. The book presented Frank Lloyd Wright in the image of Jesus Christ, and the apprentices as his apostles. "The tears of his suffering and sorrow were illuminated by love," she wrote of her husband. "The forgiveness of his heart was so formidable that he had not a glimmer of resentment against his enemies. . . . His spirit grew to a limitless stature. . . . [t]he world received his benediction in art and architecture." And, just as Christ was ahead of his time, so it was with this other savior.

The Taliesin Associated Architects could never duplicate Wright's godlike creative energy, but as his disciples, they would carry on his principles. Her husband, Olgivanna wrote, had left behind "inspired architects who continue to build on the principles of Organic Architecture founded by him. . . . Nobody is ashamed to say, 'I am a follower of Christ or a follower of Christ's principles.'" And Mrs. Wright, not the apostles, would take responsibility for guarding those principles.

Among Wright's followers, though, there was little agreement on just what those principles were, or how they should be applied. Without the master there to guide them, many former apprentices were flummoxed when asked to explain the tenets of organic architecture. Indeed, even Wright had once confessed to some apprentices that the word "organic" was nothing more than what advertisers called a "hook."

AT THE OUTSET there was plenty of work—several years' worth, in fact. Just before his death Wright had landed two major jobs, both for college campuses. For one of them, the Grady Gammage Auditorium for Arizona State University in nearby Tempe, Wright had left only a sketch, recycling his unbuilt design for the Baghdad Opera House.

The Gammage would be a test of both TAA's fealty to the master and its self-reliance. The task of making the Baghdad extravaganza buildable, while remaining faithful to Wright's vision, became more difficult when the university asked the Taliesin architects to add a 40,000-square-foot music school to the building. Torn between their dead master's dream and the needs of their very-much-alive client, Wes Peters tried to do both. As even the junior apprentices knew, compromise never came naturally to Peters, a resourceful engineer and a designer who had trouble knowing when to stop.

The addition of the music school turned the project's strength—Wright's original eccentric scheme for Pig Island—into its liability. The building would need to be enlarged by about 30 percent, enough to warrant a serious reexamination of the basic scheme. The client, however, wanted to preserve Wright's design. That left two choices: either enlarge the circle that formed the basis of the original design, maintaining Wright's original form but dramatically altering its scale, or connect new volumes to the circle. Peters chose the latter.

Even Wright, with the Guggenheim, had struggled with the problem of elegantly mating a circular and a rectangular volume. The Gammage presented the same challenges, and it pushed Wes Peters well beyond his design abilities. Wherever a rectangular element met a round one, the design made no attempt to relate the two. This awkwardness is most apparent in Peters's much-reduced version of the enormous arch in Wright's original Baghdad design. For the Tempe auditorium, Peters transformed it into a functionally dubious bridge from the parking lot into the upper lobby of the theater. Where the archway meets the glass windows of the lobby, a giant arching tube of steel terminates, incredibly, just inches in front of a giant pane of glass.

In another unfortunate deviation from Wright's vision of a garden-encircled Baghdad Opera House, Taliesin's architects surrounded their building with acres of blacktop, running almost up to the building itself. Here in the Arizona desert, Wright's metaphoric garden of Eden became a sea of asphalt and cars. As Joni Mitchell sang a few years later, they had paved paradise and put up a parking lot.

IF OLGIVANNA RELIED on Wes for architectural matters, for personal comfort she depended on one of her Gurdjieff students, Dr. Joseph Rorke. The doctor and his wife, Beatrice, were members of the Pittsburgh group when Frank asked the physician to become Taliesin's house doctor. In 1958, Rorke moved his practice to Phoenix and his family to Taliesin West. Their daughter, Shawn, remembers her father selling everything, including all her toys except a Raggedy Ann doll.

Rorke's wife had severe psychological problems, and they only worsened at Taliesin. Olgivanna thought her too disruptive. Rorke tried everything to help his wife, sending her to the Mayo Clinic, moving his family off campus. But the couple soon divorced.

"Dr. Joe," as he was known, became Olgivanna's stalwart and confidant. She remained his spiritual advisor. Soon after he split with his wife, Rorke mentioned to Olgivanna that Shawn seemed to be playing with her doll too much. Olgivanna suggested he take it away. He did.

After Wright's death, Olgivanna took an extra room next to Rorke's, a retreat—off limits to the apprentices—where she could read and write. Young Shawn was criticized constantly by the woman she called "Gana," for laughing too loudly or wearing the wrong clothes. Then her father was given a room, adjoining Olgivanna's, inside the main house. Rorke's "assignment," as he put it, was to extricate her from Taliesin's burdens. He accompanied her on daily walks and drove her into town to shop and for meals. The two went shopping almost every day. He closed his Phoenix practice to spend more time with her, and lavished her with gifts: jewels from Czar Nicholas's collection, a ring with six-carat cabochon rubies and emeralds, a mink stole he designed and made himself. "They might as well have been married," Shawn remarked.

NOW THAT WRIGHT was gone, Olgivanna's thirty-five-year-old vision for Taliesin could finally be implemented without opposition. As it happened, though, the dual crises of running an architecture practice without her husband and clearing a $6 million tax bill must have been overwhelming.

With all her energies focused on Taliesin's survival, Olgivanna disbanded her outside Gurdjieffian groups soon after Wright's death. Just as Gurdjieff had flushed out his followers when he wanted to write, Olgivanna now told her Chicago group they had "failed" her, without ever explaining how. She offered to continue seeing people on an individual basis at Taliesin, but the outside groups and their weekend visits to Taliesin were over.

Olgivanna no longer needed an outside Gurdjieffian community, or secret conclaves inside Taliesin; now the whole compound was her stage, the Fellowship her audience. Indeed, by now Taliesin was home to quite a few apprentices who had come expressly to work with her. For years, she had conducted her "philosophy" lectures *sub rosa*, often during Frank's naptime. Now it was she who gave the official Sunday morning talks. And, along with Iovanna, she made the sacred dances even more central to the Fellowship. The Taliesin Festival of Music and Dance, begun in 1957, was expanded to five performances each spring. Now everybody took part—dancing, singing, playing, making beautiful sets and ornate costumes. Iovanna was forever summoning apprentices out of the drafting room. Rehearsals went on throughout the night. For three months every year, the drafting room more or less shut down.

While her mother composed new music, Iovanna choreographed new dance pieces on themes ranging from the American experience (*American Montage*) to the work of her father's favorite poet (an adaptation of William Blake's *Urizen*). Sometimes Olgivanna would adapt music for her daughter's dances; sometimes Iovanna choreographed to her mother's compositions.

Though Iovanna sometimes had to shriek at her charges to make it happen, the results were often spectacular, remembered as magical evenings with inventive and often remarkable staging. Within the larger Gurdjieff world, Olgivanna's new dances were seen as even greater deviations from "the work," mounted purely for her personal gain. Dushka Howarth, now based in New York, felt that Olgivanna and Iovanna were putting on "half-assed things and calling them Gurdjieff." The networks in New York and London saw Olgivanna as a kind of "bastard offshoot," and relations with Taliesin grew distant and hostile. Olgivanna dismissed it all as simple jealousy; after all, her work was attracting large audiences and getting good notices in the newspapers.

Despite her success, though, Iovanna was not faring well. She had often been the object of her father's anger. Now, with his death, her accumulated rage began to seep out. She grew to consider her father "profoundly unattractive," she later admitted. "I could never understand how my mother could marry him. To look at him, he's no taller than poor Paul Newman. I often felt that my father imposed on my mother, loading on her his disappointments." It enraged her that her father had been so miserly, refusing to buy her mother the jewels and couture she loved. "He was ugly about it," she claimed. She was convinced that the Fellowship was really her mother's doing, that Wright himself had never really appreciated it.

After her father's death, Iovanna began a downward spiral, drinking heavily to help her sleep. Olgivanna cast about desperately for a solution, but the usual answers—marriage, the movements—had failed her already. Perhaps, she thought, a baby might help her daughter get a grip on herself.

Children were never really welcomed at Taliesin, and less so as Wright

Iovanna, circa 1970

grew older. By the 1950s, babies and toddlers were kept in a tent at the far-thest edge of camp in Arizona, where the women took turns caring for them out of sight and earshot. When Wright came walking by, children would be shooed out of the way. By the late 1950s, applicants with children were being turned away altogether.

For her own daughter, though, Olgivanna would make an exception. Not long after her father's death, Iovanna became involved with apprentice Andrew Binnie. Olgivanna didn't think much of Binnie, and she tried to persuade the very wealthy and very gay ex-apprentice Edgar Kaufmann Jr. to marry her daughter instead. But Kaufmann declined, and Iovanna mar-ried Binnie. In 1960 she gave birth to a daughter named Eve, but her fourth marriage fared no better than the first three. When the baby was little more than a year old, Iovanna's marriage crumbled and Binnie left the Fellow-ship.

GENE MASSELINK STROVE mightily to serve Mrs. Wright, although his own health was beginning to deteriorate. After a hip replacement in 1952, in his early forties, he was able to reduce his office workload when Olgi-vanna recruited a new apprentice, former army paymaster Richard Carney, to help.

Gene's past performance in running Taliesin's office, though, was coming back to haunt him. It was his bookkeeping, after all, that had failed to im-press the government's tax auditor, as Taliesin's attorney scolded Gene just two weeks before Wright's death. "I find," he wrote, "that if I forward copies [of tax records] to you 'artists', you always misplace them, lose them, etc., and in any event, they are never available to me when necessary the following year." Most painfully, it was Gene who had managed things for Taliesin when the tax case went to court, resulting in a devastating defeat. Given the Wrights' financial practices, it was hard to blame him. But now they were struggling to come up with the $6 million, and Gene took it hard.

If there was one thing going well for Gene, it was his art. Olgivanna had gone out of her way over the years to find him work painting murals and other outside projects. The Annunciation Greek Orthodox Church near Mil-waukee, Wright's "flying saucer," provided Gene with a wonderful opportu-nity. The groundbreaking on the building happened just a month after Wright died, and Gene was one of many apprentices who were taken by the story of the modest Greek immigrants who'd raised the money to build it. Olgivanna had convinced Frank to give Gene the job of painting the icons for the gold "iconostasis," a large screen between the sanctuary and the nave. When the church rejected his first efforts as too abstract, he began painting bright, vivid blue-and-gold portraits of the infant Messiah and the crucified Christ.

Gene was still completing the icons when the church opened in July 1961. When the parishioners arrived each Sunday, they would find one or another of the panels missing. Unable to paint in the church itself, Gene commuted almost daily from Spring Green to Milwaukee with a panel strapped to the back of his 190SL Mercedes-Benz a car paid for with proceeds from his outside painting commissions. He came to view the Milwaukee icons as the culmination of his work as an artist; he even contemplated converting to Greek Orthodoxy.

With all the work on his plate, Gene was sleeping little, grabbing baloney or bread-and-ketchup sandwiches on the run. The recent passing of his mother had also taken its toll. But nobody seemed to notice. Born with a congenital heart condition, he had recently suffered a small heart attack. Yet still he pushed his body to its limit.

One July day in 1962, Iovanna fought with Gene for choosing her dead sister Svetlana's image as the model for his portrait of the Virgin Mary. (The fact that he modeled the baby Jesus after Iovanna's daughter, Eve, was little consolation.) Later, he was in his small Taliesin studio, struggling with a rendering of the archangel Gabriel's visit to Mary, when he felt a pain in his chest. He had no nitroglycerin nearby, having been too busy to stop at the Dodgeville pharmacy. The pain was so great that he sent Dick Carney to Mrs. Wright's room for a tranquillizer. Gene's father, who happened to be visiting, was working outside trimming trees; he rushed to his son's side.

Gene died in his father's arms. He was only fifty-one.

"I wish I could die," Olgivanna sobbed. "The soul of your sister," she confided to Iovanna, "has flown to Gene."

OLGIVANNA MAY HAVE loved Gene, but business was business. Masselink was one of the apprentices who had bought property around Taliesin at Wright's urging, and the Foundation had an option to repurchase the "collateral farm" at a mutually agreeable price if Gene should "withdraw his services from the foundation or die."

As far as Olgivanna was concerned, that "mutually agreeable price" had already been paid. She went to Gene's grieving father claiming that his son's eighty acres were owed to the Foundation as compensation for the car she claimed they had provided Gene, and for medical expenses related to his broken hip and heart condition. The elder Masselink was astonished. His son had dedicated his life to Taliesin, and now she was trying to appropriate what amounted to his life savings after his death.

Taliesin also kept possession of Gene's paintings. Apparently, she even sold Gene's valuable Hiroshige print, on whose margin her husband had written, "to my secretary '38 FLLW." After all, there were still a lot of taxes to pay.

Gene's father was bitter, but he declined to take the matter to court. Other pieces of his legacy met a similar dispiriting fate: The icons he had painted so lovingly for the Greek Orthodox church in Milwaukee had left the parishioners cold, and in 1988 they would finally be removed. But another of his designs did appear on the cover of Olgivanna's next book, *The Roots of Life*, in 1963. She dedicated it "to the memory of Eugene Masselink," adding, "There was no conflict between his faith and his life."

"JOHNNY, WE NEED your assistance." With Gene gone, Olgivanna needed another inside man she could trust, and she turned to Johnny Hill. *House Beautiful* offered to double his salary, but Johnny left his luxurious East Side apartment and came marching home to Taliesin. He just couldn't say no to Mrs. Wright.

In some respects, the call was a relief. The years of cigarette-and-martini lunches, adrift in Manhattan's ugliness, had given his senses a beating. Hill had become something of an alcoholic, and at Taliesin he hoped to purify himself. Johnny also knew that his patron Elizabeth Gordon's days at *House Beautiful* were numbered. Gordon, he recalled, "was the front person. I could hide behind her." Once she left, he had no interest in staying.

Two months after Gene's death, Johnny took his place as secretary, joining Wes and Olgivanna in the Taliesin triumvirate. Mrs. Wright knew she needed Johnny, but she had agreed to bring him back only at the insistence of Foundation lawyer Orme Lewis. It was a gamble: Unlike Gene Masselink, who was easily controlled, Johnny had grown confident during his years in the outside world—as architectural editor of one of America's leading magazines, no less.

To keep Johnny in line, Olgivanna had her trusted protégé Dick Carney stay on as his assistant. "I know that God is in heaven," Carney once remarked. "But for me, now at this stage of my development, Mrs. Wright is my God." Through Carney, Johnny recalled, "Mrs. Wright could run everything. . . . She built him into what he is."

After Wright's death, Olgivanna had arranged and rearranged a cluster of gay men—Gene Masselink, Dick Carney, Bruce Pfeiffer, now Johnny Hill—around her as her agents. Unlike Gurdjieff, who believed that gays were poor candidates for spiritual development, she had come to see them as endowed with aesthetic gifts. She nurtured them, sought to develop their talents, and tried to mold them to her will. "Who's going to hang out around a strong woman like Mrs. Wright but a gay man?" mused Adrienne Schiffner, who was close to this inner circle. If these men hadn't come to Taliesin, she added, "they would have been left behind."

Adrienne was surely thinking of her friend Bruce Pfeiffer. Since his arrival in 1949, Pfeiffer had been a special charge of Olgivanna's. In turn he had become her devoté, her musical arranger, and the director of the chorus. He made her breakfast, baked her pastries, made her applesauce from scratch. After Wright's death, Bruce campaigned for the job of running Taliesin's archives. In 1963 he finally got his wish. He would build on what David Wheatley and Jack Howe had started, preserving the invaluable collection of drawings, photographs, writings, and correspondence.

Pfeiffer had arrived during the traumatic year of Howe's show trial, when Olgivanna was desperate to make Taliesin straight. Five years later, in 1954, she was pleased when Pfeiffer himself married a woman, apprentice Betty Scott. "So the miracles are still within our reach," Olgivanna wrote to her brother. After the marriage's predictable end, she finally asked Bruce directly: Was he homosexual or heterosexual? The former, Pfeiffer told her. That was fine; "it's just in you," she told him.

After nearly all her attempts to marry off gay apprentices had failed, Olgivanna finally concluded that homosexuality was largely inherited and abandoned her experiments with conversion. Now she demanded only that gay relationships be discreet. The apprentices didn't always comply. Once, when she came upon two men having sex outdoors, she "reminded" the surprised couple of the policy. Olgivanna found any public display of eroticism unseemly. Spying one straight couple arriving for breakfast hand in hand, she remarked acidly to Pfeiffer, "Look at them; they are still dripping."

Taliesin's gayness may have been dropping off Olgivanna's list of concerns, but it was still a topic of conversation among the locals and the architecture-student network. Stories filtered out of young arrivals being hustled in their tents at night by the older apprentices. Longtime Spring Green area resident Eloise Fritz, a friend of the Wrights, admitted that she didn't want her own son going there. Mr. Wright had brought a lot of "real masculine energy" to Taliesin, but now, she believed, "it wasn't a sound moral place to be."

IN WES PETERS, Johnny Hill, and Jack Howe, Mrs. Wright had a formidable core group to reckon with. The first could calculate and build, the second color and decorate, the third draw and effortlessly mimic Wright's forms. None of them was a great architectural designer, but they knew one another's skills, trusted one another, and had spent decades building a working solidarity. Olgivanna would have to show them who was boss.

On July 4, 1963, Jack Howe left the drafting room for his regular morning meeting with Olgivanna to discuss his studio work. When he got there, she had another subject to discuss: him. He was not an architect, she told him, and never would be. It was a "shattering scolding," Jack's wife wrote in her diary at the time. Olgivanna would tell others she had asked Jack to leave, but she hadn't. She had simply detonated a ton of emotional explosives, a technique she had seen Gurdjieff use when he wanted to clear the decks of unwanted followers.

Howe had no intention of leaving, but neither would he succumb to her manipulations. "J. H. H. Declaration of Independence," he wrote in his diary afterward.

Olgivanna told Wes Peters that there were other draftsmen who could fill Jack's shoes, but Wes knew better. Peters, too, was getting pressure to leave—from his mother and his sister, who had been trying to extricate him from Taliesin for decades. Now that Wright was gone, they started berating him for sacrificing his talent for the right to play the dead king's son-in-law. Even his son Brandoch urged him to leave and start his own practice in California.

Peters stayed put, the same Taliesin fixture he had been for decades. Svetlana's death was a blood debt he would work the rest of his life to repay. And yet Mrs. Wright still couldn't bring herself to trust him completely, appointing a spy to report back what he was saying and doing.

FRANK LLOYD WRIGHT had tinkered incessantly with the design of his Taliesins, and now Olgivanna was doing the same. Wright had purchased a set of Chinese carpets for the living room in Wisconsin, but died before they were installed. Olgivanna decided to replace them with carpets matching those designed for Wright's 1957 Hoffman house. Johnny Hill, who had done the interiors for that house, thought it was a real mistake: From their colors to the scale of their outsized patterns, they were all wrong for the space.

Wright had taken great care in designing the natural stone wall in Taliesin's living room, matching it to the stone piers in the four corners. Olgivanna had a better idea: She had the wall plastered and covered with gold leaf. Johnny was aghast.

Olgivanna's heavy-handed touch was most evident at Taliesin West, which she made her base of operations. That itself defied her husband's wishes. "If anything happens to me," Wright had told Wes near the end of his life, "concentrate the activity in Wisconsin." For Olgivanna, though, Taliesin was always Mamah Cheney's house. The Arizona complex was hers alone.

Olgivanna made extensive changes to the desert complex, which she claimed her husband considered just a "rough charcoal sketch." Olgivanna dreamed of finishing off the building with a new eastern wing; Kamal Amin, for one, was so taken aback that he actually refused to participate in its design or construction. Johnny Hill wasn't any happier: To his eye, Olgivanna's alterations took Wright's "rugged, masculine, barbaric kind of a creation" and remade it as an elegant, feminine place.

GENE MASSELINK HAD been the peacemaker, the one apprentice who knew both of the Wrights well enough to serve as the intermediary between them and the others. Without him, Taliesin was controlled more and more by Olgivanna's sometimes brutal machinations. The Fellowship was still fractured in two camps; the likes of Hill and Howe, Mr. Wright's people, felt they were fighting a losing battle with apprentices like Pfeiffer and Carney who worshipped his widow.

Johnny Hill was allowed to maintain his position at Taliesin, but at a price—his psyche. Mrs. Wright started a campaign to shatter his confidence by demeaning his skills, his style, his very look. It was a strategy she had learned from Gurdjieff, one designed to bring about rebirth by breaking down the conventional self one puts out for show. Olgivanna took special care to cut him off from his old source of self-esteem, the publishing world, forbidding him from responding to the editors and journalists who tried to interview him about his life back at Taliesin.

She had already begun her similar campaign to push Jack Howe out, but finishing the job would take some doing. Jack couldn't stomach her, but he was determined to remain at Taliesin until the projects Wright had personally designed were all completed. In frustration, Olgivanna went after Jack's wife, Lu Howe. One June day in 1964, Lu was too sick to come to her job as a typist in the Taliesin office. After a day or so, Olgivanna called and demanded that she return to work. She didn't feel well enough, Lu replied. Olgivanna told her to see Dr. Rorke, but Lu demurred.

When Olgivanna called again to complain about Lu's behavior, Jack did something nobody did: He hung up on Mrs. Wright. Unbeknownst to her, the Howes had already decided to leave Taliesin as soon as Wright's projects were completed. Jack soldiered on for another year while Lu continued to work under Olgivanna's watchful eye.

In 1964, exactly a year to the day after Howe proclaimed his "independence," he informed Olgivanna that they were leaving. At first she didn't believe him. When the couple told Wes Peters, he rubbed his hands together feverishly, upset at the thought of losing his good friend and the most talented draftsman in the place. Taliesin needed him, Wes protested. *He* needed him. Besides, he warned, Jack would never make it in the competitive outside world.

The apprentices had been preparing to leave for Paris on a three-week

European caravan in rented Citröen station wagons. Wes convinced Olgi-vanna to let the Howes join them, and their decision was kept secret until they returned from Europe. "Have you changed your mind?" she asked Jack at a gathering of the entire community as she announced their departure. When he said he hadn't, she turned to the assembled apprentices and assured them that there would be no difficulty getting along without Jack.

Aaron Green, a former apprentice visiting at the time, was stunned; after all, he had seen firsthand what Howe meant to the studio. Olgivanna's hand-picked replacement, John Rattenbury, would never measure up.

Green was one of the rare alumni who were still welcome at Taliesin, and with good reason. In 1957, he had a line on a big civic job, a government center for Marin County, just across the Golden Gate Bridge from his San Francisco office. Instead of trying to go it alone, though, he had brought in Wright. By the time Jack Howe decided to quit, the Marin Civic Center was under construc-tion, with Green's office managing the project. Howe asked Green to hire him on to help, and Green agreed—if Olgivanna approved. She did. Jack Howe would see the Marin Civic Center through, fulfilling his promise at last: When the complex opened in 1966, it was Wright's last active project to be completed.

Taliesin would never regain the productivity it enjoyed under Jack Howe.

OLGIVANNA DID AT least one thing right. She figured out how to trade on her husband's name. She threw big parties at Taliesin for wealthy guests, benefactors, and potential clients. And they treated her like royalty, as she ap-parently expected. Leah Adler, Steven Spielberg's mother, was working in a Scottsdale shop one day when Olgivanna arrived with her Fellowship en-tourage. Adler made the mistake of asking if she needed any help. "I haven't spoken to you!" Olgivanna snapped.

The widow's networking efforts did lead to commissions. There was a studio for Clare Boothe Luce, the congressperson, former ambassador, and wife of Henry Luce, the founder of *Time*. And there were less glamorous jobs: a Scottsdale Lutheran church, a small medical building in Spring Green, a mortuary in California, a scattering of houses here and there.

THE ARCHITECTS OF Taliesin, Olgivanna declared in her 1963 book *Roots of Life*, "are continuing to design on the principle of Organic Architecture founded by Frank Lloyd Wright. . . ." Their buildings were "marked with a character of their own," she averred, "though naturally bearing the touch of the master who inspired them."

No one would deny that the Lincoln Income Life Insurance building had "a character of its own." If there was a "touch of the master" about it, though, it was not easy to find. Wes Peters responded to the company's call for a sixteen-story office building in Louisville, Kentucky, by pulling out a set of unused sketches for a hotel Wright had designed for India in the 1940s. Ignoring the cultural chasm between Wright's original and his new site, Wes made it the loose basis for his new design.

Seeking to minimize the amount of steel in the building, Peters suspended all but the uppermost floors of the building from steel cables fixed at the top. The idea was clever, but what came next was outrageous. From this elegantly efficient structural system, Wes dangled a monstrously heavy concrete "sunscreen." Covering all four sides of the building, nearly the full height of the tower, the screen was only minimally effective at blocking the sun, but did a terrific job of blocking what would have been expansive views from inside the offices.

A former Taliesin apprentice who happened on the building one day was flummoxed by its ineptness. He was not alone. Locals called it "the doily building," "the concrete Kleenex box," and "the ugliest building in Louisville."

Louis Weihle, one of the most capable architects left at Taliesin, was so discouraged by the design direction under Wes that he left soon thereafter.

"SHE WANTED THE work out, she wanted the money in," apprentice David Dodge recalled of Olgivanna. But it wasn't that easy. With the Lincoln Tower, the Gammage Auditorium, other college buildings, and a number of houses on the boards, TAA had been busy—but not profitable enough to support two estates and dozens of apprentices. Wes and Olgivanna needed a real moneymaker; they could no longer gamble the fate of the Fellowship on the uncertainties of client work.

In 1966, the year the Lincoln Tower opened, the government put Frank Lloyd Wright's image on a postage stamp. In his lifetime, of course, they had had little use for this social radical, who had dreamed of remaking the United States as a vast landscape of Broadacre Cities. Despite the years of time and effort Wright had expended on his failed Broadacre dream, now Olgivanna and Wes decided to implement their own corporate variation of his "collateral farms" plan. Their scheme was different, but it had one thing in common with Wright's original vision: the difficulty of assembing a vast real estate development with minimal funds. If they could pull it off, it would mean ten years of work for TAA, and a permanent buffer for the Foundation's finances.

Olgivanna and Wes formed the Wisconsin Recreation Development Corporation to launch a project they called "The Spring Green," a bold $50- million commercial development on four thousand acres of Taliesin land. They would doubly benefit from the plan—first by selling the land, then by arranging for TAA to be the sole provider of architecture and planning services. To those who saw Wright's methodical accumulation of the old Lloyd Jones farms as either a sentimental gesture or a political program, the plan was a betrayal.

At length, a buyer did emerge for the property—ironically, the son-in-law of the very first businessman who had resisted Wright's pressure to bankroll a Broadacre City. Married to Hib Johnson's daughter, Williard Keland was a former executive at Johnson Wax.

Taliesin Associated Architects dove into the massive effort, promoted as a reincarnation of Broadacre City. The Spring Green, the *Minneapolis Tribune* announced in a May 1968 column, "is confidently expected to unfold as a billboardless, neonless, elegantly groomed nature-first thing under the esthetic aegis of the late Frank Lloyd Wright. . . ." Yet the site plan suggested that its designers saw the development less as a home for a certain way of life than as a place to play, featuring a ski resort and a golf course.

The proposed architecture of The Spring Green was a mixed bag. The restaurant was a genuine Wright creation, designed in his last years as a teahouse for Taliesin visitors; its foundations had already been poured when he died. But then there was the ski lodge, dubbed the "Wintergreen." Bravely eschewing the typical alpine clichés, Wes and TAA proposed a huge precast-concrete structure lifted in the air on Johnson Wax–style columns. Rather than creating the impression that the building was growing out of the ground, though, the design floated on the columns, which recalled the Le Corbusier *pilotes* Wright had always derided. Defying all practicalities in snow country, Peters also gave the Wintergreen a flat roof. The aesthetic awkwardness of the whole affair was, alas, typical of his work.

The site planning was also bizarre. On relatively flat terrain flanking both banks of the Wisconsin River, Peters's site plan transgressed all of Wright's rules. While Wright himself had used a circular lot, Peters proved indifferent to the natural features of the land, superimposing two perfectly circular roads on the topography, a design that could have been understood only from the air. The site plan did have a certain kinship to Gurdjieff's enneagram—a fact that must have pleased Olgivanna, if no one else.

Only the restaurant was built before the extravagant project went bust.

"WES IS MORE," Wright had often joked, and he was right: Wes Peters loved excess. Like Olgivanna, Wes used the color gold whenever he could. When the talented apprentice Ling Po saw Wes reaching for the bottle of gold ink, he sometimes hid the drawings they were working on until the moment had passed. Johnny Hill interceded as well, toning down that extra bit of circular decoration, those gaudy colors.

But when Iranian royalty came calling with a $6 million budget, there was no holding Wes back. Taliesin's biggest and most remunerative project in the early post-Wright days was the Pearl Palace for Princess Shams, the Shah's eldest daughter by his first wife. The project, to be built on a salt marsh in northern Iran, was brokered by a former apprentice, Nezam Amery, whose father was Shah during the First World War. TAA started work on the commission in 1965; the work would continue for the next eight years.

The first design presentation to the Princess was to take place at Lake Como in Italy. The studio busied itself preparing concept drawings, inked perspectives done in the manner of Persian miniatures. It was a calculated gamble. They knew that the Princess's taste for things American had helped them get the job. Even the royal family's children had had their noses fixed to appear less Iranian. When the Princess saw the drawings, she got up and left the room without saying a word. The Taliesin contingent—Wes Peters, Ling Po, Johnny Hill, and Nezam Amery—sat there perplexed. Amery was beside himself with worry. Soon the Princess returned, daubing her kohl-darkened eyes, and apologized. It looked, she told them, just like what a palace should be.

Wes turned the Pearl Palace into an astoundingly complex project that took over much of the studio. For two summers, Olgivanna even relocated the entire Fellowship to Lugarno, Switzerland, presumably to be closer to the site and their client.

Peters's design for the palace was inspired by the same source as Wright's Baghdad Opera House—*The Thousand and One Nights.* As its name suggests, it was also meant to evoke the princess's most treasured jewel. The building's centerpiece was a metaphorical pearl, a translucent dome 120 feet in diameter, hovering over a reception hall whose grand curved staircase was enveloped in a series of round glass discs. Circles were everywhere in the project—right down to the Princess's circular bed, whose white silk bedspread would contain so much gold and silver thread that it took two servants to turn down the covers. When the Princess was shown a chair, the architects fretted that it would be too heavy for her to move. "Don't worry," she said. "I never move a chair myself."

Every detail was custom-made—cabinet handles, dishes, furniture, and tiles. Johnny Hill did the interiors, scouring Beverly Hills with the Princess for decorator sources. Even he admits that the interiors were overdone, full of velvets and gold leaf. With its fuchsia color scheme, including an incredibly thick shag rug from San Francisco, the palace could have been the world's most expensive whorehouse. In the wake of the Iranian revolution, it was taken over by an Islamic foundation. Rumored within the country to have been designed by Wright himself, the building—now known as the Morvarid Palace—has been called one of Iran's "most prominent contemporary architectural monuments."

OLGIVANNA AND IOVANNA spent much of the 1960s at each other's throats. Olgivanna would make changes to her scores and then demand that Iovanna adapt her choreography. Iovanna would rechoreograph her pieces in turn, demanding changes in her mother's music.

Further aggravating their relationship, Olgivanna increasingly directed her emotional endearments toward other Fellowship women, especially Johnny Hill's ex-wife, Heloise, and Shawn Rorke. Now married to apprentice Vern Swaback, Heloise was Iovanna's second in command, teaching the movements on a day-to-day basis. Shawn, Dr. Rorke's beautiful daughter, starred in some of the performances.

Alcohol was no longer enough for Iovanna. Increasingly desperate for approval, she gradually added sleeping pills, phenobarbital, daprisol, diet

Lath Schiffner

pills, and amphetamines to her regimen, and soon descended into severe addiction.

Still anxious to cure her daughter's troubles, Olgivanna turned to yet another man. Charles Schiffner was a lanky former high school football player who had left Sacramento City College for Taliesin West in 1968. He had been orphaned twice over: Part Native American, he was adopted from a Reno orphanage at the age of three, but his adopted parents were now both dead, his alcoholic father having shot himself. Arriving at Taliesin a homeless youth with the look of a long-haired rock and roller, he managed to talk his way past Olgivanna's hesitations into an apprenticeship. "There are certain things that I can do," he assured her. "Believe me, I will not let you down."

At the outset, Taliesin just seemed bizarre to him. Having come to learn architecture, he found himself in black tie working as a server at the Saturday evening dinner. Hauling the garbage out at midnight, he spilled it all over himself. "What the hell am I doing here?" he wondered, looking up into the onyx night.

There were already Charleses at Taliesin, so Schiffner chose a new name: "Lather," after his shaving cream. Thinking it undignified, Olgivanna shortened it to "Lath."

Schiffner soon came to appreciate what he saw as the beautiful totality of the place, the wholeness Mrs. Wright expected of its residents. "Living in my tent, I learned the season of the brittle bush," he remembered. "I'd wake up at night and see the arc of the moon had changed. I lived with the coyotes. I saw the washes run and I saw them still." Like one of Mr. Wright's original apprentices, he experienced "a love of life that is framed by beauty. . . . I was there at a magical time."

Schiffner proved both an adventuresome designer and a seeker of deeper truths. Like all apprentices, he designed and built his own living quarters at Taliesin West—graced, in his case, by a spiky, nine-foot phallic stone that he persuaded eleven other apprentices to help him haul out and upend on his land: "my prow that faces the city," as he called it. Olgivanna would see his potential and seize it.

Iovanna would put him to the test.

₣AMILY ꟿATTERS

EVER SINCE SVETLANA'S DEATH IN 1946, Olgivanna had sought to establish contact with her daughter by occult means. And she believed that she had received messages in response.

But she needed more, and two decades after losing her daughter, she found hope in a second immigrant named Svetlana. Born in Tiflis, like her own daughter, this Svetlana struck Olgivanna as a spirit double sent by cosmic forces. There were other coincidences: Georgi Gurdjieff, whom some considered may have been Svetlana Hinzenberg's real father, had boasted of studying at a Jesuit seminary in Tiflis where this new Svetlana's father actually had studied. But the newcomer's father never became a priest. Quite the contrary: He became the leader of the Soviet Union.

Joseph Stalin's beloved only daughter, Svetlana Alliluyeva, escaped mother Russia in 1967, to a flurry of media attention. Premier Kosygin declared before the United Nations that she was a "morally unstable person and she's a sick person, and we can only pity those who wish to use her for any political aims." While she would indeed later claim to have been used, the aim wasn't even remotely political.

SVETLANA ALLILUYEVA, A red-haired, twice-divorced English-to-Russian translator, had defected during a trip to India to scatter the ashes of her common-law Indian husband on the Ganges. When her two grown children went to the airport to meet their mother's returning plane, she was not on board. Svetlana had asked for asylum from the American embassy in New Delhi.

"Hello there, everybody," a smiling Svetlana said to the mob of reporters at Kennedy Airport on April 21, 1967. "I am very happy to be here." The *New*

York Times reporter noted that "[h]er cheeks were pink, but her only make-up was dark pink lipstick. She wore no gloves, nail polish or jewelry." Svetlana was a joyful, plain-spoken woman, robust yet bookish, who was most comfortable among common folk. When a private detective was assigned to travel with her, Svetlana detached a rose she had pinned to her suit and stuck it into his sun visor.

In the months that followed, Alliluyeva was constantly in the news. Harper and Row gave her a $2.5 million advance to write a book, a figure second only to the amount Winston Churchill received for the first volume of his wartime memoirs. The publisher's stock jumped on the news of her signing, and both *Life* magazine and the *New York Times* bought serial rights. The tabloids splashed rumors that her father had placed a fortune in gold in her name in a Swiss bank before his death in 1953.

Alliluyeva herself, however, showed no appetite for the high life. She donated part of her royalties to a charitable trust to fund a hospital for the poor in India in memory of her husband. Settling into Princeton, New Jersey, she drove a four-door green Dodge without air-conditioning, and bought a small white Cape Cod house with black shutters, its living room flooded with light from the garden. "I longed to be unnoticed," she remembered, "and to sit on my porch, barefooted, at my typewriter."

She thought she would stay there forever.

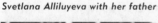

Svetlana Alliluyeva with her father

*   *   *

WITH THE PUBLICATION of *Twenty Letters to a Friend*, Svetlana began receiving letters of her own from all over the world—some of them from a certain desert compound in Arizona. Olgivanna and Iovanna were both, for their own reasons, intrigued by this newcomer's story, and they both invited her to visit Taliesin.

For Olgivanna, of course, the name itself was a talisman. From the Russian *svet*, meaning light, it is a name often given to the beautiful young maiden in Russian fairy tales. And there were other signs—the coincidences of their birthplaces, of their shared connection to the Tiflis seminary. Alliluyeva's maternal grandmother was even named Olga, Olgivanna's birth name.

Casting about for spiritual connection, Olgivanna soon became convinced that Stalin's daughter's coming was a cosmic event, a replacement for her dead daughter, Taliesin's own fairy princess.

The invitations to Taliesin started in November 1969, when dreams of big money from the Spring Green project had collapsed. The apprentices followed up with letters of their own. Olgivanna sent pictures and books showing Alliluyeva their estate, but the visual aids didn't convince her; to her, the buildings looked like "theater decorations."

Olgivanna also contacted her by phone, repeatedly. "When are you coming? When are you coming? You must come here." Olgivanna held little or nothing back from Alliluyeva, telling her of the Svetlana she had lost, returning over and over again to their shared name, to its rarity in America. "There are karmic waves which are over our heads," she explained. Soon, Olgivanna was even referring on the phone to this new Svetlana as her "daughter."

All of this made Svetlana Alliluyeva cringe, but it also intrigued her. She had grown up without a mother. In 1932, when Svetlana was just six years old, her mother, Stalin's second wife, had died violently in their Kremlin apartment after publicly standing up to him at a banquet. Her death from a gunshot wound was apparently self-inflicted, but there were also marks on her neck, and whispers of murder. In 1957, Svetlana shed the name Stalin in favor of her mother's family name, Alliluyeva. Olgivanna was born in the same year as her own mother. Perhaps, she thought, a meeting would have emotional meaning for her too.

"SVETLANA!" A WOMAN about her own age, eyes heavy with mascara and shadow, called out loudly at the Phoenix airport. The woman rushed forward and enveloped her in a hug, embarrassing Svetlana with the public display. As the two sped off across the suburbanizing desert in Iovanna's red sports car, Iovanna blurted out: "I hope YOU will be my sister!" The colors of the desert on that March day in 1970, the smell of the orange groves, the vast sunshine, all made Svetlana feel drunk.

Olgivanna, too, embraced Svetlana on their first meeting. Svetlana, who knew that Mrs. Wright was also a Slav, had expected her to look like her own mother. Yet Taliesin's slender matriarch, with her "parchment-yellow wrinkled face" and "quick sharp eyes," recalled nothing of her mother's shy beauty, her "velvet soft eyes." Rather, she reminded Svetlana of somebody else: "A very strong lady, regal widow," she wrote, "her light-brown eyes [had] that yellow wildcat spark my father used to have. . . ."

THAT FIRST NIGHT in the Taliesin West dining room—a "fantastic cave," she thought—Svetlana was seated next to a tall man wearing a sand-colored tuxedo and a ruffled lavender shirt, finished off with a pendant on a massive gold chain, a golden owl with sapphire eyes. She was a bit shocked; she had known that the "other" Svetlana had left a widower, but hadn't realized that Wes Peters was still around. She was struck by his handsome, Lincolnesque face, and attracted to his quiet reserve. He was unlike the others, who reminded her of "birds of paradise." They sat together, dining on spicy Mexican food; Peters said almost nothing.

The opulence of the setting astounded her: the polished red table, the gilded cutlery, the crystal glasses, the antique Chinese tapestries hanging on the walls. Attentive young male waiters served them course after course. "I could not guess who were those young men," she recalled, "who looked too serious and inspired to be waiters."

Olgivanna held court, directing conversation while monitoring each of her guests out of the corner of her eye. Every word she uttered was followed with rapt attention by all in attendance.

"It was like at my father's table," Svetlana recalled. "People didn't talk until he talked. He would set the subject, and he would make a joke, and everybody would say 'ha, ha, ha.' It was that way."

"I am so glad Wes and Svetlana have finally met," Olgivanna finally announced to the table. It must have been delicious to say the two names together again.

For the next several days, Wes guided her about Taliesin West, a place she found ominous, heavy, and dark, evoking "ancient graves." The low-ceilinged apprentice rooms reminded her of monk's cells. She had come to meet Olgivanna, but it was clear that she had been invited to meet Wes Peters. How was it possible, she wondered, that the chief architect could spend so much time away from work showing her around?

If Svetlana Alliluyeva didn't much care for Taliesin, she did fall under the spell of Wes Peters, whose aura of power made her feel safe. Even so, her instinct was to depart. She had good friends back in New Jersey; she had a third book in the works. She was planning a trip to Hawaii that summer. "It was the first time in my life [when I was] doing what I wanted," she recalled. "I had money." All she felt like doing was taking her dog for a drive in her Dodge, listening to the radio as the American countryside rolled by.

When Svetlana told her hostess she was ready to go, Olgivanna pressed her to remain a little longer, until Easter. Svetlana found it hard to say no.

"How do you like Wes?" Olgivanna suddenly asked, pinning her with her stare.

"I said that I liked him very much, indeed," Svetlana recalled, "avoiding her straight look, which went deep into me, searching for truth. My Father had a way of asking questions like that, and it was alarming. People would back out of his room, paralyzed by his quick intense look. So they did here." It was uncomfortable, a feeling of invasion. "This was kind of ugly, you know, because this was America, after all."

Easter at Taliesin was beautiful, a festival featuring traditional Orthodox Pascha, a sweet cheese, and a raisin cake called *koulitch*. The apprentices painted elaborately decorated Easter eggs, which were presented to each of the guests. Svetlana, though, was puzzled by the constant festivities at Taliesin— the nonstop parade of dance presentations, concerts, and picnics. She found it distasteful that the guests invited to these lavish events were always wealthy potential clients and patrons, never the artists and intelligentsia to whom she had been drawn in Moscow. And with so many social events, she wondered, how did they get their architectural work done?

Nevertheless, tucked away in the sensuous desert setting, surrounded by a community whose members all seemed to dote on her, Svetlana felt herself bending to the desires of her hostess and the charms of this handsome, Midwestern giant.

The taciturn Wes Peters was finally opening up to her. As they shared stories of lost love and missed chances, Svetlana felt the power of Peters's love for his dead wife. "He was so under the spell of his first marriage," she recalled. "It was almost a ritual thing. . . . [Wright] was like a king and he married a king's daughter."

Though the match began as another of Olgivanna's arranged-marriage schemes, Wes's feelings for this second Svetlana flowered with amazing speed. Perhaps to her surprise, Alliluyeva felt the same way. "Marriage, a conventional marriage with family, home, children," she recalled, "had been something I always wanted since my youth, yet it never worked. By now I was afraid even to think about another possibility and to try again. Yet something in this man was so sad and so decent that I was overwhelmed with compassion to him. And with that came feeling that I would do anything for him—which is love."

On April 7, 1970, just three weeks after she landed in Phoenix, the two were married.

The night before, Olgivanna had called Svetlana to her room. Wes, she explained with a grave look on her face, had a "strange weakness." He was a profligate spender, constantly buying new cars for himself, jewels for the Taliesin women, dogs and presents for the children. Many years ago, she explained, Wes had used his inheritance to buy some of the most beautiful lands around Taliesin for the Fellowship, and she was grateful for that. But he had continued to spend beyond his means, and though the Fellowship had come to his financial rescue in the past, they had reached their limit.

The man Svetlana was about to marry, Olgivanna made clear, was on the verge of bankruptcy. He would have to sell his farm to pay off his debts. "You will have to see now that he stops that! My own Svetlana was always worried about this, too!"

Wes Peters and Svetlana Alliluyeva at their wedding, 1970

Svetlana thought Mrs. Wright was saving her fiancé the embarrassment of telling her himself. "I was not used to money talk," she recalled. Astounded that the chief architect of such an apparently opulent institution was penniless, Svetlana saw instantly what she must do. "Yes, Mrs. Wright, of course, of course, it's now our debts," she told her hostess. It would be her pleasure to share the burden.

At the ceremony, which received intense publicity, Olgivanna introduced her to everybody as "my daughter, Svetlana." The apprentices showered her with jewelry. "Now I can say again, 'Svetlana and Wes!'" Olgivanna exulted.

At 2:30 that same afternoon, a quit claim deed was recorded in Dodgeville, Wisconsin, removing Wes's name from the title of the Hillside property, putting it in the name of the Foundation. Should the couple divorce, Taliesin's land could no longer become community property.

On her wedding night, Svetlana must have been unnerved to discover that Mrs. Wright's sway extended into their nuptial bedroom. It was rumored that Olgivanna convinced them to spend their wedding night in separate bedrooms. There could not have been a blunter signal of who was really in charge. Svetlana was even expected to call Olgivanna "Mother"— just as some others did.

A few days later, lawyers for the Foundation asked Svetlana if she intended to open a joint account with her husband. The question struck her as precipitous, but she shrugged it off as American money-mindedness. Her new husband had no money at all, it turned out—not even pocket cash—so Svetlana ignored her own lawyers' advice and transferred her total savings into a joint bank account in Arizona. As a wedding present, she paid off all her new husband's personal debts, half a million dollars in total, and cleared his farm, Aldebaran, of all encumbrances.

"I wanted us to have together a small family property—something of our own," she recalled. "Not all those architectural novelties, but a little old-fashioned farmhouse amidst hills, woods and fields. . . . I was launched on a path of domesticity, trying to heal all old hurts of my husband."

Some men are good lovers, some good parents, others good friends, still others good husbands. At first, Svetlana believed that she had found the last in Wes Peters. She hoped to be with him for life. When he introduced her as "my wife," she recalled, "I would just swoon[;] I would just melt."

Wes bought Svetlana clothes for Taliesin's dinners and parties, cloaking her in embroidered and glittering gowns, in silks and chiffons, finished with stunning pieces of jewelry. But she squirmed in the hostess role he expected. She had married him, not Taliesin. His complaints about her behavior infuriated her. At one of Taliesin's gala dinner parties the couple argued publicly.

Svetlana's largesse seemed unlimited. She went back to Princeton t̶o̶ her home and to bring her beloved Dodge back to Taliesin. She gave the car to her new stepson, and when Wes told her that Brandoch would prefer a new Citröen, she wrote a check for it. Abandoning his career as a professional cellist, Brandoch had come back to Taliesin. He had been raised to reach for greatness, and playing in the Munich Symphony was not good enough—particularly for his grandmother. He was, Olgivanna told him, just a "stand player. You don't stack up."

Svetlana bankrolled a cattle-breeding operation at Aldebaran for Brandoch and Wes. After she invested a third of a million dollars, they lost two herds.

Svetlana had hoped to move out of their cramped quarters at Taliesin—where there wasn't even room to make a cup of coffee—and make Aldebaran their family home. She stayed off their terrace during daylight hours, avoiding the tourists who sometimes hovered there hoping to see or even photograph the daughter of Joseph Stalin. And she disliked the enforced community lifestyle at the Fellowship—the meals together, the comradeship in which Wes expected her to participate. She did, however, dutifully handle her chores—washing dishes, cleaning tables, tending the gardens.

The two spent more and more time apart; preoccupied by the palace in Iran, Wes seemed to like it that way.

WHEN SVETLANA RETURNED from Princeton, a chill had set in; she could feel it. "Nobody smiled at me. Mrs. Wright had no time for me." It would never have occurred to Svetlana that money might have something to do with it.

But it did. Shortly after they were married, Olgivanna had commented in passing that Svetlana might consider transferring all her personal assets to the Frank Lloyd Wright Foundation. "You will be one of our benefactors," she had suggested. Svetlana was assured that she would always be well looked-after, that she could live out her life here.

Olgivanna didn't wait for an answer. When Svetlana was in Princeton settling her affairs, she discovered that Taliesin's attorneys had contacted her lawyer requesting that her Alliluyeva Trust give the Foundation a yearly grant of $40,000. "I felt," she said, "there was some kind of mistake because they imagined me more wealthy than I was." The trust, which financed a hospital in India, did not have that kind of money.

Olgivanna, she realized, had accepted the tabloid rumors at face value. "You see," she said many years later, "to put it bluntly in the American way—I was invited to finance the institution. There was this terrible [impression] created by the media or the State Department, I don't know by who, my

iss banks which allegedly my father left for me. My fa-
money for me. He was of communist inclinations; he
private wealth." She bluntly refused Olgivanna's request
an explanation from Wes. "My dear," he replied, "Mrs.
you. You try to stay good friends with her. Because if you don't
eet a tragedy."

Initially Olgivanna had approached Svetlana only to pay Peters's debts. And that, to Olgivanna's fury, was all that had been done with his new wife's money. Soon, however, Svetlana was furious with both of them—her hostess and her new husband. Perusing Wes's cancelled checks, she found he was using her money to buy dresses for the apprentice girls at Taliesin.

Money wasn't the only issue between the two women. Not only had Svetlana refused to call her "Mother," but she wouldn't share her secrets. When the older woman tried to interrogate her about her sex life, Svetlana refused to talk about such matters, rebuffing her overtures with fierce shame. Why not? Olgivanna asked. Everybody here sought her counsel about their personal lives. Mrs. Wright was disappointed that Svetlana had revealed herself to be so "conventional."

JUNE 8, 1970, brought the usual celebration of Wright's birthday. "Mr. Wright is with us. He hears us," Olgivanna exclaimed to the hundreds of guests, just as she often did to the apprentices in the drafting room. The guests greeted her declaration with silence.

"Who would like to speak about our Fellowship and its work?" she asked, looking directly at Svetlana.

Svetlana did not move. If forced, she would talk about her pleasure in marrying her husband, but not the community.

"Whom would the spirit move?" Olgivanna insisted, looking again at Wes's new bride.

Svetlana understood what she was being asked. But she wouldn't oblige.

Barbara Kaiser, Kamal Amin's fiancée and heir to the Kaiser Aluminum fortune, stood up to say something gracious. Svetlana had been saved.

TO ADD TO Olgivanna's consternation, Stalin's daughter was getting all the attention, from both visitors to Taliesin and the press. Olgivanna was consumed with jealousy. "I'm throwing Svetlana out," she announced to a visiting friend one day after Svetlana hung up on her. "It's never going to work."

Terrified that he would have to go with her, Wes objected. Olgivanna relented.

Having come to America dreaming of starting a family in a house with a white picket fence, Svetlana found herself in what she now saw as a cross between a feudal manor and a Soviet labor camp. "Architects were paid miserable salary, or not paid at all. . . . There was NO individual income for anyone. Architects were working with no weekends, no yearly vacations, and actually no holidays: because on big national holidays they had to entertain guests, cook for a party of 200, serve meals, play music, dance before the audience and also do their work some time."

Svetlana saw fear among the apprentices, not unlike the fear Soviet citizens had once felt toward her father. She also saw all the familiar signs of a personality cult. In her father's case at least there was an embalmed body to worship. At Taliesin, she recalled, "Wright's portrait looked from every corner, but he himself was not here." Neither was there any architectural creativity, she thought, just a "re-hashing of his old designs, making 'Wright-style' projects."

"Why had I to come to this weird place," she recalled thinking, "where everything reminded me [of] what I have run away from? This primitive communism under a dictator."

Having resisted Olgivanna herself, Svetlana was dismayed at how completely her apparently powerful husband deferred to her, never once daring to express an opinion, let alone cross her, in public. "Wes had no authority," she recalled. "All decisions belonged to the widow, even if [they] concerned very special architectural matters." How could it be, she wondered, for "a big man like him to fear a little old lady with wrinkled parchment face?"

And while Wes attended to Olgivanna's every whim, he showed no interest in his wife, never even read her books. He was uninterested in anything beyond Taliesin; the two found very little to talk about when they were alone. Only when he was far from Olgivanna's judgmental eye, driving the open road during their annual migrations between the two Taliesins, did things change. Then Wes opened up, reciting ditties, drawing on his vast store of American historical knowledge to describe the sites along the way. She loved him then.

OLGIVANNA WAS MAKING one of her surprise visits to the apprentices' rooms when she stepped into the one "Lath" Schiffner had just finished decorating for himself. Iovanna's long-haired paramour was using an old toilet as his chair, and his walls were covered with posters of the Beatles, the Grateful Dead, and Jefferson Airplane. He knew he was in for it. "Posters of women, I can understand," Mrs. Wright said as she left his room, "but posters of men?" Lath took down the posters, and dropped his youthful rebellion along with them. It was time "to generate something new," he recalled thinking.

Olgivanna took to the ruggedly handsome young man, who felt he had found a family "closer than an organic or natural family" in Taliesin. "Mrs. Wright is like a mother to us all," he told a reporter for *Life* magazine. "She is the best counselor in the world and can talk to us about all sorts of problems. If people have trouble understanding her, they haven't really arrived yet."

Lath's "arrival" included a full immersion into the Gurdjieff work. With Iovanna, now forty-five, teaching him the movements, and Olgivanna offering instruction in the philosophy, he felt his energies all shift. He danced the part of "Man" in Iovanna's *Time Upon Time*. The whole experience reshaped who he was, he recalled, and hence his ability to be an architect.

It seemed to Lath that Taliesin's architecture was "evolving . . . into a new form" under Mrs. Wright's influence. There wasn't a project on the boards, he felt, that didn't have "a certain glow to it." He was not surprised. Olgivanna had often been summoned into the drafting room by her husband, she told him, to ask her opinion about a new design. When she didn't approve of something, Olgivanna told Schiffner, her husband would "rant and rave and say, 'What do you know about architecture? You don't know anything.' And then she would come in the next morning and it would be totally changed."

But it wasn't just a color or detail here and there. Lath was convinced of Olgivanna's claim that by introducing Wright to Gurdjieff, she had fundamentally transformed his architecture. As a result, the young man believed, Wright was able to move beyond the masculine geometries of the Prairie houses and the Unity Temple to more fluid forms, to draw on the ways of the heart, rather than the abstractions of his head. One indicator of this change was Wright's increasing use of the compass, balancing the rectilinear with the circular. Under Olgivanna's influence, Lath observed, Wright was able to draw on his feminine side. Even the rectilinear Fallingwater seemed to show her influence. Look closely, Lath advised, and you can see the "love that is in that work." "See, if the Bauhaus had Mrs. Wright, maybe we'd have a different International Style architecture. It wouldn't be so intellectual and so cubistic."

Olgivanna dubbed Lath her "spiritual son." She also encouraged his budding relationship with her daughter. Lath read bedtime stories to Iovanna's little daughter, Eve, and each day the little girl would place flowers on his drawing board. He was also given a rare leave to go with Iovanna on a drive to California. At the time, Iovanna was still living with another apprentice, Michael Sutton, whom she had been sleeping with on and off for fifteen years. But Lath, twenty years her junior, was different; he was someone she could fall in love with. Sutton tried to put a stop to it, confronting Schiffner in an attempt to scare him off.

Schiffner wasn't deterred. He was taken by Iovanna's fierce creativity, her force, both artistic and erotic. He continued dancing in her mythic choreographies, including a well-received show at San Francisco's Grace Cathedral in May 1971. He spent the night constructing the set and fell asleep next to the altar. "I fell in love with life. I fell in love with the energy that Taliesin was giving me, with the expansion of my consciousness, with the understanding and appreciation of what a human being is. It was love. . . . That's what kept me going."

Lath composed and framed a poem to Iovanna "whose faith is my strength":

> . . . If the world knew
> the genius that veins through the blood of Iovanna
> They would know
> the grace of God
> and the cause of God
> And the course of poetry.

A MIRACLE HAD occurred: At forty-four, Svetlana Peters was pregnant. She glowed with the knowledge. Wes rushed off ebulliently to tell Mrs. Wright, but when he returned the joy was gone. How could he have been so stupid to have gotten his wife pregnant? Olgivanna had rebuked him. Babies were a nuisance, distracting and diverting energy from the work. Women of Svetlana's age, she informed him, didn't give birth in America.

"Are you not going to do something about it?" Wes asked his wife timidly a few days later. She would have this baby no matter what, she replied. "Why do dictators always interfere?" she rebuked her husband, and then answered her own question: "Well, because such is the nature of all dictators."

Her words inevitably worked their way back to Mrs. Wright. Somewhere along the way Olgivanna had gotten the mistaken impression that Svetlana's godfather was ambassador George Kennan, the architect of America's policy of Soviet "containment," and now she asked Kennan to convince Svetlana to get an abortion. When he refused, she even threatened to come to Princeton to argue her case.

Even so, Wes was quietly pleased that he was going to be a father again, and the discord between the pair soon evaporated. Olgivanna, however, was livid. "I think she was annoyed seeing us happy," Svetlana recalled. "She was cutting Wes with an old rusty saw. She was cutting him in pieces and he just couldn't stand it."

Wes and his underlings did some sawing themselves, adding closets, a kitchenette, and a roof over the balcony to ready their studio apartment for the baby. But they couldn't get a washing machine—only Mrs. Wright was allowed that luxury. When the work was finished, Wes came to Svetlana with a bill for

$30,000—a high price for the work, and perhaps not coincidentally the exact amount the Foundation had asked from her as an annual donation. The check was drawn on their joint account, but he made sure it was she who signed it.

HAVING DELIVERED IOVANNA'S baby, and knowing that Svetlana would get little help from anyone at Taliesin, her obstetrician advised her to have it elsewhere. As she entered her ninth month, Wes took her to Mill Valley, California, where his sister Marge lived with her husband, the famed semanticist Samuel Hayakawa, then the president of San Francisco State University. Marge didn't mince words with Svetlana. "He's working like a slave and they don't pay him," she said of Wes, but he would never leave.

Olga Margedant Peters was born on May 21, 1971. When Svetlana's contractions began, Wes was at a meeting in nearby San Francisco; Hayakawa drove her to the hospital. Wes didn't arrive until after the baby was born, and when he did, he had a television crew with him. Wes was thrilled to have a girl at last. Svetlana was annoyed at his late arrival and his entourage.

When the threesome returned to Spring Green, Olgivanna was pleased to learn that Wes had named the girl Olga, after her. Then Svetlana informed Mrs. Wright that she had in fact been named for Olga Alliluyeva, her grandmother.

Svetlana was hoping that the family could now move to Aldebaran, whose revival as a working cattle farm she had financed—with a new silo, a big herd of cows, and a prize bull from Colorado. Wes, however, was set on living with the rest of the Fellowship, and he asked Svetlana to stay at Taliesin and leave her stepson behind at the farm. Brandoch needed his privacy, Wes explained.

Trapped at Taliesin, Svetlana began acting the part of the Russian dissident, complaining about how unfairly overworked the apprentices were. Once friendly to her, the "exploited labor" were ordered to stop visiting her—except to ask her to return their wedding gifts, which they explained had actually belonged to Taliesin. Iovanna was just plain rude, demanding the return of a turquoise pin and a set of large pearls.

One night, with Wes away yet again on business, Svetlana was invited to a private dinner with Olgivanna, Iovanna, and Kamal Amin. Svetlana was worried about Wes. "He works too hard all the time; he is going to die," she announced at the table.

"So are you," Iovanna growled through clenched teeth.

Before the winter departure for Arizona, Olgivanna invited Svetlana to her room for a personal audience. What was it that she so disliked about Taliesin? the matron asked. Svetlana assured her that there was nothing wrong, that she was sure everything would be all right.

According to Svetlana, Olgivanna suddenly reached forward, grabbed her hands, and pulled her "so close that there was almost no space between us." When Svetlana tried to pull free, Olgivanna held on. "She stared into my eyes and would not let me take mine away; then she began to breathe deeply and slowly, still staring." In Olgivanna's grip—held tight by her hands, her eyes, her very breath—Svetlana felt her will slipping away, as if she were being possessed.

Finally Svetlana broke. Her face flooded with tears. And then she did something she would never have done normally: She kissed the old woman's hands. Only then did Olgivanna release Svetlana.

"One never forgets such moments," Olgivanna told her.

Svetlana couldn't understand her own behavior. After all, she had stood up to Joseph Stalin. She had once thought of herself as being made of harder stuff.

AFTER THE ENCOUNTER, Svetlana sat in her room trembling and weeping. "Mrs. Wright loves you," Wes told her without a hint of outrage, "but you are unable to respond to her in the same way. She is very much upset by that. She loves everybody here like a mother." They were reaching an impasse. "You have not understood this place at all," he said. "It is a privilege to live at Taliesin, the best way of life imaginable. I thought I gave you this chance by our marriage. If you do not appreciate that, I do not know what our future will be."

Svetlana took baby Olga and drove out in the countryside. After all she had gone through in the Soviet Union, she vowed, she would not "make a robot" of her daughter at Taliesin, a place where children were so unwelcome.

And then one afternoon Svetlana stopped across the road at the Unity Chapel cemetery—and saw the name "Svetlana Peters" beautifully lettered on one of grave markers. "Oh my god," she thought. "That's how it will finish with me." Next to the grave was that of little Daniel Peters, the boy who died with the first Svetlana in the shallow wash. Olga, she thought, looked just like Daniel had as a baby. She began to fear for her own baby's life. It did not seem beyond Olgivanna to engineer an accident. "I think," she said, "she could just kill us, throw us in the lake. . . . She was that kind of person."

Svetlana decided that Olga must be baptized, "for protection." There was, she believed, "some kind of evil lurking around." Wes was pleased; Wright's Greek Orthodox Church of the Annunciation near Milwaukee was about to celebrate the tenth anniversary of its completion, and the Orthodox Church's American archbishop was coming to consecrate it. A baptism for the daughter of its chief engineer would be a happy addition to the festivities. And it was doubly fitting that the child's mother was Stalin's daughter—a symbol of the victory of Orthodox Christianity over Communism.

The entire Fellowship came to Milwaukee for the baptism. The altar was washed in wine and rose water; the building itself was anointed with baptismal oil. As they thrice dipped baby Olga into the waters beneath the gold-flecked dome, Svetlana was presented with a pair of uncanny visions: an icon of the Holy Virgin that Gene Masselink had modeled on the dead Svetlana, and a baby Jesus that appeared to be based on young Daniel, who so resembled her own baby.

When the joyful Peters family returned to Taliesin late that night, Wes received a summons from Mrs. Wright. When he returned, he was ashen. He sat down limply, holding his head in his hands; Svetlana could see he was on the verge of tears. "We have ruined this celebration," he told Svetlana. "She blames me; she blames us. Our baby was in the front of the whole thing, while Frank Lloyd Wright was forgotten. His building was not celebrated. Your baby was celebrated."

For Svetlana, that was the end. She pleaded with Wes's friends Don and Virginia Lovness, who happened to be visiting, to take her and the baby with them when they left. "Someone tried to burn Taliesin before," she told Virginia, "and they didn't do a good job. But I'm going to burn it down, and I'll do a good job." Taking the threat seriously, Virginia warned Olgivanna—who immediately hired a guard to protect the estate—and brought in a doctor to look after Wes's anguished wife.

Svetlana sequestered herself and Olga in her room. Fearing for her baby's safety, she never let her out of her sight; Wes had to bring in food for her. Though she made the winter 1971 trip to Arizona, she refused to accompany Wes to the all-important Taliesin Christmas dinner. Later, Olgivanna came in bare feet to the Peters's room to give Svetlana a Christmas present of diamond earrings. Svetlana refused to take them, shouting, "You cannot buy my friendship!"

"I'll kill her! I'll kill her!" Iovanna roared when she heard.

OLGIVANNA WANTED HER out, and finally Wes was ready. When Svetlana asked him again to move away from Taliesin, he agreed. They found a little house in Paradise Valley, fifteen minutes' drive from Taliesin West. When she moved in, Wes told her that he would be staying at Taliesin. The whole house-hunting exercise had been a ruse to get her off the premises and set the stage for divorce.

Wes didn't even have the nerve to tell Svetlana himself. She first heard the news from reporters who came to the house looking for a response to a statement from Taliesin confirming that Wes wanted a divorce. Wes told friends he no longer loved her; some longtime apprentices were starting to see him as pathetic. "Wes Peters approaches the age of 60," Edgar Tafel wrote to Jack Howe, "and he cannot have any feelings of his own without consulting his superiors."

Svetlana was outraged. "I believe in private property," she told a reporter from the *Arizona Republic*. At Taliesin, however, "they live a communal life. . . . They share their incomes, their food, their living. Everyone works, including the children. That's why I left Russia."

Wes was outraged. "Everybody is here by choice, not compulsion. Svetlana failed to separate this from totalitarianism. This is the quintessence of democracy. . . . Frank Lloyd Wright taught a higher degree of individuality than anyone I knew. . . . Of course, there is leadership."

Iovanna was outraged. "Nobody rejected her at all. It was she who rejected and was so suspicious." Svetlana's book, she claimed, "had been shadow written by somebody in the government. . . . She was a murderer's daughter."

Svetlana's lawyer was outraged. Wes continued writing checks on their joint account, which contained only his wife's money. By the time a final accounting was completed, two thirds of Svetlana's $1.2 million savings were gone. At least, her attorney advised, she should demand the farm she had financed in return.

All talk of cosmic convergence aside, Svetlana concluded, Olgivanna had invited her to Taliesin for one reason only: to get her money.

In May 1973, Wes Peters filed for divorce. Svetlana's attorney wanted to sue for alimony; Taliesin would have to pay. "I was advised by the lawyer," Svetlana recalled, "to take all my money, to get Aldebaran, to get this, get that, actually to crush the man. I didn't do that."

Wes granted her complete custody of Olga, but gave her no child support. Svetlana did ask that Wes pay a small monthly amount into a college fund for his daughter, but he didn't. Wes had no money, and never would.

IN THE SAME month in 1971 when Svetlana fled Taliesin with her newborn daughter, one of Taliesin's own—a young man whose very name made him an emblem for the community—tried to escape back into Taliesin from the outside world. Olgivanna would not make it easy.

Tal Davison, named for Taliesin, had been trying for months to make his way on the outside, but each time he returned he was in worse shape. No wonder: The twenty-year-old son of Kay and Davy Davison, he had been raised to think of himself as a problem. The demands of parenting were irreconcilable with the demands of serving Olgivanna. Kay often tried to solve the problem by locking young Tal in a tiny room, sometimes for as long as six hours. This worked until he learned to take the hinges off the door from the inside. Desperate to attract his mother's attention, he once cut up her clothes with pinking shears.

Kay had largely deferred decisions about Tal's upbringing to Olgivanna, but that was cold comfort for him; Mrs. Wright often singled him out for blame when things went wrong. Tal actually fared better than his sister Celeste, seven years his junior, who was sent away to a residential hospital as a girl after developing polio. After two years there, with few visits from her parents, Celeste returned to Taliesin with her legs in braces. When she broke one of them while in the first grade at a local school, she was sent away again, this time to a special school in Denver. Dealing with the sickly child, Olgivanna insisted, was interfering with her parents' duties, particularly Kay's. Celeste remained in Denver for the next six years.

Tal Davison, one of Taliesin's tragic lost boys

Mrs. Wright rode young Tal for his childish shenanigans. Mr. Wright made him feel lacking in another way: Whenever he encountered Tal, the imposing architect would ask him what he'd done that day that was creative. The boy always found himself groping for an answer. Sometimes he just stood there saying nothing.

Tal entered his teens the year *Rebel Without a Cause* came out. Directed by former apprentice Nicholas Ray, the movie starred James Dean as an aimless teenager hell-bent on trouble. Tal looked a bit like Dean, and he identified with him, showing his own rebellious streak by hanging around Taliesin in sandals and open shirts to show off his chest. He even attended Taliesin's Saturday and Sunday evening events without the mandated formal wear. When Tal finally decided on a direction in life, it was acting: He knew he was funny, and thought he could parlay that into a career on-screen.

In the winter of 1961, at nineteen, Tal met Diane Snodgrass, one of those town girls Mrs. Wright had forbidden the boys to date. Diane was the sixteen-year-old daughter of an Arizona train engineer who had little income, but lots of children and enough love for everybody. Tal would take his new sweetheart up the long dirt road to Taliesin West in his father's Lincoln convertible and sneak her in. The other boys Diane knew just drank a few beers, but Tal kept a vodka bottle in the canvas folds of the Lincoln's top. They made out in Tal's tent and watched the stars.

Olgivanna was determined to bridle this rebel. That summer, as his parents joined the migration back to Wisconsin, she forced Tal to remain behind to suffer the scorching desert heat.

But this punishment worked no better than any of the others she had tried. So, in a move that would have appalled her husband—but not her mother, the general—Olgivanna made a last-ditch effort to instill some discipline in the nineteen-year-old: She forced him to sign up for the Air Force. America's air war in Vietnam and Laos was just beginning. When Tal shipped out, neither his father nor his mother showed up; he was taken to the station by the Snodgrass family. After a stint in Spain, he was transferred to England, where he married a black woman who bore him a son before they divorced.

After his discharge, Tal returned to Taliesin, a source of hot meals, the only home he knew. His sister, Celeste, wasn't doing well either. At sixteen she had married a Taliesin hired man and moved with him to Florida, but her new husband had died in a car crash a few months later. When she called her father asking him to come pick her up, Olgivanna intervened, instructing Kay to tell Celeste to get a job.

Tal's father, Davy, almost succumbed to "sentimentality" and rushed to be with Celeste, he later wrote Olgivanna. "But then your sound advice came to me through Kay and I realized instantly, despite all the turmoil inside, how absolutely right you were. All I could say was 'Thank God for Mrs. Wright.'"

TAL RETURNED FROM the Air Force in 1969, in time for Taliesin's Easter celebration. There he met Anna Bogdanovich, a fetching seventeen-year-old girl visiting for the summer from Scottsdale; the two were taken with each other. He was "a lovely, lovely young man," remembered Anna, whose brother was the young film critic and director Peter Bogdanovich. But she also recalled how he trembled ever so slightly and took valium to calm himself down. The two of them spent much of that summer together in Spring Green.

Anna found it strange how all the apprentices stood whenever Mrs. Wright walked into the room, sitting down again only after she took her seat. Tal told her he considered Olgivanna a "grand despot," but she could tell he was afraid of her, that he didn't feel he measured up.

Anna Bogdanovich left Spring Green early, thinking of returning to her old boyfriend. By the time Tal appeared in Arizona the following winter, though, Anna had decided on him. So she was shocked to receive a call from the emergency room: Tal had tried to kill himself by taking almost a hundred valium tablets. When she rushed to the hospital, she found Kay in the foyer. Kay walked over to her and slapped her face, hard. "You almost killed my boy," she spat at her.

The suicide attempt ended the romance.

All the pills and alcohol had permanently damaged Tal's brain. His parents had him briefly institutionalized. "You are there to protect yourself from harm," his mother wrote him, "until you are strong enough to go out in the world and have the will power to resist drugs and alcohol and be strong enough to go without sex without going to pieces."

When he got out, Tal made his way to Los Angeles for what turned out to be a short stint at USC film school. While there, he added Quaaludes and marijuana to his regular intake of vodka. Before long, he was in freefall.

In 1971, Tal returned to Scottsdale and asked Olgivanna for permission to move back to Taliesin. She refused. La Don Van Noy, a friend and ex-apprentice living nearby, took him in, dried him out, and got him a job in construction. They loved going out into the desert to shoot together, but Tal had pawned his shotgun; Van Noy loaned him the money to get it back.

A short time later, Tal was waiting at the Phoenix airport—another new girlfriend was about to arrive from Switzerland—when he became anxious. He started drinking, then took some drugs, probably Quaaludes, hoping to calm his nerves before she arrived. When her plane touched down, he was so stoned that the only thing she felt was revulsion. She fled, checking into a hotel without him.

Devastated, Tal went back to his room at La Don's place, and placed a desperate phone call. He had never felt so bad, so worthless, he told Mrs. Wright on the phone. His life was pointless, he told her. He wanted to kill himself.

Well, if you feel that way, Olgivanna replied, maybe you should do it.

Olgivanna's words seem almost unbelievably cruel. But it was also a Gurdjieffian technique to deliver a "shock," a sudden, painful jolt of judgment and insult, in order to induce what the master called "self-remembering," to help the listener reach beyond the disordered maelstrom of the personality and reach the true "I." Tal Davison was clearly off track, captured by his sexual and emotional selves. But Gurdjieff himself had sent a few of his adepts over the brink in just this fashion, and Olgivanna had disapproved of Madame de Salzmann's severe directives after they led one of her pupils to commit suicide.

Tal got off the phone, reached out beyond the long shotgun barrel pointing into his chest, and pulled the trigger.

When Diane Snodgrass's Taliesin apprentice boyfriend discovered the body and called Taliesin, nobody would come down from the hill to help her. Diane, Tal's first real love, came and cleaned up the blood herself. He had shot himself in the chest, she thought, to avoid ruining that handsome face of his. Tal Davison was twenty-nine years old.

Van Noy, who was on vacation at the time, regretted lending Tal the money to get his shotgun out of hock. A psychiatric social worker friend of Tal's, who had contemplated having him hospitalized, regretted that she had not acted on her professional judgment. Diane Snodgrass, who had renewed her friendship with Tal, had finally told him she loved him just two weeks before he took his life. She wished she had told him earlier. "If you had told me this before," he had replied, "I might have turned out differently."

But there were two people who showed no regret, accepted no responsibility. Shortly after Tal's body was found, Olgivanna and Kay stormed into the home of Anna Bogdanovich, who had not seen Tal for more than a year. Anna wasn't there, but her mother was. "Mrs. Wright and my mother," Celeste recalled, "railed against Anna Bogdanovich, who was this young little chickadee who didn't have a clue about what was going on." Tal's "two mothers" laid responsibility for the death at her daughter's feet. Mrs. Bogdanovich threw them out, and never told her daughter of the encounter.

Memorial services for Fellowship members were always held at Taliesin. Not this one. At the funeral in town, a rageful Diane Snodgrass had to grip the chapel bench in front of her to contain herself. She wouldn't talk to Mrs. Wright, couldn't even look at her. Celeste, who was at college in Hawaii, never even made it to her brother's funeral. Her parents didn't notify her about it until a week afterward. Then, when she pleaded for plane fare home, her father replied, "You better not show your face. It will be too complicated."

When Tal's mother, Kay, died in 1996, John Rattenbury, her final apprentice husband, composed a tribute. To her last moment on earth, he wrote, Kay "felt guilty that her devotion to Mrs. Wright often didn't allow her to spend more time raising her family."

Olgivanna prided herself on her ability to remake those apprentices who were willing to submit to her interrogations and her discipline. But how successful had she really been in recreating people, one apprentice asked her? What about Kay, who had cycled through four husbands?

She was such poor material to begin with, Olgivanna replied.

THE YEAR AFTER Tal's suicide, 1972, Iovanna had a nervous breakdown. There was no spring festival at Taliesin that year. Concerned about her daughter's welfare, Olgivanna called Lath into the "swan cove," the fabled Taliesin West site where she held her imperial audiences. "Counting the swans," the apprentice called them. Was he sure he still wanted to marry Iovanna? Yes, he answered, "because in marrying her, I'm also marrying the life I love."

"I thought that I would be able to help Iovanna," he recalled, "and also very idealistically, in helping with Iovanna, I would also be helping the Fellowship. . . ." In October 1972, Lath became Iovanna's fifth husband.

Jack Howe wrote former apprentice Curtis Besinger with the news, trying to remember which number husband it was. "I don't know," Curtis replied, "I lost track of Iovanna's 'boyfriends,' amours, husbands, and 'vaginal swabs.' Poor dear, she inherited neither her mother's—nor her father's—talents. And only their worst characteristics!"

For Lath Schiffner, the marriage was both a spiritual odyssey and a personal service.

FOUR YEARS AFTER Tal's death, Taliesin lost another apprentice child. Johnny Hill and Heloise's son, Christopher, had been taking drugs. As a senior in high school, he took a Taliesin truck without asking. The truck turned out to have no brakes, and he crashed it; he was arrested and had to go to court. A few months later, he put on a tuxedo, got into his Volkswagen, and drove off to a formal dinner. He never arrived. Someone later found the burned-out shell of a VW nearby; the body inside was apparently burned beyond recognition. He was only identified when Heloise saw his ears, which had stuck out so much that Heloise had had them pinned back. To honor his memory, Heloise changed her last name to Christa.

The following year, burdened with guilt over his inadequate fathering, Johnny Hill received the final blow. He and Cornelia Brierly were working on an addition to the Arizona Biltmore Hotel, a building that Wright had consulted on in 1929, and which had become a regular source of work for TAA after a recent fire. Hill was responsible for the design of the interiors, but as usual Olgivanna was taking official credit for his work. Johnny and Cornelia were in the Wisconsin studio sorting through fabric samples when Mrs. Wright called. "How dare you be working on the Biltmore interiors?" she raged at Hill. "Kay should be doing that!" She commanded him to send Kay the presentation at once.

Cornelia watched Hill wilt before her eyes. Johnny was a nationally recognized designer; this was his usual domain. Kay Rattenbury had no real qualification for this kind of work—other than her absolute devotion to Mrs. Wright, and her marriage to John Rattenbury, the project head.

Hill sunk into a depression from which he never recovered. He would spend the rest of his life dependent on medication—first lithium, then a string of antidepressants. He lost interest in writing and, eventually, design. Some years later, when an apprentice requested some of his drawings for an exhibit, he confessed that he had burned his portfolio. Olgivanna had convinced him that he had done nothing of importance.

Wright's death had robbed Johnny Hill of his sense of purpose. "I've often thought since that I should have died when he did," he once said, "because I didn't go on. . . ."

After receiving Johnny and Cornelia's Biltmore design, Kay radically reworked it. Years later, in 1992, the previous owners of the Biltmore repurchased the hotel; they tore out Kay's work and hired a Los Angeles design firm to restore the interiors to something closer to what Frank Lloyd Wright might have done.

IOVANNA HAD HOPED her marriage to Lath would be "gay and free." It wasn't. She couldn't stop her drinking or drug use, particularly her intake of speed. Unable to save her, Lath began to withdraw, hanging around the drafting room in the evenings, sometimes just watching football on TV. In turn, Iovanna started going out on her own, dancing with strangers in cowboy bars. Small but extraordinary powerful, she sometimes took out her anger on her ex-football-player husband, beating him up and then sending him out to live in his old self-made apprentice shelter in the desert.

Her motherly resources spent, her Gurdjieffian techniques useless, Olgivanna now took the desperate step of sending her daughter away to the first of many hospitals and clinics in America and Europe, with Lath often in tow.

Iovanna was diagnosed with manic depression, a form of illness that follows genetic tracks. If one parent has it, the child has more than a 25 percent chance of being affected. If both parents have it, the probability rises to 75 percent.

Iovanna Lloyd Wright has a history of mental illness on both sides of her family. Her maternal grandmother was manic-depressive, one of Olgivanna's concerns when she considered aborting Iovanna. And Olgivanna knew there was insanity on her husband's side, too. Wright's mother certainly had violent, hysterical attacks, and even pleaded with her husband, William, to put her in an asylum. But William's own peripatetic career, the way he moved his family from place to place and mastered so many fields without ever really succeeding at any of them, also suggests a manic-depressive streak. And Iovanna was not the only child of Frank Lloyd Wright to suffer manic depression. His son Lloyd, according to Eric Lloyd Wright, also suffered from the disorder.

And what of the great architect himself? Frank Lloyd Wright had nearly all the classic symptoms of manic behavior: the bursts of energy, the cocksure agility and speed of thought, the inspired ebullience always shadowed by a streak of irritability. Manics spend too much; they're prone to sexual escapades; their talk is grandiose; they take reckless chances. The energy coursing through a manic personality enables some to grasp complex situations, to sort through associations at light speed, to visualize correspondences and imagine extraordinary solutions.

Of such stuff is artistic genius often made. Artists of all kinds—poets and writers, but also musicians and architects—are especially likely to suffer such mood disorders. It is out of this passionate sensibility that many of our greatest cultural achievements have emerged.

LATH SCHIFFNER FOUND the doctors useless to help Iovanna. "They hadn't a clue what the Taliesin experience was about," he recalled. "They hadn't a clue what the relationship with Mrs. Wright was." For the aspiring architect, who by 1973 had become a designer and project manager for TAA, shepherding his wife from institution to institution was a huge sacrifice. He did it for Olgivanna, but also the love of Iovanna; he believed he could help bring her around. "She had the ability, the fortitude, to carry it on after Mrs. Wright's death." That he might then become Taliesin's heir apparent was unspoken.

In 1974, Iovanna wrote to Jenkin Lloyd Jones, Richard's son. "If I am one of the last of the daughters of the pioneers, it stands to reason that you are one of the last of the sons of the pioneers." Iovanna proposed that the two join forces to restore the family chapel and add life-size, bronze statues of the family. "I see Richard with bible in hand, arms spread wide, preaching. Mary next to him, her eyes, upward, holding the body of Nellie. . . . Jenkin holding a bible close standing on the side nearest the entrance, his young son Richard looking up at him. Have I forgotten anyone?"

She also wrote to Anthony Quinn, the failed Taliesin applicant turned internationally celebrated actor, proposing that he make a motion picture on her father. "You have no idea how you've moved me with your letter and the reminder of your father's affection for me," Quinn responded. "He changed the whole course of my life." Iovanna should write the script around her relationship with him, he suggested—"the dramatic conflict that you witnessed, that you experienced with him." Although he admitted he looked nothing like Wright, he would be happy to play the man.

Iovanna completed her last dance composition around this time. In the piece, called simply *Poem,* a female figure of happiness dances with the sprites, until suddenly the dancers freeze. A figure of death marks her forehead with a black cross. Unable to remove the ominous sign, she feigns happiness. Understanding that she is doomed, the sprites bow to her. She collapses in death.

In 1976, in anticipation of the next year's Taliesin Festival, Iovanna wrote to actor Martin Sheen asking him to do the "poetic narration" for a series of dramatic scenes she had planned based on the writings of William Blake and Omar Khayyam. When Olgivanna canceled the festival, the project foundered.

By now, Iovanna was striking out wildly. One day she stomped into the drafting room, seized a drawing off the boards, and ripped it into pieces. It represented one hundred hours of work.

Later the same year she was sent off for yet another hospitalization, this time to Hartford, Connecticut. As she languished in bed, clinically depressed, her troubled mind finally settled on an ideal man, a misunderstood hero for whom she would make an ideal wife—at least in fantasy. Her father would not have approved: After all, he had condemned the man in a 1957 television interview with Mike Wallace, predicting that young people would eventually abandon his primitive rock and roll for the pleasures of organic architecture.

Iovanna had fallen in virtual love with Elvis Presley, now a drug-addicted recluse himself. Surrounded by Bach and Beethoven at Taliesin, Iovanna had never before heard his music. At the hospital, though, Elvis became Iovanna's solace, and she danced her blues away in the lounge, even in the bathroom. "Rock and roll is here forever," she wrote in her unpublished autobiography. "One of the best things the government could do would be to wire all hospitals and jails with the music of Elvis."

She returned to Taliesin, and to the cycle of booze and pills, driving wildly through the deserts, getting arrested for driving under the influence. Then it was back to another hospital to start the process again. Lath held on through it all, traipsing back and forth to clinics, hoping for a turnaround, trying to please Mrs. Wright and serve the greater cause. In 1978, he was promoted to staff architect.

But Iovanna could not be saved. Her rage expanded beyond even Olgivanna's ability to cope. She attacked her mother twice, once with a meat cleaver, narrowly missing murdering her. Lath arranged to have her committed for the long term, but Olgivanna backed out at the last minute, unwilling to do that to her daughter. The troubled couple would carry on as husband and wife, shuttling between clinics and Taliesin, for a decade. "In the early years, I had a great sense that she was a great woman with great power," Schiffner recalled. But eventually it all got to be too much. "That was ten years that almost killed me."

COUPLINGS AT TALIESIN—Wes and Svetlana Alliluyeva, Johnny and Heloise, Heloise and Vern Swaback, Lath and Iovanna, Kay and nearly everyone—were often Olgivanna's experiments. Nearly all of them failed. But in the early 1980s, out of the ruins of two arranged relationships, there emerged a spontaneous and successful one: Lath Schiffner and Adrienne Burchett.

Burchett had been married before, in Panama. At twenty-four, a divorcée with two daughters, she moved back to Scottsdale, where she had been raised by a mother who was once a schoolmate of Iovanna's. Adrienne was working in an art gallery when Mrs. Wright called to invite her to tea.

"You really have everything," Olgivanna told her. "We just need to put it into place." Within the year, this beautiful, charming, cultured young woman was married to Olgivanna's trusted lieutenant, Richard Carney, then Taliesin's forty-eight-year-old treasurer.

Adrienne and Dick both followed Olgivanna's Gurdjieffian teachings eagerly, striving to develop a "permanent I." Both felt blessed that she was willing to work with them. "She was in people's lives," Adrienne recalled, "but she didn't actually work with everybody there. She did choose. And they didn't even know if they were being worked with or not."

Adrienne was being worked with. As Olgivanna knew, but Adrienne didn't, Dick Carney was gay. His obvious lack of interest in their sex life drove Adrienne into outside assignations in the desert, and ultimately, in great secrecy, into the arms of her despondent counterpart, Lath Schiffner.

Carney never disclosed his secret, but Olgivanna did. In 1981, furious about Adrienne's behavior, she sat the young woman down and revealed that her husband was homosexual. In that instant, the marriage was over.

Before long Lath Schiffner also had an announcement to make, and he made it to Iovanna and her mother together: He was in love with another woman. After the two women guessed all of Taliesin's single girls, he finally revealed that it was Adrienne Carney. They exploded. Mrs. Wright demanded that Lath and Adrienne reconsider their relationship. Iovanna blamed Carney for being unable to satisfy his woman.

Olgivanna tried reasoning with Adrienne. There was a "higher purpose" to their union, she argued. Her husband was in line to become the CEO of Taliesin. He should have "a pretty wife with two lovely children . . . that was what she wanted," Adrienne recalled. "I knew how to pour tea." Adrienne would not let Mrs. Wright work on her again. Taliesin had a double divorce—Adrienne and Dick, Lath and Iovanna.

In 1982, Olgivanna amended the Foundation's articles of incorporation to remove Iovanna as a trustee. Adrienne's plunge in status was just as dramatic, if less consequential. As Carney's wife, she had always been seated at Mrs. Wright's table with the invited guests at the Saturday evening formal dinners. Now she was put to work serving the diners at the same table where she once sat. Mrs. Wright kept a Fellowship list with each person ranked in terms of their stature in the community. As Carney's wife, she had been listed near the top; now Olgivanna drew a slash through her name and repositioned her near the bottom, with the newest recruits.

Lath and Adrienne were determined to leave. Olgivanna tried to argue with them, reminding them that Taliesin was an ideal and as such required sacrifice from its inhabitants. She had endured pains to remain with Gurdjieff and then with Mr. Wright. Why shouldn't Adrienne do the same? "It was kind of off the path of my destiny to leave," Adrienne remembered Olgivanna advising her sternly.

But leave she did, in January 1983, and Lath Schiffner went with her. Adrienne had loved Mrs. Wright and she had loved her back. Yet now Olgivanna wouldn't speak to either of them. On the day of their departure, "nobody said goodbye to us, nothing."

Iovanna warned Lath that he and his new love were stepping down into a "mediocre world." Indeed, moving out into workaday Arizona, with its unstoppable suburban expansion, was disorienting to them both. "It's very tough," Lath recalled, "when you come back [into the world] and nothing seems to be as beautiful, or nicely done. You've got a closet full of long dresses and tuxedos. You're used to Saturday evenings, living in a certain way. You're used to music. Even though you go to concerts, it's not the same. And it takes quite a while. I think for a lot of people being at Taliesin was the defining moment of their lives and they were never able to capture that again."

SPIRITS IN THE WALL

BY THE LATE WINTER OF 1983, Olgivanna had started to slip away. When she could no longer see well enough, her most trusted confidantes read to her. To the embarrassment of one, she was particularly fond of homosexual erotica. When her sight failed completely, she relied on her memory of the table settings to preserve the illusion that she could see the apprentices she talked with at dinner—much as her father, the blind judge, had used his total recall of the law to "read" his rulings.

By the time former apprentice Edgar Tafel came to dinner in 1984, she was able to make only a brief appearance. Mrs. Wright was in a "sad condition," he recalled. At one Saturday dinner the following year, she was too weakened by a series of small strokes to participate at all. Later in the evening the attendees stood as she was escorted into the living room to hear a musical performance, her proud frame now noticeably shrunken. Passing her former son-in-law Charles Schiffner, she somehow sensed his presence. "Hello Lath," she said and then embraced him. It would be the last time he saw her.

One day Bruce Pfeiffer went up to tell her it was lunchtime. "Lunch, dinner," she replied, "it doesn't matter. It's all darkness now."

Almost sixty years had passed since the Montenegrin teenager had approached Georgi Gurdjieff in Tiflis, seeking immortality. Whether or not she still expected to live on in another plane, the inevitable death of her body made her angry. "She couldn't stand having me talk about anybody who died," Pfeiffer recalled of her last months. "I couldn't mention Mr. Wright's name."

Iovanna was not around to see her mother's decline. After Lath walked out, she had taken a portrait of her father and a cache of jewelry and fled to Paris. In the city where Gurdjieff had instructed her in the mysteries, she steadily sold off and drank away the jewels, sleeping with bartenders, taxi drivers, a turbaned cook who bedded her in the back of the restaurant, one of her hospital interns. She walked the streets at night. Finding herself in ever smaller and more tawdry hotel rooms, she even lived for a time in a house in Marseilles that also served as a brothel. Finally Iovanna was shipped back and installed for two years in the Silver Hill Hospital in Connecticut. Her mother was not yet too weak to visit her, but she refused nonetheless. "I was on the other side of the world," Iovanna remembered.

ON MARCH 1, 1985, Olgivanna Lloyd Wright died in a Scottsdale hospital. The cause of death was tuberculosis, which she had likely carried since her days tending Katherine Mansfield at the Prieuré. The night before she died, apprentice Ralph Williamsen had served her dinner. Afterward, when all the apprentices were tested for exposure to the disease, he was the only one to test positive. It was a proud moment for Williamsen, who would spend the following year on a course of protective medication. "That was some wonderful ritual," he recalled. "I loved taking the pill, sort of in her memory."

When Edgar Tafel arrived for the funeral, he was greeted by a security guard and a sign at the Taliesin West entrance, CLOSED TODAY. The living room was filled with flowers. The casket, set at a Wrightian sixty-degree angle from the fireplace, was draped in Cherokee red velour. To Tafel, Olgivanna appeared to be sleeping in the casket. Apprentices milled around the room, some wearing sunglasses to hide their tears.

At four o'clock, the members of the Taliesin chorus entered and arranged themselves behind the casket. Bruce Pfeiffer led them in Mrs. Wright's favorite songs, including a Serbian hymn and "Vaya Con Dios." After a brief silence, Iovanna read an excerpt from her mother's book *Roots of Life*. Iovanna was enraged at the way her mother's life had ended. Her mother "had always devoted herself to God," she said. "Why did He turn his back on her at the end of her life? . . . I will never forgive God for that."

After a minister read prayers, the short service concluded with one of Olgivanna's own compositions, played by apprentice Effie Casey on the violin and Pfeiffer on the piano. The mourners were then ushered outside into the evening's cool desert air.

As the apprentices and guests stood watching, eight pallbearers carried the coffin to a white hearse. Edgar Tafel cried as it drove off to the crematorium.

Diane Snodgrass, Tal Davison's first real love, felt a rush of delight when she got the news. "The wicked witch is dead," she thought.

DR. RORKE WAS the only one with Olgivanna when she died. He had been there when her husband passed away, too, bearing witness that there were no last words, no final requests. This time was different. Emerging from her hospital room, Rorke announced to the grieving apprentices that Mrs. Wright had asked that her husband's body be dug up and cremated, and that the ashes be brought from Wisconsin to Arizona to be mixed with Olgivanna's and interred at Taliesin West.

As the closest surviving relative, Iovanna would have to sign off before her father's body could be moved. She didn't want to do it. Only after Olgivanna's closest confidantes pressured her did she acquiesce. Wright's other children were outraged at the idea. Their father had loved the valley, and his body had lain there peacefully for over a quarter of a century. "More dramatic elsewhere, perhaps more strange, more thrilling, more grand," he once wrote, "but nothing that picks you up in its arms and so gently, almost lovingly, cradles you as do these southwestern Wisconsin hills." After all, he had even planned his own mausoleum for the site. He expected to spend eternity there.

Olgivanna, though, had never liked Wright's original Taliesin, and she was clearly bothered by the idea of lying thousands of miles from her husband when Mamah Cheney was just a few feet away from him. Frank had never shared Taliesin West with another woman, and it was there that Olgivanna wanted Frank to rest eternally, mixed with her own ashes.

After Iovanna signed the papers, the undertaker, at four in the morning, snuck out to the little cemetery. The twenty-six-year-old corpse was said to be in remarkable condition. Nearby farmers notified the press, who tailed the hearse on its way to the crematory. The undertaker flew with the ashes to Arizona instead of sending them through the mail as usual. "Not somebody like that," his wife recalled of the decision.

When Jack Howe heard about the exhumation, he felt a deep sense of betrayal. His loyalty to Wright was expressed daily in his small but well-respected architecture practice in Minneapolis. He was doing what he had always been able to do—produce Frank Lloyd Wright houses with little help from the master. He had long planned to donate his valuable Wright drawings and manuscripts to the University of Minnesota, but after the grisly doings at Spring Green, he changed his mind. "Something of Mr. Wright's belongs in Wisconsin," he said, and gave the collection to the Wisconsin Historical Society.

The controversy rankled for decades. In 2001, a former apprentice published a poem in the *Taliesin Fellows Newsletter.*

> *Who was it who, after lying in the cold damp ground for 25 years*
> *And after hearing the clink of beer bottles and drunken voices above his*
> * grave,*

May have called out to his beloved wife
To take him to a warm dry place?

TO THE SURPRISE of many, Olgivanna had kept the Taliesin Fellowship alive for a quarter of a century beyond her husband's death. The question now was, what would happen when she died? "If we can manage Taliesin without Mr. Wright," she had declared, "how much more easily can it be done without me. Taliesin not only survived the death of Mr. Wright, it went far beyond. It will be all right."

She was wrong. The vacuum left by her death was immediately apparent. After the hearse pulled out, the Fellowship gathered in Taliesin's dining room for dinner. For the first time, Tafel recalled, the seating arrangement was informal, the discussion just small talk. Tafel had to prod the apprentices to make any gesture to mark Olgivanna's passing.

On the way home from the funeral dinner, Tafel was unnerved. "Maybe I felt it was what purgatory could be," he wrote Bob Mosher about that evening, "or that the past was done."

AFTER OLGIVANNA'S PASSING, Iovanna remembered, the senior apprentices argued over who would sit in her mother's chair at dinner. In his will, Wright had spelled out a chain of succession: The Fellowship would pass to Olgivanna after his own death, and then to Iovanna after Olgivanna's. But madness had broken the chain. With no viable heir, the Fellowship increasingly became a religion of the dead. The many writings and recordings of the Wrights became the Word, the drawings the iconography. Sunday breakfasts still featured Wright's sermons on organic architecture, members of the Fellowship eating in silence as his mellifluous voice filled the room from a tape recorder. In the drafting room, the pencils were guided not so much by organic principles, as Wright had hoped, as by the resurrection of his stylistic motifs. And new apprentices continued to arrive, a miracle unto itself.

After Mr. Wright's death, Bruce Pfeiffer had attacked the piles of drawings and photographs, the taped reels of speeches and Fellowship talks, organizing, transcribing, publishing, and preserving them to create a repository of infinite value to architects, scholars, and curators. He would do likewise for Mrs. Wright, starting by cataloging her clothing. At first two of her loyal assistants guarded her huge, overstuffed closets from any such violation, but when they finally relented Pfeiffer made a meticulous review of the shimmering golden fabrics and big loud prints. Every single dress, sweater, and blouse had lingerie straps sewn into them to keep the bra straps from slipping. The finest items included a rack of Pucci couture gowns, some of which she had altered using cheaper fabrics. There was row after row of fur coats, as well as three bakers' boxes stuffed with fine jewelry. More than one hundred items of clothing were carefully wrapped and stored in the archives alongside one of the most valuable architectural drawing collections in the world.

IN 1987, FOR the very first time, former apprentices gathered at Taliesin West for a reunion. They had been unwelcome while Olgivanna was alive, so the event offered a kind of giddy collective catharsis. But many were shocked when they saw what Mrs. Wright had done to the place. "What had been a work of art," one recalled, "now had all the ambiance of a second rate motel."

Perhaps most offensive was the transformation of the family quarters at Taliesin West. Curtis Besinger, by then a professor of architecture, was speechless when he first came into the "cove." "There was a set of 1955 Heritage-Henredon dining furniture plunked in the center of the room," he recalled. A portrait of Olgivanna hung over the fireplace, he observed, "in lower middle class bozo fashion." Near the theater, she had installed a gas-fed, fire-breathing dragon.

Her general neglect of the Wisconsin Taliesin had left it relatively unscathed. "For that," Besinger noted, "we should be thankful." But Olgivanna had done some damage there as well, and now that she was gone Johnny Hill set about undoing all of her renovations. He replaced the carpets she had had made with the Chinese carpets Mr. Wright had originally ordered. Her walled garden and moon gate were bulldozed away, along with the swimming pool she'd put in near the house. In the last years of his life, Hill restored the living room at Taliesin West with the furnishings Mr. Wright had installed before his death.

AS HILL WORKED away on his restoration projects, Wes Peters focused on the future. When Olgivanna died, the Fellowship was already on its way to becoming an Arizona developer. A new project, to be called Taliesin Gates, was announced to the public just two weeks later. Though small compared to The Spring Green, their failed Wisconsin venture, Taliesin Gates would leave an even bigger scar on the Foundation's finances.

When it began in the 1930s, Taliesin West was the only major habitation in the high desert outside of Scottsdale; now the town was both a resort and a wealthy Phoenix suburb. Tract housing had been closing in since at least the 1970s, and in an attempt to control the aesthetics of Taliesin's western approach, in 1982 Wes spearheaded an ambitious real estate development at the base of the hills. Taliesin Gates, of course, was also an unabashed scheme to cash in on what Mr. Wright had derided as the "unearned increment." With the edge of posh Scottsdale now nipping at the edges of their once-remote property, the potential for good old-fashioned profit seemed enormous.

Under Peters's enthusiastic leadership, Taliesin allocated twenty-four acres of its own land and bought fifty more adjacent acres. To raise the money, the Foundation had to dig deep, even selling some of Wright's drawings. The Foundation formed the Taliesin Gates Development Corporation with plans to build sixty-two homes. Lucky buyers would have a choice: Either have one of Taliesin's architects design their homes, or choose an unbuilt original by Wright himself. Either way, work would be generated for the studio.

Taliesin Gates was designed to accommodate roughly one family per acre, the same ratio Wright had proposed for Broadacre City. The promotional brochure brazenly identified the project with the long-dead architect. "Residents of Taliesin Gates," it claimed, "will share an intimacy with not only their own home, but also with Taliesin and the Frank Lloyd Wright ideal."

The Taliesin architects built one model home and a gatehouse. The 4,300-square-foot "Focus House"—based on the saguaro cactus—was a typically awkward Peters design, but bad design has rarely been a real deterrent in an active housing market. The real problem was that its design would have made it incredibly costly to build. When the model home finally went on the market in 1987, its asking price was $1.6 million—far more than comparable houses in the area. When the real estate market took an untimely downturn before the model home could be sold, Taliesin Gates went bust, and the Foundation sold the land to a company who built a conventionally mediocre tract development.

In the process, the Fellowship somehow managed to lose ten million dollars—the kind of loss that might cripple even most professional developers, much less a financially marginal operation like Taliesin. In its aftermath they hectored patrons, clients, and friends for financial support. Elizabeth Gordon refused to make a contribution. "Let 'em sink or swim on their own," she told Curtis Besinger. To stay afloat, the Foundation sold off another batch of Wright's drawings, $3 million worth.

"I've come to the conclusion that the best thing that could happen to Taliesin West," Besinger wrote a fellow ex-apprentice, "would be for it to be allowed to become the 'handsome ruin' that Mr. Wright stated that it would make."

Wes took the fall for Taliesin Gates. Even before Olgivanna died, he had been tottering. Once, while they were eating alone in the private dining room, she began pestering him to eat his dessert. "Mrs. Wright," he was overheard to say, "I am trying to lose weight, please don't make me eat it." When she insisted, he began to cry.

Taliesin Gates was not even his final humiliation. Without Olgivanna there to support her son-in-law, the Board of the Frank Lloyd Wright Foundation stripped him of the title of chief architect. One by one, they took away his responsibilities. By the end, Peters was reduced to asking Dick Carney, the new head man, for pocket money.

In 1990, Wes Peters had several mild heart attacks. On July 17, 1991, he died.

Wearing a Navajo necklace his father had presented to his mother, Brandoch delivered one of the eulogies. Among other things, he described how a visitor from MIT had come across a formula, while reviewing his father's Fallingwater engineering, that he thought had been solved only recently—by computer.

His beautiful, now tattooed daughter Olga, Joseph Stalin's granddaughter, was never informed about her father's memorial. She still cries about missing it.

Her mother, Svetlana, still wonders how Wes Peters felt about her. "He never said that he loved me," she says. And while he certainly loved Olga, he never provided for her; in fact, he unwittingly became a further drag on her finances. When Olga applied for college aid, she was denied because the reviewers disbelieved a claim she made on her application—that her father's income, as Taliesin's chief architect, was zero.

FOR DECADES, FRANK and Olgivanna had pretended the Fellowship was a school. Under Dick Carney it finally become one: the Frank Lloyd Wright School of Architecture. In Wright's contrarian footsteps, he and the other "faculty" bristled at the conventions of traditional education. To receive accreditation, they were required to hold classes, but instead of using the name, they dubbed the gatherings "GLO," for group learning opportunities.

The Foundation also sought income by licensing Wright's image and designs for merchandise of all kinds. In museum stores around America, one can find Frank Lloyd Wright coffee mugs, business card holders, doormats—almost anything on which his image could be stamped or one of his designs adapted. One of the biggest sellers was a Christmas necktie Johnny Hill based on a fabric Wright had designed. To package it, Hill had a wooden box made with a small red glazed tile with Wright's initials. By 2001, the program was generating more than a million dollars a year. Taliesin even sold a photograph of Wright to The Gap, for an ad that declared, "Even Frank Lloyd Wright wore khakis."

The Foundation also created a tour program for both Taliesins, where, for a fee, docents regale groups of camera-bearing tourists with the official version of the Frank Lloyd Wright story. Should this be thought an unseemly betrayal of the master's wishes, recall that Wright himself had instituted such a program in the Fellowship's early years, and for the same reason.

What the visitors saw was increasingly decrepit. The stone walkways at

Spring Green were sinking, the unpainted wood rotting, the masonry crumbling. Wright had never installed gutters on the building—he enjoyed the icicles too much—and as a result the water eventually ate away the roof structure.

In 1987, Dick Carney convinced the governor of Wisconsin to create a commission to preserve Taliesin. Concerned about the Foundation's large debt, he was worried about maintaining his local architectural treasure. Through the years, the house had become a trap for water running off the hillside, making the ground soggy and causing the hill itself to shift. Taliesin's walls began to tilt in odd directions; the whole house threatened to slide off its "brow." Taliesin did not have the tens of millions it would take to restore the building. And the damage continued: One stormy night in 1998, the great oak in the tea circle crashed into Wright's office, causing extensive damage.

Taliesin West, where Frank and Olgivanna found their final resting place, has fared somewhat better. Blessed by the desert climate and rugged stone construction, the compound has survived the wear and tear of 125,000 visitors each year better than its eastern sibling. The couple themselves are buried in a wall of the house—indeed, a wall passed by visitors on the tour, though its precise location is known only to members of the Fellowship. Cornelia Brierly's daughter Indira Berndtson, who still works and lives at Taliesin, says she doesn't pay her respects at the burial site. "There is no need to," she declares in her soft, matter-of-fact voice. "Mr. and Mrs. Wright are with me wherever I go."

FOUNDED DURING THE depression, the Taliesin Fellowship was born of the premise that if Wright could not get his buildings built, at least he could build men who could build them later. During Wright's lifetime, ironically, the Fellowship did a better job making architecture than making architects. Even Wes Peters opposed the idea of a book showcasing the architectural work of the former apprentices, telling John Geiger it was so bad as to be embarrassing.

There were notable exceptions, of course, but not many. Of the thousands of apprentices who came through Taliesin, only a few went on to achieve significant professional recognition. The most acclaimed apprentice was Fay Jones, a recipient of the American Institute of Architects' prestigious Gold Medal; he had served only three months at Taliesin. John Lautner created an interesting body of work, mostly in California. The list of significant architects isn't much longer than that. In contrast, in his years at Harvard, Walter Gropius produced many important architects—I. M. Pei, Paul Rudolph, Philip Johnson. The Bauhaus, the school he founded before leaving Europe in the 1930s, likewise produced quite a few important designers.

And even those ex-apprentices with talent faced long odds. A Taliesin "diploma" not only brought little respect within the profession, it was often treated with scorn. The market for organic architecture was tiny. Often the only road into the profession was through one of the few former apprentice firms. After leaving Taliesin, Lath Schiffner and Verne Swaback each formed such practices in Arizona, following in the footsteps of Louis Wiehle in Los Angeles, Aaron Green in San Francisco, and Jack Howe in Minneapolis. Wright had always drilled into every departing apprentice a clear message: If you can't find the opportunity to design within "the principles," you'll be better off digging ditches. Some did just that.

For those who stayed at Taliesin, manual labor might have been more lucrative. The studio barely scraped by after Olgivanna's death, and by the time a much watered-down version of Wright's Monona Terrace project in Madison was completed in 1997, the flow of new work had all but dried up. There were new efforts to generate income from Wright's architecture, including the "legacy program," where clients were offered authentic unbuilt Wright designs at a hefty price. Still, most years the architectural practice lost money, and by the turn of the century the Foundation itself was teetering on the verge of bankruptcy.

Tourists still make the pilgrimage to Wright's two Taliesins each year. But what they find there may seem increasingly like a ghost town. In 2004, the architecture practice was severed from the Foundation; by October 2005 the Frank Lloyd Wright School of Architecture had lost the majority of its faculty, and its eight remaining students saw their hard-earned accreditation threatened.

Amid these prolonged struggles, however, Taliesin has succeeded gloriously in one mission: as a repository of the records of Wright's remarkable body of work. The collection of Wright's drawings and papers at Taliesin West represents the largest archive in the country devoted to a single artist.

LATH SCHIFFNER REMAINED Olgivanna's spiritual son. The Fellowship, he believed, had had cosmic significance. "The genius of Taliesin was that it was able to be an esoteric school," he declared, "and have all of the appearance of not being one, and not scaring people away." Taliesin was a major power center, he believed, the Wrights a medium through which a singular source of energy came to earth, teaching human beings to pursue beauty as a spiritual path. This energy drew apprentices, clients, and friends who often could only dimly explain their attraction, but who grew to understand each other nonetheless. And the same force created an irrational repulsion on the part of those who could not respond.

Gurdjieff and Wright, Schiffner suspects, were part of the same short burst of light, a cosmic "release of information" at the beginning of the twentieth century, "which is just now starting to make a true impact in society as a whole.

"This is the purpose that Taliesin served," he says today. "It was a rung on the ladder, part of the awareness and the creativity that is necessary for us to move in the future. The golden era that I knew at Taliesin does not exist anymore. The door is closed."

AN HEIRLESS HOUSE

AS A GIRL, IOVANNA LOVED the stories of Edgar Allan Poe. Best of all was "The Fall of the House of Usher," also a favorite of her father's. In this tale of Gothic horror, the Usher family house harbors an "oppressive secret." Roderick, the family's last man-child, has no one to carry on his name. His sister, Madeline, is entombed alive, and by his own hand. Then, incredibly, the girl emerges from the crypt; her brother dies; and the house crumbles from fissures within, sinking into a dank marsh, an heirless house that disappears without a trace.

Now, in her mid-seventies, in her room at Las Encinas, Rosa thinks of the story once more. She is telling about a winter picnic her father called in the first years of the Fellowship, when she was just a little girl. As Wright took the apprentices out in the dry frigid night to watch the moon rise, she rode in the wagon at her father's feet. Bundled in blankets, huddling close for warmth, the apprentices roasted meat over an open fire whose orange sparks rose toward the paper-white stars.

That night, Rosa recalls, she had told the apprentices her own version of Poe's tale, making up what she couldn't remember. Her version had the young men shaking with laughter.

"Usher," she recounted, "was a very exciting man, who lived in a huge house with lots of angles in it. He spent all day and all night sitting in a large chair in front of a fireplace that had no fire." Usher needed a friend—a friend like her. One day the house began emitting strange noises, as it began to crack and crumble. "Usher sat so long," she told the apprentices, "that he wore out the chair and then he wore out the whole house. Some of the angles survived. But Usher did not die, you see, he was dreaming of me all the time as his perfect wife. So when I go home tonight, I will marry Usher and I will write Edgar Allan Poe."

After finishing her story, Iovanna fell asleep. One of the apprentices carried her to the wagon, and when she awoke she was in her bed at home.

Rosa still remembers hoping to meet a man like Usher someday, a man with a fireplace where they could roast marshmallows together. She would keep him warm. Her love would finally be enough.

As for the story she told that night? The apprentices must have thought she wanted "Usher's fate to happen to Taliesin," she says.

WELL, THERE'S A leak in this old building. . . . We're going to move to a better home. Rosa is crooning for us, a song by Elvis Presley, her imaginary mate, a rebel like her, another soul who eventually slipped beyond despair. Elvis, of course, died from a drug overdose. Iovanna is still alive, after a fashion. As we sit with her in her hospital room, the soup cold on her cafeteria tray, it is all too apparent that she will never see a "better home."

Frank and Olgivanna's only child has had six last names and two firsts. She was Iovanna until she renamed herself Rosa, perhaps after the flower her mother brought her every birthday. "I wanted to be like her," she tells us. "Not my father, no. Like her." Yet she also twice tried to kill this mother, whose followers had now commandeered Taliesin. "I thought that maybe if I changed my name my destiny would improve." It didn't.

Rosa Wright insists on the authority of her bloodline. After her mother died, she tried to demand a voice in the Taliesin community, whose respect she had squandered through her years of self-abuse, sexual escapades, and imperious rages. Each change in the management of Taliesin provoked her snarling contempt. "The senior apprentices," she claims, "let the Midway Barn go to hell and used it as a dumping ground for baby carriages, whiskey bottles, clothing, what have you." She was particularly irked at Johnny Hill for deciding that the house should be the same as it was after the "gruesome death" of her father.

The penumbra of high culture that had made the Fellowship so special has fallen away, she laments. The music, the dancing, the readings, the Saturday night formal dinners and Sunday morning breakfast talks—all have been allowed to atrophy. And she dismisses the architectural talent of those who assumed command after her mother's death. "They can't design. They're just out of it," she declares. "I split with them entirely in what they were doing. There were three of them, all homosexuals—Dick Carney, Bruce Pfeiffer, and John Hill—they were all against me."

With Olgivanna gone, there was no one left to shield her from the apprentices she affronted. There was no one to honor her mother's promise that she would always be able to come home. When her own daughter, Eve, warned her that the new powers at the Fellowship would try to keep her away, Iovanna had reacted in disbelief.

But Eve was right. When Iovanna came back after her mother's death, she could not control herself, and she could not be controlled. She once called for "a man" to come to her room to help her get out of the shower. When a woman showed up instead, she got out by herself and flopped on the bed in a sulk. As if her shrieking weren't bad enough, she threw things at those who provoked her ire. Handling her required too much patience, diverted time and attention from the business of Taliesin. Potential apprentices and clients had to be shielded from her unpredictable tirades.

Iovanna was unhinged, and her madness gave the Taliesin Fellowship occasion to push Frank and Olgivanna's only child from her lifelong home. In 1990, under pressure from Dick Carney and the reigning forces at Taliesin, Iovanna voluntarily checked herself into Las Encinas. What seemed to her at the time a temporary expedient, a way to get a grip, to recover her balance in the aftermath of her mother's death, stretched into an indefinite sentence, an end game. "The homos did it," she proclaims. "They won."

Iovanna became increasingly desperate. "You enjoy the luxury of many admiring people around you," she wrote Carney from the hospital in 1994. "I have only medicine and I hate it. You are not going to lock me up in this pathological dump any longer. . . . How I miss the gentle, loving voice of my Mother, just the opposite of yours." From another letter, in 1996: "You have no right morally to bar me from my home. You are simply following the course of all history. When the King and Queen were dead, the courtiers either beheaded them or drove them out into the world without food and water."

Nobody wanted her; she had no place to go. Frank and Olgivanna's daughter was allowed back to Taliesin for vacations twice a year. During her visits she invariably attacked apprentices verbally and sometimes physically, and she became progressively less welcome. "She can be dangerous," Johnny Hill recalled. "She's strong. And I've always worried that she would set the place on fire in some kind of a rage." Once there, she did not want to leave; it took two or three men to force her into the car to take her to the Phoenix airport, pushing her into the back seat until the doors were locked and the car could speed off. Some apprentices made a point of leaving Taliesin when Iovanna was expected. Even Johnny Hill found it sad. "The poor thing is not allowed to come to her home when she needs it most."

Diagnosed as a manic depressive—or a bipolar personality, in the more current lingo—Iovanna became ensconced at Las Encinas. Taliesin paid her way, using assets that may have been hers in the first place. In her periods of extreme mania, she became extraordinarily surly and enraged, threatening the staff and sometimes other patients. Once, as she was being escorted through an office, she grabbed a huge IBM typewriter and threw it across the room. At times likes this, she was taken to the hospital's lockup facility until she could recover a rough equilibrium. It was in this facility that we first interviewed her, the three of us alone together in her room, the door left open as required by the hospital. When Rosa asked if we were afraid to be alone with her, we had assumed the frail little woman was joking.

Over the course of many months, she told us her story, and whatever her demons may have been, her memory proved remarkable; nearly all her recollections were confirmed by others. Manic depressives often function at a high level, but the illness can also be severely debilitating, sometimes leading to suicide. Over the years, drug therapies have grown increasingly effective. Most sufferers cycle out of mental hospitals and residential treatment centers into group homes or back into the world. It is very unusual for a manic depressive patient to be confined for so long.

For well over a decade, though, Rosa was closeted in a bungalow at Las Encinas. And, though she has since been moved—to a different, more austere California facility—we can still picture her in that small but elaborate bungalow, on a Chinese chair draped in red silk, in a room she has decorated to evoke Taliesin. There she sits behind a dark screen door that keeps out the flies, drinking weak coffee, always waiting—for a visitor, for the next meal, for a hair appointment, for the next day to pass. Each day brings a new drama. She complains that her proud collection of cowboy boots and leather coats is constantly being pilfered, that her spare cash is being siphoned off by the staff. Compared to many senior homes or mental hospitals, this is a luxurious affair. But in contrast to the sculpted stone walls and handsomely framed azure skies of Taliesin, Las Encinas is hell to Iovanna Lloyd Wright.

"They wanted—were determined—to have me to stay here permanently," she tells us of the three men she sees as her tormentors. "They were determined to get rid of me and put me in a hospital that would keep me for a long time. I represented competition."

When she first arrived here, Iovanna could have left whenever she felt she was ready. But the truth is that she has never been ready to go home again. Today, by a judge's decree, Rosa is under a conservatorship. Her nephew Eric, her father's grandson, has the ultimate say over where she lives; an attorney controls her finances. She is resigned to the fact that Taliesin does not want her. "For ten years I would go back," she remembered, "and they were so nasty. I don't think I'm going back again."

Having lived her entire life within a communal order, she does not enjoy living by herself. But no relatives or friends have stepped forth to shoulder the burden, to take a chance on her. For a long time, her daughter Eve—once an aspiring actress, a schoolteacher, then an expatriate in Nicaragua—wouldn't even give her mother her phone number.

Rosa maintains her sitting room as a kind of shrine. On its walls are large drawings of her father and mother, their faces completely filling the picture frames. On a low table, she has gold statuettes her father crafted himself. Also on prominent display are photos of her father's rivals: Next to her bed she keeps a framed picture of Georgi Gurdjieff, without whom there would have been no Taliesin Fellowship, and, therefore, almost certainly no Fallingwater, no Johnson Wax or Guggenheim Museum. And in her main room she keeps a treasured picture of Elvis, the sensuous hero of rock and roll, the man whose primitive crooning was dismissed by her father on national television.

There is an acid smell of urine in her room, whose walls have been painted rose at her request. Dirty towels are piled on the floor. She complains about the institutional food, about her drug dosage, about her psychiatrist, whom she sees as self-promoting. "He knows the truth and he doesn't want it talked about," she insists, "what went wrong with Taliesin. . . . He has a pathological desire to keep me here." She wants a lawyer to reestablish her right to live in Taliesin, who will contest her father and mother's will. There was another will, she claims, in which she was more richly provided for. She is certain that there has been some nefarious business, that she has been cheated.

We have just sat down for another long talk. Unprompted, Rosa begins to speak right through us, as if she is addressing another presence in the room. "Mr. Gurdjieff, you have forgotten me completely." Tears form in her uplifted eyes. "You have left me in this awful place to die. . . . I'm burning in the night until I simply burn out."

ACKNOWLEDGMENTS

WRITING ABOUT WRIGHT AND THE Taliesin Fellowship is a humbling task, one that involves trawling not just through vast archives of documents, photographs, and drawings, and mountains of secondary scholarship, but through the cliques that still divide the Wright community—through an ocean of memories, vignettes, and rumors, of life stories whose meanings are still at stake in a recounting of the collective dream space that was Taliesin.

We are grateful to the many organizations that dug deeply into their archives to help us. The Frank Lloyd Wright Archives deserve special thanks for making available thousands of documents, including many that had never been provided to previous researchers. And their photo archivist, Oskar Munoz, has earned special mention for expending great effort and considerable care in securing photographs.

Many other individuals became invaluable. Former apprentice John Geiger, in addition to being always available for a quick answer, shed an extraordinarily helpful light on which apprentice produced each drawing and gave us access to his personal correspondence. Barbara Bezat at the University of Minnesota Libraries went out of her way in providing drawings from their Jack Howe collection. Julie Wigg generously made available her Jerome Blum images. Scott Elliott let us dip into his trove of William Marlin materials. Amy Hutchins at the University of Pennsylvania went well beyond the call in searching the Margaret Naumburg Papers. Sociologist Lisa McCormick slogged through the Jean Toomer papers for us at Yale's Beinecke Rare Book and Manuscript Library, and Chrissy Speer plumbed the Charles Ashbee archives at Cambridge University. Alison Ward and Melissa Winn helped at an early stage with secondary sources on G. I. Gurdjieff. Nathan Roller did newspaper work at UCSB.

We are indebted to many former Taliesin residents and apprentices for giving generously of their time. Iovanna Lloyd Wright, Eric Lloyd Wright, Pedro Guerrero, Jim Charlton, Celeste Davison, Jay Pace, Kamal Amin, and Jane Gale Sheain deserve special thanks. Mary Jane Hamilton directed us to important sources, especially Eloise Fritz. We are indebted to Robert Graves for arranging the rare opportunity to interview Svetlana Alliluyeva (Peters), and to Ms. Peters for enduring the recounting of her days at Taliesin.

David Rubenson gave generously of his time assisting with German language materials; Shinya Yamada did the same for Japanese texts. Phil Freshman and Marcia Wright provided welcome hospitality in Minneapolis and Madison.

We are especially grateful to have had the opportunity to interview two members of the Fellowship's 1932 "freshman class," Edgar Tafel and Abrom (Abe) Dombar. Dombar's family not only arrived en masse to share their memories during the interview, but kindly took the time to provide documents.

To understand Taliesin in its intellectual context, we needed to move far beyond the architectural domain. Gurdjieff scholar Paul Beekman Taylor was our invaluable guide through the mysteries of a man who relished remaining a mystery. Jack Holzhueter steered us in several new directions, including through the unknown waters of gay Taliesin. Dance historian Suzanne Carbonneau generously provided us background on the dance world of the 1920s and a copy of the program for the night the Wrights first met. Amy Wlodarski, at the Eastman School of Music, provided us insight about the structure of Beethoven's music. Other scholars who have guided us include Kathleen Lawrence, Tom Carlson, Enrique Vivoni, and Kate Saltzman-Li. Psychiatrist Lee Sadja of the UCLA Neuropsychiatric Hospital gave us his valuable expertise on bipolar disorder.

We are deeply indebted to those who reviewed our manuscript. The collective efforts of Paul Beekman Taylor, Jack Holzthueter, Alan Hess, Franklin Toker, Kamal Amin, Alan Crawford, Robert Twombly, and Helen Friedland provided valuable insights and saved us from not a few embarrassments.

This project began when we were Getty Scholars at the Getty Research Institute researching the impact of Wright's Broadacre City on Crestwood Hills in Los Angeles, one of the largest cooperative modernist housing projects ever attempted. For our exquisitely stimulating time there, we thank Michael Roth, Charles Salas, Sabine Schlosser, Robert Dawidoff, Dana Cuff, Phil Ethington, Becky Nicolaides, Linda Hart, and Carolyn See. Also at the Getty Research Institute, we thank Mark Henderson of Special Collections, and Wim de Wit for his personal recollections of Hendrik Wijdeveld. The institute's collection of Wright's letters and reproductions of drawings has been invaluable.

Harold Zellman would like to thank the staff of his architecture practice for tolerating a boss whose head was often preoccupied with architectural urgencies long ago resolved. Roberta Willens deserves special mention for her years directly assisting on the book while simultaneously juggling her other responsibilities.

We have had the inestimable benefit of one of the most exacting and incisive editors with whom it has ever been our privilege to work—Cal Morgan. And though this book took years longer than anyone had predicted—or contracted for—Judith Regan's commitment was unwavering.

The publication of the hardback edition has brought us many communications from former Taliesin residents, relatives of Frank Llyold Wright, professional Wright historians, and amateur Wright scholars. We are especially grateful to those who took the time to point out factual errors. This Harper Perennial paperback edition has been corrected accordingly. Notwithstanding an army of copy editors who worked on the hardback edition, punctuation and grammar errors slipped through. We owe a special thanks to Phil Freshman for his meticulous copyedits.

As a cultural sociologist and an architect, we have given a decade of our lives to this book. Through thousands of hours spent together in airport terminals, chop houses and cheap hotels, sources' kitchens and archival reading rooms, we entered each other's lives and very different working worlds. As we sleuthed, learned, laughed, and fought over words and interpretations, we forged our own kind of fellowship, which made the journey immensely gratifying and the book much better than either of us could have done alone. We wrote every chapter collaboratively; our author credit is strictly alphabetical.

We have been fortunate to have had the support of our families—Debra and Gail, our wives; Hannah, Laura, Reuben, and Sarah, our children—who cheered us on, provided us refuge from our labors, and sometimes each other, and endured our passionate quest, believing that one day we would have something that might "count us one."

CITATIONS

Research for this book was based on hundreds of our original interviews; the correspondence files of Frank Lloyd Wright with his family, clients, and apprentices at the Frank Lloyd Wright Archives at Taliesin West, Arizona; and the oral histories executed primarily by archivist Indira Berndtson. Portions of the archives of William Marlin, one of Wright's deceased biographers, were provided to us both by the Taliesin Archives and Scott Elliott, a dealer in Wright materials. Unless otherwise noted, all references to the Marlin papers are from the Taliesin Archives. We have also been granted access to the correspondence files of former apprentices and depositories at other universities in the United States and abroad. All correspondence to and from apprentice John Geiger is from his personal files. Unless otherwise noted, all other correspondence, documents, and interviews are from the Frank Lloyd Wright Archives and/or the Getty Research Institute and copyrighted by the Frank Lloyd Wright Foundation. To conserve space, we have used the abbreviations FLW for Frank Lloyd Wright, OLW for Olgivanna Lloyd Wright, and ILW for Iovanna Lloyd Wright.

PROLOGUE: ROSA

"It's a miracle . . ." This and all quotations in prologue from authors' interview with Iovanna Lloyd Wright, January 21, 2000.

CHAPTER 1: THE ARCHITECT OF PROPHECY

3 *"[T]he familiar strains . . ."* We have drawn on various editions of Wright's autobiography, particularly those of 1932 and 1943 and his unpublished drafts at the Getty Research Institute. In the 1932 edition, Wright leaves the impression that his mood resulted from remorse at abandoning his family. FLW, *An Autobiography* (New York: Longmans, Green and Co., 1932), 364. The importance of the "ideal" appears only in the 1943 edition (New York: Buell, Sloan and Pearce,

1943), 366. The capitalization of "Ideal" first appeared in the 1977 reissue purportedly based on Wright's notes (New York: Horizon Press), 392.

4 *"one of the truly great things . . ."* FLW, "The Art and Craft of the Machine," 1901, in Bruce Brooks Pfeiffer, ed., *Collected Writings, Volume 1, 1894–1930* (New York: Rizzoli in association with the Frank Lloyd Wright Foundation, 1992), 60.

4 *"Architecture is dead . . ."* Victor Hugo, *Notre-Dame de Paris*, translated by Alban Krailsheimer (New York: Oxford University Press, 1993), 204.

5 *Frank's father . . .* Further sources for Wright's youth include Hope Rogers, *Grandpa Wright* (Vinton, Iowa: Inkspot Press, 1976); Elizabeth Wright Heller, *The Story of My Life* (Des Moines: State Historical Society of Iowa, unpub-

lished ms, 1929); Maginel Wright Barney, *The Valley of the God-Almighty Joneses* (Spring Green, Wisconsin: Unity Chapel Publications, 1965); Olgivanna Lloyd Wright, *Frank Lloyd Wright: His Life, His Work, His Words* (New York: Horizon, 1966); Meryle Secrest, *Frank Lloyd Wright* (New York: Knopf, 1993); Robert C. Twombly, *Frank Lloyd Wright: His Life and His Architecture* (New York: Wiley Interscience, 1979); Brendan Gill, *Many Masks: A Life of Frank Lloyd Wright* (New York: Putnam, 1987).

8 *Artistic genius,* . . . Emerson, "Self-Reliance," in Carl Bode, ed., *The Portable Emerson* (New York: Penguin, 1981), 145. On the Wrights' Transcendentalism, see David Michael Hertz, *Angels of Reality: Emersonian Unfoldings in Wright, Stevens and Ives* (Carbondale: Southern Illinois University Press, 1993), and O. B. Frothingham, *Transcendentalism in New England* (New York: Putnam, 1876).

9 . . . *such sentimental architects* . . . FLW, *An Autobiography,* 1932, 88, 240.

9 *"erotic foolishness"* FLW, *An Autobiography,* 1932, 183.

9 *And Anna was humiliated* . . . Anna Wright to FLW, May 28, 1887.

10 *In adulthood* . . . "There is a good deal of sadness back of all this bravado and though you may not know it, I too have fought a good fight." FLW to Richard Lloyd Jones, December 5, 1928.

11 *Anna responded* . . . According to William's divorce testimony, it was in March 1883 that his wife expelled him from her bed and told him she hated him. Circuit Clerk Files, *William C. Wright vs. Anna L. Wright,* cited in Thomas S. Hines, "Frank Lloyd Wright—the Madison Years," *Journal of the Society of Architectural Historians,* Vol. 26, 1967, 227–33, 229.

12 *But Frank must have made sure* . . . OLW, *Frank Lloyd Wright,* 1966, 20. In his last book, *A Testament* (New York: Bramhall House, 1957), 17, in a section entitled "The Seed," Wright linked his reading of Hugo's *Notre Dame* to his pawning of "[m]y father's Gibbon's *Rome* and Plutarch's *Lives* (see Alcibiades) and the mink cape collar my mother had sewed to my overcoat financed the enterprise." In 1958, while showing the apprentices a copy of Grant Manson's *Frank Lloyd Wright to 1910: The First Golden Age,* he complained that the author "didn't make me live, as Plutarch did Alcibiades." Grant Carpen-

ter Manson, *Frank Lloyd Wright to 1910: The First Golden Age* (New York: Reinhold, 1958). Letter from Arthur Stopes, *Journal of the Taliesin Fellows,* Issue 7, Summer, 1992, 22.

12 *"unmanly fondness"* Plutarch, *The Lives of the Noble Grecians and Romans,* trans. John Dryden (New York: Modern Library, 1992, 233–62, 235; Eva Cantarella, *Bisexuality in the Ancient World,* trans. Cormac Ó Cuilleanáin (New Haven: Yale University Press, 1992).

12 *Frank read of how Alcibiades loved* . . . Plutarch, *The Lives,* 244; FLW, *An Autobiography,* 1932, 56.

13 *Aligning oneself with the delicate powers* . . . Caroline van Eck, *Organicism in Nineteenth Century Architecture* (Amsterdam: Architecture & Natura Press, 1994). On romantic genius, see Carl Pletsch, *Young Nietzsche: Becoming a Genius* (New York: Free Press, 1991).

15 *"I have been very sad* . . ." Anna Wright to FLW, June 26, 1887.

17 . . . *Wright's "Ideal" since childhood.* This was surely a logical boast, as Viollet-le-Duc's *Dictionaire Raissonné*—which Wright called the only book on architecture worth reading—had not yet appeared in English, and Wright had only a semester of college French. Narciso G. Menocal, *Architecture as Nature: The Transcendentalist Idea of Louis Sullivan* (Madison, Wisconsin: University of Wisconsin Press, 1981), 24.

17 *"Father used to tell me* . . ." Anna Wright to FLW, April 21, 1887.

17 *"Don't let our enemy* . . ." Anna Wright to FLW, May 28, 1887.

17 *But her son wasn't listening.* William Connelly, *Louis Sullivan: The Shaping of American Architecture* (New York: Horizon Press, 1960), 116–17.

18 *Sullivan, whose own photographs* . . . Robert Twombly, *Louis Sullivan: His Life and Work* (Chicago: University of Chicago Press, 1986), 201–2; John Lloyd Wright, *My Father, Frank Lloyd Wright* (New York: Dover, 1992), 147.

18 *In private moments, Sullivan also bragged* . . . George Nelson, "An Evening at the New School for Social Research, 1980," in Edgar Tafel, *About Wright: An Album of Recollections by Those Who Knew Frank Lloyd Wright* (New York: Wiley, 1993), 232.

18 *Rather, the evidence suggests* . . . Twombly, *Louis Sullivan*, 1986, 214, 399–403; Menocal, *Architecture as Nature*, 1981, 185. According to Scott Elliott, a longtime dealer in Wright and Sullivan materials, after Sullivan died George Elmslie went through his papers and burned anything with intimate or erotic content. Authors' phone interview, Benton Harbor, Michigan, February 17, 2004. See also Louis H. Sullivan, *The Autobiography of an Idea* (New York: Dover, 1956 [1924]), 206–11.

18 *In* Leaves of Grass *and elsewhere* . . . George Chauncey, *Gay New York: Gender, Urban Culture and the Making of the Gay Male World, 1890–1940* (New York: Basic Books, 1994), 104–5.

18–19 *"I, too," Sullivan penned Whitman* . . . Twombly, *Louis Sullivan*, 1986, 214.

19 *"She's awfully fond of me* . . ." FLW, *An Autobiography*, 1932, 85.

20 *"I was scared to death* . . ." FLW to Jim Thomson, 1939, undated.

20 *"That place* . . ." H. Allen Brooks, *The Prairie School: Frank Lloyd Wright and His Midwest Contemporaries* (New York: Norton, 1972), 43.

21 *"To deny that men of genius* . . ." FLW, "Architect, Architecture, and the Client" (1896) and "The Architect and the Machine" (1894), in Bruce Pfeiffer, ed., *Collected Writings, Volume 1*, 1992, 29 and 20.

21 *The Northwestern speech* . . . FLW, "The Architect and the Machine," 1894.

21 *"There is not,* . . ." FLW, "A Philosophy of Fine Art" (1900), in Pfeiffer, ed., *Collected Writings, Volume 1*, 1992, 39.

25 *A wiry man* . . . Alan Crawford, *C. R. Ashbee: Architect, Designer and Romantic Socialist* (New Haven: Yale University Press, 1985). On his wife, Felicity Ashbee, *Janet Ashbee: Love, Marriage, and the Arts and Crafts Movement* (New York: Syracuse University Press, 2002). Charles Ashbee to FLW, May 9, 1939.

26 *"It is not new* . . ." Ashbee, *Chapters in Workshop Reconstruction and Citizenship*, London, 1894.

26 *"The burning activity* . . ." *CRA Journal*, December 7, 1900, Cambridge University Library, C. R. Ashbee Archives.

26 *"I know of no one* . . ." FLW to Charles Ashbee, January 1902, in Alan Crawford, "Ten Letters from Frank Lloyd Wright to Charles Robert Ashbee," *Architectural History*, Vol. 13, 1970, 64–76, 65. "I think there was perhaps some special electricity between the two," Crawford wrote the authors on August 20, 2004, "something Whitmanic—that would carry the literary and American and sublimated aspects of it. . . ."

26 *It was probably Wright* . . . Crawford, *C. R. Ashbee*, 1985, 99, 104-110-111; FLW, "The Architect," 45–53; Pfeiffer, ed., *Frank Lloyd Wright, Volume 1*, 1992, 51.

27 *As Wright's five-year-old son,* . . . Robert Llewellyn Wright, "Letters to His Children on His Childhood," Marlin papers.

27 *In 1903, the architect* . . . Authors' interview with James de Long, October 20, 2000. The date varies among scholars; several cite 1905.

28 *As his cousin Richard* . . . Richard Lloyd Jones to FLW, November 26, 1928.

28 *Cheney became a follower* . . . On Key, see Thorbjörn Lengborn, "Ellen Key (1849–1926)," *Prospects: The Quarterly Review of Comparative Education* (Paris: UNESCO, International Bureau of Education), vol. XXIII, no. 3/4, 1993, 825–37; Ellen Key, *Love and Ethics* (New York: B. W. Huebsch, 1911).

29 *Janet Ashbee knew* . . . Of the Sicilian priests, Ashbee wrote, "Oh but the faces of the priests! . . . There are troops of them about here in long black petticoats and black beaver hats. I feel as if I wanted to strip them, whip them, and then wash them in the water of paganism again . . ." Crawford, *C. R. Ashbee*, 1985, 143.

29 *"I feel in the background* . . ." journal entry, December 21, 1908, Felicity Ashbee, *Janet Ashbee: Love, Marriage, and the Arts and Crafts Movement* (New York: Syracuse University Press, 2002), 121–22.

29 *Ashbee and Wright* . . . Robert Twombly, *Louis Sullivan: His Life and Work* (Chicago: University of Chicago Press, 1986), 396–97; Secrest, *Frank Lloyd Wright*, 1993, 160–61.

29 *"No temptation to 'desert'* . . ." FLW to Charles Ashbee, January 3, 1909, in Crawford, "Ten Letters from Frank Lloyd Wright," 1970, 66.

29 *"I am leaving the office* . . ." FLW to Darwin Martin, September 16, 1909. Quoted courtesy of the University Archives, University at Buffalo, State University of New York.

30 *At just the moment he was deciding* . . . Brooks, *The Prairie School*, 1972, 344.

30 *The region's simply structured . . .* Authors' interview with Franco D'Ayala Valva, December 25, 2002. Valva claims they also shaped Wright's residential architecture.

30 *"I think you will believe . . ."* FLW to Charles Ashbee, March 31, 1910, "The Ashbee Papers," Marlin papers. This letter was suppressed by Olgivanna Wright when Ashbee's biography was written. Charles Ashbee to FLW (draft), April 13, 1910, Cambridge University Ashbee archives.

31 *"the rare lady . . ."* FLW to Charles Ashbee, July 8, 1910, in Crawford, "Ten Letters from Frank Lloyd Wright," 1971, 67; Crawford to the authors, August 20, 2004.

31 *This belief in a broader . . .* Wright also had connections to other utopian workshops, including Elbert Green Hubbard's Roycroft Shop and Press in East Aurora, New York. Hubbard had been part-owner of the Larkin Company, an early client, which Ashbee also visited. Donald Leslie Johnson, *Frank Lloyd Wright Versus America: The 1930's* (Cambridge: MIT Press, 1990), 47–51.

31 *"a pure bit of sentiment . . ."* Crawford, *C. R. Ashbee*, 1985, 154.

31 *Ashbee's own designs— . . .* "International Arts and Crafts," exhibit at the Victoria and Albert Museum, March 17–July 24, 2005, London.

31 *He arrived back . . .* Marlin, "Frank Lloyd Wright: The First Space Man," unpublished.

31 *"Each morning . . ."* Catherine Wright to Janet Ashbee, October 12, 1910; FLW to Charles Ashbee, July 8, 1910.

33 *Indeed, in buying . . .* Marlin, "Frank Lloyd Wright: The First Space Man."

33 *"a small farm up country . . ."* Anthony Alofsin, "Taliesin I: A Catalogue of Drawings and Photographs," in Narciso G. Menocal, ed., *Taliesin 1911–1914*, Wright Studies, Volume One (Carbondale and Edwardsville: Southern Illinois University Press, 1992), 98.

33 *But its highlight . . .* Neil Levine, *The Architecture of Frank Lloyd Wright* (Princeton: Princeton University Press, 1996), 104.

36 *Wright named his house . . .* Anthony Alofsin, "Taliesin: 'To Fashion Worlds in Little,'" Narciso G. Menocal, *Wright Studies, Volume 1*, 1992, 44–65. See also Levine, *The Architecture of Frank Lloyd Wright*, 1996, 96–98.

37 *Twenty years later . . .* Authors' interview with Henry Herold, May 8, 2000, and Jim Charl-

ton, "A Life," *Journal of the Taliesin Fellows*, Spring 1999.

37 *A letter from his daughter . . .* Frances Wright to FLW, November 19, 1911.

37 *"[I]t is like living on the edge . . ."* Catherine Wright to Janet Ashbee, July 1913.

37 *Carlton asked for gasoline . . .* "Murderer of Seven: Sets Fire to Country Home of Frank Lloyd Wright Near Spring Green," *Weekly Home News*, August 20, 1914.

38 *"You black son of a bitch."* Barbara Fritz to Robert Twombly, June 22, 1979, Marlin papers. She was told this by her father, Herb Fritz, who survived the fire.

38 *"His face . . ."* J. L. Wright, *My Father, Frank Lloyd Wright*, 1992, 83.

39 *"Rejoice," she wrote . . .* Miriam Noel and FLW: December 12–25, 1914.

40 *Wright was wearing . . .* Penny Fowler, unpublished essay on Wright's clothing, provided to the authors.

40 *Her money allowed . . .* Marlin, "Frank Lloyd Wright: The First Space Man."

40 *"his poses and all his talk . . ."* Ashbee, *Janet Ashbee*, 2002, 143–144.

40 *"I love your work"* Charles Ashbee to FLW, February 25 and April 29, 1916.

40 *Wright was devastated.* FLW, "The Natural House," in Pfeiffer, ed., *Frank Lloyd Wright Collected Writings*, Vol. 5, 1995, 127.

CHAPTER 2: THE GENERAL'S DAUGHTER

42 *Olga Ivanova Lazovich Hinzenberg . . .* For our portrait of Olgivanna Lloyd Wright we have drawn on a draft of an unpublished, undated, unpaginated manuscript of Mrs. Frank Lloyd Wright, *Autobiography*; some of her correspondence; our interviews in 1999 and 2000 with Iovanna Wright, and Iovanna's own unpublished, undated autobiography, *My Life*. See also Bruce Brooks Pfeiffer, "Olgivanna Lloyd Wright: Her Life, Her Words, Her Works," *When Past Is Future: Frank Lloyd Wright's Taliesin Legacy Continues* (Taliesin Fellows, Architrave, and the Pittsburgh History and Landmarks Foundation, 1999).

42 *. . . She was born in 1897.* Olgivanna's year of birth is a subject of considerable dispute among Wright scholars. Her birth date varies by as much as four years depending on the source.

Brendan Gill is skeptical about her claim to have been twenty-six when she met Wright in 1924, which would make her birth year 1897 (*Many Masks*, 1987, 290). Secrest, without citing a source, gives her birth date as December 27, 1898 (*Frank Lloyd Wright*, 1992, 303). Myron A. Marty and Shirley L. Marty put the date in 1899 in *Frank Lloyd Wright's Taliesin Fellowship* (Kirksville, Missouri: Truman State University Press, 1999), 291. Olgivanna's *New York Times* obituary also listed her birth year as 1898. Social Security records, however, list her date of birth as December 27, 1896. Immigration documents reveal that her first husband, Valdemar Hinzenberg, was twenty-eight when they met in 1916. If he was truly ten years her senior, as he claimed, that would mean she was born in 1898. In her autobiography, Olgivanna herself would claim to have been sixteen when she met Hinzenberg, making her birth year 1900, but Bruce Pfeiffer told the authors that Olgivanna was not sure of her own birth year. We adopt 1897 as a convention.

46 *"elimination of the insignificant"* Hertz, *Angels of Reality*, 1993, 137–56.

46 *"His genius is just unbelievable . . ."* Toh Endo, *The Shadow of the Imperial Hotel: Architect Arata Endo's Life* (Tokyo: Kosaido Publishing, 1997), 9–10. Translated for the authors by Shinya Yamada.

47 *On September 27, . . .* Svetlana Hinzenberg was born September 27, 1917, according to Indira Berndtson of the FLW Archives. For a detailed discussion of the debate over this date, see chapter 18, notes.

47 *"struck something deep . . ."* OLW, *Autobiography.*

47 *The couple was actually considering . . .* Kamal Amin, *Reflections from the Shining Brow: My Years with Frank Lloyd Wright and Olgivanna Lazovich* (Santa Barbara: Fithian Press, 2004), 54–55.

48 *"looking for something . . ."* OLW, *Autobiography.*

49 *The school would house . . .* Anna Wright to FLW: 1919 (undated); November 27, 1920; March 2, 1921.

49 *Wright had come into . . .* Twombly, *Frank Lloyd Wright*, 1979, 139, 177–78. See also FLW, "The Taliesin Fellowship," Bruce Pfeiffer, ed., *Collected Writings*, Volume 3, *1931–1939* (New York: Rizzoli, 1993), 159.

49 *A school of sorts had just opened . . .* On Gurdjieff, see James Webb, *The Harmonious Circle: The Lives and Work of G. I. Gurdjieff, P. D. Ouspensky, and Their Followers* (New York: G.P. Putnam's Sons, 1980); James Moore, *Gurdjieff: A Biography* (Shaftesbury, Element Books, 1999); William Patrick Patterson, *Struggle of the Magicians: Exploring the Teacher-Student Relationship* (Fairfax, California: Arete Communications, 1996). Webb argues that Gurdjieff's interest in esoteric Buddhism came via Theosophy, as did the concept of the "astral body" and the laws of seven and three, which appear in Madame Blavatsky's *Secret Doctrine* (1888) (pp. 36, 530–33). Gurdjieff also took Blavatsky's four bodies of man, and modeled Beelzebub on Blavatsky's heroic Lucifer, the fallen angel. See also Sophia Wellbeloved, *Gurdjieff: The Key Concepts* (London: Routledge, 2003), 205–6, and Kathleen Riordan Speeth, *The Gurdjieff Work* (New York: Tarcher/Putnam, 1989).

51 *"purity of execution" . . .* G. I. Gurdjieff, *Meetings with Remarkable Men* (London: Penguin, 1963), pp. 161–63.

51 *"teach dancing same . . ."* John G. Bennett, *Gurdjieff: Making a New World* (New York: Harper and Row, 1973), 105.

51 *"Ass is projector . . ."* Solita Solano, "Notes from 1935–1940," FLW Archives.

51 *De Hartmann had written . . .* Thomas de Hartmann, *Our Life With Gurdjieff* (London: Penguin, 1972), 3; C. S. Nott, *Teachings of Gurdjieff: A Pupil's Journal* (London: Penguin, 1990), 9; "Music for Movements," a review of de Hartmann's music, by Darell Ang, inkpot.com/classical/gurdmovements.html; Moore, *Gurdjieff*, 1999, 92–93.

52 *Some thought they were mad; . . .* Elizaveta de Stjernvall, *Across the Caucuses* [sic] *with G. I. Gurdjieff*, unpublished, translated by Paul Taylor, 1997.

52 *"Georgivanitch, most of all . . ."* OLW, *Autobiography*; Nott, *Teachings of Gurdjieff*, 1990, 84.

52 *He likely absorbed . . .* Bennett, *Gurdjieff: Making a New World* (Bennett Publishing Co., 1992), 185–200. See, David Gordon White, *Kiss of the Yogini: 'Tantric Sex' in Its South Asian Contexts* (Chicago: University of Chicago, 2003). On "higher" bodies, see P. D. Ouspensky, *In Search of the Miraculous* (New York: Harcourt Brace, 1949), 180.

52 *During the Last Supper,* . . . Ouspensky, *In Search of the Miraculous,* 1949, 97–98.

53 *By changing the impressions* . . . Well-beloved, *Gurdjieff,* 2003, 97–100, 207–11.

53 *"If one knows how to eat . . ."* Jessmin and Dushka Howarth, "It's Up to Ourselves: A Mother, a Daughter, and Gurdjieff," *Gurdjieff International Review,* Vol. 7, No. 1, Fall 2003; www.gurdjieff.org/howarth2.htm.

54 *In man, Gurdjieff maintained,* . . . Bennett, *Gurdjieff,* 1992, 191–192. These ideas are also explored, often obliquely and in language that may frustrate casual readers, in Gurdjieff, *Beelzebub's Tales to His Grandson* (New York: Penguin/Arkana, 1999 [1950]).

56 *Many said he could look* . . . Ouspensky, *In Search of the Miraculous,* 1949, 7; J. G. Bennett, *Witness* (London: Hodder and Stoughton, 1962), 121.

57 *Still stuck in Tiflis* . . . Interview with Wes Peters, June 16, 1988.

57 *Perhaps, she thought,* . . . OLW, *Autobiography.*

59 *Such knowledge, she knew,* . . . P. D. Ouspensky, *The Psychology of Man's Possible Evolution* (New York: Knopf, 1954), 280; Speeth, *The Gurdjieff Work,* 1989, 71–72.

59 *Her brother Vlado* . . . Amin, *Reflections from Shining Brow,* 2004, 57.

59 *With Olgivanna now encumbered* . . . OLW, *Autobiography.*

60 *And he attracted* . . . Paul Beekman Taylor, *Gurdjieff and Orage: Brothers in Elysium* (York Beach, ME: Welser Books, 2001), 92.

60 *To make matters worse* . . . Gurdjieff rotated the women chosen for this job so that their children would not be spoiled by their mothers. Nicholas de Val, *Daddy Gurdjieff,* unpublished MS, translated by Paul Taylor, 1997, Paul Taylor papers. See also Lincoln Kirstein, *Mosaic* (New York: Farrar, Straus and Giroux, 1994), 129.

61 *Meals included* . . . Luba Gurdjieff Everitt with Marina C. Bear, *Gurdjieff: A Memoir with Recipes* (Berkeley: Ten Speed Press, 1993), 20; De Val, *Daddy Gurdjieff,* 1997.

61 *Only through voluntary* . . . Nott, *Teachings of Gurdjieff,* 1990, 50.

61 *As the students performed* . . . Bennett, *Witness,* 1997, 89; Webb, *The Harmonious Circle,* 1980, 239; de Hartmann, *Our Life with Mr. Gurdjieff,* 1972, 105.

61 *The disheveled state* . . . Fritz Peters, *My Journey with a Mystic* (Laguna Niguel, California: Tale Weaver Publishing, 1986), 32.

63 *He sired at least six* . . . Authors' interview with Paul Taylor, Los Angeles, March 11, 2001. Paul Beekman Taylor, *Shadows of Heaven* (York Beach, S. Weiser, 1998), 143–44. Though in 1929 Gurdjieff threatened Olga de Hartmann that something bad would happen to her husband if she did not respond to his sexual demands, she remained a loyal follower. De Hartmann, *Our Life with Mr. Gurdjieff,* 1964, 131. See also Moore, *Gurdjieff,* 1999, 233–34. The de Stjern-valls had been with Gurdjieff in Russia from the start. The doctor's wife, Elizabeta de Stjernvall, took the master's insemination as confirmation of Rasputin's prophesy that she would give birth to a single child. De Val, *My Mother and Her Wish to Have a Child: Her Own Account of Her Meetings with Rasputin,* translated by Paul Taylor, 1997.

63 *He was so impressed,* . . . Moore, *Gurdjieff,* 1999, 351–52; Kirstein, *Mosaic,* 1994, 127, 152; Kirstein, "A Memoir: At the Prieuré des Basses Loges, Fontainebleau," *Raritan 2,* Fall, 1982.

64 *Gurdjieff, Kirstein later wrote,* . . . Kirstein, *Mosaic,* 1994, 151. The teaching of George Balanchine, Kirstein's collaborator, also included explicit Gurdjieffian elements. Erik Hawkins, a student of Martha Graham, likewise drew explicitly on Gurdjieffian elements. Authors' phone interview with Kathleen Lawrence, Boston, January 10, 2002.

64 *And the circle* . . . Sir Isaac Newton also built analogies between the intervals of the musical scale, the optical spectrum, and planetary distances. As Gurdjieff pointed out, dividing any number from one to six by the number seven produces exactly the same digits in the same sequence ($1/7 = .142857$). Connecting these six numbers on the circumference of the circle, in that order, produces the six central points of the enneagram. Ouspensky, *In Search of the Miraculous,* 1949, 288–89.

65 *He called this six-pointed star* . . . The clearest description of Gurdjieff's understanding of the enneagram appears in Ouspensky, *In Search of the Miraculous,* 1949, 278–98.

65 *Hailed as London's* . . . Taylor, *Gurdjieff and Orage,* 2001, 10–20; Webb, *The Harmonious Circle;* Tim Gibbons, *Rooms in the Darwin Hotel:*

Studies in English Literary Criticism and Ideas 1880–1920 (University of Western Australia Press, 1973), pp. 100–103; John Carswell, *Lives and Letters* (London: Faber and Faber, 1978), 123.

66 *"In the depths of despair, . . ."* Nott, *Teachings of Gurdjieff*, 1990, 28.

66 *"But it is a wonderful experience . . ."* Taylor, *Gurdjieff and Orage*, 2001, 77.

66 *Gurdjieff's "work" . . .* Taylor, *Shadows of Heaven*, 1998, 98.

67 *The last three stages . . .* Bennett, *Gurdjieff*, 1992, 120–22; William Patterson, *Ladies of the Rope: Gurdjieff's Special Left Bank Women's Group* (Fairfax, California: Arete Publications, 1999), 51.

67 *"cosmic anatomy"* John Middleton Murry, *Katherine Mansfield's Letters to John Middleton Murry, 1913–1922* (New York: Knopf, 1951), 642; Katherine Mansfield, *The Letters of Katherine Mansfield, Volume II*, J. Middleton Murry, ed. (New York: Knopf, 1929), 454.

67 *"I have a suspicion, . . ."* Katherine Mansfield, *Journal of Katherine Mansfield*, J. Middleton Murry, *Katherine Mansfield's Letters to John Middleton Murry*, 1951.

67 *When a pot . . .* Everitt and Bear, *Luba Gurdjieff*, 1993, 4, 20.

68 *"I want to learn something . . ."* Katherine Mansfield to J. M. Murry, October 26, 1922, Mansfield, *The Letters, Volume II*, 1929, 511.

68 *"I do feel* absolutely confident . . ." Katherine Mansfield to J. M. Murry, October 18, 1922, in Murry, *Katherine Mansfield's Letters*, 1951, 677. Mansfield to Dorothy Brett, October 9, 1922 and October 15, 1922, in Mansfield, *The Letters, Volume II*, 1929, 502, 507.

68 *Olgivanna was entranced . . .* OLW, "The Last Days of Katherine Mansfield," *The Bookman*, March 1931, Vol. LXXII, No. 1, 6–13, 7.

68 *"But her glance was so lovely . . ."* Katherine Mansfield to J. M. Murry, October 20, 1922, Murry, *Katherine Mansfield's Letters*, 1951, 678.

68 *"Friendship," Mansfield wrote . . .* "Katherine Mansfield to J. M. Murry, cited in Webb, *The Harmonious Circle*, 1980, 248.

68 *"Your body," she told her . . .* OLW, *Autobiography*; OLW, "The Last Days of Katherine Mansfield," *The Bookman*, 1931, 8.

68 *For a month . . .* Webb, *The Harmonious Circle*, 1980, 249.

69 *"[I]f we're allowed . . ."* Katherine Mansfield to J. M. Murry, Boxing Day, 1922, Mansfield, *The Letters, Volume II*, 1929, 515; Mansfield, *Journal*, 1927, 255–56.

69 *"If within three months . . ."* Gurdjieff, *Life Is Real Only Then: When 'I Am'* (New York: Dutton, 1981), 30.

69 *The French, Gurdjieff concluded, . . .* Gurdjieff, *Beelzebub's Tales to His Grandson*, 1999, 945.

70 *As far back as Constantinople, . . .* Webb, *The Harmonious Circle*, 1980, 176. Paul Beekman Taylor, *Gurdjieff's America: Mediating the Miraculous* (London: Lighthouse Editions Limited, 2004).

70 *His plan seems to have been . . .* Gurdjieff, *Meetings with Remarkable Men*, 1985, 292

71 *What he didn't reveal . . .* Secrest, *Frank Lloyd Wright*, 1993, 283.

71 *As Olgivanna helped . . .* Everitt and Bear, *Luba Gurdjieff*, 1993, 23; de Val, *Daddy Gurdjieff*, 1997.

71 *Olgivanna put her fork . . .* James Auer and Claudia Looze interview with Eve Lloyd, 1992; OLW, *Autobiography*.

CHAPTER 3: PARALLEL LINES

72 *Located at the base . . .* Gorham Munson, *The Awakening Twenties* (Baton Rouge: Louisiana State University, 1985), 256.

72 *As editors . . .* Margaret Anderson, *My Thirty Years War: The Autobiography, Beginnings and Battles to 1930* (New York: Horizon Press, 1969); Webb, *The Harmonious Circle*, 1980; Taylor, *Gurdjieff and Orage*, 2001; Holly A. Baggett, *Dear Tiny Heart: Letters of Jane Heap and Florence Reynolds* (New York: New York University Press, 2000).

73 *"be ashamed to ask help . . ."* Anderson, *My Thirty Years War*, 1969, 69.

74 *"The Institute . . ."* Nott, *Teachings of Gurdjieff*, 1982.

74 *"superreal . . . I am in on the front row . . ."* Jane Heap to Florence Reynolds, February 1, 1924, in Baggett, *Dear Tiny Heart*, 2000, 94.

74 *"Gurdjieff is coming!"* Munson, *The Awakening Twenties*, 1985, 208.

74 *Ouspensky now ran his own group . . .* Carswell, *Lives and Letters*, 1978, 171.

75 *When he greeted . . .* Connelly, *Louis Sullivan*, 1960, 262, 287–88.

75 *"I have much to tell you . . ."* Twombly, *Louis Sullivan*, 1986, 429.

75 *To raise cash,* . . . Authors' phone interview with Scott Elliott, February 18, 2004. Elliott acquired the text from the Burnham estate.

75 *Llewellyn was shocked . . .* Robert Llewellyn Wright, "Letter to His Children on His Childhood," March 26, 1986, unpublished, Marlin papers.

75 *Both understood . . .* Claude Bragdon, *The Secret Springs: An Autobiography* (London: A. Dakers, Ltd., 1938), 158–59; *More Lives than One* (New York: Knopf, 1938), 293.

75 *"[I]t was the great good fortune . . ."* Bragdon, *The Secret Springs*, 1938, 150–51.

76 *A strange thing . . .* Bragdon, *More Lives than One*, 1938, 293, 301

77 *Olgivanna, who listed her occupation . . .* Authors' interview with Dushka Howarth, December 29, 2003; immigration records generously provided by Howarth.

77 *Valdemar had earlier . . .* Interview with Wes Peters, June 16, 1988.

77 *"She looked lovely . . ."* OLW, *Autobiography.*

78 *"From my seat . . ."* Margaret Anderson, *The Unknowable Gurdjieff* (London: Arkana, 1962), 77.

78 *"like a hutchful . . ."* Bragdon, *More Lives than One*, 1938, 323.

78 *"seemed to reside . . ."* Anderson, *The Unknowable Gurdjieff*, 1962, 78.

78 *"Now dear . . ."* Jane Heap to Florence Reynolds, February 1, 1924, Baggett, ed., *Dear Tiny Heart*, 2000, 93.

79 *The second house . . .* "The Gale House at Oak Park built in wood and plaster was its progenitor as to general type." *Sixty Years of Living Architecture: The Work of Frank Lloyd Wright* (New York: Solomon R. Guggenheim Museum, 1953), 14.

79 *"Straightaway I made up my mind . . ."* Wright, *An Autobiography*, 1943, p. 507.

79 *"poor tortured soul . . ."* FLW to Miriam Noel, undated, Marlin papers.

80 *"Loving," she wrote . . .* FLW, *An Autobiography*, 1943, 507.

80 *"Perhaps," Wright later revealed . . .* FLW, *Autobiography*, 1942, p. 507.

80 *When she discovered Gurdjieff . . .* Harold Simonson, *Zona Gale* (New York: Twayne Publishers Inc., 1962), 99.

80 *"The Asiatic dances . . ."* Zona Gale, letter to the *New York Times*, February 28, 1924.

81 *The evening's dance demonstrations . . .* On the performances, see Louise Welch, *Orage with Gurdjieff in America* (London: Routledge and Kegan Paul, 1982), 5–6. See also Webb, *The Harmonious Circle*, 1980, 268–269; Taylor, *Gurdjieff and Orage*, 2001, 47. On Bragdon's reaction, see Bragdon, *More Lives than One*, 1938, 322–323; Webb, *The Harmonious Circle*, 1980, 269; August Derleth, *Still Small Voice: The Biography of Zona Gale* (New York: D. Appleton-Century Company, Inc., 1940).

81 *Toomer, who once identified himself . . .* Robert C. Twombly, "A Disciple's Odyssey: Jean Toomer's Gurdjieffian Career," Jack Salzman, ed., *Prospects: An Annual of American Cultural Studies*, 1976, 437–62, 441.

82 *One of the most important . . .* Emily Hahn, *Mabel: A Biography of Mabel Dodge Luhan* (Boston: Houghton, Mifflin Company, 1977), 180.

82 *"to know that it is a rotten, . . ."* Webb, *The Harmonious Circle*, 1980, 339.

82 *"Gurdjieff's statement . . ."* Anderson, *The Unknowable Gurdjieff*, 1962, 81.

82–83 *"It's surprising, . . ."* Taylor, *Gurdjieff and Orage*, 2001, 55.

83 *"Zona is still . . ."* Taylor, *Gurdjieff's America: Mediating the Miraculous* (London: Lighthouse Editions, 2004), 55.

83 *After paying the bills . . .* Jasmin Howarth, Dushka's mother, could not understand how Gurdjieff could leave her there in this condition. Authors' interview with Dushka Howarth, December 29, 2003.

83 *On April 8, 1924 . . .* Taylor, *Gurdjieff in America*, 2004, 60.

84 *"The book, . . ."* FLW, *Genius and the Mobocracy*, 1949, in Pfeiffer, ed., *Collected Writings, Volume 4*, 367–8, and Louis H. Sullivan, *The Autobiography of an Idea* (New York: Dover, 1956 [1924]), 289–90.

84 *"There it is, Frank . . ."* Authors' interview with William Patrick, May 10, 2000. See also Connelly, *Louis Sullivan*, 1960, 303.

84 *"high act of courage"* Louis H. Sullivan, "Concerning the Imperial Hotel. Tokyo, Japan," *Architectural Record*, April 1923, 333–52. See also Twombly, *Louis Sullivan*, 1986, 439–40.

85 *Wright, who always suspected . . .* FLW, "Louis Henry Sullivan: Beloved Master," in Pfeiffer, ed. *Collected Writings, Volume 1*, 1992, 193–96. In a marginal note beside his portrait in his son John's memoir, Frank wrote: "What a horrible looking monster!" Wright, *My Father Who Is on Earth*, 1994, 195.

85 *In her diary, Heap wrote . . .* Patterson, *Ladies of the Rope*, 1999, 45. On Heap's use of "playing," see Baggett, ed., *Dear Tiny Heart*, 2000, 96, 99. Jane Heap to Florence Reynolds, June 17, 1924, in Baggett, ed., *Dear Tiny Heart*, 2000, 94–95. On Rothermere's financial role, see Webb, *The Harmonious Circle*, 1980, 225.

85 *The movie director . . .* Secrest, *Frank Lloyd Wright*, 1992, 311.

86 *"Orage said many harsh things . . ."* Jane Heap to Florence Reynolds, June 25, 1924, in Baggett, ed., *Dear Tiny Heart*, 2000, 96. On dating the departures of Olgivanna, Heap, and Orage, see Taylor, *Gurdjieff's America*, 2004, 62

86 *But more likely . . .* Margaret Naumberg, "Talk with Olg.," February 19, 1925, Margaret Naumberg Papers, Rare Book and Manuscript Library, University of Pennsylvania.

86 *"I'll have to give . . ."* Jane Heap to Florence Reynolds, July 2, 1924, Baggett, *Dear Tiny Heart*, 2000, 97–98.

86 *There they met up . . .* Glenda Dawn Goss, *Music and the Moderns: The Life and Works of Carol Robinson* (Metuchen, New Jersey: Scarecrow Press, 1993), 55–57. Heap writes to Reynolds on October 22, 1924: "Carol is in love with an Englishman who may take the room, don't tell anyone. It might get to her people and spoil everything for her—God's I'm glad—if it will get rid of some of her insupportable virginities." Baggett, ed., *Dear Tiny Heart*, 2000, 102. Presumably "her people" are lesbians who would look awry at this development. Jane Heap to Florence Reynolds: June 28 and July 24, 1922, Baggett, ed., *Dear Tiny Heart*, 2000, 77, 79.

87 *"Olgivanna was in the kitchen . . ."* Patterson, *Ladies of the Rope*, 1999, 52, 54.

87 *"Never such thing again . . ."* Webb, *The Harmonious Circle*, 1980, 321.

88 *"[I]t was hushed . . ."* Baggett, *Dear Tiny Heart*, 2000, July 19, 1924, 98.

88 *"I've so many heart affairs . . ."* Baggett, *Dear Tiny Heart*, 2000, August 12, 1924, 100.

88 *Gurdjieff, in fact, . . .* Thomas de Hartmann, *Our Life With Mr. Gurdjieff*, 1972, 120–121; Patterson, *Struggle of the Magicians*, 1996, 111–112. Gurdjieff insisted that he had not fallen back into the orbit of the law of the accident. G.I. Gurdjieff, *Life Is Real Only Then: When "I Am"* (New York: Triangle Editions, 1975), 1.

88 *"I still wonder whether . . ."* Patterson, *Struggle of the Magicians*, 1996, 111–12.

88 *"Olgivanna liked me yesterday"* Baggett, *Dear Tiny Heart*, 2000, August 12, 1924, 100.

89 *"It was the last chord . . ."* Nott, *Teachings of Gurdjieff*, 1990, 80–8; Patterson, *Struggle of the Magicians*, 1996, 112.

89 *"It was in the year 223 . . ."* Gurdjieff, *Beelzebub's Tales to His Grandson*, 1999, 51.

89 *"Now, inside of me . . ."* Nott, *Teachings of Gurdjieff*, 1990, 83–84; Patterson, *Struggle of the Magicians*, 1996, 114–15; De Val, *Daddy Gurdjieff*, 1997; Bennett, *Gurdjieff*, 1990, 128.

90 *At midnight, distraught, . . .* Naumberg, "Talk with Olga," February 19, 1925.

90 *The master's once-promising . . .* Amin, *Reflections from the Shining Brow*, 2004, 60; OLW, *Autobiography*.

90 *From there she should go . . .* Taylor, *Gurdjieff in America*, 2004, 70–71, 108–9.

90 *"[Y]our daughter needs . . ."* OLW, *Autobiography*; Secrest, *Frank Lloyd Wright*, 1993, 31.

91 *He promised . . .* OLW, *Autobiography*.

91 *"O she talked . . ."* Jane Heap to Florence Reynolds, postmarked October 22, 1924, Baggett, ed., *Dear Tiny Heart*, 2000, 102–3.

91 *"new faith"* Twombly, *Louis Sullivan*, 1986, 438–42. Rather than a new faith, Sullivan was simply working the logic of Romanticism and German idealism. Both Goethe and Hegel used the logic of the seed. In his 1797 "The Metamorphosis of Plants," which Wright read, Goethe spoke of the "mystical law" proclaimed by the multitude of flowers, a law contained in "the force in the seed; a germ of the future . . ." Hegel used the seed in his *Phenomenology of Spirit*, as an example of dialectical logic, in which the life's unity is maintained and yet transformed despite negation through disintegration. For both Goethe and Emerson, man was a cocreator with God; for Hegel, man was an embodiment of the spirit animating the world, and necessary to its self-actualization. Sullivan was influenced by both Hegel and Goethe. Menocal, *Architecture as Nature*, 1981.

91 *"co-creators"* van Eck, *Organicism in Nineteenth Century Architecture*, 1994, 263.

91 *And Louis Sullivan saw Frank* . . . Sullivan, "Concerning the Imperial Hotel," 1923, 344.

92 *"I think* . . ." Harvey Einbinder, *An American Genius: Frank Lloyd Wright* (New York: Philosophical Library, 1986), 220.

CHAPTER 4: THE MAD GENIUS OF THE PIG BRISTLES AND MR. BELLYBUTTON

93 *Frank Lloyd Wright was alone.* Gill, *Many Masks*, 1987, 277–78; Wright, *An Autobiography*, 1943, 508.

93 *He had a contract* . . . FLW to Lloyd Wright, September 15, 1924, UCLA Special Collections.

94 *"All his hopes* . . ." Dione Neutra, *Richard Neutra: Promise and Fulfillment, 1919–1932* (Carbondale: Southern Illinois University Press, 1986), 126.

94 *Before arriving in town* . . . *Chicago Tribune*, November 27, 1924.

94 *Along with Olgivanna* . . . Olgivanna wrote that she arrived in New York two months before meeting Wright. Mrs. Frank Lloyd Wright, *The Roots of Life* (New York: Horizon Press, 1963), 126. That would place her arrival around October 1, 1924. The actual date, based on the ship's manifest—courtesy of Paul Beekman Taylor and Michael Benham—was October 31. The authors are grateful to Michael Benham for sharing his research on ship passenger lists. See also OLW, *Autobiography*.

94 *Olgivanna was on assignment* . . : "Mrs. Wright was given the charge to start a group in America. . . . Gurdjieff said, 'You've been with me seven years now. You've learned everything that you can. It's time for you to go to America and start a group.'" Authors' interview with Charles Schiffner, January 30, 2002. Schiffner, Olgivanna's son-in-law, was told this directly by her. Amin similarly claims that Olgivanna came to America with "an agenda" to start a Gurdjieff community. *Reflections from the Shining Brow*, 2004, 14–15, 60.

94 *Olgivanna would be responsible* . . . Taylor, *Gurdjieff in America*, 2004, 70–71; Taylor to the authors, e-mail, February 29, 2004; OLW, *Autobiography*.

94 *Olgivanna was in no hurry* . . . Moore, *Gurdjieff*, 1999, 211.

94–95 *"Little knots of people* . . ." Webb, *The Harmonious Circle*, 1980, 301–2.

95 *The complex chain* . . . Paul Taylor to authors, e-mail, January 5, 2003. There is no evidence of any relationship among Olgivanna, Jerome Blum, and Waldo Frank, other than through Gurdjieff connections. Olgivanna had been friends with Frank's wife, Margaret Naumberg, in January or February of the same year, but Waldo Frank was out of the country. When he returned to New York in July 1924, Olgivanna had already returned to France with the rest of the group. Later in the year Waldo joined one of Orage's groups. Blum most likely knew Waldo through their mutual friend Theodore Dreiser, or perhaps through Carol Robinson, another Gurdjieff follower.

95 *Jerry Blum was a brilliant colorist* . . . Jerome Blum, *Life Answered*, unpublished, undated autobiography; *Catalogue of an Exhibition of Paintings by Jerome Blum with a foreword by Theodore Dreiser*, January 28–February 9, 1929, Anderson Galleries, New York. Blum knew a number of people who attended Orage's groups, including his closest friends, Dreiser and Anderson. Blum also knew two of Orage's students among the musical avant-garde, composer Edgar Varèse and Carol Robinson.

95 *"I would ask* . . ." Sherwood Anderson, brochure for exhibition at the Delphic Studios, New York, November–December 1933; Frances Blum, undated memoir, Jerome Blum papers, Smithsonian Institution.

96 *By then, she later told* . . . In an oral history videotaped ten years after Olgivanna's death, her closest confidante, Kay Rattenbury, recalled the story as told to her by Olgivanna. "And it turned out," Kay said, "that their seats were next to each other and Mr. Wright was with a friend of Mrs. Wright." Allan Roth interview with Kay Rattenbury, October 5, 1994.

96 *Though Olgivanna had other friends* . . . FLW, *An Autobiography*, 1943, 511; Naumberg, "Talk with Olgo," February 19, 1925.

96 *". . . I had to have more in my life* . . ." OLW, *Autobiography*.

96 *"God," she prayed* . . . OLW, *Autobiography*. While the manuscript gives no specific dates, this must have occurred on November 22, 1924, the only day, weather records reveal, of significant rainfall during her stay in New York.

96 *"mad genius-of-the-pig-bristles"* Jerry just "happened in," Wright recalled. *An Autobiography*, 1943, 507–8. According to Secrest, Wright too had just been in New York, arriving there on November 25, 1924, just five days before Blum found him at the Congress Hotel (*Frank Lloyd Wright*, 1992, 313). This offers the tantalizing possibility that Wright may have just encountered some of his Gurdjieff Institute friends there, perhaps Zona Gale, which could have led to the subsequent encounter with Olgivanna. The authors, however, have found no information confirming whom Wright saw in New York.

Blum made a point of staying close to friends, like Anderson and Dreiser, but apparently exchanged no letters during this period with Wright. In an autobiography dealing specifically with this period in Chicago, Blum never mentions Wright. Nor does he appear in a biography by his second wife, Frances, based on Blum's own notes. The Jerome Blum Papers, Smithsonian Institution. Frank called Blum "Jerry of auld-lang-syne" in *An Autobiography*, 1943, 508.

96 *Blum as "rather terrifying"* . . . On November 12, 1940, two years before Wright wrote those words for his autobiography, Blum had written to Wright from the Rockland State Asylum for the Insane in upstate New York, where he had been admitted as a paranoid schizophrenic after a breakdown. Frances Blum to Theodore Dreiser, August 23, 1936, Annenberg Rare Book and Manuscript Library, University of Pennsylvania. Blum, who had just read about Frank's MoMA show, wanted Wright to solicit the museum's help in getting him released. There is no record that Wright ever replied. The only other letter Wright ever got from Blum had come years before, shortly after the Midway was finished, and eight years before his surprise visit to Wright in the hotel. Wright apparently didn't reply to that one either.

97 *The performance had been arranged* . . . Bolm may very well have known Wright. He came to Chicago in the same year that his frequent dance partner Anna Pavlova had been brought to the city to dance at Wright's Midway Gardens. Bolm was part of a Russian ballet circle centered on the impresario Sergei Diaghilev, who also produced Thomas de Hartmann's ballet *The Pink Flower* (starring Karsavina) before

de Hartmann began working with Gurdjieff. Webb, *The Harmonious Circle*, 1980, 284.

97 *Bolm had helped Gurdjieff* . . . Taylor, *Gurdjieff in America*, 2004, 45, 56; Gurdjieff, *Beelzebub's Tales to his Grandson*, 1999, 935–6. Gurdjieff used only nicknames in the book. Adolph Bolm was identified as Mr. Bellybutton in Moore, *Gurdjieff*, 1999, 203.

97 *But a greater contribution* . . . One reason to believe that Olgivanna's meeting with Wright was planned by Gurdjieff's followers concerns the box seats where they met. Seats in private boxes were almost invariably held by one party, either sold by subscription or made available as house seats for those, like Bolm, who were involved with the performance. That Wright and Hinzenberg met in a "private box" was confirmed by Taliesin Fellowship member Cornelia Brierly, *Tales of Taliesin*, 2000, 7. Those seated in the same box would almost certainly have procured their seats from the same source. Adolph Bolm had a connection with both Olgivanna and Jerome Blum, and very likely provided their seats. Given that Blum's two tickets were for the same box, they were also more than likely received from Bolm.

97 *Frank attributed* . . . In his memoir Wright contends that Olgivanna moved away out of fear (*An Autobiography*, 1943, 509). Since Olgivanna is known to have participated actively in the writing of Wright's book, it's quite possible that she gave her husband the idea that she was afraid of Blum—contradicting her later comment to Kay Rattenbury that Blum was a friend.

98 *"Suddenly in my unhappy state, . . ."* FLW, *An Autobiography*, 1943, 509.

98 *Providence, Olgivanna wrote* . . . OLW, *Frank Lloyd Wright*, 1966, 73. Bruce Brooks Pfeiffer, "Olgivanna Lloyd Wright: Her Life, Her Words, Her Works," 1999; Amin, *Reflections from the Shining Brow*, 2004, 62; Wright, *An Autobiography*, 1943, 509–10.

99 *"occult powers . . . by means of formulas . . ."* Louis H. Sullivan, *A System of Architectural Ornament According with a Philosophy of Man's Powers* (New York: Eakins Press, 1967 [1924]).

100 *"He liked her,"* Naumberg, "Talk with Olgo," February 19, 1925; Amin, *Reflections from the Shining Brow*, 2004, 63.

100 *Neither Gurdjieff nor Orage* . . . Taylor, *Shadows of Heaven*, 1998, 157.

101 *Valdemar had fallen...* Naumberg, "Talk with Olg.," February 19, 1925.

101 *Frank offered to design...* Marlin, "Frank Lloyd Wright: The First Space Man."

101, 102 *"special fur cap... The Cadillac..."* Letter from Richard Neutra to Lilly Mueller Niedermann, January 1925; Neutra, *Richard Neutra*, 1986, 135–36.

According to Jack Holtzheuter, Wright had been in a brief relationship starting around October 1924 with a university student also named Mary. Neutra's reference to "present sweetheart" and the "American," however, suggests that this Mary was indeed Olgivanna.

102 *"Such beautiful things,..."* Naumberg, "Talk with Olg.," February 19, 1925.

102 *"magnificently painted screens..."* Dione Neutra to her parents, July 1924, in Neutra, *Richard Neutra*, 1986, 127.

102 *"Olgivanna, from this time on..."* James Auer, interview with OLW, *Milwaukee Journal*, August 24, 1980, reprinted in Patrick J. Meehan, ed., *Frank Lloyd Wright Remembered* (Washington, D.C.: Preservation Press, 1991), 217.

102 *"Olgivanna," he crowed...* FLW, *An Autobiography*, 1943, 512. The story of Frank and Olgivanna's fateful meeting is curiously missing from the autobiography's 1932 edition. All of Wright's other future wives and lovers—even Miriam, whom he came to despise—were introduced in long, detailed, romantic passages. Not Olgivanna. Even when their memories were freshest—when Olgivanna was all but coauthoring the manuscript, her arrival was reduced to two simple words: "Came Olgivanna." Coincidence or not, the story of their meeting appeared only after Alfred Orage was dead and Jerry Blum locked away in an insane asylum.

103 *"It was somewhat painful,"* Dione Neutra to her parents, July 1924, Neutra, *Richard Neutra*, 1986, 126.

103 *"My life in a worldly sense..."* James Auer, interview with OLW, *Milwaukee Journal*, August 24, 1980, reprinted in Meehan, ed., *Frank Lloyd Wright Remembered*, 1991, 217.

103 *Her loyalty to him,...* Authors' interviews with Charles Schiffner, October 30 and December 14, 2000;

103 *"she never lost sight..."* Amin, *Reflections from the Shining Brow*, 2004, 63.

103 *Just days before,...* Taylor, *Gurdjieff and Orage*, 2001, 99.

103 *More to the point,...* FLW, *An Autobiography*, 1977, 532.

103 *"Olgivanna Hinzenberg was discussed..."* Jessie Orage, diary entry, provided to the authors by Paul Taylor.

103 *Orage didn't particularly cotton...* Naumberg, "Talk with Olg.," February 19, 1925.

104 *Though Olgivanna later acknowledged...* Amin, *Reflections from the Shining Brow*, 2004, 63.

104 *Just two weeks after...* Twombly, *Frank Lloyd Wright*, 1979, 186. According to Twombly, Wright followed Olgivanna to New York, "all the while wooing her vigorously." In contrast, in his autobiography, Wright suggests the relationship was solidified before the New York trip.

104 *"Carl's fairy tale..."* FLW, *An Autobiography*, 1943, 512.

105 *But Olgivanna was a big girl...* Jessie Orage, diary entry, provided to the authors by Paul Taylor via e-mail, January 16, 2002.

105 *Although Gurdjieff looked...* Ouspensky, *In Search of the Miraculous*, 1949, 134–38.

105 *"Real art..."* Nott, *Teachings of Gurdjieff*, 1961, 67; Speeth, *The Gurdjieff Work*, 1989), 90.

106 *The next day,...* Orage had his students write a detailed accounting of a day's events "imagined as the unrolling of a cinema film." See Webb, *The Harmonious Circle*, 1980, 307. The idea was to see everything from the perspective of a disinterested observer. Naumberg's "film" of Olgivanna's visit, quoted here, preserves the exchanges between the two in remarkable detail. Naumberg, "Talk with Olg," February 19, 1925. Orage's January 1925 meeting schedule was provided by Paul Taylor, December 23, 2002.

109 *"Thinking he had pushed..."* *Milwaukee Journal*, April 23, 1925.

109 *"A poor trustee..."* FLW, *An Autobiography*, 1943, 262.

109 *"The fire knocked me flat..."* Secrest, *Frank Lloyd Wright*, 1993, 316.

109 *"It is people like you..."* Author's interview with Dori Roy, December 12, 2000. If full term, the baby, born December 2, 1925, was probably conceived between mid-February and early March, making Olgivanna about six weeks pregnant (pregnancy timing starts with the date

of the first missed menstruation, not conception) around the time of the mid-April fire at Taliesin.

110 *"more philosophical"* The essay, "To My European Co-Workers," was first drafted in January 1925 but replaced with a draft "of a more philosophical sort" in October 1925. Donald Langmead and Donald Leslie Johnson, *Architectural Excursions: Frank Lloyd Wright, Holland and Europe* (Westport, Conn: Greenwood Press, 2000), 95. FLW, "To My European Co-Workers," in *Wendigen*, 1925. Pfeiffer, ed., *Collected Writings, Volume 1*, 1992, 207–8.

110 *"was happily married..."* Margaret Naumberg to Jean Toomer, June 30, 1925, Yale Collection of American Literature.

111 *Recalling the meeting...* Paul Taylor to the authors, e-mail, March 7, 2002. Taylor discovered the reference to the Chicago meeting in a draft of Jean Toomer's unpublished autobiography. See also Taylor, *Gurdjief's America*, 2004, 104, 109.

111 *As the reporters...* FLW, original unpaginated manuscript for the 1932 edition of *An Autobiography*, Getty Research Institute.

112 *"You're as big..."* ILW, *My Life*, 17.

112 *As Olgivanna may well...* Authors' interview with Paul Taylor, December 19, 2001. Olgivanna may indeed have been thinking of Gurdjieff in choosing Iovanna's name. As Olgivanna may have learned in Kabbalah studies with Gurdjieff in Constantinople, the names Ivana, Ivane, Iva, and Ivanna all mean "gift from God" in Hebrew etymology. The root *Iv* refers back to the Eve of Genesis, a figure with special meaning to Gurdjieff. See Chapter 18, notes.

112 *Olgivanna left in...* FLW, original unpaginated manuscript for the 1932 edition of *An Autobiography*, Getty Research Institute. Text deleted from the published version.

112 *Whatever was happening...* Taylor, *Shadows of Heaven*, 1998, 81.

113 *"I need you..."* Mabel Dodge Luhan to Jean Toomer, undated, Yale Collection of American Literature.

113 *Within days of...* Lois Rudnick, *Mabel Dodge Luhan: New Woman, New Worlds* (Albuquerque, New Mexico: University of New Mexico Press, 1984), 228.

113 *But Tony Luhan...* Margaret Naumberg to Jean Toomer, December 26, 1925, Yale Collection of American Literature.

113 *"opportunity for exercising..."* Jean Toomer to Gurdjieff, January 10, 1926.

113 *"I regret, ..."* Gurdjieff to Mabel Dodge Luhan, February 1, 1926, Yale Collection of American Literature.

114 *"I lost what..."* OLW to Maude Devine, January 12, 1927, Olgivanna Lloyd Wright Letters, 1926–1931, to Maude E. Devine, M0518, Dept. of Special Collections, Stanford University Libraries, Stanford, Calif.

114 *"I am still his wife..."* Twombly, *Frank Lloyd Wright*, 1979, 188; Secrest, *Frank Lloyd Wright*, 1993, 327–32.

115 *The project was Olgivanna's...* Authors' interview with ILW, August 16, 2000.

116 *"Svet, Svet..."* Susan Smith, "Grandson of Wright Offers His Memories," *Wisconsin State Journal*, December 14, 2003.

116 *"Hearst the Bastard..."* Authors' interview with ILW, August 16, 2000.

116 *Perhaps influenced...* Smith, "Grandson of Wright Offers His Memories," December 14, 2003.

116 *She even thought...* Authors' phone interview with Scott Elliott, February 17, 2004. Elliott, who acquired the Darwin Martin letters, reports that Olgivanna confided her suicidal feelings to Martin's wife

116 *Jean Toomer was now...* Taylor, *Shadows of Heaven*, 1998, 89–115.

116 *The "Olgivanna business..."* Notes on the Orage correspondence provided to the authors by Paul Taylor, April 3, 2002. Though Toomer's specific concern about Olgivanna was not recorded by Jessie, he appears to have been thinking of her arrest and hospitalization.

116 *Toomer renewed...* Rudnick, *Mabel Dodge Luhan*, 1984, 229; Alfred Orage to Jean Toomer: December 6, 1926 and January 17, 1927.

116–17 *"I've never for a moment..."* Jean Toomer to Mabel Dodge Luhan in Rudnick, *Mabel Dodge Luhan, New Woman, New Worlds*, 1984, 229.

117 *"Do you still love yourself..."* Mabel Dodge Luhan to Jean Toomer, November 26, 1927, Yale Collection of American Literature.

117 *Valdemar had dropped...* Twombly, *Frank Lloyd Wright*, 1979, 190. Ferdinand Schevill to OLW, January 22, 1927.

117 *"Whenever I go..."* OLW to Svetlana Hinzenberg, 1926.

117 *"out of step . . ."* Ferdinand Schevill to FLW, December 19, 1926.

117 *"Why since the baby was born, . . ."* OLW to Maude Devine, January 12, 1927, Olgivanna Lloyd Wright Letters, 1926–1931, to Maude E. Devine, M0518, Dept. of Special Collections, Stanford University Libraries, Stanford, California.

118 *"They are happy . . ."* OLW to Maude Devine, December 22, 1926, Olgivanna Lloyd Wright Letters, 1926–1931, to Maude E. Devine, M0518, Dept. of Special Collections, Stanford University Libraries, Stanford, California.

118 *"And this is my crime!"* Theodore Turak, "Mr. Wright and Mrs. Coonley," in Richard Guy Wilson and Sidney Robinson, ed., *Modern Architecture in America* (Ames, Iowa State University Press, 1991), 160.

118 *"I wish I could see you!"* OLW to Svetlana Hinzenberg, Elmwood School, Chicago: December 22, 1926 and October 3 and 9, 1927.

119 *"see to it that Svetlana . . ."* Ferdinand Schevill to OLW, January 13 and February 16, 1927.

119 *"every child is like that"* OLW to Ferdinand Schevill, January 13, 1927.

119 *Frank's close friend, . . .* Alexander Woollcott to Colonel William Joseph Donovan, January 16, 1927.

119 *"His ego, . . ."* Donald L. Miller, *Lewis Mumford: A Life* (Pittsburgh: University of Pittsburgh Press, 1989), 185.

119 *"so natural and reasonable . . ."* FLW to Alexander Woollcott, late 1928 or early 1929, undated.

120 *"For four months . . ."* FLW, "The Pictures We Make," in Pfeiffer, ed., *Collected Writings, Volume 1*, 1992, 215–24.

121 *"It is not plain . . ."* Alfred Orage to Jean Toomer, March 25, 1927, Yale Collection of American Literature.

121 *"Money is our object . . ."* Taylor, *Shadows of Heaven*, 2001, 133.

121 *This time the meeting . . .* From notes on Alfred Orage's diary provided to the authors by Paul Taylor.

121 *Olgivanna thought Toomer . . .* Paul Taylor to authors, e-mail, April 23, 2001. Taylor was told that this subject was discussed by Fritz Peters, and of Olgivanna's opinion of Toomer by Moore.

122 *In fact, Gurdjieff had been forced . . .* Alfred Orage to Jean Toomer, March 25 and April 16, 1927, Yale Collection of American Literature.

122 *He asked about Jean . . .* Taylor, *Shadows of Heaven*, 2001, 121.

122 *"The top o' the morning . . ."* Ferdinand Schevill to FLW, March 8, 1927.

122 *"I don't know where . . ."* OLW to Maude Devine, April 2, 1927, Olgivanna Lloyd Wright Letters, 1926–1931, to Maude E. Devine, M0518, Dept. of Special Collections, Stanford University Libraries, Stanford, Calif.

122 *To conform . . .* Secrest, *Frank Lloyd Wright*, 1992, 338. Ferdinand Schevill to FLW, September 19, 1928.

122 *"Mr. Wright is leaving . . ."* OLW to Maude Devine, May 13, 1927, Olgivanna Lloyd Wright Letters, 1926–1931, to Maude E. Devine, M0518, Dept. of Special Collections, Stanford University Libraries, Stanford, California.

122 *While in Chicago, . . .* Webb, *The Harmonious Circle*, 1980, 425.

122 *"All the wrongs . . ."* Capital Times, October 1927.

123 *"all history is the dirty product . . ."* FLW to Harold Kemp, September 13, 1927.

123 *Olgivanna worried . . .* OLW to Maude Devine, July 18, 1927, Olgivanna Lloyd Wright Letters, 1926–1931, to Maude E. Devine, M0518, Dept. of Special Collections, Stanford University Libraries, Stanford, California.

123 *"We found everything . . ."* OLW to Svetlana Hinzenberg at Hillcrest School, Beaver Dam, Wisconsin, October 9, 1927.

124 *"A primitive instinct . . ."* Alexander Woollcott and FLW: December 3 and 7, 1927.

124 *"The economy of Taliesin . . ."* FLW Archives, document dated 1927.

CHAPTER 5: FRANK LLOYD WRIGHT, SCHOOLMASTER

129 *"You covet attention . . ."* Richard Lloyd Jones to FLW, November 26, 1928.

129 *(Dickie's own idea . . .* Memorie Knox, "Oklahoma mulls reparations for 'Black Wall St. Massacre,'" *The Final Call*, online edition, http://www.finalcall.com/national/tulsa_03-13-2001.htm.

131 *"was an undefiled-by-irrigation . . ."* FLW, *An Autobiography*, 1943, 306.

131 *"greeted us warmly . . ."* Neutra, *Richard Neutra*, 1986, 166–67.

133 *"I decided,"* she later explained . . . Secrest, *Frank Lloyd Wright*, 1992, 340.

133 *"I hesitate . . ."* FLW to Phillip LaFollette, August 13, 1928.

133 won a *"heroic victory"* . . . Ferdinand Schevill to FLW, September 20, 1928.

134 *"I think you understand . . ."* FLW to Siegfried Scharfe, December 2, 1928.

134 *"This is the most beautiful . . ."* Langmead and Johnson, *Architectural Excursions*, 2000, 136; FLW to Ferdinand Schevill, December 11, 1928.

134 *"urgent matters . . ."* FLW to Phillip La Follette, March, 4, 1929.

135 *"ingenious, inventive . . ."* FLW, "The Hillside Home School of the Allied Arts," 39–49, Pfeiffer, ed., *Collected Writings, Volume 3*, 1993, 40.

136 *"You are authorized . . ."* Philip La Follette to FLW, November 10, 1928.

136 She was remarkably assertive . . . FLW to Jens Jensen, December 8, 1928.

137 Wright acknowledged . . . Authors' interview with Iovanna Wright, who was so informed by both her mother and her father. August 16, 2000.

137 *"This creative-instinct . . ."* FLW to Jens Jensen, December 8, 1928.

137 Having taught her husband . . . FLW, *An Autobiography*, 1943, 370.

137 *"has been tried . . ."* Franz Aust to FLW, December 7, 1928.

138 Wright's maiden aunts . . . Mary Ellen Chase, *A Goodly Fellowship* (New York: The Macmillan Company, 1939), 94.

138 *"a demon in human form"* Einbinder, *An American Genius*, 1986, 244.

138 *"great moral obligation . . ."* FLW to Ferdinand Schevill: November 16 and December 7, 1928; Barney, *The Valley of the God-Almighty Joneses*, 1965, 122.

138 *"a charming and graceful compliment . . ."* FLW to Hendrik Wijdeveld, October 30, 1925.

138 *"Perhaps Mr. Wijdeveld . . ."* OLW, *Frank Lloyd Wright*, 1966, 77.

139 It was a bitter cold . . . Vladimir Karfik, interview with Bruce Pfeiffer, Richard Carney, and John Hill, 1991.

139 *"[C]ome along dear Ferdinand . . ."* FLW to Ferdinand Schevill, December 7, 1928.

139 *"Oh, Holy simplicity . . ."* Ferdinand Schevill to FLW, November 26, 1928.

139 He made sure . . . Bruce Brooks Pfeiffer and Robert Wojtowicz, "Introduction," *Frank Lloyd Wright + Lewis Mumford: Thirty Years of Correspondence* (New York: Princeton Architectural Press, 2001), 11; Lewis Mumford, *Sticks and Stones: A Study of American Architecture and Civilization* (New York: Dover, 1955 [1924]).

140 *"stark and naked and severe"* FLW, "The Words Functional and Functionalism. Architectural Degeneracy—The Esthete Affirmation," Sunday morning talk, July 18, 1953, FLW Archives.

140 *"a kind of digest . . ."* Ferdinand Schevill to FLW, December 15, 1928.

140 *"Division of Architecture . . ."* Ferdinand Schevill, "Summarized Statement of the Project of a School of Allied Arts at Hillside. Wisconsin," undated, FLW Archives.

140–41 *"I was so disappointed . . ."* Lloyd Wright to FLW, circa 1928; "The Hillside Home School of the Allied Arts," in Pfeiffer, ed., *Collected Writings, Volume 3*, 1993, 48.

141 *"I have . . . considered . . ."* Heinrich Klumb to FLW, July 29, 1928.

141 When Klumb arrived . . . Authors' interview with Enrique Vivoni, December 23, 2000. Vivoni, who knew Klumb and has organized the Klumb archive, told us that Klumb "went up in 1928 and he was interviewed by Wright and with that interview, the Taliesin Fellowship began." Wright, he explained, "started hiring people to establish a Fellowship."

141 With the exception of two Americans . . . Enrique Vivoni to the authors, e-mail, July 9, 2003.

142 *"This is the year . . ."* Ferdinand Schevill to FLW, January 2, 1929.

142 *"the most beautiful part . . ."* FLW to Alexander Woollcott, undated (after Christmas 1928).

142 *"battered up but still . . ."* FLW to Lewis Mumford, January 7, 1929, in Pfeiffer and Wojtowicz, *Frank Lloyd Wright + Lewis Mumford: Thirty Years of Correspondence*, 2001, 62.

142 *"we [had] coke to burn . . ."* FLW to Philip LaFollette, March 3, 1929.

143 *"delighted"* M. Cochius to FLW, February 4, 1929, in Langmead and Johnson, *Architectural Excursions*, 2000, 136. Hendrik Wijdeveld to FLW, telegram, March 4, 1929.

144 *"If your plans . . ."* Hendrik Wijdeveld to FLW, April 22, 1929.

144 *"still some distance away . . ."* Wright did not date his letter to Wijdeveld. A handwritten "Ap. 30" on the typed letter appears to be an archivist's note. Alofsin dates it April 1, 1929, but that appears wrong; based on a reference to Wijdeveld's last "cablegram" that Wright received "some months ago in the desert," our best guess is April 30, 1929.

144 *"Clearly, under this contract . . ."* FLW to Phillip La Follette, March 18, 1929.

144 *"more shallow than it should be . . ."* FLW to Lewis Mumford, August 6, 1929, in Pfeiffer and Wojtowicz, *Frank Lloyd Wright + Lewis Mumford: Thirty Years of Correspondence*, 2001, 77.

144 *"You have in Olgivanna . . ."* Richard Lloyd Jones to FLW, April 19, 1929.

145 *"The city is a prison . . ."* Einbinder, *An American Genius*, 1986, 251–3.

146 *And now Wright . . .* Phillip La Follette to Darwin Martin, Ben Page, and Ferdinand Schevil, June 5, 1929; FLW to Werner Moser, July 25, 1929.

146 *"to keep the wolf . . ."* FLW to Lloyd Wright, October 29, 1929; Hines, "The Blessing and the Curse," 1998.

146 *"inane fiddling with philosophy . . ."* Franz Aust to FLW, December 17, 1929.

147 *The following month, . . .* George Cronin to Bruce Pfeiffer, July 9, 1988.

147 *"Frank Wright was neither"* Authors' interview with Eric Saarinen, October 25, 2004.

148 *"Nothing that International Style . . ."* Clarissa Mendez, *Of Surface and Shadow*, master's thesis, College of Architecture and Urban Studies, Virginia Polytechnic and State University, April 1997.

148 *"style center . . . The first thing to do . . ."* FLW, *The Future of Architecture* (New York: Mentor, 1953), 150; "Modern Architecture, Being the Kahn Lectures," *Collected Writings, Volume 2, 1930–1932* (New York: Rizzoli, 1992).

149 *And it was in the basement kitchen . . .* Heller, *The Story of My Life*, 1929, 14.

150 *"Your ways are Wright's ways, . . ."* Langmead and Johnson, *Architectural Excursions*, 2000, 140.

150 *"A stream of joyful words . . ."* Henry Klumb to FLW, May 27, 1931.

150 *Back in Wisconsin . . .* On the MoMA show see Twombly, *Power and Style*, 67–68; Franz Schulze, *Philip Johnson: Life and Work* (Chicago: University of Chicago Press, 1994), 47–48; FLW to Lewis Mumford, January 7, 1929; Pfeiffer and Wojtowicz, *Frank Lloyd Wright + Lewis Mumford: Thirty Years of Correspondence*, 2001, 61–63, 104; Terrence Riley, *The International Style: Exhibit 15 and the Museum of Modern Art* (New York: Rizzoli, 1992), 10, 14–15; Henry-Russell Hitchcock and Philip Johnson, *The International Style: Architecture Since 1922* (New York: Norton, [1932] 1966); Henry-Russell Hitchcock, "Foreword to the 1966 Edition," 21, in Hitchcock and Johnson, *The International Style* (New York: Norton, 1995).

151 *Philip Johnson "will come West . . ."* Lewis Mumford to FLW, March 29, 1931, Pfeiffer and Wojtowicz, *Frank Lloyd Wright + Lewis Mumford: Thirty Years of Correspondence*, 2001, 104.

151 *"the style and nothing but . . ."* Riley, *The International Style*, 1992, 26.

151 *"more akin to the men . . ."* Hitchcock and Johnson, *The International Style*, [1932] 1966, 27.

151 *"surface and mass . . . coroner's jury"* FLW to Lewis Mumford, January 27, 1929, *Frank Lloyd Wright + Lewis Mumford: Thirty Years of Correspondence*, 2001, 61–63.

152 *"the bastard begotten . . ."* *Architectural Forum*, Vol. 68, January 1938, 100.

152 *"was a great pioneer . . ."* Donald L. Miller, *Lewis Mumford: A Life* (Pittsburgh: University of Pittsburgh Press, 1989), 183.

152–53 *"fall into raptures . . ."* Lewis Mumford to FLW, May 11, 1928, in Pfeiffer and Wojtowicz, *Frank Lloyd Wright + Lewis Mumford: Thirty Years of Correspondence*, 2001, 52.

153 *"full-aged unfortunate people . . ."* Taylor, *Gurdjieff in America*, 2004, 141; see also Webb, *The Harmonious Circle*, 1980, 370; Taylor, *Shadows of Heaven*, 1998, 151; Brian Joseph Benson and Mabel Mayle Dillard, *Jean Toomer* (Boston: Twayne Publishers, 1980), 39; Charles Scruggs and Lee VanDermarr, *Jean Toomer and the Terrors of American History* (Philadelphia:

University of Pennsylvania Press, 1998), 211; Taylor, *Shadows of Heaven*, 1998, 151. Brownell and Wright would cowrite *Architecture and Modern Life* (New York and London: Harper and Bros., 1937). Zona Gale to Jean Toomer, July 1, 1931, Yale Collection of American Literature.

153 *"in a particular way . . . Something awful happened . . ."* Authors' interview with Paul Taylor, March 11, 2001. Claude Bragdon was identified by James Moore as being with "a prominent woman novelist" when Gurdjieff performed this feat. *Gurdjieff*, 1999, 248. The two were Gale and Bragdon, according to Rom Landau, *God Is My Adventure: A Book on Modern Mystics, Masters and Teachers* (New York: Knopf, 1936), 188–89, though he does not identify Gale or Bragdon by name, undoubtedly in the interest of discretion. Gale is called "one of our great novelists" and Bragdon a "companion" to Gurdjieff. Landau interviewed Bragdon extensively for other parts of the book. Moreover, this same "companion" describes witnessing Gurdjieff being identified as a Russian agent by writer Achmed Abdullah. Webb also discusses the event, and notes that "the man was probably Bragdon and the woman Zona Gale." *The Harmonious Circle*, 1980, 420. The incident is identical to one Bragdon himself relates in his autobiography. *More Lives Than One*, 1938, 323. One piece of the dialogue, however, is absolutely unbelievable—that Gale did not know who caused her orgasm.

154 *During his time in Portage, . . .* On Toomer's Portage experiment, see Patterson, *Struggle of the Magicians*, 1996, 157; Twombly, "A Disciple's Odyssey," 1976, 454–455; Taylor, *Shadows of Heaven*, 1998, 151–152.

154 *"Negro Poet . . ."* Scruggs and VanDemarr, *Jean Toomer*, 1998, 216.

154 *"As I see America . . ."* "Just Americans," *Time*, March 28, 1932, cited in Taylor, *Shadows of Heaven*, 1998, 152.

155 *Toomer was in serious trouble, . . .* Authors' phone interview with Robert Twombly, November 2003; Moore, *Gurdjieff*, 1999, 244; Taylor, *Shadows of Heaven*, 1998, 151. Writing about Toomer's Portage experiment, Twombly notes that "[s]uch a conspicuous undertaking only fifty miles away, virtually coinciding with the Mansfield article and the Hillside pamphlet, undoubtedly reinforced their plans for the Fel-

lowship." "Organic Living," *Wisconsin Magazine of History*, Winter 1974–5, 126–139, 136–137; *The Bookman*, LXXIII(1), March 1931, New York, 6–13.

155 *"A school is forming . . ."* FLW to Hendrik Wijdeveld, April 6, 1931.

155 *"Chicago school overwhelming . . ."* Wijdeveld to FLW, telegram, April 16, 1931.

156 *"WRIGHT, TALIESIN, WIJDEVELD, ART-SCHOOL, . . ."* Wijdeveld to FLW, April 11, 1931.

156 *The year before, . . .* Stahl's Association of Arts and Industries appears to be the well-endowed Allied Arts and Industries organization Wright referred to in his letter to Wijdeveld. Norma Stahl to FLW, November 14, 1930.

156 *"I want you to see . . ."* FLW to Norma Stahl, April 17, 1931.

157 *In a sure sign . . .* Karl E. Jensen to Hendrik Wijdeveld, June 15, 1931; FLW to Wijdeveld, August 13, 1931.

157 *"I have only been unwilling . . ."* FLW to Hendrik Wijdeveld, August 13, 1931.

157 *"I feel the burden . . ."* Hendrik Wijdeveld to FLW, August 26, 1931. The date of June 1931 given for this letter in Langmead and Johnson, *Architectural Excursions*, 2000, 141, is wrong.

158 *"Consider earnestly proposal, . . ."* Hendrik Wijdeveld to FLW, telegram, September 5, 1931.

158 *At the end of October 1931, . . .* FLW to Charles Morgan, October 8, 1931.

CHAPTER 6: A STATION FOR THE FLIGHT OF THE SOUL

159 *"That counts you one . . ."* OLW, *The Work of Frank Lloyd Wright: The Wendingen Edition* (New York: Horizon Press, 1965), republication of Hendrik Wijdeveld, *A Life-Work of the American Architect Frank Lloyd Wright* (1925).

159 *"Could life undergo . . ."* Langmead and Johnson, *Architectural Excursions*, 2000, 143.

159 *Wright was surprised . . .* FLW to Lewis Mumford, December 9, 1931, in Pfeiffer and Wojtowicz, *Frank Lloyd Wright + Lewis Mumford: Thirty Years of Correspondence*, 2001, 117–18.

159 *"all found recognition, . . ."* Henrik Wijdeveld, "An International Guild," 1931, republished in Longmead and Johnson, *Architectural Excursions*, 2000, 199.

160 *To make matters worse, . . .* Authors' interview with Enrique Vivoni, director, Archivo de Arquitectura y Construcción de la Universidad de Puerto Rico, December 23, 2002.

160 *Iovanna, nearly six now, . . .* Authors' interview with ILW, August 16, 2000.

161 *"the privilege of participation . . ."* FLW and Wijdeveld, "The Taliesin Fellowship," November 1, 1931.

161 *The book's title, . . .* FLW, *The Disappearing City* (New York: William Farquhar Payson, 1932).

161 *"a tomb that will mark . . ."* "Skyscraper Passing Says Frank L. Wright," *New York Times,* November, 14, 1931.

162–63 *"It is in fact and principle . . ."* Lloyd Wright to FLW, 1932, Though undated, the letter mentions Olgivanna's illness and that Schindler was not included in the MoMA show, which suggests a date around this time.

163 *"The various enterprises . . ."* "Agreement for the founding and conduct of the proposed Taliesin Fellowship—by and between Frank Lloyd Wright and H. Th. Wijdeveld," typed document, hand-dated November 1931. There is no record of a signed agreement.

163 *"The thing has as many . . ."* FLW to Lewis Mumford, January 10, 1932, in Pfeiffer and Wojtowicz, *Frank Lloyd Wright + Lewis Mumford: Thirty Years of Correspondence,* 2001, 122; FLW to Lewis Mumford, January 19, 1932.

163 *"Settled plans and contract . . ."* Hendrik Wijdeveld to Ellen Wijdeveld, December 5, 1931, reprinted in Longmead and Johnson, *Architectural Excursions,* 2000, 144.

164 *"beautiful time at Taliesin . . ."* Hendrik Wijdeveld to FLW, December 9, 1931.

164 *"Dutchy has gone home . . ."* FLW to Lewis Mumford, December 9, 1931, Pfeiffer and Wojtowicz, *Frank Lloyd Wright + Lewis Mumford: Thirty Years of Correspondence,* 2001, 117–118.

164 *"We have done nothing . . ."* FLW to Lloyd Wright, January 2, 1932.

164 *"I had a wonderful time . . ."* Hendrik Wijdeveld to FLW, January 1, 1932.

164 *"I am sending you . . ."* FLW, "specimen letter," January 26, 1932.

165 *"the matron of . . ."* "Agreement for the founding and conduct of the proposed Taliesin Fellowship," November 1931.

165 *After Wijdeveld left . . .* Secrest, *Frank Lloyd Wright,* 1992, 399.

165 *"a ball of shit"* Taylor, *Shadows of Heaven,* 1998, 146; Taylor, *Gurdjieff's America,* 2004, 150.

165 *"I had certain qualifications; . . ."* FLW, *An Autobiography,* 1943, 389, 394.

165 *"The Fellowship aims first . . ."* Longmead and Johnson, *Architectural Excursions,* 2000, 209.

166 *"an inexhaustible supply . . ."* Amin, *Reflections from the Shining Brow,* 2004, 64.

166 *"A Station for the Flight . . ."* FLW, *An Autobiography,* 1943, 389.

166 *"pushing themselves . . .* Lloyd Wright to FLW, undated, 1931.

166 *"Both of you . . ."* FLW to Rudolph Schindler, June 3, 1931.

166 *"The internationalists, . . ."* Lloyd Wright to FLW, undated, January 1932.

167 *"Will try to get . . ."* FLW to OLW, telegram, January 24, 1932.

167 *"Leaving Los Angeles . . ."* FLW to OLW, telegram, January 30, 1932.

167 *"My way has been . . ."* FLW to Philip Johnson, telegram, January 18, 1932.

167 *"I am going . . ."* FLW to Philip Johnson, January 19, 1932.

167 *"worthless here . . ."* FLW to Lewis Mumford, January 19, 1932; Thomas S. Hines, *Richard Neutra and the Search for Modern Architecture* (Berkeley: University of California Press, 1994), 55.

168 *"Olgivanna alongside Schindler, . . ."* FLW to Lloyd Wright, January 2, 1932.

168 *"As for company, . . ."* Lewis Mumford to FLW, telegram, January 21, 1932, in Pfeiffer and Wojtowicz, *Frank Lloyd Wright + Lewis Mumford: Thirty Years of Correspondence,* 2001, 131.

168 *"For God's sake . . ."* Lloyd Wright to FLW, undated, 1932.

168 *"health house . . . without question . . ."* Henry-Russell Hitchcock, *Modern Architecture* (New York: Museum of Modern Art, 1932), 157–60.

168 *"Believe me, Philip . . ."* FLW to Philip Johnson, January 19, 1932.

168 *"In short, Philip, . . ."* FLW to Philip Johnson, April 19, 1932.

168 *The international style architects . . .* Wright was also thinking of Schindler, whom he

once denounced as a "pus-bag of treachery" for claiming creative input into the Barnsdall house in Los Angeles. Frank opened a letter to Schindler with the words "[o]ut in front, with your naked sentiments in your hand at last": FLW to Rudolph Schindler, June 19, 1931.

168 *"To the Neuter"* "To the Neuter," January 13, 1932. In a February 3, 2003, e-mail to the authors, Margo Stipe of the FLW Archives informed us that the essay was edited quite a bit, but there is no evidence that it was ever submitted for publication.

169 *"To tell the truth . . ."* FLW to Lewis Mumford, February 2, 1932, in Pfeiffer and Wojtowicz, *Frank Lloyd Wright + Lewis Mumford: Thirty Years of Correspondence*, 2001, 137.

169 *"We have at this time . . ."* FLW to Lewis Mumford, February 1, 1932.

169 *Creative people . . ."* Lewis Mumford to FLW, February 6, 1932, in Pfeiffer and Wojtowicz, *Frank Lloyd Wright + Lewis Mumford: Thirty Years of Correspondence*, 2001, 139–140.

169 *"Ignoring his friend's . . ."* Secrest, *Frank Lloyd Wright*, 1992, 398.

169 *"Everywhere Youth is rocking . . ."* FLW, *An Autobiography*, 1943, 398.

170 *"The articles in the paper . . ."* Alice Warner to FLW, January 2, 1932. Karl Jensen wrote back immediately, "As soon as we receive the printed programme for the Hillside Art School from Holland we will send you a copy." At this point, Wright obviously thought Wijdeveld would be handling production of the prospectus.

170 *"Predilection for what . . ."* "Application for Fellowship," FLW Archives, no date. In a February 7, 2003, e-mail to the authors, archivist Indira Berndtson notes that this was taken from the Franklin Porter collection, a sepia prospectus marked "1st".

170 *With no real expectation . . .* Franklin Toker, *Fallingwater Rising: Frank Lloyd Wright, E.J. Kaufmann, and America's Most Extraordinary House* (New York: Knopf, 2003), 30; "The Taliesin Fellowship," 157–166, Pfeiffer, ed., *Collected Writings, 1931–1939*, 1993, 163.

170 *"The home life . . ."* Wijdeveld's 1931 proposal reads: "The home life is simple and very regular. Meals in common, fixed hours for works, recreation and sleep. For each worker an apartment of his own for private study and sleeping."

Langmead and Johnson, *Architectural Excursions*, 2000, 204. Wright's first prospectus reads: "The home life will be simple. Meals in common. Fixed hours for work, recreation and sleep. Each worker will have his or her own room for study and rest." *The Taliesin Fellowship*, Franklin Porter collection. undated, FLW Archives.

171 *"After that we might . . ."* This letter from Wijdeveld to Wright was dated in the European fashion "8-2-1932," causing Wright's archivists to misread the note and date it as August 2 instead of February 8. This evidently led Langmead and Johnson, whose account of these events is otherwise exemplary, to conclude that the return of Wright's exhibition materials being held by Wijdeveld triggered Wright's letter informing him that he would no longer be the school's director.

171 *"F. L. Wright Tells . . ."* "F.L. Wright Tells of His Stormy Life," *New York Times*, March 30, 1932.

171–72 *"I have longed . . ."* FLW, *An Autobiography*, 1932, 328.

172 *"I wish you . . ."* FLW to Charles Ashbee, July 27, 1932.

172 *"insurmountable . . ."* OLW, *Frank Lloyd Wright*, 1966, 79.

172 *So it could hardly . . .* An alternate source for the name "Broadacre City" is cited in Einbinder, *An American Genius*, 1986. ". . . he took its name from Broad Acre, the title of a ranch near his Ocatillo camp" (p. 263). It's also possible that the coincidence of the ranch's name and Wijdeveld's had special meaning for Wright.

CHAPTER 7: EVERYTHING TO DREAM

177 *"Whenever Architect . . ."* *Time*, September 5, 1932.

177 *"Dear Mr. Wright, . . ."* James Gehr to FLW, September 14, 1932.

177 *"I read so much . . ."* Grace Mundt to FLW, September 18, 1932.

178 *Six-feet-four . . .* Transcriptions of letters between Wes Peters and his parents: October 19, November 23, and December 26, 1930; April 16 and June 15, 1931. Marlin papers, Scott Elliott collection. Unless otherwise noted, letters credited to the Marlin/Elliott collection are transcriptions.

178 *"With all due respects . . ."* Wes Peters to his parents, April 16, 1931, Marlin Papers, Scott Elliott collection.

178 *"I doubt if you realize . . ."* Mr. Peters to Wes Peters, December 15, 1930, Marlin Papers, Scott Elliott collection.

178 *"All the streets . . ."* Wes Peters to Mr. Peters, December 26, 1930.

179 *After opening windows . . .* Authors' interview with Edgar Tafel, June 27, 2003.

179 *When Wes and the others . . .* Authors' interview with ILW, January 26, 2000. Peters told Iovanna this story; she claimed he was not "profoundly affected" by the event. While nobody has confirmed the story, the entire period (June 1931 to July 1932) is missing in his collected correspondence. Marlin papers, Scott Elliott collection. While Peters' large and ordered files of personal correspondence were carefully stripped of letters from this period, nothing indicates that he was anything but satisfied with his education at MIT. And while many of his classmates were flunking out, he was headed for a brilliant finish. MIT was not able to locate records on Peter's leaving.

179 *"Oh, don't touch . . ."* Tafel, *About Wright,* 1993, 158.

179 *In July 1932 . . .* Secrest suggests June 1932 in *Frank Lloyd Wright,* 1993, 593. Karl Jensen invites Peters to come to Taliesin in a letter of July 17 or July 24: Marlin papers, Scott Elliott collection. Peters finished his second year at MIT, leaving in June 1932. Authors' correspondence with Connie Scribner, Assistant Registrar, MIT, May 21, 2003.

180 *"I loved . . ."* Interview with William Wesley Peters, 1967–1968.

180 *"Dad and I . . ."* Mrs. Peters to Wes Peters, undated, Marlin papers, Scott Elliott collection.

181 *"I was talking . . ."* Authors' interview with Edgar Tafel, September 22, 2000.

181 *"Believe we can . . ."* Tafel, *Years with Frank Lloyd Wright,* 1985, 15–17.

182 *"handsome man . . ."* Abrom Dombar, *Abrom Dombar, Autobiography,* April 29, 1995, compiled by his children and unpublished. Abrom Dombar private papers.

182 *"Rent," he had . . .* FLW, *An Autobiography,* 1932, 315.

182 *"the money-changers . . ."* Tafel, *About Wright,* 1993, 61.

184 *"no closer to . . ."* Yen Liang, "First Apprentice," in Tafel, *About Wright,* 1993, 128–129.

185 *"It was like . . ."* Tafel, *Years with Frank Lloyd Wright,* 1985, 20, 141.

187 *"That young man . . ."* OLW, *Frank Lloyd Wright,* 1966, 81.

187 *Jack Howe went . . .* Tafel, *About Wright,* 1993, 123–124; Meehan, ed., *Frank Lloyd Wright Remembered,* 1991, 116.

187 *All but one . . .* Indira Berndtson and Greg Williams, interview with Herb Fritz, February 15, 1970.

187 *He had previously . . .* Authors' interview with Eloise Fritz, who was told this both by her husband and her draftsman father-in-law: December 15, 1999.

187 *Most of the foreigners . . .* "Charter Applicants," undated printed sheet, Abrom Dombar papers. "Charter applicants for Fellowship accepted and at work in temporary quarters at Taliesin October 25, 1932," includes Karl E. Jensen, Heinrich Klumb, Else Klumb, Yuan Hsi Kuo, and Rudolph Mock.

187 *Now, however, Wright . . .* Betty J. Blum, interview with Alfred Caldwell, 1987, Chicago Architects Oral History Project, Art Institute of Chicago. 37; FLW, *An Autobiography,* 1943, 260.

188 *These men were given . . .* Interviews with Wes Peters, 1967–1968.

188 *"We had to learn . . ."* Tafel, *Years with Frank Lloyd Wright,* 1979, 161.

188 *The novel . . .* FLW, *An Autobiography,* 1943, 446; Johann Wolfgang von Goethe, *Wilhelm Meister's Apprenticeship,* trans. Eric A. Blackall (New York: Suhrkamp Publishers, 1989), 16–17. At the dedication of the First Unitarian Society Church on August 28, 1951, for example, Wright told the apprentices that only Goethe was more important than Ralph Waldo Emerson. At a Sunday lecture on January 23, 1955, he told the apprentices that it had been his favorite book.

189 *. . . Wright always remembered . . .* "[F]ellowship was taking its course in apprenticeship in the offices of Adler and Sullivan in the Auditorium Tower," he wrote in his autobiography about this moment, doubtless thinking of the triad he now sought to establish at Taliesin. FLW, *An Autobiography,* 1943, 104.

189 *"listen to music . . ."* OLW, *Frank Lloyd Wright,* 1966, 134.

189 *Karl Jensen wrote...* Karl Jensen to the National Theatre Supply Co., October 5, 1932.

189 *"Here it was..."* FLW, *An Autobiography*, 1943, 446.

189 *Wright was forced...* Tafel, *Years with Frank Lloyd Wright*, 1979, 140.

189 *"Wait a minute..."* OLW, *Frank Lloyd Wright*, 1966, 81.

190 *"[S]ince I had..."* Dombar, *Abrom Dombar*, 1995.

190 *"Long caravans..."* Neutra, *Richard Neutra*, 1986, 128; Randolph C. Henning, ed., *"At Taliesin": Newspaper Columns by Frank Lloyd Wright and the Taliesin Fellowship, 1934–1937* (Carbondale and Edwardsville: Southern Illinois University Press, 1992), 47.

190 *"we'd rush to town..."* Interview with Cornelia Brierly, May 12, 1989.

191 *A girl, he joked,...* FLW, "At Taliesin," September 20, 1934, Henning, ed., *"At Taliesin,"* 1992, 79.

191 *Workers and apprentices quarried...* Interviews with Wes Peters, 1967–1968.

191 *Asked to slaughter...* Tafel, *Years with Frank Lloyd Wright*, 1979.

192 *Instead he had young...* Brierly, *Tales of Taliesin*, 1999, 12.

192 *"My God!..."* Indira Berndtson and Greg Williams, interview with Wes Peters, Bob Mosher, and Victor Cusack, April 7, 1992.

192 *"tonic to the lungs..."* "At Taliesin," *The Capital Times*, May 1, 1934, Abe Dombar papers.

192 *Some apprentices made...* Tafel, *Years with Frank Lloyd Wright*, 1979, 145; Eugene Masselink, "At Taliesin," February 2, 1934, in Henning, *"At Taliesin,"* 1992, 19.

192 *"Joy in work..."* FLW, "At Taliesin," September 30, 1934, in Henning, *"At Taliesin,"* 1992, 78–79.

193 *"If you get yourself..."* Edgar Tafel to Wes Peters, March 16, 1934, Marlin papers, Scott Elliott collection.

193 *"He published..."* Yen Liang to Wes Peters, 1933, Marlin papers, Scott Elliott collection.

193 *It would take a day...* Interviews with Wes Peters, 1967–1968.

193 *One female apprentice...* Brierly, *Tales of Taliesin*, 1999, 16.

193 *Others were assigned...* Indira Berndtson and Greg Williams, interview with Wes Peters, Bob Mosher, and Victor Cusack, April 7, 1992.

194 *Wright took his meals...* Authors' interview with O. P. Reed, July 15, 1999. Reed was told this by Olgivanna, for whom he later arranged the evaluations and sale of some of Taliesin's art collection.

194 *She used simple...* Brierly, *Tales of Taliesin*, 1999, 10.

194 *No more drawing-board..."* FLW, *An Autobiography*, 1943, 401.

195 *"I hope you are..."* Letter from Abe Dombar to Beck and Ben Dombar, January, 1933, Dombar papers.

196 *...Yvonne stripped naked...* Dombar, *Abrom Dombar*, 1995.

196 *"We would spend..."* Authors' interview with Abrom Dombar, September 17, 2000.

197 *Sometimes, to make a point,...* Authors' interview with O. P. Reed, who appraised all 20,000 drawings at Taliesin, July 15, 1999.

197 *"In a sense..."* Tafel, *Years with Frank Lloyd Wright*, 1979, 164.

197 *"Fourteen thousand..."* Front page, undated, 1932, FLW Archives.

197 *"wore lavender trousers, ..."* Tafel, *About Wright*, 1993, 48, 156, 222.

197 *"I do it..."* George Goodwin, interview with Philip Johnson, July 27, 1992.

198 *While the plans...* Levine, *The Architecture of Frank Lloyd Wright*, 1996, 220.

198 *"And Ralph Adams Cram..."* Cram was a famous proponent of the Gothic revival movement. Wright adored Gothic architecture, but Wright felt he made the unpardonable sin of copying the style rather than creating something new from its core principles.

199 *And then he began...* Neil Levine, interview with Wes Peters, April 5, 1990. Peters's recollection that this song was sung just after raising the roof may be off, given that Jack Howe had yet to ascend to head of the drafting room.

199 *"I felt in duty bound..."* Wright, *An Autobiography*, 1943, 399.

199 *"We are desperate here..."* FLW to George T. Bye, May 16, 1932.

200 *When the police...* Dombar, *Abrom Dombar*, 1995; interview notes with Wes Peters, March 8, 1988.

200 *In the spring of 1933...* Abrom Dombar, "1933–34 'Crises!' at Taliesin," undated notes provided by Dombar to the authors, Dombar papers.

200 *"I have not been able . . ."* FLW to Wijde-veld, April 7, 1933.

201 *"We miss the man . . ."* Heinrich Klumb to Hendrik Wijdeveld, April 11, 1933, Getty Research Institute. Translated from the German by Gudrun Hausegger.

201 *Though he agonized . . .* Langmead and Johnson, *Architectural Excursions*, 2000, 152

CHAPTER 8: FLIGHT

203 *With a strong handshake . . .* Clare Crane to Sue Scheutz, January 7, 2002.

203 *"To Svet . . ."* Correspondence between Wes Peters and Svetlana Wright quoted from transcriptions in the Marlin papers, Scott Elliott collection, and from original correspondence at the FLW Archives: Wes Peters to Svetlana Wright, April 7, 1933, April 2, 1934.

204 *The clique . . .* Tafel, *Years with Frank Lloyd Wright*, 1979, 139, 143.

204 *"Mr. Wright came upon . . ."* Indira Berndtson and Greg Williams, interview with Kay Rattenbury, January 16, 1990.

204 *"smooth it out . . ."* Indira Berndtson and Greg Williams interview with Wes Peters, June 15, 1988.

204–5 *"Don't, Daddy Frank . . ."* Authors' interview with ILW, January 14, 2000; William Marlin interview with Iovanna Wright, May 17, 1988. In Marlin's interview, Iovanna dates the incident to 1933, when she would have been seven; in her own autobiography, she says she was about five when it happened. *My Life*, 25.

205 *"Initially . . ."* Tafel, *About Wright*, 1993, 161–62; Indira Berndtson and Greg Williams, interview with Wes Peters, June 15, 1988.

206 *It "took the life . . ."* Robert Bishop to Mendel Glickman, November 4, 1933.

206 *The son of a dentist, . . .* O. P. Reed, *Eugene Masselink: His Art and Life at Frank Lloyd Wright's Taliesin*, unpublished manuscript, 1999, 28; Gene Masselink to FLW: October 11 and 17, 1932; authors' interview with O. P. Reed, July 15, 1999; Karl Jensen to Gene Masselink, November 28, 1932; Ben Masselink, *Gene*, 1996, unpublished, 107.

208 *"You have talent, . . ."* ILW, "Reverence for Life," eulogy at the funeral of Eugene Masselink, FLW Archives. See also Reed, *Eugene Masselink*, 1999, 29; Eugene Masselink to Karl Jensen, March 12, 1933.

209 *"The next thing . . ."* Reed, *Eugene Masselink*, 1999, 30–31.

209 *"My dear Masselink . . ."* FLW and Gene Masselink: August 20 and September 9, 1933.

209 *Nancy Willey, . . .* Indira Berndtson, interview with Nancy Willey, February 15, 1995; Alvin Rosenbaum, *Usonia: Frank Lloyd Wright's Design for America* (Washington, D.C. : Preservation Press, 1993), 102–4.

209 *"Mr. Wright called me . . ."* Authors' interview with Abe Dombar, September 17, 2000.

210 *"Damn fools! . . ."* ILW, *My Life*; authors' interview with ILW, July 24, 2000.

210 *And she was a sensuous . . .* Authors' phone interview with Jane Gale Sheain, February 26, 2002; authors' interview with ILW, July 24, 2000; authors' phone interview with Clare Crane, who lived in the Taliesin household in the early 1940s, June 28, 2004.

210 *"I am leaving him . . ."* ILW, *My Life*, 27–28.

211 *"Until now . . ."* Abe Dombar, "At Taliesin," February 9, 1934, 20–22, in Henning, *"At Taliesin,"* 1992.

211 *And when, for the room-warming party . . .* Authors' interview with ILW, August 16, 2000.

211 *When she got angry . . .* Maggie Valentine, interview with John Hill, July 19, 1993, Frank Lloyd Wright Design Heritage Program of the Frank Lloyd Wright Oral History Program, completed under the auspices of the Oral History Program University of California, Los Angeles, and the State Historical Society of Wisconsin, 1997, The Regents of the University of California.

211 *Wright burned . . .* Abe Dombar to Becky Dombar, February 1934, Dombar papers.

211 *"Spider man, . . ."* ILW, *My Life*, 16–21; FLW, *An Autobiography*, 1932, 366.

212 *"I don't think . . ."* Dombar, *Abrom Dombar*, 1995.

212 *Betty and Louise . . .* Correspondence among Svetlana and Wes Peters and their friends from Marlin's transcriptions, Scott Elliott collection, and original correspondence at the FLW Archives: Edgar Tafel to Svetlana Peters, March 15, 1934; Louise Dees-Porch to Svetlana Wright, undated, probably late 1933; Louise Dees-Porch to Svetlana Wright, November 6, 1933; Svetlana Wright to Wes Peters, un-

dated; Dees Porch or Elizabeth Weber to Wes Peters, January 20, 1934; Yen Liang to Wes Peters, 1933; Jack Howe to Svetlana Wright, 1933. See also *Memories of Svetlana Peters* by Margaret Jean Evans, January 16, 1999, Sue Schuetz personal archives.

212 *"I am sorry . . ."* FLW to Wes Peters, September 15, 1933.

213 *"I have resolved . . ."* Wes Peters and Svetlana Wright correspondence: pre-Christmas 1933; December 12, 1933; early January 1934; February 8, February 9, March 23, August 3, 1934; Mrs. Peters to Wes Peters, 1933; Yen Liang to Wes Peters, 1933; Elizabeth Weber to Wes Peters, undated; Olgivanna to Svetlana Wright, undated; Dees Porch or Elizabeth Weber to Wes Peters, January 20, 1934.

215 *"After all, . . ."* Svetlana Wright to Wes Peters, Christmas 1933. Svetlana was not alone in her judgment of her mother. Elizabeth Weber noted at the same time in a letter to Wes Peters, "After all, the situation is not entirely of Mrs. Wright's making—it is far from a happy one for her. I have a feeling that she is going to take pride in Svetlana's independence and strength as contrasted with her own weakness and position of utter dependence. Not now—the cuts are still open—but ultimately I am sure it will be so." Elizabeth Weber to Wes Peters, early 1934.

215 *Before leaving . . .* Elizabeth Weber to Wes Peters, early 1934.

216 *"Don't you feel . . ."* Wes Peters and Svetlana Wright correspondence: late 1933 or early 1934; December 31, 1933; January 3, January 5, 1934; Yen Liang to Wes Peters, January 3, 1934; Louise Dees-Porch to Svetlana Wright, January 10, 1934.

217 *Instead she was thinking . . .* Svetlana Wright and Wes Peters: February 1, February 12, February 15, March 4, March 23, May 15, 1934.

218 *"Lo! On the Horizon . . ."* Rosenbaum, *Usonia*, 1993, 106; Indira Berndtson, interview with Nancy Willey, February 15, 1995.

219 *"He believes . . ."* Yen Liang to Wes Peters, March 16, 1934; letter from Wes Peters to Svetlana Wright, March 19, 1934.

219 *At the Crees', . . .* Margaret Jean Evans, "Memories of Svetlana Peters," January 16, 1999; Svetlana Wright to Wes Peters, June 28, 1934.

219–20 *If Svetlana returned . . .* Edgar Tafel to Wes Peters, March 16, 1934; Svetlana Wright to Wes Peters, March 23, 1934; Edgar Tafel to Svetlana Wright, March 15, 1934; Wes Peters and Svetlana Wright: March 20 and March 23, 1934.

220 *"Mother just left . . ."* Svetlana Wright and Wes Peters: April 7, 9, and 14, 1934.

220 *Encouraged by the caviar . . .* Edgar Tafel to Svetlana Wright, April 11, 1934.

220 *"Oh Svet, Grrrrr . . ."* Wes Peters and Svetlana Wright: April 11 and 16, 1934.

221 *Wright took Abe . . .* Dombar, *Abrom Dombar*, 1995; Abe Dombar to the authors, e-mail, July 11, 2003.

222 *But Dombar had learned . . .* Authors' interview with ILW, August 16, 2000; authors' interview with Abrom Dombar, September 17, 2000.

222 *"She made us . . ."* Henning, ed., "At Taliesin," 1992, 46; Abrom Dombar to Becky Dombar, June 1934; Dombar, *Abrom Dombar*, 1995.

222 *Wright then offered . . .* Authors' interview with ILW, August 16, 2000.

223 *"I began to feel . . ."* Abe Dombar, unpublished notes, 1946, Dombar papers.

CHAPTER 9: COMINGS AND GOINGS

225 *"backstage gossip . . ."* Authors' interview with Enrique Vivoni, December 23, 2000.

225 *"I decided . . ."* http://www.universia.pr/klumb/i_crono.html.

225 *"I knew where . . ."* Meehan, ed., *Frank Lloyd Wright Remembered*, 1991, 127–29.

226 *" 'darky' stories . . ."* Interview with Jack Howe, March 25, 1991.

226 *Wright told . . .* FLW, *An Autobiography*, 1943, 422; David Hertz, whose work we discovered later, also points to a parallel with Beethoven, in *Angels of Reality*, 1993, 243–56.

226 *"When you listen . . ."* Bruce Brooks Pfeiffer, *Frank Lloyd Wright: His Living Voice* (Fresno: California State Univesity Press, 1987), 70.

226 *"integral ornament . . ."* The previous symphonic form, as in Mozart, had followed a certain structure: exposition, second exposition, development, recapitulation. Beethoven, in contrast, developed a new form: exposition, exposition, development, recapitulation, coda. The coda was exactly the same length as the first exposition, which it recapitulated. This eliminated the line of symmetry between the two exposi-

tions and the development and recapitulation in the previous symphonic form. Authors' interview with Amy Wlodarski, Eastman School of Music, July 14, 2002. See also *New Grove Dictionary of Music* (New York: Macmillan, 2000), and letter to authors from Lisa McCormick, Department of Sociology, Yale University, November 17, 2003.

226 *"little dissensions..."* Karl Jensen to FLW, September 14, 1933; Tafel, *About Wright*, 1993, 156–157. Lloyd Wright wrote to his father disapproving of Jensen's having "dropped a few sorry words about the Jewish contingent just before I left. That is, if nothing worse, an exceedingly stupid attitude to hold. As a matter of fact . . . the best of them will be your best aides and most promising material. Let's hope the general sweep and progress of the work will wipe out that mean attitude at Taliesin." Hines, "The Blessing and the Curse," 1998.

227 *"dutiful buffoon . . ."* Wes Peters to Svetlana Wright, March 15, 1934, Marlin papers, Scott Elliott collection.

227 *"From an authentic..."* "At Taliesin," August 2, 1934, Henning, ed. *"At Taliesin,"* 1992, 67. Wright usually reviewed and often edited these columns.

227 *"The woman..."* FLW to Karl Jensen, November 26, 1934.

229 *"quiet, silky, silky way"* Indira Berndtson, interview with Nancy Willey, February 15, 1995.

229 *"dragg[ing] his voice..."* Masselink, *Gene*, 1996, 71.

229 *"a radiance..."* FLW to Svetlana Peters, 1941, William Marlin papers

229 *"Gene was the..."* authors' interview with ILW, January 14, 2000; authors' interview with O. P. Reed, July 15, 1999.

229 *Forbidden by his father...* Masselink, *Gene*, 1996; Reed, *Eugene Masselink*, 1999, 37, 112; Secrest, *Frank Lloyd Wright*, 1993, 507.

230 *"Lists..."* Eugene Masselink, *"I Have a Little List,"* August 4, 1935, in Henning, ed., *"At Taliesin,"* 1992, 147–148.

230 *"We don't need..."* authors' interview with O. P. Reed, July 15, 1999.

231 *"I saw clearer..."* Eugene Masselink, "At Taliesin," September 26, 1935, Henning, ed., 1992, *"At Taliesin,"* 160–162; Dombar, "1933–34 'Crises!' at Taliesin," Dombar personal notes, 1995.

232 *"The common man..."* "FLLW Sunday Morning Chats," FLW Archives. The informal talks began in 1934. Henning, ed., *"At Taliesin,"* 1992, 18.

232 *Before the feature...* Eugene Masselink, "At Taliesin," February 2, 1934, Henning, ed., *"At Taliesin,"* 1992, 18–20; Dombar, *Abrom Dombar*, 1995; Cornelia Brierly, "The Early Years," *Journal of the Taliesin Fellows*, Vol. 3, No. 4, Fall, 1992.

232 *"The Theater..."* Yen Liang to Wes Peters, transcription, 1933, Marlin papers, Scott Elliott collection.

232 *In November 1935...* Authors' phone interview with Edgar Tafel, July 18, 2003; Taylor, *Shadows of Heaven*, 1998, 119; *Gurdjieff and Orage*, 2001, 100, 106, 139.

232 *"You cannot imagine..."* Ron Ramdin, *Paul Robeson: The Man and His Mission* (London: Peter Owen, 1987), 85.

232 *On Wright's return...* James Auer and Claudia Looze, interview with Cornelia Brierly, 1992; Brierly, *Tales of Taliesin*, 1999, 71–72.

233 *The apprentices also organized...* Authors' interview with O. P. Reed, July 15, 1999.

233 *"establish drama as architecture..."* Nicholas Ray, "At Taliesin," Henning, ed., *"At Taliesin,"* 1992, 25–28, 32–34.

234 *But Rogue...* Abrom Dombar, "1933–34 'Crises!' at Taliesin," undated notes. Wright's two wolfhounds would later kill a dozen sheep and be "gotten rid of." Tafel, *About Wright*, 1993, 164–65. In a July 5, 2003 e-mail to the authors, Dombar recalls that it was Mrs. Wright who issued the order.

234 *"I went to look..."* Bruce Pfeiffer, *Frank Lloyd Wright: Letters to Apprentices* (Fresno: Press at California State University, 1982), 85.

234 *"Why do you..."* Anthony Quinn with Daniel Paisner, *One Man Tango* (New York: HarperCollins, 1995), 82–86.

236 *"Let your hair..."* "FLLW Sunday Morning Chats," FLW Archives.

236 *"You know very well..."* Yen Liang to Wes Peters, May 22, 1934, Marlin papers, Scott Elliott collection.

236 *He was enthralled...* Sullivan, *A System of Architectural Ornament*, 1924; interview with Cornelia Brierly, May 9, 1989; Dombar, *Abrom Dombar*, 1995.

237 *"You have ruined..."* Authors' interview with James de Long, October 20, 2000.

237 *"The Guernsey . . ."* Authors' conversation with Bruce Pfeiffer, May 27, 2004. Olgivanna's desire to replace the Holstein may have had other motivations: Wright had written of seeing Mamah Cheney's death and the burning of Taliesin foreshadowed a few months before—in a storm in which a valuable Holstein, a Maplecroft, was also struck down by lightning. FLW, *An Autobiography*, 1932, 192.

238 *"to save alcohol"* Tafel, *About Wright*, 1993, 250.

CHAPTER 10: SORCERERS' APPRENTICES

239 *"Taliesin was much honored . . ."* Henning, ed., *"At Taliesin,"* 1992, 65.

239 *Having lost . . .* Taylor, *Gurdjieff's America*, 2004, pp.152–54

239 *Olgivanna used . . .* Robert C. Twombly is the only architectural historian to give the relation between Gurdjieff and the the Fellowship serious consideration. "Organic Living: Frank Lloyd Wright's Taliesin Fellowship and Georgi Gurdjieff's Institute for the Harmonious Development of Man," *Wisconsin Magazine of History*, Vol. 58, No. 2, Winter, 1974–1975, 126–39.

239 *Even though some, . . .* Jack Howe describes dropping a Jell-O dessert mold at Sunday night dinner: "Now—all this efficiency and correlation of faculties at the mercy of a stubbed toe was replaced by the feeling one has when his heart sinks to all his toes and they all feel like two big ones." Henning, ed., *"At Taliesin,"* 1992, 146.

240 *"He had grown fat . . ."* Webb, *The Harmonious Circle*, 1980, 421.

240 *Toomer, now living . . .* Taylor, *Gurdjieff's America*, 2004, 154–55; Taylor, *Shadows of Heaven*, 1998, 157; Moore, *Gurdjieff*, 1999, 252.

240 *"would knock the roof off . . ."* Tafel, *Years with Frank Lloyd. Wright*, 1979, 139; Henning, ed., *"At Taliesin,"*1992, 64.

240 *"The last two days . . ."* Svetlana Wright to Wes Peters, undated, 1934, Marlin papers, Scott Elliott collection and FLW Archives.

241 *"Well, Mr. Gurdjieff . . ."* C. S. Nott, *Further Teachings of Gurdjieff: Journey Through this World* (London: Routledge and Kegan Paul, 1978), 151–52.

241 *"The conversation turned . . ."* Henning, *"At Taliesin,"* 1992, 68.

241 *Back in their private quarters . . .* Secrest, *Frank Lloyd Wright*, 1992, 430.

242 *Through Jean Toomer . . .* Moore, *Gurdjieff*, 1999, 253; Taylor, *Shadows of Heaven*, 1998, 157; Taylor, *Gurdjieff's America*, 2004, 154.

242 *"apples and bananas . . ."* Notes from a letter from Svetlana Wright to Wes Peters, September 28, 1934, Marlin papers, Scott Elliott collection.

242 *"massive sense of . . ."* FLW, "At Taliesin," *The Capital Times*, August 26, 1934, cited in Twombly, 1974–1975, 137, and in Moore, *Gurdjieff*, 1999, 253.

242 *"Olgivanna and I . . ."* FLW to Georgi Gurdjieff, September 10, 1932; Taylor, *Shadows of Heaven*,1998, 57.

242 *"had my thoughts . . ."* Transcripts and letters between Wes Peters and Svetlana Wright, July 29; August 16, 21, 29, 30, and 31; September 1, 1934: Marlin papers, Scott Elliott collection and FLW Archives.

243 *Alternatively, Gurdjieff suggested . . .* Transcript of letter from Elizabeth Weber to Wes Peters, January 1934, from Svetlana Wright to Wes Peters, 1934, Marlin papers, Scott Elliott collection.

243 *"The inflated pig!"* Wes Peters to Svetlana Wright, September 1, 1934, Marlin papers, Scott Elliott collection. *"How I wish . . ."* Transcript of letter from OLW to Svetlana Wright, September 3, 1934, Marlin papers, Scott Elliott collection.

244 *"We are rather tired . . ."* FLW to "My dear Georgivnitch," November 14, 1934.

244 *Olgivanna and Frank were aghast . . .* Sue Scheutz to the authors, e-mail, May 11, 2005, based on Scheutz's notes from interview with ILW.

245 *"anybody appears light . . ."* OLW to Svetlana Wright, September 3, 1934, Marlin papers, Scott Elliott collection.

245 *"I feel entirely cured . . ."* Notes from a letter from Svetlana Wright to Wes Peters, undated, Marlin papers.

245 *"girlish whim . . ."* Notes from letter from Svetlana Wright to Wes Peters, September 7, 1934.

245 *"I know the powerful . . ."* Wes Peters to Svetlana Wright, September 5, 1934, Marlin papers, Scott Elliott collection.

245 *"It is strange . . ."* Gurdjieff to OLW, undated, translated from the Russian. Date is in-

ferred from the fact that it is written from the Leighton home in New York and that Gurdjieff makes it clear that he has just seen Olgivanna, who has written to him in the city.

246 *"I am so weak..."* Svetlana Wright to Wes Peters, October 5, 1934, Marlin Papers, Scott Elliott collection.

246 *"Brace up..."* Transcript of telegram from Wes Peters to Svetlana Wright, October 6, 1934, Marlin papers, Scott Elliott collection.

246 *Gurdjieff came to Chicago...* Svetlana Wright to Wes Peters, October 16, 1934, and notes concerning letter, Marlin papers, Scott Elliott collection and FLW Archives.

246 *"I am not going..."* OLW to Svetlana Wright, October 25, 1934, Marlin papers, Scott Elliott collection.

246 *"I could go back..."* Svetlana Wright to Wes Peters, November 20, 1934, Marlin Papers, Scott Elliott collection.

246 *"I think you..."* Wes Peters to Svetlana Wright, November 21 and 22, 1934, and January 1935, Marlin papers, Scott Elliott collection.

247 *"I couldn't read..."* ILW, *My Life*, unpublished, 135.

247 *"She really liked..."* Authors' interview with Barbara Dresser, June 4, 2000.

248 *"My boys'll..."* Authors' interview with Eloise Fritz, December 15, 1999.

248 *"Ah, now I understand"* Authors' interview with Adrienne Carney Schiffner, December 12, 2000; Secrest, *Frank Lloyd Wright*, 1993, 430; authors' interview with Charles Schiffner, January 30, 2002.

CHAPTER 11: SOMETHING TO DO

253 *"Cornelia Brierly arrived..."* Henning, ed., *At Taliesin*, 1992, 82.

253 *The twenty-two-year-old...* Interview with Cornelia Brierly, May 12, 1989.

253 *The boy...* Jimmy Drought to Svetlana Wright, September 26, 1934, Marlin papers, Scott Elliott collection; Henning, *"At Taliesin,"* 1992, 82; Toker, *Fallingwater Rising*, 2003, 360; Svetlana Wright to Wes Peters, November 20, 1934, Marlin papers, Scott Elliott collection.

254 *"disconnected from the thoughts..."* Edgar Kaufmann Jr., *Fallingwater: A Frank Lloyd Wright Country House* (New York: Abbeville Press, 1986), 36.

254 *"like the first trickle"* Donald Hoffman, *Frank Lloyd Wright's Fallingwater: The House and Its History* (New York: Dover, 1978), 11.

254 *It had managed...* Toker, *Fallingwater Rising*, 2003, 50.

254 *The Pittsburgh socialite...* Indira Berndtson and Greg Williams, interview with Robert Mosher, April 7, 1991.

254 *But Kaufmann...* Roger Friedland and Donald Palmer, "Park Place and Main Street: Business and the Urban Power Structure," *Annual Review of Sociology*, Vol. 10, (Palo Alto, California: Annual Reviews, Inc., 1984), 393–416.

254 *"Could I do anything..."* Hoffman, *Frank Lloyd Wright's Fallingwater*, 1978, 12.

254 *"is jewish..."* Toker, *Fallingwater Rising*, 2003, 118–23, 367–68.

255 *"I was interested..."* Hoffman, *Frank Lloyd Wright's Fallingwater*, 1978, 12.

255 *"They are very very..."* Svetlana Wright to Wes Peters, November 20, 1934, Marlin papers, Scott Elliott collection.

255 *Wright was attracted...* Toker, *Fallingwater Rising*, 2003, 129.

255 *"Something interesting..."* Authors' phone interview with Edgar Tafel, July 18, 2003.

255 *"Well," Kaufmann interjected...* Indira Berndtson and Greg Williams, interview with Robert Mosher, April 7, 1991; Edgar Tafel, *Years with Frank Lloyd Wright*, 1979, 2–3; Hoffmann, *Frank Lloyd Wright's Fallingwater*, 1978, 12.

257 *Like Junior's joining...* Toker, *Fallingwater Rising*, 2003, 124.

257 *"Let me know..."* authors' phone interview with Edgar Tafel, July 18, 2003.

257 *"showed that romance..."* FLW, "At Taliesin," in Henning, ed., *"At Taliesin,"* 1992, 87–88.

258 *"Talestine"* Abrom Dombar, unpublished autobiography.

258 *Before, only two...* Tafel, *About Wright*, 1993, 105–106. *"has a son here..."* Tafel, *About Wright*, 1993, 106.

258 *Junior suggested...* Hoffmann, *Frank Lloyd Wright's Fallingwater*, 1978, 12–13; Levine, *The Architecture of Frank Lloyd Wright*, 1996, 226–27; Kevin Gray, "Modern Gothic," *Men's Fashions of the Times*, September 23, 2001.

258 *"You love this waterfall..."* Levine, *Frank Lloyd Wright*, 1996, 227.

259 *But Klumb and another...* Authors' interview with Enrique Vivoni, December 23, 2000.

259 *"It would be difficult..."* Henry Klumb and FLW: November 25 and December 2, 1934.

259 *Klumb would...* Enrique Vivoni Farage, *Hacia una modernidad tropical: la obra de Henry Klumb, 1928–1984,* http://www.periferia.org/publications/obraklumb.

260 *Back at Taliesin...* Tafel, *About Wright,* 1993, 107.

260 *"So many irresponsibles..."* Tafel, *About Wright,* 1993, 106–10.

260 *Socializing credit...* Taylor, *Gurdjieff and Orage,* 2001, 187, 195. Orage had coined the term "social credit" for C. H. Douglas's ideas. See http://www.douglassocialcredit.com/social-credit/background.html. Brian Burkiss and Frances Hutchinson, "Major Douglas' Proposals for a National Dividend: A Logical Successor to the Wage," Department of Social and Economic Studies, University of Bradford, United Kingdom. http://www.thirdway.org/files/articles/natdiv1.html.

260 *"transfer work..."* Taylor, *Gurdjieff and Orage,* 2001, 195.

260 *"Poor Orage..."* C. S. Nott, *Further Teachings of Gurdjieff: Journey Through This World* (London: Routledge and Kegan Paul, 1978), 53–54.

261 *"I have been writing..."* Tafel, *About Wright,* 1993, 106, 110.

261 *"To overidealize..."* Dombar, *Abrom Dombar,* 1995.

261 *"In spite of his..."* Tafel, *About Wright,* 1993, 106–7.

262 *"To hell with Christmas..."* FLW to Henry Klumb, December 2, c. 1932 or 1933.

262 *"Gad but Mr. Wright..."* Tafel, *About Wright,* 1993, 109.

262 *When word of the Taliesin...* Henning, ed., *"At Taliesin,"* 1992, 136; Brierly, *Tales of Taliesin,* 1989, 26.

263 *He also later...* Wright, *An Autobiography,* 1943, 406.

263 *"Hebrew boy..."* Dombar, *Abrom Dombar,* 1995.

263 *"To start 30 people..."* Dombar, *Abrom Dombar,* 1995.

263 *"Mrs. Wright,"* Gene wrote... Henning, ed., *At Taliesin,* 1992, 107.

264 *Wright blushed...* Authors' interview with Abrom Dombar, September 17, 2000. *"Pic-tures of the house..."* Henning, ed., *"At Taliesin,"* 1992, 108.

266 *"It's an exciting..."* Interview with Cornelia Brierly, May 9, 1989; Brierly, *Taliesin Tales,* 1999, 26; Cornelia Brierly, Henning, ed., *"At Taliesin,"* 1992, 110–12.

267 *"extremely jealous"* Tim Wright, interview with Cornelia Brierly, November 12, 1993.

267 *At Oak Park...* David Van Zanten, "Schooling the Prairie School: Wright's Early Style as a Communicable System," in Carol R. Bolon, Robert S. Nelson and Linda Seidel, eds., *The Nature of Frank Lloyd Wright* (Chicago: University of Chicago Press, 1988), 78–79; FLW, "Women in the Arts," Pfeiffer, ed., *Frank Lloyd Wright,* 1987, 69.

267 *Olgivanna actively worked...* Abrom Dombar to authors, e-mail, July 9, 2003. Dombar, one of the first apprentices to be called into the drafting room to work on a project, recalled that Mrs. Wright "kept the women separately." He recalls that there were no women in the drafting room during his time there, between September 1932 and September 1935.

267 *Indeed, she suspected...* Tim Wright, interview with Cornelia Brierly, November 12, 1993.

267 *As a result, women...* According to former apprentice John Geiger, Diane Pierson left by October 1932; Elizabeth Bauer by April 1933; Alma Olson by June 1933; Elizabeth Weber, Louise Dees-Porch, and Yvonne Lagier by December 1933.

268 *"family and friends..."* Dombar, *Abrom Dombar,* 1995.

268 *"Ocatillo"—the camp...* FLW, *An Autobiography,* 1943, 311.

268 *Everything worth stealing...* Brierly, *Taliesin Tales,* 1999, 29.

269 *"We pile ourselves..."* Interview with Cornelia Brierly, May 9, 1989. *"Last night..."* Tafel, *About Wright,* 1993, 114. *If that didn't work...* Interview with Kay Rattenbury, no date.

269 *"Fred, you're wasting..."* Brierly, *Tales of Taliesin,* 1999, 28–29.

270 *"At exactly midnight..."* Reed, *Gene Masselink,* 1999, 73–76.

270 *"The picture-artist...* anonymous author, in Henning, ed., *"At Taliesin,"* 1992, 120.

271 *"It is the swellest..."* Reed, *Gene Masselink,* 1999, 70.

271 *"The magnum opus..."* Henning, ed., *"At Taliesin,"* 1992, 104.

271 *"model is now..."* Hoffman, *Frank Lloyd Wright's Fallingwater*, 1993, 14.

271 *"Junior is sagging..."* Tafel, *About Wright*, 1993, 114; Kaufmann, *Fallingwater*, 1986, 38–39.

271 *"whippoorwill..."* Toker, *Fallingwater Rising*, 2003, 370, 459.

271 *And Junior's homosexuality...* Authors' interview with Eric Lloyd Wright, July 16, 1999; Dombar, *Abrom Dombar*, 1995. Dombar does not mention that homosexuality was at issue, but does note that Wright was angry at his friend and that Kaufmann had to leave the Fellowship. Although Dombar was close friends with Kaufmann, he did not remember what Kaufmann and Wright fought about. Dombar to the authors, e-mail, July 10, 2003.

271 *"all our eggs..."* Henning, ed., *"At Taliesin,"* 1992, 122; Tafel, *About Wright*, 1993, 148; Dombar, *Abrom Dombar*, 1995.

272 *"I have not forgotten..."* Edgar Kaufmann Jr. to FLW, 1935.

272 *To his gay colleagues,...* Authors' interview with Philip Johnson, May 3, 2000.

272 *"I cannot help..."* Edgar Kaufmann Jr. to FLW, 1935.

272 *"Mr. Wright,"* Mosher replied... Tafel, *About Wright*, 1993, 148–150.

273 *"News of Broadacre City's..."* Henning, ed., *"At Taliesin,"* 1992, 123, 127–28.

273 *Svetlana had written...* Margaret Jean Evans, memories of Svetlana Peters, January 16, 1999, Sue Schuetz papers, FLW Archives.

273 *"I feel so sorry..."* Julia Siberiakova to OLW, undated, translated from the Russian.

273 *"Mark Twain!"* Interview with Wes Peters, June 16, 1988.

273 *"to make our life..."* Wes Peters to Svetlana Wright, March 10, 1935, transcript in Marlin papers, Scott Elliott collection.

274 *Now in 1935...* Viva German Young Schneider (b. 1901) was the daughter of Albert German of the A. D. German Warehouse, Richland Center, Wisconsin (1915). Celeste Davison to the authors, e-mail, March 7, 2005.

274 *During her childhood...* Authors' interviews with Celeste Davison: May 7, 2000; March 3, 2005, by phone.

274 *"The minute I saw it..."* Indira Berndtson, interview with Kay Rattenbury, July 15, 1987.

275 *It had been nine months...* Neil Levine, "The Temporal Dimension of Fallingwater," in Narciso G. Menocal, ed., *Fallingwater and Pittsburgh, Wright Studies, Volume 2* (Carbondale and Edwardsville: Southern Illinois University Press, 2000), 32.

275 *"Come along E. J...."* Tafel, *Years with Frank Lloyd Wright*, 1979, 1–3.

276 *"Every line he drew..."* Hoffmann, *Frank Lloyd Wright's Fallingwater*, 1993, 17.

276 *"thought-built"* Maggie Valentine, interview with Alvin Louis Wiehle, UCLA Oral History Collection, 1996, 109.

276 *In early accounts...* Hoffmann, *Frank Lloyd Wright's Fallingwater*, 1993, 17, 26.

277 *"Come over here...* Indira Berndtson and Greg William interview with Robert Mosher, April 7, 1991. Tokker maintains that the house was not known as Fallingwater until much later.

277 *"You don't mean..."* Toker claims that Wright already had a clear concept in his head in July 1935, long before drawing it and before Kaufmann arrived at Taliesin. *Fallingwater Rising*, 2003, 141.

CHAPTER 12: THE TEST

279 *"[C]losets are rotten..."* Gill, *Many Masks*, 1987, 340–43.

279 *"He is, but..."* Tafel, *About Wright*, 1993, 257.

279 *They had finished...* Authors' phone interview with Edgar Tafel, July 18, 2003.

279 *For a time...* Gene Masselink, April 22, 1936, Henning, ed., *"At Taliesin,"* 1992, 190; interview with Cornelia Brierly, May 9, 1989; OLW, *Frank Lloyd Wright*, 1966, 108; Indira Berndtson and Greg Williams, interview with Kay Rattenbury, July 13, 1989; OLW, *The Shining Brow* (New York: Horizon, 1960), 95–96.

280 *"Goddamn you..."* Interview with Cornelia Brierly, May 9, 1989.

280 *"Let someone else..."* OLW, *Frank Lloyd Wright*, 1966, 108.

280 *"I am the Postmistress..."* Gene Masselink, April 22, 1936, Henning, ed., *"At Taliesin,"* 1992, 190.

280 *"There we were..."* Indira Berndtson and Greg Williams, interview with Kay Rattenbury, July 13, 1989.

281 *"Providence,"* Olgivanna *remarked...* OLW, *Frank Lloyd Wright,* 1966, 96.

281 *Wright's jutting decks...* Toker, *Fallingwater Rising,* 2003, 176–78.

282 *"the Internationalists..."* Interview with Cornelia Brierly, July 30, 1992.

282 *"You people are crazy"* Authors' phone interview with Scott Elliott, May 17, 2004. Elliott was told this by Mosher, who was present when it was proposed to Kaufmann. Toker maintains that Kaufmann rejected the idea. *Fallingwater Rising,* 2003, 224. Edgar Kaufmann Jr. denied Mosher's account.

282 *"The youth..."* FLW, *An Autobiography,* 1943, 56; "The Passing of the Cornice" (1931), in Pfeiffer, ed., *Collected Writings, Volume 2,* 1992, 42.

283 *"Nature,"* he told... Neil Levine, "The Temporal Dimension of Fallingwater," Narciso G. Menocal, ed., *Fallingwater and Pittsburgh* (Wright studies, vol. 2), 2000, 37.

283 *Wright knew this...* Andrew Saint to the authors, e-mail, March 1, 2005.

284 *And it was a good thing...* Wright publicly pinned his claim to engineering genius on the notion that his foundation concept for the Imperial Hotel had spared it from destruction when almost everything else seemed to be leveled by the Tokyo earthquake of 1923. However, a recent study has shown that the hotel fared about the same as reinforced concrete structures with conventional pile foundations. Wright's floating foundation was one of the reasons it was eventually demolished in the 1960s. Andrew Saint, "Frank Lloyd Wright and Paul Mueller: the architect and his builder of choice," *Architecture Research Quarterly,* v. 7, No. 2, 2003, 157–67.

284 *Just before the Fellowship...* Interview with Jack Howe, February 19, 1991; interview with Wes Peters, June 15, 1988.

284 *"Mrs. Wright's queenly behavior..."* Iris Herzfeld, interview with Herzfeld Glickman's daughter. Mendel Glickman, August 15, 1997.

284 *"Wright did not show anti-Semitism..."* Iris Herzfeld, interview with Mendel Glickman, August 15, 1997.

285 *"I've bought the nails..."* FLW to Svetlana and Wes Peters, July 7, 1936, Marlin papers. This letter suggests that despite earlier visits, which other authors took to be their homecoming, Wright considered this their real return. See, for instance, Secrest, *Frank Lloyd Wright,* 1993, 436.

285 *"I frankly didn't..."* Indira Berndtson and Greg Williams, interview with Wes Peters, June 15 and 16, 1988.

285 *"struggling, fighting,..."* Svetlana Wright to Wes Peters, 1937, Marlin papers, Scott Elliott collection.

285 *It was then...* Indira Berndtson and Greg Williams, interview with Wes Peters, Bob Mosher, and Victor Cusack, April 7, 1991.

285 *By now, Svetlana...* Indira Berndtson and Greg Williams, interview with Kay Rattenbury, January 16, 1990.

286 *When Wes finally...* Noverre Musson, "Svetlana and Wes," unpublished manuscript, FLW Archives; Herb Fritz, "At Taliesin," in Henning, ed., *"At Taliesin,"* 1992, 135; Margaret Jean Evans, memories of Svetlana Peters, January 16, 1999.

286 *"was such despair..."* OLW to Svetlana Peters, June 9, 1937, Marlin papers, Scott Elliott collection.

286 *For the apprentices,...* Noverre Musson, "Svetlana and Wes," unpublished manuscript; Indira Berndtson and Greg Williams, interview with Kay Rattenbury, January 16, 1990.

286 *"exercised more Christian..."* Interview with Iris Herzfeld, August 15, 1997; interview with Cornelia Brierly, May 12, 1989.

287 *Wright summarily changed...* Authors' phone interview with Edgar Tafel, July 18, 2003; Abrom Dombar to the authors, e-mail, July 17, 2003.

287 *Kaufmann apologized...* Hoffmann, *Frank Lloyd Wright's Fallingwater,* 1978, 24.

288 *Not a few builders,...* Besinger, *Working with Mr. Wright,* 1997, 31.

288 *Over the years,...* Authors' interview with Shawn Davis, October 28, 2000.

289 *"Go home and bury..."* Authors' interview with Abram Dombar, September 17, 2000.

289 *"neck into the money-yoke..."* FLW to Abe Dombar, 1935, undated, Pfeiffer, ed., *Letters to Apprentices,* 1982, 69.

289 *"Abe,"* Wright *warned...* Dombar, *Abrom Dombar,* 1995.

290 *When Dombar phoned* . . . Abrom Dombar to Donald Hoffmann, April 4, 1975, Dombar personal correspondence; Dombar, *Abrom Dombar*, 1995.

290 *The discontent* . . . Toker, *Fallingwater Rising*, 2003, 205.

290 *"Mr. Wright says . . ."* Tafel, *Years with Frank Lloyd Wright*, 1979, 85.

290 *"We hiked," Mosher recalled* . . . Tafel, *About Wright*.

291 *"Wright had warned them* . . . Dombar, *Abrom Dombar*, 1995.

292 *Mosher took it on* . . . Hoffmann, *Frank Lloyd Wright's Fallingwater*, 1978, 33–34; Kaufmann, *Fallingwater*, 1986, 46–51.

292 *"If you've not noticed it . . ."* Kaufmann, *Fallingwater*, 1986, 48–49.

292 *"If you are paying . . ."* FLW to Edgar Kaufmann Sr., August 26, 1936; Kaufmann, *Fallingwater*, 1985, 46; Kaufmann to FLW, August 28, 1936.

293 *"I was in disgrace . . ."* Hoffmann, *Frank Lloyd Wright's Fallingwater*, 1978, 39; FLW to Kaufmann, August 31, 1936, Bruce Pfeiffer, ed., *Frank Lloyd Wright: Letters to Clients* (Fresno: The Press at California State University, 1986), 99.

293 *"Take him away . . ."* Wright, *An Autobiography*, 1943, 448.

293 *Any experienced builder* . . . Hoffmann, *Frank Lloyd Wright's Fallingwater*, 1978, 33–34.

293 *"Oh my God . . ."* Authors' phone interview with Edgar Tafel, July 18, 2003. See also Hoffmann, *Frank Lloyd Wright's Fallingwater*, 1978, 42; Toker 215–16.

295 *Completely ignoring* . . . Lembly, "Saving Fallingwater," 2003, Kaufmann, *Fallingwater*, 1978, 51; Hoffmann, *Frank Lloyd Wright's Fallingwater*, 1978, 33–34.

295 *Steel does weigh* . . . Authors' interview with Steven Mezey, structural engineer, July 17, 2003.

295 *But the stronger replacements* . . . Western Pennsylvania Conservancy, Fallingwater web site: "The Building." http://www.wpconline .org/fallingwater/building.

295 *"This may be an obsession . . ."* Robert Lusk to FLW, January 13, 1936.

296 *"They may shock you . . ."* FLW to Robert Lusk, March 10, 1936.

296 *Wright filled them* . . . Interviews with Wes Peters, 1967–1968.

296 *Years later he would recall* . . . The Usonian house was an integral part of Wright's vision of Broadacre City. Most scholars assume that Broadacre never went anywhere. In fact, a piece of it was attempted in the scrub hills of Los Angeles. See Harold Zellman and Roger Friedland, "Broadacre in Brentwood: The Politics of Architectural Aesthetics," Michael Roth and Charles Salas, ed., *Looking for LA*, Los Angeles: Getty Research Institute, 2001, 167–210. See also Harold Zellman and Roger Friedland, *The Bride Stripped Bare: Frank Lloyd Wright, Crestwood Hills and the Politics of modernism*, forthcoming.

297 *The Lusks were denied* . . . Robert Lusk to FLW, July 8, 1936.

297 *"We have had an estimate . . ."* Mrs. C. H. Hoult to FLW, April 8, 1936.

297 *"But if you are . . ."* FLW to Mrs. C. H. Hoult, May 8, 1936.

297 *"It's all right boys . . ."* Jonathan Lipman, *Frank Lloyd Wright and the Johnson Wax Buildings* (New York, Rizzoli, 1986), 14.

297 *Matson's plans* . . . Mark Hertzberg, *Wright in Racine* (Petaluma, Pomegranate, 2004), 53–54; Lipman, *Frank Lloyd Wright and the Johnson Wax Buildings*, 1986, 7.

298 *"He wore a tweed . . ."* Authors' interview with Ben Masselink, April 5, 1999; interviews with Wes Peters, 1967–1968.

299 *"Something always happens . . ."* Tafel, *About Wright*, 1993, 245.

299 *"The architect," he told* . . . Tafel, *Years With Frank Lloyd Wright*, 1979, 176; Barney, *The Valley of the God-Almighty Joneses*, 1965.

300 *"Would you really . . ."* Herbert Jacobs with Katherine Jacobs, *Building with Frank Lloyd Wright* (San Francisco: Chronicle Books, 1978).

300 *"The average builder . . ."* Bennie Dombar, "At Taliesin," in Henning, ed., *"At Taliesin,"* 1992, 258.

300 *"You were the King . . ."* Nancy Snyder, interview with Ben Masselink, April 5, 1992.

301 *He would put a stack* . . . Indira Berndtson, interview with Yen Liang, October 4, 1999.

301 *A few minutes later* . . . Authors' interview with Ben Masselink, January 24, 1997, Los Angeles, California; letter from Ben Masselink

to Bruce Pfeiffer, June 17, 1988; Herb Fritz, Henning, ed., "At Taliesin," 1992, 138.

301 *Wright, of course* . . . Tafel, *Years with Frank Lloyd Wright*, 1979, 176.

302 *"While overcoming . . ."* FLW to Wes Peters, November 11, 1949, Marlin papers; Secrest, *Frank Lloyd Wright*, 1993, 438. Iowa county records show only that a portion of the SW quarter under the Hillside School buildings was transferred to Olgivanna.

302 *In so doing* . . . Author's interview with ILW, July 24, 2000.

302 *Though he was running* . . . Indira Berndtson and Greg Williams, interview with Kay Rattenbury, January 16, 1990.

302 *"Not enough steel . . ."* Indira Berndtson and Greg Williams interview with Wes Peters, Bob Mosher, Victor Cusack, April 7, 1991; Brierly, *Taliesin Tales*, 1999, 42.

303 *"How is father . . ."* Lloyd Wright to FLW, telegram, January 1, 1937.

303 *Finally, after days* . . . Secrest, *Frank Lloyd Wright*, 1993, 450.

303 *To signal his gratitude* . . . OLW to Robert Mosher, August 6, 1967.

CHAPTER 13: PARADISE VALLEY

304 *"Mr. Wright," read* . . . Tafel, *Years with Frank Lloyd Wright*, 1979, 178.

305 *"[W]e can all blame . . ."* J. R. Ramsey to FLW, February 25, 1937.

305 *"We are on the spot . . ."* Toker, *Fallingwater Rising*, 2003, 221–22; FLW to Glickman, January 2, 1937.

305 *Tafel, Peters, and* . . . unnamed contractor to J. R. Ramsey, February 25, 1937.

306 *"Have Edgar and Wes . . ."* FLW to Gene Masselink, March 18, 1937.

306 *"[T]here could be . . ."* FLW, *An Autobiography*, 1943, 306.

306 *On that trip* . . . Levine, *The Architecture of Frank Lloyd Wright*, 1996, 258.

306 *Olgivanna, too* . . . Milena Slonovich to OLW, March 19, 1937.

306 *"I love every stone . . ."* OLW to Svetlana Peters, March 25, 1937.

307 *And he had promised* . . . OLW, *The Shining Brow*, 1960, 93; Brierly, *Tales of Taliesin*, 2000, 43.

307 *Wright was taken* . . . OLW to Svetlana Peters, March 25, 1937.

307 *"Get land, . . ."* OLW to Svetlana Peters, March 25, 1937; Indira Berndtson and Greg Williams, interview with Kay Rattenbury, July 13, 1989.

307 *"With Christianity* . . . Baker Brownell and FLW, *Architecture and Modern Life*, 1937, 61–62.

307 *"that he would not . . ."* Wright, "What the Cause of Architecture Needs Most," *Collected Writings*, 1993, 265–266.

308 *At noon on Saturday* . . . Eugene Masselink to William T. Evjue, March 17, 1937; Henning, ed., "At Taliesin," 1992, 230; District Attorney George Larkin to Hill, Miller, and Hill, March 11, 1937.

308 *The day before* . . . Eugene Masselink to James H. Hill, March 16, 1937.

308 *"There isn't much . . ."* J. H. Hill to Eugene Masselink, March 19 and 31, 1937.

309 *Running from Taliesin* . . . Authors' interview with Ben Masselink, April 5, 1999.

309 *As a get-well present* . . . John Geiger to Curtis Besinger, March 18, 1988, John Geiger personal correspondence..

309 *"It was a fairly . . ."* Masselink, Henning, ed., "At Taliesin," 1992, 267.

309 *For years after* . . . Reed, *Eugene Masselink*, 1999, 87.

309 *"I feel as though . . ."* Richard Armor to FLW, June 20, 1937.

310 *"Somber, forest-abstract . . ."* FLW and Baker Brownell, *Architecture and Modern Life*, 1937, New York and London: Harper and Brothers, 40–41.

311 *The authorities finally* . . . Lipman, *Frank Lloyd Wright and the Johnson Wax Buildings*, 1986, 46.

311 *"We will construct . . ."* Tafel, *Years with Frank Lloyd Wright*, 1979, 176.

311 *His bravado unchecked* . . . Toker, *Fallingwater Rising*, 2003, 220; Carter Manny to Edgar Tafel, August 10, 1987.

313 *"Well I guess that's enough . . ."* Lipman, *Frank Lloyd Wright and the Johnson Wax Buildings*, 1986, 62.

313 *The impact* . . . Lipman, *Frank Lloyd Wright and the Johnson Wax Buildings*, 1986, 62.

313 *Their additional height*... Interview with Wes Peters, 1967–1968; Johnson Wax construction drawings, Getty Research Institute.

313 *The Russians, he was sure*... Donald Leslie Johnson, *Frank Lloyd Wright Versus America: The 1930's* (Cambridge, Mass: MIT Press, 1990), 179–230.

314 *For Olgivanna, who*... OLW to Svetlana Peters, June 9, 1937, Marlin papers, Scott Elliott collection.

314 *"[I]magine what that meant..."* FLW to Svetlana Peters, June 14, 1937, Marlin papers.

314 *"Give my love..."* FLW to Svetlana Peters, June 14, 1937, Marlin papers.

314 *"We've got to work together..."* James Auer and Claudia Looz, interview with Kay Rattenbury, 1992.

314 *"You had better..."* OLW, *Our House* (New York: Horizon Press, 1959), 38.

315 *Instead they called*... Johnson, *Frank Lloyd Wright Versus America*, 1990, 190–92, 226–27.

315 *"The fact that..."* Johnson, *Frank Lloyd Wright Versus America*, 1990, 226.

316 *"If Comrade Stalin..."* Johnson, *Frank Lloyd Wright Versus America*, 1990, 317.

316 *"We wonder if..."* Henning, ed., *"At Taliesin,"* 1992, 271.

316 *"This 'red' menace..."* Henning, ed., *"At Taliesin,"* 1992, 271.

317 *"of any use..."* FLW to Virginia Burdick, December 7, 1937.

317 *"I think he would enjoy..."* FLW to Alexander Portnoff, October 25, 1937.

317 *"I have no curiosity..."* FLW to Franz Aust, November 5, 1937.

318 *"Mr. Wright, it's a pleasure..."* Tafel, *Years with Frank Lloyd Wright*, 1979, 66.

318 *"were left equally..."* Henning, ed., *"At Taliesin,"* 1992, 275.

318 *"shuts himself up..."* Pfeiffer, *Frank Lloyd Wright*, 1987, 70.

318 *It was one of the happiest*... Toker, *Fallingwater Rising*, 2003, 226.

318 *While Unity's plan*... Kevin Nute, *Frank Lloyd Wright in Japan* (London and New York: Routledge, 1993), 149–50.

319 *"Now," he told a friend*... Pfeiffer, *Letters to Apprentices*, 1982, 31.

319 *"I am banking..."* Dr. A. J. Chandler to FLW, September 2, 1937.

319 *"ever-moving in caravan..."* Levine, *The Architecture of Frank Lloyd Wright*, 1996, 258.

320 *"On a mesa..."* FLW, *An Autobiography*, 1943, 452.

320 *"I always liked Phoenix*... OLW, *The Shining Brow*, 1960, 99.

320 *"WEATHER WARM..."* Pfeiffer, *Letters to Apprentices*, 1982, 30.

320 *It wouldn't hurt Johnson Wax*... Lipman, *Frank Lloyd Wright and the Johnson Wax Buildings*, 1986, 75–6.

320 *"embarrassing for me, to say the least...."* Jonathan Lipman, *Frank Lloyd Wright and the Johnson Wax Buildings*, 1986, p. 76.

321 *There was "no water*... Indira Berndtson and Greg Williams interview with Kay Rattenbury, July 13, 1989.

321 *"a look over the rim..."* FLW, *An Autobiography*, 1943, 452–54.

321 *"We had to carry it..."* Indira Berndtson and Greg Williams, interview with Kay Rattenbury, July 13, 1989.

322 *Wright laid out*... Herb Fritz, Henning, ed., *"At Taliesin,"* 1992, 141; interview with Wes Peters, Bob Mosher, and Victor Cusack, April 7, 1991.

323 *He returned empty-handed*... Eugene Masselink to Universal Credit Co., March 12, 1936.

323 *"There must be some limit..."* FLW to R. E. Campion, June 27, 1938.

323 *"full settlement"* Eugene Masselink to V. Ennis, March 2, 1936.

323 *"to defeat us..."* FLW to V. Ennis, May 19, 1936.

323 *"A major rule..."* FLW, *An Autobiography*, 1943, 452.

323 *"Building progresses..."* Lipman, *Frank Lloyd Wright and the Johnson Wax Buildings*, 1986, 73.

324 *"Your 'crab' received..."* Lipman, *Frank Lloyd Wright and the Johnson Wax Buildings*, 1986, 73.

324 *"That was all right..."* Tafel, *Years with Frank Lloyd Wright*, 1979, 165.

325 *"The builders were ready..."* Interview with Wes Peters, 1967–1968. Lipman's account is slightly different: In his verison Peters worked "around the clock" for two days on the reinforcement calculations. *Frank*

Lloyd Wright and the Johnson Wax Buildings, 1986, 75.

325 *"Would it be too much . . ."* Samuel Tafel and FLW: August 24 and September 1, 1937, Tafel, *About Wright*, 1993, 10–11.

325 *"The greatest architect . . ." "*Usonian Architect," *Time*, January 17, 1938, 29–32.

326 *"fifth symphony . . ."* Herb Fritz, Henning, ed., *"At Taliesin,"* 1992, 137; Toker, *Fallingwater Rising*, 2003, 255.

326 *Between Edgar Tafel's competent work . . .* Lipman, *Frank Lloyd Wright and the Johnson Wax Buildings*, 1986, 77.

327 *"how nice the house was . . ."* Authors' interview with Edgar Tafel, June 27, 2003.

328 *"You snitched! . . ."* Lipman, *Frank Lloyd Wright and the Johnson Wax Buildings*, 1986, 80–83.

328 *Before leaving for Los Angeles . . .* Lipman, *Frank Lloyd Wright and the Johnson Wax Buildings*, 1986, p. 83.

328 *"Officer," Wright said . . .* Tafel, *Years with Frank Lloyd Wright*, 1979, 179–80.

328 *"in no way inferior . . ."* Lipman, *Frank Lloyd Wright and the Johnson Wax Buildings*, 1986, p. 182.

329 *"into small enough units . . ."* George Goodwin, interview with Philip Johnson, July 27, 1992.

329 *"Any photograph . . ."* Tafel, *Years with Frank Lloyd Wright*, 179.

329 *"was one man . . ."* Authors' interview with Victor Cusack, May 19, 2000.

330 *"Young man, beard the lion . . ."* Indira Berndtson and Greg Williams, interview with Wes Peters, Bob Mosher, and Victor Cusack, April 7, 1991.

330 *"hitch-hike his way . . ."* Alexander Woollcott to FLW, March 25, 1938.

330 *"Desire conference with you . . ."* Ludd Spivey to FLW, April 11, 1938.

330 *"[I]f you'll design . . ."* Florida Southern College website (www.flsouthern.edu/fllwctr/history.htm).

330 *"I don't know what to do . . ."* Wes Peters to Svetlana Peters: November 1938 or 1939, November 28, 1939, Marlin papers, Scott Elliott collection.

330–31 *The Florida Southern master plan . . .* Florida Southern College, www.flsouthern.edu/fllwctr/history.htm.

331 *He even purchased . . .* Notes from a letter from the Rudolph Wurlitzer Co. to Svetlana Peters, September 26, 1940, Marlin papers, Scott Elliott collection.

331 *If not for the publicity . . .* Maggie Valentine, interview with John Hill, July 15, 19, 30 and 31, 1995, UCLA Oral History Collection; Brierly, *Tales of Taliesin*, 1999, 113–14.

332 *"Well, I don't know . . ."* Maggie Valentine, interview with John Hill, 1997.

332 *"I knew so little . . ."* Jane Margolies, interview with John Hill, March 26, 1992.

332 *"I had never let go . . ."* Maggie Valentine, interview with John Hill, July 15, 1993.

332 *"We had no idea . . ."* Authors' interview with Ben Masselink, April 5, 1999.

333 *"No theatrical entrance . . ."* Brierly, *Tales of Taliesin*, 1999, 114.

333 *"Well, you've got . . ."* Maggie Valentine, interview with John Hill, July 15, 1993.

334 *"One of the things . . ."* Elizabeth Gordon to the authors, winter 1998; Maggie Valentine, interviews with John Hill, July 19, 30, and 31, 1993.

334 *"She was so used . . ."* Maggie Valentine, interview with John Hill, March 26, 1992.

334 *"I was getting . . ."* Authors' interview with ILW, February 19, 2000.

334 *"They will ship . . ."* Wes Peters to Svetlana Peters, November 28, 1939, Marlin papers, Scott Elliott collection.

334 *"get through being thirteen . . ."* Maggie Valentine, interview with John Hill, 1997.

334 *"I remember . . ."* Authors' interview with ILW, August 16, 2000.

335 *Two days after . . .* Interview with Jack Howe, March 5, 1991.

335 *"Arizona character . . ."* FLW, *An Autobiography*, 1943, 309.

335 *"[O]ut there . . ."* FLW, *The Future of Architecture* (New York: Horizon, 1953), 19. Quotation is from a transcript of a May 17, 1953, NBC telecast of a Hugh Downs interview; *Frank Lloyd Wright's Taliesin West: A CD-ROM with introduction and overview by Bruce Brooks Pfeiffer*, Los Angeles, California, in-D Press, 2002.

336 *"And how our boys . . ."* FLW, *An Autobiography*, 1943, 454–455.

336–37 *"The canvas overhead . . ."* FLW, *The Future of Architecture*, 1953, 255–6.

337 *"Frequently visitors..."* FLW, *An Auto-biography*, 1943, 455.

337 *"there will be..."* Svetlana Peters to Jim Thompson, 1939.

337 *Johnny had had to be dragged...* Maggie Valentine, interview with John Hill, 1997, 206.

338 *The offering of drawings...* Indira Berndt-son to the authors, e-mail, February 22, 2005.

338 *"Why by helium balloons..."* William Patrick to the authors, e-mail, March 5 and 6, 2005; John Geiger to the authors, e-mail, February 25, 2005.

338 *The problem was...* Authors' interview with Jim Charlton, February 15, 1997.

338 *"Well, there is nothing new..."* William Patrick to the authors, e-mail, March 5, 2005.

338 *"God, I do not want..."* Amin, *Reflections from the Shining Brow*, 2004, 261.

339 *"I tried unsuccessfully...* Tafel, *About Wright*, 1993, 133.

340 *"Hardships toward...* FLW, *An Autobi-ography*, 1943, 455.

340 *"When the Indians...* Tafel, *Years with Frank Lloyd Wright*, 1979, 196.

340 *"What a romantic..."* Baker Brownell and Frank Lloyd Wright, *The Architecture of Modern Life* (New York: Harper and Brothers, 1937), 39. They were mistaken: The story is Chinese in origin.

CHAPTER 14: LITTLE AMERICA FIRST

345 *The magazine was deluged...* Jacobs, *Building with Frank Lloyd Wright*, 1978, 51, 56.

345 *Hoping to stimulate...* "Eight Houses For Modern Living," *Life*, September 26, 1938.

346 *Yet not every apprentice...* Tafel, *Years with Frank Lloyd Wright*, 1979, 191.

346 *"I know the farmers..."* Ben Masselink, "Picnicking with Frank Lloyd Wright," *Journal of the Taliesin Fellows*, Vol. 7, No. 1, Winter 1996.

346 *"A fine spot..."* Ben Masselink, "Pick-nicking with Frank Lloyd Wright," *Journal of the Taliesin Fellows*, Winter, 1996, Vol. 7, No. 1, 11–17.

347 *"I should think..."* Betty Blum, interview with William Turk Priestley (Chicago: Chicago Architects Oral History Project, Ernest R. Graham Study Center for Architectural Drawings, 1995, revised 2003); Betty Blum, interview with Bertrand Goldberg (Chicago: Chicago Architects Oral History Project, 1992, revised 2001).

347 *"Now there, boys..."* Blum, interview with Bertrand Goldberg, 1992, revised 2001.

347 *"Ladies and gentlemen...* National Historic Landmark Nomination. S. R. Crowne Hall, http://www.cr.nps.gov/nhl/designations/samples/il/crown.pdf.

347–48 *"Since you choose..."* FLW to Henry-Russell Hitchcock, undated.

348 *was—incredibly—the first...* John Geiger to Curtis Besinger, August 1, 1986.

348 *While Hitchcock was reviewing...* Authors' phone interview with Scott Elliott, February 2004.

348 *"Oh, Frank,..."* Indira Berndtson and Greg Williams, interview with Wes Peters, Bob Mosher, and Victor Cusack, April 7, 1992.

348 *"The lands of my dreams..."* FLW, *An Autobiography*, 1932,

348 *Indeed, he was inspired...* Bertrand Goldberg, a young American architecture student, accompanied Mies to Taliesin and translated for him. When he complained in German about Wright's "silly romanticism," Mies snapped at him: "Shut up, Goldberg. Just be grateful it's here." Blum, interview with Goldberg, 1992, revised 2001.

348 *"Boldest stroke..."* "The Fate of Europe Sends No. 1 Briton to Hitler's House," *Life*, September 26, 1938.

349 *"When I got here..."* FLW, "An Organic Architecture," 1939, 311, 325, 331

349 *"Like Marie Antoinette..."* Andrew Saint, "Wright and Great Britain," 121–46, in Anthony Alofsin, ed., *Frank Lloyd Wright: Europe and Beyond* (Berkeley: University of California Press, 1999), 135.

349 *"Horrors on an enormous..."* Moore, *Gurdjieff*, 1999, 268, 277; OLW to Svetlana Peters, April 23, 1939; Office Memorandum to Director, FLW FBI file, February 11, 1955, provided to the authors under the Freedom of Information Act; authors' interview with Dushka Howarth, December 29, 2003.

349 *"Half the world..."* "Notes taken by Solita Solano (Kanari) from 1935–1940," July 24, 1937, FLW Archives.

349 *When the Wrights arrived...* Patterson, *Ladies of the Rope*, 1999.

350 *"You know, you are a..."* Rob Baker, "No Harem: Gurdjieff and the Women of The Rope," *Gurdjieff International Review*, Winter 1997–1998,

Vol. I, No. 2., http://www.gurdjieff.org/G.1-2.htm. Baker incorrectly dates this evening in May 1937, rather than 1939, as witnessed by C. S. Nott; see Nott's *Further Teachings of Gurdjieff*, 1978, 139. OLW to Svetlana from the Cunard *Queen Mary* bound for Europe, April 23, 1939, indicates a meeting with Gurdjieff planned for May 26, 1939.

351 *Olgivanna would later claim* . . . Pfeiffer, *The Crowning Decade*, 1989, 121–122. "There was one period, peculiarly enough, I believe it may have been somewhere between the ages of 70 and 75, where he required less of sex contact."

351 *In the meantime* . . . In 1990, Scott Elliott, a prominent dealer in Wright materials, was at a major New York show when he was approached by a heavily made-up woman in her eighties, with false eyelashes and a big, peacock-blue chiffon scarf holding down a large bouffant wig. When she pulled a letter out of her purse and thrust it into his hands, Elliott—who had handled countless Wright drawings and letters—instantly recognized Wright's handwriting. The letter, signed "Frank," was a love letter from the architect to the woman, Mary La Follette, the youngest daughter of Wright's ally and friend, the progressive congressman Robert La Follette. Mary eventually allowed Elliott to read her entire trove of thirty or so steamy, though not graphic, letters, replete with images of the two of them flowing into each other. Later, by chance, a copy of Louis Sullivan's *Kindergarten Chats* fell into Elliott's hands, bearing the following inscription in Wright's hand: "To Mary La Follette Xmas 1936." Authors' interviews with Scott Elliott, February 17 and May 17, 2004.

352 *"this hysterical chatter* . . ." Leonard Mosley, *Lindbergh: A Biography* (New York: Doubleday, 1976), 269.

352 *Lindbergh was an American hero* . . . Sailing in 1939 on a ship with a number of Jews fleeing Hitler, he had written in his diary: "A few Jews add strength and character to a country, but too many create chaos. And we are getting too many." Politicized Jew hatred, he was sure, would come to America, too. "It is too bad," he wrote, "because a few Jews of the right type are, I believe, an asset to any country. . . . If an anti-Semitic movement starts in the United States, it may go far. It will certainly affect the good Jews along with the others." A. Scott Berg, *Lindbergh* (New York: G.P. Putnam's Sons, 1998), 393.

352 *"reduce the strength* . . ." Berg, *Lindbergh*, 1998, 376, 394.

352 *"We all knew you could fly* . . . FLW to Charles Lindbergh, May 24, 1940. Wright offered a slightly different wording in his 1943 autobiography: "We knew you could fly straight, but now when everywhere is equivocation and cowardice you not only think straight but you dare speak straight." FLW, *An Autobiography*, 1943, 500.

352 *"so that his inner life* . . ." Nott, *Further Teachings of Gurdjieff*, 1978, 151, 156.

352 *"In the evening* . . ." Taliesin Junior Fellowship, undated.

353 *"half in love"* Clare Crane, "Svetlana Wright Peters and the Taliesin Junior Fellowship"; authors' phone interview with Clare Crane, June 28, 2004.

354 *The Frank Lloyd Wright Foundation never* . . . Commissioner of Internal Revenue Service to FLW, March 31, 1942, Marlin papers, Scott Elliott collection.

354 *"Why do the English* . . ." Nott, *Further Teachings of Gurdjieff*, 1978, 153.

354 *"quite a reputation* . . ." Bill Kauffman, "JFK, Frank Lloyd Wright, and Gerald Ford Did What?" *American Enterprise Online*, January 2000; Charles Lindbergh to FLW (American First Committee "loyal supporter"), June 28, 1941.

355 *Wright raved* . . . Authors' phone interview with Pedro Guerrero, December 1, 2003.

355 *Henry Ford, another anti-Semite* . . . "The international financiers are behind all war," Ford had told a reporter in 1920. "They are what is called the International Jew—German Jews, French Jews, English Jews, American Jews. I believe that in all these countries except our own the Jewish financier is supreme. . . . Here, the Jew is a threat."

355 *When the architect appeared* . . . Conrad Nagel Brown, "The Continental Chop Top," *Inland Architect*, 1997, 9. Additional details of the transaction from Motor Trend magazine online (www.motortrend.com).

355 *But none from the Fellowship* . . . Besinger, *Working with Mr. Wright*, 1997, 95.

355 *"Wake up America* . . ." FLW, "Wake Up America!", *Christian Century*, November 13, 1940, in Pfeiffer, ed., *Collected Writings: Volume 4*, 1994, 39–43.

355 *"Jew him down"* Authors' phone interview with Pedro Guerrero, December 1, 2003.

357 *Long after his death* ... Authors' interview with Aaron Green, January 1, 1999.

357 *"over his dead body"* Alleged by an informant in a letter to U.S. attorney John J. Boyle. "Frank Lloyd Wright Sedition," July 17, 1943, FLW FBI file.

357 *"True defense for us ..."* FLW, "Wake Up America," in *Collected Writings: Volume 4*, 42.

357 *Gene Masselink, Herb and Eloise Fritz* ... Secrest, *Frank Lloyd Wright*, 1993, 439.

358 *"Wes coveted it ..."* FLW, *An Autobiography*, 1943, 466–67.

358 *Under Wes's coordination* ... Wes Peters to FLW, undated, Marlin papers.

358 *Between the apprentice farms* ... Secrest, *Frank Lloyd Wright*, 1993, 438–39.

358 *For Svetlana, it meant* ... Interview with Bob May, February 2, 1996.

358 *"Taliesin's first real extension ..."* FLW, *An Autobiography*, 1943, 467.

358 *It was Kay* ... Authors' phone interview with Clare Crane, June 28, 2004. Crane was living inside the household at the time.

358 *"And I just scrunched ..."* Indira Berndtson and Greg Williams, interview with Kay Rattenbury, January 16, 1990. The quotation marks around "beating" are from the transcription; the videotape of the interview reveals no basis for the quotes.

359 *She charged Kay with* ... The letter refers to the apprentice only as "Ted."

360 *"Human congestion ..."* There is some date confusion here. Pfeiffer dates this article to February 1941; in his autobiography, Wright dates it to January 1942. FLW, *An Autobiography*, 1943, 538.

360 *"live again ..."* FLW, *An Autobiography*, 1943, 540.

360 *"national objective ..."* Eugene Masselink to Colonel Lindbergh, March 27, 1941.

360 *"Each member ..."* Wright even asked a member of the local draft board whether his apprentices might get a break for occupational deferment. This was in conjunction with his interest in doing war workers' housing in Massachusetts. "Frank Lloyd Wright Sedition," March 3, 1943, FLW FBI file 25-2326.

361 *... a military invasion of his own* ... Meehan, *Frank Lloyd Wright Remembered*, 1991, 76–87, 140–147.

361 *Between the draft* ... FLW, "Our Work," February 1941, *Taliesin*, in Pfeiffer, ed., 1994, 69.

361 *"quite indispensable ..."* Jack Howe to Mrs. C. W. Howe, February 19, 1940, Lu Howe personal correspondence.

362 *"The best defense ..."* FLW, "Good Afternoon, Editor Evjue," *The Capital Times*, May 29, 1941.

362 *"an out-and-out ..."* FLW, "Of What Use Is a Great Navy with No Place to Hide?" *Taliesin Square-Paper*, May 15, 1941.

362 *"What a spectacle! ..."* Lewis Mumford to FLW, May 30, 1941, 181–82, in Pfeiffer and Wojtowicz, *Frank Lloyd Wright+Lewis Mumford: Thirty Years of Correspondence*, 2001.

362 *"Time will discover you ..."* FLW to Lewis Mumford, June 3, 1941, 183–84, in Pfeiffer and Wojtowicz, *Frank Lloyd Wright+Lewis Mumford: Thirty Years of Correspondence*, 2001.

363 *"all work is ..."* Wright, "Our Work," February 1941, 69; Tafel, *Years With Frank Lloyd Wright*, 1979, 206–207.

363 *By the summer of 1941* ... Jack Howe to Mrs. C. W. Howe, July 14, 1941, Lu Howe personal correspondence.

363 *"I can't stay ..."* Tafel, *Years with Frank Lloyd Wright*, 1979, 207.

363 *"I hope you and Sally ..."* FLW to Edgar Tafel, January 13, 1942, Tafel, *About Wright*, 1993, 14.

364 *On Wright's new national map* ... Wright placed the capital of the state of Usonia in Denver, the capital of the entire country on the Mississippi just north of St. Louis.

365 *"should be opposing ..."* Berg, *Lindbergh*, 1998, 427.

365 *"the innumerable four-year ..."* FLW, "The American Quality," in *Scribner's Commentator*, October 1941, 35–46.

365 *Wright told Howe to stay* ... Jack Howe to Mrs. C. W. Howe, May 14, 1941; Mrs. C.W. Howe to Jack Howe, May 30, 1941, Lu Howe personal correspondence.

365 *The Wrights had been awfully nice* ... Jack Howe to Mrs. C. W. Howe, October 6, 1941, Howe personal correspondence.

365–66 *"He pointed out ..."* Jack Howe to Mrs. C. W. Howe, November 1941, Howe personal correspondence.

366 *With his attentions* . . . Eugene Masselink to Jack Waxler, December 8, 1943.

366 *"I bought you . . ."* Tafel, *About Wright*, 1993, 134. *"Iovanna in New York"* FLW to ILW, December 25, 1943.

366 *On December 7, 1941* . . . Besinger, *Working with Mr. Wright*, 1997, 123.

366 *Though Pedro Guerrero* . . . Authors' interview with Pedro Guerrero, December 16, 1999. Wright's support for draft resistance apparently never stopped. Memo from D. J. Sullivan to J. Belmont, "Subject: Security Matter X, Conscientious Objector," June 27, 1954, FLW FBI File.

366 *Jim would fly* . . . Jim Charlton papers. Charlton's account of his war record was checked by his client and friend, Richard de Mille. This contradicts the statement made in the memoirs of Charlton's former lover and friend, Christopher Isherwood, in his *Diaries, Volume One, 1939–1960* (New York: HarperCollins, 1997).

367 *"Taliesin had a son . . ."* FLW, *An Autobiography*, 1943, 467.

367 *Wright not only rented* . . . Jack Howe to Mrs. C. W. Howe: January 14 and April 16, 1942, Lu Howe personal correspondence.

367 *. . . drawings for demountable houses* . . . Besinger, *Working with Mr. Wright*, 1997, 124–125.

367 *"I think you boys . . ."* Eugene Masselink to Herbert Fritz, January 8, 1943; Washington City News Service, December 21, 1947, FLW FBI File; "Frank Lloyd Wright Demands Out of Judge in Draft Fight," *New York Herald Tribune*, December 20, 1942.

368 *The FBI interviewed* . . . FLW FBI file 25-2326.

368 *"And then if we were . . ."* Authors' phone interview with Pedro Guerrero, December 1, 2003.

368 *When agents* . . . Authors' interview with O. P. Reed, July 15, 1999.

368 *"The boys who shoot . . ."* An anonymous informant's letter to the FBI, October 25, 1943, FLW FBI File.

368 *In the fall of 1942* . . . Roland Reisley with John Timpane, *Usonia New York: Building a Community with Frank Lloyd Wright* (New York: Princeton Architectural Press, 2001). This community, which was ultimately built, has been mistakenly identified by some architectural historians as the only realization of Broadacre, despite the much larger and more extensive effort in West Los Angeles chronicled in Harold Zellman and Roger Friedland, "Broadacre in Brentwood: The Politics of Architectural Aesthetics," in Michael Roth and Charles Salas, *Looking for LA* (Getty Research Institute, 2001), 167–210.

368 *"In this day of destruction . . ."* David Henken and FLW: July 17 and August 14, 1942.

369 *With his all-too-convenient* . . . Besinger, *Working with Mr. Wright*, 1997, 140–41.

369 *"Whether we like it* . . . FLW to Henning Waterston, undated.

369 *We were to live* . . . Fritz, Henning, ed., *"At Taliesin,"* 1992, 146.

369 *Wright's Broadacre City* . . . Interview with Wes Peters, 1967.

369 *Fritz's farm,* . . . Authors' interview with Eloise Fritz, December 15, 1999.

370 *Wright even talked* . . . Jack Howe to Mrs. C. W. Howe, April 1, 1942, Lu Howe personal correspondence.

370 *"To the American Eagle . . ."* FLW, *An Autobiography*, 1943, 500–501.

370 *Roosevelt wouldn't let* . . . Mosley, *Lindbergh*, 1976, 322–323; Receipt for Registered Article 876, January 23, 1943, Getty Research Institute.

370 *When she finally admitted* . . . Mr. C. W. Howe to Jack Howe, June 3, 1942, Lu Howe personal correspondence.

371 *What the country needed* . . . Jack Howe to Mr. C. W. Howe, June 7, 1942, Lu Howe personal correspondence.

371 *He had been fortunate* . . . Jack Howe to Mrs. C. W. Howe, September 16, 1942, Lu Howe personal correspondence.

371 *Howe's request* . . . Jack Howe to Major General Louis B. Hershey, director, Selective Service System, undated, Howe personal correspondence.

371 *Jack came away* . . . Jack Howe to Mr. and Mrs. C. W. Howe, January 19, 1943, Lu Howe personal correspondence.

371 *To the truly committed* . . . Jack Howe to Bill Howe, February 6, 1943, Lu Howe personal correspondence.

371 *If it continued* . . . Jack Howe to Mrs. C. W. Howe, February 13, 1943, Howe personal correspondence.

372 *... are now a national hero*... FLW to Joe X, January 30, 1943.

372 *Wright followed up*... "Broadacre City Petition, 1943," John Sergeant, *Frank Lloyd Wright's Usonian Houses: Designs for Moderate Cost One-Family Homes* (New York: Whitney Library of Design, 1976), 201; FLW and Walter Gropius: February 6 and 9, 1943.

373 *Wright calculated*... Jack Howe to Mrs. C. W. Howe, March 3, 1943, Lu Howe personal correspondence.

373 *Kay visited them*... Jack Howe to Mr. and Mrs. C. W. Howe, June 18, 1943, Lu Howe personal correspondence.

373 *One of America's own sons*... OLW to Alexander Woollcott, June 19, 1943.

373 *"I should hate..."* Jack Howe to Mrs. C. W. Howe, June 30, 1943, Lu Howe personal correspondence.

CHAPTER 15: SPACE LOVERS

374 *Copper magnate*... Joan M. Lukach, *Hilla Rebay: In Search of the Spirit in Art* (New York: George Braziller, 1983), 54, 66–83; Bruce Hooten, interview with Hilla Rebay, 1966, *Smithsonian Archives of American Art*, www.aaa.si.edu/oralhist/rebay66.htm.

374 *Rebay believed*... Lukach, *Hilla Rebay*, 1983, 96, 144.

375 *The contessa found*... Lukach, *Hilla Rebay*, 1983, 44–46, 182.

375 *Suddenly, one of Wright's books*... ILW, *My Life*, undated, 216. Lukach suggests that Irene Guggenheim recommended Wright: *Hilla Rebay*, 1983, 183.

375 *Having never seen*... Lukach, *Hilla Rebay*, 1983, 186.

375 *"Organic architecture," she read*... FLW, *An Autobiography*, 1943, 472.

376 *That charge was dropped*... Lomask, *Seed Money*, 1964, 178; John H. Davis, *The Guggenheims: An American Epic* (New York: William Morrow and Co., 1978), 213.

376 *I need a fighter*... Hilla Rebay to FLW, June 1, 1943, Bruce Brooks Pfeiffer, *Frank Lloyd Wright: The Guggenheim Correspondence* (Fresno and Carbondale: The Press at California State University and Southern Illinois University Press, 1986), 4.

376 *"Mr Guggenheim is 82 years old..."* Hilla Rebay to FLW, June 14, 1943.

376 *Guggenheim trusted*... Hilla Rebay to FLW, July 18, 1943; Solomon Guggenheim to FLW, June 29, 1943.

376 *The museum was a thrilling*... Jack Howe to FLW, July 7, 1943.

377 *"We've got the Guggenheim..."* FLW to Jack Howe, July 27, 1943, Lu Howe personal correspondence.

377 *"You are a son..."* FLW to Jack Howe, August 31, 1943, Lu Howe personal correspondence.

377 *"The hero business..."* Jack Howe to FLW, July 29, 1943, FLW Archives; Jack Howe to Mr. and Mrs. C. W. Howe, July 27, 1943; Jack Howe to Mrs. C. W. Howe, August 13, 1943; Jack Howe to Miss Elizabeth Howe, March 3, 1944, Lu Howe personal correspondence.

377 *"inviolate inner strength..."* FLW, "Address at Sandstone Prison," 1942, 106–8, in Pfeiffer, ed., *Collected Writings, Volume 4*, 1994.

377 *"Several fellows claim..."* Jack Howe to Mr. and Mrs. C. W. Howe, July 27, 1943, Lu Howe personal correspondence.

378 *... who had read both Steiner*... Langmead and Johnson, *Architectural Excursions*, 2000, 62. See also Susan R. Henderson, "Architecture and Theosophy: An Introduction," *Architronic*, Vol. 7, No. 2, 1–4, 1998. Indira Berndtson to the authors, November 21, 2003. Mrs. Wright's library contains a large number of mystical works, including those of Madame Blavatasky and Rudolph Steiner.

378 *Small groups at Taliesin*... Maggie Valentine, interview with John Hill, 1997, 269.

378 *His son Lloyd*... Hilla Rebay to FLW, September 1, 1943, and November 1943.

379 *"bound to earth..."* Hilla Rebay and FLW: August 12 and 16, 1943.

379 *"new and higher..."* FLW, *When Democracy Builds* (Chicago: University of Chicago Press, 1945), 48–49; Hilla Rebay to FLW, August 12, 1943.

380 *She had long dreamed*... Lukach, *Hilla Rebay*, 1983, 62; Levine, *The Architecture of Frank Lloyd Wright*, 1996, 489.

380 *Wright sent her*... Authors' interview with ILW, January 14, 2000.

380 *"You are not going to..."* Maggie Valentine, interview with John Hill, July 19, 1993, UCLA Oral History Program; ILW, *My Life*, 130.

380 *"accomplishment"* ILW to FLW, November 29, 1943; ILW, *My Life*, 130.

381 *"innate sense of music"* FLW, *An Autobiography*, 1943, 467; interview with Cornelia Brierly, July 30, 1992.

381 *"Taliesin is a great place . . ."* FLW to ILW, November 6, 1943.

381 *"learn about the holy . . ."* Hilla Rebay to FLW, August 19, 1943.

381 *"Let us forget . . ."* Hilla Rebay to FLW, June 23, 1943, cited in Lukach, *Hilla Rebay*, 1983, 186.

382 *"humanity . . ."* FLW to Hilla Rebay, August 16, 1943.

382 *"Go and find out . . ."* Hilla Rebay to FLW, August 19, 1943.

382 *"Way back there . . ."* FLW to Hilla Rebay, August 25, 1943.

382 *Wright sent Rebay . . .* Hilla Rebay to FLW, September 1, 1943; Hilla Rebay to OLW, November 4, 1943; FLW to Hilla Rebay, September 24, 1943.

382 *. . . shared their respective . . .* Hilla Rebay to Frank Lloyd Wright, July 29, 1943 and November 1943. Hilla went out and listened to Gurdjieff's music, which she liked. Hilla Rebay to OLW, October 6, 1946.

382 *Guggenheim's curator . . .* Lukach, *Hilla Rebay*, 1983, 174, 180–81; Masselink, *Gene*, 1996, 108–9; Reed, *Eugene Masselink*, 1999, 110–111.

383 *"I've had a hard time . . ."* FLW to Hilla Rebay, July 29, 1943.

383 *"just plain common sense"* Hilla Rebay to FLW, May 20, 1944; *"Don't call me . . ."* "The Guggenheim Museum," *Frank Lloyd Wright Quarterly*, Vol. 3, No. 3, Summer 1992, 6.

383 *"The remodeling job . . ."* Jack Howe to FLW, July 29, 1943.

383 *"I cannot tell you . . ."* ILW to FLW, circa October 1943.

383 *"She should be competent . . ."* FLW to ILW, November 6, 1943, in ILW, *My Life*, 349.

384 *"such an ugly city . . ."* ILW to FLW, October 25, November 4, and December 14, 1943.

384 *Her concert grand . . .* Indeed, in 1941 he had already received a telegram reading "Arrears on harp. $186. Not received. Why?" ME. Coolbaugh, Lyon and Healy, Inc. to FLW; ILW to FLW, November 5, 1943.

384 *"Please don't expect . . ."* ILW to FLW, November 29, 1943.

384 *"I was practically . . ."* ILW to FLW, January 29, 1944.

384 *Wright had once admired . . .* Edgar Tafel, "The New Tenements," December 5, 1935, Henning, ed., *"At Taliesin,"* 1992, 168. Whatever his feelings about its appropriateness for his daughter, Wright's opinion of Debussy's music must have changed; in 1932, he had listed the composer among his favorites. "Books That Have Meant Most To Me," Pfeiffer, ed., *Frank Lloyd Wright Collected Writings, Volume 3*, 1993, 64.

384 *When Iovanna reported . . .* ILW to FLW, November 29, 1943, and January 19, 1944.

384 *"You have convinced her . . ."* FLW to Marcel Grandjany, December 7, 1943. Wright also forbade Ravel. Authors' interview with ILW, August 16, 2000.

384 *"You could do her . . ."* FLW to Hilla Rebay, November 20, 1943.

385 *"The sidewalk crowd . . ."* FLW to Solomon Guggenheim, July 14, 1943.

385 *"negro dangerous Harlem . . ."* Hilla Rebay to FLW, July 18, 1943.

385 *But Rebay envisioned . . .* Levine, *The Architecture of Frank Lloyd Wright*, 1996, 320–321.

385 *"Frankly . . ."* Hilla Rebay to FLW, August 12, 1943. The building should not be "crawling in wide extensions." Lukach, *Hilla Rebay*, 1983, 187; Levine, *Frank Lloyd Wright*, 1996, 320–21; see also FLW to Solomon Guggenheim, December 31, 1943.

385 *"inner uplift"* Hilla Rebay to FLW, August or September 1943.

385 *"That fall, he began . . ."* FLW to Hilla Rebay, November 5, 1943.

385 *"I hope we can get . . ."* FLW to Hilla Rebay, December 18, 1943.

386 *"Vell," she said . . .* ILW, *My Life*, 217.

386 *"Stuck in Manhattan . . ."* ILW, *My Life*, 44; Herb Fritz, Henning, ed., *"At Taliesin,"* 1992, 132.

386 *"Expecting Guggenheim . . ."* Besinger, *Working with Mr. Wright*, 1997, 146–48; FLW to Jack Howe, August 31, 1943, Lu Howe personal correspondence.

386 *"I realize very well . . ."* ILW to FLW, December 6, 1943.

387 *"Taliesin missed you . . ."* FLW to ILW, January 5, 1944; ILW to FLW, January 29, 1944; FLW to ILW, February 14, 1944, Marlin papers.

387 *"It must be pretty tough . . ."* FLW to Jack Howe, December 24, 1943, Lu Howe personal correspondence.

387 *"The fantasy called . . .* FLW to Davy Davison and Jack Howe, January 5, 1944, Lu Howe personal correspondence.

387 *"it was very difficult . . ."* Authors' interview with Eric Lloyd Wright, July 16, 1999.

387 *Just by reading . . .* Jack Howe to Mr. and Mrs. C. W. Howe, December 30, 1943, and February 16, 1944, Lu Howe personal correspondence.

388 *"go where we please"* FLW to Hilla Rebay, telegram, December 30, 1943.

388 *"Don't like perpendicular . . ."* Hilla Rebay to FLW, telegram, January 3, 1944.

388 *"spacious horizontality . . ."* FLW to Hilla Rebay, telegram, January 3, 1944; FLW to Hilla Rebay, January 4, 1944.

388 *But Guggenheim was expecting . . .* Levine, *The Architecture of Frank Lloyd Wright*, 1996, 321.

388 *Then, in another sketch . . .* John Hill remembers a square one with level floors as well. Maggie Valentine, interview with John Hill, UCLA Oral History Program, 1997, 158.

389 *As a Theosophist . . .* Lukach, *Hilla Rebay*, 1983, 144–45. In her *Secret Doctrine*, Blavatsky writes, "The immutable law of Nature is ETERNAL MOTION, cyclic and spiral, therefore progressive even in its seeming retrogression. The one divine Principle, the nameless THAT of Vedas, is the universal total, which, neither in its spiritual aspects and emanations, nor in its physical atoms, can ever be at 'absolute rest' except during the 'Nights' of Brahma." H. Blavatsky, *The Secret Doctrine, Volume II*, Theosophical University Press, 44.

389 *a concept derived . . .* Wright may well have heard of Gurdjieff's comparison of America to Babylon, the ancient society Beelzebub describes to his grandson as a turning point in human history from true knowledge to false philosophy. Taylor, *Gurdjieff in America*, 2004.

389 *Wright not only labeled . . .* Levine, *Frank Lloyd Wright*, 1996, 324, 326.

389 *"the cosmic wave . . ."* William H. Jordy, *American Buildings and Their Architects: The Impact of European modernism in the Mid-Twentieth Century* (New York: Oxford University Press, 1972), 330–332.

389 *"curving wave . . ."* Levine, *The Architecture of Frank Lloyd Wright*, 1996, 356. Olgivanna,

too, would explain that she felt as if "I were standing on the shore watching the ocean waves rising and falling, never breaking." *Our House*, 1959, 301.

389 *"I hear you are . . ."* ILW to FLW, January 12, 1944.

389 *"I find the antique . . ."* FLW to Hilla Rebay, January 26, 1944, Pfeiffer, *Frank Lloyd Wright: The Guggenheim Correspondence*, 1986, 42.

389 *With Rebay and Guggenheim . . .* Hilla Rebay to FLW, February 1944.

390 *In one letter . . .* Levine, *The Architecture of Frank Lloyd Wright*, 1996, 323–24.

390 *"But for heaven's sake . . ."* Hilla Rebay to FLW, early February 1944.

390 *. . . but to Theosophists . . .* Lukach, *Hilla Rebay*, 1983, 191.

390 *"The Sun is the soul . . ."* FLW to Hilla Rebay, February 6, 1944.

390 *Rebay had long hated . . .* "I cannot imagine why," she wrote, even before meeting Wright, "they have not yet found a way to get away from the staircase which disturbs the unit[y] of a house." Hilla Rebay to Moholy-Nagy, May 28, 1943, in Lukach, *Hilla Rebay*, 1983, 182. Rebay would later claim to have generated the idea that became the building's signature. "I explained to him what I wanted, a museum that goes slowly up. No staircase, no interruptions." Bruce Hooten, interview with Hilla Rebay, 1966, *Smithsonian Archives of American Art*. There is a design in one of her later letters, but it is a rectangular structure. Hilla Rebay to FLW, early February 1944. She told apprentice Curtis Besinger the same thing, and he believed her: *Working With Mr. Wright*, 1997, 229.

390 *"Give them what . . ."* Hill, *Oral History*, 1997, 158.

390 *"You may be shocked . . ."* FLW to Hilla Rebay, February 19, 1944.

391 *"What a great man . . ."* Bruce Hooten, interview with Hilla Rebay, *Smithsonian Archives of American Art*, 1966.

391 *"I have boundless . . ."* OLW to Hilla Rebay, December 6, 1943.

CHAPTER 16: SPACE WARRIORS

392 *Guggenheim was not like her . . .* Hilla Rebay to FLW, July 29, 1943.

393 *In face of his insecurity . . .* "He made three drawings of the museum and it was

mother who chose the round one," she said. Authors' interview with ILW, February 13, 2000.

393 *The natural form* . . . Authors' interview with Charles Schiffner, October 30, 2000. Describing the Guggenheim's ascending ramp, Wright told *Architectural Forum* that it would be constructed "like that of a sea-shell being carried throughout from the outer walls." Levine, *The Architecture of Frank Lloyd Wright*, 1996, 328. See also his comparison to a "chambered nautilus," 340.

393 " *'nervous' state* . . ." FLW to Hilla Rebay, July 6, 1944.

393 *"I need you two* . . ." FLW to Jack Howe, April 10, 1944.

393 *With two years left* . . . Jack Howe to Eugene Masselink, June 11, 1944.

393 *"slave labor"* Jack Howe to Mr. and Mrs. C. W. Howe, June 20, 1944, Lu Howe personal correspondence.

393 *"I may sound cool* . . ." Jack Howe to FLW, July 9, 1944.

393 *Aldebaran was on its way* . . . Percentage Allotment, undated memo, probably 1943; letter from Wes Peters to Frederick Heckel, secretary of the Bio-Dynamic Farms and Gardeners Association, February 4, 1944, Marlin papers, Scott Elliott collection.

393 *When he came across* . . . Wes Peters to FLW, undated, probably 1944.

393 *"I suggest if you have* . . ." FLW to Svetlana Peters, April 11, 1941, Marlin papers. The date, in Wright's hand, is likely erroneous: Svetlana was not pregnant in 1941, and there is no known miscarriage or abortion. The letter also refers to Tal Davison, who was not born until February 13, 1942. In addition, a response from Wes states that Wes has been working with Wright for more than ten years. Wes came to work with Wright in 1932. Wright's letter also refers to Davy Davison being imprisoned in Sandstone, something that had not yet happened in 1941. Both William Marlin and FLW archivist Indira Berndston concluded that it was written in 1944.

394 *"abominable* . . . *It is hard* . . ." OLW to Svetlana Peters: April 19 and 18, 1944.

394 *He sent Svetlana* . . . Vladimir Hinzenberg to Svetlana Peters, March 31, 1944, Marlin papers.

394 *"The time is coming* . . ." FLW to Wes Peters, undated.

394 *"It is a very great sorrow* . . ." Wes Peters to FLW, undated: This is the letter noted above, rebutting charges Wright made in his erroneously dated "April 11, 1941" letter to Svetlana.

394 *"I allow you were* . . ." FLW to Wes Peters, undated. Wright is working on the Oboler house layout, which started in the drafting room in 1940. Marlin papers. However, 1944 is also a probable date, for it was in that year that Wright told Gene Masselink to come up with the accounting with Wes Peters.

394 *Cash was tight* . . . OLW to Svetlana Peters, April 25, 1944; FLW to Gene Masselink, 1944.

395 *"How callow* . . ." FLW to Wes Peters, undated, probably 1944, Marlin papers .

395 *"I have no son* . . . FLW to Wes Peters, undated, probably 1944, Marlin papers .

395 *"The affair has drifted* . . ." FLW to Gene Masselink, 1944.

395 *"I am awfully sorry* . . ." Svetlana to FLW, 1944.

395 *"By this time* . . ." FLW to Svetlana Peters, probably April 11, 1944.

396 *Wes celebrated* . . . Gene Masselink to Svetlana Peters, Marlin Papers, FLW Archives, undated.

396 *"I hope Wes* . . ." FLW to Svetlana Peters, May 8, 1944.

396 *I have assigned* . . . Unsigned letter to Lt. Col. Mann and David Williamson, June 15, 1944.

397 *Jack Howe was still trying* . . . Jack Howe, Application for Parole, July 25, 1944.

397 *"Mr. Wright, I knew* . . ." FLW to Harry Guggenheim, May 14, 1952, in Pfeiffer, *Frank Lloyd Wright: The Guggenheim Correspondence*, 1986, 49, 169.

397 *"I couldn't imagine* . . ." Maggie Valentine, interview with John Hill, 1995, 162.

397 *"Mr. Wright had more* . . ." Indira Berndtson and Greg Williams, interview with Wes Peters, December 29, 1989.

397 *"way beyond our* . . ." FLW to Jack Howe: August 17 and 18, 1944, Lu Howe personal correspondence.

398 *"How honorable* . . ." ILW, *My Life*, 226.

398 . . . *the structure of the saguaro* . . . Wes Peters interviews, 1967 and 1968. Peters estimated that 75–80 percent of all engineering was done by him, the rest by Mendel Glickman.

398 *To Wright, these struts . . .* Jordy, *American Buildings and Their Architects*, 1972, 313. In 1946, he brought in an outside engineer, Jaroslav Polivka, to help him in that task. Levine, *The Architecture of Frank Lloyd Wright*, 1996, 486.

399 *What had begun . . .* Jordy, *American Buildings and Their Architects*, 1972, 325–28; Levine, *The Architecture of Frank Lloyd Wright*, 1996, 328; Lewis Mumford, "What Hath Wright Wrought?" *The New Yorker*, December 5, 1959.

399 *They would be lit . . .* FLW to Hilla Rebay, August 27, 1946, Pfeiffer, ed., *The Guggenheim Correspondence*, 1986, 88

399 *"look awful . . ."* Hilla Rebay to FLW, incomplete letter, July–August 1944; Lukach, *Hilla Rebay*, 1983, 192–93. Rebay also proposed using the little bays on the ramp as a domestic space where people could view paintings that they might rent and take home. Maggie Valentine, interview with John Hill, June 5, 1995, UCLA Oral History Program.

400 *He promised . . .* Hilla Rebay to FLW, February 14, 1945; Pfeiffer, *Frank Lloyd Wright: The Guggenheim Correspondence*, 1986, 57.

400 *"Olgivanna, I love you . . ."* Hilla Rebay to OLW, February 14, 1945.

400 *"But, no, I am told . . ."* Hilla Rebay to FLW, February 14, 1945.

400 *"You have a sense . . ."* FLW to Hilla Rebay, February 19, 1945.

400 *"An unconscious feeling . . ."* Hendrik Wijdeveld to FLW, February 27, 1945; Langmead and Johnson, *Architectural Excursions*, 2000, 163.

401 *"Yours was a swell . . ."* FLW to Jack Howe, July 30, 1945, Lu Howe personal correspondence.

401 *"I fear . . ."* Jack Howe to FLW, August 1, 1945.

401 *Though he grudgingly . . .* "Frank Lloyd Wright's Daughter, Iovanna, Is Married to Lieut Howe," March 23, 1945, Marlin papers.

402 *"Of course I have . . ."* FLW to ILW, undated, Marlin papers.

402 *"He expects perfection . . ."* Hilla Rebay to FLW, undated, circal fall 1945.

402 *"the Good Spirit . . ."* FLW to Hilla Rebay, May 12, 1945, Pfeiffer, *Frank Lloyd Wright: The Guggenheim Correspondence*, 1986, 60.

403 *. . . Guggenheim personally . . .* Pfeiffer, *Frank Lloyd Wright: The Guggenheim Correspondence*, 1986, 53.

403 *"The daring dean . . ."* "Art Museum a la Wright," *Time*, July 23, 1945.

403 *"Somewhere in transit . . ."* Levine, *The Architecture of Frank Lloyd Wright*, 1996, 328; Besinger, *Working with Mr. Wright*, 1987, 178–79.

403 *"How you did . . ."* Jack Howe to FLW, October 23, 1945.

404 *"big, white . . ."* "Art Optimistic Ziggurat," *Time*, October, 1, 1945.

404 *"Museum that Drycleans"* Jack Howe to Eugene Masselink, July 12, 1945.

404 *"Knowing how much . . .* Rebay to FLW.

404 *Rebay convinced . . .* Hilla Rebay to FLW, October 28, 1945; ILW, *My Life*, 220.

404 *"Absolutely marvelous . . ."* Pfeiffer, *Frank Lloyd Wright: The Guggenheim Correspondence*, 1986, 75.

404 *Hilla Rebay was not. . . .* "This building is devoted to a higher decoration than nature, to finer flowers—each wall should be *devoted* to some lovely paintings['] influence. The art will be dominant in this task and not let architecture predominate . . ." Lukach, *Hilla Rebay*, 1983, 198.

405 *"You can't. . . ."* Indira Berndtson and Greg Williams, interview with Wes Peters, December 27, 1989.

406 *"My goodness . . ."* OLW to Svetlana Peters, May 10, 1944; OLW to Gene Masselink, March 6, 1947. "Mr. Wright and I still argue about Ayn Rand's *Fountainhead*. He loves it and wants me to love it. So you better read it."

406 *"It is only . . ."* Michael S. Berliner, ed., *Letters of Ayn Rand* (New York: Dutton, 1995), 109.

406 *"It was like . . ."* Barbara Branden, *The Passion of Ayn Rand* (Garden City, N.Y.: Doubleday, 1986), 191–92.

406 *"wants other men . . ."* Ayn Rand, journal entry, April 13, 1946, David Harriman, ed., *Journals of Ayn Rand* (New York: Dutton, 1997), 410–14

406 *At one point . . .* Interview with Jack Howe, March 12, 1991.

407 *"My one hope . . ."* Jack Howe to FLW and OLW, December 25, 1945.

CHAPTER 17: A FRESH START

411 *On a warm Saturday . . .* Manny Carter diary, March 9, 1946.

411 *"Free! Free!..."* Jack Howe to Gene Masselink, undated.

411 *"Why didn't you..."* Pedro Guerrero, "Photographing Frank Lloyd Wright," *Journal of the Taliesin Fellows*, Vol. 3, No. 3, Summer, 1992; authors' phone interview with Clare Crane, June 28, 2004.

412 *After her return...* Authors' interview with ILW, August 16, 2000.

412 *"image of what..."* Curtis Besinger to John Geiger, October 20, 1988.

412 *"what this thing God..."* Authors' interview with James and Barbara Dresser, June 4, 2000.

412 *"heresy or breach..."* Manny Carter to William Marlin, undated; Manny Carter diary, March 13–14, 1946.

413 *"Sometimes..."* James Auer and Claudia Looz, interview with Kay Rattenbury, 1992.

413 *"You don't do that..."* ILW, *My Life*, 66; authors' interview with ILW, February 19, 2000.

413 *"My father was insulting..."* William Marlin, interview with ILW, May 17, 1988.

413 *I couldn't take it..."* William Marlin, interview with ILW, May 17, 1988; ILW, *My Life*, 129. Iovanna says she was nineteen or twenty at the time, which would place this event in 1945 or 1946. In Marlin's interview, she dates this incident to when Wright was around seventy-five years old, or 1942.

414 *"I think I saved..."* Authors' interview with ILW, August 16, 2000.

414 *He was the one man...* Authors' interview with O. P. Reed, July 15, 1999.

414 *"was completely..."* ILW, *My Life*, 66.

414 *"I wouldn't have..."* Authors' interviews with ILW, February 13 and 19, 2000.

415 *And often...* James Auer and Claudia Looz, interview with Kay Rattenbury, 1992.

415 *"It was like* Jules and Jim ..." Nancy Snyder, interview with Ben Masselink, April 5, 1992.

415 *One of the new crop...* Authors' interview with Jim de Long, January 11, 2001.

415 *The Jeep swerved...* Kay Rattenbury claimed that Daniel, who was sitting in Brandoch's lap, started to climb out and Svetlana reached out suddenly to keep him from slipping out of the jeep. James Auer and Claudia Looz interview with Kay Rattenbury, 1992.

415 *"Won't you please..."* Interview with Mrs. Glenn Richardson, wife of the station owner, August 16, 1990.

415 *Driving madly...* Authors' interview with O. P. Reed, July 15, 1999.

415 *"It can't be that bad..."* Secrest, *Frank Lloyd Wright*, 1993, 519.

417 *As Johnny Hill...* John Hill to his parents, 1946.

417 *The father, she confided...* Celeste Davison, Kay's daughter, was told this by her mother. Authors' interview with Celeste Davison, May 7, 2000. Peters's second wife, Svetlana Alliluyeva, reports that Peters told her of the pregnancy, but never mentioned the idea that Masselink was the father. Martha Schad, *Stalins Tochter* (Lübbe, 2004, 302).

417 *"The weeks move..."* Gene Masselink to "Jim," October 16, 1946.

417 *"She never knew..."* Gene Masselink to Vladimir Hinzenberg, October 19, 1946.

417 *Each morning...* Authors' interview with ILW, July 24, 2000.

417 *"He was the only..."* Notes from a dinner with Don and Virginia Lovness, April 12, 1982, FLW Archives.

417 *"She must always..."* OLW to Gene Masselink, December 2, 1946, Plaza Hotel, New York.

417 *She stopped wearing...* James Auer and Claudia Looz, interview with Kay Rattenbury, 1992.

417 *And when Mansinh...* Authors' phone interview with John Geiger, November 6, 2000.

417 *"Your wife says..."* Authors' interviews with ILW, July 24 and August 16, 2000.

CHAPTER 18: A USONIAN IN PARIS

418 *With his wife gone...* Ed Wolpert, interview with Brandoch Peters, January 14, 1992.

418 *"I am so glad..."* OLW to Wes Peters, November 23, 1946.

418 *Svetlana's mother...* Curtis Besinger to John Geiger, July 16, 1992; Secrest, *Frank Lloyd Wright*, 1993, 519.

418 *"I grow numb..."* OLW to Gene Masselink, March 6, 1947.

418 *"something disrespectful..."* ILW, *My Life*, 127.

419 *Roland Rebay...* FLW to Solomon Guggenheim, July 1, 1949, Pfeiffer, ed., *Guggenheim Correspondence*, 1986, 125.

419 *"There is no conscience..."* ILW, *My Life*, 172–73, 302.

419 *"You rat..."* Authors' interview with a former apprentice who has requested anonymity.

420 *On that day...* Quit Claim deed, September 3, 1947, Kathryn Smith papers.

421 *"[F]ind a form..."* Hendrik Wijdeveld to FLW, October 13, 1947.

421 *"You are one..."* FLW to Hendrik Wijdeveld, October 21, 1947.

421 *"I did a lot..."* ILW, *My Life*, 132–33.

422 *They were Gurdjieff's...* Authors' phone interview with Dushka Howarth, April 6, 2005; James Auer and Claudia Looz, interview with Kay Rattenbury, 1992; Patterson, *Struggle of the Magicians*, 1996, 215; Taylor, *Shadows of Heaven*, 1998, 172.

422 *"very evident"* Secrest, *Frank Lloyd Wright*, 1993, 510–11.

422 *"Were I to judge..."* OLW to Vlado and Sophie Lazovich, May 28, 1948.

422 *"if I felt..."* *Time*, February 9, 1948.

423 *Like his fictional...* Taylor, *Gurdjieff in America*, 2004; Jessmin and Dushka Howarth, *It's Up to Ourselves: A Mother, A Daughter, G. I. Gurdjieff, and Others*, unpublished manuscript, 1998.

423 *"My words will..."* authors' interview with Dushka Howarth, December 29, 2003.

423 *"into another dimension..."* OLW to Carol Robinson, September 7, 1948.

424 *"104 sons..."* *Capital Times*, September 9, 1934, cited in Taylor's *Gurdjieff in America*, 2004, 199. FLW's unpublished eulogy for Gurdjieff, 1949, Marlin papers.

424 *"really been initiated..."* Whitall N. Perry, *Gurdjieff: In Light of Tradition* (Pates Manor: Perennial Books, 1978), 76.

424 *"But Frank..."* authors' interview with ILW, February 13, 2000.

424 *In August 1948...* Bennett, *Witness*, 1997, 196–97.

424 *Four months later...* One of the six was Tania Savitsky, the newly married granddaughter of Madame Ouspensky, whose husband, Gurdjieff's early errant and most popular protégé, had recently passed on. Savitsky had just married Tom Forman, a British émigré who was the estate manager at Ouspensky's farm: Jessmin and Dushka Howarth, "It's Up to Ourselves," unpublished, 1998. Authors' phone interview with Dushka Howarth, November 27,

2001. See also Gurdjieff's recruitment of Nicholas de Stjernvall as his houseboy and of another son, Michel de Salzmann. Du Val, *Daddy Gurdjieff*, 1997.

424 *"This is your father"* Jessmin and Dushka Howarth, "It's Up to Ourselves," unpublished, 1998; Taylor, *Shadows of Heaven*, 1998, 133–134.

424 *"How could you..."* Authors' phone interview with Dushka Howarth, April 26 and November 27, 2001.

424 *And Gurdjieff claimed...* Authors' interview with Dushka Howarth, December 29, 2003.

425 *Olgivanna's reaction to Eve...* Svetlana Hinzenberg's paternity remains in question. In her unpublished autobiography, Olgivanna maintained that her daughter's father was Valdemar Hinzenberg, and that she was born before she met Gurdjieff in Tiflis in 1919. Available legal records put Hinzenberg and Olgivanna's wedding on January 31, 1917, and the baby's birth on September 27, 1917, exactly nine months later.

In that chaotic moment of revolution, however, it would have been easy to falsify Svetlana's birthdate to legitimize her paternity. Olgivanna's autobiography strangely omits the child's birth, noting only that Olgivanna was nineteen at the time. But in what year was Olgivanna nineteen? As noted above, Olgivanna's birth year has been variously cited as 1898, 1897, and 1896 (as per her Social Security records). The latter date would make her two years older—and, if indeed she was nineteen when she gave birth—would mean that her baby was conceived before she met both Hinzenberg and even Gurdjieff.

In her autobiography, Olgivanna says that Svetlana was three when she first met Gurdjieff in 1919. It's hard to imagine a mother forgetting her first daughter's age at this critical moment. This would put Svetlana's birth not in Tiflis in 1917, but in Moscow in mid-1916, and suggest that Olgivanna was either pregnant or already had a child when she married Hinzenberg.

One possibility is that Svetlana's birthdate was falsified to conceal a premarital pregnancy with Hinzenberg (Secrest, *Frank Lloyd Wright*, 1993, 307). Olgivanna herself claimed that when Hinzenberg was courting her in Moscow she was not in love with him, rarely saw him, and cried through the wedding: OLW, *An Autobiography*, and Allan Roth, interview with Kay Rattenbury, October 5, 1994.

Hinzenberg showed little or no paternal feeling during the child's earliest years. He was absent during his wife's entire pregnancy, and apparently willing to let his toddler follow his wife into a cultish community. Only when Olgivanna sent the child away, and then again when filing for divorce, did he attempt to claim custody—strangely, without success. Hinzenberg did hire an attorney when he thought the child's welfare was being endangered by his ex-wife's relationship with Wright. But Olgivanna did not seek him out when Svetlana died.

Many of Olgivanna's Gurdjieff contemporaries—those who knew either Gurdjieff in Russia or Olgivanna in Tiflis or Paris—were certain that Svetlana was Gurdjieff's child. Among them are Dr. Leonid Stjernvall; his son, Nikolai Stjernvall, the product of his wife's sexual union with Gurdjieff; Natalie de Salzmann, Jeanne and Alexandre's de Salzmann's daughter; Lonia Savitsky and Jessmin Howarth, whose daughter Dushka was likewise Gurdjieff's daughter. Authors' interviews with Dushka Howarth, April 26, 2001, and Paul Taylor, January 3, 2001.

Is it possible? Perhaps. Olgivanna spent the years 1915 and 1916 in Moscow, returning to the Caucasus in 1917 after the revolution. In 1916, Olgivanna was an eighteen-year-old drama student in Moscow; Gurdjieff took up residence in Moscow the same year, and began recruiting a network of followers (Moore, *Gurdjieff*, 1999, 324–25; Elizabeta de Sternvall, *Across the Caucuses* [sic] *with G.I. Gurdjieff*, unpublished, translated by Paul Taylor, 1997). Olgivanna could have met Gurdjieff in Moscow in 1916, not in Tiflis in 1919. Some of those who believe that Gurdjieff was Svetlana's father were, in fact, in Moscow with Gurdjieff at this time. However, no evidence yet confirms that Olgivanna and Gurdjieff actually met before Svetlana's birth.

425 *"Mr. Gurdjieff . . ."* ILW, *My Life*, 141.

425 *They spoke in Russian* . . . James Auer and Claudia Looz, interview with Kay Rattenbury, 1992.

425 *"Tell, Mr. Director* . . . William J. Welch, *What Happened in Between: A Doctor's Story* (New York: George Braziller, 1972), 122–23.

425 *"In that case . . ."* ILW, *My Life*, 145.

425 *More than a decade* . . . Allan Roth, interview with Kay Rattenbury, October 5, 1994.

425 *"I, seven times . . ."* Moore, *Gurdjieff*, 1999, 307; Welch, *What Happened in Between*, 1972, 127.

426 *"No, has to be . . . "* Authors' interview with Dushka Howarth, December 30, 2003; Beth McCorkle, *The Gurdjieff Years 1929–1949: Recollections of Louise March* (New York, The Work Study Association), 1990, 87.

426 *Gurdjieff's place* . . . The requests for groups were documented in Du Val, *Daddy Gurdjieff*, 1997. Many visitors came to Gurdjieff to be cured, paying him handsomely. During Iovanna's time there, he claimed to have cured a paralytic Russian, for which he was paid 50,000 French francs. Bennett, *Witness*, 1997, 217.

426 *Whatever their paternity* . . . Authors' interview with Paul Taylor, March 11, 2001. When Iovanna later give birth to a daughter, she would name her Eve—the very name Gurdjieff had chosen for one of his illegitimate daughters, Eve Taylor, in tribute to a woman named Evdokia, one of the great loves of his life. Evdokia is also the name of a figure in an epic ballad from the eastern border of Byzantium. In the ballad, Evdokia's husband, Basil, half-Greek, half-Arab, is the courageous son of an Arab emir, a border warrior who carried off the daughter of a Greek general, then converted to Christianity. Basil himself falls in love with Evdokia, carrying her off, defeating her brothers who pursue him without harming them. Basil and Evdokia rule their common lands together. Gurdjieff, half-Greek, half-Armenian who hovered on the borderlands himself, would have easily identified.

426 *"Was like a . . ."* Madame de Salzmann to OLW, May 10, 1949; authors' phone interview with Dushka Howarth, April 26, 2001.

427 *"I had a . . ."* ILW, *My Life*, 148, 158.

427 *"She took it . . ."* authors' phone interview with Eve Chavalier, née Taylor, February 3, 2004.

427 *"subjectively hopeless . . ."* Bennett, *Witness*, 1997, 200.

427 *"I think that as well . . ."* ILW, *My Life*, 152.

427 *With Jeanne de Salzmann improvising . . .* Wim van Dulleman, "The History of Gurdjieff Movements," 2002, http://www.gurdjieff-movements.net/sub_newsletter/gurdjieffmovements_history.pdf.

427 *"You like to sing, . . ."* Authors' phone interview with Dushka Howarth, April 26, 2001; Taylor, *Shadows of Heaven*, 1998, 175.

428 *"STOP!" Gurdjieff yelled . . .* ILW, *My Life*, 149.

428 *She sent liqueur-filled . . .* ILW, "Eugene Masselink: The Artist with Reverence for Life," eulogy for November 30, 1962, Marlin papers.

CHAPTER 19: THE SEX CLUBS

429 *"Members of the Fellowship . . ."* Pfeiffer, ed., *Letters to Apprentices*, 1982, 63–64.

429 *. . . locals used to hide . . .* Authors' interview with Eloise Fritz, December 15, 1999.

431 *. . . she considered it an expression . . .* "[Y]ou can express it like insects meeting casually in the night," she told apprentice Kamal Amin, "thus squandering this valuable energy. Or you can behave like a man. For this you need to be working toward being a complete person within. That means intense work on yourself. In terms of life here at Taliesin, it means long hours of consistent hard work free from resistance." Amin, *Reflections from the Shining Brow*, 2004, 42.

431 *And she took an intense . . .* Authors' phone interview with Kamal Amin, June 26, 2004.

431 *"every position . . ."* Dushka Howarth, letter to Jessmin Howarth based on Dushka's personal interview with OLW, 1953; authors' phone interview with Dushka Howarth, March 22, 2004.

431 *Many an apprentice . . .* Svetlana Alliluyeva, *The Faraway Music*, unpublished draft, 1983–1986, 94.

431 *And not just any orgasm . . .* Taylor, *Gurdjieff in America*, 2004, 171.

431 *"seek each other out . . ."* Authors' interview with Louis Wiehle, July 23, 1999.

431 *Even Gurdjieff had taught . . .* Gurdjieff, *Beelzebub's Tales to His Grandson*, 1964, 382–83.

431 *She had the selected apprentices . . .* Authors' interview with James de Long, October 20, 2000.

431 *Olgivanna was comfortable . . .* Authors' interview with Kamal Amin, May 29, 2004.

432 *. . . Howe became so forward . . .* Authors' interview with Eloise Fritz, December 15, 1999. In the late 1930s, Fritz said, Howe's reputation was such that her husband Herbert was the only one who would. "He's one of this guys that just can go through the den of them, and come out pure as a lily white. Some people are just protected that way."

432 *Howe was especially . . .* Authors' interview with O. P. Reed, July 15, 1999; authors' interview with Victor Cusack, July 3, 2002.

433 *"Pansy Patch . . ."* Authors' conversation with Bruce Pfeiffer, October 30, 2000.

433 *"I always enjoy . . ."* FLW to Philip Johnson, telegram, September 25, 1946.

434 *"I fell in love . . ."* Authors' interview with Philip Johnson, May 3, 2000.

434 *"I had them all"* Authors' interview with a source who has requested anonymity.

434 *"help keep the boys . . ."* Jane Sheain to the authors, June 1, 2004.

434 *"We were in . . ."* Authors' interview with James and Barbara Dresser, June 4, 2000.

435 *"Jack grew very . . ."* Indira Berndtson, interview with Don Erickson, March 23, 1994.

435 *"a love colony"* Dombar, *Abrom Dombar*, 1995.

435 *"happened to know . . ."* Authors' interview with Lois Davidson Gottlieb, April 5, 2002.

435 *"The rumor . . ."* Authors' interview with Eric Lloyd Wright, July 15, 1999.

435 *"Now is the time . . ."* Indira Berndtson, interview with Don Erickson, February 23, 1994.

436 *"We've got this . . ."* Authors' interview with Lois Davidson Gottlieb, April 5, 2002.

436 *His eyes swelling . . .* Authors' interview with William Patrick, May 7, 2000.

436 *More than one writer . . .* Gill, *Many Masks*, 1987, 63l; Shand-Tucci, *Boston Bohemia*, 1995, 279.

436 *"I always loved . . ."* FLW, *An Autobiography*, 1932, 262.

436 *In the 1930s . . .* Besinger, *Working with Mr. Wright*, 1997, 49.

436 *Sullivan felt that his own . . .* Sullivan was influenced by the eighteenth-century Swedish mystic Emanuel Swedenborg's idea that the universe was composed of two transcendent principles, the rational masculine and the emotional feminine. Menocal, *Architecture as Nature*, 1981, 24–36.

437 *. . . overlay masculine geometries . . .* "Wright, *My Father Who Is on Earth*, 1994, 29; FLW to Lewis Mumford, July 7, 1930, Pfeiffer and Wojtowicz, *Frank Lloyd Wright + Lewis Mumford: Thirty Years of Correspondence*, 2001, 91.

437 *"It is better to die..."* FLW, *An Autobiography*, 1932, 359.

437 *Despite his wife's protests...* William Patrick to the authors, e-mail, March 6, 2005.

437 *"You are trying..."* Authors' interview with Lois Davidson Gottlieb, April 5, 2002.

438 *But those who had revealed...* William Patrick to the authors, e-mail, March 10, 2005.

438 *A number of the new recruits...* Besinger, *Working with Mr. Wright*, 1997, 199.

438 *... stomped out...* Authors' interviews with Eric Lloyd Wright, July 16, 1999, and James Dresser, June 4, 2000.

438 *"should be shamed..."* OLW, *Our House*, 1959, 117.

438 *Mrs. Wright even resolved...* William Patrick to the authors, e-mail, March 10, 2005.

438 *It was time...* Authors' interview with Eric Lloyd Wright, July 16, 1999.

438 *"Ok,"* Wright had replied... FLW to Douglas MacAgy, ca. February, 1949.

438 *"I think I'll bring it up...* Frank Lloyd Wright and Margaret Sanger talk to the Fellowship," March 9, 1952.

439 *"We heard that term...* Transcript of the Western Round Table on Modern Art, San Francisco Art Association, April 8. 1949, San Francisco, California, Huntington Library, Pasadena, California.

439 *"But no man..."* Wright also used the concept of "refreshment" when speaking about "painter architects" like Michelangelo, whom he supposedly despised. "We are refreshed," he told his apprentices, "not from the realm of builders, experienced builders, but we are refreshed from the realm of the painter, well, the aesthete in many lines." In Wright's view, aestheticism, a painterly approach to architecture that values appearances above all, robbed architecture of its depth, its capacity to operate in the third dimension. FLW, "The words Functional and Functionalism. Architectural degeneracy—The Esthete Affirmation." Sunday morning talk, July 18, 1953.

440 *"strutting around..."* Tafel, *About Wright*, 1993, 107, 109.

440 *... Wright had felt compelled...* William Patrick to the authors, e-mail, March 6, 2005.

440 *"It is not so long..."* FLW to Cecil Corwin, November 20, 1932.

441 *Ever since Walt Whitman...* Shand-Tucci, *Boston Bohemia*, 1995. It was this "male" homosexuality that attracted the poet Federico Garcia Lorca, visiting New York in 1929. Dinitia Smith, "Garcia Lorca's Rich Summer in New York," *International Herald Tribune*, July 5, 2000.

441 *"Old Walt..."* FLW, "Books that Have Meant Most to Me," Pfeiffer, ed., *Collected Writings, Volume 3*, 1993, 63. *"it is so easy..."* Indira Berndtson interview with Nancy Willey, February 15, 1995.

441 *"tried with all his might..."* "Bruce Goff, 1904–1982," *Artists Represented*, http://www.architechgallery.com/arch_info/artists_pages/bruce_goff.html.

441 *"There but for the grace..."* Jay Pace, who worked with Bruce Goff after leaving Taliesin in 1963, was told of these interchanges by Goff. Authors' interview with Jay Pace, May 28, 2004.

442 *Spying the book...* Peter Blake, *Master Builders: Le Corbusier/Mies Van Der Rohe/Frank Lloyd Wright* (New York: W.W. Norton, 1960), 288–89.

442 *"Frahnk, Frahnk..."* Authors' phone interview with Jane Gale Sheain, February 25, 2002.

442 *"Sex,"* Olgivanna once told... John Geiger to the authors, e-mail, January 26, 2005.

442 *Men without proper consciousness...* Wellbeloved, *Gurdjieff*, 2003, 191.

442 *When he was aroused...* Bruce Brooks Pfeiffer, *Frank Lloyd Wright: The Crowning Decade* (Fresno, California: The Press at California State University, 1989), 122.

442 *She delighted...* Don Lovness recounted this "to [his] amazement." William Marlin, notes on conversation with Lovness, April 1983, Marlin papers.

442 *... her husband's sexual stamina...* Authors' interview with Jim de Long, October 20, 2000.

442 *"Geniuses are oversexed..."* Authors' interview with ILW February 19, 2000.

442–43 *"fucked his wife..."* Authors' interview with Ben Masselink, January 24, 1997.

443 *"I can do everything..."* Elizabeth Gordon to the authors, winter 1998.

443 *"Look at what..."* Authors' interview with Peter Blake, May 2, 2000; Peter Blake, *No Place Like Utopia: Modern Architecture and the Company We Kept* (New York: Norton, 1993), 57.

443 *When Wright kicked...* Authors' interview with Paolo Soleri, December 17, 1999.

445 *"You couldn't swish..."* Authors' interview with Shawn Rorke Davis, October 28, 2000.

445 *"You always have to..."* Authors' interview with Lois Davidson Gottlieb, April 5, 2002.

445 *"He made a more beautiful..."* Thomas S. Hines, "Photography, Architecture, and the Coming to Oneself: Edmund Teske and Frank Lloyd Wright," in Charles G. Salas and Michael S. Roth, *Looking for Los Angeles: Architecture, Film, Photography, and the Urban Landscape* (Los Angeles: Getty Publications, 2001), 211–246.

445 *"Here's a playmate..."* Authors' interview with Jim Charlton, February 15, 1997.

445 *... but Olgivanna concluded...* Authors' interview with Kamal Amin, May 29, 2004.

445 *... Masselink's only serious...* Authors' interviews with O. P. Reed, July 15, 1999, and Jane Gale Sheain, February 26, 2002. In Sheain's four years at Taliesin she never saw Gene with a woman.

445 *"Your letters..."* Johnny Hill to Gene Masselink, April 12, 1951.

445 *"Adonis"* Brierly, *Tales of Taliesin*, 1999, 115.

446 *When Richard Carney...* Maggie Valentine, interview with John Hill, July 30, 1995.

446 *The one notable exception...* "Do you think that his relationship with Lu was in part a response to your grandmother's demands?" we asked Eric Lloyd Wright. "Oh yah," he replied. Authors' interview, July 15, 1999.

446 *Soon after his trial...* Authors' interview with Eloise Fritz, December 15, 1999, and Eric Lloyd Wright, July 16, 1999.

446 Her *"demeaning" interview...* Lu Howe to the authors: June 24 and August 22, 2005.

446 *... an adaptation...* Authors' interview with James de Long, October 20, 2000.

446 *... and most apprentices lasted...* Jay Pace, who has maintained a database of every apprentice who ever worked at Taliesin, concluded that most apprentices stayed for one year. Authors' interview with Jay Pace, May 28, 2004.

446–47 *"Mrs. Wright had..."* Nancy Snyder, interview with Ben Masselink, April 5, 1992.

447 *... he found her sitting...* Authors' interview with Pedro Guerrero, October 29, 2000.

447 *"We all wanted to fuck her..."* Authors' interview with Ben Masselink, April 5, 1999.

447 *Pfeiffer's wealthy father...* Authors' interview with Edgar Tafel, September, 2000; authors' phone interview with Jane Gale Sheain, April 25, 2004.

447 *"She was the first person..."* Authors' interview with Louis Wiehle, July 23, 1999.

447 *"Bruce, why don't you cut..."* Authors' conversation with Bruce Pfeiffer, December 17, 1999.

447 *"a little bit of conversion"* Authors' interview with Louis Wiehle, July 23, 1999.

CHAPTER 20: A NEW CALF AT TALIESIN

448 *"astonishing progress..."* Madame de Salzmann to OLW, May 10, 1949.

448 *On occasion...* De Val, *Daddy Gurdjieff*, 1997; Gurdjieff, *Luba Gurdjieff*, 1993, 30.

448 *... like a dog...* Authors' phone interview with Dushka Howarth, April 26, 2001.

449 *"Tell him that such place..."* Bennett, *Eyewitness*, 1997, 215.

449 *... was pleased to learn...* Madame de Salzmann to OLW, May 10, 1949; Bennett, *Eyewitness*, 1997, 208.

451 *"For years, I have waited..."* FLW to Hilla Rebay, June 23, 1949, in Pfeiffer, *Frank Lloyd Wright: The Guggenheim Correspondence*, 1986, 123.

451 *"The House of..."* OLW, *Frank Lloyd Wright*, 1966, 162.

451 *Yet instead...* Lukach, *Hilla Rebay*, 1983, 205.

451 *In mid-October...* FLW to Harry Guggenheim, May 14, 1952, Pfeiffer, *The Guggenheim Correspondence*, 1986, 100, 121, 170; Lukach, *Hilla Rebay*, 1983, 205.

452 *"Occasionally one of these..."* John Geiger to Ginny Kazor, April 5, 2000.

452 *"That old, vague nausea..."* ILW, *My Life*, 164.

452 *All puffed up...* Besinger, *Working with Mr. Wright*, 1987, 201.

452 *"The movements you will learn..."* ILW, *My Life*, 165.

452 *When Gurdjieff sailed...* Authors' phone interview with Dushka Howarth, April 27, 2001.

452 *One of the stops...* Moore, *Gurdjieff*, 1999, 300. On September 9, 1948, Gurdjieff announced that he wanted to prepare eighteen people—three rows of six—for a demonstration of his latest movements in New York. According to correspondence in the Taliesin files, Olgivanna

possessed a letter of April 11, 1946, from Madame de Salzmann to a Mr. Whitcomb, indicating that Gurdjieff had planned to come to New York in 1946 with four people, and requesting affidavits that he would be financially supported while in the United States. The existence of this letter in her files suggests that she not only knew about Gurdjieff's plans to come to America, but also may have helped try to secure his passage.

452 *"We know all about . . ."* OLW to Madame Ouspensky, telegram, October 11, 1950, and OLW to Mrs. De Hartmann, June 1, 1953; Patterson, *Struggle of the Magicians*, 1996, 181; Olga de Hartmann to OLW, October 7, 1949.

453 *"Very, very bad pain"* Solito Solano, undated, addressed "For Everyone," www.gurdjieff-bibliography.com.

453 *"Bravo America"* Jeanne de Salzmann to OLW, November 18, 1949; Moore, *Gurdjieff*, 1999, 314.

453 *"Mr. Gurdjieff is dead."* ILW, *My Life*, 166.

453 *"looked lovely . . ."* John Geiger to the authors, e-mail, November 11, 2002.

453 *"Real men . . ."* FLW, unpublished eulogy, Marlin papers.

454 *"He looked as handsome . . ."* Patterson, *Struggle of the Magicians*, 1996, 225.

454 *"God and all his angels . . ."* Olja de Hartmann to OLW, early November 1949; De Hartmann, *Our Life with Mr. Gurdjieff*, 1964, 134.

454 *"alone without him . . ."* Olja de Hartmann to OLW: 1949 and October 7, 1949; Thomas de Hartmann to OLW, October 1949; Nott, *Teachings of Gurdjieff*, 1961, 120.

454 *His will was silent . . .* Davis, *The Guggenheims*, 1978, 204; Pfeiffer, *The Guggenheim Correspondence*, 1986, 102–3, 127.

455 *"So may I suggest . . ."* FLW to Hilla Rebay, October 24, 1949, in Pfeiffer, *Frank Lloyd Wright: The Guggenheim Correspondence*, 1986, 124.

455 *"No carping . . ."* Lukach, *Hilla Rebay*, 1983, 132–35, 206.

455 *In an unprecedented gesture . . .* Wright did not follow through because he spent all the money refurbishing Taliesin West—giving the "buildings here and there in Arizona some semblance of prestige and thrift," as he put it. FLW to Wes Peters, November 15, 1949, William Marlin papers.

455 *"I want to look that . . ."* FLW to Wes Peters, November 15, 1949, Marlin papers.

456 *"Every G-damn effort . . ."* FLW to Wes Peters, August 7, 1948, Marlin papers.

456 *According to Peters's son . . .* Authors' phone interview with Brandoch Peters, May 30, 2000.

456 *"My dear dear Olga . . ."* Jeanne de Salzmann to OLW, November 18, 1949, translated from the Russian.

456–57 *"All over the world . . ."* Peter Brook, *Threads of Time* (Washington, DC: Counterpoint, 1998), 109.

457 *"I am so happy . . ."* Jeanne de Salzmann to OLW: November 18, 1949, and January 3, 1950, translated from the Russian.

457 *Olgivanna was elated . . .* Olja de Hartmann to OLW, 1949.

457 *Wright even paid . . .* Thomas de Hartmann to OLW, October 1949.

457 *With her was Lise . . .* Jeanne de Salzmann to OLW, November 18, 1949, and December 16, 1949, translated from the Russian..

457 *Still others . . .* Authors' interview with John Geiger, February 19, 2000; Besinger, *Working with Mr. Wright*, 1997, 213–14.

457 *. . . an angry apprentice . . .* Authors' phone interview with John Geiger, February 20, 2002.

457 *"Tell your husband . . ."* "Everything seems awful, senseless, not human. He has a treasure as well as his creation as the life of the Fellowship. If he does not keep it as an organism the spirit will disappear!" Jeanne de Salzmann to OLW, Monday night, undated.

457 *"Olga we must . . ."* Jeanne de Salzmann to OLW, March 25, 1950.

457 *Determined to prevent . . .* Jessmin Howarth, "Remember Inner Work," *Gurdjieff International Review*, www.gurdjieff.org/howarth1.htm; Dushka Howarth, "It's Up to Ourselves," unpublished, Chapter 23.

458 *He forbade his wife . . .* Authors' interview with ILW, February 13, 2000.

458 *"I wish I could be near . . ."* Jeanne de Salzmann to OLW, June 1, 1950.

458 *"You have a sexuality . . ."* ILW, *My Life*, 169.

458 *But Iovanna was repulsed . . .* ILW, *My Life*, 169.

458 *"just another phase . . ."* FLW, Sunday morning talk to the apprentices, October 29, 1950.

459 *When she instituted* . . . Authors' phone interview with Kamal Amin, June 26, 2004.

459 *. . . she also had reason* . . . This is the understanding of David Dodge, an apprentice in 1951, and still a member of the Fellowship as of 2005. Authors' interview with David Dodge, October 27, 2000.

459 *"This is our day . . ."* FLW, Sunday morning talk to the apprentices, October 29, 1950.

459–60 *. . . twenty-two new arrivals* . . . John Geiger helped identify those who joined for the Gurdjieff program.

460 *"completed enneagram"* Thomas de Hartmann to OLW, Friday, Easter Week, no date. Unlike Iovanna, Curtis Besinger places this performance on Easter 1950: *Working with Mr. Wright*, 1987, 214.

460 *"I've never seen . . ."* ILW, *My Life*, 174.

460 *They started holding* . . . Besinger, *Working with Mr. Wright*, 1987, 219.

460 *In August 1951* . . . FLW, "Dedication of the First Unitarian Society Church," Madison, Wisconsin, August 28, 1951.

461 *"to detect and watch . . ."* Ralph Waldo Emerson, "Self-Reliance," 138–64, in Carl Bode, ed., *The Portable Emerson* (New York: Penguin, 1981), 139.

461 *"my daughter and . . ."* FLW, "Bill Doudna's Spotlight," *The Capital Times*, November 3, 1951, Section 2, 3.

461 *"exercises that even he was doing . . ."* Authors' interview with ILW, February 19, 2000.

461 *"thinking of Taliesin . . ."* Authors' interview with Rupert Pole, February 25, 2000.

461 *"For the first time . . ."* ILW, *My Life*, 175.

461 *"The young people . . ."* Olja de Hartmann to OLW, undated.

461 *"Do whatever you want . . ."* Thomas de Hartmann to OLW, 1953.

462 *. . . providing Olgivanna and Iovanna* . . . Olja and Thomas de Hartmann to OLW, undated and October 1949; ILW, *My Life*, unpublished, 173.

462 *"I think you amazingly . . ."* Elizabeta Stjernvall to OLW, April 30, 1954.

462 *Gurdjieff's chosen successor* . . . Wim van Dulleman, "The History of Gurdjieff Movements," 2002, http://www.gurdjieff-movements .net/sub_newsletter/gurdjieffmovements_history .pdf.

462 *"I wish to stay . . ."* Madame de Salzmann to OLW, March 25, 1950.

462 *Not as knowledgeable* . . . Authors' phone interview with Dushka Howarth, July 3, 2004.

462 *For now De Salzmann* . . . Madame de Salzmann to OLW, February 1951; Indira Berndtson to the authors, e-mail, March 20, 2005; Susan Thompson to Dushka Howarth, e-mail, April 8, 2005; Madame de Salzmann to FLW, March 31, 1951.

462 *"before they will . . ."* Jeanne de Salzmann to OLW, February 1951.

462 *"You know she . . ."* Jeanne de Salzmann to FLW, March 31, 1951.

462 *At the very least* . . . Jeanne de Salzmann to OLW, April 26, 1950.

463 *"Dante wanted . . ."* *Time*, April 14, 1952.

463 *"have just started . . ."* Kamal Amin to the authors, e-mail, February 23, 2005.

463 *She told more than a few* . . . Authors' interview with Celeste Davison, May 7, 2000.

463 *"To his followers . . ."* *Time*, July 1, 1946.

463 *"first mighty Craftsman . . ."* Louis H. Sullivan, *The Autobiography of An Idea* (London: Dover, 1956), 234–5.

463 *"I never could see . . ."* FLW, Talk to the Fellowship, Tape No. 93; "The Guggenheim Museum: Wright Has the Last Word," *Frank Lloyd Wright Quarterly*, Summer 1992, Vol. 3, No. 3. 8.

464 *During their stay* . . . Authors' interview with Eloise Fritz, December 15, 1999.

464 *Though her mother was wary* . . . Authors' phone interviews with Dushka Howarth: April 26, 2001, and February 13, 2002.

464 *. . . Iovanna now demanded* . . . Besinger, *Working with Mr. Wright*, 1987, 245.

464 *"I lose the heaviest . . ."* FLW to ILW, undated, Marlin papers.

465 *"at the insistence . . ."* Curtis Besinger to John Geiger, December 28, 1991.

465 *"They just have to freeze . . ."* Authors' interview with David Dodge, October 27, 2000.

465 *"still a child . . ."* Jeanne de Salzmann to OLW, September 28, 1952.

465 *"I was pairing off . . ."* ILW, *My Life*, 172; authors' interview with David Dodge, October 27, 2000.

465 *"You are not . . ."* Authors' phone interview with John Geiger, February 22, 2002.

466 *When Iovanna went to launch* . . . Besinger, *Working with Mr. Wright*, 1987, 245.

466 *She gave her students . . .* Indira Berndtson, phone interview with Anna Durco, July 13, 1998.

466 *Sometimes Iovanna slipped out . . .* William Marlin notes, citing a letter from ILW to Mr. Ludwig, March 3, 1953, Marlin papers.

466 *Wright eventually relented . . .* Authors' phone interview with Jane Gale Sheain, February 26, 2002.

466 *She expected the wealthy . . .* Amin, *Reflections from the Shining Brow*, 2004, 109.

466 *As they wound their way . . .* Indira Berndtson, phone interviews with Anna Durco, July 13, 1998, and with Jane Gale Sheain, July 15, 1998.

466 *Many were friendless . . .* Indira Berndtson, phone interview with Jane Gale Sheain, July 15, 1998.

466 *Almost fifty years . . .* Authors' interview with Lois Barnes, May 8, 2000.

466 *. . . Gurdjieff's "awakening" process . . .* Fritz, "At Taliesin," in Henning, ed., *"At Taliesin,"* 1992, 135.

467 *"Oh, that mask . . ."* Indira Berndtson, phone interview with Anna Durco, July 13, 1998.

467 *Kay Davison would inform . . .* Authors' phone interview with Jane Sheain, May 23, 2004.

467 *"would be just burning . . ."* Indira Berndtson, interview with Mary Stanton, December 21, 1993.

468 *"one infinite mind . . ."* United Church of Religious Science Web page (www.religiousscience.org/ucrs_site/philosophy/spiritual.html).

468 *The apprentices were put to work . . .* Besinger, *Working with Mr. Wright*, 1987, 251.

469 *. . . incorporating Gurdjieff's law . . .* Authors' interview with O. P. Reed, July 15, 1999.

469 *Solomon Guggenheim's estate . . .* John H. Davis, *The Guggenheims: An American Epic* (New York: William Morrow and Co., 1978), 225.

469 *. . . the entire city block . . .* Besinger, *Working with Mr. Wright*, 1987, 228, 234–35.

469 *"He had the emotions . . ."* Authors' interviews with ILW: February 13 and 19, 2000.

470 *"I don't want to leave . . ."* ILW, *My Life*, 177–78.

471 *she had been chronically depressed . . .* Menocal, *Falingwater and Pittsburgh*, 2004, 104.

471 *"Your mother needs . . ."* Gray, "Modern Gothic," *Men's Fashions of the Times*, September 23, 2001.

CHAPTER 21: LAWS OF BEAUTY

475 *"entire career . . ."* ILW, *My Life*, 220.

475 *"Niemeyer knows no more . . ."* FLW, Talk to the Apprentices, August 31, 1958.

475 *After discovering . . .* Levine, *The Architecture of Frank Lloyd Wright*, 1996, 341.

476 *"in the interest . . ."* FLW to the Trustees of the Solomon R. Guggenheim Gallery, December 15, 1952, in Pfeiffer, ed., *Frank Lloyd Wright: The Guggenheim Correspondence*, 1986, 177–78.

476 *With America's red scare . . .* FLW FBI File, Volumes I and II. In 1944, for instance, an FBI report on the League of American Writers' drive to create a cabinet Department of Arts and Letters notes that Wright, "who has no sympathies for Communism," caused a furor at a leadership meeting when he stated that the only way to get such a thing done was to get Roosevelt out of the Oval Office. "League of American Writers," Los Angeles, July 4, 1944.

476 *"Which is most dangerous . . ."* FLW, "Force Is a Heresy," *Wisconsin Athenaean*, September 1951, 43–44, in Pfeiffer, ed., *Collected Writings*, Volume 5, 1949–1959 (New York: Rizzoli, 1995).

477 *In the 1940s . . .* "Artkino Pictures, Inc." "Internal Security Registration Act," October 23, 1945. "It was the custom at Artkino to ship a film to Taliesin Hall when it was not in demand and not booked by anyone else." Wright FBI file. Maggie Valentine, interview with John Lautner, Oral History Program, UCLA, Frank Lloyd Wright Archives.

477 *As early as 1948 . . . Unamerican Activities in California, 1948, 1949, Communist Front Organizations*, Sacramento, 1948 and 1949; "Notables Ask Parole for Hollywood 8," *Daily Worker*, December 22, 1950; "Rally Tomorrow for Russian War Aid," *Sunday Worker*, October 26, 1941, all in Wright FBI file.

477 *The draft contretemps . . .* SAC, Milwaukee, December 17, 1942; see also D. J. Sullivan to Mr. Belmont, memo, June 27, 1954, Wright FBI file.

477 *"if you raise . . ."* FLW, "Civilization Without Culture," Talk to the Apprentices, February 25, 1951.

477 *In January 1953 . . .* "Emergency Civil Liberties Committee," Internal Security, 4/15/53. Wright FBI file.

477 *"Romanticism in architecture . . ."* FLW, "Architecture as Mother Art," Talk to the Fellowship, January 4, 1953.

479 *Though the magazine . . .* Authors' phone interview with former *House Beautiful* writer Marva Shearer, November 16, 2001.

479 *It was also the first . . .* Diane Maddex, *Frank Lloyd Wright's House Beautiful* (New York: Hearst Books, 2000), 22–23.

480 *"I have decided . . ."* Elizabeth Gordon, "The Threat to the Next America," *House Beautiful*, April 1953, 126–30, 250–51.

481 *"Grandmother, what big . . ."* George Howe to Elizabeth Gordon, March 27, 1953, Frank Lloyd Wright Archives.

481 *"You know . . ."* Authors' phone interview with Elizabeth Gordon, winter 1998.

481 *Both Johnson and his fellow . . .* Authors' interviews with Philip Johnson, May 3, 2000, and Peter Blake, May 2, 2000.

481 *They were especially appalled . . .* Elizabeth Gordon to FLW, July 9, 1953.

481 *"We thought she was . . ."* Authors' interview with Philip Johnson, May 3, 2000.

481 *"Surprised and delighted . . ."* FLW to Elizabeth Gordon, telegram, March 24, 1953; Jane Margolies, interview with John Hill, March 26, 1992; Gordon, "The Threat to the Next America," 1953, 251.

482 *"been describing the play . . ."* FLW to Elizabeth Gordon, March 25, 1953.

482 *"was a streetcar . . ."* Elizabeth Gordon to the authors, winter 1998.

482 *"If we are to succeed . . ."* FLW, "Preface," May 9, 1953.

482 *"I have a feeling . . ."* Maggie Valentine, interview with John Hill, June 5, 1995, UCLA Oral History Program; Marston Fitch to the authors, e-mail, June 30, 1997.

482 *"I have something . . ."* authors' phone interview with Marva Shearer, November 16, 2001.

483 *On December 8, 1953 . . .* FLW to Harry Guggenheim, telegram, December 8, 1953, Pfeiffer, *Guggenheim Correspondence*, 1986, 191.

483 *But when the plan checkers . . .* Indira Berndtson and Greg Williams, interview with Wes Peters, December 29, 1989; Jordy, *The Im-*pact of European modernism in Mid-Twentieth Century, 1972, 328–29; Levine, *The Architecture of Frank Lloyd Wright*, 1996, 341–42.

483 *The idea satisfied . . .* John Geiger, who has studied and catalogued drawings produced at Taliesin between 1932 and 1959—with an emphasis on determining which apprentice drew them—examined the plan, section, and details of the dome produced between 1955 and 1956. See Figure 330 and 331 in Levine, *The Architecture of Frank Lloyd Wright*, 1996, 344. "I do see Wes's hand," Geiger concluded. "The extension, the supporting ribs to form the skylight ribs could well be Wes and Mendel. . . . The geometry of the skylight with the lunette seems to be to be 100% Wes. The dropped center panel has some precedent in Midway Gardens. But the pattern looks like Peters." John Geiger to the authors, e-mail, April 25, 2002.

484 *Wright's input . . .* Louise Wiehle Oral History, UCLA Oral History Program, 1996, 125.

484 *He was also a homosexual . . .* Simon Callow, *Charles Laughton: A Difficult Actor* (New York: Grove Press, 1987), 5, 27, 278–79.

484 *Though rarely comfortable . . .* Callow, *Charles Laughton*, 1987, 232.

484 *"Frank," he said . . .* Indira Berndtson, interview with Wes Peters, September 24, 1989.

484 *"He read it like . . ."* "Frank Lloyd Wright and Hollywood," *Frank Lloyd Wright Quarterly*, Winter 1993, Vol. 4, No. 1, pp. 5–13, p. 9.

485 *While the apprentices slept . . .* Authors' interview with Jay Pace, January 31, 2002; Besinger, *Working with Mr. Wright*, 1987, 247–49; authors' phone interview with Jane Gale Sheain, February 26, 2002.

485 *"This is Johnny . . ."* Maggie Valentine interview with John Hill, July 15, 1993 and June 6, 1995, UCLA Oral History Program; OLW to Elizabeth Gordon, telegram, June 9, 1953.

485 *"All in all . . ."* Elizabeth Gordon to FLW, July 9, 1953.

485 *She also took the young gay man . . .* "It was a full-fledged affair and . . . it played itself out. It didn't make any difference fortunately. I mean, we were so interested in other things that that was kind of a passion phase, yeah. But it was great fun." Maggie Valentine, interview with John Hill, June 5, 1995, UCLA Oral History Program.

485 "I trusted him . . ." Authors' phone interview with Elizabeth Gordon, 1999. Gordon's view of homosexuals as disloyal, particularly to their lovers, was confirmed by Marva Shearer, one of her contributors. Authors' phone interview, November 16, 2001.

485 "They're mean . . . Maggie Valentine interview with John Hill, June 6, 1995, UCLA Oral History Program.

486 To make matters worse . . . William Marlin, notes from a March 3, 1953, letter from an unnamed author to a member of the Chicago Gurdjieff group, Marlin papers .

486 As early as 1947 . . . Time, March 17, 1947.

486 The exhibition put apprentice . . . Besinger, Working with Mr. Wright, 1987, 250–63; authors' phone interview with John Geiger, February 20, 2002.

487 . . . Henken seemed . . . Roland Reisley, Usonia New York: Building a Community with Frank Lloyd Wright (Princeton: Princeton University Press, 2001); Leonard Wisniewski, "Wisniewski on Wright," January 24, 2004, http://www.davidalanbadger.com/DIRECTORY/wisniewski/v6-i1.html.

487 . . . she cleared the studio . . . Authors' interview with John Geiger, February 19, 2000; Besinger, Working with Mr. Wright, 1987, 250–61.

487 . . . even violating . . . John Geiger to the authors, e-mail, March 16, 2005; Maggie Valentine, interview with John Hill, June 6, 1995.

487 She instructed . . . John Geiger to the authors, e-mail, March 20, 2005.

488 "You have married . . ." Counterattack, October 30, 1953, Wright FBI file.

488 "Let your beard . . ." Pedro Guerrero to the authors, April 17, 2004. Guerrero obtained a copy of the letter from Henken.

488 . . . the substitute pianist . . . Besinger, Working with Mr. Wright, 1987, 260.

488 "flat cardboard compositions . . ." Lewis Mumford, Sketches from Life: The Autobiography of Lewis Mumford, The Early Years (New York: The Dial Press, 1982), 21, 437; Miller, Lewis Mumford, 1989, 188, 190.

489 What in heaven's name . . . Curtis Besinger to John Geiger, February 7, 1987; Besinger, Working with Mr. Wright, 1987, 260.

489 . . . a conciliatory letter . . . "He too kept living . . ." Jeanne de Salzmann and OLW: July 17 and July 21, 1953.

489 . . . Olgivanna saw it . . . Authors' phone interviews with Jane Gale Sheain, June 6, 2004, and Kamal Amin, June 26, 2004; ILW, My Life, 287; authors' interview with Charles Schiffner, January 30, 2002.

489–90 "Miss," he told . . . Authors' interview with David Dodge, October 27, 2000.

490 "In the moving . . ." Music, Ritual Exercises and Temple Dances by Georges Gurdjieff, program for the presentation by Members of the Taliesin Fellowship Under the Auspices of the Art Institute of Chicago at the Goodman Theatre, November 3, 1953, FLW Archives.

490 "You know that old saying . . ." ILW, My Life, 181.

490 "The dancing . . ." Herman Kogan, "Taliesin Dancing Grim, Stiff," Chicago Sun-Times, November 4, 1953.

490 "The reviews . . ." Authors' interview with David Dodge, October 27, 2000.

490 "The program notes . . ." Authors' phone interview with Dushka Howarth, February 13, 2002.

490 A number of Gurdjieff's . . . Authors' phone interview with Dushka Howarth, February 13, 2002. Howarth was asked by Jeanne de Salzmann to train the dancers for movies documenting the work.

491 "I am simply horrified . . ." Ethel Merston to Jessmin Howarth, 1953, personal correspondence of Dushka Howarth; authors' phone interview with Dushka Howarth, March 20, 2004.

491 Schumacher liked . . . Maggie Valentine, interview with John Hill, July 25, 1995.

491 "Now why, David . . ." FLW to David Henken, February 15, 1954, Pedro Guerrero personal files.

491 When Steinway . . . Curtis Besinger to John Geiger, November 9, 1991.

492 "He felt so . . ." Authors' interview with Philip Johnson, May 3, 2000.

492 "socially presentable . . ." Jane Margolies, interview with John Hill, March 26, 1992.

492 "It cost a fortune . . ." Maggie Valentine, interview with John Hill, June 5, 1995.

492 "Frank Lloyd Wright is . . ." Ann Barzel, "Taliesin Fails on Gurdjieff," Chicago American, November 4, 1953.

493 Iovanna was devastated . . . Amin, Reflections from the Shining Brow, 2004, 89.

493 *"She was ready to kill..."* Authors' phone interview with Kamal Amin, July 13, 2004.

493 *"They didn't like it..."* Authors' phone interview with Heloise Christa, April 23, 2004.

493 *"The young people..."* OLW to Sophie Mumford, April 2, 1954, in Pfeiffer and Wojtowicz, 2001, 252.

493 *"Many [of them]..."* OLW, *Our House*, 1959, 98.

493 *To the chagrin...* Curtis Besinger letter to John Geiger, February 7, 1987; authors' phone interview with Dushka Howarth, March 20, 2004; Marty and Marty, *Frank Lloyd Wright's Taliesin Fellowship*, 1999, 155.

493 *She accused her...* Authors' conversation with Bruce Pfeiffer, January 31, 2002. Pfeiffer maintains that Olgivanna had all of Gurdjieff's music. Unbeknownst to de Salzmann, Gurdjieff had asked Carol Robinson to transcribe the music, which Olgivanna had obtained. De Hartmann's correspondence makes it clear that she could easily have obtained Gurdjieff's music from him as well. Iovanna says just this in her unpublished autobiography. David Dodge, who also sometimes played piano for Mrs. Wright, contends that copyright claims from the Gurdjieffians pushed Mrs. Wright to compose her own music.

493 *"Well," she told..."* Authors' interview with David Dodge, October 27, 2000.

493 *"Give that to Iovanna"* Kamal Amin to the authors, e-mail, February 24, 2005.

493–94 *Using two of her...* According to Besinger, the two apprentices who pushed the design changes were Dick Carney and Steve Oyakawa. *Working with Mr. Wright*, 1987, 266.

494 *"I've been fighting..."* Wong's recollections are from his letter to John Geiger, spring 1999; Kathryn Smith, *Frank Lloyd Wright's Taliesin and Taliesin West* (New York: Abrams, 1997), 119. Smith says the last performance occurred in 1970; David Dodge, who participated in the music, claims the later date. Authors' interview with David Dodge, October 27, 2000.

494 *"was only a scaffolding..."* Besinger, *Working with Mr. Wright*, 1997, 267.

494 *In June 1954, a handful...* "Trip to Europe Follows Wedding of Iovanna Wright," *Weekly Home News*, June 24, 1954, Marlin papers.

494 *... her daughter could use...* Maggie Valentine, interview with John Hill, June 6, 1995.

494 *"trusted mother's wisdom"* ILW, *My Life*, 239.

494 *... the woman Frank Lloyd Wright expected...* Authors' interview with Kamal Amin, May 29, 2004.

495 *"The little Philly-Johnson..."* FLW to Arthur Pieper, December 27, 1954, Marlin papers.

495 *At one point...* Maggie Valentine, interview with John Hill, June 5, 1995.

495 *"Our survival lies...* OLW, *The Struggle Within* (New York: Horizon, 1955), 12.

496 *"a Jew, a real Jew"* Authors' interview with Franco D'Ayala, December 24–25, 2002.

496 *"Well, gentlemen..."* FLW, Talk to the Fellowship, March 14, 1954.

496 *Tapped to redecorate...* Pfeiffer, *Frank Lloyd Wright: The Guggenheim Correspondence*, 1986, 195–96; Jane Margolies, interview with John Hill, March 26, 1992.

496 *... he refused to have it...* Maggie Valentine, interview with John Hill, June 5, 1995, UCLA Oral History Program.

496 *Georgia O'Keeffe...* Indira Berndtson and Greg Williams, interview with Wes Peters, December 29, 1989.

497 *... Monroe turned...* Maggie Valentine, interviews with John Hill: June 4 and 29, 1995; "Frank Lloyd Wright and Hollywood," *Frank Lloyd Wright Quarterly*, Vol. 4, No. 1, Winter, 1993, 5–12.

497 *"Hello, Mr. Wright..."* Jordy, *The Impact of European modernism in the Mid-Twentieth Century*, 1972, 317.

497 *... spraying a material...* Jordy, *The Impact of European modernism in the Mid-Twentieth Century*, 1972, 318–20.

498 *It was an inspired stroke...* FLW to Harry Guggenheim, October 1, 1954, Pfeiffer, *Frank Lloyd Wright: The Guggenheim Correspondence*, 1986, 207.

498 *The engineers would have...* Indira Berndtson and Greg Williams, interview with Wes Peters, December 29, 1989.

498 *They concocted...* Authors' interview with Jay Pace, May 28, 2004. Pace was told this by his friend Wes Peters years after the fact.

CHAPTER 22: HEADING FOR THE COSMOS

499 *"You must now..."* Hilla Rebay and FLW: February 28, March 9, December 22, 1953.

499 *"utter degeneracy"* Franz Schulze, *Philip Johnson: Life and Work*, (Chicago: University of Chicago Press, 1994), 92; Frank Lloyd Wright and Margaret Sanger, Talk to the Fellowship, March 9, 1952, Frank Lloyd Wright Archives.

499–500 *... set about trying...* Davis, *The Guggenheims*, 1978, 226.

500 *"required circumference..."* "The Guggenheim Museum: Wright Has the Last Word." *Frank Lloyd Wright Quarterly*, Summer 1992, Vol. 3, No. 3. 8.

500 *In a gesture...* OLW, *Frank Lloyd Wright*, 1966, 167.

500 *"toilets of the Racquet Club..."* Davis, *The Guggenheims*, 1978, 226.

500 *"For an Irishman..."* Authors' phone interview with Kamal Amin, May 31, 2004.

500 *"That's Gropius..."* Tafel, *About Wright*, 1993, 57.

500 *In a generous...* Schulze, *Philip Johnson*, 1994, 242–43; Indira Berndtson and Greg Williams, interview with Wes Peters, December 29, 1989.

501 *"... the Wright Foundation..."* John Edgar Hoover to N. D. Hathaway, director, Investigation Service, Veterans Administration, April 1, 1954, FLW FBI file.

501 *The "students"...* SAC, Phoenix, March 16, 1954, FLW FBI file.

502 *"Now is the time..."* FLW to Abe Dombar, June 5, 1952, Dombar papers.

502 *Olgivanna readied...* Marty and Marty, *Frank Lloyd Wright's Taliesin Fellowship*, 1999, 159.

502 *Architectural training...* Twombly, *Frank Lloyd Wright*, 1979, 377–78.

502 *Some inside Taliesin...* O. P. Reed to the authors, e-mail, August 13, 2002.

502 *"For God's sake..."* Draft pages by OLW, Marlin papers.

502 *"reincarnated, reborn, different"* Draft pages by OLW, Marlin papers.

502–503 *... planned to live at the Plaza...* Twombly, *Frank Lloyd Wright*, 1979, 379.

503 *... she had been keeping copies...* Authors' interview with O. P. Reed, July 15, 1999.

503 *Didn't they love...* Draft pages by OLW, Marlin papers.

503 *"Your eye for a site..."* Berg, *Lindbergh*, 1998, 496.

503 *"I assume that an architect..."* C. Mark Hamilton, "The Air Force Academy Chapel: A Persistent Form in the Face of Controversy," http://architronic.saed.kent.edu/v4n2 /v4n2.03p02 .html.

504 *"This is not..."* Authors' phone interview with Kamal Amin, June 26, 2004.

504 *"From now on..."* Vlado Lazovich to OLW, July 14, 1955.

504 *"Uncle Vlado handles us..."* Text from Charles Montooth, August 16, 1955.

505 *"What is this..."* Bruce Pfeiffer, ed., *Frank Lloyd Wright: The Crowning Decade 1949–1959* (Fresno: The Press at California State University, Fresno, 1989), 112–17.

505 *"a certain superiority..."* OLW, *The Struggle Within*, 1955, 102, 117.

505 *"Yes," Wright said...* Wright, *The Struggle Within*, 1955.

506 *"archeseum..."* Lomask, *Seed Money*, 1964, 183.

506 *"indicates a callous..."* Levine, *The Architecture of Frank Lloyd Wright*, 1996, 347.

506 *"rectangular frame..."* "The Guggenheim Museum," 5–9, *Frank Lloyd Wright Quarterly*, Summer, 1992, Vol. 3, No. 3. 9.

506 *"The Museum itself..."* FLW to Wes Peters, telegram, March 16, 1956, in *Letters to Apprentices*, 1982, 182–83.

507 *"Your boss is..."* Indira Berndtson and Greg Williams, interview with Wes Peters, December 27, 1989.

507 *After Western Union...* Authors' interview with Tom Casey, June 5, 2000.

507 *Using a string...* Indira Berndtson and Greg Williams, interview with Wes Peters, December 29, 1989.

509 *"John could take three stones..."* Elizabeth Gordon to Indira Berndtson, September 17, 1996.

509 *Johnny brought his close friend...* Maggie Valentine, interview with John Hill, July 29, 1995; OLW, unpublished autobiography fragments, Marlin papers.

509 *Wright had allowed...* Marty and Marty, *Frank Lloyd Wright's Taliesin Fellowship*, 1999, 156.

509 *"These works of art..."* Cited in ILW, "Eugene Masselink," November 30, 1962, Marlin papers.

510 *... "Joel" sounded Jewish...* Maggie Valentine interview with John Hill, June 5 and June 6, 1995.

510 *"A Room to Be Alone In"* "House Beautiful Room," http://www.fairplex.com/fp/Foundations/MillardSheets/catalog.asp, Fairplex: The Millard Sheets Gallery. In a later letter (Elizabeth Gordon to Indira Berndtson, September 17, 1996), Gordon estimates 350,000 visitors. In Maggie Valentine's interview of June 5, 1995, Hill estimates more than a million.

510 *"Look carefully ..."* Maggie Valentine, interview with John Hill, June 5, 1995.

510 *And even though ...* Elizabeth Gordon to FLW, September 29, 1955.

511 *"intrude on the ..."* Curtis Besinger to John Geiger: December 9, 1991, and November 16, 1988. Besinger wrote: "At the time that I left only Tom Casey was doing much work in the drafting room. Everyone else, who is now there, was waiting attendance on Mrs. Wright."

511 *If he would just let her ...* Curtis Besinger to John Geiger: March 11, 1986, and undated.

511 *His well-publicized ...* Terry Reksten, *Rattenbury* (Victoria, British Columbia: Sono Nis Press, 1978).

511 *... his younger colleague's ...* Kamal Amin to the authors, e-mail, March 7, 2005; Curtis Besinger to John Geiger: March 11, 1986, and August 28, 1989.

511 *"So there I sat ..."* Curtis Besinger to John Geiger, December 1986 and January 20, 1990.

511 *"For the first time ..."* Curtis Besinger to John Geiger, December 24, 1988. This meeting took place in August 1955, the same month that Besinger's departure from the Fellowship became public.

512 *"What you will receive ..."* Amin, *Reflections from the Shining Brow*, 2004, 107; authors' interview with Jane Gale Sheain, May 24, 2004.

512 *"Franco,"* Olgivanna chided ... Authors' interview with Franco D'Ayala Valva, December 26, 2002.

512 *"I see we have ..."* Authors' interview with Nick Devenney, May 29, 2004.

512 *"She told her weekend students ..."* "And he knew what I was doing," she recalled. Indira Berndtson, phone interview with Jane Gale Sheain, July 15, 1998.

512 *"You belong here"* Authors' phone interviews with Jane Gale Sheain: April 25 and May 23, 2004.

513 *once even pushing ...* Authors' interview with ILW, August 16, 2000.

513 *... sometimes even refusing ...* Authors' interview with David Dodge, October 27, 2000.

513 *"I cannot believe ..."* Author's interview with James de Long, October 20, 2000.

513 *But Olgivanna reserved ...* Authors' phone interview with Jane Gale Sheain, April 25, 2004.

514 *Instead of scolding ...* Authors' phone interview with Kamal Amin, June 26, 2004. Amin was told this by Olgivanna.

514 *The inaugural performance ...* Anna Durco, who joined the Chicago group in 1956, is certain that there were no movements until Olgivanna and Iovanna decided to have another public performance. Indira Berndtson, phone interview of Anna Durco, July 13, 1998.

514 *... slated to sing ...* Indira Berndtson, phone interview of Jane Gale Sheain, July 15, 1998.

515 *"I don't want you ..."* Amin, *Reflections from the Shining Brow*, 2004, 111–12.

515 *In the first dance ...* OLW, *Our House*, 1959, 101.

515 *"She wanted you ..."* Authors' phone interview with Jane Sheain, May 2, 2004.

515 *"tasks" and "shocks"* Indira Berndtson, phone interview with Anna Durco, July 13, 1998.

516 *"Mrs. Wright got me ..."* Authors' phone interview with Jane Sheain, April 25, 2004.

516 *"Well, Kay ..."* Celeste Davison to the authors, e-mail, March 7, 2005; authors' phone interview with Jane Gale Sheain, May 24, 2004.

516 *"The merry wives ..."* Authors' interview with John Geiger, February 19, 2000. *An exquisite dancer ...* Marty and Marty, *Frank Lloyd Wright's Taliesin Fellowship*, 1999, 163.

516 *"If you listen ..."* John Geiger to the authors, e-mail, January 28, 2005.

517 *Heloise fell in love ...* Authors' phone interview with Jane Gale Sheain, February 26, 2002.

517 *"Heloise and I ..."* Maggie Valentine, interview with John Hill, July 29, 1995.

517 *... Olgivanna was disturbed ...* Authors' interview with Eloise Fritz, December 15, 1999.

517 *"I do not like ..."* John Hill to Gene Masselink, April 12, 1951.

517 *"Can you make decisions?"* Maggie Valentine, interview with John Hill, July 29, 1995.

517 *Ferdinand Scheville ...* FLW to Ferdinand Schevill, October 15, 1952.

517 *"mere contributor ..."* James Cate and FLW: March 25 and April 2, 1957; Indira Berndtson to the authors, e-mail, November 21, 2002.

518 *"I felt really..."* Jeffrey Aronin, interview with FLW, May 1, 1957.

518 *"radiations"* OLW to Vlado and Sophie Lazovich, June 11, 1957.

518 *Working with the circular*... Levine, *The Architecture of Frank Lloyd Wright*, 1996, 397.

520 *"Mrs. Wright," she recalled*... Indira Berndtson, phone interview with Anna Durco, July 13, 1998.

521 *"He looked up..."* Bruce Brooks Pfeiffer, *The Crowning Decade: 1949–1959*, 1989, 178–79.

521 *"It appears that aliens*... From www .milwaukeecollegelife.com. Architectural historian Kenneth Frampton saw this in much of Wright's late work. "... Wright continued to develop a curious kind of science-fiction architecture which, judging from the exotic style of his late renderings, seemed intended for occupation by some extraterrestrial species (*Modern Architecture: A Critical History*, 1980, 189).

522 *... an outside contributor*... John Gurda, *New World Odyssey: Annunciation Greek Orthodox Church and Frank Lloyd Wright* (Milwaukee: The Milwaukee Hellenic Community, 1986), 57. In 1998, the pastor had a gilded metal cross placed on top of the church.

522 *Almost no one*... Perhaps mercifully, the church is sometimes ignored by serious architecture writers. Neil Levine's *The Architecture of Frank Lloyd Wright*, 1996, relegates it to a footnote on historicism in Wright's later works, 500, n. 147.

522 *The projects of Walter Gropius*... FLW, Talk at San Rafael High School, San Rafael, California, July 1957, www.geocities.com/SoHo/-1469/flw_iraq.html.

523 *"This morning the architect..."* John Ottenheimer, "The Final Resting Place," *Taliesin Fellows Newsletter*, July 15, 2003.

CHAPTER 23: SUCCESSION

524 *He beckoned*... Authors' interview with O. P. Reed, July 15, 1999.

524 *"Why didn't you..."* Secrest, *Frank Lloyd Wright*, 1992, 563.

524 *"Balloons flew everywhere..."* OLW, *The Shining Brow*, 1960, 118–19.

525 *"And then," Green recalled*... Robert Green, *Frank Lloyd Wright Architecture Design Style*, www.robertgreen.com.

525 *The performers*... Indira Berndtson and Greg William, interview with Kamal Amin, July 29, 1992; authors' interviews with Walter Madeiros, April 28, 2001 and May 12, 2002.

525 *"The pain..."* ILW, *My Life*, 254.

525 *The doctors wouldn't increase*... Authors' interview with Walter Madeiros, November 12, 2002.

526 *... as Olgivanna slept*... Marty and Marty, *Frank Lloyd Wright's Taliesin Fellowship*, 1999, 104.

526 *Dr. Rorke would blame*... Authors' interview with Jay Pace, January 31, 2002; OLW to Svetlana Wright, October 12, 1934, Marlin papers, Scott Elliott collection.

526 *"You will not be alone..."* ILW, *My Life*, 254–55.

526 *An apprentice was assigned*... Indira Berndtson, interview with William Osgood, March 1, 2002.

526 *"Frank Lloyd Wright, regarded..."* "Frank Lloyd Wright Dies; Famed Architect Was 89," *New York Times*, April 10, 1959.

526 *It was the only time*... Lu Howe to authors, May 18, 2005.

526 *"I felt a terrible loss..."* Indira Berndtson and Greg William, interview with Kamal Amin, July 29, 1992.

526 *... another decade in him*... Marty and Marty, *Frank Lloyd Wright's Taliesin Fellowship*, 1999, 103; authors' phone interview with Walter Madeiros, November 12, 2002.

527 *After a short service*... Goss, *Music and the Moderns*, 1993, 43; Indira Berndtson, interview with Charles Montooth, October 11, 2000.

527 *Olgivanna suddenly ordered*... Robert Green, Frank Lloyd Wright Architecture Design Style www.robertgreen.com; authors' phone interview with Walter Madeiros, November 12, 2002.

527 *... a client's corporate plane*... Indira Berndtson, interview with William Osgood, March 1, 2002.

527 *The hole awaiting him*... Green, *Frank Lloyd Wright Architecture Design Style*.

527 *... Was all nature* ... ILW, "Will Mankind Listen?," *My Life*, 260; authors' interview with Michael Sutton, May 25, 2004.

528 *He left Taliesin*... Authors' interview with Eric Lloyd Wright, August 2, 2001; Curtis Besinger to John Geiger, January 6, 1977.

529 *"are alleged to have been . . ."* Van J. Ferris, United States Treasury Department, to Frank Lloyd Wright Foundation c/o Mr. William W. Peters, May 18, 1959.

530 *"He looked like . . ."* Green, *Frank Lloyd Wright Architecture Design Style.*

531 *Olgivanna, who had lost . . .* "Re FLLW Death," notes from Indira Berndtson.

531 *"you kept feeling . . ."* Marty and Marty, *Frank Lloyd Wright's Taliesin Fellowship,* 1999, 103.

531 *"represented the great . . ."* OLW, *The Shining Brow,* 1960, 138.

531 *"built an immortal chapter . . ."* OLW, *The Shining Brow,* 1960, 130–38.

531 *"Oh, Katy . . ."* Pfeiffer, *The Crowning Decade,* 1989, 188.

531 *Taliesin, it stated . . .* Curtis Besinger to John Geiger, September 23, 1988. Curtis was asked to sign this document by Gene Masselink.

531 *. . . Wright also wrote a will . . .* John Geiger to Curtis Besinger, March 28, 1988.

532 *. . . in conversation with client . . .* Meehan, *Frank Lloyd Wright Remembered,* 1991.

532 *Surely, he told her . . .* Authors' conversation with Bruce Pfeiffer, July 29, 2001. According to O. P. Reed, who has seen the letter, Wright instructed his wife to terminate the Fellowship upon his death. "One of his last letters said that after he died, 'I don't want you to have a Fellowship.' You don't know that," he told us, "but that's in a letter that exists." Authors' interview with O. P. Reed, July 15, 1999.

532 *"religious . . . kind of thing"* Maggie Valentine, interview with John Hill, July 30, 1995, UCLA Oral History Program.

532 *Wouldn't it be better . . .* Curtis Besinger to John Geiger, December 22, 1984. Besinger, an apprentice who also worked for Elizabeth Gordon as architectural editor, sent a copy of this letter to the Taliesin Archives. In 1988, while preparing his own book, he wrote Gordon asking permission to use it. "I don't want to get involved," she replied. "I don't want to get involved. That was thirty years ago. Why bring it up now? Why make a mess of it?" Curtis Besinger to John Geiger, December 24, 1988.

532 *"Your views on the . . ."* FLW to Lewis Mumford, May 22, 1958, Pfeiffer and Wojtowicz, *Frank Lloyd Wright + Lewis Mumford: Thirty Years of Correspondence,* 2001, 273.

532 *"sooner or later . . ."* OLW, *Our House,* 1959, 17.

533 *"If the wife . . ."* OLW, *The Shining Brow,* 1960, 17.

533 *The day after the birthday . . .* Tafel, *About Wright,* 1993, 293–95.

534 *Wes had bounced . . .* Randolph Conners to William Wesley Peters, March 27, 1959, Getty Research Institute.

534 *Georgia O'Keeffe . . .* Indira Berndtson and Greg Williams, interview with Wes Peters, December 29, 1989.

534 *. . . she continued her plan . . .* O. P. Reed, who appraised Taliesin's collections and helped arrange the sale of their Asian art, remarked, "They're helpless. They're helpless people . . . God." Authors' interview, July 15, 1999.

534 *At first she envisioned creating . . .* Authors' interview with Don and Virginia Lovness, September 18, 2000.

534 *. . . that idea . . .* Kamal Amin to the authors, e-mail, April 7, 2005.

534 *But she would sell . . .* Marty and Marty, *Frank Lloyd Wright's Taliesin Fellowship,* 1999, 105–106; Indira Berndtson to the authors, e-mail, April 12, 2005.

534 *Wright left behind . . .* John Rattenbury, *A Living Architecture: Frank Lloyd Wright and Taliesin Architects* (San Francisco: Pomegranate Communications, 2000), 77.

535 *invite comparison with a urinal* Lomask, *Seed Money,* 1964, 200–201.

535 *The "miracle on Fifth Avenue" . . .* OLW, *The Shining Brow,* 1960, 181.

535 *One no-show . . .* Davis, *The Guggenheims,* 1978, 228.

535 *"When I die . . ."* Lomask, *Seed Money,* 1964, 175.

535 *"The Frank Lloyd Wright Foundation . . ."* Its "architects" included Wes Peters, John Howe, Allen Davison, Kenneth Lockhart, Eugene Masselink, and Mendel Glickman. Aaron Green was the San Francisco representative, Charles Montooth in Phoenix, and Stephen Oyakawa in Honolulu. *House Beautiful,* October 1959, 266; OLW to Dr. W. L. Stucky, April 24, 1959.

537 *"We hope you will return . . ."* Langmead and Johnson, *Architectural Excursions,* 2000, 170–71.

537 *"It is as if nature . . ."* Lewis Mumford to Hendrik Wijdeveld, April 28, 1959, in Landg-

mead and Johnson, *Architectural Excursions*, 2000, 170–71.

537 *"grew to the stature . . ."* OLW, *Our House*, 1959, 59.

537 *Olgivanna marked Peters's . . .* Alliluyeva, *The Faraway Music*, 1986, 109.

537 *Indeed, he had spent . . .* Authors' phone interview with John Geiger, November 1, 2003.

537 *He sported an . . .* Indira Berndtson, video interview with Mary Stanton, December 21, 1993.

537 *. . . sixty Eames chairs . . .* Authors' interview with O. P. Reed, July 15, 1999.

538 *. . . his own architectural license . . .* Indira Berndtson and Greg Williams, interview with Wes Peters, May 15, 1991.

538 *"His devotion to Mr. Wright . . ."* OLW, *Our House*, 1959, 59.

538 *"So infinite . . . House Beautiful, Your Heritage from Frank Lloyd Wright*, special volume, Vol. 101, No. 10, *l*, October, 1959, 212, 275, 277.

CHAPTER 24: GRANDOMANIA

543 *"In my life . . ."* OLW, *The Roots of Life*, 1963, 142–45.

543 *. . . her husband's work . . .* Authors' phone interview with Kamal Amin, July 13, 2004.

543 *. . . she still sought his advice telepathically . . .* Taylor, *Gurdjieff in America*, 2004, 154.

543 William Wesley Peters . . . "Fellowship List" and "Seating Arrangements for Trip to Arizona," both dated October 1959.

543 *. . . tales of King Arthur . . .* Authors' interview with Svetlana Peters, June 6, 2000; Amin, *Reflections from the Shining Brow*, 2004, 161.

544 *. . . his name alone . . .* Authors' interview with Kamal Amin, May 29, 2004.

544 *"He was headstrong . . ."* Maggie Valentine, interview with John Hill, 1997, 88, UCLA Oral History Program.

544 *Peters had assured . . .* Authors' interview with Kamal Amin, May 29, 2004; Maggie Valentine, interview with John Hill, July 30, 1995, UCLA Oral History Program; Indira Berndtson, interview with Charles Montooth, October 11, 2000.

544 *Almost everything . . .* John Geiger to Curtis Besinger, August 27, 1987.

544 *Some architects had to cancel . . .* Authors' interview with Roger and Anna Coor, February 1, 2002.

544 *Jack Howe, much to his disappointment . . .* "Jack thought he should have been made chief architect," Johnny Hill told John Geiger. John Geiger to Curtis Besinger, August 21, 1989.

544 *. . . she handed him a sketch . . .* Frances Nemtin, *Frank Lloyd Wright and Taliesin* (Rohnert Park, California: Pomegranate Press, 2000), 52–53; authors' interview with then-apprentice Michael Sutton (who saw Mrs. Wright hand him the sketch and who worked on the masonry in the garden), July 29, 2001; authors' interview with Lu Howe, Jack's wife, who remembered her husband's displeasure, August 1, 2001.

545 *Others suspected . . .* John Geiger, who has studied Wright's drawing style in the period, certainly thinks so. "I have examined the drawing of Mrs. Wright's garden and moon gate in Nemtin's book and do not think it is by Mr. Wright. He never scribbled; he knew what he was drawing and described it with the fewest necessary lines. The 7 or 8 lines in the lower right hand corner to describe a wall of the garden [are] just too diffuse to be Wright. . . . It looks to me like a Rattenbury/Olgivanna scam." John Geiger to the authors, e-mail, October 5, 2001.

545 *"When a drawing . . ."* OLW, *Frank Lloyd Wright*, 1966, 89.

545 *"whole presentation . . ."* Authors' interview with Anna and Roger Coor, February 1, 2002.

545 *"So many build . . .* OLW, *Our House*, 1959, 183.

545 *"constructively and with kindness"* Meehan, ed., *Frank Lloyd Wright Remembered*, 1991, 130.

545 *Now he threw himself . . .* Authors' phone interview with John Geiger, February 20, 2002. Geiger learned this from Wheatley himself, who claims that it is his handwriting on the drawings.

545 *"June 8, 1869 will forever . . ."* OLW, *The Shining Brow*, 1960, 15–17.

546 *Indeed, even Wright had . . .* John Geiger to Curtis Besinger, March 28, 1988. Wright suggested they might use "bionic" instead.

547 *. . . a functionally dubious bridge . . .* The archway originally marked the main entrance of the campus, but the university moved the main entrance to the campus so that the large archway no longer had the same significance. Jack Howe to

Allen Brooks, September 5, 1966, Lu Howe personal correspondence.

547 *The doctor and his wife* . . . Authors' interview with Shawn Rorke Davis, October 28, 2000.

547 . . . *Shawn seemed to be playing* . . . Authors' interview with Suzy Pace, July 25, 2001.

548 . . . *they had "failed" her* . . . Indira Berndtson, phone interview with Anna Durco, July 13, 1998.

548 *The Taliesin Festival* . . . Smith, *Frank Lloyd Wright's Taliesin*, 1997, 128; Marty and Marty, *Frank Lloyd Wright's Taliesin Fellowship*, 1999, 155; authors' interview with David Dodge, October 27, 2000.

548 *Sometimes Olgivanna would adapt* . . . Authors' interview with Charles Schiffner, January 30, 2002.

549 *"half-assed things* . . . Authors' phone interview with Dushka Howarth, April 26, 2001.

549 *"bastard offshoot . . ."* Authors' phone interviews with Jane Gale Sheain, February 26, 2002 and June 6, 2004.

549 *"profoundly unattractive . . ."* Authors' interviews with ILW, February 19 and August 16, 2000.

549 *Perhaps, she thought, a baby* . . . Authors' interview with Eloise Fritz, December 15, 1999.

550 *When Wright came walking* . . . Indira Berndtson, interview with Mary Stanton, December 21, 1993.

550 *But Kaufmann declined* . . . Edgar Kaufmann Jr. had told this to Edgar Tafel: Curtis Besinger to John Geiger, December 1989.

550 *"I find," he wrote* . . . Randolph R. Conners to Gene Masselink, March 25, 1959.

550 *But now they were struggling* . . . Indira Berndtson to authors, e-mail, April 12, 2005.

550 *Olgivanna had convinced Frank* . . . Olgivanna was particularly invested in this church. When apprentice Alvin Wiehle designed a cross for it that was intended to be plastic, Wes had it cast in concrete. Mrs. Wright was outraged by the switch, and gave them both a dressing down. John Geiger to Curtis Besinger, August 27, 1987.

550 *When the church rejected* . . . "The faces and clothing were poor art nouveau and not up to his great draftsmanship," declared O. P. Reed, his biographer. O. P. Reed to the authors, e-mail, August 2, 2002. "I think he tried to adapt Russian icons with organic art and the result was awful": O. P. Reed to the authors, e-mail, July 31, 2002.

551 *When the parishioners* . . . Gurda, *New World Odyssey*, 1986, 100–101.

551 *"I wish I could die"* Authors' interview with O. P. Reed, July 15, 1999.

551 *"The soul of your sister . . ."* Authors' interview with ILW, August 16, 2000.

551 *Masselink was one* . . . Authors' interview with Eloise Fritz, December 15, 1999.

551 *"withdraw his services . . ."* Document dated 1944, Getty Research Institute.

551 *She went to Gene's grieving father* . . . Authors' interview with Eloise Fritz, December 15, 1999.

552 *"to my secretary . . ."* John Geiger inferred as much after seeing it in a Los Angeles museum exhibit. Curtis Besinger and John Geiger: March 14 and 18, 1988.

552 *The icons he had painted* . . . In 1977, the church decided not to follow Gene's preliminary sketches for stained-glass lunette windows ringing the church's upper level. The pastor finally removed Masselink's icons from the iconostasis in 1998, replacing them with iconographically correct traditional icons. "Signs of the Times," *Criterion*, Autumn 2001, http://divinity.uchicago.edu/research/criterion/autumn2001/article2.html.

552 *"to the memory . . ."* OLW, *The Roots of Life*, 1963.

552 *"Johnny, we need . . ."* Authors' interview with Anna and Roger Coor, February 1, 2002.

552 *"was the front person . . ."* Maggie Valentine, interviews with John Hill: June 5 and 6, 1995, UCLA Oral History Program.

552 . . . *she had agreed to bring him back* . . . Maggie Valentine, interview with John Hill, July 30, 1995, UCLA Oral History Program.

552 *"I know that God . . ."* Amin, *Reflections from the Shining Brow*, 2004, 66.

552 *"Mrs. Wright could run . . ."* Maggie Valentine, interview with John Hill, July 30, 1995.

552–53 *"Who's going to hang out . . ."* Authors' interview with Adrienne Schiffner, December 12, 2000.

553 *He made her breakfast* . . . Authors' interview with Don and Virginia Lovness, September 18, 2000; interview with Don and Virginia Lovness, April 15, 1996.

553 *"So the miracles . . ."* OLW to Vlado and Sophie Lazovich, May 29, 1954.

553 *Was he homosexual*... Authors' conversation with Bruce Pfeiffer, October 30, 2000.

553 *"it's just in you..."* Authors' conversation with Bruce Pfeiffer, December 17, 1999.

553 *"reminded" the surprised couple*... One of the two, whom she had already warned about public dalliances, was later expelled. Authors' interview with Dr. Joseph Rorke, October 30, 2000.

553 *"Look at them..."* Authors' conversation with Bruce Pfeiffer, October 30, 2000.

553 *"real masculine energy..."* Authors' interview with Eloise Fritz, December 15, 1999.

553 *Olgivanna would have to*... Kamal Amin writes, "After Mr. Wright's passing, architecture was viewed [as] the only source of income. She did not appreciate what all the fuss was about when the concept of integrity became associated with a certain look, proportion, or dimension in a building." *Reflections from the Shining Brow*, 2004, 148.

554 *Olgivanna would tell others*... Maggie Valentine, interview with John Hill, July 30, 1995, UCLA Oral History Program.

554 *... but she hadn't*... Authors' phone interview with Lu Howe, May 21, 2003. There is no mention in Lu or Jack Howe's personal diaries of being asked to leave. Lu Howe is emphatic that Olgivanna never asked her husband to leave. Lu Howe's diary entry reads for July 4, 1963: "A lousy day. Jack got a shattering scolding from Mrs. Wright regarding his architectural design and the drafting room work."

554 *"J. H. H. Declaration..."* Authors' phone interview with Lu Howe, May 21, 2003.

554 *Olgivanna told Wes*... Authors' interview with Michael Sutton, July 29, 2001.

554 *Now that Wright was gone*... Authors' interview with Svetlana Peters, June 6, 2000; authors' phone interview with Brandoch Peters, May 30, 2000.

554 *... appointing a spy*... Amin, *Reflections from the Shining Brow*, 2004, 163; authors' phone interview with Kamal Amin, July 13, 2004. Amin is certain that Peters knew nothing of her attempts to spy on him.

554 *She had the wall plastered*... Curtis Besinger to John Geiger, July 16, 1992; Maggie Valentine, interview with John Hill, July 5, 1995, UCLA Oral History Program.

554 *"If anything happens..."* Curtis Besinger to John Geiger, December 22, 1984.

554 *"rough charcoal sketch"* Curtis Besinger to John Geiger, December 22, 1984; authors' interview with Kamal Amin, October 29, 2000.

555 *"rugged, masculine..."* Maggie Valentine, interview with John Hill, July 5, 1995, UCLA Oral History Program.

555 *Jack couldn't stomach*... Authors' interview with Jay Pace, director of development, Taliesin School of Architecture, July 25, 2001. Jay was told this by Jack. Authors' interview with Terry Sewell, July 28, 2001.

555 *At first she didn't*... Lu Howe, private diary entry, Lu Howe personal collection; authors' phone interview with Lu Howe, May 21, 2003.

555 *The apprentices had been preparing*... Marty and Marty, *Frank Lloyd Wright's Taliesin Fellowship*, 1999, 206.

556 *Howe asked Green*... Authors' phone interview with Lu Howe, August 1, 2001.

556 *Taliesin would never regain*... Maggie Valentine, interview with John Hill, July 30, 1995, UCLA Oral History Program.

556 *She threw big parties*... Alliluyeva, *The Faraway Music*, 1986, 97.

556 *"I haven't spoken..."* Authors' interview with Leah Adler, March 2, 2004.

556 *"marked with a character..."* OLW, *The Roots of Life*, 1963, 142–45.

557 *A former Taliesin apprentice*... Authors' phone interview with John Geiger, October 31, 2002.

557 *"the doily building..."* http://www.geocities.com/SoHo/1469/kaden.html.

557 *"She wanted the work out..."* Authors' interview with David Dodge, October 10, 2000.

558 *To those who saw*... Authors' phone interview with Kathryn Smith, October 8, 2002.

558 *"is confidently expected..."* *Minneapolis Tribune*, May 17, 1968.

558 *"Wes is more..."* Amin, *Reflections from the Shining Brow*, 2004, 161; authors' interview with Roger Coor, February 1, 2002.

559 *The first design presentation*... Maggie Valentine, interview with John Hill, July 31, 1995, UCLA Oral History Program.

559 *"Don't worry..."* Authors' interview with Roger Coor, February 1, 2002.

560 *"most prominent..."* Mark Hertzberg, "Prairie's creator returns to oversee another expansion," *Journal Times*, March 2004.

560 *Shawn, Dr. Rorke's beautiful daughter* . . . Authors' phone interviews with Jane Gale Sheain, February 26, 2002, and Shawn Rorke Davis, October 28, 2000.

560 *Alcohol was no longer* . . . Authors' interview with Charles Schiffner, October 30, 2000.

561 *He had been orphaned* . . . William Marlin, interview with ILW, May 17, 1988.

561 *"There are certain things . . ."* Authors' interview with Charles Schiffner, October 30, 2000.

561 *"Lather"* Loudon Wainwright, "Guardian of a Great Legacy," *Life*, June 11, 1971.

CHAPTER 25: FAMILY MATTERS

562 *And she believed* . . . Alliluyeva, *The Faraway Music*, 1986, 104.

562 *"morally unstable person . . ."* "News Conference Held by Premier Kosygin at the United Nations," *New York Times*, June 26, 1967, 17.

562 *"Hello there, everybody . . ."* *Time*, April 28, 1967.

563 *The tabloids* . . . Authors' interview with Svetlana Peters, June 6, 2000.

563 *"I longed to be . . ."* Svetlana Alliluyeva, *The Faraway Music*, 1986 revision, unpublished, Svetlana Peters papers, 20, 39.

564 *"When are you coming? . . ."* Authors' interview with Svetlana Peters, June 6, 2000.

564 *She had grown up* . . . Brian Moynahan, *The Russian Century* (London: Seven Dials, 1994), 171.

564 *In 1932, when Svetlana* . . . Alliluyeva, *The Faraway Music*, 1986, 152. "Hey, you, have a drink," Stalin had shouted. "Don't dare talk to me like that!" Nadezhda had replied, running from the table. According to Moynahan, she later shot herself in her apartment in the Kremlin. *The Russian Century*, 1994, 178.

565 *"I hope YOU . . ."* Alliluyeva, *The Faraway Music*, 1986, 73–77.

565 *"It was like . . ."* Authors' interview with Svetlana Peters, June 6, 2000.

565 *"I am so glad . . ."* "That meant that I was already engaged, you know. It was finished. It was finished." Authors' interview with Svetlana Peters, June 6, 2000.

566 *"How do you like . . ."* Alliluyeva, *Faraway Music*, 1986, 79; authors' interview with Svetlana Peters, June 6, 2000.

566 *"He was so under . . ."* Authors' interview with Svetlana Peters, June 6, 2000.

567 *"strange weakness"* Authors' interview with O. P. Reed, July 15, 1999; Tafel, *About Wright*, 1993, 164.

567 *"You will have to see . . ."* Authors' interview with Svetlana Peters, June 6, 2000.

568 *"Now I can say . . ."* "Personalities: The Saga of Stalin's 'Little Sparrow,'" *Time*, January 28, 1985.

568 *At 2:30 that same afternoon* . . . Quit claim deed filed April 4, 1970, Iowa County land records.

568 *Somehow Olgivanna* . . . Authors' interview with O. P. Reed, November 8, 1999.

568 *A few days later* . . . Authors' interview with Svetlana Peters, June 6, 2000.

568 *As a wedding present* . . . Authors' phone interview with Svetlana Peters, June 14, 2000.

568 *"I wanted us . . ."* Alliluyeva, *The Faraway Music*, 1986, 84.

568 *"I would just swoon . . ."* Authors' interview with Svetlana Peters, June 6, 2000.

568 *Just a month after* . . . "Personalities: The Saga of Stalin's 'Little Sparrow,'" *Time*, January 28, 1985.

569 *She gave the car* . . . Authors' phone interview with Svetlana Peters, June 14, 2000.

569 *"stand player . . ."* Authors' phone interview with Jack Holzheuter, July 30, 2005.

569 *After she invested* . . . Authors' phone interview with Svetlana Peters, June 14, 2000.

569 *"Nobody smiled at me . . ."* Authors' interview with Svetlana Peters, June 6, 2000.

569 *"You will be one . . ."* Authors' phone interview with Svetlana Peters, June 14, 2000.

569 *"I felt . . ."* Authors' interview with Svetlana Peters, June 6, 2000.

570 *"My dear . . ."* Alliluyeva, *The Faraway Music*, 1986, 88.

570 *Soon, however, Svetlana* . . . Authors' interview with Svetlana Peters, June 6, 2000.

570 *Perusing Wes's cancelled checks* . . . Interview with Don and Virginia Lovness, April 15, 1996.

570 *"conventional"* Authors' interview with Svetlana Peters, June 6, 2000; Alliluyeva, *The Faraway Music*, 1986, 95.

570 *"Mr. Wright is here . . ."* Authors' interview with Svetlana Peters, June 6, 2000.

570 *Olgivanna was consumed . . .* Authors' interview with Patty Kaeser, October 28, 2000.

570 *"I'm throwing Svetlana out . . ."* Interview with Don and Virginia Lovness, April 15, 1996.

571 *"Architects were paid . . ."* Alliluyeva, *The Faraway Music*, 1986, 94, 97, 102, 105.

571 *"Wes had no . . ."* Alliluyeva, *The Faraway Music*, original manuscript dated 1983–1986, 79, Svetlana Peters papers.

571 *"Posters of women . . ."* Authors' interview with Charles Schiffner, October 30, 2001.

572 *"closer than an organic . . ."* Loudon Wainwright, "Guardian of a Great Legacy," *Life*, June 11, 1971.

572 *Lath was convinced that . . .* Authors' interview with Charles Schiffner, October 30, 2000. Iovanna also claimed that her mother influenced her father's major buildings. Interview with William Marlin, March 17, 1988.

572 *"love that is in . . .* Authors' interviews with Charles Schiffner, December 14, 2000, and January 30, 2002.

572 *She also encouraged . . .* Alliluyeva, *The Faraway Music*, 1986.

572 *. . . each day the little girl . . .* ILW, *My Life*, 249.

573 *"I fell in love . . ."* Authors' interview with Charles Schiffner, January 30, 2002.

573 *Lath composed and framed . . .* Poem at the Sun Trap, Taliesin West, January 2002.

573 *"Are you not . . ."* Authors' interview with Svetlana Peters, June 6, 2000.

574 *The check was drawn . . .* Authors' phone interview with Svetlana Peters, June 14, 2000.

574 *"He's working like . . ."* Authors' interview with Svetlana Peters, June 14, 2000.

574 *Then Svetlana informed . . .* Authors' interview with Svetlana Peters, June 6, 2000.

574 *"He works too hard . . ."* Amin, *Reflections from the Shining Brow*, 2004, 223.

574 *"Oh my god . . ."* Authors' interview with Svetlana Peters, June 6, 2000.

575–76 *And it was doubly . . .* Gurda, *New World Odyssey*, 1986, 112.

576 *"We have ruined . . .* Authors' interview with Svetlana Peters, June 6, 2000.

576 *"Someone tried to burn . . ."* Interview with Don and Virginia Lovness, April 15, 1996.

576 *Fearing for her baby's . . .* Authors' interview with Svetlana Peters, June 6, 2000.

576 *"You cannot buy . . ."* Interview with Don and Virginia Lovness, April 15, 1996.

577 *"Wes Peters approaches . . ."* Edgar Tafel to Jack Howe, March 8, 1972, Lu Howe personal correspondence.

577 *"I believe in private . . ."* Peter Kihss, "Stalin's Daughter Leaves Her Husband," *New York Times*, February 23, 1972.

577 *"Everybody is here . . ."* "Stalin Daughter Disputes Husband on Separation," *New York Times*, February 24, 1972.

577 *"Nobody rejected her . . ."* Authors' interview with ILW, July 24, 2000.

577 *"I was advised . . ."* Authors' interview with Svetlana Peters, June 6, 2000.

578 *This worked until . . .* Authors' interview with Celeste Davison, May 7, 2000.

579 *Whenever he encountered Tal . . .* Authors' interview with Diane Snodgrass Bickford, February 2, 2002.

579 *After a stint in Spain . . .* Authors' phone interview with Anna Bogdanovich, February 11, 2002.

579 *When she called her father . . .* Authors' phone interview with Celeste Davison, February 6, 2002.

579–80 *"But then your sound advice . . ."* Davy Davison to OLW, May 2, 1965, Celeste Davison papers.

580 *"a lovely, lovely . . ."* Authors' phone interviews with Anna Bogdanovich, February 11, 2002, and Diane Bickford, February 2, 2002.

580 *"You almost killed . . ."* Authors' phone interview with Anna Bogdanovich, February 11, 2002.

580 *"You are there . . ."* Kay Davison to Tal Davison, August 15, 1970, Celeste Davison papers.

581 *Well, if you feel that way . . .* The source of this, a Taliesin insider who has asked for anonymity, heard it from another member of the Fellowship who was in a position to know. Those who found Tal's body have not mentioned a suicide note. Van Noy was on vacation when Tal committed suicide, so he could not have overheard the conversation. The implication is that somebody heard Olgivanna Wright talking with Tal. That Tal would have called Mrs. Wright one last time for her blessing, her expiation, has been

confirmed by one of his closest friends at the time, Diane Snodgrass Bickford.

581 *But it was also . . .* Webb, *The Harmonious Circle*, 1980, 147–48.

581 *. . . Olgivanna had disapproved . . .* Authors' conversation with Bruce Pfeiffer, January 31, 2002.

581 *"If you had told me . . ."* Authors' interview with Diane Snodgrass Bickford, February 2, 2002.

581 *"Mrs. Wright and my mother . . ."* Authors' interview with Celeste Davison, May 5, 2000. Unwilling to burden her daughter, Anna's mother took this secret to her grave. Authors' phone interview with Anna Bogdanovich, February 12, 2002.

582 *"You better not . . ."* Authors' phone interview with Celeste Davison, February 5, 2002.

582 *"felt guilty that . . ."* John Rattenbury, "In Celebration of Kay," December 9, 1996.

582 *She was such poor material . . .* Curtis Besinger to John Geiger, May 20, 1987.

582 *. . . Iovanna had a nervous breakdown . . .* This according to Frances Nemtin. Curtis Besinger to John Geiger, December 26, 1972.

582 *"because in marrying her . . ."* Authors' interview with Charles Schiffner, December 14, 2000.

582 *"I don't know . . ."* Curtis Besinger to John Geiger, December 26, 1972.

582 *. . . got into his Volkswagen . . .* Authors' phone interview with Jane Gale Sheain, February 6, 2002.

583 *"How dare you . . ."* Authors' phone interview with John Geiger, June 23, 2005; Curtis Besinger to John Geiger, December 4, 1989.

583 *"I've often thought since . . ."* Maggie Valentine, interview with John Hill, July 30, 1995.

583 *After receiving Johnny and Cornelia's . . .* Indira Berndtson to the authors, e-mail, June 28, 2005, based on her conversations with Cornelia Brierly and John Rattenbury.

583 *She couldn't stop . . .* William Marlin interview with ILW, March 17, 1988.

583 *. . . she sometimes took out her anger . . .* Authors' interview with Jay Pace, July 25, 2001.

584 *Iovanna was diagnosed . . .* Authors' phone interview with Kamal Amin, June 26, 2004.

584 *If both parents . . .* Kay Redfield Jamison, *Touched with Fire: Manic-Depressive Illness*

and the Artistic Temperament (New York: Free Press, 1993), 194.

584 *. . . she considered aborting . . .* Interview with Doris Roy, December 12, 2000. Doris Roy came to Taliesin from Olgivanna's Gurdjieffian circle in Chicago in 1958; Olgivanna told her this story.

584 *. . . even pleaded with her husband, William . . .* Heller, *The Story of My Life*, 1929, 45. "She had her usual spells of mad hysterics and acted like a raving maniac and told Father to send for the officer and take her to the Asylum, and I used to wish he would. Poor man, he led a wretched existence."

584 *But William's own peripatetic career . . .* Authors' interview with Lee Sadja, psychiatrist, ward head at UCLA's Neuropsychiatric Institute, June 12, 2001.

584 *His son Lloyd . . .* Authors' interview with Eric Lloyd Wright, August 2, 2001.

584 *the bursts of energy . . .* Jamison, *Touched with Fire*, 1993, 28.

584 *Manics spend too much . . .* Authors' interview with Lee Sadja, June 12, 2001.

584 *Artists of all kinds . . .* A. Juda, "The Relationship Between Highest Mental Capacity and Psychic Abnormalities," *American Journal of Psychiatry*, 106 (1949), 296–307; A. M. Ludwig, "Creative Achievement and Psychopathology: Comparisons Among Professions," *American Journal of Psychotherapy*, 46 (1992), 330–56; C. Martindale, *The Clockwork Muse: The Predictability of Artistic Change* (New York: Basic Books, 1990); W. H. Trethowan, "Music and Mental Disorder," M. Critchley and R. E. Henson, eds., *Music and the Brain* (London: Heinemann, 1977), 398–442. See also Jamison, *Touched with Fire*, 1993, 49–99. Roughly 1 percent of the general population has manic-depression; architects, for instance, have a rate of manic-depression of 17 percent. See Jamison, 1993, 60.

584 *"They hadn't a clue . . ."* Authors' interviews with Charles Schiffner, October 20 and December 14, 2000.

584–85 *"If I am one of . . ."* Iovanna Schiffner to Jenkin Lloyd Jones, March 28, 1974.

585 *"You have no idea . . ."* Anthony Quinn to Iovanna Schiffner, June 10, 1975, Marlin papers.

585 *In 1976, in anticipation . . .* Iovanna Schiffner to Martin Sheen, November 19, 1976.

585 *One day she stomped* . . . John Geiger to Curtis Besinger, July 14, 1990.

585 *"Rock and roll* . . ." ILW, *My Life*, 254.

586 *She attacked her mother* . . . Authors' interviews with Charles Schiffner, October 30, 2000, and Shawn Rorke, October 28, 2000.

586 *Lath arranged* . . . Authors' interview with Charles Schiffner, December 14, 2000.

586 *"In the early years* . . ." Authors' interview with Charles Schiffner, October 30, 2000.

586 *"You really have everything* . . ." Authors' interview with Adrienne Schiffner, December 12, 2000.

587 *In 1982, Olgivanna* . . . Amendments to the Frank Lloyd Wright Foundation Articles of Incorporation, May 18, 1982.

587 *"mediocre world* . . ." Authors' interview with Adrienne Schiffner, December 12, 2000.

CHAPTER 26: SPIRITS IN THE WALL

588 *To the embarrassment* . . . Authors' conversation with Bruce Pfeiffer, December 17, 1999.

588 *"sad condition"* Tafel, *About Wright*, 1993, 305.

588 *"Hello Lath* . . ."* Marty and Marty, *Frank Lloyd Wright's Taliesin Fellowship*, 1999, 106–7.

589 *"I was on the other side* . . ." Author's interview with ILW, July 24, 2000.

589 *"That was some* . . ." Authors' interview with Ralph Williamsen, August 2, 2000.

589 *"had always devoted* . . ." ILW, *My Life*, 46.

589 *"The wicked witch* . . ." Authors' interview with Diane Snodgrass Bickford, February 2, 2002.

590 *"More dramatic elsewhere* . . . FLW, "Why I Love Wisconsin," *Wisconsin Magazine*, 1932, reprinted in Frederick Gutheim, ed., *Frank Lloyd Wright: On Architecture* (New York: Universal Library, 1941), 158.

590 *After Iovanna signed the papers* . . . Authors' interview with Viola Richardson, May 24, 2007.

590 *"Who was it who* . . ." Frank Laraway, *Taliesin Fellows Newsletter*, No. 3, April 15, 2001.

591 *"Maybe I felt* . . ." Tafel, *About Wright*, 1993, 2007.

591 *After Olgivanna's passing* . . . Authors' interview with ILW, January 21, 2000.

591 *He would do likewise* . . . Authors' interview with a Taliesin resident who wishes to remain anonymous.

592 *"What had been* . . ." Anonymous source to the authors, e-mail, June 8, 2004.

592 *"There was a set* . . ." Curtis Besinger to John Geiger, September 19, 1987.

592 *"For that,"* *Besinger noted* . . . Curtis Besinger to John Geiger, June 17, 1992.

592 *He replaced the carpets* . . . Authors' phone interview with John Geiger, July 6, 2001.

592 *In the last years* . . . Brierly, *Taliesin Tales*, 1999, 117.

593 *Under Peters's enthusiastic leadership* . . . Lawrence W. Cheek, "Spirit of Frank Lloyd Wright Still Pervades Taliesin West," *Architecture*, December 1987, 19–20.

593 *To raise the money* . . . John Geiger to Curtis Besinger, October 16, 1986.

593 *"Let 'em sink* . . ." Curtis Besinger to John Geiger, December 24, 1988.

593 *To stay afloat* . . . Curtis Besinger to John Geiger, May 29, 1987. "I'm enclosing a copy of a list of drawings which were being sold recently. Edgar T. sent the list." On December 12, 1987, in response to a letter from Wes Peters soliciting funds, Edgar Tafel wrote: "Since $3,000,000.00 was raised thru sales of original drawings of Mr. Wright's, where has the money gone? Reports were monies would be used for restoration of Taliesin."

593 *"I've come to the conclusion* . . ." Curtis Besinger to John Geiger, November 29, 1987.

593 *"Mrs. Wright,"* *he was overheard* . . . Authors' interview with Jay Pace, July 26, 2001.

594 *By the end, Peters* . . . Authors' interview with Svetlana Peters, June 6, 2000.

594 *Among other things* . . . Brandoch Peters's eulogy for his father; authors' phone interview with Brandoch Peters, May 30, 2000.

594 *She still cries* . . . Authors' interview with Olga Peters, June 5, 2000.

594 *"He never said* . . ." Authors' interview with Svetlana Peters, June 6, 2000.

594 *By 2001, the program* . . . James Auer, "Turmoil at Taliesin: Nature's forces are putting Wright masterpiece at risk," *JA On Line*, *Milwaukee Journal Sentinel*, November 9, 2002.

595 *Concerned about the Foundation's* . . . Curtis Besinger to John Geiger, October 4, 1988; Auer, "Turmoil at Taliesin," November 9, 2002; Juliet Williams, "Doing the Wright Thing with Taliesin Poses a Daunting

Challenge for Preservationists," May 24, 2004, *Pittsburgh Post-Gazette*.

595 *"There is no need to . . ."* Authors' interview with Indira Berndtson, 1997. *Even Wes Peters . . .* John Geiger to Curtis Besinger, May 4, 1989. Robert Twombly is more brutal: "The work produced by Wright's students and firm since his death in 1959 is imitative (of him), redundant, involuted, imprisoned by its own theories, unrelated to social and architectural change, and is received with amused tolerance even by conservatives in the profession." "Organic Living: Frank Lloyd Wright's Taliesin Fellowship and Georgi Gurdjieff's Institute for the Harmonious Development of Man," *Wisconsin Magazine of History*, Winter 1974–1975, 126–39, 134.

596 *"The genius of Taliesin . . ."* Authors' interview with Charles Schiffner, January 30, 2002.

CHAPTER 27: AN HEIRLESS HOUSE

599 *"Usher," she recounted . . .* ILW, *My Life*, 52; authors' interviews with ILW, January 21 and 26, July 24, August 16, 2000.

600 *"I wanted to be like her . . ."* authors' interview with ILW, August 16, 2000.

600 *"I thought that maybe . . ."* authors' interview with ILW, January 26, 2000.

600 *"I split with them entirely . . ."* authors' interview with ILW, January 21, 2000.

601 *She once called for a "man" . . .* Jack Holzhueter to the authors, e-mail, May 30, 2000.

601 *"The homos did it . . ."* Authors' interview with ILW, February 13, 2000.

601 *"You enjoy the luxury . . ."* ILW to Richard Carney: August 25, 1994, and May 4, 1995.

601 *"She can be dangerous . . ."* Maggie Valentine, interview with John Hill, July 19, 1993, UCLA Oral History Program, 1997.

601 *"The poor thing . . ."* Maggie Valentine, interview with John Hill, July 19, 1993, UCLA Oral History Program, 1997.

601–2 *Once, as she was being escorted . . .* Authors' interview with Steve Lamb, December 22, 1999.

602 *"They wanted—were determined . . ."* Authors' interview with ILW, July 24, 2000.

602 *"For ten years . . ."* Authors' interview with ILW, February 13, 2000.

603 *"He knows the truth . . ."* Authors' interview with ILW, January 21, 2000.

603 *"Mr. Gurdjieff, you have forgotten . . ."* Authors' interview with ILW, February 13, 2000.

ꟼΠDΣX

CREDITS